Vera Menchik

Vera Menchik

*A Biography of the First
Women's World Chess Champion,
with 350 Games*

ROBERT B. TANNER

McFarland & Company, Inc., Publishers
Jefferson, North Carolina

FIRST EDITION, *first printing*

LIBRARY OF CONGRESS CATALOGUING-IN-PUBLICATION DATA

Names: Tanner, Robert B., author.
Title: Vera Menchik : a biography of the first women's world
chess champion, with 350 complete games / Robert B. Tanner.
Description: Jefferson, North Carolina : McFarland & Company, Inc.,
Publishers, 2016. | Includes bibliographical references and index.
Identifiers: LCCN 2015050044 | ISBN 9780786496020
(library binding : alk. paper) ∞
Subjects: LCSH: Menchik, Vera, 1906–1944. | Chess players—
Great Britain—Biography. | Women chess players—Great Britain—
Biography. | Chess—Collections of games.
Classification: LCC GV1439.M4 T36 2016 | DDC 794.1092—dc23
LC record available at http://lccn.loc.gov/2015050044

BRITISH LIBRARY CATALOGUING DATA ARE AVAILABLE

ISBN (print) 978-0-7864-9602-0
ISBN (ebook) 978-1-4766-2498-3

Edited by Robert Franklin
Designed by Robert Franklin and Susan Ham
Typeset by Susan Ham

Printed in the United States of America

*McFarland & Company, Inc., Publishers
Box 611, Jefferson, North Carolina 28640
www.mcfarlandpub.com*

To my father, Paul M. Tanner,
who taught me how to play chess,
and to my wife Elizabeth Tanner,
who insisted that I finish this project
and who has supported me every inch of the way

Acknowledgments

In a work of this nature there is no way to thank everyone who contributed, but to not give credit to the following people would be unconscionable. I received substantial help from the late Alice Loranth and the staff of the John G. White Collection of Chess and Orientalia at the Cleveland Public Library. More recently, Pam Eyerdam and her staff at the library, including Kelly Ross Brown and Michael Jacobs have helped with various finishing touches. The trips I made there hunting down and copying materials are among the most enjoyable of my chess career. In addition, I have been fortunate to have had access to the English National Chess Library in Hastings, the British National Library, the Salt Lake City Public Library, the library of NM Craig Madsen and the University of Utah Library.

Correspondents who were invaluable in tracking down material were Jan Kalendovský and Jan Orna (Czechoslovakia), Mr. L. Polden (Australia), Roy Morris (Scotland), T.G. Whitworth and W. Goerke (England), Val Zemitis and Dale Brandreth (U.S.A.). I honor Glenn Peterson of *Chess Life* and the late Ken Whyld for his help in his *British Chess Magazine* column "Quotes & Queries." IM John Donaldson provided much assistance and WGM Jennifer Shahade's encouragement was greatly appreciated.

A treat was the short time I was able to spend at the Hastings Chess Club where I was made to feel very welcome and was able to view several of Vera's awards as well as documents and photographs pertaining to her career.

Persons who have undertaken translations for me include my wife, Elizabeth Tanner, and Hans Morrow (German), NM Sergey Akhpatelov and GM Igor Ivanov (Russian), Audrey Colletti (Esperanto) and Dr. Hilda Parker (Czech). A special thank-you is offered to the memory of Irena Otorabova who translated all the non-technical material in Jan Kalendovský's 1986 book. Although we had only communicated by phone and letter, her death in 1991 was a very personal loss to me.

Table of Contents

List of Illustrations

Abbreviations Used

B.C.F.	British Chess Federation
BCM	*British Chess Magazine*
CS	*Československý Šach* / Czechoslovakian Chess
Chess	*Chess Magazine*, Sutton Coldfield
EST	Edwart Samuel Tinsley
FIDE	Fédération International des Echecs / World Chess Federation
GM	(International) Grandmaster
HSLO	*Hastings & St. Leonard's Observer*
IA	International Arbiter
IM	International Master
NCC	National Chess Center
QCH	*Quarterly for Chess History*
SCQ	*Social Chess Quarterly* magazine
RT	Robert Tanner
USCF	United States Chess Federation
VM	Vera Menchik
WRM	W. Ritson Morry
WSZ	*Wiener Schach-Zeitung* / Vienna Chess Magazine

PART I.
VERA MENCHIK

1. Introduction

Although matters have been changing with the advent of the Polgars and others there is still a conception that, as a rule, women cannot play good chess. I can only surmise that this is due to the fragile male ego and society's pressure on women to not be competitive. As recently as 1937, none of the chess clubs in Boston allowed female members. Former U.S. Women's Champion Mona Karff finally persuaded the Commonwealth Club to admit women in 1938.

It is my hope that this book about Vera Menchik will bring this unique chess personality to life for a new generation. This I aim to do by two means: first, to create an historical record of the games of the first female chess master and women's world champion. Even though she lived most of her life in England, and despite the fact that most of her available games were first published in English, there is no readily accessible comprehensive source of those games for most players or historians. The two works extant are both rare and in foreign languages. Elizaveta Bikova's 1957 Russian biography is, without question, the most comprehensive work on Miss Menchik, but it has only 93 games, is lacking a lot about her personal life and is difficult to come by. In 1986, Jan Kalendovský compiled a collection in Czech of 94 Menchik games as well as a copy of Salo Flohr's brief biography of her. Thanks to Chessbase and the Internet, almost 300 of her games are now available if one searches, but there is no particular context. These games are not only interesting in their own right, but they are demonstrative of much of the play of the 1920s and 1930s.

Given the paucity of biographical information, I have tried to let Vera and her opponents speak for themselves. I have used their annotations and comments to bring to life as many of her games as possible. Generally I have segregated material relating to specific tournaments to the relevant area of the games sections. Such information is included in the biography only when it is pertinent to the larger story. To do otherwise would be to give undue prominence to such items.

In this book, I wanted to publish every game that can be found. Of necessity, I have fallen far short of the impossible goal of "every game she played" but with more than 350 complete games the present work is the best effort yet. I have included in the events section games where I have a name, color, round and result, even if it is only a partial game or even just a note as to what opening was played.

My second intention has been to provide a role model for other chess players, men and women. I have included as comprehensive a biography as I could assemble as well as a wide ranging sample of Vera's own writings. If Vera wasn't the best player of her day, she was certainly competitive as an international master and absolutely dominated chess in her unique arena (women's chess) as no champion has before or since. She was proof that you can be an innovator and competitor, yet still be admired in both your own era as well as through posterity.

Unfortunately, many of the available photographs are of too poor quality to use and for some I was unable to track down ownership rights and permission. The result is a smaller than intended but, I hope, adequate grouping. In a few cases, I have chosen to use lesser quality shots which illustrate important parts of her life.

As a chess instructor myself, I have been astounded at how little knowledge the majority of modern players have of the history of our sport. It is not unusual to find players with Elo ratings over 2000 who cannot name all of the World Champions or even their own national champion. Ask a 1500 player who Frank Marshall, George Thomas or Salo Flohr were and you are met with a blank stare. Vera Menchik, as well as those above, played a huge role and should be recognized. Chess is not just a game, but a culture with a myriad of aspects in which to dabble.

I have used Jeremy Gaige's definitive *Chess Personalia* as my bible for spelling of names and life dates. Crosstables have mostly been taken from Gino Di Felice's books with assistance from other sources when needed. The few exceptions to the above have been noted and explained. Crosstables contain the most correct spellings of names possible, regardless of any variances in the source material.

The majority of the games have at least some annotations. Given the level of play of middle level masters of the late 1920s through the early 1940s it made little sense to comment on the games through the eyes of a modern master—especially in the openings. I chose to use annotations by her contemporaries where possible. This means that a lot of her games are commented on by the editors and contributors of *British Chess Magazine* and *Chess* magazine and above all by herself. In addition we are fortunate to have detailed notes by Alekhine, who wrote a book on London 1932 and even listed two of her games in *My Best Games 1924–1937*[1]; Flohr, Keres, Mieses and others. I have included notes on other games based on results of Fritz 5.32 and have also, at times, made corrections to the notes of others when computer analysis has shown that they have suffered oversights. Needless to say as I have discovered errors in previous works, there will be errors in this one. They are my responsibility alone.

Missing Games

As is inevitable there have been a substantial number of game scores and even a few crosstables that have eluded me. Most are from her early career, but there are also a good number of games with major personalities in some of her most important tournaments. Anyone possessing information on the following items is encouraged to send copies with any appropriate source documentation to me for future editions of this work.

1. Scarborough 1923: Crosstable; Thomas and six others
2. Hastings 1923-24: Crosstable (1st Class, Section A); Meynott, Wright, Reeve, Riley, Joyce, Lees, Hamilton-Russell games
3. Hastings 1924-25: McLean, Barlow, Graham, Brown, Jones, Agnes Stevenson games
4. Edith Price Match #1: Games: 1, 2, 3 & 5
5. Edith Price Match #2: Games: 2, 3 & 5
6. Stratford on Avon 1925: All games

7. Hastings 1925-26: Stevenson, Bolland, Goldstein, Berger, Jesty, Holmes, Morrison, Packer games
8. London Girls' 1926: All games
9. Hastings 1926-27: Milner-Barry, Watt, Illingworth, Littlejohn, Winter, Barlow, Howell-Smith, Rutherford games
10. London Girls' 1927: All games
11. Tunbridge Wells 1927: All games
12. Hastings 1927-28: SaloLandau, Rellstab, Jackson, Illingworth, Lean games
13. Cheltenham 1928: MacDonald, Littlejohn, Parsons, Bolland, Fry, Powell games
14. Scarborough 1928: Thomas, Winter, Berger, Wenman, Colle, Michell, Saunders games
15. Tenby 1928: All games
16. Hastings 1928-29: Steiner, Price, Znosko-Borovsky, Jackson, Noteboom, Sapira, Milner-Barry, P. Sergeant games
17. Paris 1929: Leon Schwartzmann games
18. Hastings 1929-30: Price, Maróczy, Takács, E. Sergeant games
19. Hastings Club Championship 1930: Crosstable & all games
20. Hastings 1930: All games
21. Canterbury 1930: Thomas, Seitz, Price games
22. Hastings 1930-31: Yates, Tylor, Price, Colle, Winter games
23. Antwerp Match Tournament: All games
24. Worcester 1931: Jackson, Seitz, Jacobs, Cross, Watts, Stronach, Rhodes games
25. Hastings 1931-32: Jackson, Thomas games
26. Cambridge 1932: Tylor, Yates, Thomas games
27. London 1932 (B.C.F. Champ.): Cross, Heath, Stronach, Wallis, Jacobs, Reeves games
28. Mnicho Hradiště 1933: Zinner, Foltys, Opočenský, May, Pokorný games
29. Groningen 1934: All games
30. Sonja Graf match 1934: Games 3 & 4
31. Amsterdam 1934: All games
32. Semilich 1934: Hadac, Paroulek, Matejka, Skrbek, Kovarik, Blazej games
33. Yarmouth 1935: Seitz, Conde, Fajarowicz, Klein, Wood, Butcher, Prins, Ivanoff, Kitto games
34. Margate 1936: Lundin, Thomas, Ståhlberg, Milner-Barry, Tylor games
35. Nottingham 1936: Tsukerman, Reynolds, Abrahams, Opočenský, Mallison, Lenton, Wood, Watts, Craddock, Coggan games
36. London 1937: Wheatcroft, Craddock, Parr, Berger games
37. Znosko-Borovsky Match 1937: Games 1, 2, 3, 4
38. Bournemouth 1938: All games
39. Brighton 1938: Alexander, Golombek, E. Sergeant, Milner-Barry, Thomas, Tylor, Aitkin, Lenton, Parr, Mallison games
40. Plymouth 1938: List, Milner-Barry, Mallison, Wheatcroft, Bruce games
41. Montevideo 1939: Hounie Fleurquin, Alfredo, Roux Cabral, Gulla games
42. London 1939: All games
43. London Easter 1940: Golombek, Schenk, Thomas, Morry, Podhorzer, Collins, Mieses games
44. Mieses Match 1942: Games: 2, 8, 10
45. Sidcup 1942: Podger, Brierley games
46. London Women's World Champs 1927: All Games
47. Hamburg Women's World Champs 1930: Wolf-Kalmar, Beskow (2 games each); Henschel, Stevenson (1 game each)
48. Folkstone Women's World Champs 1933: Gilchrist, Benini, Schwartmann, d'Autrement, Harun (2 games each); Price, Michell (1 game each)
49. Warsaw Women's World Champs 1935: All games except Gerlecka
50. Graf World Championship 1937: Games 1, 3, 5, 6, 9, 10, 11, 12, 13, 15, 16
51. Stockholm Women's World Champs 1937: Harum, Mellbye, Karff, Benini, Farago, Lauberte, Anderssen, Thomson, Roodzant, Gilchrist games

2. Prologue

Before it is possible to understand the importance of a player such as Vera Menchik, it is necessary to understand a little of what a woman's role in chess was prior to Vera's joining it. In its earliest European form, during the Middle Ages, chess was a game played almost exclusively by the upper classes.

> Skill in play was esteemed in a knight as an accomplishment befitting his rank and position, and while knowledge of chess is attributed to almost every character of rank in the romances, the heroes are regularly credited with a very high degree of proficiency. Nor was the game confined to the male sex alone: the noble's daughter learnt chess beside her brother, and grew up every whit as fond of the game as, or even better than, the knights of her acquaintance.[2]

Although there were not any tournaments or clubs to attend, single chess playing knights were allowed to play chess in their lady love's chambers. Strangely enough this custom, to some degree, carried on right through the 18th century. It is well known that Benjamin Franklin, while stationed in Paris, frequently played chess with a Madame Brillon in her bathroom until all hours of the morning.[3]

Needless to say there were women who played chess in the early 19th century; they just didn't play in the tournaments or clubs of the day; not that they weren't competent to do so; we wouldn't even know, because they were invisible! Let us focus primarily on the English speaking world for the present.

The first mention of women in the *British Chess Magazine* (the BCM; de facto journal of record for the world until recently) is on page 290 of the August-September 1881 issue where Misses Bridgewater, Wildman and Arkwell are listed as part of a group of singers—not players—who sang at the conclusion of the Birmingham vs. Nottingham match. Miss F.F. Beechley received recognition on page 359 of that journal for getting an honorable mention in a two-move problem competition. These are the only women amongst hundreds of men to be mentioned for their "chess" achievements in that year!

It was only in 1872 that Mary Rudge was allowed to join the Bristol Chess Club. William Steinitz, a proponent of female membership in all chess clubs, noted, "The Chess Circle of Turin, Italy has, by modification of its statute books permitted the wives and daughters of members to frequent the Club rooms and to participate in their tournaments. This is as it should be...."[4] Yet not until 1938 was the Manhattan Chess Club opened to female members.[5] Of course the women were not about to be denied a place to play and clubs were opened for Ladies only: The "Women's Club" in New York City opened in 1894 and the "Ladies' Club" in London premiered in 1895. A strange irony occurred in 1898 with the opening of the Gambit. During most of its 60 years of existence, only men were allowed to join despite the fact its owner, for most of that time, was a top British lady player, Edith Price.

Since women were not allowed to compete with the men—too stressful for the women—or the men depending on your perspective—they started holding their own events. The beginning was in 1884 when the Sussex (England) Chess Association sponsored the first women's tournament, which was won by a Miss Parvess. Three years later Miss Thorold won a challenge cup sponsored by the Counties Chess Association. This event was an annual fixture in England until 1893, when the association was dissolved.

One of the most famous of all tournaments is Hastings 1895. In conjunction with the Premier Section there was a women's section—oft thought in error to be the first all women's tournaments. First prize went to Lady Edith Margaret Thomas, mother of the British Champion and IM Sir George Thomas of later years.

By 1897, the Ladies' Club in London had grown to 100 members and hosted the first International Women's Tournament. With 20 players representing nine countries one could make an argument that the winner has a moral right to the title of women's world chess champion along the same lines as that of Adolph Anderssen after he won the great London 1851 tournament. To top it off, Mary Rudge (England) scored 18½ out of 19—a very Menchik-like score. It is generally thought that Miss Rudge was a strong Class II player by the end of her career so we can get an idea of the strength of the competition. Following is a nice game of hers from this event.

(A) Mary Rudge–Thomas [B01]
London International Women's, 1897
[*New York Daily Tribune*, July 25, 1897]

1. e4 d5 2. e×d5 ♕×d5 3. ♘c3 ♕d8 4. d4 ♗f5 5. ♗e3 e6 6. ♗b5+ c6 7. ♗c4 ♘f6 8. ♘ge2 ♗e7 9. ♘g3 ♗g6 10. a3 ♘bd7 11. 0-0 0-0 12. f4 ♘d5 13. ♗×d5 c×d5 *(see diagram)*

After 13. ... c×d5

14. f5 ef5 15. ♘×d5 ♗g5 16. ♘×f5 ♗×e3+ 17. ♘d×e3 ♗×f5 18. ♘×f5 f6 19. ♕g4 g6 20. c3 ♕h8 21. ♘d6 ♕c7 22. ♕g3 ♕c6 23. ♖ae1 f5 24. ♖e6 ♕d5 25. ♖fe1 ♘f6 26. ♕e5 ♕×e5 27. d×e5 ♘d5 28. ♖d1 ♘f4 29. ♖e7 ♔g8 30. g3 ♘h5 31. ♖×b7 ♖fd8 32. ♖d4 a5 33. ♖c4 a4 34. ♖cc7 *(see diagram)*

34. ... ♖ab8 35. ♖×b8 ♖×b8 36. ♖c8+ ♖×c8 37. ♘×c8 ♔f7 38. ♘b6 ♔e6 39. ♘×a4 ♔×e5 40. c4 ♘f6 41. b4 ♔d6 42. c5+ ♔c6 43. ♘c3 ♘d7 44. ♔f2 ♘e5 45. ♔e2 h6 46. a4 g5 47. a5 g4 48. a6 ♔c7 49. b5 ♔b8 50. b6 ♘c6 51. ♘b5 h5 52. a7+ ♔b7 53. ♘c7 ♘×a7 54. b×a7 1-0

Finishing second was Miss L.M. Fagan (Italy) at 15½ points and Miss Thorold (England) at 14 points took third place. Miss Fagan may have been the first woman to compete

After 34. ♖cc7

in a mixed gender event when she played in an 1882 event at the Bombay Sports Club. Evidently there was opposition to her competing and a compromise was reached where she was allowed to play as long as all of her games were played off site. She went +12 −0 =0 and was given a signed photograph of each opponent and an album in which to hold them.

This seems to have been a turning point for women in chess. A year later a women's event was held in The Hague and other countries were not far behind.

In 1904 the newly formed British Chess Federation hosted a women's championship section as part of the congress they held in Hastings. Taking first with three points to spare was Miss Kate B. Finn, age 33, of London who scored +10 =1. A large article about her on pages 399–400 of the 1904 issue of the *BCM*, with her picture, makes for quite interesting reading. This was the first substantial coverage of a female player. It would not be surpassed for many years—probably 1929.

In reviewing the 1904 *BCM*, we start seeing a small but regular number of female players competing in the British counties club matches. Of course women rarely competed against men in tournaments. In the B.C.F. Hastings Congress of 1904, not counting the Ladies' Section, there were 17 women competing out of 183 participants—all of them in the second class and below levels. Actually this was a number that would be greater than average for a long time.

Other early entries for women into the male bastions would be when Frideswide Beechey became the first woman to write a chess column in December 1882. The first chess book by a woman was *The ABC of Chess, by a Lady.* The lady was H.I. Cooke although researchers seem to have found nothing about her.

We now arrive at 1923—the beginning of Vera's career: No woman has played against a master level player in tournament competition. There have been a few minor female chess columnists and a few low to mid-level chess problem solvers. Many of the top level clubs do not allow female members. A very high number of the prominent women personalities (players and organizers) are associated with more prominent husbands. Most journals at the time when referring to a woman either use the term "Miss" or Mrs. "Husband's Name."

On the other hand we now had women who had achieved class I and II playing status (Elo 1600–2000 possibly) and, on occasion, get to play against men in lower level tournaments and in club matches.[6]

3. A Biographical Sketch

Vera Franceva Menchikova was born on February 16, 1906, in Moscow, to František and Olga Illingworth Menchik. Relatively little is known of her parents. Her father, a Czech, was born in Bystra nad Jizerou, Bohemia. He was the manager of several estates owned by Russian nobles while his wife worked as a governess for the same employers. Mrs. Menchik's parents were Arthur Wellington and Marie Illingworth. Arthur was a cotton manufacturer who died in Moscow. We don't know where Arthur and Marie met, were born or were married.[7] Most references list Vera's mother as English, but whether she was born in England is at this stage a matter of conjecture.

The period of her life spent in Russia and the Soviet Union is very sketchy. According to Vlastimil Fiala, Vera and her sister Olga were caught in Stockholm, Sweden, in 1914 at the start of the First World War, making it difficult to return to their home. The family of four lived in a six room Moscow flat where Vera's father taught her to play chess at the age of nine. Her early education was in a private school for girls; later she attended a public school. It was at the public school where it is likely that Vera played in her first chess tournament at age 14. Although the tournament was not completed, Vera would have finished in no less than second place.

After the revolution of 1917, they were required to share their home with others. She told several friends how she and her sister Olga were banned by their father from going to the basement of the building which had dirt floors and was occupied by the very poor. According to Brian Denman, Vera's father owned a mill which was confiscated in the unrest of the revolution and the family was ejected from their home. Vera's grandmother, Mrs. Illingworth, left Moscow and walked to the British Consul where she was able to get assistance to return to England, settling in Hastings. The rest of the Menchik family struggled to make ends meet by sweeping snow and other such duties.

In the autumn of 1921, the Menchiks left the Soviet Union. For whatever reason, the marriage of František and Olga broke up, with the father returning to Bohemia. Vera maintained contact with him via letters and met with him at Carlsbad, Czechoslovakia, in 1929 and probably on other trips to that country. Olga took her two daughters to St. Leonard's, England, not far from Hastings, where they lived with their maternal grandmother at 13 St. John's Road. The home is a four-story row house built in the 1880s. Although currently rather dilapidated and converted into four unit flats, at the time it was considered a rather desirable neighborhood. It was also in England that Olga dropped the "ova" at the end of her name which has the English meaning of "daughter of" in Russian. As a result, we find her listed with last names of Menchikova, Menchik and Stevenson depending on the era and the part of the world.

Vera was by nature a shy person and immersed herself in chess partially due to her poor English. In an article, she wrote, "I have often been asked, what made me think seriously about chess? ... In different circumstances I might never spend time in such a way, but chess is a quiet game and therefore the best hobby for a person who cannot speak the language."[8] Salo Flohr notes, as of 1933, that Vera spoke quite good English although not as good as her Russian and that she did not know the Czech language at all![9] By 1923, the family had settled in and Vera joined the Hastings Chess Club on March 18 of that year.

The home of Vera's grandmother, Marie Illingworth, where Vera, her sister Olga, and her mother, also named Olga, lived from the time they moved to England until Vera moved to London in the 1930s. At the time this was considered to be a nice neighborhood, but over the years the houses have been subdivided into apartments rather worn.

We first find her in a chess journal on page 242 of the 1923 *British Chess Magazine*, where she is listed as drawing with H.M. Baldrey on Board 28 of the Hastings vs. Brighton match. Her first chess coach was James A.J. Drewitt (1873–1931). Vera herself credited Professor Drewitt with her understanding the secrets of the closed openings. She played him in at least two tournaments (Tunbridge Wells 1927 and Hastings 1930—and probably in club tournaments) and lost both games. At the time she joined the Hastings club she was considered a weak second class player, possibly a "C" player by present-day U.S. standards.

About this time the great Hungarian grandmaster Géza Maróczy was lecturing at the club. It was Vera's good fortune to start taking private lessons from him. Although we have no way of knowing what went into her lessons, an article in *The Times* indicated that she had received her tuition in the form of 20 games. Maróczy and Vera had a mutual admiration for the rest of her life. A number of sources have attributed her positional style as well as many of her openings to GM Maróczy. Maróczy's observation was that she was, "Every inch a master."

British chess, now, and more so in the mid–20th century, is the home of a well organized regimen of team matches between clubs and counties. Vera served her chess apprenticeship playing for the Hastings Chess Club and Sussex County teams. In the 1920s she played in more than 15 club matches per year that it has been possible to document through Hastings CC records, the *BCM* and local papers. This is in addition to the regular activities at the club. Her first match was on Board 26 of the Hastings club against the English Boys team. She was Black and lost. Her first serious match was against H.M. Baldry in the Sexton Cup. Presciently, her future time pressure problems were foreshadowed by the fact that the game had to be adjudicated since it went past the scheduled completion time.

Vera put a lot of effort into these games, as shown by the fact that although the teams on which she played were not much more than average in strength she scored better than 83.75 percent in her games throughout that period. In that time she rose from playing on team boards in the twenties to the teens by 1925; by 1930 she was playing boards one and two. On June 27, 1925, the *Hastings and St. Leonard's Observer* offered "Further congratulations to Miss Menchik who has not only won the Bradley

Vera Menchik at age 16—this, along with the studio photograph of c. 1936, is one of the two most well known portraits of Menchik, and was taken shortly after winning the British Girl's Championship in 1922 (*Chess Review*, June 1969).

Marten Cup,[10] but also the Bogner Cup for the best score in 1st class matches, her total being 11 out of 13 made up of 10 wins, 2 draws and one loss, probably the best score ever for this cup."

Vera represented Hastings until at least 1934; Sussex County until 1937; and in the last years the county of Kent. The present author, sadly, found only five of her county and club games; these constituted a very large part of her output.

For many years, Hastings has held a prestigious place in chess. In 1895, what was arguably the strongest tournament up to that time was held there. Starting in 1920, Hastings hosted an annual Christmas Congress that has been attended by most of the world's top players. Two months after commencing lessons with GM Maróczy, Vera was admitted into the 1st Class section of the 1923-24 Hastings Christmas Congress. Vera later was to state that she did poorly, although she did draw with Edith Price, the British Ladies' Champion. In fact, she scored 3½ points out of 9 and proved herself to be a (marginal) first class player. Not being of British citizenship, however, she was ineligible to compete in the British Ladies' Championship.

The following year she scored 5 out of 7 in the 1st Class and took second place. She again drew with Miss Price; this time in a playoff for the Hastings top woman title as they were in separate sections. In a stereotypically sporting British gesture Miss Price suggested a match. Two five-game matches were played in 1925 with Vera winning both by scores of 3 out of 5.

In 1926-27 she was elevated to the Major Reserve Section where she scored +5 –1 =3 and tied for first place. This was her first victory in a "men's" tournament of high quality. In 1929, she played in the Premier section for the first of six times. Not until 1963 did another woman (Nona Gaprindashvili) play in the Premier Section at Hastings.

The year 1925 also saw Vera take second place in the 1st Class of the Stratford tournament. From that point, she became an avid chess player, competing not only in open and invitational tournaments, but in the British county and club matches.

One needs only to glance through British chess columns to see that Vera was considered to be something special by the time she won the London Girls' Championships in 1926 and 1927. It was at the first of these girls' tournaments, held in London at the Imperial Club, that she gave her first recorded simultaneous exhibition. She won 9 games while losing and drawing 2 each, including a loss to the father of Muriel Brown who was one of her tournament victims. This was the first tournament in which Vera was lionized by the press. According to the *British Chess Magazine*, no fewer than 23 press photographers were on hand for the opening ceremonies, with eight more arriving later in the day! The *Sussex Daily News* of August 1, 1927, described Vera as "...a short homely girl and her unbobbed hair is combed back from the forehead. She has a winsome smile and regular features. She speaks broken English." Vera finished the day at 10:30 p.m. when she reported on the results over the B.B.C. radio system.

In 1927 Vera first made chess history when she won the Women's World Chess Championship, held in London. As with all other such events prior to World War II, it was held in conjunction with the chess Olympiad. At that time, no one considered that there was adequate interest for a women's Olympiad. Entry for the 12 player event was £1 with prizes for first through fourth place of £20, £15, £10, and £5. By 2013 standards that works out to a $42 entry fee and a first prize of $840—comparable to many modern open events although there was a two week time investment. Her score of +10 =1 was almost laughably easy.[11]

Originally the women's event was simply one of several subsidiary sections of the tournament with no special status attached to it. However, on page 200 of the 1927 BCM the organizers indicated that, "It is hoped to persuade the FIDE to nominate the winner of this event their first Women's Champion." Sad to say, according to David Jarrett, the FIDE records prior to 1944 were destroyed in Amsterdam in a bombing. Thus we again rely on BCM to learn that, "It was agreed that Article 3 of the rules of the FIDE should be altered to include a Women's Championship of the FIDE, and this was made retrospective so as to award the title to the winner of the Women's Tournament of the London Congress, 1927."[12]

Although she had a faintly more challenging time when she defended her title in 1930, in Hamburg, scoring +6 –1 =1, her overall results in these tournaments demonstrated a dominance that no other World Chess Champion has approached. In seven title tournaments, she scored +78 –1 =4 (96.3%)! In addition to the FIDE title events, Vera played two matches against Sonja Graf, her strongest challenger. Although some writers, including the FIDE website, have claimed both events were for the title, only the 1937 match, held in Semmering,

Austria, was a title event. If that score was added to her tournament results, then Vera's total record in World Championship competition would be +87 –3 =9.

The year 1928 was a time of growth for Vera. In the club championship she scored 7 of 8 in the preliminaries and finished the event with 11½ out of 14 to place equal 2nd place with her mentor J.A.J. Drewitt after E.M. Jackson who had 12½ points. She also started developing a reputation as a teacher and lecturer when she gave a talk on the French Defense to about 30 Hastings Chess Club members that lasted for an hour and 35 minutes.[13] Also in that year Vera was asked to take part in an event of 21 players in the United States. At least at that time the organizers expected (hoped) to include Lasker, Capablanca and Alekhine. Needless to say nothing came of the venture, but it did show that she was considered a draw even in the Americas.[14]

Generally, her participation in the Premier section of the Scarborough 1928 tournament is considered to be the first time a woman played in a master level event. After her attractive win over Yates the *London Observer* quoted the new world champion, Alexander Alekhine, as saying, "She is without a doubt a phenomenon, and her victory over Yates in the first round will be historical."[15]

It was in 1929 that she set the chess world afire when she scored +3 –0 =4 at Ramsgate, placing equal second with Rubinstein, half a point behind Capablanca and ahead of Koltanowski, Maróczy, Thomas, Winter and Yates. The congress was divided into 13 sections, and more than 10 women played. The top section was comprised of seven British masters and seven foreign masters. Vera, still not having British citizenship, represented the foreign contingent. In the first round, she beat Sir George Thomas, who had just won his eleventh London Championship. She then drew three games before winning an uphill battle against Mitchell and defeating Price. In the last round, she had a hard fought draw to take equal second place only one-half point behind Capablanca, equal with the great Rubinstein and ahead of her teacher, GM Maróczy. Capablanca called her, "the only woman who plays as a man."[16]

In 1929, as a result of the Ramsgate event, invitations started coming and Vera played in tournaments throughout Europe: Paris, Carlsbad, Barcelona, and the championship section in Hastings! Shortly thereafter, in 1930, the Hastings C.C. Championship was annexed to her resume with the score of 11½–½.

Also in 1929, she was the first woman to compete in a major international grandmaster tournament when she played at Carlsbad. Although she came in last place, it was at that event that the legendary "Menchik Club" was founded. Even in the past 40 years I have seen the difficulties women chess players must endure. Times have gotten better, but in Vera's era it was much worse than now. On the eve of the Carlsbad tourney, Hans Kmoch said, "If Menchik gains more than three points I will join women's ballet." Menchik took pity on Kmoch and scored exactly three points. After the first round, which she lost to Frederick Yates, Albert Becker proposed that anyone who lost to Vera should be inducted as a member of the "Vera Menchik Club." Those players who drew with her would become candidate members of the club. In the third round, Vera played well and Becker became the club's charter member! For a while Dr. Max Euwe, the future World Champion, was recognized as the Menchik club's "president," because of his score against Vera of +1 –2 =1. More deserving may be IM George Thomas, several-time British champion, who lost no fewer than 9 games and drew 13 games with her.[17]

In 1931, an opportunity arose for Vera to take a position as a coach for the Empire Social

Two time British Champion and International Master Sir George Thomas in simultaneous play at Royal Northern Hospital in London, circa 1930. Vera had a lifetime winning record against Sir George, who was her most frequent serious opponent (John G. White Chess Collection, Cleveland Public Library).

Club in Bayswater, a suburb of London. There is some speculation that she may have lived at least part-time in London, given the commute to Hastings. She earned a living by giving chess lessons, editing the short lived journal *Social Chess* with William Winter, as well as playing in tournaments and acting as host for several clubs. Although chess was her main avocation she had many interests. These included travel (what better interest for a chess player?), as well as literature, tennis, music and the study of human nature. Two of her favorite authors were Anton Chekhov and Katherine Mansfield. She placed a high value on friendships and maintained close contact with those fortunate enough to be included in that circle.

This was also the year in which she won her second game from Max Euwe. It is said that after this game Dr. Euwe's wife came to find out who this femme fatale was. No doubt it was quickly evident that the good doctor was not succumbing to the plump Miss Menchik's wiles and the two ladies got along quite amicably.

At the conclusion of the Sussex vs. Kent match on December 2, 1933, Vera was presented with a check in recognition of her wonderful success in the Women's World Championships and her able support in the County Matches; also for the work she did for the Empire Social Club. Her short and "well-considered" reply thanked all those who had associated themselves with the gift.[18]

The year 1934 involved little play in England aside from the Hastings events, but it did entail a fair amount of travel out of the country. After Hastings she played in small tournaments in Groningen and Amsterdam with a four game match against the German, Sonja Graf, sandwiched in between in Rotterdam. This later is of some interest and the source of a little confusion. A few sources (most notably Richard Eales in *Chess: The History of a Game*) list it as a World Championship match but the evidence is quite convincing that this was not the case. Sonja had been tutored by the famous Siegbert Tarrasch and was the only notable woman, besides Vera, to play in "men's" tournaments as well as to make a living of sorts out of chess. Still, Sonja had no track record to speak of at this time. Vera lost the first game, before winning three consecutive games to win the match. It is possible that this match was put together as a prelude to the Amsterdam event where the two women played in "different but equal" sections of the tournament. While in Holland, Elizaveta Bikova indicates that she played 16 simultaneous exhibitions with a combined score of +238 −54 =83.

Following her play in the Netherlands she traveled to the Balkans where she competed in Maribor and Semily. The former event is generally held up as one of her best results; placing third behind Pirc, and Lajos Steiner, but ahead of Spielmann, Milan Vidmar, Jr., and Rejfir among others.

Upon the death of Mrs. Illingworth, Vera's grandmother, in late 1934, the family moved to the London (Westminster) suburb of Bayswater. It seems that Vera had taken on the role of the "head of household" for the family as her grandmother's cemetery plot is listed as being owned by Vera and she apparently handled the details of the obituary and death certificate.

In 1935 Miss Menchik played with very poor results in the famous Moscow tournament. Certainly she was one of the weakest players in this super tournament, but stories by other participants, as well as her own writings, indicate that she was highly distracted by social factors. She had returned to her birthplace after 14 years and engaged in too much visiting and cultural activity to play up to par.

There is a well known anecdote from this event. In Moscow, Salo Flohr had indicated that he was going to become world champion shortly. When several players expressed skepticism he explained. "Euwe will win the title from Alekhine, Menchik will then beat Euwe (she had a +2 −1 =1 score against him), then I will beat Menchik." Everyone was quite amused when Miss Menchik held Flohr to a draw the next day. Ultimately this prevented Flohr from taking clear first place in the tournament!

Prior to 1937 Vera had won the Women's World Championship five times with a combined score of +45 −1 =2. No one was considered to be in the same league with her. Then, starting in 1934, Sonja Graf started making a name for herself. Herr Zimdin, a chess enthusiast who owned the palatial Pahhans Hotel in Kemeri, decided to underwrite a match for the Women's World Championship between the two women in Semmering, Austria.[19]

B.H. Wood, editor of *Chess* magazine and a good friend of Vera, gave a lengthy prematch analysis in the June 1934 issue of his magazine. Following is an extract thereof.

Death certificate of Marie Illingworth, Vera Menchik's grandmother, on 29 November 1934 from a stroke.

The forthcoming match for the women's world championship between Miss Vera Menchik and Miss Sonja Graf is of outstanding interest. Not only because the two contestants stand so obviously head and shoulders above all their feminine competitors; ... but especially because of their striking contrast in manners, dress, temperament and particularly style. Euwe might well have dispensed with the first chapter of his new book in which he attempts to differentiate "Strategy" from "Tactics," referring his readers instead first to Miss Menchik's play with the remark: "This is strategy," then to Miss Graf's "This is tactics."

Both err. Miss Menchik is a little too cautious.... Miss Graf goes to the opposite extreme. ... Miss Menchik likes a close game, Miss Graf an open. A pawn down in an equal position, Miss Menchik would rarely escape loss. A pawn down in an equal position, Miss Graf is no more likely to lose—than if she were a pawn up!

Sonja Graf is the gay, the volatile; Miss Menchik the quiet and homely. Sonja Graf smokes endlessly; in the rare intervals between cigarettes she violently chews sweets. Between moves she rushes round the room, exchanging a few words with all and sundry, at the board her hair is disheveled, her face drawn and anxious, and her whole bearing tense to the point of painfulness....

Miss Menchik on the other hand sits, plum and placid, her hands folded before her, not a muscle twitching through hours of play. We cannot remember having seen her smoking a cigarette. Her play rarely departs from a steady standard of solidity....

The result...? The odds? The chances are probably three to two that Miss Menchik will win....[20]

Wood then states that Vera's game has shown an "imperceptible falling off," although Sonja has not fulfilled her early promise. He finishes with the observation, "the rivalry between the two is extraordinarily intense—they are *not* on good terms with each other—and there will be no quarter given on either side." For those who wondered what the official FIDE stance towards the match was, FIDE President Alexander Rueb wrote, "The match is a private one, but under FIDE's auspices. The World Championship is connected with it, but only until the Stockholm tournament. The match is not for the cup [the Hamilton-Russell Cup]; the Stockholm tournament is for both."[21]

Needless to say Vera won by the lopsided score of +9 –2 =5. She then went on to win the Stockholm 1937 Women's Championships by a score of +14 –0—4 points ahead of the runner-up Miss Benini and 5 ahead of the third place finisher Sonja Graf.

Whether or not Wood was correct in the Vera was suffering an "imperceptible falling off" of form is certainly a matter of opinion. I don't know how one detects the imperceptible, but I tend to agree with him. That being said, she certainly continued to study and learn her craft. In a remembrance of Harry Golombek's he writes, "She knew her theory extremely well: openings as well as endgames. So I was a little surprised when in 1939 Vera Menchik asked me to give her some lessons in the Sicilian Defense. But she was always striving for more knowledge."

On October 19, 1937, she married Rufus

Vera Menchik (circa 1937) (John G. White Chess Collection, Cleveland Public Library).

Henry Streatfield Stevenson[22]; 28 years her senior, he was a chess personality of moderate strength in play and considerable repute as an administrator (see Appendices 6 and 7). Mr. Stevenson's first wife, Agnes Lawson Stevenson, was one of Britain's premier women players and was killed when she walked into a moving propeller. She was at the time in Warsaw on her way to the 1935 Women's World Championship. Vera moved to her husband's home of 47 Gauden Road in Clapham, a suburb of London. Mr. Stevenson seems to have been in chronic ill health from the start. After accepting her invitation to play in Hastings 1937-38, Vera had to withdraw to nurse her husband through an illness. Mr. Stevenson died from a heart attack on 10 February 1943. Although they were married only a short time, there was a strong bond between them. When Mr. Stevenson died, it took several months before she was able to pull herself together, according to her close friend Margaret Hilton Brown. Vera continued to reside in the Clapham home after her husband's death and was joined by her mother and sister.

After Vera's marriage, her sister Olga also was married (December 1938) and became Olga

Rubery. Interestingly, Olga met her husband while taking Esperanto lessons—a new "artificial" language, and one in which a fairly large manuscript of Vera's life was written. Later, in 1967, Vera's world championship medal was displayed in Hastings, courtesy of her niece. So far I have not been able to determine whether this was a child of Olga's, a child of her husband, Clifford Rubery's or a more distant relative.

One advantage of Vera's marriage was that she finally became a British citizen, which allowed her to compete in the British Championship—scoring 5½/11 in her debut as the first woman to compete in the national championships. In 1938 she was selected to represent Britain in its match against Holland. The Buenos Aires Women's World Championship of 1939, was the only time that she represented England; previously she was listed as a Russian in 1927 and as a Czechoslovakian in the Championships from 1931 through 1937.

Shortly before leaving to play in South America she participated in a living chess display at Wandle Park to aid the Croyden General Hospital. She drew her game with Imre König. Other participants included British champions Alexander and Golombek as well as Elaine Saunders.

The trip to Buenos Aires must have been an exciting one for Vera. With most of the rest of the British contingent she traveled to Amsterdam where they boarded the *Piriapolis* for South America. Although most of the players did well, both Vera and Harry Golombek found themselves somewhat affected by seasickness. Much of Vera's time was spent playing bridge with various masters including C.H.O'D. Alexander, Gideon Ståhlberg and Vasja Petrov among others. Throughout the Olympiad the players expressed much gratitude with their reception—excepting their initial arrival in Buenos Aires, where they had their eyelids "twisted back in a search for negro blood."[23]

In this, her last world championship, Vera's score, as usual, is dominating. The event was not without its rocky moments though. Against the American Mona Karff, Vera dropped the exchange on move six and required a little help to gain the point. Near the end of the tournament in a very exciting game against her perennial opponent Sonja Graf, she was completely lost in the endgame, but her adversary missed the line. A reversal of that one game would have left the players in a tie for first. Graf later said it haunted her for the rest of her life.

Vera (right) with her sister Olga, also a candidate for the world title (circa 1927).

1937. Marriage solemnized at *the* REGISTER OFFICE in the
District of WANDSWORTH. in the METROPOLITAN BOROUGH OF WANDSWORTH.

No.	When Married	Name and Surname	Age	Condition	Rank or Profession	Residence at the time of Marriage	Father's Name and Surname	Rank or Profession of Father
250	Nineteenth October 1937	Rufus Henry Streatfield Stevenson	59 years	Widower	Pharmacist	47 Cambon Road Clapham	Rufus Stevenson (deceased)	Accountant
		Vera Menchikova	31 years	Spinster	Professional Chess Player	47 Cambon Road Clapham	Franz Menchikova (deceased)	Mill Owner

Married in the REGISTER OFFICE according to the Rites and Ceremonies of the _____ by certificate before by me,

This Marriage was solemnized between us, R. H. S. Stevenson / Vera Menchikova — in the Presence of us, Olga Menchikova / Beatrice E Jamieson — W. A. Fleming Registrar / H. E. Plott Spt. Registrar

	REGISTRATION DISTRICT				WANDSWORTH			
1944	DEATH in the Sub-district of Clapham				in the Metropolitan Borough of Wandsworth			

Columns:—	1	2	3	4	5	6	7	8	9
No.	When and where died	Name and surname	Sex	Age	Occupation	Cause of death	Signature, description and residence of informant	When registered	Signature of registrar
198	Twenty sixth June 1944 47 Cambon Road	Vera Stevenson	Female	38 years	Widow of Rufus Henry Streatfield Stevenson a Clerk	Due to War Operations	Certificate received from R. H. Jervan Town Clerk Wandsworth Borough Council	Thirtieth June 1944	A. H. Liston Deputy Registrar

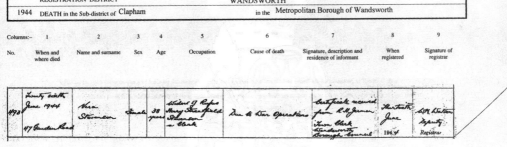

Top: Marriage registry of Rufus Henry Streatfield Stevenson and Vera Menchikova on 19 October 1937. *Bottom:* Death certificate of Vera (Menchik) Stevenson on 26 June 1944. Cause of death listed as "Due to War Operations."

World War II broke out in Europe in the middle of the Buenos Aires Olympiad and Women's World Championship. Although the British Olympiad team withdrew from competition, Vera stayed to finish winning her seventh championship tournament. At the request of a British official, Vera, B.H. Wood and Harry Golombek stayed to compete in a Montevideo, Uruguay, tournament held to benefit the British Red Cross. Vera placed third in this event; Alekhine took top honors with Golombek in second, a half point ahead of Vera.[24] The three British players then returned to Europe on a sister ship of the *Piriapolis*. Little could she know that this would be her last international tournament. After returning to London, she would never again leave Britain.

The war was a tough time for the entire world. The professional chess player was no exception. People like Vera had to cobble together a living from many sources: simultaneous exhibitions and lectures, writing, lessons and, least of all, tournaments. Much discussion was held over whether a 1940 British championship should or could be held. In a survey of the top players there was a general consensus that it would be appropriate to have a championship, but that they weren't sure about the feasibility of such a venture. Vera was among the more skeptical in her response. "I really do not know if there is a big demand for it among players of lower classes ... it is very doubtful indeed if I myself could play while the war is on, anywhere away from London."

Vera Menchik's World Championship medal (left) and the "Vera Menchik Medal" awarded by the Hastings Chess Club in her honor.

One thing Vera had in common with former world champion Lasker was that she enjoyed contract bridge and earned money by giving lessons in it. The going rate was 3 schillings, six-pence (or nearly $8 in 2016) according to her advertisement in *Chess*. This leads to the unanswered question as to what Vera's financial resources were. We have no information about jobs held by members of her living family, but given her travels and activities it is doubtful that she was fully reliant on her chess income alone—it just didn't pay that well. In September 1939, she was named to run the National Chess Center.[25] Sadly, that project ended when the center was destroyed in an aerial bomb attack almost exactly one year later. In 1942, Vera was the first woman to play a serious match against an acknowledged grandmaster, Jacques Mieses. Vera of course was 41 years younger than the 77 year old Mieses, but her victory by a score of +4 −1 =5 was still highly thought of. He had, after all, been one of the world's top 10 players in about 1900 (see game 5 of their match for an exciting game with notes by VM). As with most of the country, she helped where she could in the war effort. She was active in the Women's Voluntary Service

(W.V.S.). Besides giving simultaneous exhibitions for the military, she volunteered in other ways available to women of the time such as hospital work, playing games with and visiting the wounded, etc. At one point she put together a program to teach chess and write columns for the army, but it was shot down by headquarters as being too serious!

Very little is known of Vera's personal life. That she was well liked by nearly all members of the chess community is well documented. Not only do we have dozens of testimonials written after her death, one only need look at the nature of her tournament invitations. Although Vera was a strong player, it is rare that a player can place in the bottom half of tournaments such as Hastings year after year and still be invited. This can be attributed to her being a novelty and nominally adding to the international flavor of the events, but the bottom line is she was very popular.

There were of course a few contrarians. B.H. Wood made comments about animosity between Sonja Graf and Vera, but the most interesting item is a letter from E.S. Tinsley, chess columnist of *The Times*, to GM Erich Eliskases:

London 22-July-1936

Dear Mr. Eliskases,
Many thanks for your notes and the results to hand, and I am obliged to you for the information about Frydman. I was too full up tonight to use his game against Petrov, for I am getting games from Zandvoort as well.

I ought to have told you at first that I did not want one of his [*sic*] Miss Menchik's games, for my experience is they are always dull. She is a good player, for a woman, but had been very lucky against many good players in this country. Also, and this is strictly between ourselves, she is not at all a popular person in this country, for reasons I can perhaps tell you when we meet. So we are not giving her an inch of advertisement in our papers, probably much to her dislike!

Yours sincerely
E.S. Tinsley.

There were others who never got personal, but frequently seemed to make a point of diminishing Vera's abilities in their writings, often relating it to her femaleness or how "they" were better than she. A notable example was Harry Golombek, who never was able to write about her without mentioning her poor record against him and commenting on her lack of imagination. The easiest example to find is his entry about Vera in *Golombek's Encyclopedia of Chess*. A more unique item was his comment in *The Times* (London) of January 26, 1980, where he writes, "I won many games against the Women's World Champion, Vera Menchik. That was 42 years ago, but I can still see the murderous look that came over her usually benign face when I was engaged in beating her for the seventh time. I think it was in the British Championship in Brighton."

As has been noted, chess was only one of Vera's interests. Julius du Mont, noted that, "Philosophically she was a dialectician and an agnostic; it was the only option available given the answers that reason gives."[26] To that end, she was very interested in how peoples' lives are impacted by chance and she studied human nature intensively, albeit informally. Not one to push her view on others, she only asked for her view to be considered. She was quite shy away from the board, but instilled a tremendous sense of affection and admiration in those who got to know her. Although she took pride in being British and representing her new country, she always felt an affinity for Russia. Du Mont, who discussed her agnosticism in an obituary, stated that she was a Christian in the best sense of the word.

Vera Menchik, along with her sister and mother, died on 26 June 1944 during a Nazi air raid. The family took refuge in the basement, rather than going to the backyard or the neighborhood bomb shelters. A V-1 rocket demolished the home with a direct hit; leaving the shelter in the backyard of their London home unscathed. Joint cremation of the family took place on Tuesday, July 4, 1944, at the Strathan Park Crematorium. Not only was the family wiped out, but so were her trophies and virtually all her personal records. One apparent exception was the gold medal which she was awarded to commemorate her triumph in the World Ladies' Championships from 1927–1939. This medal was first seen after her death when in 1970 it was borrowed for an exhibition from Vera's niece and brother-in-law.[27] Currently it is on display along with a few other awards of Vera's at the Hastings Chess Club.

Vera's last event was the championship of the Southern Counties Chess Union. It was an elimination tournament and she had won her first three games, qualifying for the semifinals. Her next game was to have been played on June 27th.

It is a common pastime in any sport to speculate on how the greats in history would fare if alive today. With that in mind I went to a few websites to see what comments others had made regarding Vera's playing ability. It was not with great surprise that I found the term "dull" bandied about a lot as well as a feeling by some that she was at best a "190 player" to use British terminology (equivalent in rough terms to about 2150 using FIDE ratings which in the U.S. is a strong expert or a very low master). The reasons varied, but comments included the dullness alluded to above and that she did not sacrifice much. That of course does not mesh with Professor Arpad Elo's listing her five year peak rating at 2350,[28] which equates to a low level IM or, by USCF standards, a borderline senior master.

There is little doubt that Vera's choice of openings, notably the French Defense and Queen's Gambit as Black and d-pawn openings as White, led to games that are not exceptionally interesting to a large (especially weaker) portion of the chess community. Unless a player of those positional games has the winning results of Karpov or Petrosian, the rank and file of the chess world will often dismiss them. Vera, good as she was, certainly was not in that category. Vera also made what would, by today's standards, be considered a large number of errors or blunders in her games. This caused me to look at a lot of games played by other IM and GM level players of the 1930s. I discovered that large errors were quite common in the games of most of the IM level players although the GMs had far fewer blunders.

It seems that the IMs of the 1930s generally had a solid positional sense (if not as polished as exists now) even by modern standards and their tactical acumen was not of a much lower standard than similar players of the 21st century. What was missing, aside from a century of study and theory, was consistency. I attribute this in large part to fewer opportunities to play strong competition in tournaments and clubs as well as the distractions of making a living outside of the chess world. Although most of the GMs were full time professionals (notable exceptions being Euwe and Maróczy), the same was not true of many of the IM level players. While the chess professional existed at the IM level (e.g., F.D. Yates and William Winter) it was much less common than today; fewer players to pay for individual lessons and virtually no scholastic programs which are the bread and butter of today's low master.

In Vera's case, many observers have commented on how she was more interested in the people around her and having a well rounded life than in eating and breathing chess. In her two biggest events this may have played a major role in her final results. At Carlsbad 1929 she was visiting her paternal heritage for the first time as well as visiting her father after a break of almost a decade. At Moscow 1935 she had the conflict of working as a player while spending a substantial amount of time at theaters, museums and otherwise immersing herself in the city of her childhood. Obviously the average competition at both of these events was stronger than other events in which she played, but factors like this had to creep in.

It is virtually impossible to compare players of different eras. As Isaac Newton stated, "If I have seen further than others it is because I have stood on the shoulders of giants." Today's players have too many advantages over those of a century ago: opening theory, games by the best players of the past to study, more tournaments and clubs, and of course computers—and that is just a start. What we do know is that:

- She played some tremendous games that received praise from Alekhine, Capablanca, Euwe and more. Examples include her wins against Yates (Scarborough 1928), Euwe (Hastings 1930-31), Sultan Khan (Hastings 1931-32) among others.
- She scored +2 –1 =1 against Max Euwe shortly before he won the world championship.
- She was, according to Arpad Elo, a strong master—an IM of her day. To that end she had a five year peak of a 2350 Elo. That was calculated in 1978 and the consensus is that there has been rating inflation since then.
- Against George Thomas (an IM who had a five year peak Elo rating of 2470) she had a winning score out of over two dozen games—despite his finishing above her in 16 of the 25 round robins in which they competed.
- Her lifetime record against recognized World Champions was 2½–21½ or 10.4 percent.
- Her lifetime record against recognized GMs was 29–83 or 25.9 percent.
- Her lifetime record against recognized IMs was 63–72 or 46.7 percent.

How would Vera do in today's chess environment? Without access to modern theory it is reasonable to assume the answer would not be promising. However, if we take Professor Elo at his word, it is reasonable to expect that given access to modern tools of study and improvement, a player of the past would reach a similar level of accomplishment in relationship to their new peers as they did in their actual career. The above listing is enough to convince me of the legitimacy of listing Vera as of International Master strength. To think that such a player would be merely of expert or borderline master strength is patently untenable.

During a visit to the site of her home at Gauden Road, one is struck by the contrast between the impersonal concrete block of a structure that replaced the destroyed homes and with the very attractive houses which still remain on either side of it. It seemed a most poignant indictment of war.

This book is intended as a picture of Vera and her life where we can look at the master and the person. About her style of play it is enough to state that it was generally restrained and positional in style. It was popular for years to believe that women could not be tacticians and that they played without imagination. This perception was certainly exacerbated by remembrances of Julius du Mont (editor of the *BCM*) and GM Henry Golombek who admired her personality but tended to dismiss her originality and imagination. Alekhine and Capablanca, on the other hand, gave her strong praise and saw tremendous potential in her play. Maybe a world champion does not worry about comparisons with the mortals.

Although still better known by chess historians than players, recognition has come to Vera. In 1957 the reigning Women's World Champion, Elizaveta Bikova, wrote Vera's first biography. Unfortunately for a large part of the world, it is only available in Russian and is out of print. It consists of a modest number of games with notes, and a number of remembrances by important players, but very little hard biographical material, and it is something of a Soviet propaganda piece of the times.

A biography of Vera—not an easy task under any circumstances—is almost impossible given the lack of remaining first or secondhand sources. What is discernible is that she was no Alekhine who breathed, lived and died chess. For Vera, chess seems to have been a means to an end. Like most serious chess players her vision changed. A 1929 quote in Bikova's book is, "Formerly I played to amuse myself, then to study, but now I play to create." Vera enjoyed people, traveling and challenging herself. In an interview in 19XX in the *Sussex Daily News* she said, "Once I played chess every day, but lately I have not been so constant to the game. I do not live and dream chess. That would be too fixed. It is nice to turn to tennis, and I spend a lot of time modeling clay."[29]

Over the years Vera has slowly regained some of her richly deserved recognition. The Women's Chess Olympiad (which commenced in 1957) championship cup is titled the "Vera Menchik Cup." FIDE declared 1994 to be the "Year of Vera Menchik" in commemoration of the 50th anniversary of her death. That same year, the British Chess Federation and the Kent County Chess Association sponsored a tournament to commemorate the occasion; many more minor memorial events have been held over the years. In 1996, Czechoslovakia printed a postage stamp in her memory. Finally, in 2011, Vera was inducted as the 16th member of the World Chess Hall of Fame in St. Louis, Missouri, USA.[30]

4. Eulogies

Although all sources indicate her as being kindly and having a mild personality, she was intensely curious about life and the thoughts of people around her. A few excerpts from reminiscences at the time of her death are enlightening. First is Julius du Mont, then Margaret Hilton Brown, one of Vera's closest friends in the last six years of her life, who wrote an illuminating portrait of Vera.

Julius du Mont

[S]he had the combative, tenacious nature so often found in good chess players; for chess is a battle of wits, the fight is what most of us love in chess. Vera was, however, seldom assertive, a fault not uncommon in chess players. She sat placidly at the chess board, never causing even mild irritation by any of those nervous mannerisms that may always be seen in any chess room, the peripatetic fever being the most prominent. A light flush would rise in her face when the position would grow difficult, or when she was short of time on her clock—and that was recurrent according to the time-limit.

Away from the chess board she would readily talk of other subjects, and her great interest was in persons, in their actions and behavior under the strain and stress of the unruly passions; in the molding of their lives under the inscrutable dictates of chance; in the twists and turns of a mind warped perhaps by a casual incident long ago. Of course she was a pagan,[31] a thinking one, who had asked and found only the answers that reasoning gave. She judged kindly and never inflicted upon others her own opinions or beliefs: she asked only that these should be heard as one side of an argument, for she enjoyed a dialectical bout.

I shall remember her more for the woman as I knew her over many cups of coffee and, as I understand the word, a Christian....[32]

Margaret Hilton Brown

I first met Vera Menchik (Mrs. Stevenson) at an informal Chess Congress at Bournemouth in 1938. As soon as I was introduced to her I knew that we should be friends, she was interested in so many things outside chess, so anxious to hear of other people's lives, and had so much to tell of her own. She told me how when she was about eleven years old, at the time of the Russian Revolution, she was living with her father, mother and sister Olga in a six room flat in Moscow and how a notice was served on her father to the effect that he must share his rooms or give up most of them. People "from below" came up, bringing their goats and fowls with them. Vera told me that "below" in the basement of their flats, was a forbidden land to her sister and herself, and of course extra fascinating on that account. Apparently many people lived in these basements in great poverty; "they had earth floors and the children were terribly dirty and ill cared-for."

I asked Vera what struck her most when first she came to England. She said at once, "The way the milk bottles can be left outside houses; that would be impossible in Russia—they would be stolen."[33]

When I had a chess lesson we often had lunch together afterwards and went to a play or film. Here I think I should say, what a splendid and patient teacher Vera Menchik was, most encouraging, but she was not pleased at twice made mistakes....

Vera enjoyed everything we went to except an occasional Russian play. That was because the pronunciation of the Russian names was all wrong—"much too slow."

I often went to the house in Gauden Road, a large old fashioned basement house. There was a nice garden—for London. I remember remarking on the number of chess boards, chessmen and chess trophies Vera had. She said wistfully, "I wish people would present me with something else; I could think of so many things I would prefer...."

She was most interested in young chess players, and in young people generally; not that she was old herself! My son, aged nineteen, and she were friends. They never talked chess but ragged a bit together. They talked languages and she used to tell us how to pronounce many Russian and Polish words. Vera told me she sometimes felt shy with people of nineteen but that was not so with Geordie, "for, he draws me out." I like to think it was so, for I really believe, apart from the chess world, Vera Menchik often felt shy. That will be hardly credible to those who have seen her only at a display or playing in a match.[34]

Gideon Ståhlberg

Vera Menchik was relaxed in both her wins and losses. When an opponent won a good game she was the first to congratulate him.... I met her later in at least three tournaments and during a sea journey to Argentina in 1939. We played bridge daily during the trip. She made this trip unforgettable for me and other participants of the chess Olympics of 1939 due to her great humor and charm.

Thomas Olsen

When, in 1936 I searched on a hot summer's day for the City of London Chess Club in the quiet courts of Doctor's Commons, I was imbued with desire to improve my chess. Latter, in a dark quiet room with boards and me positioned around the walls, J.H. Blake gave me two pieces of advice. One was to join the Metropolitan Chess Club and the other was to have lessons from Miss Vera Menchik.

I have never regretted taking that advice, although both the club and the player are now, alas, no more. The Metropolitan may resume its activities when peace comes but Vera Menchik will never again grace a conversation or congress with her quick penetrating humor, her rich brown eyes and neat, shingled head. That she who faced the blitz undaunted should now, in the last days of the war, be struck down, is a catastrophe for British chess and a heavy blow to her friends. Her place was unique in the world and it was this country's good fortune that her home was here. Not only was she a player of the first rank who had more than once beaten Euwe and more than held her own with the first English players; she had a special gift for teaching.

Before her marriage to Mr. Stevenson she lived with her mother and sister in a flat in Bayswater. I remember very clearly my early visits there that led to friendship with my wife and myself. A steep, narrow stair painted green led up to the landing where, hands clasped before her, Vera Menchik would be waiting. I was usually a few minutes late and was firmly scolded and then we went into her room with the board set on a table and the gas fire popping in the corner. After less than a dozen lessons with her my playing ability had doubled itself.

But Miss Menchik's conversation was as entrancing as her chess play. She was widely read and widely traveled. Her favorite authors were Katherine Mansfield and Chekhov. Whatever turn the talk took she had something interesting and enlightening to say. And she never forgot her friends. From Austria and elsewhere occasional postcards would arrive to report her progress. At congresses, where she met many friends from this country and abroad, she never neglected to have a word with each. She had a just appreciation of her own position in the chess world but she was always modest. I never heard her make any malicious remarks about her opponents, a thing that could not be said of all the masters. At the National Chess Center in its setting of warm lights, soft carpets and beautiful boards and pieces she was the perfect hostess. When it was lost through enemy action she bore the disaster bravely and looked forward to its rebirth.

She had perfected the art of living. Chess genius as she was she did not allow the game to rule out everything else and her interests were extensive. Her life had not always been easy but she never gave way and her integrity was always maintained. Her example was a good one. In the records of her games, in the memory of those who played with her and learnt from her she will live on. It is to be hoped that a memorial volume of her games may be produced and the looked for revival of the National Chess Center will not be complete without some special tribute there to one who, like her husband, did so much for British and world chess.[35]

PART II.
HER GAMES, EVENTS AND CROSSTABLES

The Apprentice:
The Early Events, 1923–1928

Scarborough 1923

4th–6th Place	George Thomas	Points 5/9
7th–8th Place	Vera Menchik	4½/9

Hastings 1923-1924
(1st Class—Section A)
December 27, 1923–January 4, 1924

7th–8th Place	Vera Menchik	Points 3½/9

Vera garnered a fair amount of coverage in *The Times* (London) commentary regarding the tournament. On December 27: "First-class tournament 'Section A' is again quite interesting for Miss Price, the British Lady Champion, is the outstanding figure." Two days later, the same source noted that Vera had won her first game, but was in trouble in the second game and that her real test would be when she played Miss Price in the fourth round.

1 Menchik–J.W. Danahay
Hastings 1923-24 1st Class, Section A (1), December 27, 1923
[D52] *Queen's Gambit Declined, Cambridge Springs Variation*

1. c4 e6 2. d4 d5 3. ♘c3 ♘f6 4. ♗g5 ♘bd7 5. e3 c6 6. ♘f3 ♕a5 7. ♗×f6 ♘×f6 8. ♘d2 ♗e7 9. ♗d3 d×c4 10. ♘×c4 ♕h5 11. 0-0 b5 12. ♘e5 ♕×d1 13. ♖f×d1 ♗b7 14. ♘e4 0-0 15. ♖ac1 ♖ac8 16. ♘c5 ♗×c5 17. ♖×c5 ♘d5 18. ♖dc1 f6 19. ♘×c6 ♖×c6 20. ♖×c6 ♗×c6 21. ♖×c6 ♘b4 22. ♖c3 ♘×a2 23. ♖a3 ♘b4 24. ♗×b5 a6 25. ♗×a6 ♖b8 26. ♗c4 ♔f7 27. ♖a7+ ♔g6 28. ♗×e6 ♘d3 29. b3 ♖b6 30. ♗f7+ ♔h6 31. ♗d5 ♘c1 32. ♖a3 ♘e2+ 33. ♔f1 ♘c3 34. ♗c4 ♘e4 35. ♔e2 ♖b4 36. f3 ♘c3+ 37. ♔d3 1-0 (Source: Game #50, p. 54 L. Toth)

(R01) S. Meynott–Menchik
Hastings 1923-24; 1st Class, Section A (2), December 28, 1923
½–½

(R02) Menchik–G. Wright

Hastings 1923-24; 1st Class, Section A (3), December 29, 1923

0–1

2　Edith Price–Menchik

Hastings 1923-24; 1st Class, Section A (4), December 29, 1923

[A14] *French, Classical Variation*

This is an interesting game as it shows Vera in competition with her first rival in their first known game. They played in later Hastings tournaments, in two matches and in Women's World Championship events. Needless to say Menchik ended up outclassing Price, but at the start it was pretty even.

After 31. ... h6

1. e4 e6 2. d4 d5 3. ♘c3 ♘f6 4. ♗g5 ♗e7 5. e5 ♘fd7 6. ♗e3 c5 7. f4 c×d4 8. ♗×d4 ♘c6 9. ♘f3 ♘×d4 10. ♘×d4 0-0 11. ♗d3 ♘c5 12. ♗e2 ♗d7 13. 0-0 ♖c8 14. ♔h1 ♕b6 15. ♘b3 ♘×b3 16. a×b3 f6 17. f5 f×e5 18. f×e6 ♖×f1+ 19. ♗×f1 ♕×e6 20. ♘×d5 ♗c5 21. b4 ♗d4 22. c4 b5 23. ♕b3 b×c4 24. ♗×c4 ♔h8 25. ♖f1 ♕d6 26. ♘c3 ♖f8 27. ♖d1 ♕g6 28. ♘e2 ♖f2 29. ♘g3 ♖×b2 30. ♕f3 ♕e8 31. ♖f1 h6 *(see diagram)*

32. ♗d3? 32. ♕f8+ ♕×f8 33. ♖×f8+ ♔h7 34. ♗d3+ **32. ... ♔g8?** 32. ... ♕g8 **33. ♕e4** 33. ♕d5+ ♗e6 34. ♕e4 ♖f2 35. ♖×f2 ♗×f2 36. ♕h7+ ♔f8 37. ♕h8+ ♔e7 38. ♕×g7+ ♕f7 39. ♕×e5± **33. ... ♖f2 34. ♕h7+ ♔f8 35. ♖×f2+ ♗×f2 36. ♗g6?** ♕e6 **37. ♘e4** ♗e3 38. ♗h5 ♕g8 39. ♕g6 ♕e6? 39. ... ♕c4 is the best move 40. ♕g3 ♗d4 41. ♕a3 ♕e7 41. ... ♕c4 42. ♘c5 ♗×c5 43. b×c5 ♗c6 44. ♕b3 ♕b7 45. ♕a2 ♗e4 46. ♕f2+ ♔g8 47. h3 ♗d5 48. ♔h2 e4 49. ♕f4 a5 50. ♕d6 ♕a8 51. ♗e8 ♕×e8 52. ♕×d5+ ♕f7 53. ♕a8+ ♕f8 54. ♕×a5 ♕f4+ 55. ♔g1 ♕c1+ 56. ♔f2 ♕c2+ 57. ♔g3 e3 58. ♕d8+ ♔h7 *(see diagram)* 59. ♕f8? 59. ♕d4 ♕f2+ 60. ♔h2 ♕d2 61. ♕e4+ ♔g8 62. c6 ♕d6+ 63. ♔g1= **59. ... e2** 59. ... ♕e4 60. ♕f1 e2 61. ♕e1 ♕e3+ 62. ♔h2 ♕f4+ 63. ♔g1 ♕d4+ 64. ♔h2 ♕d1–+ **60. ♔f2 ♕d1 ½–½** (Game score: *Glasgow Herald,* January 19, 1924; notes by RT)

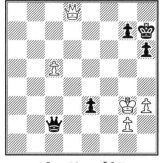

After 58. ... ♔h7

(R03) Menchik–A.H. Reeve

Hastings 1923-24; 1st Class, Section A (5), December 31, 1923

This game went into adjournment. **1–0**

(R04) F.A. Riley–Menchik

Hastings 1923-24; 1st Class, Section A (6), January 1, 1924

(R05) Menchik–F.A. Joyce

Hastings 1923-24; 1st Class, Section A (7), January 2, 1924

(R06) Menchik–S.P. Lees
Hastings 1923-24; 1st Class, Section A (8), January 3, 1924

(R07) F.G. Hamilton-Russell–Menchik
Hastings 1923-24; 1st Class, Section A (9), January 4, 1924

Hastings 1924-1925

(1st Class—Section 2)
December 27, 1924–January 2, 1925

		1	2	3	4	5	6	7	8	Points	Place
1	McLean, L.	•	=	=	1	1	1	1	1	6	1
2	Menchik, Vera	=	•	1	=	0	1	1	1	5	2
3	King, W.H.	=	0	•	0	1	=	1	1	4	3
4	Barlow, A.D.	0	=	1	•	0	1	1	0	3½	4
5	Graham, R.D.	0	1	0	1	•	0	1	0	3	5
6	Brown, R.H.	0	0	=	0	1	•	0	1	2½	6
7	Jones, E.M.	0	0	0	0	0	1	•	1	2	7–8
8	Stevenson, Agnes	0	0	0	1	1	0	0	•	2	7–8

After the tournament Vera engaged in a one game playoff with Edith Price, who took second place in Section 1 of the 1st glass. The game ended as a draw and led to two matches later in the year.

3 W.H. King–Menchik
Hastings 1924-25 1st Class. (7), January 2, 1925
[D10] *Slav Defense*

1. d4 d5 2. c4 c6 3. e3 ♘f6 4. ♘c3 ♘bd7 5. ♕c2 g6 6. ♗d2 ♗g7 7. c×d5 ♘×d5 8. ♘×d5 c×d5 9. ♘e2 0-0 10. ♘c3 ♘f6 11. ♗d3 a6 12. 0-0 b5 13. b4 ♕d6 14. a4 b×a4 15. ♘×a4 e5 16. d×e5 ♕×e5 17. ♘c5 ♘g4 18. f4 ♕e7 19. ♖ae1 ♖e8 20. h3 ♘h6 21. ♗c3 ♗×c3 22. ♕×c3 ♕d6 23. e4 d×e4 24. ♘×e4 ♕b6+ 25. ♔h1 ♖e6 26. ♘f6+ ♖×f6 27. ♖e8+ ♔g7 28. g4 ♗b7+ 29. ♔h2 ♖×e8 30. g5 ♕c6 31. ♕×f6+ ♕×f6 32. g×f6+ ♔×f6 0-1

Edith Price vs. Menchik, Match 1, 1925

April 20–24, 1925

	1	2	3	4	5	Pts
Menchik, Vera	0	=	1	1	=	3
Price, Edith	1	=	0	0	=	2

After the Hastings Tournament of 1924-25 where Menchik and Price took second place in their respective Class 1 sections, they played a game to determine their relative placement—it ended as a draw. Price then offered to play a match with Menchik to determine their relative abilities. The match would not be for the British title as Vera was still not a citizen of that

Miss Edith Price, British Women's Chess Champion (left), vs. Vera Menchik, in 1925 Match (John G. White Chess Collection, Cleveland Public Library).

country. Following is a commentary from the April 25, 1925, issue of the *Hastings and St. Leonard's Observer.*

Two matches were also played at the Hastings Chess Club, probably the first of their kind between lady chess players. The most important was a match between Miss Price, the Lady Chess Champion of Great Britain and Miss Menchik of Hastings. Miss Price has won the British Ladies' Chess Championship three years in succession....

Play commenced at 9:30 a.m. on Monday and considerable interest was shown by spectators. Miss Menchik had the White pieces in the first game which proved a long one. The first game was adjourned at 1:30 p.m. and continued for two hours in the evening when Miss Price won it. The second game (played on Tuesday) also proved a long one. Like the first it was adjourned at 1:30 p.m., the position being much in Miss Menchik's favor, but after a long sitting Miss Price managed to draw. The third game soon developed into a position much in Miss Menchik's favor and she won it, thus bringing the scores level, 1½ each. The fourth game was the best of the series. Miss Menchik having the black forces, played a French defense, which Miss Price met by a line of play known as Alekhine's Attack in which she eventually gave up a piece. The attack did not succeed and Miss Menchik won a fine game. In game five a queen's pawn opening was well played on both sides. The game was drawn at the 70th move leaving Miss Menchik the winner of the match by 3–2.

Played concurrently was a match between Mrs. Agnes Stevenson, a past British Ladies Champion and Miss Musgrave. Miss Stevenson won the first three games before losing and then drawing one game each.

(R08) Menchik–Edith Price
Match 1 Hastings (1), April 20, 1925
0–1

(R09) Edith Price–Menchik
Match 1 Hastings (2), April 21, 1925
½–½

(R10) Menchik–Edith Price
Match 1 Hastings (3), April 22, 1925
1–0

4 Edith Price–Menchik
Match 1 Hastings (4), April 23, 1925
[A16] *French, Classical Variation*

1. e4 e6 2. d4 d5 3. ♘c3 ♘f6 4. ♗g5 ♗e7 5. e5 ♘fd7 6. h4 c5 7. ♗×e7 ♔×e7 8. ♘b5 ♘c6 9. c3 a6 10. ♘d6 c×d4 11. f4 d×c3 12. b×c3 ♛a5 13. ♕d2 ♘c5 14. ♖c1 b5 15. ♘f3 ♘b7 16. ♘×b7 ♗×b7 17. ♗d3 f5 18. 0–0 ♛b6+ 19. ♔h1 h6 20. ♕e1 ♖ag8 21. ♖b1 ♛a5 22. ♕d2 g5 23. ♕f2 g×f4 24. ♕c5+ ♔f7 25. ♗×f5 e×f5 26. ♕×d5+ ♔e8 27. ♕e6+ ♘e7 28. ♖bd1 ♗c8 29. ♕f6 ♛×a2 30. ♖d2 ♛e6 31. ♘d4 ♛×f6 32. e×f6 ♘g6 33. h5 ♘f8 34. ♘c6 ♘e6 35. ♘e7 ♔f7 36. ♘×g8 ♖×g8 37. ♖d6 ♔×f6 38. ♖c6 ♗b7 39. ♖×e6+ ♔×e6 40. ♖f2 ♖×g2 0–1

(R11) Menchik–Edith Price
Match 1 Hastings (5), April 24, 1925
½–½

Edith Price vs. Menchik, Match 2, 1925

June 6–11, 1925

	1	2	3	4	5	Pts
Menchik, Vera	0	1	1	0	1	3
Price, Edith	1	0	0	1	0	2

5 Edith Price–Menchik
Match 2 Hastings (1), June 6, 1925
[C14] *French, Classical Variation*

1. e4 e6 2. d4 d5 3. ♘c3 ♘f6 4. ♗g5 ♗e7 5. e5 ♘fd7 6. h4 c5 7. ♗×e7 ♔×e7 8. ♘b5 c×d4 9. f4 ♛a5+ 10. ♔f2 ♘c5 11. ♘f3 ♘e4+ 12. ♔g1 ♗d7 13. ♘b×d4 ♘c6 14. c3 ♛b6 15. ♖b1 ♖af8 16. ♗d3 f5 17. ♕e1 h6 18. ♖h3 ♗e8 19. h5 ♗f7 20. ♔h2 ♖hg8 21. ♘×c6+ b×c6 22. ♘d4 c5 23. ♘f3 c4 24. ♗×e4 f×e4 25. ♘d4 ♗e8 26. b4 g5 27. h×g6 ♖×g6 28. ♕h4+ ♔d7 29. ♖g3 ♖fg8 30. ♖×g6 ♖×g6 31. ♕f2 ♛d8 32. f5 e×f5 33. ♕×f5+ ♔c7 34. ♘e6+ ♖×e6 35. ♕×e6 ♛h4+ 36. ♔g1 e3 37. ♕d6+ ♔b7 38. ♕×d5+ ♗c6 39. ♕f7+ ♔c8 40. b5 ♗a8 41. ♕f8+ ♔c7 42. ♕c5+ ♔b8 43. ♕×e3 ♛g4 44. ♕f2 ♗e4 45. ♖f1 ♗d3 46. ♕f8+ ♔c7 47. ♖f7+ 1–0

(R12) Menchik–Edith Price
Match 2 Hastings (2), June 8, 1925
1–0

(R13) Edith Price–Menchik
Match 2 Hastings (3), June 9, 1925
0–1

6 Menchik–Edith Price
Match 2 Hastings (4), October 6, 1925
[D02] *Queen Pawn Opening*

1. d4 c5 2. c3 e6 3. ♘f3 d5 4. ♗f4 ♘f6 5. e3 ♘c6 6. ♘bd2 ♗e7 7. ♗d3 ♗d7 8. 0–0
c4 9. ♗c2 ♘h5 10. ♘e5 ♘×f4 11. e×f4 g6 12. ♘df3 ♕c7 13. g3 f6 14. ♘×d7 ♕×d7
15. ♖e1 0–0–0 16. ♕e2 ♕c7 17. ♕×e6+ ♔b8 18. ♗a4 ♖d6 19. ♕e2 ♗d8 20. ♗×c6
♕×c6 21. ♕c2 ♕c8 22. ♔g2 ♖g8 23. b3 ♖c6 24. ♖ab1 h6 25. ♖e3 g5 26. f×g5 h×g5
27. b×c4 ♖×c4 28. ♕h7 ♗c7 29. ♕f7 f5 30. ♕×d5 ♗b6 31. ♘e5 ♖c7 32. ♕b5 f4
33. ♖d3 ♖h8 34. ♘f3 ♕h3+ 35. ♔g1 g4 36. ♘g5 ♕×h2+ 37. ♔f1 ♕h1+ 38. ♔e2
♖e7+ 39. ♔d2 ♕g2 40. ♔c2 ♕×f2+ 41. ♖d2 ♕×g3 42. ♖d3 ♕f2+ 43. ♔b3 ♕e2
44. ♖b2 ♕f1 45. ♖dd2 ♕c4+ 46. ♔c2 ♕×c3+ 47. ♔d1 ♕c1+ 0–1 (Source: *Times Literary
Supplement*)

(R14) Edith Price–Menchik
Match 2 Hastings (5), June 11, 1925
0–1

Stratford on Avon 1925
(B Section)
August 17–29, 1925

	1	2	3	4	5	6	7	8	9	10	11	12	Pts	Place
1 Thomas, George A.	•	0	1	=	1	0	1	1	1	1	1	1	8½	1
2 Menchik, Vera	1	•	1	=	=	1	=	=	1	1	0	1	8	2
3 Cooper, W.A.	0	0	•	1	1	=	=	0	1	1	1	1	7	3
4 Rutherford, Dr. V.H.	=	=	0	•	1	0	=	1	=	=	1	1	6½	4
5 Greenhalgh, Rev. W.R.	0	=	0	0	•	1	=	=	=	1	1	1	6	5
6 Hulbert, A.P.L.	1	0	=	1	0	•	1	0	=	=	0	1	5½	6
7 Holloway, E.	0	=	=	=	=	0	•	1	0	1	1	0	5	7–8
8 Solomon, F.	0	=	1	0	=	1	0	•	1	0	=	=	5	7–8
9 Vine, Lt. Leslie	0	0	0	=	=	=	1	0	•	0	1	1	4½	9
10 Burton-Eckett, E.	0	0	0	=	0	=	0	1	1	•	0	1	4	10
11 Wilkinson, F.	0	1	0	0	0	1	0	=	0	1	•	0	3½	11
12 Smith, Dr. E.H.	0	0	0	0	0	0	1	=	0	0	1	•	2½	12

Miss Menchik won £8 ($543 in 2016 dollars[36]) for her second place finish.[37]

Hastings 1925-1926
(Major Tourney)
December 28, 1925–January 5, 1926

		1	2	3	4	5	6	7	8	9	10	Points	Place
1	Teller, Alfred	•	1	=	1	=	1	1	1	1	=	7½	1
2	Stephenson, H.J.	0	•	1	1	1	0	=	=	1	1	6	2
3	Bolland, P.D.	=	0	•	0	1	1	1	=	=	1	5½	3
4	Goldstein, Maurice E.	0	0	1	•	0	=	1	=	1	1	5	4
5	Berger, Victor	=	0	0	1	•	0	=	=	1	1	4½	5–6
6	Jesty, E.T.	0	1	0	=	1	•	0	1	1	0	4½	5–6
7	Holmes, N.B.	0	=	0	0	=	1	•	0	0	1	3	7–10
8	Menchik, Vera	0	=	=	=	=	0	1	•	0	0	3	7–10
9	Morrison, John Harold	0	0	=	0	0	0	1	1	•	=	3	7–10
10	Packer, G.F.H.	=	0	0	0	0	1	0	1	=	•	3	7–10

Menchik's elevation to the Major Class section did not go unnoticed. The *Hastings and St. Leonard's Observer* of 2 January 1926 (generally a solid supporter of Vera) wrote, "The Major tourney for the first time includes a lady player, Miss Menchik, the Young Russian lady, at Hastings. Miss Menchik won her first game, but up to the fifth round had only scored 1½ points out of a possible five, so at present it cannot be said that her appearance in so high a class is justified." It seems that such a score is far from disastrous for a first effort and makes one wonder if the article, which had no byline, was taken from a release from *The Times* which never was supportive of Vera.

(R15) N.B. Holmes–Menchik
Hastings 1925-26 Major (1), December 28, 1925
0–1

(R16) Menchik–E.T. Jesty
Hastings 1925-26 Major (2), December 29, 1925
0–1

(R17) Victor Berger–Menchik
Hastings 1925-26 Major (3), December 30, 1925
½–½

(R18) Menchik–John H. Morrison
Hastings 1925-26 Major (4), December 30, 1925
0–1

(R19) G.F.H. Packer–Menchik
Hastings 1925-26 Major (5), December 31, 1925
1–0

(R20) Menchik–P.D. Bolland
Hastings 1925-26 Major (6), January 1, 1926
½–½

(R21) Maurice E. Goldstein–Menchik
Hastings 1925-26 Major (7), January 2, 1926
½–½

7 Menchik–Alfred Teller
Hastings 1925-26 Major (8), January 3, 1926
[D40] *Queen's Gambit Declined, Semi-Tarrasch Variation*

1. d4 ♘f6 2. c4 e6 3. ♘f3 d5 4. ♘c3 d×c4 5. e3 c5 6. ♗×c4 a6 7. 0-0 ♘c6 8. a3 b5 9. ♗a2 ♗e7 10. ♘e2 ♗b7 11. d×c5 ♕×d1 12. ♖×d1 ♗×c5 13. b4 ♗b6 14. ♗b2 ♔e7 15. ♖ac1 ♖ac8 16. h3 ♖hd8 17. ♖×d8 ♖×d8 18. ♘fd4 ♘×d4 19. ♗×d4 ♗×d4 20. ♘×d4 ♖c8 21. ♖×c8 ♗×c8 22. ♗b1 ♘d5 23. ♔f1 g6 24. ♔e1 f5 25. ♔d2 e5 26. ♘b3 ♔d6 27. ♘c5 a5 28. ♘d3 e4 29. ♘f4 a×b4 30. ♘×d5 ♔×d5 31. a×b4 ♔c4 32. ♔c2 ♔×b4 33. ♔b2 ♗e6 34. ♗c2 g5 35. g3 h6 36. h4 g×h4 37. g×h4 ♔c4 38. ♗d1 b4 39. ♗e2+ ♔d5 40. ♗d1 ♔e5 41. ♗b3 ♗×b3 42. ♔×b3 ♔f6 0–1

(R22) H.J. Stephenson–Menchik
Hastings 1925-26 Major (9), January 4, 1926
½–½

London Girls' Championship, 1926
January 12–16, 1926

		1	2	3	4	5	Pts	Place
1	Menchik, Vera	•	1	1	1	1	4	1
2	Brown, Muriel	0	•	1	0	1	2	2–3
3	Menchik, Olga	0	0	•	1	1	2	2–3
4	Spencer, B.J.	0	1	0	•	d	1½	4
5	Green, A.I.	0	0	0	d	•	½	5

By the time of the first London Girls' Championship there was no doubt as to who the winner would be. She was already competing in the second highest section of the Hastings Christmas tournaments and was the most experienced under 21 girl in the nation.

Hastings 1926-1927
(Major Reserves Tourney)
December 28, 1926–January 6, 1927

		1	2	3	4	5	6	7	8	9	10	Points	Place
1	Menchik, Vera	•	=	1	=	1	1	0	1	1	=	6½	1–2
2	Milner-Barry, Philip S.	=	•	1	=	0	1	=	1	1	1	6½	1–2
3	Watt, J.A.	0	0	•	=	1	1	1	0	1	1	5½	3
4	Illingworth, Leonard	=	=	=	•	=	0	=	=	1	1	5	4–5
5	Littlejohn, P.C.	0	1	0	=	•	0	=	1	1	1	5	4–5
6	Lean, R.E.	0	0	0	1	1	•	0	=	1	1	4½	6
7	Winter, William	1	d	0	=	=	1	•	0	0	=	4	7
8	Barlow, Henry S.	0	0	1	=	0	=	1	•	=	0	3½	8
9	Howell-Smith	0	0	0	0	0	0	1	=	•	1	2½	9
10	Rutherford, Dr. V.H.	=	0	0	0	0	0	=	1	0	•	2	10

8 R.E. Lean–Menchik [C01]
Hastings 1926-27 Hastings, 1926

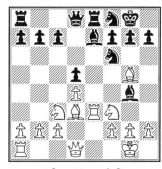

After 10. ... ♘f8

White in this game was the champion of Brighton, England. Already Vera Menchik was being touted as the best woman player in the world. This was one of her first published games, but the truth is that White almost forced Menchik to win due to his insistence on his unsound e-file attack. **1. e4 e6 2. ♘c3 d5 3. d4 ♘f6 4. ♗g5 ♗e7 5. e×d5 e×d5 6. ♘f3 0-0 7. ♗d3 ♖e8 8. 0-0 ♗g4 9. ♖e1 ♘bd7 10. ♖e3** Until now White has opened well, but his attack on the e-file is a mistake. Black can and does frustrate it by ♘e6. White's resulting loss of material is fatal, and he should have abandoned the attack to Black, acknowledging his 10th move to be a mistake. **10. ... ♘f8** *(see diagram)*

11. ♕e2? [The only move is 11. ♗×f6 giving Black the option of liquidating with ♗×f6 or creating weaknesses with the doubling on the f file by g×f6—RT] **11. ... ♘e6 12. ♖e1?** [12. ♕d2 c5 13. ♗b5 ♖f8 was better, but it's not always possible to save a game that has already been compromised—RT] **12. ... ♗×f3 13. g×f3 ♘×g5 14. f4 ♘e6 15. ♕f3 ♘×d4 16. ♕h3 ♘e6 17. ♕h4 d4 18. ♖h3 d×c3 19. ♗×h7+ ♔f8 20. ♗e4 ♕d2 21. ♕h8+ ♘g8 22. ♖he3 ♗c5 23. ♖3e2 ♕×e2 24. ♖×e2 ♘×f4 25. ♖e1 c×b2 26. ♕h7 ♖e5 0-1** (Source: *Chess Amateur*, March 1927, #2041; *L'Echequier*, February 1927, p. 571; notes based on those of Soultanbéieff [additional notes by RT])

London Girl's Championship, 1927
January 11–15, 1927

		1	2	3	4	5	6	Pts	Place
1	Menchik, Vera	•	1	1	1	1	1	5	1
2	Menchik, Olga	0	•	1	d	1	1	3½	2
3	Gregory, R.	0	0	•	1	1	1	3	3
4	Hazeldon,	0	d	0	•	d	1	2	4
5	Brown, Muriel	0	0	0	d	•	1	1½	5
6	Green, A.I.	0	0	0	0	0	•	0	6

This was Vera's last year competing in the London Girl's Tournament as a month later she turned 21 and was no longer eligible. Olga, who had taken or tied for second in 1926 and 1927, tied for first the next year, but lost the title in a playoff. Vera of course would win the world women's title later in 1927.

Tunbridge Wells, 1927
(21st Kent County Chess Association—Major Tournament)
April 16–23, 1927

		1	2	3	4	5	6	7	8	Points	Place
1	Drewitt, John Arthur J.	•	=	=	1	1	1	1	1	6	1
2	Morrison, John Harold	=	•	0	1	=	1	1	1	5	2–3
3	Winter, William	=	1	•	=	1	1	1	0	5	2–3
4	Jesty, E.T.	0	0	=	•	1	1	1	1	4½	4
5	Menchik, Vera	0	=	0	0	•	1	=	=	2½	5
6	Lean, R.E.	0	0	0	0	0	•	1	1	2	6
7	Howell-Smith, S.G.	0	0	0	0	=	0	•	1	1½	7–8
8	O'Hanlon, John J.	0	0	1	0	=	0	0	•	1½	7–8

Hastings 1927-1928

(Major Open A)
December 28, 1927–January 6, 1928

		1	2	3	4	5	6	7	8	9	10	Points	Place
1	Koltanowski, George	•	0	=	=	1	1	1	1	1	1	7	1–2
2	Baratz, Abraham	1	•	=	1	=	1	0	1	1	1	7	1–2
3	Landau, Salo	=	=	•	=	1	0	=	1	1	1	6	3
4	Rellstab, Ludwig	=	0	=	•	1	1	0	=	1	1	5½	4
5	Jackson, Edward M.	0	=	0	0	•	1	=	1	1	1	5	5
6	Smith, Stephen F.	0	0	1	0	0	•	1	=	1	1	4½	6
7	Menchik, Vera	0	1	=	1	=	0	•	0	1	0	4	7
8	Illingworth, Leonard	0	0	0	=	0	=	1	•	0	=	2½	8
9	Lean, R.E.	0	0	0	0	0	0	0	1	•	1	2	9
10	Rivkine, J.W.	0	0	0	0	0	0	1	=	0	•	1½	10

Prizes in the 1920s were a bit different than they are now. Hastings in 1927-28 paid £15 to the winner of the top (Premier) section. Further prizes were £12, £8 and £5 with 10 shillings per win for non–prize winners. In the Major section in which Menchik played prizes were £10, £7 and £4 with 10 shillings per win for non–prize winners. Of course there was no entry and generally at least some expenses were covered. A few very prominent players received appearance fees. For this event Menchik received winnings of £2 ... or about $135 in 2016 money using the consumer price index.

9 Abraham Baratz–Menchik
Hastings 1927-28 Major A, 1927
[A06] *Irregular Opening*

This is Menchik's first win over an acknowledged master.

1. b3 d5 2. ♗b2 ♘f6 3. e3 g6 4. ♘f3 [4. f4 would maintain a stronger hold on the center, but White is apparently striving for eccentricity—RT] **4. ... ♗g7 5. h3 0–0 6. g4?** Feeble, weakening and pointless. If he expects to terrify his opponent he is soon taught a bitter lesson. **6. ... c5 7. ♗g2 ♘c6 8. d3 ♗d7 9. ♘bd2 ♕c7** In contrast to her opponent, Black develops simply and effectively. **10. ♘f1 ♖fd8 11. ♘g3 ♘xg4! 12. hxg4** [If now 12. ♗xg7 ♘xe3 and Black is a clear two pawns to the good—RT] **12. ... ♗xb2 13. ♖b1 ♗c3+ 14. ♘d2 ♘e5 15. ♗f3** [Not 15. f3 because of 15. ... ♘xd3+—RT] **15. ... ♕a5** With the brutal threat of 16. ... ♗xd2+ or 16. ... ♘xf3+ winning a piece in either event. **16. ♘gf1 ♕xa2** This is not vulgar pawn-grabbing, as Black threatens ... ♘xf3+ 18. ♕xf3 ♕xa1+ **17. ♗e2 ♕a5** [17. ... ♗xg4 was also possible; but Black is content with her booty—RT] **18. f4 ♘c6 19. ♔f2 ♕c7! 20. ♗f3 d4! 21. ♘e4 dxe3+ 22. ♔g3** [If 22. ♔xe3 ♗d4+ White's game is in ruins—RT] **22. ... ♗g7 23. ♘xe3 ♗e8** So that if 24. ♘xc5? ♗d4 **24. ♕f1 h6! 25. c3?** *(see diagram)*

After 25. c3

Overlooking the threat. **25. ...** ♕×**f4+!!** For if 26. ♔×f4 ♗e5 mate. An artistic conception. **26.** ♔**f2** ♘**e5** White resigns. He has been battered from pillar to post. 0–1 (Notes by *BCM* 1928 #5949; Reinfeld, *British Chess Masters Past and Present*; *Chess*, August 1944 #1801 [additional notes by RT])

10 Menchik–George Koltanowski
Hastings 1927-28 Major A, 1927
[E60] *King's Indian Defense*

1. d4 ♘f6 2. c4 g6 3. g3 ♗g7 4. ♗g2 0-0 5. e4 d6 6. ♘e2 c5 7. d5 ♗g4 8. h3 ♗d7 9. 0-0 b5! 10. c×b5 ♗×b5 11. ♘a3 a6 12. ♔h2 ♘bd7 13. ♖b1 ♖b8 14. f4 ♘e8 15. ♖f2 ♘b6 16. b4 ♗a4 *(see diagram)*

After 16. ... ♗a4

    17. ♘c2? As every beginner knows it is better to pin your opponent's pieces than your own! 17. ♕e1 maintains a small edge **17. ... ♘d7 18. ♗d2 ♕b6 19. ♖f1 a5 20. a3??** 20. b5 is the best try **c×b4 21. a×b4 ♕c7** After 22. ♖c1 ♗b7. **0–1** (Source: *L'Echiquier*, April 1928 #616 p. 895; notes by RT)

11 J.W. Rivkine–Menchik
Hastings 1927-28 Major A, 1927
[C13] *French Defense*

1. e4 e6 2. d4 d5 3. ♘c3 ♘f6 4. ♗g5 d×e4 5. ♘×e4 ♘bd7 6. ♘f3 ♗e7 7. ♘g3 0-0 8. ♗d3 c5 9. c3 c×d4 10. ♘×d4 h6 11. h4 ♘c5 12. ♗c2 ♕d5 13. ♗e3 ♖d8 14. ♕e2 b6 15. c4 ♕b7 15. ... ♕×g2!? 16. 0–0–0 ♕b7 **16. 0-0 ♗d7 17. b4 ♘a6 18. a3 ♘c7 19. ♘h5 ♘×h5 20. ♕×h5 ♘e8 21. ♗×h6 g×h6 22. ♕×h6 ♘f6 23. ♖fe1 ♕c7 24. ♖e3??** 24. ♘f3 ♗f8 25. ♕×f6+− **24. ... ♗a4??** 24. ... ♕h2+!! 25. ♔f1 (25. ♔×h2 ♘g4+ 26. ♔g1 ♘×h6–+) 25. ... ♗f8 **25. ♖g3+ ♕×g3 26. f×g3 ♖×d4 27. ♗×a4 ♖×c4 28. ♖f1 ♘g4 29. ♕h5 ♖f8 30. ♗b3 ♖d4 31. ♖f4 1-0** (Notes by RT)

12 Stephen Smith–Menchik
Hastings 1927-28 Major A, 1927
[B08] *Pirc Defense*

1. e4 ♘c6 2. ♘c3 ♘f6 3. d4 d6 4. ♘f3 g6 5. ♗e2 ♗g7 6. 0-0 0-0 7. d5 ♘b8 8. ♗e3 c5 9. h3 h6 10. ♕d2 ♔h7 11. ♘h2 b6 12. ♘g4 ♘×g4 13. h×g4 ♗a6 14. g3 ♗×e2 15. ♕×e2 ♘d7 16. ♔g2 ♖h8 17. ♖h1 ♔g8 18. g5 h×g5 19. ♖×h8+ ♗×h8 20. ♗×g5 b5 21. ♖h1 b4 22. ♘d1 ♗f6 23. ♕g4 *(see diagram)*

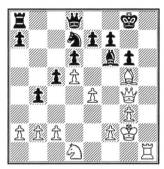

After 23. ♕g4

    23. ... ♗×g5? Putting a quick end to the game. [23. ... ♗g7 24. ♘e3—RT] **24. ♕×g5 ♕f8 25. ♕h4 ♔g7 26. ♘e3 e5 27. ♘f5+ 1-0**

Cheltenham 1928

(Major Division)
April 7–14, 1928

	1	2	3	4	5	6	7	8	Points	Place
1 Menchik, V.	•	1	1	=	1	1	1	1	6½	1
2 MacDonald, E.	0	•	1	1	=	0	1	1	4½	2
3 Smith, Stephen F.	0	0	•	=	1	1	=	1	4	3
4 Littlejohn, P.C.	=	0	=	•	0	1	1	=	3½	4–5
5 Parsons, H.	0	=	0	1	•	1	=	=	3½	4–5
6 Bolland, C.F.	0	1	0	0	0	•	1	0	2	6–7
7 Fry, W.J.	0	0	=	0	=	0	•	1	2	6–7
8 Powell, G.W.	0	0	0	=	=	1	0	•	2	6–7

Vera's sister Olga scored 2½ out of 9 points in the Class II section. According to BCM (May 1928, p. 192) the tournament was played at a time control of 17 moves in 60 minutes.

13 Stephen Smith–Menchik
Cheltenham—Major, 1928
[C11] *French, Classical Variation*

After 14. ♖b1

In this game Menchik takes revenge on S. Smith who defeated her a few months earlier in Hastings when she played the epitome of a hypermodern defense. This time Vera essays a French Defense and seizes control with a pretty pawn push on the 14th move.

1. e4 e6 2. d4 d5 3. ♘c3 ♘f6 4. e5 ♘fd7 5. ♘ce2 c5 6. c3 ♘c6 7. f4 ♕b6N 8. ♘f3 f6 9. g3 c×d4 10. c×d4 f×e5 11. f×e5 ♗b4+ 12. ♘c3 0-0 13. ♗f4 ♗e7 14. ♖b1 *(see diagram)*

52 years later Ghindi played the following in Bucharest, as did Anand against Sisniega in Philadelphia 1987: 14. a3 **14. ... g5!** **15. ♗×g5** Best is 15. ♘a4 ♗b4+ 16. ♗d2 ♗×d2+ 17. ♕×d2 ♕b4 18. ♕×b4 ♘×b4=; 15. ♗e3? ♘d×e5 16. ♘×e5 ♘×e5∓; 15. ♗d2 ♘×d4 16. ♘×d4 ♕×d4–+ **15. ... ♘d×e5 16. ♘×e5 ♗×g5 17. ♘×c6 b×c6 18. ♕g4** 18. ♗d3 **18. ... h6 19. h4 e5 20. ♕e2 e×d4 21. h×g5 ♗f5 22. ♕h5??** White's game is in dire straits, but best is 22. ♗h3 **22. ... d×c3 23. ♕×h6 ♕e3+ 24. ♗e2 ♕d2+ 25. ♔f2 ♗×b1 26. ♕g1 ♕e1+ 27. ♔h2 ♕×e2+ 28. ♔h3 ♗f5+ 29. ♔h4 ♕g4 mate 0-1** (Notes by RT)

Master Level Events, 1928–1944

Scarborough 1928
May 26–June 2, 1928

		1	2	3	4	5	6	7	8	9	10	Pts	Place
1.	Winter, William	•	1	0	1	=	1	1	1	=	1	7	1
2.	Colle, Edgar	0	•	=	1	=	=	=	1	1	1	6	2
3.	Michell, Reginald P.	1	=	•	1	0	=	=	0	1	1	5½	3
4.	Saunders, Harold	0	0	0	•	1	0	1	1	1	1	5	4–6
5.	Thomas, George A.	=	=	1	0	•	0	0	1	1	1	5	4–6
6.	Yates, Frederick D.	0	=	=	1	1	•	1	0	0	1	5	4–6
7.	Berger, Victor	0	=	=	0	1	0	•	=	1	1	4½	7–8
8.	Menchik, Vera	0	0	1	0	0	1	=	•	1	1	4½	7–8
9.	Schubert, František	=	0	0	0	0	1	0	0	•	1	2½	9
10.	Wenman, Francis P.	0	0	0	0	0	0	0	0	0	•	0	10

The dates, colors, openings and notes on adjournments are taken from *The Times* (London), May 28 to June 2, 1928.

On the first day of the tournament *The Times* wrote in reference to Miss Menchik's participation, "It [the Premier Section] would have been even stronger if the organizers had been able to secure the entries of Messrs. S. Mlotkowski [*sic*] and N.T. Whitaker, two very well known American players, but they found themselves unable to compete. The organizers therefore paid Miss Menchik the compliment of placing her in the Premier Tournament. The first idea was for her to play in the Major Tournament. Here she is meeting players of far greater strength than those she encountered at Cheltenham, and the improvement she has made in the last few years will be tested to the uttermost."

The *British Chess Magazine* noted that this was her first appearance in the ranks of the masters—referring to her competing in the Premier Section.

14 Menchik–Frederick D. Yates
Scarborough (1), May 26, 1928
[A50] *Queen's Fianchetto Defense*

1. d4 ♘f6 2. c4 g6 This defense was well suited to the fighting style of Yates who never tried to draw a game throughout his whole career. He scored some notable wins with it, most famous of which was his brilliancy game against Alekhine at Carlsbad 1923, a game which deserves to be far better known than it is. **3. g3** Menchik's style, however, was quite different. She was a purely positional player and did not go in for flamboyant combination play. The exploitation of positional advantages was much more to her taste, and she could handle the ending with excellent skill, as witness the games with Euwe and Sultan Khan in this issue. The reason for this was that she was the pupil of Maróczy, who was one of the world's leading endgame players of his time. The text move eventually proved instrumental in discrediting [!?—RT] the King's Indian, and although today it is fashionable to lead into the Grünfeld Defense by 3. ♘c3 d4 4. ♕b3, etc., the position is much more likely to yield White winning chances, provided he is prepared to "sit on the splice" and wait for his superiority in space to fructify. **3. ... ♗g7 4. ♗g2 0-0** [Nowadays 4. ... d5 is often preferred but after 5. cxd5 ♘xd5 6. e4 etc., White has an excellent center and can build up a free, well developed game without fear of interruption—RT] **5. e4** This, followed by 6. ♘e2 constitutes the Rubinstein System. The idea is to seize the center quickly and maintain an octopus-like grip. ♘c3 is not necessary to the plan and so is reserved until later. **5. ... d6 6. ♘e2 ♘c6** Burn's idea offering two tempi to provoke d5, thereafter he would be able to play his queen's knight to c5 (after the restraining move ... a5) and attack the center. [In the present position, however, the move 6. ... e5 is possible since 7. dxe5 dxe5 8. ♕xd8 ♖xd8 clearly gives White nothing and relieves Black's cramped position, whilst after 7. d5 ♘bd7; and Black has saved a lot of time. White, would, therefore, probably play neither lines and prefer 7. 0-0 leaving Black the option of surrendering the center by 7. ... exd4 8. ♘xd4 ♖e8 9. ♘c3 with a playable but cramped game, or simply playing 7. ... ♗bd7 when his development would be somewhat crowded but quite solid—RT] **7. 0-0 e5 8. d5 ♘b8** [The claims of 8. ... ♘e7 followed by ♘d7 leaving the way clear for ... f5 are to be lightly dismissed, but never appear to have been seriously considered in master practice—RT] **9. ♘bc3** A more or less standard position has now been reached in which Black must try to counterattack by posting his queen's knight at c5 and eventually playing ♘e8 and ... f4; whilst White must prepare to conquer the square b4 for a pawn to drive away the Black knight from c5, and thereafter an attack on the queen's side by c5, etc., would be the strategic necessity. That the game does not entirely pursue this ideal strategic course is due to the subsequent errors by Black who risks too much in trying to win at all costs. **9. ... ♘bd7 10. h3** In order to permit ♗e3 without the annoyance of ♘g4 in reply. **10. ... a5 11. ♔h2** This, however, is not at once necessary. [It is more important to attend to the task of forcing b4 as soon as Black plays ♘c5. 11. ♗e3 ♘c5 12. b3 (12. a3 a4!) 12. ... b6 13. a3 etc., is more correct. If Black plays 11. ... b6 12. a3 is playable—RT] **11. ... ♘c5 12. ♗e3 b6** This is usual but not absolutely necessary. 12. ... ♘e8 is worth considering so as to play ... f5 before White can secure the advance of his b-pawn. Should White reply with 13. ♗xc5 dxc5 14. f4 ♘d6! 15. ♕d3 f5 and Black can exchange the e and f pawns after which his two bishops would be a potent factor in the ending. **13. ♕d2** *(see diagram)*

After 13. ♕d2

[Again inaccurate. Strictly correct is 13. b3 etc., the queen remaining at d1 until c4 has been played so as to hold the Black knight from b3 or a4. It is, of course, very easy to criticize White's play in the light of present day theory, which more or less completely analyzed out this variation, but it must be remembered that when this game was played the subtleties of this line were still comparatively unknown to the masters who have themselves to learn their theory by hard work and sometimes bitter experience in actual play—RT] **13. ... a4 14. ♖ab1 ♘h5 15. b4 a×b3 16. a×b3 f5 17. f4** On the other hand Fairhurst remarks of this move, "the compact array of the White forces is better able than Black to stand the opening up of the position which now occurs. White's pieces are all on the right squares and Black was ill advised to precipitate the breaking up of the position by this 16th move." It is very easy for the annotator to be unwittingly influenced by the results of a game and to take the line of least resistance by assuming all the winner's moves were correct and many of the loser's bad. We are only too conscious of our own shortcomings in this respect, and the unpleasant shocks we have sustained from those unkind enough to read our notes and lie in wait for a game in which to disprove them. Correspondence play is a cruel school in this respect. Reverting to the present position, before White's 17th move let us with a properly critical state of mind examine the strengths and weaknesses of the respective situations. There is, to use Nimzowitsch's terminology, a pawn-chain consisting of the king's and queen's pawns. The correct course for Black is to attack the base at White's e4 by ... f5l whilst White should aim at c4–c5 to attack Black's base. Nimzowitsch demonstrated that attack on the head of the chain is ineffective until the base has been properly undermined. Black has, in fact, attacked the base first and also holds the open a-file for the moment, but this latter point is rather two-edged since if he concentrates on the f-file White could take the a-file with effect. On the other hand White wants to drive the Black knight on c5 so as to advance on c5. The logical objectives for White to aim at, therefore seem to be (a) to protect her base as securely as possible and (b) to keep Black's queen's knight in a restricted position after driving it away. Viewed from this aspect the move now chosen looks incongruous and unless it really does force open the position advantageously as Fairhurst implies it is not the correct play. [Best in fact was 17. f3! and if 17. ... f×e4 18. f×e4 ♖×f1 19. ♗×f1 ♘f6 20. ♕c2 ♗d7 21. b4 ♘a4 22. ♘d1 and now White threatens to maneuver the queen's knight to f2 and d53 with the threat of c5. By this means White would get the best out of the position, but the text should not force the win at all—RT] **17. ... f×e4??** This is the real mistake, for hereafter his knight is driven into the backwoods. No doubt he was trading on what he supposed to be his opponent's inexperience, but it truly is inexplicable that he should make the one move which Blacks a valuable exchange square for his knight. [Correct was 17. ... e×f4 18. ♘×f4 ♘×f4 19. ♗×f4 (19. g×f4 ♘×e4 20. ♘×e4 f×e4 21. ♗×e4 ♕h4 22. ♗g2 ♗f5; 19. ♖×f4 ♗e5 20. ♖f2 ♘×e4 21. ♘×e4 f×e4 22. ♗×e4 ♕h4! and wins) 19. ... ♘×e4 (not 19. ... ♗×c3 20. ♕×c3 ♘×e4 21. ♗×e4 f×e4 22. ♗h6 and wins) 20. ♘×e4 f×e4 21. ♗×e4 ♗f5 and Black's game is quite satisfactory, but the chances of a draw would be considerable and Black probably avoided this variation for this reason only—RT] **18. b4 e×f4 19. ♘×f4 ♘×f4 20. g×f4!** At first sight this looks very risky since a pawn is left isolated, but White realizes that after the normal 20. ♗×e4 Black would be able to play 20. ... ♘d7; followed by ... ♘e5; when his hold upon the square e5 would enable him to establish an unassailable game. Black can now get no good squares for his knight. **20. ... ♘a4** This leaves the knight on the edge with no squares for his retirement. Black thus remains virtually a piece down in the vital theater. [Comparatively better was 20. ... ♘b7 21. ♘×e4 ♗f5 and Black can fight; if 20. ... ♘d7 21. ♘×e4 h6 (forced for 22. ♘g5 is a most powerful threat) 22. ♘g3 ♘f6 23. f5! ♗×f5 24. ♘×f5 g×f5 25. ♖×f5 ♔h7 (forced or the h-pawn is lost) 26. ♖bf1 with a manifestly crushing advantage.—RT] **21. ♘×e4 ♗f5 22. ♗d4** Necessary against the threat of

22. ... ♗xe4 23. ♗xe4 ♘c3 etc. It settles the immediate future of the Black knight. **22. ... ♕d7** [No better would be 22. ... ♗xd4 23. ♕xd4 ♗xe4 (23. ... ♕h4 24. ♖be1 ♖ae8 25. ♖a1! ♖a8 26. ♖a2 and there is no defense to the threat of ♕a1) 24. ♗xe4 and Black has no good defense to the threat of f5 followed by ♖g1 and an attack in the g-file—RT] **23. ♖be1 h6** [Again 23. ... ♗xe4 24. ♗xe4 leaves White the devastating threat of f5. The text is forced to prevent 24. ♘b5 and ♘e6—RT] **24. ♘g3 ♔h7** He must meet the threat of 25. ♘xf5 gxf5 26. ♖g1 etc. **25. ♘xf5 gxf5** [25. ... ♖xf5 26. ♗e4 ♖ff8 (or 26. ... ♖h5 27. ♕g2 ♕f7 28. ♖g1 etc.) 27. ♖g1 (not 27. ♕g2 ♗xd4 etc.)—RT] **26. ♗f3!** Decisive. He has no good reply to the threats of ♗h5 and ♖e6. He chooses the best answer. **26. ... ♖ae8 27. ♗h5 ♖e4** [27. ... ♖xe1 28. ♖xe1 would leave him defenseless against the threat of ♖e6 followed by ♕g2—RT] **28. ♖xe4 fxe4 29. ♖g1 ♗xd4** [Fairhurst mentions the following variations: 29. ... ♗f6 30. ♕g2 ♗xd4 31. ♕g6+ ♔h8 32. ♕xh6+ ♔h7 33. ♕xf8+ ♕g8 34. ♕xg8 mate; 29. ... ♖g8 30. ♕g2 and Black has no reply to ♕g6+ followed by ♕xg6 mate, for if 30. ... ♕f5 31. ♗g6+, etc.—RT] **30. ♗g6+ ♔h8** [No better is 30. ... ♔g8 31. ♕xd4 and the discovered check is killing—RT] **31. ♕xd4+ ♕g7** [31. ... ♔g8 32. ♗f5+ ♔f7 33. ♕g7+ and mates—RT] No better is **32. ♕xg7+ ♔xg7 33. ♗e8+ ♔h8 34. ♗xa4** The concluding attack from move 18 was conducted in irreproachable style by Menchik, and most masters would have been more than satisfied to make such a debut. **1–0** (Source: *Chess*, August 1944 #1796; notes by WRM [additional notes by RT])

(R23) George Alan Thomas–Menchik
Scarborough (2), February 5, 1928
French Defense 1–0

(R24) William Winter–Menchik
Scarborough (3), February 5, 1928
Queen Pawn Opening 1–0

(R25) Menchik–Victor Berger
Scarborough (4), February 5, 1928
Réti Opening—game adjourned ½–½

(R26) Menchik–Francis Wenman
Scarborough (5), February 5, 1928
Réti Opening—game adjourned 1–0

(R27) Menchik–Edgar Colle
Scarborough (6), February 5, 1928
60 Moves—Queen Pawn Opening 0–1

(R28) Reginald Michell–Menchik
Scarborough (7), February 6, 1928
Queen Pawn Opening—game adjourned
0–1

(R29) Harold Saunders–Menchik
Scarborough (8), February 6, 1928
43 moves—Queen Pawn 1–0

15 Menchik–František Schubert
Scarborough (9), February 6, 1928
[D35] *Queen's Gambit Declined, Exchange*

1. d4 d5 2. c4 e6 3. ♘c3 ♘f6 4. ♘f3 ♘bd7 5. c×d5 e×d5
6. ♗f4 c6 7. e3 ♘e4 8. ♕c2 ♘df6 9. ♗d3 ♘×c3 10. b×c3
♗e7 11. 0–0 0–0 12. ♖ab1 h6 13. h3 ♗d6 14. ♘e5 ♕c7
15. c4 c5 16. ♖fc1 c×d4 17. e×d4 b6 18. ♕d1 ♕e7
19. ♘c6 ♕c7 20. ♗×d6 ♕×d6 21. ♘e5 d×c4 22. ♗×c4
♗b7 23. ♖b3 ♖ad8 24. ♖d3? ♘d5? 25. ♕g4 ♘f6
26. ♕h4 ♘e4 27. ♖e1 ♘g5 28. f4 ♘h7 29. ♖g3 ♕×d4+
30. ♔h2 ♘g5 31. ♖e2 *(see diagram)*

    31. ... ♖d6? [31. ... ♖c8—RT] **32. ♖d3 ♕c5 33. ♖×d6
♕×d6 34. f×g5 b5 35. ♗b3 h×g5 36. ♕×g5 a5 37. ♕d2
♕c7 38. ♕c2 ♕b8 39. ♕f5 ♕c7 40. ♖c2 1–0** (Source:
www.Chessgames.com)

After 31. ♖e2

Tenby 1928
(21st B.C.F. Congress—Major Open)
July 2–13, 1928

	1	2	3	4	5	6	7	8	9	10	11	12	Pts	Place
1. Koltanowski, George	•	=	=	=	1	=	1	1	1	1	1	1	9	1–2
2. Seitz, Jakob A.	=	•	=	=	1	1	1	1	1	=	1	1	9	1–2
3. Znosko-Borovsky, Eugene	=	=	•	1	0	1	=	1	1	1	1	1	8½	3
4. Noteboom, Daniël	=	=	0	•	=	=	=	1	1	1	1	1	7½	4
5. Milner-Barry, Philip S.	0	0	1	=	•	1	0	=	1	1	1	1	7	5
6. Menchik, Vera	=	0	0	=	0	•	=	1	1	1	1	1	6½	6
7. Jackson, Edward M.	0	0	=	=	1	=	•	=	1	=	1	=	6	7
8. Holloway, Edith M.	0	0	0	0	=	0	=	•	0	1	0	1	3	8–10
9. Lacy-Hulbert, A.P.	0	0	0	0	0	0	0	1	•	0	1	1	3	8–10
10. Littlejohn, P.C.	0	=	0	0	0	0	=	0	1	•	0	1	3	8–10
11. Wright, G.	0	0	0	0	0	0	0	1	0	1	•	=	2½	11
12. Dewing, Leslie Charles	0	0	0	0	0	0	=	0	0	0	=	•	1	12

Times were different then. For the Tenby Congress a time control of 36 moves in two hours was set with 18 moves per hour thereafter. The concern noted in BCM was whether the faster time control would diminish the quality of play. The "official Director of the Tourneys" was R.H.S. Stevenson who would in nine years become Vera's husband. Her results were a little disappointing to some and her play a bit labored—an interesting observation as her percentage in Tenby was a bit higher than in Scarborough and she demolished the bottom of the field while scoring 25 percent against the top four. So far, the chess world does not have her games to review!

No game scores known.

Hastings 1928-1929

Premier Reserve Section
December 27, 1928–January 5, 1929

	1	2	3	4	5	6	7	8	9	10	Pts	Place
1. Steiner, Herman	•	1	=	=	1	1	1	1	1	1	8	1
2. Price, Hubert E.	0	•	=	1	1	=	0	1	1	1	6	2
3. Rejfíř, Josef	=	=	•	=	0	1	1	0	1	1	5½	3
4. Znosko-Borovsky, Eugene	=	0	=	•	1	d	0	1	=	1	5	4
5. Jackson, Edward M.	0	0	1	0	•	1	1	0	=	1	4½	5–7
6. Noteboom, Daniël	0	=	0	=	0	•	=	1	1	1	4½	5–7
7. Sapira, Emanuel J.	0	1	0	1	0	=	•	1	0	1	4½	5–7
8. Menchik, Vera	0	0	1	0	1	0	0	•	=	1	3½	8–9
9. Milner-Barry, Philip S.	0	0	0	=	=	0	1	=	•	1	3½	8–9
10. Sergeant, Philip W.	0	0	0	0	0	0	0	0	0	•	0	10

16 Menchik–Josef Rejfíř
Hastings 1928-29 Premier Reserve (6), 1928

[E38] *Queen's Gambit Declined, Ragozin Variation*

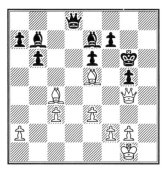

After 26. ... ♔g6

1. d4 ♘f6 2. c4 e6 3. ♘c3 ♗b4 4. ♕c2 c5 5. ♘f3 ♘c6 6. dxc5 ♗xc5 7. ♗f4 d5! 8. e3 0-0 9. ♗e2 dxc4 10. ♗xc4 ♘b4! 11. ♕e2 ♘bd5 12. 0-0! ♘xc3 13. bxc3 b6 14. ♖fd1 ♕e7 15. ♗g5 h6 16. ♗h4 ♗b7 17. ♘e5!! g5 18. ♗g3 ♖fd8? 19. ♘g4! ♘xg4 20. ♕xg4 ♖xd1 21. ♖xd1 ♖d8 22. ♖xd8+ ♕xd8 23. h4 ♔g7? 24. ♗f4! [24. ♗e5+?! f6 25. ♕xe6 fxe5 26. ♕f7+ ♔h8 27. ♕xb7—RT] **24. ... ♗e7 25. hxg5 hxg5? 26. ♗e5+ ♔g6** *(see diagram)* **27. ♗e2! ♗f6??** [27. ... f6 28. ♕h5+ ♔g7 29. ♕xg5+ ♔h7—RT] **28. ♕h5+ ♔f5 29. f4 ♗xe5 30. ♗d3+!! ♕xd3 31. ♕h7+ ♔f6 32. fxe5+! 1-0** (Source: *BCM* #6122)

Kent Congress at Ramsgate 1929

March 30–April 6, 1929

Foreign Team	GT	FY	RM	TT	WW	ES	HP	Points	Place
1. Capablanca, José R.	=	=	1	=	1	1	1	5½	1–3
2. Menchik, Vera	1	=	1	=	=	=	1	5	2–3
3. Rubinstein, Akiba	=	=	=	1	1	1	=	5	2–3
4. Koltanowski, George	=	=	=	=	1	=	1	4½	4–5
5. Maróczy, Géza	0	1	=	1	=	=	1	4½	4–5
6. Soultanbéieff, Victor I.	0	1	1	=	=	1	0	4	6
7. Znosko-Borovsky, Eugene	1	0	0	=	0	=	1	3	8–9

World Champion José R. Capablanca (John G. White Chess Collection, Cleveland Public Library).

British Team	Pts	Place
Thomas, Sir George (GT)	3½	7
Yates, Fredrick D. (FY)	3	8–9
Michell, Reginald P. (RM)	2½	10–12
Tylor, Theodore (TT)	2½	10–12
Winter, William (WW)	2½	10–12
Sergeant, Edward G. (ES)	2	13
Price, Hubert E. (HP)	1½	14

The 22nd Kent County Chess Association tournament in Ramsgate thrust Vera onto the international chess scene in a big way. The reason for the unusual format was to prepare for the Hamilton-Russell Cup. As of the February issue of BCM the foreign contingent list included Capablanca, Koltanowski, Maróczy, Soultanbéieff and Dr. A. Vajda. When the later withdrew and Rubinstein, Menchik and Znosko-Borovsky were added is anybody's guess.[38] The festival opened with a "living chess" display with boys dressed in white and red costumes; with hats appropriate for their respective pieces. After a game by a couple of the local dignitaries, Capablanca defeated Sir George Thomas and, lastly, Menchik lost with White against B.H. Lohmann in 29 moves.

17 Menchik–B. Lohmann
Living Chess Game, Ramsgate, March 30, 1929
[A29] *English Opening*

1. c4 e5 2. ♘c3 ♘f6 3. ♘f3 ♘c6 4. g3 ♗c5 5. ♗g2 0-0 6. 0-0 d6 7. a3 ♗e6 8. d3 ♕d7 9. b4 ♗b6 10. ♗b2 a6 11. ♖c1 ♗h3 12. ♘d5 ♘×d5 13. c×d5 ♘e7 14. ♕b3 ♗×g2 15. ♔×g2 ♖ac8 16. d4 ♘g6 17. d×e5 ♘×e5 18. ♘×e5 d×e5 19. ♗×e5 ♖fe8 20. f4 ♕f5 21. ♕f3 f6 22. ♗b2 ♖e3 23. ♕f2 ♕e4+ 24. ♔h3 ♖×e2 25. ♕×b6 c×b6 26. ♖×c8+ ♔f7 27. ♖c7+ ♔g6 28. f5+ ♔h5 29. ♖g1 ♕g4 mate 0-1 (Source: *Sunday Referee*, 7 April 1929; Gillam: *Ramsgate 1929: QCH* 10, p. 396)

The tournament itself was organized as a 13 section event with 110 players—more than 10 of which were women. The main section, designated as a "Team Practice Tournament," consisted of two sections: The English team and the Foreign team, which included Menchik. The tournament was run on the Scheveningen System, with the players on each team playing all the players from the opposing team.

In the first round of the event Sir George Thomas played rather without purpose and lost to Menchik, setting the tone for the event. In the second game Tylor built up a nice game against her, but by delaying his attack found himself having to defend, and after adjournment the game ended as a draw. The next two games, against Winter and Yates, also ended as fairly bland draws.

Round five saw Menchik and Michell get into a complicated game which ended on move 31 after Michell dropped a queen for two minor pieces. A round later Menchik added another win to her score when Price, in a better position, got over eager and made a flawed sacrifice.

The final round was important as Menchik was only one-half point behind Capablanca on the score table and even with Rubinstein. In the event all three of them had to settle for draws leaving Capablanca in first place. Even so, for Vera to come in equal second only a half point behind the former world champion, equal with Rubinstein and ahead of her coach, Géza Maróczy was spectacular. Capablanca stated that she was "the only woman who plays as a man."[39]

Strangely a number of the games from this event appeared to have been lost and it is was only due to the efforts of A.J. Gillam that we finally got a booklet of the tournament. Evidently Edward Samuel Tinsley, the chess editor of *The Times* (and who was not fond of Vera as noted elsewhere) copied all of the games in notebooks. Those notebooks were discovered after his death and turned over to Harry Golombek, the new *Times* chess editor and prominent British chess personality. Mr. Gilliam finally was able to obtain copies of the manuscripts and has produced a number of historically important tournament monographs. Notes to the games (below) appear to be those of Mr. Tinsley, who was not a strong player.

18 Menchik–George Alan Thomas
Ramsgate (1), March 30, 1929
[D78] *Neo-Grünfeld*

1. d4 ♘f6 2. c4 g6 3. g3 d5 4. ♗g2 ♗g7 5. ♘f3 0-0 6. 0-0 d×c4 7. ♘a3 c6 8. ♘×c4 ♘bd7 9. ♕c2 ♘b6 10. ♘cd2 A clever positional move ensuring the pawn advance to e4. **10. ... ♘e8 11. ♘b3 ♘d6 12. e4 ♘d7 13. ♗e3 ♘e8** Black's aimless knight moves allow Vera to complete her development with a spatial advantage to boot. [If 13. ... e5 14. d×e5 ♘×e5 15. ♘×e5 ♗×e5 16. f4 ♗g7 17. ♖ad1 ♕c7 18. ♗c5 ♖d8 19. ♕d2 ♗f8 20. e5 and wins a piece. Black must therefore abandon all hope of freeing his position—RT] **14. ♖ad1 ♕c7**

15. ♖c1 Again cleverly played, as if Black's queen goes back to d8, then ♖fd1, having gained a move. The text threatens d5. **15. ... b6** A desperate attempt to develop, but although some complications ensue, Black now loses a pawn. **16. ♗f4!** *(see diagram)*

After 16. ♗f4

[Of course, if 16. ♕×c6 ♕×c6 17. ♖×c6 ♗b7 recovering the pawn with a good game—RT] **16. ... e5** [If 16. ... ♘d6 17. e5 ♘f5 18. e6 and wins; or 16. ... ♕b7 17. e5 ♘b8 (best) 18. d5! and should win.; and lastly, if 16. ... ♕d8 17. ♕×c6 and wins—RT] **17. d×e5 ♘×e5 18. ♘×e5 ♗×e5 19. ♗×e5 ♕×e5 20. ♕×c6 ♖b8 21. ♕c3 ♕e7 22. ♘d4 ♗b7 23. ♘c6 ♗×c6 24. ♕×c6** White has systematically simplified the position and with a pawn to the good has an excellent chance of winning the end-game. **24. ... ♘g7 25. ♕c7 ♕b4 26. ♕c3 ♕e7 27. ♖fd1 ♘e6 28. ♕e5 ♖fd8 29. ♗h3** Bringing about an endgame with two rooks each. **29. ... ♖e8 30. ♗×e6 ♕×e6 31. ♕×e6 ♖×e6 32. ♖c7** Retaining the initiative and offering the exchange of the e-pawn for the opposing a-pawn. **32. ... a5 33. ♖dd7 ♖f6** [Perhaps 33. ... ♖f8 34. f3 was a little better, but White with a pawn up and control of the seventh rank would win—RT] **34. e5** Forceful play, which soon leads to a win. **34. ... ♖f5 35. e6! f×e6** [Black is compelled to accept the "Greek gifts," for if 35. ... ♖f8 36. e7 ♖e8 37. ♖d8—RT] **36. ♖g7+ ♔f8 37. ♖×h7 ♔g8 38. ♖cg7+ ♔f8 39. ♖×g6 ♖d8 40. ♖h8+ ♔f7 41. ♖×d8 ♔×g6 42. ♖d6** Black must lose another pawn, and White will then have four pawns more. An object lesson, in simple and forceful play by the lady champion. **42. ... ♖b5 1–0** (Source: Gilliam, AJ; *Ramsgate 1929*; *Chess Amateur*, W.A. Fairhurst, June 1929; notes by EST [additional notes by RT])

19 Theodore Tylor–Menchik
Ramsgate (2), April 1, 1929
[B72] *Sicilian Defense*

1. e4 c5 A rare Sicilian by Menchik in a mixed gender event as she consistently preferred the French. **2. ♘f3 ♘c6 3. d4 c×d4 4. ♘×d4 ♘f6 5. ♘c3 d6 6. ♗e2 g6 7. ♗e3 ♗g7 8. ♕d2 ♘g4 9. ♘×c6 b×c6 10. ♗×g4 ♗×g4 11. ♗d4 0–0 12. ♗×g7 ♔×g7 13. f3 ♗e6 14. h4 h5 15. 0–0–0 ♕a5 16. b3 ♖a3+ 17. ♔b1 a5 18. ♘a4 ♕b4 19. ♕e3 ♖fb8 20. ♔a1 ♕b5 21. ♕c3+ f6 22. ♖dg1 ♕e5 23. ♕×e5 f×e5 24. c4 c5 25. ♘c3 ♗d7 26. ♖b1 ♗c6 27. ♖b2 ♖b4 28. a3 ♖b7 29. ♔b1 ♖ab8 30. ♔c2 ♔f7 31. ♖hb1 ♔g7 32. ♘a2 ♔f7 33. ♔c3 ♔f6 34. b4 a×b4+ 35. a×b4 c×b4+ 36. ♘×b4 ♖c8 ½–½** (Source: Gilliam, AJ; *Ramsgate 1929*)

20 Menchik–William Winter
Ramsgate (3), April 2, 1929
[E37] *Nimzo-Indian, Classical*

1. d4 ♘f6 2. c4 e6 3. ♘c3 ♗b4 4. ♕c2 d5 5. a3 ♗×c3+ 6. ♕×c3 ♘e4 7. ♕c2 c5 8. d×c5 ♘c6 9. ♘f3 Black would meet 9. b4? with 9. ... ♕f6 **9. ... ♕a5+ 10. ♗d2 ♘×c5 11. e3 ♘×d2 12. ♘×d2 ♗d7 13. b4 ♕e7 14. ♕b2 0–0 15. ♗e2 d×c4 16. ♘×c4 b5 17. ♘e5 ♘×e5 18. ♕×e5 a5 19. ♗f3** Not 19. ♗×b5 ♗×b5 20. ♕×b5 a×b4 21. a4 ♖fb8 **19. ... ♖a7 20. b×a5 ♖c8** If 20. ... ♖×a5 there would follow 21. ♕c7 ♕d8 22. ♕d6 **21. a6 ♕c5 22. ♕×c5 ♖×c5 23. ♗b7 ♗c6 ½–½** (Source: Gilliam, AJ; *Ramsgate 1929*; notes by RT)

21 Frederick D. Yates–Menchik
Ramsgate (4), April 3, 1929

[A48] *King's Indian Defense*

Few chances were taken in this game with both players offering and taking every opportunity to trade down.

1. d4 ♘f6 2. ♘f3 g6 3. h3 ♗g7 4. ♗f4 c5 5. e3 0-0 6. ♘bd2 d6 7. c3 ♘bd7 8. ♗e2 b6 9. 0-0 ♗b7 10. ♕c2 ♖c8 11. ♖ad1 ♕c7 12. ♗h2 ♕c6 13. ♘e1 b5 14. ♗f3 ♕b6 15. ♗×b7 ♕×b7 16. ♕d3 ♕d5 17. ♕b1 c×d4 18. c×d4 ♘b6 19. ♘ef3 ♘c4 20. ♖fe1 ♘×d2 21. ♘×d2 ♖c6 22. ♘b3 ♕e4 23. ♕×e4 ♘×e4 24. f3 ♘f6 25. ♖c1 ♖fc8 *(see diagram)*

½-½ (Source: Gilliam, AJ; *Ramsgate 1929*)

Final position

22 Menchik–Reginald Michell
Ramsgate (5), April 4, 1929

[D13] *Réti Opening*

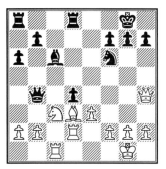

After 22. ♕h4

1. ♘f3 d5 2. c4 c6 3. c×d5 c×d5 4. d4 ♘c6 5. ♘c3 ♘f6 6. ♗f4 e6 7. e3 ♗d6 8. ♗×d6 ♕×d6 9. ♗d3 0-0 10. 0-0 ♖d8 11. ♖c1 ♗d7 12. ♕e2 ♗e8 13. ♘b5! ♕b8 14. ♖fd1 a6 15. ♘c3 ♕d6 16. ♘d2 White threatens f4 followed by ♘f3 and ♘e5 with a strong attacking position. **16. ... e5 17. d×e5 ♘×e5 18. ♘f3 ♘×f3+** Black should not take the ♗f3 as White will later be able to play ♘d4. **19. ♕×f3 ♗c6 20. ♕h3 ♕b4 21. ♖d2 d4? 22. ♕h4!** *(see diagram)*
    22. ... d×c3? [22. ... ♕b6 23. e×d4 ♖×d4? 24. ♗×h7+; 22. ... ♖d7 23. e×d4 ♖ad8 24. ♖cd1!; 22. ... ♖d6!?; 22. ... ♔h8 23. ♗b1! and the d4 pawn cannot be defended further (23. ♘b1 ♕b6 24. e4 etc.)—RT] **23. ♗×h7+!** [23. ♕×b4 c×d2 24. ♕×d2 ♗b5 25. ♖c3 ♘e4 26. ♕c2 ♘×c3 27. ♗×h7+ ♔h8 28. b×c3 g6 wins the bishop because of 29. ♗×g6 f×g6 30. ♕×g6 ♖d1 mate—RT] **23. ... ♘×h7 24. ♖×d8+! ♖×d8 25. ♕×b4** [Naturally not 25. ♕×d8+ ♘f8—RT] **25. ... c2 26. ♕e1** The c2 pawn cannot be maintained. **26. ... ♗e4 27. f3 ♗d3 28. ♕d2 ♘f8 29. ♖×c2 ♘e6 30. ♖c1 ♗f5 31. ♕a5 1-0** (Source: Gilliam, AJ; *Ramsgate 1929*; notes by EST [additional notes by RT])

23 Hubert Price–Menchik
Ramsgate (6), April 5, 1929

[E73] *King's Indian Defense*

1. d4 ♘f6 2. c4 g6 3. ♘c3 ♗g7 4. e4 d6 5. ♗e2 0-0 6. ♗e3 ♘c6 7. h3 e5 8. d5 ♘e7 9. ♕d2 ♘d7 10. g4 ♘c5 11. ♗×c5 d×c5 12. 0-0-0 b6 13. ♘f3 ♔h8? 14. ♖dg1 ♗d7 15. h4 f6? 15. ... h6 16. h5 ♖g8 17. h×g6? 17. g5!! f5 18. h6 ♗f8 19. ♘b1 f×e4 20. ♘×e5 ♗e8 21. ♕c3 ♗g7 22. h×g7+ ♖×g7+– 17. ... ♘×g6 *(see diagram)*

After 17. ... ♘×g6

18. ♖×h7+? 18. g5 ♘f4 19. g6 h6 20. ♘e1 and Black still wins **18. … ♔×h7 19. ♖h1+ ♘h4 20. ♖×h4+ ♔g6 21. d6?!** 21. ♕e3 ♖h8 22. ♖×h8 ♕×h8 23. g5 **21. … c6 22. ♔c2 ♖h8 23. ♘d1 ♗h6 24. ♘e3 ♗g5 25. ♖h5 ♗×e3 26. ♕×e3 ♗e6 27. ♘h4+ ♔f7 28. g5 ♖×h5 29. ♗×h5+ ♔g7 30. g×f6+ ♔×f6 31. ♕g3+ ♔h6 32. ♗g6 ♕f4 33. ♘f5+ ♗×f5 34. ♕×f4+ e×f4 35. ♗×f5 ♔g5 36. ♔d3 ♔f6** *(see diagram)*

37. ♔e2 ♔e5 38. d7 b5 39. b3 a5 40. ♔d3 ♔d6 41. ♔e2 b×c4 42. b×c4 a4 43. ♔f3 ♔e5 44. ♗g4 ♖b8 45. ♗f5 a3 46. ♗g4 ♔d6 47. ♔×f4 ♔e7 48. ♔g5 ♖b2 49. f4 ♖×a2 50. f5 ♖f2 51. e5 ♖×f5+ 52. ♗×f5 a2 53. ♔g6 a1♕ 0–1 (Source: Gilliam, AJ; *Ramsgate 1929*; notes by RT)

After 36. … ♔f6

24 Edward G. Sergeant–Menchik
Ramsgate (7), April 6, 1929
[C14] *French, Classical*

1. e4 e6 2. d4 d5 3. ♘c3 ♘f6 4. ♗g5 ♗e7 5. e5 ♘fd7 6. ♗×e7 ♕×e7 7. ♘b5 ♘b6 8. c3 a6 9. ♘a3 c5 10. ♘f3 ♗d7 11. ♗d3 ♘a4 12. ♕d2 ♘c6 13. d×c5 ♘×c5 14. 0–0 ♘×d3 15. ♕×d3 0–0 16. ♖ae1 b5 17. ♘c2 h6 18. ♘fd4 ♘×d4 19. ♕×d4 ♖fc8 20. ♖e3 a5 21. ♖g3 ♖c4 22. ♕d2 ♔h7 23. ♘e3 ♖c7 24. ♘g4 ♖ac8 25. ♕f4 ♖c4 26. ♕f3 ♖g8 [26. … b4? 27. ♘f6+ g×f6 28. e×f6—RT] **27. ♖e1 b4 28. ♕d3+ ♔h8 29. ♕e3 ♖e4 30. ♕d2 b×c3 31. b×c3 ♖×e1+** [31. … ♕g5 32. ♘e3 ♕×e5∓—RT] **32. ♕×e1 ♖c8 33. h3 ♖c4 34. ♖f3 ½–½** (Source: Gilliam, AJ; *Ramsgate 1929*)

Paris 1929
June 15–30, 1929

		1	2	3	4	5	6	7	8	9	10	11	12	Points	Place
1.	Tartakower, Saviely	•	1	=	=	=	=	1	=	1	1	1	=	8	1
2.	Baratz, Abraham	0	•	=	=	=	1	=	0	1	1	1	1	7	2–4
3.	Colle, Edgar	=	=	•	0	1	1	1	=	=	1	0	1	7	2–4
4.	Znosko-Borovsky, Eugene	=	=	1	•	1	1	0	=	=	=	=	1	7	2–4
5.	Tsukerman, Iosif I.	=	=	0	0	•	1	0	1	=	=	1	1	6	5–6
6.	Thomas, George A.	=	0	0	0	0	•	1	=	1	1	1	1	6	5–6
7.	Lazard, Frédéric D.	0	=	0	1	1	0	•	=	1	=	0	1	5½	7
8.	Koltanowski, George	=	1	=	=	0	=	=	•	0	=	1	0	5	8–9
9.	Schwartzmann, Leon I.	0	0	=	=	=	0	0	1	•	=	1	1	5	8–9
10.	Seitz, Jakob A.	0	0	0	=	=	0	=	=	=	•	1	1	4½	10
11.	Menchik, Vera	0	0	1	=	0	0	1	0	0	0	•	=	3	11
12.	Duchamp, Marcel	=	0	0	0	0	0	0	1	0	0	=	•	2	12

Thanks to the Ramsgate success, invitations to international tournaments became available. The first of these events was the Paris International of June 1929. The tournament was organized by a committee of Soviet expatriots and covered extensively by the French "Russian expatriot" newspaper *Poslednie Novosti* every other day. Also providing coverage were the French journals, *La Stratégie* and *Excelsior* as well as *The Times* of London with E.S. Tinsley in attendance. The event was held at the Café Harola on Place des Abesses. Prizes were awarded ranging from 1,200 francs for first to 200 francs for sixth with cash awards for wins and draws by nonprize winners.[40]

In describing the players, all of the men were listed, followed by

> And then ... one representative of the gentle sex. Miss V. Menchik, a player with a great talent, who will humble many representatives of the stronger sex. Photographers surround her, ignoring any discretion (these great artists of the dailies ignore the fact that players and women players need periods of rest and quiet.) A flash, a smile and one "thank you Madam" for the women's world champion.[41]

Although Vera's score was less than triumphant, she did have the sensational "success," to quote the press of the day, of defeating Edgar Colle and Frédéric Lazard (Belgian and Paris champions respectively) and drawing with Eugene Znosko-Borovsky and Marcel Duchamp. Both of who were vital to the holding of the event; the former being a strong former Russian and the latter being one of the world's foremost artists. A detailed account of the event is told in volume two of Vlastimil Fiala's chess biography of Marcel Duchamp (1887–1968).

25 Menchik–Eugene Znosko-Borovsky
Paris (1), June 15, 1929

[E11] *Bogo-Indian Defense*

Although the press made a big deal over this first round result, there really is not too much to be said. Menchik played solidly and Znosko-Borovsky took no steps to create any real imbalances.

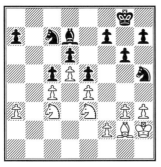

Final position

1. d4 ♘f6 2. c4 e6 3. ♘f3 ♗b4+ 4. ♗d2 ♕e7 5. ♕c2 b6 6. a3 ♗×d2+ 7. ♘b×d2 ♗b7 8. g3 d6 9. ♗g2 ♘bd7 10. 0-0 0-0 11. e4 e5 12. ♖fe1 ♖fe8 13. ♖ad1 g6 14. h3 c5 15. d5 ♘h5 16. ♘f1 ♕f8 17. ♘e3 ♕g7 18. ♘h4 ♘df6 19. ♔h2 ♗c8 20. b4 ♗d7 21. b×c5 b×c5 22. ♘f3 ♖ab8 23. ♖b1 ♕f8 24. ♘d2 ♖×b1 25. ♖×b1 ♖b8 26. ♖b2 ♕d8 27. ♖×b8 ♕×b8 28. ♕b1 ♕×b1 29. ♘×b1 ♘e8 30. ♘c3 ♘c7 *(see diagram)*

½–½ (Source: Fiala, *Chess Biography of Marcel Duchamp*, 2004)

26 Abraham Baratz–Menchik
Paris (2), June 16, 1929

[D61] *Queen's Gambit Declined Classical*

1. d4 d5 2. c4 e6 3. ♘c3 ♘f6 4. ♗g5 ♘bd7 5. e3 ♗e7 6. ♘f3 0-0 7. ♕c2 h6 8. ♗h4 c5 9. c×d5 e×d5 10. ♗e2 ♖e8 11. 0-0 a6 12. ♖fd1 c4 13. a4 ♕c7 14. ♘e5 ♘×e5 15. d×e5 ♕×e5 16. ♗×f6 ♗×f6 17. ♘×d5 ♗e6?± 17. ... ♕×b2= 18. ♕×c4 *(see diagram)*

18. ... ♗×d5? 18. ... ♕×b2= 19. ♕×d5 ♕×b2 20. ♗c4 ♖e7 21. ♖ab1 ♕e5?! 21. ... ♕c2 22. ♖×b7 at this point Baratz firmly took control of the game. Though Menchik defended stolidly, no more chances to get back into it were given. 22. ... ♕×d5 23. ♗×d5 ♖a7 24. ♖b6 a5 25. ♖c1

After 18. ♕×c4

♖ec7 26. ♗c6 ♖a8 27. ♕f1 ♖ac8 28. ♔e2 ♗e7 29. ♖c4 ♗b4 30. g4 ♔f8 31. h4 ♗e7 32. h5 ♗b4 33. f4 ♗e7 34. e4 ♗d8 35. ♔d3 ♗e7 36. ♗d5 ♖×c4 37. ♗×c4 ♖d8+ 38. ♗d5 ♖d7 39. ♔c4 ♗d8 40. ♖a6 ♖c7+ 41. ♗c6 ♖c8 42. ♔d5 ♗c7 43. e5 ♖d8+ 44. ♔e4 ♖d1 45. ♖a8+ ♖d8 46. ♖a6 ♖d1 47. ♗d5 ♖e1+ 48. ♔f5 ♖d1 49. ♖a7 ♖×d5 50. ♖×c7 ♖d4 51. ♖c8+ ♔e7 52. ♖g8 ♖×a4 53. ♖×g7 ♖b4 54. ♖g8 ♖b5 55. ♖a8 ♔d7 56. g5 ♔e7 57. g×h6 1–0 (Source: Fiala, *Chess Biography of Marcel Duchamp*, 2004; notes by RT)

27 Menchik–Jakob Adolf Seitz
Paris (3), June 20, 1929
[D30] *Queen's Gambit Declined*

Vera played without a strong plan at the start and with modest errors on moves 13 and 14 she fell into inferiority which she was not able to extract herself despite long resistance.

1. d4 d5 2. c4 e6 3. ♘f3 ♘d7 4. ♗f4 d×c4 5. ♕a4 ♗d6 6. ♗g5 f6 7. ♗d2 ♘e7 8. e4 0–0 9. ♕×c4 ♔h8 10. ♘c3 e5 11. ♘b5 e×d4 12. ♘×d6 c×d6 13. ♕×d4?! [13. ♘×d4— RT] **13. ... ♘c5 14. ♗c4?** [14. ♗f4 ♖e8∓—RT] **14. ... ♘c6 15. ♕e3 ♖e8 16. ♗d3 ♘×d3+ 17. ♕×d3 d5 18. ♗e3 d×e4 19. ♕×d8 ♖×d8 20. ♘d2 f5 21. 0–0 ♗e6 22. ♖fc1 ♖d3 23. ♘f1 ♖ad8 24. ♘g3 h6 25. h4 ♔h7 26. ♘e2 ♖3d6 27. ♔h2 ♗f7 28. ♖c5 g6 29. h5 g5 30. ♖×f5 ♗×h5 31. ♘g3 ♗g6 32. ♖c5 ♖8d7 33. a3 b6 34. ♖c3 ♘e7 35. ♖c4 ♘d5 36. ♘×e4 ♖e6 37. ♘g3 ♘×e3 38. f×e3 ♖×e3 39. ♖ac1 h5 40. ♖c7 ♖ee7 41. ♖×d7 ♖×d7 42. ♖e1 h4 43. ♘f1 ♖f7 44. ♔g1 ♔h6 45. ♖e5 ♖f5 46. ♖e7 ♖b5 47. ♖e2 g4 48. ♖d2 ♔g5 49. ♘e3 ♗e4 50. b4 ♔f4 51. ♘c4 ♖d5** (*see diagram*)
0–1 (Source: Fiala, *Chess Biography of Marcel Duchamp*, 2004)

Final position

28 George Koltanowski–Menchik
Paris (4), June 21, 1929
[D31] *Semi-Slav*

1. d4 d5 2. c4 c6 Despite the prevalence of the Slav at this time and in the upcoming World Championships by Max Euwe, this was a rate essaying of this opening by Menchik who mostly played the Queen's Gambit Declined. **3. e3 ♘f6 4. ♘c3 e6 5. c×d5 e×d5 6. ♗d3 ♗d6 7. ♘f3 ♗g4 8. h3 ♗h5 9. ♕c2 ♘bd7 10. ♗d2 ♖c8 11. ♘e5 ♗g6!?** [The line 11. ... ♘×e5 12. d×e5 ♗×e5 13. f4 ♗×c3 14. ♗×c3 ♘d7 leads to a cramped position with little play for Black; better appears to be 11. ... ♗×e5 12. d×e5 ♘×e5 13. ♗f5 ♗g6∓—RT] **12. f4 ♗×d3 13. ♕×d3 0–0 14. 0–0 ♘e8?! 15. g4 ♗×e5 16. f×e5 ♘c7 17. ♘a4 ♘e6 18. ♔g2 b6 19. ♖ac1 c5 20. ♘c3** (*see diagram*)

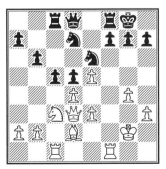

After 20. ♘c3

20. ... c4? This move serves no purpose other than to force the White queen to its best square and essentially end the game. [Play 20. ... ♘c7 and we still have a game—RT] **21. ♕f5 ♘c7 22. e4 d×e4 23. ♘×e4 f6 24. ♗b4 ♘d5 25. ♕e6+ 1–0** (Source: Fiala, *Chess Biography of Marcel Duchamp*, 2004; *Poslednie Novosti*, June 21, 1929 [additional notes by RT])

29　Menchik–Saviely Tartakower

Paris (5), June 23, 1929

[A51] *Budapest Gambit, Fajarowicz Variation*

**1. d4 ♘f6 2. c4 e5 3. ♘f3 e4 4. ♘fd2 d5 5. c×d5 ♕×d5
6. e3 ♗b4 7. ♘c3 ♗×c3 8. b×c3 0-0 9. ♕b3 ♕g5 10. ♗a3
♖e8 11. g3 b6 12. ♗g2 ♗a6 13. c4 ♘c6 14. ♕c3 ♖ad8
15. 0-0 h5** *(see diagram)*

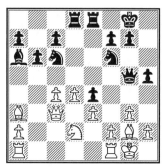

After 15. ... h5

This is one of Menchik's few lines in the ECO (A51 foot-
note 1) and is evaluated as –/+. Fritz 12 is more inclined to
call it even. At any rate this declined line of the Budapest is
quite rare. **16. f4 e×f3 17. ♖×f3 ♘g4 18. ♘f1** [Better is
18. ♘b3 ♗b7 19. ♗c1—RT] **18. ... ♘a5 19. h3 ♘f6 20. ♘d2 ♗b7 21. d5 c6 22. e4 ♘×e4
23. ♘×e4 ♖×e4 24. ♗c1 ♕g6 25. ♗f1 c×d5 26. ♗d3 d×c4 27. ♗×e4 ♖d1+ 28. ♔f2
♕×e4 29. ♗h6 ♕×f3+ 30. ♕×f3 ♗×f3 31. ♖×d1 ♗×d1 0-1** (Source: Fiala, *Chess Biography
of Marcel Duchamp*, 2004; *La Stratégie*, 1929, p. 155; *L'Echequier*, 1929, p. 291 [additional note by RT])

30　Menchik–Iosef Tsukerman

Paris (6), June 24, 1929

[D61] *Queen's Gambit Declined, Classical*

**1. d4 ♘f6 2. c4 e6 3. ♘c3 d5 4. ♗g5 ♘bd7 5. e3 ♗e7 6. ♘f3 c6 7. ♕c2 0-0 8. ♖d1
a6 9. ♗d3 b5 10. c×d5 c×d5 11. 0-0 ♗b7 12. ♘e5 ♖c8 13. ♕b1 h6 14. ♗×f6 g×f6
15. ♘×d7 ♕×d7 16. e4 b4 17. ♘e2 ♗d6 18. f4 d×e4 19. ♗×e4 f5 20. ♗×b7 ♕×b7
21. d5 ♖fd8 22. d×e6 f×e6 23. ♔h1 ♗f8 24. ♘d4 ♖d6 25. ♘f3 ♕e4 26. ♖fe1 ♕×f4
27. ♖×d6 ♗×d6 28. ♕d3 ♖c1 29. g3 ♖×e1+ 30. ♘×e1 ♕f2 31. ♘f3 ♗c5 32. b3 a5
33. ♕d8+ ♗f8 34. ♘d2 ♔f7 35. ♕d3 ♗c5 36. ♘f3 ♔e7 37. ♕d1 ♕×a2 38. ♘e5 a4
39. b×a4 ♕d5+ 40. ♕×d5 e×d5 41. ♘f3 ♗e3 42. ♘e1 b3 43. ♘d3 ♗d4 0-1** (Source:
Fiala, *Chess Biography of Marcel Duchamp*, 2004)

31　Frédéric Lazard–Menchik

Paris (7), June 25, 1929

[C30] *King's Gambit Declined*

This has to be one of the craziest games ever between two masters of the 20th century in
a major event. One can only assume that Lazard had an opinion similar to that of Becker in
Carlsbad—and he paid the price. Menchik's essaying of From's Gambit certainly led to a wild
game.... Neither C30 nor A02, we do know that White quickly gave away both the initiative
and space and seemed hell bent on trying to use sheer uncon-
trolled power to force his will on her. **1. f4 e5?! 2. f×e5 d6
3. ♘f3 d×e5 4. e4 ♘f6 5. ♘c3 ♘c6 6. d3 ♗g4 7. ♗e3
♕d7 8. ♗e2 0-0-0 9. 0-0 ♔b8 10. a3 ♗×f3 11. ♖×f3?!**
11. ♗×f3 **11. ... ♘d4 12. ♖f1 ♗c5 13. ♔h1 ♗b6** 13. ...
♘b3!? **14. ♗g5 ♕c6 15. ♗h5 ♖hf8 16. ♘d5 ♘×d5
17. e×d5 ♖×d5 18. c3** Better is 18. ♗e7 ♖h8 19. c3 **18. ...
g6 19. ♗g4 h5 20. ♗×h5?** why commit to a long term loss.
Despite being in trouble, White still had play with c4. **20. ...
g×h5 21. c×d4 ♕g6 22. h4 ♖×d4 23. ♕e1 ♕×d3?** 23. ...
f6–+ **24. ♕×e5 ♕e4** *(see diagram)*

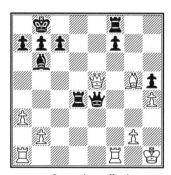

After 24. ... ♕e4

25. ☐×f7?? 25. ☐ae1 ♕e5 (Not 25. ... ♕×h4+ 26. ♗×h4 ☐×h4+ 27. ♔h2 ☐×h2+ 28. ♔×h2±) 26. ☐×e5 c6= **25. ... ♕×h4+ 26. ♗×h4 ☐×h4+ 27. ♔h2 ☐×h2+ 28. ♔×h2 ☐×f7 29. ☐e1 ♔c8 30. ☐e5 ♗d4 31. ☐×h5 ♗×b2 32. ☐h3 c5 33. g4 c4 34. g5 ♗e5+ 35. ♔g2 c3 0–1** (Source: Fiala, *Chess Biography of Marcel Duchamp*, 2004; *La Stratégie*; notes by RT)

32 Menchik–Edgar Colle
Paris (8), June 27, 1929
[E43] *Nimzo-Indian, Rubinstein Variation*

1. d4 ♘f6 2. c4 e6 3. ♘c3 ♗b4 4. e3 ♗×c3+ 5. b×c3 b6 6. ♗d3 ♗b7 7. ♘f3 ♘e4 8. ♕c2 f5 9. 0-0 0-0 10. ♘d2 ♕h4 11. f3 ♘f6 12. ☐b1 ♘c6 13. ♕d1 ♕h8 14. ♕e1 ♕h5 15. ♕g3 d6 16. ♗a3 ☐fe8 17. c5 ♕h6 18. ♕f2?! 18. f4 d×c5 19. ♗×c5= **18. ... d×c5 19. ♗×c5 ♘d5 20. ♗a3 ♘×e3 21. ☐fe1 ♘d5 22. c4?** 22. ♘f1 ♘×c3 23. ☐bc1 ♘d5 24. ♗b5∓ **22. ... ♘f4 23. ♗f1 ♘×d4?** 23. ... e5 24. d5 ♘d4∓ **24. ♕×d4 ☐ad8** *(see diagram)*

After 24. ... ☐ad8

25. ♕e3 ☐×d2 26. ♗c1 ☐ed8 27. ♗×d2 ☐×d2 28. ♔h1 ☐×a2 29. ☐bd1 ♔g8 30. ☐d8+ ♔f7 31. ☐d7+ ♔g6 32. ☐×c7 ♕g5 33. ♕e5 ♔h6 34. ☐×g7 ♕×g7 35. ♕×f4+ ♔h5 36. ☐×e6 ☐×g2 37. ♕×f5+ ♔h4 38. ♕f4+ ♔h5 39. ☐e5+ 1–0 (Source: Fiala, *Chess Biography of Marcel Duchamp*, 2004; *L'Echequier*, 1929, p. 291; notes by RT)

33 Marcel Duchamp–Menchik
Paris (9), June 28, 1929
[D13] *Slav, Exchange*

When one looks for the reason Duchamp threw away his winning chances in this game it may have been because of his duties as one of the organizers. Of course Menchik may have made more than one poor move due to her sightseeing. Everyone has an excuse!

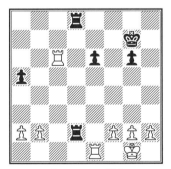

After 29. ... ☐d2

1. d4 d5 2. c4 c6 3. c×d5 c×d5 4. ♘f3 ♘c6 5. ♘c3 ♘f6 6. ♗f4 e6 7. e3 ♗d6 8. ♗×d6 ♕×d6 9. ♗d3 0-0 10. 0-0 ☐d8 11. ♘b5 ♕b8 12. ☐c1 ♗d7 13. ♕e2 a6 14. ♘c3 ♕d6 15. e4 d×e4 16. ♘×e4 ♘×e4 17. ♕×e4 g6 18. ♕h4 ♔g7 19. ♘g5 h6?? [19. ... h5—RT] **20. ♕×h6+ ♔×h6 21. ♘×f7+ ♔g7 22. ♘×d6 ♘b4 23. ♗e4 ♗c6 24. ♗×c6 b×c6 25. ☐c4 ☐×d6 26. ☐×b4 a5 27. ☐c4 ☐ad8 28. ☐e1 ☐×d4 29. ☐×c6 ☐d2** *(see diagram)* **30. g3?** [30. ☐b6 ☐f8 31. ☐f1±—RT] **30. ... ☐f8 31. f4 ☐h8 32. h4 ☐b8 33. b3 ☐×a2 34. ☐e×e6 ☐×b3 35. ☐×g6+ ♔f7 36. ☐b6 ☐d3 37. ☐bd6 ☐b3 ½–½** (Source: Fiala, *Chess Biography of Marcel Duchamp*, 2004; *Excelsior*, June 30, 1929; *La Stratégie*, 1929, p. 172)

(R30) Menchik–Leon Schwartzmann
Paris (10), June 29, 1929
Game not available 0–1

34 George Alan Thomas–Menchik
Paris (11), June 30, 1929
[D46] *Semi-Slav*

This game shows that Vera could not only win miniatures against Thomas, but lose them as well. The nature of the loss, however (she had the advantage until her last move), presents one of the conundrums of her play. She could blunder to anyone at anytime. One can only speculate as to the reason.

1. d4 d5 2. ♘f3 ♘f6 3. c4 c6 4. e3 e6 5. ♗d3 ♘bd7 6. 0–0 ♗e7 7. ♘bd2 0–0 8. e4 d×e4 9. ♘×e4 b6 10. ♕e2 ♗b7 11. ♖d1 ♕c7 12. ♗g5 c5 13. ♖ac1 ♔h8 14. ♗b1 ♖ad8 15. ♘c3?! c×d4 16. ♘b5 ♕b8 17. ♘b×d4 h6 18. ♗×f6 ♘×f6 19. ♘e5 *(see diagram)*

After 19. ♘e5

19. ... ♕a8?? [19. ... ♗d6∓—RT] **20. ♘×e6 1–0** (Source: Fiala, *Chess Biography of Marcel Duchamp*, 2004; *Excelsior*, June 30, 1929; *La Stratégie*, 1929, p. 172)

Carlsbad 1929
July 31–August 28, 1929

	1	2	3	4	5	6	7	8	9	10	11	12	13	14	15	16	17	18	19	20	21	22	Pts.	Place
1. Nimzowitsch, Aron	•	=	1	=	=	1	1	1	=	=	1	=	=	1	=	1	0	1	=	1	=	1	15	1
2. Capablanca, José	=	•	0	=	1	=	=	=	=	=	1	1	1	=	1	0	1	1	1	1	=	1	14½	2–3
3. Spielmann, Rudolf	0	1	•	0	=	=	=	=	1	0	=	1	1	=	1	1	=	1	1	1	1	1	14½	2–3
4. Rubinstein, Akiba	=	=	1	•	=	=	=	=	1	1	1	=	=	=	1	=	=	1	=	0	=	1	13½	4
5. Becker, Albert	=	0	=	=	•	1	1	1	0	0	1	=	=	=	=	1	=	1	1	=	0		12	5–7
6. Euwe, Machgielis	0	=	=	=	0	•	0	=	=	1	=	1	=	1	=	=	1	=	=	1	1		12	5–7
7. Vidmar, Milan, Sr.	0	=	=	=	0	1	•	=	=	=	=	1	=	1	0	=	=	0	1	1	1	1	12	5–7
8. Bogoljubow, Efim D.	0	=	=	=	0	=	=	•	=	=	=	1	0	0	1	1	1	0	=	1	1	1	11½	8
9. Grünfeld, Ernst F.	=	=	0	0	1	=	=	=	•	=	=	1	0	1	=	=	0	1	=	1	=	1	11	9
10. Canal, Esteban	=	=	1	0	1	0	=	=	=	•	1	0	0	=	=	=	0	1	0	=	1	1	10½	10–11
11. Matisons, Hermanis	0	0	=	0	0	=	=	=	=	0	•	1	1	1	0	1	1	1	=	0	=	1	10½	10–11
12. Colle, Edgar	=	0	0	=	=	0	0	0	1	1	0	•	1	=	1	0	=	0	1	1	1		10	12–15
13. Maróczy, Géza	=	0	0	=	=	=	1	0	1	0	0	•	=	0	0	1	1	1	=	1		10	12–15
14. Tartakower, Saviely	0	=	=	=	=	0	1	=	0	=	=	•	=	=	=	=	=	=	1		10	12–15
15. Treybal, Karel	=	0	0	0	=	0	1	0	=	=	1	0	1	=	•	=	=	0	1	1	=	1	10	12–15
16. Sämisch, Friedrich	0	1	0	=	=	=	=	=	0	1	=	0	=	1	=	•	=	0	=	=	1	0	9½	16–17
17. Yates, Frederick D.	1	0	=	=	0	=	=	0	0	1	0	0	0	=	=	=	•	1	=	1	1	1	9½	16–17
18. Johner, Paul F.	0	0	0	0	=	0	1	1	=	0	0	1	=	=	1	1	0	•	=	0	=	1	9	18–19
19. Marshall, Frank J.	=	0	0	=	0	=	0	=	0	1	=	0	=	0	=	=	=	=	•	1	1	1	9	18–19
20. Gilg, Karl	0	0	0	1	0	=	0	0	=	=	1	1	0	=	0	=	=	1	0	•	=	=	8	20
21. Thomas, George A.	=	=	0	=	=	0	0	0	0	0	=	0	=	=	=	0	0	=	0	=	•	1	6	21
22. Menchik, Vera	0	0	0	0	1	0	0	0	=	0	0	0	0	0	0	1	0	0	0	=	0	•	3	22

Carlsbad 1929 was the strongest post–World War I tournament up to its time. With the exception of World Champion Alekhine, who was preparing for his first title defense against Bogoljubow, and Emanuel Lasker, all of the top players were there. Prizes ranged from 20,000

Kronen for first place (about £125) to 3,000 for eighth place. The tournament was held at the Kurhaus for the first eight games before moving to the more modern and luxurious Hotel Imperial. The time control was a generous 30 moves in two hours followed by 15 moves per hour.

Spielmann jumped to an early lead, but in the end Nimzowitsch was out ahead. Capablanca started slowly as was his want, but worked himself into contention for the title only to lose a late game to Spielmann. After the tournament Nimzowitsch wrote a well received book about the event, but it is very limited in games and gives almost no human interest material. The games can be found in Jack Spence's old books, but anyone wanting much information is best served by chess articles in the chess press or mainstream media.

Alekhine in an article about the tournament made reference to Menchik as follows:

> I have suspended final judgment so far about Miss Vera Menchik of Russia, because the greatest caution and objectivity in criticism are necessary regarding anyone so extraordinary. However, after 15 rounds it is certain that she is an absolute exception in her sex. She is so highly talented for chess that with further work and experience at tournaments she will surely succeed in developing from her present stage of an average player into a high classed international champion.
>
> She indisputably has attained her three points against the strong masters, but it is little known to the public that she has also attained superior positions against Euwe, Treybal, Colle and Dr. Vidmar. She was beaten by Dr. Vidmar only after a nine hour match. It is the chess world's duty to grant her every possibility for development.[42]

It was, of course, at this event that the famous Vera Menchik Club was formed at the ill-advised instigation of Alburt Becker. (See Appendix 1.)

35 Frederick D. Yates–Menchik
Carlsbad (1), July 31, 1929

[C14] *French, Classical*

1. e4 e6 2. d4 d5 3. ♘c3 ♘f6 4. ♗g5 ♗e7 5. e5 ♘fd7 6. ♗×e7 ♕×e7 7. ♕d2 a6 8. ♘d1 c5 9. c3 ♘c6 10. f4 0-0 11. ♘f3 b5 12. ♗d3 ♘b6 13. 0-0 ♗d7 14. ♕f2 f6 15. e×f6 ♖×f6 16. g3 c×d4 17. c×d4 ♘b4 18. ♗b1 ♖c8 19. ♘e3 ♘c4 20. ♘g4 ♖ff8 21. ♖e1 ♘d6 22. ♘ge5 g6 23. ♘g5 ♖f6 24. ♘g4 ♖ff8 25. ♕g2 ♘c6 26. ♕f2 ♘e8 27. h4 ♘f6 28. ♘h2 ♕b4 29. ♘gf3 ♔g7 30. a3 ♕d6 31. ♗d3 ♖c7 32. ♖e2 ♖fc8 33. ♖ae1 ♘d8 34. ♕e3 ♗e8 35. ♘e5 ♘d7 36. ♘hg4 ♔h8 37. ♖h2 ♕f8 38. ♘×d7 ♖×d7 39. ♘e5 (*see diagram*)

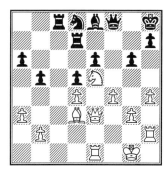

After 39. ♘e5

39. ... ♖g7? 39. ... ♖dc7± **40. ♘f3?!** 40. ♖c1 ♖gc7 41. ♖×c7 ♖×c7 42. ♖c2± **40. ... ♕d6 41. ♘g5 ♗f7?!** 41. ... ♖gc7 42. ♔h1± **42. ♘×f7+** 42. ♖c2!? ♖×c2 43. ♗×c2 **42. ... ♖×f7 43. h5 g×h5 44. ♖×h5 ♖g7 45. ♔f2 ♕f8** No better is 45. ... ♖cc7 46. ♖eh1 b4 47. ♖h6+– **46. ♕e5 ♔g8 47. ♖eh1 ♖cc7 48. ♖g5 ♖×g5 49. ♕×c7 ♖g7 50. ♗×h7+ ♔h8 51. ♕e5 ♕e7 52. ♖h6 1-0** (Source: Spence, *Carlsbad 1929*, 1956; notes by RT)

36 Paul F. Johner–Menchik
Carlsbad (2), August 1, 1929

[D63] *Queen's Gambit Declined, Classical*

1. d4 d5 2. c4 e6 3. ♘c3 ♘f6 4. ♗g5 ♘bd7 5. e3 ♗e7 6. ♘f3 0-0 7. ♖c1 b6 8. c×d5 e×d5 9. ♕a4 c5? [9. ... ♗b7 10. ♗d3 c5±—RT] **10. ♕c6 ♖b8 11. ♘×d5 ♘×d5 12. ♕×d5**

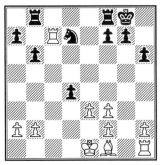

After 18. Rc7

♗b7 13. ♗×e7 ♕×e7 14. ♕g5 ♕×g5 15. ♘×g5 h6 16. ♘f3 ♗×f3 17. g×f3 c×d4 18. Rc7 *(see diagram)*

18. ... ♘e5?! [18. ... Rfd8!? 19. e×d4 (19. R×a7?! Rbc8 20. e×d4 ♘f8 21. Rb7? (21. Ra4 ♘e6 22. Rc4 ♘×d4 23. R×c8 R×c8=) 21. ... R×d4∓) 19. ... ♘f6 20. ♗c4 Rbc8 21. ♗×f7+ ♔f8 22. R×c8 R×c8 23. ♗b3±—RT] 19. f4 ♘g6 20. R×a7 Rbc8 21. ♔d2 d×e3+ 22. f×e3 Rfd8+ 23. ♗d3 Rc6 24. ♔e2 ♘f8?! 25. Rd1 ♘e6 26. ♗e4 R×d1 27. ♔×d1 Rc5 28. Ra8+ ♘f8 29. Rb8 Rb5 30. ♔c2 g6 31. ♔c3 ♔g7 32. b4 Rh5 33. R×b6 R×h2 34. a4 Ra2 35. a5 ♘e6 36. ♗d5 Ra3+ 37. ♗b3 1-0 (Source: Spence, *Carlsbad 1929*, 1956)

37 Menchik–Alburt Becker
[A85] Dutch Defense by transposition

1. d4 d5 2. Nf3 Nf6 3. c4 c6 4. Nc3 e6 5. e3 Ne4 An independent idea. 6. Bd3 [A terrible faux-pas would be 6. N×e4 d×e4 7. Ne5 (better in any event 7. Nd2 f5) 7. ... Bb4+ 8. Bd2 B×d2+ 9. Q×d2 f6 10. Ng4 h5 appropriating the knight—RT] 6. ... f5 This deferred stonewall formation leads to a difficult game for Black. It is playable in this position because White's QB also remains shut in. 7. Ne5 Counter-stonewall. A splendid idea, 7. ... Qh4 [More enterprising than 7. ... Qf6—RT] 8. 0–0 Nd7 9. f4 Be7 10. Bd2 N×e5 A less assertive continuation is 10. ... 0–0. 11. d×e5 [Better than 11. f×e5 which would enlarge Black's field of action—RT] 11. ... Bc5 12. B×e4 f×e4 [12. ... d×e4 13. b4 B×b4 14. N×e4—RT] 13. Qb3 Threat: 14. c×d5 e×d5 15. ♘×d5 winning a pawn. 13. ... Qd8 [Not 13. ... 0–0 14. c×d5 e×d5 (or 14. ... c×d5 15. N×d5 etc.; or 14. ... R×f4 15. Na4 and wins.) 15. N×e4 etc.; against 13. ... Qe7 14. Na4 as in the text, would still prevent Black from castling, e.g. 14. ... 0–0 15. N×c5 Q×c5 16. Bb4 etc.—RT] 14. Na4 Be7 15. Bb4 b6 16. B×e7 Q×e7 17. c×d5 e×d5 Hoping to obtain a well balanced position by ♗b7 and c5, but White prevents this important advance of the c-pawn. Better would be 17. ... c×d5 with a cramped but playable game. 18. Rac1 Bb7 [After 18. ... Ba6 White would not play 19. R×c6 B×f1 20. Q×d5 Rd8 21. Qb3 Rd3 etc., but simply 19. Rfd1 maintaining the pressure—RT] 19. Nc3 Qf7 Overprotecting the d-pawn with a view to 20. ... c5. He can play neither 19. ... 0–0 nor 19. ... ♕e3, on account of ♘×e4 20. Qb4 Rd8 [20. ... Qe7 because of 21. Q×e7+ K×e7 22. N×d5+ c×d5 23. Rc7+ followed by R×b7.; Nor would 20. ... Qf8 21. Q×f8+ R×f8 be desirable 22. b4 etc.; whilst 20. ... 0–0–0 is too provocative; against 20. ... c5 the liquidation by 21. Qb5+ Qd7 22. Q×d7+ K×d7 23. Rfd1 Ke6 24. b4 Rhc8 25. Nb5 would still keep the Black forces at bay—RT] 21. Rfd1 Ba8 [Not yet 21. ... Qe7 by reason of 22. Qa4 winning a pawn; best now or on the next move is 21. ... h5 followed by Rh6—RT] 22. h3 Qe7 an illusory relief. 23. Q×e7+ K×e7 24. b4 Rd7 [If 24. ... Rc8 in order to play the key move ... c5; then—RT] 25. Rd2 Rhd8 26. Ne2 Rc8 27. Rdc2 *(see diagram)*

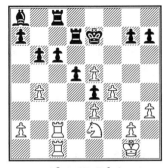

After 27. Rdc2

27. ... Rdc7 28. Nd4 The mobile knight is manifestly superior to the imprisoned bishop. 28. ... g6 [28. ... c5 29. f5—RT] 29. Nb5 Rd7 30. Kf2 [Methodical procedure. The hasty 30. Nd6 would allow the liberating sacrifice of the exchange by 30. ... R×d6 31. e×d6+ K×d6 and Black's position becomes

tenable—RT] **30. … h6** Black is reduced to makeshift moves. If his rook on c8 moves, 31. ♘d4 wins the dc pawn. If 31. ♖dd8, then equally 31. ♘d4, and if 30. … ♖b7 31. ♘d6, etc. Finally, if 30. … ♗b7 31. ♘×a7 ♖a8 32. ♘×c6+ ♗×c6 33. ♖×c6 ♖×a2+ 34. ♖1c2 with a definite advantage. **31. g4** Preparing the breakthrough. **31. … a6 32. Nd4 Rdc7 33. f5** The deluge! **33. … g5 34. Kg3 Bb7** [If 34. … c5 35. Ne6—RT] **35. h4 g×h4+** Or else there follows 36. h×g5 h×g5 37. ♖h1, a turning maneuver which wins easily. **36. K×h4 Kf7 37. Kh5 a5** Desperation. **38. b×a5 b×a5 39. Nb5 Rd7 40. e6+ 1–0** (Source: Spence, *Carlsbad 1929*, 1956; notes by S. Tartakower in *500 Master Games of Chess* [additional notes by RT])

38 Max Euwe–Menchik
Carlsbad (4), August 4, 1929
[D55] *Queen's Gambit Declined*

As much as anyone, Euwe is responsible for Menchik's historical reputation. She had a lifetime record of +2 –1 =1 against him and in this, their first game, she had a winning position for some time and even later missed a draw.

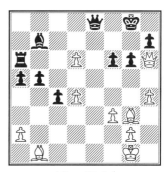

After 28. h4

1. d4 d5 2. c4 e6 3. ♘c3 ♘f6 4. ♗g5 ♘bd7 5. e3 ♗e7 6. ♘f3 0–0 7. ♖c1 b6 8. c×d5 e×d5 9. ♗d3 ♗b7 10. 0–0 c5 11. ♕e2 ♘e4 12. ♗f4 ♘×c3 13. b×c3 c4 14. ♗b1 b5 15. ♘e5 a5 16. ♕f3 ♘×e5 17. ♗×e5 ♖a6 18. ♕h3 g6 19. ♕h6 f6 20. ♗g3 ♕e8 21. f3 ♗a3 22. ♖ce1?! ♗b2 23. e4 ♗×c3 24. e×d5 ♗×e1 25. ♖×e1 ♕f7 26. d6 ♖e8 27. ♖×e8+ ♕×e8 28. h4 *(see diagram)*
      28. … ♗d5?! 28. … ♕f8 29. ♕f4 (29. ♕×f8+ ♔×f8 30. h5 g×h5 31. ♗f5 ♗c6 32. d5 ♗×d5 33. d7 ♔e7 34. ♗c7 ♖a8–+) 29. … ♗c8–+ **29. h5 ♖a7?** 29. … ♗f7 30. h×g6 ♗×g6 31. ♗×g6 ♕×g6 32. d7 ♕×h6 33. d8♕+ ♕f8∓ **30. h×g6 h×g6 31. ♗×g6 ♕e6 32. ♕f4 ♗c6 33. ♗f5 ♕f7 34. ♕g4+ ♕g7 35. ♗e6+ ♔f8 36. ♕h4 b4??** 36. … ♗d7 37. ♗f4 ♔e8 38. ♗×d7+ ♔×d7= **37. ♗f4 ♔e8 38. ♕h5+ ♔d8 39. ♕c5 ♖a6 40. d5 f5 41. d×c6 ♕a1+ 42. ♔h2 ♕h8+ 43. ♔g3 ♕g7+ 44. ♔h4 ♕h7+ 45. ♔g5 ♕g7+ 46. ♔×f5 ♕h7+ 47. ♔g4 1–0** (Source: Spence, *Carlsbad 1929*, 1956; notes by RT)

39 Menchik–Karel Treybal
Carlsbad (5), August 5, 1929
[D38] *Queen's Gambit Declined, Ragozin Defense*

After 43. … ♖d6

1. d4 d5 2. ♘f3 ♘f6 3. c4 e6 4. ♗g5 h6 5. ♗×f6 ♗b4+ 6. ♘c3 ♗×c3+ 7. b×c3 ♕×f6 8. ♕b3 c6 9. e3 ♘d7 10. ♗e2 0–0 11. c×d5 e×d5 12. 0–0 g6 13. a4 ♕d6 14. c4 d×c4 15. ♗×c4 ♘b6 16. ♗d3 ♗e6 17. ♕b1 ♔g7 18. ♘e5 ♘d5 19. ♖c1 ♗c8 20. ♕b2 ♖b8 21. ♖ab1 ♗e6 22. a5 ♘e7 23. e4 f6 24. ♘f3 ♖fd8 25. h3 ♕f4 26. ♕b4 ♕d6 27. ♕×d6 ♖×d6 28. ♗c4 28. ♔f1!? **28. … ♗×c4 29. ♖×c4 ♕f7 30. ♖cb4 ♖d7 31. ♔f1 ♘c8 32. ♘e1** Better is 32. ♖c1 **32. … ♘d6 33. f3 f5 33. … ♘b5! 34. ♘d3 ♔g7 35. ♘e5 ♖c7 36. ♘c4 ♘b5 37. e×f5 g×f5 38. ♘e3 ♖f7 39. ♖c1 ♖e8 40. ♔f2 a6 41. ♖c5 f4 42. ♘g4 ♖d8 43. ♖h5 ♖d6** *(see diagram)*

44. ♖h4? 44. ♘e5 ♖e7∓ **44. ... ♖e7?!** 44. ... ♖f5 **45. d5 c×d5 46. ♖×f4 d4 47. ♖e4 ♖×e4 48. f×e4 ♘c3 49. e5 ♖d5 50. e6 ♘e4+ 51. ♔f3 ♘g5+ 52. ♔e2 d3+ 53. ♔d1 ♘e4?** Best is 53. ... ♖×a5 **54. e7?** 54. ♘e3 ♖e5 55. ♘f5+ ♔g6 56. ♘d4 and Black will have to fight all over again to get his win **54. ... ♖×a5 55. ♔c1 d2+ 56. ♔c2 ♖c5+ 0–1** (Source: Spence, *Carlsbad 1929*, 1956; notes by RT)

40   Aron Nimzowitsch–Menchik
Carlsbad (6), August 6, 1929
[C02] *French, Advance*

With mentors like Maróczy and, indirectly, Tarrasch it is no wonder that Menchik was not really comfortable in the hypermodern genre. The closest she came was the occasional essaying of the King's Indian or Grünfeld. In this game she faced Nimzowitsch playing his own variation of an old line of the French Defense.

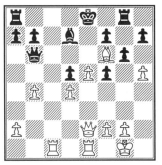
After 22. c×d4

1. e4 e6 2. d4 d5 3. e5 c5 4. ♕g4 The Nimzowitsch Variation **4. ... c×d4 5. ♘f3 ♘c6 6. ♗d3 ♕a5+ 7. ♘bd2 ♘ge7 8. 0-0 ♘g6 9. ♖e1 ♗e7?!** 9. ... ♕c7 **10. h4 ♗f8 11. h5 ♘ge7 12. ♘b3 ♕c7 13. ♘b×d4 ♘×d4 14. ♘×d4 ♗d7 15. ♗g5 g6 16. ♖ac1 ♘f5 17. ♗f6 ♖g8 18. ♗×f5 e×f5 19. ♕e2 ♕b6 20. c3 ♗c5 21. b4 ♗×d4 22. c×d4** *(see diagram)*
    22. ... ♗e6? 22. ... g×h5! 23. ♕×h5 ♗e6 24. ♕×h7 ♔d7 25. ♖ed1= **23. ♖c5?!** 23. h6 **23. ... ♕d7?** see move 22. **24. ♕f3 ♕×b4 25. ♖×d5+ ♔e8 26. ♖c1 ♗×d5 27. ♕×d5 ♕b6 28. ♕f3 g×h5??** 28. ... a5 29. h6± **29. ♕a3 ♕e6 30. ♖c7 1–0** (Source: Spence, *Carlsbad 1929*, 1956; notes by RT)

41   Menchik–José Raúl Capablanca
Carlsbad (7), August 7, 1929
[A50] *Queen's Fianchetto Defense*

1. d4 ♘f6 2. ♘f3 b6 3. g3 ♗b7 4. ♗g2 c5 5. c4 c×d4 6. 0-0 ♕c7 7. ♕×d4 ♘c6 8. ♕f4 e5 9. ♕d2 e4 10. ♘g5 ♘e5 *(see diagram)*

11. ♘c3? an incomprehensible error. How is one supposed to give Capablanca a free pawn and live? Further, the calculations of not being able to not regain it are not difficult. [Either 11. b3 h6 12. ♘h3; or 11. ♕f4 ♗d6 12. ♘×e4 ♘×e4 13. ♗×e4 ♘×c4 14. ♕g4 are called for—RT] **11. ... ♘×c4 12. ♕d4?! d5 13. b3 ♗c5?** Continuing the slide. **14. ♘b5 ♕c6 15. ♕c3 ♕×b5 16. b×c4 ♕×c4 17. ♕e5+ ♔f8 18. ♗f4 ♕a4 19. ♖fd1 ♕e8 20. ♕b2 h6 21. ♘h3**

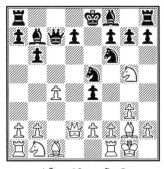
After 10. ... ♘e5

♘g4 22. ♖ac1 ♗c6 23. e3 ♔g8 24. ♕e2 f5 25. f3 ♘f6 26. g4 e×f3 27. ♗×f3 f×g4 28. ♗×g4 ♕g6 29. ♘f2 h5 0–1 (Source: Spence, *Carlsbad 1929*, 1956)

42   Hermanis Matisons–Menchik
Carlsbad (8), August 9, 1929
[B25] *Sicilian, Closed*

In this, one of the few Sicilians played by Menchik, Matisons sidestepped her presumed preparations by essaying the closed variation. By move 16 nothing had left the board, but Matisons had built a massive phalanx of pawns, while Menchik maneuvered her pieces behind her own lines. The computer finds it even, but in real life human competition it was a tough tightrope to walk.

1. e4 c5 2. ♘c3 ♘c6 3. g3 ♘f6 4. ♗g2 g6 5. ♘ge2 ♗g7 6. 0–0 d6 7. d3 ♗d7 8. ♘d5 0–0 9. c3 ♖c8 10. ♘e3 ♕b6 11. f4 e6 12. h3 ♘e7 13. g4 ♕h8 14. ♘g3 ♕c7 15. g5 ♘fg8 16. h4 f5 17. h5 *(see diagram)*

17. ... ♖f7? 18. e×f5 e×f5 19. h6 ♗f8 20. c4 ♘c6 21. b4 ♘ge7 22. ♗b2+ ♔g8 23. b5 ♘d8 24. ♕d2 ♘e6 25. ♘e2 d5 26. ♘×d5 ♘×d5 27. ♗×d5 ♖e7 28. ♖ae1 ♕f7 29. ♘c1 ♕b6 30. ♘b3 ♕e8 31. ♗f6 ♖f7 32. ♗×e6 ♗×e6 33. ♖×e6+ 1–0 (Source: Spence, *Carlsbad 1929*, 1956)

After 17. h5

43 Menchik–Ernst Grünfeld
Carlsbad (9), August 10, 1929
[E14] *Queen's Indian Defense Classical*

An intriguing game where nothing happens, then Black sprints towards a nonexistent win.

After 28. e4

1. d4 ♘f6 2. ♘f3 e6 3. c4 b6 4. e3 ♗b7 5. ♗d3 ♗b4+ 6. ♗d2 ♗×d2+ 7. ♘b×d2 d6 8. 0–0 ♘bd7 9. ♕c2 c5 10. ♘e4 ♕c7 11. ♖fd1 0–0 12. d×c5 d×c5 13. ♖d2 h6 14. ♖ad1 ♖fd8 15. h3 ♗c6 16. ♘h2 ♔f8 17. ♘f1 ♘e8 18. ♘fg3 ♘df6 19. ♘×f6 ♘×f6 20. ♗f1 ♔e7 21. ♕c3 ♖×d2 22. ♕×d2 h5 23. ♘e2 ♗a4 24. b3 ♗c6 25. ♘c3 a6 26. ♗e2 ♖h8 27. f3 g5 28. e4 *(see diagram)*

28. ... ♕f4 29. ♕×f4 g×f4 30. ♔f2 h4 31. ♗d3 ♖d8 32. ♗c2 ♖×d1 33. ♗×d1 ♘d6 34. ♗c2 ♔e5 35. ♘e2 ♘h5 36. ♗d3 ♗e8 37. ♔e1 ♘g3 38. ♘c3 ♘d4 39. ♔d2 f6 40. ♘b1 ♗g6 41. ♘a3 ♔e5 42. ♘c2 ♗e8 43. ♘e1 ♔d6 44. ♘c2 ♗d7 45. ♘a3 ♘h5 46. ♘b1 ♗c6 47. ♘c3 ♘g7 48. ♗c2 ♘h5 49. ♗d3 ♔c7 50. ♔e1 ♔d7 51. ♔d1 ♔e7 52. ♔e1 ♔f7 53. ♔d2 ♗d7 54. ♔e1 ♔e7 55. ♔d1 ♔d6 56. ♔d2 ♗c6 57. ♘e2 ♔e5 58. ♘c3 ♘g7 59. ♘e2 ♘e8 60. ♘c3 ♘d6 61. a3 ♘c8 62. ♘e2 ♔e7 63. ♔c3 ♗e8 64. ♗c2 ♗g6 65. ♘c1 ♔d6 66. ♘e2 e5 67. ♔d2 ♘c6 68. ♗d3 ♗f7 69. ♔c3 ♗e6 70. ♔d2 ♘a5 71. ♔c3 ♔c6 72. ♘c1 ♘b7 73. ♘e2 ♘d6 74. ♔d2 b5 75. ♔c3 ♔b6 76. ♘c1 ♘f7 77. ♗f1 ♘d8 78. b4 ♘b7 79. ♘b3 ♗f7 80. ♗e2 ♗e8 81. c×b5 a×b5 82. ♘×c5 ♘×c5 83. b×c5+ ♔×c5 84. ♗f1 ♗d7 85. ♗d3 ♗e6 86. ♗e2 f5 87. e×f5 ♗×f5 88. ♗d1 ♗e6 89. ♗e2 ♗d5 90. ♗d3 ♗a2 91. ♗e2 ♗b1 92. ♗d1 e4 93. f×e4 ♗×e4 94. ♗f3 ♔d5 95. ♔b4 ♗×f3 96. g×f3 ♔d4 97. ♔×b5 ♔e3 98. a4 ♔×f3 99. a5 ♔g3 100. a6 f3 101. a7 f2 102. a8♕ f1♕+ 103. ♔c5 ♕c1+ 104. ♔d6 ♕d1+ 105. ♔e5 ♕e2+ 106. ♕e4 ♕h5+ 107. ♔d4 ♕d1+ 108. ♔e3 ♕g1+ 109. ♔d3 ♕×h3 110. ♕f3+ ♕g3 *(see diagram)*

111. ♔e3 ½–½ (Source: Spence, *Carlsbad 1929*, 1956)

After 110. ... ♕g3

44   Frank James Marshall–Menchik
Carlsbad (10), August 11, 1929

[D32] *Queen's Gambit Declined, Tarrasch Defense*

One gets the feeling that Menchik is in a bit of shell shock by this game. She's had her share of chances so far in the tournament, but has choked most of the time. In this game she seems to be going through the motions without really looking at what her opponent is doing.

1. d4 c5 2. e3 d5 3. c4 e6 4. c×d5 e×d5 5. ♘c3 ♘f6 6. ♘f3 ♗e7 7. d×c5 0-0 8. ♗e2 ♗×c5 9. 0-0 ♘c6 10. a3 ♗e6 11. b4 ♗d6 12. ♗b2 ♖c8 13. ♖c1 ♕e7 14. ♘b5 ♗b8 15. ♘bd4 ♗d7 16. ♘×c6 ♖×c6 17. ♖×c6 *(see diagram)*

After 17. ♖×c6

17. ... ♗×c6? 17. ... b×c6± **18. ♗×f6 ♕×f6 19. b5 ♗d7 20. ♕×d5 ♗g4** 20. ... ♗c8 21. ♖d1 ♕e7± **21. ♕×b7 ♕d6 22. g3?** 22. ♕a6+− **22. ... ♕×a3 23. ♘d4 ♗×e2 24. ♘×e2 ♗e5 25. ♖d1 ♕a2 26. ♔f1 g6 27. ♕d5 ♕×d5 28. ♖×d5 ♗g7 29. f4 ♖b8 30. e4 ♖b6 31. e5 a6 32. b×a6 ♖×a6 33. ♖d8+ ♗f8 34. g4 ♔g7 35. f5?!** 35. ♖d7 **35. ... g×f5 36. g×f5 ♗c5 37. ♘g3 ♖a4 38. ♔g2 ♗b6?** 38. ... ♕h6 39. ♔h3 ♖a6± **39. f6+ ♔h6 40. e6 f×e6 41. f7 ♖a2+ 42. ♔h3 ♗c5 43. f8♕+ ♗×f8 44. ♖×f8 ♔g7 45. ♖f4 ♖b2 46. ♘e4 h6 47. ♖f6 ♖b6 48. ♔g4 ♖b2 49. h4 e5 50. ♖e6 ♖g2+ 51. ♔h5 ♖h2 52. ♖g6+ 1-0** (Source: Spence, *Carlsbad 1929*, 1956; notes by RT)

45   Menchik–Fritz Sämisch
Carlsbad (11), August 13, 1929

[A96] *Dutch, Classical*

1. ♘f3 e6 2. c4 f5 3. g3 ♘f6 4. ♗g2 ♗e7 5. 0-0 0-0 6. d4 d6 7. ♘c3 c6 8. ♕c2 ♘a6 9. a3 ♘c7 10. b3 ♕e8 11. e4 f×e4 12. ♘×e4 ♕g6 13. ♘×f6+ g×f6 14. ♕×g6+ h×g6 15. ♘h4 ♔f7 16. f4 ♗d7 17. ♗b2 ♖ab8 18. a4 b6 19. ♘f3 ♖fc8 20. ♗a3 c5 21. ♖fe1 a6 22. ♖ad1 ♖d8 23. ♖d3 ♗c6 24. ♘d2 ♗×g2 25. ♔×g2 b5 25. ... c×d4!? 26. ♖×d4 d5 **26. ♘e4 f5 27. ♘d2 b4?!** Locking his queen side pawns up and eliminating any play on that wing. **28. ♗b2 ♗f6 29. ♘f3 a5 30. ♗a1 ♘a6 31. ♖de3 ♖e8 32. d5 ♘c7 33. d×e6+ ♖×e6 34. ♖×e6 ♘×e6 35. ♗×f6 ♔×f6** *(see diagram)*

After 35. ... ♔×f6

36. ♖d1 ♖d8 37. ♖d3 ♘c7 Better is 37. ... ♔e7 **38. ♘e5 ♘e8 39. h3 g5 40. ♘c6 ♖d7?** 41. f×g5+ ♔×g5 **42. ♘e5?** 42. ♘×a5! ♘f6 43. h4+ ♔g4 44. ♘c6 f4 45. a5+− **42. ... ♖c7 43. ♘f3+ ♔f6 44. ♘h4 ♖e7 45. ♖f3** Better is 45. ♔f3 **45. ... ♖e5 46. g4 ♘g7 47. ♔f2 d5 48. c×d5 ♖×d5 49. ♔e2 ♔g5 50. ♘×f5 ♘e6 51. h4+ ♔f6 52. ♘e3+ ♔e5 53. ♖f5+ ♔e4 54. ♖×d5 ♘f4+ 55. ♔d2 1-0** (Source: Spence, *Carlsbad 1929*, 1956; notes by RT)

46 Karl Gilg–Menchik
Carlsbad (12), August 14, 1929

[E90] *King's Indian Defense*

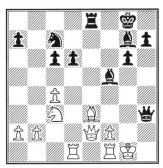

After 24. ⌗e3

1. d4 ♘f6 2. ♘f3 g6 3. c4 ♗g7 4. ♘c3 0-0 5. e4 d6 6. ♗d3 ♘c6 7. d5 ♘b8 8. 0-0 e5 9. d×e6 f×e6 10. e5 ♘g4 11. ♗g5 ♕d7 12. e×d6 c×d6 13. h3 ♘f6 14. ♗c2 ♘c6 15. ♕d2 ♘e8 16. ⌗ad1 ⌗×f3 17. g×f3 e5 18. ♗a4 ♕×h3 19. ♗×c6 b×c6 20. ♕d3 ♗f5 21. ♕e2 ♘c7 22. f4? e×f4 22. ... ♘e6! 23. ⌗fe1 e×f4 24. ⌗d3 ♕×d3 25. ♕×d3 ♗×d3 26. ⌗×e6 ♗e5 and wins **23. ♗×f4 ⌗e8 24. ♗e3** *(see diagram)*

    24. ... ♘e6?! 24. ... c5! To prevent White playing ⌗d4. 25. ⌗d2 ♗×c3 26. b×c3 ⌗e4 27. f3 ♕g3+ 28. ♕g2 ♕×g2+ 29. ♔×g2 ⌗×e3 and wins **25. ♗c1 ♘c7 26. ♗e3 ♘e6** 26. ... c5 etc. as above **27. ♗c1** After 27. ... ⌗e7 Black still has a win! ½–½ (Source: Spence, *Carlsbad 1929*, 1956; notes by RT)

47 Menchik–Edgar Colle
Carlsbad (13), August 15, 1929

[D02] *Queen's Pawn Game*

1. ♘f3 d5 2. d4 ♘c6 3. ♗f4 ♗g4 4. e3 e6 5. c4 ♗b4+ 6. ♘c3 ♘ge7 7. ⌗c1 0-0 8. h3 ♗×f3 9. ♕×f3 ♘g6 10. c×d5 e×d5 11. ♗d3 ♘×f4 12. ♕×f4 ♘e7 13. 0-0 c6 14. ♕h4 f5 15. ♘e2 ♕e8 16. ♕g3 ♘g6 *(see diagram)*

    17. ♔h1?! 17. a3 ♗e7 holds the position better **17. ...** ♕e7 **18. ♘f4 ♘h4 19. ♘e6 ♗d6 20. ♕g5 ♕×e6 21. ♕×h4 ⌗f6 22. ♕h5 ⌗af8 23. ⌗fe1 ⌗h6 24. ♕g5?** 24. ♕f3 (the only move) **24. ... ♕f7 25. f4?** 25. ♗e2 would at least prolong the battle **25. ... ♗e7 0–1** (Source: Spence, *Carlsbad 1929*, 1956; notes by RT)

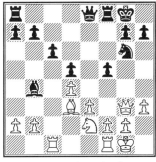

After 16. ... ♘g6

48 Milan Vidmar, Sr.–Menchik
Carlsbad (14), August 16, 1929

[A43] *Old Benoni*

1. d4 c5 2. d5 d6 3. e4 ♘f6 4. ♘c3 g6 5. f4 ♘bd7 6. ♘f3 ♕c7 7. ♕e2 ♘b6 8. a4 ♗g4 9. ♘b5 ♕b8 10. c4 a6 11. ♘c3 ♗g7 12. h3 ♗×f3 13. ♕×f3 0-0 14. ♗d3 e6 15. d×e6 f×e6 16. 0-0 ♘c8 17. g4 ♘e7 18. g5 ♘h5 19. ♕g4 ♗d4+ 20. ♔g2 ♘g7 21. ♘e2 ♘c6 22. ♘×d4 ♘×d4 23. ♗e3 ♕c8 24. ♗×d4 c×d4 25. b3 ♕c5 26. ⌗ad1 ⌗ac8 27. ⌗f2 ⌗c7 28. ⌗df1 ⌗cf7 29. h4 ♕b4 30. ♕d1 ♕a5 31. ♗c2 ♕b6 32. a5 ♕×a5 33. ♕×d4 ♕c5 34. ♕d2 a5 35. ♔h2 b6 36. ♔g2 ♘h5 37. ♗d1 ♘g7 38. ♗g4 ♕a3 39. ⌗f3 ♕c5 40. ♕d3 ⌗a7? 40. ... ♕c6= **41. ⌗d1** the only move to keep winning chances. If 41. f5 we get a rare case of 10 moves of essentially forced captures 41. ... g×f5 42. e×f5 e×f5 43. ♗×f5 ♘×f5 44. ⌗×f5 ⌗×f5 45. ⌗×f5 ♕c6+ 46. ♕d5+ ♕×d5+ 47. ⌗×d5 a4 48. b×a4 ⌗×a4 49. ⌗×d6 ⌗×c4 50. ⌗×b6= **41. ... a4 42. ♕×d6 ♕×d6 43. ⌗×d6 a×b3?** Alternatively 43. ... a3 44. ⌗d1± **44. ⌗×b6 ⌗c7 45. ⌗b×b3** Better is 45. ⌗f×b3 **45. ... ⌗×c4** *(see diagram)*

    46. ⌗be3 ⌗c2+ 47. ♔g3 ⌗c1 48. ⌗e2 ⌗g1+ 49. ♔g2 ⌗e1 50. e5 ⌗b8 51. ⌗c3

♖a1 52. ♖c6 ♖a3+ 53. ♔h2 ♖a4 54. ♖f2 ♔f7 55. ♖c7+ ♔g8 56. ♔g3 ♘f5+ 57. ♗×f5 e×f5 58. ♖fc2 ♖a3+ 59. ♖2c3 ♖×c3+ 60. ♖×c3 ♖b7 61. ♔f3 ♔g7 62. ♔e3 ♖a7 63. ♖b3 ♔f7 64. ♖b4 ♔e7 65. ♖b5 ♖d7 66. ♖b6 ♖a7 67. ♖c6 ♔d7 68. ♖d6+ ♔e7 69. h5 ♖a3+ 70. ♔d4 ♖a4+ 71. ♔e3 ♖a3+ 72. ♔d4 ♖a4+ 73. ♔d5 ♖a5+ 74. ♔c6 ♖a6+ 75. ♔c5 ♖a4 76. h×g6 h×g6 77. ♖×g6 ♖×f4 78. ♔d5 ♖a4 79. ♖g7+ ♔f8 80. ♖b7 ♖a6 81. e6 f4 82. ♔e5 f3 83. ♔f6 ♖a8 84. g6 f2 85. g7+ ♔g8 86. ♖b1 f1♕+ 87. ♖×f1 ♖a2 88. ♖e1 1–0 (Source: Spence, *Carlsbad 1929*, 1956; notes by RT)

After 45. ... ♖×c4

49   Menchik–Rudolf Spielmann

Carlsbad (15), August 18, 1929

[E23] *Nimzo-Indian Defense*

1. ♘f3 ♘f6 2. c4 c5 3. d4 e6 4. ♘c3 c×d4 5. ♘×d4 ♗b4 6. ♕b3 ♗c5 7. ♘f3 ♘c6 8. e3 0–0 9. ♗e2 d5 10. 0–0 ♘a5 11. ♕b5 b6 12. c×d5 e×d5 13. ♖d1 ♗f5 14. ♕a4 ♖c8 15. ♗a6 ♖c7 16. ♘b5 ♖e7 17. b4 ♖e4 18. ♘fd4 ♗×d4 19. ♘×d4 ♗d7 20. ♕c2 ♘c4 21. ♗×c4 d×c4 22. ♕×c4 ♕e7 23. ♗d2?! 23. ♗b2 Keeping the bishop focused on

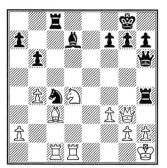

After 29. ... ♕h6

its primary target and not blocking its own pieces. **23. ... ♖c8 24. ♕b3± 23. ... ♘g4 24. ♕c7 ♖c8 25. ♕g3 ♘e5 26. f3 ♖h4 27. ♖ac1 ♘c4 28. ♗c3 ♕×e3+ 29. ♔h1 ♕h6** (see diagram)

30. ♗a1? 30. ♘b3 ♗e6 31. ♗×g7 ♕f4 32. ♕×f4 ♖×f4 33. ♗a1± **30. ... ♖h5?!** 30. ... f5= **31. ♖×c4 ♖×c4 32. ♘f5 ♕g5** (the only move) **33. ♕d6 h6 34. ♘e7+ ♔h8 35. ♕b8+ ♗c8 36. ♘×c8?!** Only a little better is 36. ♕d6 ♖×h2+ 37. ♕×h2 ♖h4 38. ♘c8 ♖×h2+ 39. ♔×h2 ♕h4+ 40. ♔g1 ♕×b4 41. ♘d6∓ **36. ... ♔h7 37. ♘×a7 ♕d2** 37. ... ♖c1 38. ♕d6 ♕g3!–+ **38. ♖g1 ♖g5** 38. ... ♖c1 39. ♗d4 ♖g5 40. g4 to avoid 40. ... ♕×g2 mate 40. ... ♖×g1+ 41. ♔×g1 ♕×d4+ and it is checkmate or the win of White's queen within a few moves **39. ♕×b6??** 39. h3 ♖c2 40. ♕h2 and any win now has become problematic **39. ... ♖×b4** 39. ... ♖c1 and mate in three **40. ♕c7 ♕×g2+ 0–1** (Source: Spence, *Carlsbad 1929*, 1956; notes by RT)

50   Géza Maróczy–Menchik

Carlsbad (16), August 19, 1929

[B01] *Scandinavian Defense*

1. e4 d5 2. e×d5 ♘f6 3. ♗b5+ ♗d7 4. ♗c4 ♗g4 5. f3 ♗f5 6. ♘c3 ♘bd7 7. d3 ♘b6 8. ♘ge2 ♘b×d5 9. ♘×d5 ♘×d5 10. ♘g3 ♗g6 11. f4 e6 12. 0–0 ♘b6 13. ♗b3 ♗c5+ 14. ♔h1 0–0 15. ♕f3 ♕c8 16. ♘e2 ♘d7 17. g4 ♘f6 18. ♘g3 h6 19. h3 c6 20. ♗d2 ♕d7 21. ♖ae1 ♖ad8 22. ♖e2 ♔h8 23. ♖g2 [23. f5!? e×f5 24. ♘×f5—RT] **23. ... ♗h7 24. h4 ♘g8 25. h5 ♘e7 26. f5 e×f5 27. ♘×f5 ♗×f5 28. g×f5 ♗d4 29. f6** (see diagram)

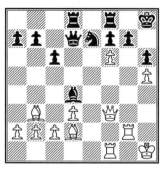

After 29. f6

29. ... ♘d5?? [29. ... ♗×f6 30. ♗×h6 ♗×b2 31. ♗e3 ♗d4 32. h6 g6≈ —RT] **30. f×g7+ ♗×g7 31. c4 ♘e7 32. ♖×g7 ♔×g7 33. ♕f6+ ♔g8 34. ♖g1+ ♘g6 35. ♖×g6+ f×g6 36. c5+ ♖f7 37. ♕×g6+ 1–0** (Source: Spence, *Carlsbad 1929*, 1956)

51 Menchik–Saviely Tartakower
Carlsbad (17), August 20, 1929

[A10] *English Opening*

1. ♘f3 b6 2. c4 ♗b7 3. ♘c3 f5 4. g3 ♘f6 5. ♗g2 g6 6. 0-0 ♗g7 7. d4 0-0 8. ♗f4 h6 9. ♕c1 g5 10. ♗d2 ♘e4 11. ♘×e4 ♗×e4 12. h4 g4 13. ♘e5 ♗×g2 14. ♔×g2 ♔h7 15. ♕c2 c5 16. ♘×g4 c×d4 17. ♘h2 ♘c6 18. e4 e6 19. e×f5 e×f5 20. ♖ae1 ♕f6 21. ♗f4 ♖ae8 22. ♘f3 ♕g6 23. ♖×e8 ♖×e8 24. ♖e1 ♖e4 25. ♕d2 ♕e6 26. b3 ♔g8 27. ♔h2 ♗f8 28. ♖×e4 ♕×e4 29. ♗g1 ♔h7 30. f3 ♕b1 31. g4 f×g4 32. f×g4 ♕e4 33. ♘h3 ♘e5 34. ♗×e5 ♕×e5+ 35. ♔g2 ♕e4+ 36. ♔f1 ♕×g4 37. ♘f4 ♕f3+ 38. ♕f2 ♕×f2+ 39. ♔×f2 ♗d6 40. ♘d3 ♔g6 41. ♔g2 ♕f5 42. ♔f3 h5 43. b4 ♗e7 44. a3 ♗×h4 45. c5 b×c5 46. ♘×c5 ♗e7 47. ♘d3 h4 48. a4 h3 49. a5 h2 50. ♔g2 ♔e4 51. ♘f2+ ♔d5 52. b5 ♗d6 0–1 (Source: Spence, *Carlsbad 1929*, 1956)

52 George Alan Thomas–Menchik
Carlsbad (18), August 22, 1929

[D60] *Queen's Gambit Declined, Classical*

1. d4 d5 2. ♘f3 ♘f6 3. c4 e6 4. ♘c3 ♘bd7 5. ♗g5 ♗e7 6. e3 0-0 7. a3 c5 8. c×d5 ♘×d5 9. ♗×e7 ♕×e7 10. ♘×d5 e×d5 11. d×c5 ♕×c5 12. ♗d3 ♘f6 13. 0-0 ♗g4 14. h3 ♗×f3 15. ♕×f3 ♕b6 16. b4 ♖ac8 17. ♖ac1 ♖c6 18. ♕f5 *(see diagram)*

After 18. ♕f5

18. ... ♖fc8?? [If only 18. ... ♕c7 and the game is by all reasonable accounts a draw, although the players may torture one another for a while—RT] **19. ♕×c8+ and mate in three. 1–0** (Source: Spence, *Carlsbad 1929*, 1956)

53 Menchik–Akiba Rubinstein
Carlsbad (19), August 23, 1929

[A31] *English Opening, Symmetrical*

Rubinstein won the sixth Brilliancy Prize of the tournament for this game.[43]

After 6. a3

1. ♘f3 ♘f6 2. c4 c5 3. d4 c×d4 4. ♘×d4 d5 This advance in the center, if it can be accomplished without harm, always give Black a free hand. Until now it was considered inadequate because of 5. c×d5 ♘×d5 6. e4, when White gains time and Black at best equalizes. **5. c×d5 a6** This move improves the whole line. If now 6. ♘c3 ♘×d5, and if 6. g3 ♕×d5, either way Black stands well. Perhaps a6 is even stronger on the fourth move, because White does not have the option of stopping the pawn advance d7–d5. Thus, the move a6 has theoretical importance. **6. a3** *(see diagram)*

More aggressive is World Champion Alekhine's suggestion

After 24. ♖×d4

of 6. e4. After the peace-loving text Black obtains full equality. **6. ...** ♘×d5 **7. g3** After this it is Black who seizes the initiative. Better was 7. e4 with equality. **7. ... e5 8.** ♘c2 ♗c5 **9.** ♗g2 ♗e6 **10. 0-0** ♘c6 **11. b4** ♗a7 **12.** ♗b2 **0-0 13.** ♘d2 ♕e7 **14.** ♘f3 ♖fd8 **15.** ♕c1 **f6 16.** ♖d1 ♖ac8 **17.** ♖b1 The idea here is not clear. Better was 17. e4, followed by 18. ♖×d8+. Now Black's attack becomes very dangerous. **17. ... e4 18.** ♘fe1 ♗g4 **19.** ♗f1 ♘e5 **20. h3** ♗h5 **21.** ♔g2 **e3 22. f4** ♘c4 **23.** ♗d4 ♗×d4 **24.** ♖×d4 *(see diagram)*

        24. ... ♘c3 **25.** ♖b3 ♘d2 **26.** ♖b2 ♗×e2 **27.** ♖×d8+ ♖×d8 **28.** ♗×e2 ♘×e2 **29.** ♕d1 ♘e4+ **30.** ♔h2 ♘f1 mate **0–1** (Source: Spence, *Carlsbad 1929*, 1956; *Shakhmaty*, September 1929, p. 168; Donaldson & Minev, *Akiba Rubinstein: The Later Years*, p. 184; notes by Akiba Rubinstein in *Shakhmaty* and reproduced in the Donaldson & Minev book)

54 Efim Bogoljubow–Menchik
Carlsbad (20), August 24, 1929

[D30] *Queen's Gambit Declined*

1. d4 e6 2. ♘f3 ♘f6 **3. c4 d5 4.** ♗g5 ♗e7 **5. e3** ♘e4 **6.** ♗×e7 ♕×e7 **7.** ♕b3 **c6 8.** ♘c3 **f5 9.** ♗e2 **0-0 10. 0-0** ♘d7 **11.** ♖ad1 ♔h8 **12.** ♕c2 ♘df6 **13.** ♘e5 ♗d7 **14. f4** ♗e8 **15.** ♘×e4 **f×e4 16. a3** ♘d7 **17. c×d5 e×d5 18. b4** ♘×e5 **19. d×e5** ♗d7 **20.** ♕c3 ♖ac8 **21.** ♖d2 ♕h4 **22.** ♕c5 **a6 23. g3** ♕h3 **24.** ♕b6 ♖b8 **25.** ♖f2 ♕e6 **26.** ♗f1 **h5 27. h3** ♕e8 **28.** ♖h2 ♔g8 **29.** ♖dg2 ♕c8 **30. g4 h×g4 31.** ♕d4 ♖f7 **32. h×g4** ♗×g4 **33.** ♖h4 ♗f5 **34.** ♖gh2 ♖f8 **35.** ♗e2 ♕e6 **36.** ♕b6 ♕d7 **37.** ♗h5 ♖fc8 **38.** ♔f2 ♕e6 **39.** ♗e2 ♕f7 **40.** ♕d4 ♖d8 **41.** ♖h5 **b6 42.** ♖2h4 **a5 43.** ♖×f5+ ♕×f5 **44.** ♗g4 ♕g6 **45.** ♗h5 **1–0** (Source: Spence, *Carlsbad 1929*, 1956)

55 Menchik–Esteban Canal
Carlsbad (21), August 26, 1929

[A31] *English Opening, Symmetrical*

A true roller coaster ride. White is winning in the first half, Black takes over, White has a draw in hand, Black wins. A fair assessment may be that time pressure played at least some role.

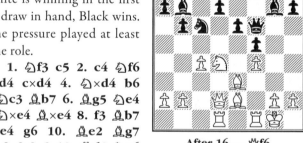

After 16. ... ♕f6

        1. ♘f3 **c5 2. c4** ♘f6 **3. d4 c×d4 4.** ♘×d4 **b6 5.** ♘c3 ♗b7 **6.** ♗g5 ♘e4 **7.** ♘×e4 ♗×e4 **8. f3** ♗b7 **9. e4 g6 10.** ♗e2 ♗g7 **11. 0-0 0-0 12.** ♕d2 ♘c6 **13.** ♗e3 **f5 14. e×f5 g×f5 15. f4 e6 16.** ♖ad1 ♕f6 *(see diagram)*

        17. ♗f3 17. ♘b5! ♖ab8 18. b4 leads to an excellent position for White **17. ...** ♘a5 **18. b3** ♖ad8 **19.** ♗×b7 ♘×b7 *(see diagram)*

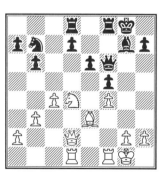

After 19. ... ♘×b7

20. ♘f3 20. ♘b5 Better fits the theme of building against the queenside **20. ... d6 21. ♕e2 ♘c5 22. ♗d4 ♕g6 23. ♗×g7 ♕×g7 24. ♘d4** 24. ♘g5 is required if White wishes to have any real chances of winning **24. ... ♕f6 25. ♖f3 ♘e4 26. ♕e1 ♖d7 27. ♘e2 d5 28. ♘c3 ♖fd8 29. c×d5** White has been retreating and playing without a real plan while Black gets his pieces coordinated. 29. ♖fd3 Would start putting pressure on Black and better get his pieces into the game **29. ... e×d5 30. ♖fd3 ♕c6 31. ♘e2 ♕f6 32. ♘d4 ♖e7 33. ♕b4**

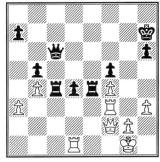

After 45. ... ♕c6

♘c5 34. ♖g3+ ♔h8 35. ♖g5? ♖e4 36. ♕d2 ♘e6 37. ♘×e6 ♕×e6 38. ♖g3 d4 39. h3 ♕d6 40. ♖f3 h6 41. ♔h1 ♔h7 42. ♔g1 b5 43. b4 ♖c8 44. a3 ♖c4 45. ♕f2 ♕c6 (*see diagram*)

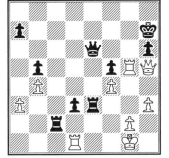

After 50. ... d3

46. ♕h4? 46. ♖fd3 and White is back in the game **46. ... ♖c2 47. ♕h5 ♕e6?** Better is 47. ... ♕d5 **48. ♖fd3 ♖ee2 49. ♖g3 ♖e3 50. ♖g5 d3** (*see diagram*)

51. ♖×f5?? 51. ♔h2 a6 52. ♖×f5 ♖×g2+ 53. ♔×g2 ♕e4+ 54. ♔h2 ♖e2+ 55. ♔g3 ♕g2+ 56. ♔h4= **51. ... ♖g3 52. ♕f7+ ♕×f7 53. ♖×f7+ ♔g6 54. ♖d7 ♖g×g2+ 55. ♔f1** Slower, but just as lost is 55. ♔h1 ♖h2+ 56. ♔g1 ♖cg2+ 57. ♔f1 d2 **55. ... ♖cf2+ 56. ♔e1 ♖e2+ 57. ♔f1 d2** (*see diagram*)

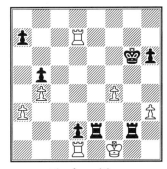

Final position

0–1 (Source: Spence, *Carlsbad 1929*, 1956; notes by RT)

Barcelona 1929

September 25–October 11, 1929

		1	2	3	4	5	6	7	8	9	10	11	12	13	14	15	Pts.	Place
1	Capablanca, José R.	•	=	1	1	1	1	1	1	1	1	1	1	1	1	1	13½	1
2	Tartakower, Saviely	=	•	1	1	=	1	=	=	1	=	1	1	1	1	1	11½	2
3	Colle, Edgar	0	0	•	1	=	1	1	=	1	1	1	1	1	1	1	11	3
4	Rey Ardid, Ramón	0	0	0	•	=	=	=	1	0	1	1	=	1	1	1	8½	4–5
5	Monticelli, Mario	0	=	=	=	•	=	1	1	0	1	=	0	1	1	1	8½	4–5
6	Golmayo de la Torrente	0	0	0	=	=	•	0	1	=	1	=	1	1	1	1	8	6
7	Yates, Frederick D.	0	=	0	0	0	1	•	=	=	=	1	1	1	1	=	7½	7
8	Menchik, Vera	0	=	=	1	0	0	=	•	1	=	=	1	1	=	0	7	8–9
9	Vilardebó-Picurena, J.	0	0	0	0	1	=	=	0	•	1	=	=	1	1	1	7	8–9
10	Marín y Llovet, Valentín	0	=	0	0	0	0	=	=	0	•	1	1	=	=	=	5	10–11
11	Soler, Plácido	0	0	0	=	=	=	0	=	=	0	•	=	=	=	1	5	10–11
12	Ribera Arnal, Angel	0	0	0	0	1	0	0	0	=	0	=	•	1	=	1	4½	12
13	Aguilera, José	0	0	0	0	0	0	0	0	0	=	=	0	•	1	1	3	13
14	Font, José María	0	0	0	0	0	0	0	=	0	=	=	=	0	•	1	3	14
15	Torres Caravaca, J.	0	0	0	0	0	0	=	1	0	=	0	0	0	0	•	2	15

This tournament was held in conjunction with the World Exhibition held in the same city that year. The Spanish had hoped to revitalize chess in their country which had been rather moribund since the time of Ruy Lopez. Although the Spanish had limited success at the time, by the late 20th century Spain had become something of a chess Mecca for the game. In this tournament, Menchik took equal eighth place to capture the last place prize.[44]

56 Joaquín Torres Caravaca–Menchik
Barcelona (1), September 25, 1929
[B74] *Sicilian, Dragon*

1. e4 c5 2. ♘f3 ♘c6 3. d4 c×d4 4. ♘×d4 ♘f6 5. ♘c3 d6 6. ♗e2 g6 7. 0-0 ♗g7 8. ♗e3 0-0 9. ♘b3 a6 10. h3 b5 11. a3 ♗b7 12. ♕e1 ♖c8 13. f4 ♘a5 14. ♘×a5 ♕×a5 15. ♗d3 ♕c7 16. ♕h4 ♖fe8 17. f5 d5 18. e5 ♕×e5 19. ♗d4 ♕d6 20. ♖ae1 ♘d7? [20. ... ♘h5∓—RT] 21. ♗×g7 ♔×g7 22. f×g6 h×g6 *(see diagram)*

    23. ♖×f7+! ♔×f7 24. ♕h7+ ♔f8 25. ♖f1+ ♘f6 26. ♗×g6 ♕e6 27. ♕h8+ 1-0 (Source: Gilliam, *Barcelona 1929*; Bachmann, *Schachjahrbuch 1929/30*)

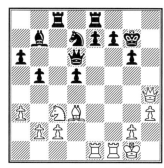

After 22. ... h×g6

57 Menchik–J. Vilardebó-Picurena
Barcelona (2), September 26, 1929
[D30] *Queen's Gambit Declined*

1. d4 d5 2. c4 e6 3. ♘f3 ♘f6 4. ♗g5 ♘bd7 5. e3 ♗b4+ 6. ♘bd2 0-0 7. ♗d3 d×c4 8. ♗×c4 ♖e8 9. 0-0 ♗×d2 10. ♕×d2 ♘e4 11. ♗×d8 ♗×d2 12. ♘×d2 ♖×d8 13. ♖fd1 e5!? 14. ♘f3 e×d4 15. ♖×d4 ♖f8 16. ♖ad1 ♘b6 17. ♗b3 ♗f5 18. ♘e5 ♗e6 19. ♗×e6 f×e6 20. e4 ♖ae8 21. f3 ♖e7 22. b3 g5 23. ♔f2 ♔g7 24. ♔e3 h5 25. h3 c5 26. ♖4d2 ♖c8 26. ... ♔f6 27. f4 ♖g7 28. ♖f2± 27. ♘d7?! 27. f4 ♔f6 28. ♖d8± 27. ... ♘d5+ 28. e×d5 e×d5+ 29. ♔f2 ♖×d7 30. ♖×d5 ♖×d5 31. ♖×d5 *(see diagram)*

After 31. ♖×d5

    31. ... ♔f6 32. h4! g×h4 33. ♖×h5 c4 34. ♖×h4 c3 35. ♖h1 ♖d8 35. ... b5 36. b4 a5 (36. ... ♖c4 37. a3 c2 38. ♖c1 ♖c3⩲) 37. b×a5 ♖a8 38. ♖c1 ♖×a5 39. ♖×c3 ♖×a2+ 40. ♔g3 ♖b2 41. ♖c6+ and we have a known win for White 36. g4 ♖d2+ 37. ♔e3 ♖×a2 38. ♖c1 a5 39. ♖×c3 b5 40. ♖c6+ ♔f7 41. ♖c5 b4 42. ♔f4 ♖a3 43. ♖g5 Best is 43. ♔e4 43. ... a4 44. b×a4 b3 45. ♖b5 ♖×a4+ 46. ♔f5 ♖a3 47. f4 ♔g7 48. ♖b7+ ♔g8 49. ♔g6 1-0 (Source: Gilliam, *Barcelona 1929*; notes by RT)

58 Frederick D. Yates–Menchik
Barcelona (3), September 27, 1929
[B02] *Alekhine's Defense*

This is a most interesting game for those looking for esoteric ways of meeting the Alekhine's. White gives up two minors for a rook and pawn. He also gained space on the kingside and had the psychological benefit of knowing what he was getting into as compensation for a possibly inferior position. At any rate this is an enjoyable game to review; especially for a draw.

1. e4 ♘f6 2. e5 ♘d5 3. ♘c3!? ♘×c3 4. d×c3 ♘c6 5. ♘f3 d6 6. ♗b5 ♗d7 7. ♕e2 e6 8. ♗f4 a6 9. ♗d3 d5 10. ♘g5 ♗c5 11. ♘×h7 ♖×h7 12. ♗×h7 ♕h4 13. ♗g3 ♕×h7 14. 0-0-0 0-0-0 15. h4 ♘e7 16. h5 ♕h6+ 17. ♔b1 ♘f5 18. ♗h2 ♗b5 19. ♕f3 d4 20. ♗f4 ♕h8 21. ♗g5 *(see diagram)*

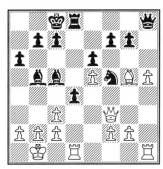

After 21. ♗g5

21. … f6 21. … ♖d7!? **22. ♗f4 ♗c6 23. ♕e2 ♖e8 24. f3 f×e5 25. ♗×e5 d×c3 26. ♕c4 ♗d6** 26. … ♕f8 Certainly a question Black has to address is, "Do I trade off my bishop pair?" **27. ♕×c3 ♗×e5 28. ♕×e5 ♕f8 29. ♖d3 ♕f7**

Final position

30. ♖hd1 ♘d6 31. g4 ♕f6 32. ♕c5 ♕b8 33. g5 ♕f5 34. ♕×f5 e×f5 35. c4 b6 36. b4 ♗a4 37. ♖×d6 c×d6 38. ♖×d6 ♔c7 39. ♖g6 ♖e7 40. h6 g×h6 41. g×h6 ♗e8 42. ♖f6 ♖e1+ 43. ♔b2 ♖h1 44. ♔c3 ♖h4 45. f4 ♗d7 46. ♔d4 ♖×f4+ 47. ♔e5 ♖h4 48. c5 b×c5 49. b×c5 f4 50. ♖×a6 ♖h5+ 50. … ♗c6 51. ♔e4 ♗c6+ 52. ♔×f4 ♖×h6 *(see diagram)*

Given that rook and bishop versus rook is a well known, albeit difficult, draw, there seems little point in fighting on given the addition of two White pawns! ½–½ (Source: Gilliam, *Barcelona 1929*; notes by RT)

59 José Aguilera–Menchik
Barcelona (4), September 28, 1929
[A50] *Queen's Fianchetto Defense*

This is a mammoth effort on the part of the players. After 17 moves all minors are gone and the complete sets of pawns are still symmetrically placed. The challenge is how can it be lost—the answer is a lack of imagination and a tendency to follow the "rules" too assiduously.

1. ♘f3 ♘f6 2. c4 g6 3. d4 ♗g7 4. g3 b6 5. ♗g2 ♗b7 6. 0-0 0-0 7. ♘c3 d6 8. ♗g5 ♘bd7 9. ♕d2 ♖e8 10. ♗h6 e6 11. ♗×g7 ♔×g7 12. ♖ad1 ♘e4 13. ♕c2 ♘×c3 14. ♕×c3 ♕f6 15. ♘e5 ♗×g2 16. ♘×d7 ♕e7 17. ♔×g2 ♕×d7 18. e4 ♕e7 19. f4 *(see diagram)*

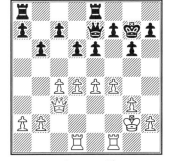

After 19. f4

Black to play and lose?? **19. … f6?!** 19. … f5 20. e×f5 e×f5 21. d5+ ♔g8 (21. … ♕f6 22. ♕×f6+ ♔×f6 23. ♖fe1 ♔f7) 22. ♖fe1 ♔g7 23. ♕×g7+ ♔×g7 24. ♔f3 ♕f7= **20. ♕f3 ♖f8** 20. … c5 21. f5 e×f5 22. e×f5 ♕e2+ 23. ♔g1 ♕×f3 24. ♖×f3 ♖e7= **21. h4 h5 22. f5 ♕f7?!** 22. … e×f5 23. e×f5 ♖ae8 24. ♖d2 ♕e4 25. ♕×e4 ♖×e4 26. f×g6 ♔×g6= **23. f×g6 ♕×g6** *(see diagram)*

After 23. … ♕×g6

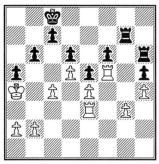

After 39. ... ♔c8

24. ♖d2 e5? 24. ... a6± 25. d5 ♖f7 26. ♕f5 ♖g8 27. ♕×g6+ ♔×g6 28. ♖f5 ♖h8 29. ♖df2 ♖h6 30. ♖2f3 ♔g7 31. ♖a3 a5 32. ♖af3 ♔f8 33. ♔f2 ♔e7 34. ♔e2 ♖g7 35. ♖e3 ♖g4 36. ♔d3 ♖g8 37. ♔c3 ♔d7 38. ♔b3 ♖g7 39. ♔a4 ♔c8?! *(see diagram)*

To quote a political statement by the IRA in reference to UK Prime Minister Margaret Thatcher, "You have to get lucky every time; we only have to get lucky once." White's position is easy to hold, Black's not nearly so. 39. ... c6!? 40. b4 a×b4 41. ♔×b4 40. ♔b5 ♔b7 41. ♖f2 ♖hg6 42. ♖ff3 ♖g8 43. a3 ♖a8 44. b3 ♖ag8 45. b4 a×b4 45. ... ♖a8 46. c5 (46. ♖f5 a×b4 47. a×b4 ♖h6 48. ♖ef3 ♖g8 49. ♖×f6 ♖×f6 50. ♖×f6 ♖×g3 51. ♖f5 ♖g4 52. ♖×h5 ♖×e4 53. ♖h8 ♖d4 54. h5 e4 55. h6 e3 and the passed pawns fall with an ensuing draw) 46. ... a×b4 47. c6+ ♔b8 48. a×b4 ♖h6 49. ♖f1 ♖g6 50. ♖ef3 ♔a7 (50. ... ♖a2 51. ♖×f6 ♖×f6 52. ♖×f6 ♖e2 53. ♖f8+ and an easy win) 51. ♖×f6 ♖×f6 (51. ... ♖×g3 52. ♖a1+ ♔b8 53. ♖f8 mate) 52. ♖×f6 ♖h8 53. ♖f7 ♔b8 54. ♔a6 ♔c8 55. ♔a7 b5 56. ♖g7 ♖e8 57. g4 h×g4 58. h5 and the win is only a few moves away 46. a×b4 ♖a8 47. ♖a3 ♖×a3 48. ♖×a3 ♖g4 49. ♖e3 ♖g8 Apparently the last chance to extract the draw. 49. ... ♔c8 50. ♖f3 ♖×e4 51. ♖×f6 ♖g4 and we have a drawn position similar to above 50. c5 b×c5 51. b×c5 ♖g4 Not 51. ... d×c5 52. ♔×c5 ♖g4 53. d6 c×d6+ 54. ♔×d6 52. c6+ ♔a7 53. ♔a5 ♔b8 54. ♖b3+ ♔c8 Not 54. ... ♔a8 55. ♖b7 ♖g7 56. ♔b4 ♖×g3 57. ♖×c7 ♖e3 58. ♖d7 ♖×e4+ 59. ♔b5 ♔b8 (59. ... ♖×h4 60. ♖d8+ ♔a7 61. c7+–) 60. ♖×d6 ♖×h4 61. ♖d8+ ♔c7 62. ♖d7+ ♔c8 63. d6 ♖d4 64. ♖c7+ ♔b8 (64. ... ♔d8 65. ♔c5 ♖d1 66. ♖h7 ♔e8 67. c7±) 65. ♖b7+ ♔c8 66. d7+ and White is victorious in all lines 55. ♖f3 ♖g6 56. ♔a6 ♔b8 No better is 56. ... ♖h6 57. ♖b3 f5 58. e×f5 ♖f6 59. ♔a7 ♔d8 60. ♖b8+ ♔e7+– 57. ♖b3+ ♔a8 58. ♖b7 ♖×g3 59. ♖×c7 ♖a3+ 60. ♔b5 ♖b3+ 61. ♔c4 ♖e3 62. ♖d7 ♖×e4+ 63. ♔b5 ♔b8 64. ♖×d6 ♖×h4 65. ♖×f6 ♖h1 66. ♖f8+ ♔c7 67. ♖f7+ ♔d8 68. c7+ 1–0 (Source: Gilliam, *Barcelona 1929*; notes by RT)

60 José Raúl Capablanca–Menchik
Barcelona (5), September 29, 1929
[B22] *Sicilian Defense 2. c3 (by transposition)*

1. e4 ♘f6 2. e5 ♘d5 3. ♘f3 d6 4. ♗c4 e6 5. 0–0 ♘b6 6. ♗b3 c5 7. c3 ♘c6 8. e×d6 ♗×d6 9. d4 c4?! 10. ♗c2 ♕c7 11. ♘bd2 ♗d7 12. ♕e2 ♘e7 13. ♘e4 ♖c8 14. ♘×d6+ ♕×d6 15. ♘e5 ♘g6 16. f4 0–0 17. ♖f3 ♗c6 This just forces the rook to go where it wishes anyway and any attack on White's kingside is more than adequately covered. 17. ... ♘d5 18. ♕f2 b5 and it will not be easy for White to penetrate 18. ♖h3 ♘d7? Still best is 18. ... ♘d5 19. ♕f2 (19. ♘×c4 ♘d×f4 20. ♗×f4 ♕×f4±) 19. ... b5 although Black's position is dicey at best 19. ♘×c4 ♕d5 20. ♘e3 ♕d6 21. ♘c4 ♕d5 22. ♘e5 *(see diagram)*

22. ... ♗b5 23. ♕e1 ♘d×e5 24. f×e5 f5 25. ♕d1 ♗c6 26. ♕e2 ♖fe8 27. ♗g5 ♘f8 28. ♖g3 b5 29. h4 ♖c7 30. h5 b4 31. ♗b3 ♕a5 32. ♖c1 ♗e4 33. ♕d2 ♖ec8 34. ♗f6 ♕b6 35. ♕g5 ♕b7 36. ♔h2 1–0 (Source: Gilliam, *Barcelona 1929*; notes by RT)

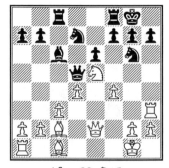

After 22. ♘e5

61 Menchik–Edgar Colle
Barcelona (6), September 30, 1929

[D07] *Queen's Gambit Declined, Chigorin Variation*

1. ♘f3 ♘c6 2. d4 d5 3. c4 ♗g4 4. ♘c3 e6 5. c×d5 e×d5 6. ♗f4 ♗×f3 7. g×f3 ♗b4 8. ♖c1 ♘ge7 9. e3 ♘g6 10. ♗g3 0-0 11. ♗d3 f5 12. f4 ♘ce7 13. a3 ♗×c3+ 14. ♖×c3 c6 15. 0-0 [15. ♕c2!? ♕d7 16. h4 ♘h8 17. h5 ♘f7 with a slight pull for White, but it was not in Menchik's nature to leave her king in the center in a position where the outcome was unclear—RT] **15. … ♘c8 16. b4 ♘d6 17. ♕e2 a6 18. a4 ♕d7 19. ♖fc1 ♖fc8 20. ♔h1 b5 21. ♕c2 h5 22. ♖×c6 h4 23. ♗×f5 ♖×c6 24. ♕×c6 ♕×f5 25. ♕×a8+ ♔h7 26. ♔g1 ♕e4 27. ♕c6 ♘c4 28. f5 ♕×f5** *(see diagram)*

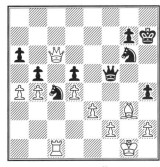

After 28. … ♕×f5

29. ♕e5?! ♕g4+ 30. ♔f1 ♘d2+ 31. ♔e1 ♘f3+ 32. ♔f1 ♘g×e5 33. d×e5 ♘×h2+ 34. ♔e1 ♘f3+ 35. ♔f1 h3 36. ♕c2+ ♔h6 37. ♕c6+ ♔g5 38. ♕c8 ♘d2+ 39. ♔e1 ♘f3+ 40. ♔f1 ½–½ (Source: Gilliam, *Barcelona 1929*)

62 José María Font–Menchik
Barcelona (7), October 2, 1929

[D35] *Queen's Gambit Declined, Exchange Variation*

After 26. … ♗×f5

1. d4 ♘f6 2. c4 e6 3. ♘c3 d5 4. e3 c5 5. ♕f3 ♘c6 6. c×d5 e×d5 7. d×c5 ♗×c5 8. ♗b5 0-0 9. ♘ge2 ♗g4 10. ♕f4 ♗d6 11. ♕g5 h6 12. ♕h4 ♘e5 13. f4 ♘g6 14. ♕g3 ♖c8 15. 0-0 ♘e7 16. ♘d4 ♘f5 17. ♘×f5 ♗×f5 18. ♖d1 ♘e4 19. ♘×e4 ♗×e4 20. ♗d2 ♕b6 21. ♗d7 ♖c2 22. b3 ♗a3 23. ♕e1 d4?! 23. … ♗b2! 24. ♖ab1 ♗c3 25. ♖bc1 ♗×d2 26. ♖×d2 ♖×c1 27. ♕×c1 ♕e3+ 28. ♔h1 ♕×f4–+ **24. ♗h3 ♕g6 25. e×d4 ♗b2 26. f5 ♗×f5** *(see diagram)*

27. ♔h1?? ♗×d4? Of course after the double oversight, Black is still winning. 27. … ♗×h3 wins an immediate piece as if 28. g×h3 ♕c6+ 29. ♔g1 ♗×d4+ **28. ♗×f5 ♕×f5 29. ♗b4? ♗c5?** 29. … ♗×a1 30. ♗×f8 ♕g4 31. ♖d2 (31. ♕f1 ♕f2 32. ♕×f2 ♕×d1+ 33. ♔g1 ♕×g1+–+) 31. … ♗c3 32. ♕d1 ♕×d1+ 33. ♖×d1 ♔×f8–+ **30. ♗×c5 ♕×c5 31. ♖ac1 ♖c8 32. ♖×c2 ♕×c2 33. ♖d2 ♕c1 34. ♖d1 ♕b2 35. ♕a5 ♕c2 36. ♖e1 ♕f2 37. ♖g1 ♖c2 38. a3 ♖b2 39. ♕d8+ ♔h7 40. ♕d3+ g6 41. ♕d5 b6 42. h3** *(see diagram)*

42. … ♕c5?? 43. ♕d1?? 43. ♕×f7+ ♔h8 44. ♖e1+– **43. … ♕c2?** 43. … ♕×a3 44. ♖f1 ♕e7 and, previous moves aside, Black should win **44. ♕d7 ♕×b3 45. ♕×a7 ♕d5 46. a4 h5 47. ♕c7 g5 48. ♕c1 ♖e2 49. ♕b1+ ♔g7 50. ♕×b6** More than likely both players were glad to put this game behind them! ½–½ (Source: Gilliam, *Barcelona 1929*; notes by RT)

After 42. h3

63   Menchik–Manuel Golmayo de la Torriente
Barcelona (8), October 3, 1929

[D60] *Queen's Gambit Declined, Classical Variation*

1. ♘f3 ♘f6 2. c4 e6 3. ♘c3 ♗e7 4. d4 d5 5. ♗g5 ♘bd7 6. e3 c6 7. ♗d3 d×c4 8. ♗×c4 0–0 9. 0–0 b5 10. ♗d3 ♗b7 11. ♕e2 a6 12. ♖fe1 b4 13. ♘e4 ♘×e4 14. ♗×e7 ♕×e7

After 46. h6

15. ♗×e4 ♘f6 16. ♗d3 ♖fc8 17. ♖ac1 c5 18. d×c5 ♖×c5 19. ♘d4 a5 20. e4 ♖×c1 21. ♖×c1 ♖d8 22. ♘c6 ♗×c6 23. ♖×c6 ♕d7 24. ♖c1 g6 25. ♗b5 ♕d2 26. ♖c8 ♔g7 27. ♖×d8 ♕×d8 28. g3 ♕d4 29. ♗d3 h5 30. h3 ♘d7 31. ♔g2 ♘c5 32. ♗b5? [32. ♗b1 ♘a4 33. b3 ♘c3 34. ♕c2‡—RT] **32. ... ♕×e4+ 33. ♕×e4 ♘×e4 34. h4 ♔f6 35. ♔f3 ♔e5 36. ♔e3 ♘d6 37. ♗f1 ♔d5 38. ♔d3 e5 39. ♗e2 f5 40. ♔c2 ♘e4 41. ♔b3 ♘c5+** [Better is 41. ... ♘×f2—RT] **42. ♔c2 ♔e4 43. ♔d2 f4 44. g4 f3 45. g×h5 f×e2 46. h6** *(see diagram)*

46. ... ♔f3 Mate in five. **0–1** (Source: Gilliam, *Barcelona 1929*)

64   Valentín Marín y Llovet–Menchik
Barcelona (9), October 4, 1929

[D05] *Colle System*

For those who enjoyed the Bill Murray movie *Groundhog Day*, this is the game for you. For eight out of nine moves (38 through 46) ♘×h7 wins.

1. d4 ♘f6 2. ♘f3 d5 3. e3 e6 4. ♗d3 c5 5. b3 c×d4 6. e×d4 ♗b4+ 7. c3 ♗d6 8. ♕e2 ♘c6 9. ♘e5 ♕e7 10. f4 ♗d7 11. 0–0 0–0 12. ♖f3 g6 13. ♖h3 ♘e8 14. ♖g3 f5 15. ♘d2 ♘×e5 16. f×e5 ♗a3 17. ♗×a3 ♕×a3 18. ♘f3 ♖f7 19. ♘g5 ♖g7 20. ♖h3 ♖c8 21. ♕d2 ♕a5 22. ♖c1 b5 23. ♗b1 ♕b6 24. ♖h6 ♖c6 25. ♕f4 ♕c7 26. ♕d2 ♗c8 27. ♖h3 ♗b7 28. ♗d3 a6 29. ♗f1 ♕a5 30. ♖e1 ♘c7 31. ♖ee3 ♘e8 32. ♖eg3 ♗c8 33. ♖h6 ♖cc7 34. ♖gh3 ♖ce7 35. ♕f4 ♕c7 36. ♕h4 ♕d7 37. ♗e2 ♘c7?? *(see diagram)*

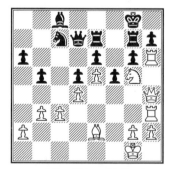

After 37. ... ♘c7

38. ♗d3? 38. ♘×h7! ♖×h7 39. ♖×g6+ ♔f8 (39. ... ♔h8 40. ♕f6+ ♖eg7 41. ♕f8+ ♖g8 42. ♕×g8 mate) 40. ♕g5 ♖eg7 41. ♖×h7 ♖×g6 42. ♕×g6+– **38. ... ♘a8??** 38. ... ♘e8‡ **39. ♗e2?** 39. ♘×h7 A second chance was given and lost **39. ... ♘b6 40. ♗f1?** 40. ♘×h7 Despite her opponent's missing ♘×h7 three times Menchik had to wait for the draw! **40. ... ♕c7 41. a3 ♗b7? 42. ♗e2** 42. ♘×h7 ♔f7 43. ♘f8 ♔e8 44. ♖h8 ♖gf7 45. ♘×e6+ and Black can resign **42. ... ♗c6 43. ♗f1?** 43. ♘×h7 Last time I'll mention it. Actually it's good up until move 46! **43. ... a5 44. ♗e2 a4 45. b4 ♗e8 46. ♗f1 ♘c4 47. ♗×c4 d×c4 48. ♔f2 ♕b7 49. ♖g3 ♕c7 50. ♔e3 ♕b7 51. ♕f4 ♕d5 52. ♕f3 ♕×f3+ 53. ♔×f3 ♗c6+ 54. ♔f4 ♔h8 55. ♘h3 ♔g8 56. ♔g5 ♔f8 57. ♘f4 ♗e4 58. ♖e3 ♔e8 59. ♖e2 ♔d7 60. ♖d2 ♔c6 ½–½** (Source: Gilliam, *Barcelona 1929*; notes by RT)

Round 10 was the bye round for Menchik

65 Menchik–Mario Monticelli
Barcelona (11), October 6, 1929

[D27] *Queen's Gambit Accepted*

After 14. ... b6

Evidently the day off (she had the 10th round bye) was not enough for Menchik to overcome her miserable games in the seventh, eighth and ninth rounds. In this game she never seemed to have a cohesive plan and dropped the exchange on move 23, causing her to resign without waiting to see what her opponent would do.

1. ♘f3 ♘f6 2. c4 e6 3. ♘c3 d5 4. d4 c6 5. e3 ♘bd7 6. ♗d3 a6 7. 0-0 d×c4 8. ♗×c4 c5 9. a4 ♗e7 10. ♕e2 c×d4 11. e×d4 ♘b6 12. ♗a2 0-0 13. ♖e1 ♘bd5 14. ♗d2 b6 *(see diagram)*

15. ♘e5?! [15. ♗c4!?—RT] **15. ... ♗b7 16. f4 ♘b4 17. ♗b1?** [When all else has been eliminated, what ever is left, however unattractive must be the truth. 17. ♗e3—RT] **17. ... ♕×d4+ 18. ♗e3 ♕×e3+ 19. ♕×e3 ♗c5 20. ♕×c5 b×c5 21. ♘e4 ♗×e4 22. ♗×e4 ♖ad8 23. ♗f3?** White resigned without waiting for Black to play ♘c2. **0–1** (Source: Gilliam, *Barcelona 1929*)

66 Ramón Rey Ardid–Menchik
Barcelona (12), October 7, 1929

[D30] *Queen's Gambit Declined*

1. d4 ♘f6 2. ♘f3 e6 3. c4 d5 4. ♗g5 ♘bd7 5. e3 ♗e7 6. ♘bd2 0-0 7. ♗d3 c5 8. 0-0 h6 9. ♗h4 b6 10. ♖c1 ♗b7 11. ♗b1? Premature. Better was 11 ♕e2 followed by ♖fd1.

After 27. ... ♘a5

11. ... ♖c8 12. ♕e2 d×c4 [12. ... ♘e4 is also possible] **13. ♘×c4 ♗e4 14. ♗×e4 ♘×e4 15. ♗×e7 ♕×e7 16. ♕d3 ♘df6 17. ♕a3 ♖fd8 18. ♕a6 c×d4 19. e×d4?** [19. ♘×d4 ♘c5 20. ♕a3 ♕b7 was better. The move played allows Black to take over the c-file] **19. ... ♖c7 20. a3 ♖dc8 21. ♘fe5 ♘d5 22. f3 ♘d2 23. ♖fd1 ♘b3 24. ♖c2 ♘a5 25. ♖dc1 ♘b3 26. ♖d1 ♔h7** [26. ... ♕g5 would be very strong. White could continue: 27. ♘×f7?! (27. h4 ♕f4 28. ♘×f7 ♕×f7 29. ♘d6 ♕d7 30. ♘×c8 ♖×c2) 27. ... ♕g6 28. ♖f2 ♕×f7 29. ♘d6 ♕d7 30. ♘×c8 ♕×c8] **27. ♕a4 ♘a5** *(see diagram)*

28. ♘×a5? After this White is lost. [He had to play 28. ♖dc1 (according to the computer, Black's suggested move is slightly worse than that actually played. Best by a fair bit is 28. ♖e1 ♕h4 29. ♖e4∓] **28. ... ♖×c2 29. ♘ac6 ♖2×c6 30. ♘×c6 ♕g5** Threatening ♘e3 or ♘f4. [Also possible was 30. ... ♕e8 31. ♖c1 ♘e7 32. ♕×a7 ♖×c6 33. ♖×c6 ♘×c6 34. ♕×b6 etc.] **31. h4 ♕g3 32. ♕c2+** There is nothing better. **32. ... f5 33. ♖c1 ♘e7 34. ♕d3 ♕f4** *(see diagram)*

0–1 (Source: Gilliam, *Barcelona 1929*; notes by VM [additional notes by RT])

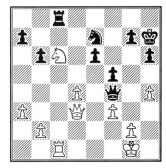

Final position

67 Menchik–Angel Ribera
Barcelona (13), October 9, 1929

[D65] *Queen's Gambit Declined, Classical*

1. ♘f3 ♘f6 2. c4 e6 3. ♘c3 d5 4. d4 ♘bd7 5. ♗g5 ♗e7 6. e3 0-0 7. ♖c1 a6 8. c×d5 e×d5 9. ♗d3 c6 10. ♕c2 ♖e8 11. 0-0 h6 12. ♗f4 ♘h5? Quite likely the losing move! **13. ♘×d5 ♘×f4** Not 13. ... c×d5 14. ♗c7 **14. ♘×f4 ♗d6 15. ♘e2 ♘f6 16. h3 ♕e7 17. ♘c3 ♘d5 18. ♘×d5 c×d5 19. ♗h7+ ♔h8 20. ♗f5 ♗d7 21. ♗×d7 ♕×d7 22. ♕d3 ♖e7 23. ♖c2 ♖ae8 24. ♖fc1 g6 25. ♘e5?!** 25. a3 **25. ... ♕e6 26. f4 ♔g7 27. ♔h1 h5 28. ♖f1 f5 29. ♖fc1 ♔h6 30. ♕e2 ♔g7 31. h4 ♔h6 32. ♕d3 ♖d8 33. ♔h2 ♔g7 34. g3 ♔h6 35. ♕b3 ♗b8 36. ♕b4 ♔g7 37. ♕a5 ♖ee8 38. ♔h3 ♖d6 39. ♕d2 ♔h6 40. ♖c3 ♔g7 41. ♕c2 ♖dd8 42. b4 ♔h6 43. ♕b3 ♖d6 44. ♖c5 ♖ed8 45. ♕c2 ♔g7 46. ♖c8 ♔h6 47. ♖×d8 ♖×d8 48. ♕c5** *(see diagram)*

After 48. ♕c5

48. ... ♗×e5 49. d×e5 d4 50. ♕c4 50. e×d4? ♕×a2 Looks nice in the short term, but leaves the White king so open as to question whether it will be possible to make it secure enough to be able to march the center pawns down the board **50. ... ♕b6** As it turns out the line played and this one are one and the same: 50. ... ♕×c4 51. ♖×c4 d3 52. ♖c1 ♔g7 53. ♔g2 **51. ♕c7 ♕×c7 52. ♖×c7 d3 53. ♖c1 ♔g7 54. ♔g2 ♔f7 55. ♔f3 ♔e6 56. ♖d1 ♖d5 57. ♖d2 ♖d8 58. a3 a5 59. b×a5 ♖d5 60. e4 ♖d4 61. e×f5+ ♔×f5 62. ♔e3 ♖e4+ 63. ♔×d3 ♖a4 64. ♖a2 ♖×a5 65. ♔d4 ♖b5 66. ♖e2 ♔e6 67. ♔c4 ♖a5 68. ♖e3 ♖a6 69. ♖b3 ♖c6+ 70. ♔d4 1-0** (Source: Gilliam, *Barcelona 1929*; notes by RT)

68 Plácido Soler–Menchik
Barcelona (14), October 10, 1929

[A80] *Dutch*

1. c3 f5 2. d4 ♘f6 3. ♘f3 e6 4. ♗g5 ♗e7 5. ♘bd2 0-0 6. ♕c2 d5 7. e3 ♘bd7 8. ♗e2 ♘e4 9. ♗×e7 ♕×e7 10. ♘×e4 f×e4 11. ♘d2 ♕h4 12. ♖f1 c5 13. h3 c4 14. g3 ♕×h3 15. 0-0-0 ♕f5 16. g4 ♕g5 17. ♔b1 b5 18. ♖de1 a5 19. f4 ♕e7 20. ♖h1 ♘b6 21. ♖h2 ♖f7 22. ♘f3 ♖a7 23. ♘e5 g6 24. ♖eh1 ♕d6 25. ♘×f7 ♖×f7 26. ♗d1 b4 27. ♖h6 ♕c7 28. ♕h2 ♖g7 29. ♕h4 a4 *(see diagram)*

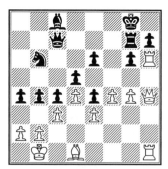

After 29. ... a4

30. ♕f6 [Much better would be 30. c×b4 with a possible line being 30. ... c3 31. b×c3 ♗a6 32. ♕f6 ♕×c3 33. ♕×e6+ ♔f8 34. ♕d6+ ♔f7 35. ♖6h2 a3 36. b5 ♕d3+ 37. ♖c2 ♕×b5+ 38. ♔a1 ♘c4 39. ♕c7+ ♔g8 40. ♕d8+ ♔f7 41. f5+——RT]

30. ... b×c3 31. ♖×h7 c2+ 32. ♗×c2 ♖×h7 33. ♕×g6+ ♔h8 34. ♕f6+ ♔g8 35. ♕g6+ ½-½ (Source: Gilliam, *Barcelona 1929*)

69 Menchik–Saviely Tartakower
Barcelona (15), October 11, 1929

[C01] *French, Exchange*

**1. d4 e6 2. e4 d5 3. e×d5 e×d5 4. ♘f3 ♗d6 5. ♗d3 ♕e7+
6. ♕e2 ♕×e2+ 7. ♗×e2 c6 8. 0–0 ♗f5 9. c3 ♘d7 10. ♗g5
♘gf6 11. ♖e1 0–0 12. ♘bd2 ♖fe8 13. ♗h4 ♗g4 14. ♗×g4
♘×g4 15. ♘f1 h6 16. ♗d2 ♖e6 17. ♘f5 ♗c7 18. f3 ♘gf6
19. ♘1g3 ♖ae8 20. ♔f2 ♘f8 21. ♖×e6 f×e6 22. ♘e3 ♘g6
23. ♘c2 e5 24. ♖e1 ♔f7 25. ♖e2 e×d4 26. ♘×d4 ♘f4
27. ♗×f4 ♗×f4 28. ♖×e8 ♘×e8 29. ♘de2 ♗c7 30. ♔e3
♘d6 31. b3 g6 32. ♔d3 ♔f6 33. ♘d4 ♘f7 34. ♔e3 ♗b6
35. ♘ge2 ♘d6 36. ♔d3 ♘f5 37. ♘×f5 ♔×f5 38. ♔d2** (*see diagram*)

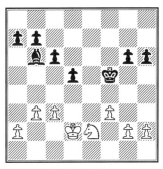

Final position

½–½ (Source: Gilliam, *Barcelona 1929*)

Hastings 1929-1930

December 27, 1929–January 4, 1930

	1	2	3	4	5	6	7	8	9	10	Points	Place
1 Capablanca, José R.	●	=	=	=	1	=	1	=	1	1	6½	1
2 Vidmar, Milan, Sr.	=	●	=	=	1	=	=	1	=	=	5½	2
3 Yates, Frederick D.	=	=	●	=	=	1	=	=	0	1	5	3
4 Maróczy, Géza	=	=	=	●	=	=	=	=	=	=	4½	4–7
5 Sergeant, Edward G.	0	0	=	=	●	1	0	1	=	1	4½	4–7
6 Takács, Sándor	=	=	0	=	0	●	=	=	1	1	4½	4–7
7 Thomas, George A.	0	=	=	=	1	=	●	1	0	=	4½	4–7
8 Winter, William	=	0	=	=	0	=	0	●	1	1	4	8
9 Menchik, Vera	0	=	1	=	=	0	1	0	●	0	3½	9
10 Price, Hubert E.	0	=	0	=	0	0	=	0	1	●	2½	10

The sponsors were not pleased with this iteration of the Christmas Congress as fully 25 out of 45 games ended as draws. Certainly this was not Menchik's fault as she only drew three of her games as opposed to the nine out of nine result by her teacher Maróczy.

Menchik's outstanding performance at Ramsgate 1929 immediately vaulted her into the first level of "British" players. That, plus her women's title and her residency in Hastings made her an attractive catch for the Premier Section of the annual Hastings Christmas Congresses. Her initial outing resulted in a ninth place showing. Although not too impressive on its face, the consensus as stated in BCM was that she played her best chess to date.

At the closing ceremony of the tournament, Menchik was presented with a cup by Lady Hamilton Russell for her victory in the Women's World Championships held earlier.

(R31) Menchik–Hubert Price
Hastings 1929-30 (1), December 27, 1929
1. d4 Not available (59 moves) **0–1**

(R32) Géza Maróczy–Menchik
Hastings 1929-30 (2), December 28, 1929
1. e4 e6 Not available ½–½

70 José Raúl Capablanca–Menchik
Hastings 1929-30 (3), December 29, 1929
[D41] *Queen's Gambit Declined, Semi-Tarrasch*

After 21. ... ♘d4

Not a game that shows off the Cuban's impeccable technique. Twice Menchik had a draw within her grasp only to let it slip away.

1. ♘f3 ♘f6 2. c4 c5 3. ♘c3 d5 4. c×d5 ♘×d5 5. g3 ♘c6 6. ♗g2 e6 7. 0-0 ♗e7 8. d4 0-0 9. ♘×d5 ♕×d5 10. ♗e3 ♕h5 11. d×c5 e5 12. ♘d2 f5 13. f4 e4 14. ♕b3+ ♔h8 15. ♖fe1 ♘d8 16. ♕c2 ♗e6 17. b4 ♘c6 18. a3 ♗f6 19. ♖ad1 ♕f7 20. ♖c1 b5?! 21. c×b6 ♘d4 (see diagram)

22. ♗×d4? Even Capablanca made mistakes. Here it was not necessary to give away the bishop pair. 22. ♕d1 seems to best maintain the advantage **22. ... ♗×d4+ 23. e3 ♗×b6 24. ♘c4 ♗×c4 25. ♕×c4 ♕×c4 26. ♖×c4 ♖ac8 27. ♗f1 g6 28. ♔f2 ♖×c4 29. ♗×c4 ♖c8 30. ♖c1 a5 31. ♔e2 a×b4 32. a×b4 ♔g7 33. h3 ♖a8 34. ♗b3 ♖a3 35. ♖c3 h5 36. g4 h×g4 37. h×g4 f×g4 38. ♔f2 ♔h6 39. ♔g3 ♗d8 40. ♔×g4 ♗f6?** 40. ... ♗e7!? 41. ♖c7 ♖×b3 42. ♖×e7 ♖×b4 43. f5 ♖b1 44. f×g6 (44. f6 ♖f1 and a draw is all that is left.) 44. ... ♔×g6 45. ♖×e4 ♔f6 and as has been known since the time of Philidor the position is drawn **41. ♖c6 ♖×b3 42. ♖×f6 ♔g7 43. ♔g5 ♖×e3 44. ♖×g6+ ♔f7 45. ♖f6+ ♔g7 46. ♖b6 ♖e1 47. ♖b7+ ♔g8 48. ♔f6 e3 49. ♖b8+ ♔h7 50. ♖e8 ♖b1 51. ♖×e3 ♖×b4 52. f5 ♖b1 53. ♔f7 ♖b7+ 54. ♖e7 ♖b6 55. f6 ♖a6 56. ♖d7 ♖a8 57. ♖e7** (see diagram)

After 57. ♖e7

57. ... ♖a6 After the game Capablanca pointed out that Vera missed 57. ... ♖b8 which leads to a draw (BCM, February 1930, p. 55) **58. ♔f8+ ♔g6 59. f7 ♖a8+ 60. ♖e8 ♖a7 61. ♖e6+ ♔h7 62. ♔e8 ♖a8+ 63. ♔e7 ♖a7+** If 63. ... ♔g7 64. ♖a6 and White wins **64. ♔f6 1–0** (Source: Wildhagen, *Capablanca*, 1963; notes by RT)

71 Menchik–Milan Vidmar, Sr.
Hastings 1929-30 (4), December 31, 1929
[D68] *Queen's Gambit Declined, Classical*

The following game may be an example of the draws that the organizers found so frustrating. Menchik maintains a slight pull most of this game. Vidmar of course was a strong master and she no doubt was in no rush to push too hard. Aside from one minor thrust around move 25 Vidmar seems content to coast throughout the game.

1. d4 ♘f6 2. c4 e6 3. ♘c3 d5 4. ♘f3 ♗e7 5. ♗g5 0-0 6. e3 ♘bd7 7. ♖c1 c6 8. ♗d3 d×c4 9. ♗×c4 ♘d5 10. ♗×e7 ♕×e7 11. 0-0 ♘×c3 12. ♖×c3 e5 13. d5 e4 14. ♘d4 c×d5 15. ♗×d5 The tournament report in BCM commented on Vidmar's gallantry in creating a nice symmetrical position when the draw became evident. It's doubtful if many women (or men) would consider that a matter of gallantry now! **15. ...** ♘f6 **16.** ♗c4 ♕e5 **17.** ♘b5 ♗g4 **18.** ♕d6 ♕h5 **19.** ♘d4 ♖ad8 **20.** ♕f4 ♕g6 **21.** ♖fc1 ♘h5 **22.** ♕c7 ♖d7 **23.** ♕a5 ♗f3 **24.** ♗f1 ♖×d4 **25.** e×d4 ♘f4 **26.** g3 ♕g4 **27.** ♕b5 h6 **28.** ♖e3 ♘h3+ **29.** ♗×h3 ♕×h3 **30.** ♕f1 ♕d7 *(see diagram)*

31. ♖×f3 [Certainly ♖×f3 locks in the draw, but is it possible that 31. ♖b3 might be worth considering?—RT]

After 30. ... ♕d7

31. ... e×f3 **32.** ♕d3 ♕d5 **33.** b3 ♖e8 **34.** h3 ♖d8 **35.** ♖c3 ♕×d4 **36.** ♕×d4 ♖×d4 **37.** ♖×f3 b5 **38.** ♖c3 ♖d2 **39.** a3 ♖a2 **40.** b4 *(see diagram)*

After 40. b4

The next 28 moves are missing. The position on move 68, however, is given on page 57 of the February 1930 *BCM*. The kingside pawns have all evaporated, leaving the a and b pawns as well as the rooks. After a couple of pawn trades the game was drawn on move 72. ½–½ (Source: *www.Chessgames.com*)

72 Menchik–Frederick D. Yates
Hastings 1929-30 (5), January 1, 1930

[D55] *Queen's Gambit Declined*

Following is a nice example of Menchik's strong positional play transposing into a precise endgame—one of her trademarks.

1. d4 d5 **2.** c4 e6 **3.** ♘c3 ♘f6 **4.** ♗g5 ♗e7 **5.** e3 0-0 **6.** ♘f3 b6 **7.** c×d5 e×d5 **8.** ♗d3 ♗b7 **9.** 0-0 ♘bd7 **10.** ♖c1 c5 **11.** d×c5 ♘×c5 **12.** ♘d4 *(see diagram)*

After 12. ♘d4

12. ... ♘fe4 **13.** ♗×e7 ♕×e7 **14.** ♗e2 ♖ad8 **15.** a3 ♕e5 **16.** ♘f3 ♕f6 **17.** ♘d4 ♖fe8 **18.** ♗b5 ♖e5 **19.** b4 ♘×c3 **20.** ♖×c3 ♘e6 **21.** ♘×e6 ♕×e6 **22.** ♖c7 ♗a8 **23.** ♕c1 ♖f8 **24.** ♗c6 ♕f5 **25.** ♗×a8 ♖×a8 **26.** ♕c2 ♕×c2 **27.** ♖×c2 ♔f8 **28.** ♖fc1 ♖ae8 **29.** ♖c8 ♖×c8 **30.** ♖×c8+ ♖e8 **31.** ♖c1 ♖e7 **32.** ♖c8+ ♖e8 **33.** ♖c1 ♖e7 **34.** ♔f1 ♖d7 **35.** ♔e2 ♔e7 **36.** ♖c8 ♖d8 **37.** ♖×d8 ♔×d8 **38.** ♔d3 ♔d7 **39.** ♔d4 ♔c6 *(see diagram)*

After 39. ... ♔c6

40. a4 a6 **41.** f4 ♔d6 **42.** g4 ♔c6 **43.** ♔e5 a5 **44.** b5+ ♔c5 **45.** f5 h6 **46.** h3 ♔b4 **47.** ♔×d5 ♔×a4 **48.** ♔c6 ♔b3 **49.** ♔×b6 a4 **50.** ♔c5 a3 **51.** b6 a2 **52.** b7 a1♕ **53.** b8♕+ *(see diagram)*

After 53. b8♕+

53. ... ♔c2 **54.** ♕h2+ ♔d3 **55.** ♕f4 ♕a5+ **56.** ♔c6 ♕a8+ **57.** ♔d7 f6 **58.** ♔e7
♕g8 **59.** ♕d4+ ♔e2 **60.** ♕d7 ♔f2 **61.** e4 [Cleaner is 61. ♔e6 ♕h8 62. ♕f7 ♔g3 63. ♔f8
♕h7 64. ♔f7—RT] **61. ...** ♔g3 **62.** ♕d3+ ♔h4 **63.** ♕f3 g5 **64.** ♔xf6 **1–0**

73 William Winter–Menchik
Hastings 1929-30 (6), January 2, 1930
[E00] *Catalan Bogo-Indian*

After 23. g4

1. d4 ♘f6 **2.** c4 e6 **3.** a3 d5 **4.** ♗g5 ♗e7 **5.** e3 h6 **6.** ♗h4
0-0 **7.** ♘c3 ♘bd7 **8.** ♘f3 ♘e4 **9.** ♗xe7 ♕xe7 **10.** ♕c2
♘xc3 **11.** ♕xc3 dxc4 **12.** ♗xc4 c5 **13.** 0-0 cxd4 **14.** exd4
♘f6 **15.** ♘e5 ♖d8 **16.** f4 ♘d5 **17.** ♕g3 ♕d6 **18.** ♖ad1
♗d7 **19.** ♗a2 ♗a4 **20.** ♖d2 ♖ac8 **21.** ♕d3 ♗d7 **22.** ♗b1
♘f6 **23.** g4 *(see diagram)*

23. ... ♗c6? [23. ... ♕b6 24. ♘xd7 ♖xd7 25. g5 ♘e8
26. gxh6 (26. ♕h7+ ♔f8 27. gxh6 ♖xd4 28. hxg7+ ♘xg7
29. ♕h8+ ♔e7 30. ♕h4+ f6∓) 26. ... g6=—RT] **24.** ♘xc6
♕xc6 **25.** g5 hxg5 **26.** fxg5 ♘e8 **27.** ♕h7+ ♔f8 **28.** ♖df2
♘d6 **29.** g6 f5 **30.** ♕h8+ ♔e7 **31.** ♕xg7+ ♔e8 **32.** ♕g8+
♔d7 **33.** ♕h7+ ♔e8 **34.** g7 **1–0** (Source: *www.Chessgames.com*)

74 Menchik–George Thomas
Hastings 1929-30 (7), January 3, 1930
[E94] *King's Indian Defense Classical*

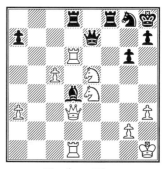

Final position

1. d4 ♘f6 **2.** c4 g6 **3.** ♘c3 ♗g7 **4.** e4 d6 **5.** ♗e2 ♘bd7
6. ♘f3 0-0 **7.** 0-0 e5 **8.** dxe5 dxe5 **9.** ♕c2 c6 **10.** h3 ♕e7
11. ♗e3 ♘h5 **12.** ♖fd1 ♘f4 **13.** ♗f1 ♘c5 **14.** b4 ♘a6
15. a3 ♗e6 **16.** c5 ♘c7 **17.** ♖d6 f5 **18.** ♘e1 fxe4 **19.** b5
♘fd5 **20.** bxc6 bxc6 **21.** ♘xe4 ♘xe3 **22.** fxe3 ♘d5
23. ♗c4 ♗h6 **24.** ♖xc6 ♗xe3+ **25.** ♔h1 ♔h8 **26.** ♘f3
♗g8 **27.** ♖d6 ♘f6 **28.** ♗xg8 ♘xg8 **29.** ♖ad1 ♖ad8
30. ♕d3 ♗d4 **31.** ♘xe5 *(see diagram)*

In this position, which is moderately favorable to Menchik, a time scramble ensued and Thomas lost enough material
to force resignation. **1–0**

(R33) Sándor Takács–Menchik
Hastings 1929-30 (8), January 4, 1930
1. c4 Not available (68 moves) **1–0**

(R34) Menchik–Edward G. Sergeant
Hastings 1929-30 Hastings (9), January 5, 1930
1. d4 Not available ½–½

Hastings Chess Club Championship 1930

Although the crosstable has eluded this author's research, Menchik played in and won,
for the only time, the Hastings Chess Club Championship with a score of +13 –0 =1.

Hastings Invitational 1930

April 14–18, 1930

		1	2	3	4	5	Pts
1	Drewitt, J. A. J.	•	=	1	1	0	2½
2	Winter, William	=	•	0	1	1	2½
3	Menchik, Vera	0	1	•	0	1	2
4	Jackson, Edward M.	0	0	1	•	=	1½
5	Tylor, Theodore H.	1	0	0	=	•	1½

The following event is not mentioned in any listing of events in which Menchik played. The tournament was organized by the Hastings Chess Club in April 1930. Originally intended to have six competitors, they were unable to find an appropriate sixth so they proceeded with five players and a bye each round. All information comes from *The Times* between 15 and 19 April 1930.

Round 1 Menchik had the bye.

(R35) Menchik–William Winter
Hastings 1930 (2), April 15, 1930

Menchik against Winter began in her usual fashion below and an exchange of the center pawns soon followed, Winter playing to keep a pawn on the queen's file and eventually hamper his opponent by bringing it to d4. The plan had to be carefully watched, for there were innumerable variations ending in disaster if not properly met. Menchik threatened an immediate mate, and Winter overlooked the further danger from an obtrusive knight in the center. This could, and should have been exchanged, the penalty for the oversight being the loss of the queen.

1. d4 d5 2. c4 e6 3. ♘f3 c6—Remaining moves not available **1–0**

A plaque at the Hastings Chess Club listing club champions. Vera is listed for her victory in 1930.

(R36) James A. J. Drewitt–Menchik
Hastings 1930 (3), April 16, 1930

Drewitt played the variation of the opening wherein White obtains a "stonewall" position with pawns at d5, c4 and e4, leaving Black very little freedom in the center. It was a long way, however, before he could obtain any material advantage, and some of the major pieces were exchanged before he saw his way to win a pawn. This involved exchanging to leave himself with a rook and six pawns, to the rook and five pawns for Menchik, and Drewitt does not usually make mistakes in an ending of this kind. He won in 43 moves.

1. d4—Remaining moves not available **1–0**

(R37) Menchik–Theodore H. Tylor
Hastings 1930 (4), April 17, 1930

The game came down to an ending with each having knight and pawns. Tylor was outplayed here and lost in 48 moves.

1. d4—Remaining moves not available **1–0**

(R38) Edward M. Jackson–Menchik
Hastings 1930 (5), April 18, 1930

Jackson was not quite happy against Menchik's defense (the Caro-Kann), for she secured some positional advantage. Jackson recovered later, however, and won in 37 moves.

1. e4 c6 2. d4 d5—Remaining moves not available **1–0**

Canterbury 1930
(23rd Kent County Association—Premier Tourney)
April 19–26, 1930

	1	2	3	4	5	6	7	8	Points	Place
1 Thomas, George	•	1	=	1	0	1	1	1	5½	1
2 Seitz, Jakob Adolf	0	•	=	=	=	1	1	1	4½	2–4
3 Winter, William	=	=	•	=	0	1	1	1	4½	2–4
4 Yates, Frederick D.	0	=	=	•	=	1	1	1	4½	2–4
5 Menchik Vera	1	=	1	=	•	0	0	=	3½	5
6 Abrahams, Gerald	0	0	0	0	1	•	1	1	3	6
7 Spencer, Edmund	0	0	0	0	1	0	•	1	2	7
8 Price, Hubert Ernest	0	0	0	0	=	0	0	•	½	8

According to *The Times* of June 21, 1930, Menchik was a last minute replacement for Saviely Tartakower who was ill. The only foreigner aside from Menchik (nominally) was Jakob Seitz of Germany. The tournament had 64 players in eight sections and was held at St. Augustine's College. Menchik played especially long games in the first round (Yates) and in the last game (Thomas); both of which had double adjournments. In the case of Thomas it was his only loss and occurred after he had clinched first place. This is another of those not infrequent cases where Menchik scored as well or better against the top of the field as against the bottom.

75 William Winter–Menchik
Canterbury (2), April 1930
[E81] *King's Indian Defense, Sämisch Variation*

Winter played the same opening as Drewitt had in Hastings the previous month, but she [Vera] had learned her lesson from that defeat and played quite a different continuation. A premature kingside attack by Winter gave her further opportunities leaving him with only bad moves to make, besides certain loss of material.[45]

1. d4 ♘f6 2. c4 g6 3. f3 c5 [The more usual alternative 3. ... d5 has the objection of leaving White with a strong center after 4. c×d5 ♘×d5 5. e4 etc. The text is not known to have been refuted—RT] **4. d5 ♗g7 5. e4 d6 6. ♘c3 0-0 7. ♗e3** He tries for a kingside attack but there seems no reason why White should not play ♗d3 followed by ♘ge2 and 0–0. The violent attacking line ♗e3, ♕d2 and 0–0–0 looks quite illogical and just because Alekhine introduced it, it does not follow that it is White's only possible way of treating the variation. **7. … ♕a5 8. ♕d2 ♖d8** Preventing the exchange threatened at h6 and preparing generally for an onslaught on the queenside. Pieces are not being locked up so as to give White a clear run on the kingside. **9. ♘ge2** [9. ♗d3 followed by ♘ge2 and 0–0 would avoid the danger of Black's threatened attack—RT] **9. … a6 10. ♘f4** A move whose object is hard to discern. He could have tried 10. ♘c1 so as to get rid of Black's queen by ♘b3, etc. and develop his other pieces by ♗d3 and 0–0. **10. … e5** White must not choose between retiring his knight to e2 or d3, permitting … b5, and loosening his hold on the center by taking the pawn. **11. d×e6 f×e6 12. g4** This has no punch here and is just a useless weakening of his kingside. [12. ♗e2 and 13. 0–0 was still reasonably good—RT] **12. … ♘c6 13. h4** Consequential but just a waste of time in view of what follows. **13. … ♘d4!** *(see diagram)*

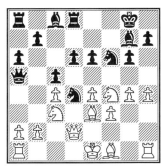
After 13. … ♘d4

Very forceful! **14. ♕f2??** [14. ♗g2 would hold the position better and would at any rate get another piece off the back rank. The text loses with breath-taking suddenness—RT] **14. … e5!** A killing blow which must have astonished White. If now 15. ♘d3 (or ♘h3) ♗×g4!! 16. f×g4 ♘×g4 17. ♕g1 (or ♕g3) ♘×e3 and wins. If 15. ♘fe2 ♗×g4 16. f×g4 ♘×e4 17. ♕g1 ♘f3+ and wins. **15. ♘fd5 ♘×d5 16. e×d5 ♖f8!** A remarkable position. There is just no defense to the double threat of 17. … ♘ or ♖×f3 and 17. ♗×g4. **0–1** (Source: *Chess*, August 1944, #1802; notes by W. Ritson Morry [additional notes by RT])

76 Menchik–Gerald Abrahams
Canterbury, April 1930
[D30] *Queen's Gambit Declined*

1. d4 d5 2. c4 e6 3. ♘f3 c6 4. e3 ♘d7 5. ♘bd2 ♘gf6 6. ♗d3 ♗d6 7. 0–0 0–0 8. e4 e5 9. ♖e1 d×e4 10. ♘×e4 ♘×e4 11. ♗×e4 f5 12. ♗c2 e4 13. ♘d2 ♕h4 14. ♘f1 ♘f6 15. ♕d2 h6 16. b3 ♗d7 *(see diagram)*

After 16. … ♗d7

17. ♗b2 Probably an error as Black has been allowed to dominate the kingside with a major attack and pawn majority. White's pieces are not well coordinated to counter in either the center or the kingside. Better seems to be 17. a3 with the goal of controlling b4 and opening the second rank for her rook **17. … ♗e8 18. h3 ♗g6 19. d5 f4 20. d×c6 ♖ad8 21. ♕a5** No better is 21. ♗×f6 ♕×f6 22. ♕d5+ ♔h8 23. c×b7 f3 24. g3 ♗×g3! and Black has a win **21. … e3 22. ♖e2 ♗×c2 23. ♖×c2 e×f2+ 24. ♔h1 f3 25. ♕f5 f×g2+ 26. ♔×g2 h5?** After 26. … b×c6 27. ♕e6+ ♔h8 28. ♖×f2 ♘e4 29. ♖×f8+ ♖×f8 and the win is straight forward *(see diagram)*

After 26. … h5

27. ♕e6+? 27. c5 ♗c7 28. ♖c4 ♘g4 29. ♕e6+ ♖f7 30. h×g4 ♖d3 31. ♕e8+ ♖f8 (Not 31. ... ♔h7 32. ♕×f7 ♖g3+ 33. ♘×g3 ♕×g3+ 34. ♔f1 ♕d3+ 35. ♔×f2) 32. ♕e6+ and we have a draw **27. ... ♔h7 28. ♖×f2 ♘e4 29. ♖×f8 ♖×f8 30. ♖d1 ♕g5+ 31. ♔h1 ♘f2 mate 0–1** (Source: Abrahams, *Not Only Chess*, p. 250; notes by RT)

77 Edmund Spencer–Menchik
Canterbury (5), April 19, 1930
[C00] *French Defense*

1. e4 e6 2. ♗b5 c5 3. c3 ♕b6 4. ♕e2 ♘f6 5. ♘a3 a6
6. ♗a4 ♘c6 7. ♘f3 ♗e7 8. 0-0 d5 9. e5 ♘d7 10. ♗c2
0-0 11. ♖d1 ♕c7 12. d4 c×d4 13. c×d4 b5 14. ♘g5 ♗×g5
15. ♗×g5 b4 16. ♖ac1? b×a3 17. ♕h5 f5 18. e×f6 ♘×f6
19. ♗×f6 g×f6 20. ♗a4 ♗d7 21. b×a3 ♕d6 22. ♖c3 (*see diagram*)

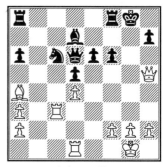

After 22. ♖c3

22. ... ♖f7?! [A better shot for good lines would be 22. ... ♗e8—RT] **23. ♖g3+ ♔f8 24. ♗c2 ♔e7 25. ♕h6 ♘d8 26. ♗×h7 ♗a4 27. ♖e1 ♔d7 28. ♗g8 ♖f8 29. ♖g7+ ♔c8 30. ♕h3 ♗d7 31. ♕c3+ ♔c7 32. ♕d2 ♕d6 33. ♖c1+** (*see diagram*)

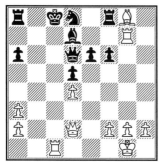

After 33. ♖c1

33. ... ♔b8?? Could this and the many second rate moves in the past 10 be time pressure? [33. ... ♘c6 should hold, although with the exposed king and the wildly asymmetrical position the result is far from a given—RT] **34. ♖×d7 ♕×d7 35. ♕b4+ ♔a7 36. ♕c5+ ♔b8 37. ♕×f8 1–0** (Source: *www.Chessgames.com*)

Scarborough 1930
June 23–July 5, 1930

		1	2	3	4	5	6	7	8	9	10	11	12	Points	Place
1	Colle, Edgar	●	=	=	=	1	=	=	1	1	1	1	1	8½	1
2	Maróczy, Géza	=	●	=	=	1	=	=	1	1	=	=	1	7½	2
3	Rubinstein, Akiba	=	=	●	0	1	=	=	1	=	=	1	1	7	3
4	Ahues, Carl O.	=	=	1	●	0	=	=	=	1	=	1	=	6½	4–5
5	Sultan Khan, Mir	0	0	0	1	●	d	1	1	1	1	0	1	6½	4–5
6	Grünfeld, Ernst F.	=	=	=	=	=	●	=	=	=	=	1	=	6	6
7	Thomas, George A.	=	=	=	=	0	=	●	=	=	=	=	1	5½	7
8	Michell, Reginald P.	0	0	0	=	0	=	=	●	1	=	1	=	4½	8–9
9	Yates, Frederick D.	0	0	=	0	0	=	=	0	●	1	1	1	4½	8–9
10	Menchik, Vera	0	=	=	=	0	=	=	=	0	●	=	=	4	10
11	Winter, William	0	=	0	0	1	0	=	0	0	=	●	=	3	11
12	Sergeant, Edward G.	0	0	0	=	0	=	0	=	0	=	=	●	2½	12

For the 23rd Annual Congress of the British Chess Federation it was decided to hold an international tournament of six foreign masters and six home players. When one of the foreign players, Saviely Tartakower, fell ill his place was filled by Menchik.

The crosstable seems to show Menchik as a solid player who is maybe lacking energy. The truth was more of a rollercoaster. After gaining a better position against Winter and a worse one against Thomas, she ended up drawing both. She then quickly traded pieces in a 17 move draw with Grünfeld. Against Colle, Menchik had at least equality only to blunder a piece after the adjournment. Solid draws against GMs Rubinstein and Maróczy were interspersed with a bizarre draw with the German Ahues where she was much better and then seemed to lose the technical abilities that were generally her forte.

78 Menchik–William Winter
Scarborough (1), June 23, 1930
[E14] *Queen's Indian*

1. d4 ♘f6 2. c4 e6 3. ♘f3 b6 4. e3 ♗b7 5. ♗d3 ♗e7 6. ♘c3 d6 7. 0-0 0-0 8. e4 c5 9. d5 ♘a6 10. ♖e1 e5 11. ♘d2 ♘c7 12. ♘f1 ♗c8 13. ♘g3 ♘fe8 14. f4 e×f4 15. ♗×f4 ♗g5 16. ♕f3 ♗×f4 17. ♕×f4 ♕f6 18. ♕×f6 ♘×f6 19. e5 d×e5 20. ♖×e5 ♖e8 21. ♖ae1 ♗d7 22. ♗f5 ♔f8 23. ♗×d7 ♘×d7 24. ♖×e8+ ♖×e8 25. ♖×e8+ ♘×e8 26. ♘ge4 ♔e7 27. b3 ♘ef6 28. ♘×f6 ♔×f6 29. ♔f2 ♔e5 30. ♔e3 f5 31. ♘b5 a5 32. g3 g5 33. ♔f3 ♘f6 34. ♘c3 ♔d4 35. ♘a4 ♘d7 36. h4 h6 37. h×g5 ½–½ (Source: Golombek, *1930 Scarborough*)

79 George Thomas–Menchik
Scarborough (2), June 24, 1930
[B13] *Caro-Kann, Exchange*

Final position

1. e4 c6 2. d4 d5 3. e×d5 c×d5 4. ♗d3 ♘f6 5. ♗f4 ♘c6 6. c3 ♗g4 7. ♘e2 e6 8. ♕b3 ♗×e2 9. ♗×e2 ♕d7 10. ♘d2 ♗e7 11. ♘f3 0-0 12. 0-0 a6 13. a4 ♖fc8 14. ♖fe1 ♗d6 15. ♗×d6 ♕×d6 16. ♗d3 ♕c7 17. ♕d1 ♖ab8 18. ♕e2 ♕f4 19. h3 ♘d7 20. g3 ♕f6 21. ♘h2 ♘f8 22. f4 ♕d8 23. ♘f3 ♕c7 24. ♔h2 ♘a5 25. ♘e5 ♘c4 26. ♘×c4 d×c4 27. ♗e4 ♘d7 28. ♗f3 ♘f6 29. ♕e5 ♕b6 30. ♖e2 ♘d7 31. ♕e3 ♕a5 32. ♖ee1 ♕b6 33. ♖e♕a5 34. ♖ee1 ♕b6 35. ♖e2 ♕a5 36. ♕d2 b5 37. ♕d1 b4 38. d5 e×d5 39. ♗×d5 ♘f6 40. ♖e5 ♘×d5 41. ♖×d5 *(see diagram)* ½–½ (Source: Golombek, *1930 Scarborough*)

80 Menchik–Ernst Grünfeld
Scarborough (3), June 25, 1930
[E14] *Grünfeld Defense*

What do you do when your opponent allows you free play and you are content to split the point? Split the point and play tennis or bridge.

1. d4 ♘f6 2. c4 e6 3. ♘f3 b6 4. e3 ♗b7 5. ♗d3 ♗b4+ 6. ♗d2 ♗×d2+ 7. ♘b×d2 d6 8. 0-0 ♘bd7 9. ♕c2 ♕e7 10. ♘e4 0-0 *(see diagram)*

11. ♘×f6+ ♘×f6 12. ♘g5 h6 13. ♘h7 ♘×h7 14. ♗×h7+ ♔h8 15. ♗e4 c5 16. ♗×b7 ♕×b7 17. d×c5 d×c5 ½–½ (Source: Golombek, *1930 Scarborough*)

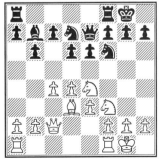
After 10. ... 0-0

81　Edgar Colle–Menchik

Scarborough (4), June 26, 1930

[B07] *Pirc Defense*

1. d4 ♘f6 2. ♘f3 g6 3. ♘bd2 ♗g7 4. e4 d6 5. ♗c4 0–0 6. 0–0 c5 7. d×c5 d×c5 8. ♕e2 ♘c6 9. ♘b3 ♕c7 10. h3 ♘d7 11. c3 ♘ce5 12. ♘×e5 ♘×e5 13. ♗f4 ♗d7 14. ♘h2 ♖ad8 15. a4 b6 16. a5 ♗c6 17. ♗b5 ♕b7?! 17. ... ♗×b5 18. ♕×b5 e6± (18. ... ♕d7 19. ♕×d7 ♖×d7=) **18. ♗a6 ♕c7 19. f4 ♘d7 20. ♘d2 b5** 20. ... b×a5!? A lot of work will

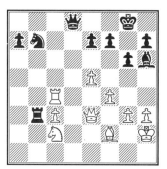

After 40. ♖c4

go into holding this pawn until it is favorable to release it, but is an interesting idea. An example of line could be as follows 21. ♗d3 a4 22. ♘c4 ♘b6 23. f5 ♕d7 24. ♖ad1 ♗b5 25. f×g6 h×g6 26. ♘e5 ♗×e5 27. ♗×b5 ♗×h2+ 28. ♔×h2 ♕e6∓ **21. ♗×b5 ♗×b5 22. ♕×b5 ♖b8 23. ♕d3 ♖×b2 24. ♘c4 ♖b3 25. e5 ♘b8 26. ♖ab1 ♖×b1 27. ♖×b1 ♖d8 28. ♕e3 ♕c6 29. ♗g3 ♕d5 30. ♕e2 ♘c6 31. ♗f2 ♗h6 32. g3 ♖b8 33. ♖d1 ♕e6 34. ♔h2 ♕c8 35. ♕e3 ♖b5 36. ♖d5 ♘×a5 37. ♘a3 ♖b3 38. ♖×c5 ♕d8 39. ♘c2 ♘b7 40. ♖c4** *(see diagram)*

40. ... ♕d1? 40. ... ♘a5 41. ♖b4 (41. ♖a4 e6 42. ♘b4 ♗f8 43. ♕×a7 ♖×c3 44. ♖×a5 ♗×b4=) 41. ... ♕c8= **41. ♘e1 ♖b2 42. ♖d4 ♕a1** 42. ... ♕e2 43. ♕×e2 ♖×e2 44. ♔g2 a5± **43. ♖b4?!** 43. e6 ♕a2∓ **43. ... a5 44. ♖×b2 ♕×b2 45. ♕b6 ♕×b6 46. ♗×b6 e6?** 46. ... ♔f8∓ **47. c4 g5 48. c5 ♘×c5 49. ♗×c5 g×f4 50. g4 ♔g7 51. h4 ♔g6 52. ♘f3 ♗g7 53. h5+ ♔h6 54. ♗e7 a4 55. ♗g5 mate 1–0** (Source: Golombek, *1930 Scarborough*; notes by RT)

82　Menchik–Reginald Pryce Michell

Scarborough (5), June 28, 1930

[E11] *Bogo-Indian Defense*

1. d4 ♘f6 2. c4 e6 3. ♘f3 ♗b4+ 4. ♗d2 ♕e7 5. ♘c3 b6 6. e3 ♗×c3 7. ♗×c3 ♘e4 8. ♕c2 ♗b7 9. ♗e2 0–0 10. 0–0 ♘×c3 11. ♕×c3 d6 12. c5 d×c5 13. d×c5 ♕×c5 14. ♕×c5 b×c5 15. ♖ac1 ♗a6 16. ♖fe1 ♗×e2 17. ♖×e2 ♘a6 18. ♘d2 ♖fd8 19. g3 ♖ab8 20. ♘b3 ♖b5 21. ♖ec2 g6 22. ♖c3 ♖db8 23. ♘×c5 ♘×c5 24. ♖×c5 ♖×b2 25. ♖×c7 ♖×a2 26. ♖c8+ ♖×c8 27. ♖×c8+ ♔g7 28. ♖c7 h5 29. h4 a5 30. ♖a7 *(see diagram)*

30. ... ♕f6 31. ♔g2 e5 32. ♔f3 ♖a4 33. e4 ♖a3+ 34. ♔g2 a4 35. ♖a6+ ♔e7 36. ♖a7+ ♔e6 37. ♖a6+ ½–½ (Source: Golombek, *1930 Scarborough*)

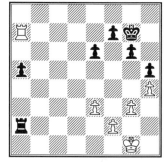

After 30. ♖a7

83　Mir Sultan Khan–Menchik

Scarborough (6), June 29, 1930

[B13] *Caro-Kann, Exchange*

1. e4 c6 2. d4 d5 3. e×d5 c×d5 4. ♗d3 ♘c6 5. c3 ♕c7 6. ♘e2 e6 7. ♗f4 ♗d6 8. ♗g3 ♘f6 9. ♘d2 0–0 10. f4 ♘h5 11. 0–0 f5 12. ♖c1 ♘×g3 13. h×g3 ♕f7 14. ♘f3 ♗e7 15. ♕c2 *(see diagram)*

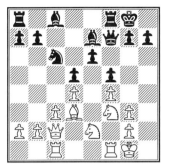

After 15. ♕c2

15. ... h6?! [15. ... ♕h5 16. ♘e5 a6=—RT] **16. g4 f×g4?** Given that White does not wish to capture on f5 and that Black has no threat on the f4 pawn, why fix the open target at e6 (blocking the bishop) and even more importantly open every White piece to the kingside attack? **17. ♘e5 ♘×e5 18. f×e5 ♕e8 19. ♗g6 ♕d8 20. ♖×f8+ ♗×f8 21. ♖f1** *(see diagram)*

21. ... ♗e7 one of the worst of a host of bad options.

After 21. ♖f1

22. ♗h7+ [22. ♗f7+ ♔h8 23. ♘f4 and mate in seven—RT] **22. ... ♔h8 23. ♘f4 g5 24. ♘g6+ ♔g7 25. ♘×e7 1–0**

(Source: Golombek, *1930 Scarborough*)

84 Menchik–Akiba Rubinstein

Scarborough (7), June 30, 1930

[D21] *Queen's Gambit Accepted*

Menchik and Akiba seemed to take this as an off day and avoided any great work—both being predisposed to trades and maintaining a symmetrical position. This was no doubt a satisfactory result for Menchik, but just aggravated Rubinstein's reputation as having declined since the war.

1. d4 d5 2. ♘f3 c5 3. c4 d×c4 4. ♘c3 a6 5. e4 c×d4 6. ♕×d4 ♕×d4 7. ♘×d4 e6 8. ♗×c4 ♗d7 9. 0-0 ♘c6 10. ♘×c6 ♗×c6 11. ♗e3 ♘f6 12. f3 ♗e7 13. ♗b3 0-0 14. ♘a4 ♘d7 15. ♘b6 ♘×b6 16. ♗×b6 ♖fc8 17. ♖fd1 ♗e8 18. ♖ac1 ♗f6 19. ♖×c8 ♖×c8 20. ♗d4 ♗×d4+ 21. ♖×d4 ♔f8 22. ♔f2 e5 23. ♖d2 ♔e7 24. ♖c2 ♖×c2+ 25. ♗×c2 a5 26. ♔e3 ♔d6 27. ♗b3 ♔c5 28. ♗d5 b5 29. ♗b3 f6 30. ♔d3 h6 31. ♗e6 b4 32. ♗c4 ♗d7 33. g4 g5 34. b3 ♗e8 35. ♔e3 ♗d7 36. ♗d3 *(see diagram)*

½–½ (Source: Golombek, *1930 Scarborough*)

Final position

85 Frederick D. Yates–Menchik

Scarborough (8), July 1, 1930

[B15] *Caro-Kann, 3.Nc3*

1. e4 c6 2. d4 d5 3. ♘c3 d×e4 4. ♘×e4 ♘f6 5. ♘×f6+ e×f6 6. c3 ♗d6 7. ♗d3 ♕c7 8. ♘e2 ♗e6 9. ♕c2 ♘d7 10. c4 g6 11. ♗d2 f5 12. ♘c3 ♘f6 13. 0-0-0 ♗f4 14. ♔b1 ♗×d2 15. ♖×d2 0-0 16. f3 ♖fd8 17. ♘e2 b5 18. c×b5 ♕a5 19. ♘c3 c×b5 20. ♗×b5 ♗×a2+ 21. ♘×a2 ♕×b5 22. ♘c3 ♕b7 23. ♖hd1 ♘d5 24. ♘×d5 ♖×d5 25. ♖d3 ♖b8 26. ♖a3 ♖b5 27. ♖d2 ♕d5 28. ♕c3 a5 29. h4 h5 30. ♕e3 ♖b4 31. ♖c3 ♖b3 31. ... a4! 32. ♖a3 ♕b5 33. ♕c3 ♖d8–+ **32. ♖dc2 a4 33. ♖c8+ ♖×c8 34. ♖×c8+** *(see diagram)*

After 34. ♖×c8+

34. ... ♔g7?? 34. ... ♔h7 35. ♕e8 ♕×d4 36. ♕×f7+ ♕g7 37. ♕×g7+ ♔×g7 38. ♖c3 (38. ♖c4 a3+− 39. ♖c2 ♖b4 40. g3−+ [40. ♔a2 a×b2 41. ♖×b2 ♖×h4−+]) 38. ... ♖b4 39. g3 f4 40. g4 h×g4 41. f×g4 f3 42. ♖×f3 ♖×g4 43. ♖h3 ♔h6 44. ♔a2 ♔h5 45. ♔a3−+ **35. ♕e8 ♖×b2+ 36. ♔×b2 ♕b3+ 37. ♔c1 ♕a3+ 38. ♔d2 ♕b4+ 39. ♔e2 1−0** (Source: Golombek, *1930 Scarborough*; notes by RT)

86   Menchik–Carl Oscar Ahues

Scarborough (9), July 3, 1930

[A53] *Old Indian*

After 17. ♗f1

This game was Menchik's for the taking except that starting on about move 27 she made one imprecise move after another. The biggest thing that can be said in Ahues' favor is that he did not get in the way of Menchik's gift of the draw.

1. d4 ♘f6 2. c4 d6 3. ♘c3 ♘c6 4. d5 ♘b8 5. e4 e5 6. d×e6 ♗×e6 7. ♘f3 ♘c6 8. ♗e2 ♗e7 9. 0−0 0−0 10. b3 ♖e8 11. ♗b2 ♗f8 12. ♘d4 ♗d7 13. f3 g6 14. ♘d5 ♗g7 15. ♖e1 h6 16. ♖c1 ♘h7 17. ♗f1 *(see diagram)*

17. ... f5?! 17. ... ♘g5 maintains the edge **18. ♘×c6 b×c6 19. ♗×g7 ♔×g7 20. ♘c3**

After 49. ... c5

♘g5 21. ♕d4+ ♕f6? 21. ... ♔h7 **22. e5 ♖×e5 23. f4 ♖×e1 24. ♕×f6+ ♔×f6 25. f×g5+ h×g5 26. ♖×e1 ♗e6 27. ♖d1 ♖e8 28. ♔f2 g4 29. ♖d2** For three moves in a row Menchik has played second rate moves that have eroded a strong advantage. **29. ... ♖h8 30. ♔g1 g5 31. g3 ♗d7 32. ♗d3 ♔e5 33. ♗b1 ♗e6 34. ♖e2+ ♔f6 35. ♖f2 ♔e5 36. ♖e2+ ♔f6 37. ♖e1 a5 38. ♗c2 ♗d7 39. ♘d1 ♖b8 40. ♘e3 ♖d8?** 40. ... f4!? **41. ♔f2?** 41. ♗×f5 ♗×f5 42. ♖f1+− **41. ... ♖h8 42. ♔g1 f4 43. ♘d1 f3 44. ♘f2 d5 45. ♗d3 ♖a8 46. ♘d1 ♗e6 47. ♘c3 ♖h8 48. c×d5 c×d5 49. ♘d1 c5** *(see diagram)* **50. ♘e3?** Last chance: 50. ♘c3 **50. ... a4 51. ♖c1 a×b3 52. a×b3 ♔e5 53. ♗f1 ♔d6 54. ♖a1 ♖b8 55. ♖a3 ♔e5 56. ♘c2 ♗f5 57. ♘e3 ♗e6 58. ♘c2 ½−½** (Source: Golombek, *1930 Scarborough*; notes by RT)

87   Géza Maróczy–Menchik

Scarborough (10), July 4, 1930

[B15] *Caro-Kann, 3.Nc3*

This is another game which coasted into a passive draw; in this case with her mentor.

1. e4 c6 2. d4 d5 3. ♘c3 d×e4 4. ♘×e4 ♘f6 5. ♘×f6+ e×f6 6. ♗c4 ♗d6 7. ♕e2+ ♕e7 8. ♕×e7+ ♔×e7 9. ♘e2 ♖e8 10. ♗f4 ♗×f4 11. ♘×f4 ♕f8+ 12. ♘e2 ♗f5 13. ♔d2 ♘d7 14. ♘g3 ♗e6 15. ♗×e6 f×e6 16. ♖ad1 e5 17. ♔c1 ♘b6 18. ♘f5 e×d4 19. ♖×d4 *(see diagram)*

19. ... ♖e2 20. ♖f1 ♖e5 21. ♘e3 ♖ae8 22. ♖fd1 ♔f7 23. b3 g6 24. c4 f5 25. g3 ♘a8 26. ♖d8 ♖×d8 27. ♖×d8 ♖e8 28. ♖×e8 ♔×e8 29. ♔d2 ½−½ (Source: Golombek, *1930 Scarborough*)

After 19. ♖×d4

88 Menchik–Edward G. Sergeant

Scarborough (11), July 5, 1930

[A09] Réti Opening

1. ♘f3 d5 2. c4 d4 3. b4 c5 4. b×c5 ♘c6 5. e3 e5 6. d3 ♗×c5 7. e4 ♘ge7 8. ♗e2 0–0 9. 0–0 ♘g6 10. ♖e1 f5 11. e×f5 ♗×f5 12. ♗g5 ♕d6 13. ♘h4 ♘×h4 14. ♗×h4 ♗b4 15. ♖f1 ♗c3 16. ♘×c3 d×c3 17. ♗f3 ♕×d3 18. ♗d5+ ♔h8 19. ♕×d3 ♗×d3 20. ♖fd1 ♗×c4 [20. ... ♗g6 21. ♗×c6 b×c6 provides better chances—RT] **21. ♗×c4 ♖f4 22. ♗d5 ♖×h4 23. ♗×c6 b×c6 24. ♖d3 ♖c4 25. ♖c1** *(see diagram)*

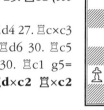

After 25. ♖c1

25. ... c2 [No better is 25. ... ♖a4 26. ♖c2 ♖d4 27. ♖c×c3 ♖ad8 28. ♖×d4 e×d4 (28. ... ♖×d4 29. ♔f1 ♖d6 30. ♖c5 ♖e6 31. ♖a5 ♖e7 32. ♖c5=) 29. ♖×c6 d3 30. ♖c1 g5= —RT] **26. ♖d2 ♖b8 27. g3 ♔g8 28. ♖d×c2 ♖×c2 29. ♖×c2**

½–½ (Source: Golombek, *1930 Scarborough*)

Hastings 1930-1931

December 29, 1930–January 7, 1931

		1	2	3	4	5	6	7	8	9	10	Points	Place
1	Euwe, Machgielis	•	=	1	1	1	=	1	0	1	1	7	1
2	Capablanca, José R.	=	•	0	=	1	=	1	1	1	1	6½	2
3	Sultan Khan, Mir	0	1	•	1	=	1	0	1	=	1	6	3
4	Michell, Reginald P.	0	=	0	•	1	1	=	1	0	1	5	4
5	Yates, Frederick D.	0	0	=	0	•	1	1	=	1	=	4½	5
6	Thomas, George A.	=	=	0	0	0	•	1	0	1	1	4	6
7	Winter, William	0	0	1	=	0	0	•	1	=	=	3½	7
8	Menchik, Vera	1	0	0	0	=	1	0	•	=	0	3	8–9
9	Tylor, Theodore H.	0	0	=	1	0	0	=	=	•	=	3	8–9
10	Colle, Edgar	0	0	0	0	=	0	=	1	=	•	2½	10

Up until this time the Christmas Congresses at Hastings were held at the Hastings Town Hall. The 1930-31 event moved to the Waverly Hotel with the assistance of J. A. Watt, a major chess supporter in England as well as proprietor of the hotel. A year later the tournament made a long term move to the White Rock Pavilion, which developed a reputation for being a rather noisy and blustery site.

The consensus being that the players in 1929-30 had drawn a bit too readily, an effort was made by the tournament committee to invite a few players with more fighting reputations. The feeling at the end was that the event was one of the most interesting and hard fought in the series.

Although Menchik might have wished for a better final score, her victory over Euwe was given worldwide coverage. *British Chess Magazine* granted Thomas the title of president of the Menchik club for his newest loss to her.[46]

Round order, colors and partial game scores are derived from *British Chess Magazine* (February 1931) as well as *The Times*.

(R39) Menchik–Frederick D. Yates
Hastings 1930–31 (1), December 29, 1930
1. d4 Not available (54 moves) ½–½
[*The Times*, 2-1-1931]

89 Max Euwe–Menchik
Hastings 1930-31 (2), December 30, 1930
[D63] *Queen's Gambit Declined Classical*

1. d4 ♘f6 2. c4 e6 3. ♘c3 d5 A common move order for Miss Menchik who rarely played the Nimzo-Indian that often follows this move order. **4. ♗g5 ♘bd7 5. e3 ♗e7 6. ♘f3 0–0 7. ♖c1 a6** The text is a very solid alternative to 7. ... c6 which gives Black the alternative of opening the c-file and maintaining the symmetry in the Exchange Variation. As played, Black at least has a pretense of imbalance in the position. **8. c×d5 e×d5 9. ♗d3 c6 10. 0–0 ♘e4 11. ♗f4** The exchanges eliminate any pull White might have. **11. ... ♘×c3 12. ♖×c3 ♖e8 13. ♕b1 ♘f8 14. b4 ♘g6 15. ♗g3 ♗d6 16. a4** Proceeding with a classical minority attack. Dr. Euwe gives a lucid account of how to handle such a process in his treatise *The Middle Game*. Black must be cautious as a timely White push to b5 could lead to fatal weaknesses. **16. ... ♗×g3 17. h×g3 ♗d7 18. ♖fc1 ♕f6 19. b5 a×b5 20. a×b5 ♖ec8** A concern of Black's is that after 21. b×c6 b×c6 she has a backward pawn that will be a target for all eternity. To prevent this she has placed her pieces so that with the exchange she will have a passed b-pawn as compensation for White's kingside majority. **21. ♕c2 ♕d8** Threatening to exchange the pawns and gain the passer. **22. b×c6 ♖×c6 23. ♖c5** [Not 23. ♖×c6 where the passed pawn gains stature as material dissipates. After the text Black is hard pressed to avoid the rook swap—RT] **23. ... ♖×c5 24. d×c5 ♖a5 25. ♕b2** *(see diagram)*

After 25. ♕b2

25. ... ♕a8 [In addition to the added control of the a-file, it's better than 25. ... ♕c7 26. ♕b6 ♕×b6 27. c×b6 ♗c6 28. ♘d4 with advantages to White in initiative, space and mobility—RT] **26. ♕b6 ♘f8 27. ♘e5 ♖a1 28. ♖b1 ♖×b1+ 29. ♗×b1 ♗e6 30. ♔h2** [30. c6 holds the draw and gives White a very slight plus. The text of ♔h2 mainly avoids queen surprises on a1 forking the knight and king as well as putting the question to Black—RT] **30. ... ♘d7 31. ♘×d7 ♗×d7 32. ♕c7?!** [Better must be 32. ♗a2 ♗c6 33. ♕c7 g6 (addressing 34. e4 which hits f7) 34. ♗b3 ♕f8 and White can still hope for more than a draw—RT] **32. ... ♕c8 33. ♕×c8+ ♗×c8 34. ♗a2 ♗e6 35. ♔g1 ♔f8 36. ♔f1 ♔e7 37. ♔e2 ♔f6 38. ♔d3 ♔e5 39. g4!? g5** Black is willing to take the draw. Not only has she struggled all game, but her opponent was one of the world's top grandmasters. Euwe, on the other hand, is determined to win ... if necessary he will take risks like his last move. Even on his next, f3 would hold the draw, but at this point he starts to self destruct. **40. g3 ♗×g4 41. f4+ g×f4 42. g×f4+ ♔f6** [Not 42. ... ♔e6 losing a tempo to e4—RT] **43. ♗×d5 ♗c8** *(see diagram)*

After 43. ... ♗c8

44. ♗f3? One can only assume that Dr. Euwe missed Black's 46th move. [Far better is 44. e4 maintaining the pressure on the b and f pawns while keeping the Black king and bishop locked up. Three plausible continuations follow. 44. ... ♔g6 **(a)** 44. ... h5 45. ♔e3 h4 46. f5 h3 47. ♔f4! and after e5 White wins; **(b)** 44. ... ♔e7 45. f5 f6 46. ♔e3 ♔d7 47. e5! f×e5 (47. ... ♔e7 48. e6) 48. ♔e4 ♔e7 (48. ... ♔c7 49. f6) 49. ♔×e5 h5 50. f6+ ♔d8 51. ♔d6 wins.; 45. f5+ ♔g7 (45. ... ♔f6 46. ♔e3 followed by ♔f4 and e4) 46. ♔e3 f6 47. ♔f4 h5 48. e5 f×e5+ 49. ♔×e5 ♔f8 50. f6 ♔e8 51. ♔d6 h4 52. ♔c7 ♗g4 53. ♔×b7 winning—RT] **44. ... ♔e7 45. ♔c4 ♔d8 46. ♔d5?** [Survivable is 46. ♔d4 f6 47. e4 followed by e5—RT] **46. ... b6 47. c6 ♔c7 48. ♔e5 ♗e6 49. f5 ♗b3 50. ♔f6 b5 51. ♔g7 b4** *(see diagram)*

52. ♔×h7? [A move pointed out later was 52. ♗h5! if 52. ... ♗c2 (if 52. ... ♗c4 53. ♔×h7 b3 54. ♗d1 ♔×c6 55. ♔g7 ♔d6 56. ♔f6! b2 57. ♗c2 ♔c5 58. ♗b1 ♔b4 59. e4 ♔c3 60. e5 ♗d3 61. ♗a2 ♔c2 62. e6 ♗c4 63. ♗×c4 b1♕ 64. e7=; if 52. ... ♔×c6 53. f6 ♗c4 54. ♗×f7 ♗×f7 55. ♔×f7 b3 56. ♔g8=) 53. ♗×f7 b3 54. ♗×b3 ♗×b3 55. ♔×h7 ♔×c6=—RT] **52. ... ♗c2 53. ♔g7 b3 54. ♗d5 b2 55. ♗a2 ♔×c6 56. f6 ♔d6 57. e4 ♗×e4 58. ♔×f7 ♗d5+ 59. ♗×d5 b1♕ 60. ♔g7 ♕g1+ 61. ♔f8 ♕×d5 0–1** (Source: *Chess*, August 1944, #1798; notes by WRM [additional notes by RT])

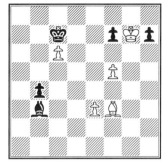

After 51. ... b4

(R40) Menchik–Theodore Tylor
Hastings 1930-31 (3), December 31, 1930

1. d4—the game went into adjournment. No game score available ½–½
[*The Times*, 2-1-1931]

(R41) Reginald Pryce Michell–Menchik
Hastings 1930-31 (4), January 1, 1931

1. e4 c6 Menchik was a pawn ahead when she lost a piece through an oversight and resigned on move 18. No game score available (18 moves) **1–0**

(R42) Menchik–Edgar Colle
Hastings 1930-31 (5), January 3, 1931

1. d4 (35 moves) Evidently Menchik got a good position— up an exchange—but lost her way in time pressure. No game score available **0–1**

90 Mir Sultan Khan–Menchik
Hastings 1930-31 (6), January 4, 1931
[E91] *King's Indian Defense Classical*

1. ♘f3 ♘f6 2. d4 g6 3. c4 ♗g7 4. ♘c3 0-0 5. e4 d6 6. ♗e2 ♘bd7 7. ♗g5 h6 8. ♗e3 ♘g4 9. ♗c1 e5 10. h3 ♘gf6 11. ♗e3 e×d4 12. ♘×d4 ♖e8 13. ♕c2 ♘c5 14. f3 ♘h5 *(see diagram)*

After 14. ... ♘h5

15. 0-0-0 [Dark squares not withstanding, Vera would have done better to castle short. 15. 0–0 ♗xh3!? (15. ... ♗xd4 16. ♘xd4 ♘e6 (16. ... ♕g5 17. ♘d5 ♘e6 18. ♗e3 ♘hf4 19. ♘xf4 ♘xf4 20. ♗xf4 ♕xf4 21. ♗d3=) 17. ♗e3=) 16. gxh3 ♗xd4 17. ♘xd4 ♕g5+ 18. ♔h1 ♘g3+ 19. ♔h2 ♘xf1+ 20. ♗xf1 ∞ —RT] **15. ... ♘g3 16. ♖he1 ♗d7 17. ♗d3 c6 18. ♕f2 ♘h5 19. g4 ♘f6 20. ♗c2 ♕b8 21. ♕d2 b5 22. ♗xh6 bxc4 23. ♗xg7 ♔xg7 24. ♘f5+ ♗xf5 25. gxf5 ♕b6 26. fxg6 ♖ab8 27. ♗b1 fxg6 28. ♖g1 ♘d3+ 29. ♗xd3 cxd3 30. ♕g2 ♕f8 31. ♖xd3 ♖e5 32. f4 ♖c5 33. ♖e1 ♘h5 34. ♖f1 ♕b5?** [34. ... ♕a6!? 35. ♕c2 d5± —RT] **35. ♖ff3 ♕c4 36. ♔b1 ♕b4 37. ♕d2 ♖c4 38. ♖f2 ♘g7 39. f5 gxf5 40. exf5 ♖h4 41. ♕g5 1-0**

91 Menchik–George Thomas
Hastings 1930-31 (7), January 5, 1931
[A34] *English, Symmetrical Variation*

For whatever reason E. S. Tinsley, the chess columnist at *The Times* (London) showed an antipathy towards Menchik. Following is his comment from the day after this game. "Why Thomas so often plays so weakly against Miss Menchik is difficult to understand, but again today a few indifferent moves by him gave her the better position. This was maintained and 35 moves saw the end." The BCM on the other hand granted Thomas the title of President of the "Vera Menchik Club."

After 34. a3

1. ♘f3 ♘f6 2. c4 e6 3. g3 c5 4. ♗g2 ♘c6 5. 0-0 d5 6. cxd5 ♘xd5 7. ♘c3 ♗e7 8. d4 ♘xc3 9. bxc3 0-0 10. ♖b1 ♕a5 11. ♕c2 h6 12. e4 cxd4 13. cxd4 ♖d8 14. ♗d2 ♗b4 15. ♗xb4 ♘xb4 16. ♕c4 ♘c6 17. ♖fd1 ♘e7 18. ♘e5 ♖d6 19. ♕e2 ♕d8 20. ♕e3 b6 21. ♘c4 ♖d7 22. ♘e5 ♖d6 23. ♕f4 f6 24. ♘f3 e5 25. ♕e3 ♔h7?! 26. d5 ♗g4 27. ♖dc1 ♗xf3 28. ♗xf3 ♖d7 29. ♗g4 ♖c7 30. ♖xc7 ♕xc7 31. ♖c1 ♕d6 32. ♗e6 a6 33. ♕c3 ♖a7 34. a3 *(see diagram)*

34. ... ♔h8? [34. ... ♖a8± —RT] **35. ♕b4** The game was adjourned here, but Thomas resigned before resumption. **1-0** (Source: *www.Chessgames.com*)

(R43) William Winter–Menchik
Hastings 1930-31 (8), January 6, 1931
BCM states that Menchik put up a good fight until right at the end of the session when she made an elementary blunder and lost on the 43rd move. No game score available **1-0**

92 Menchik–José Raúl Capablanca
Hastings 1930-31 (9), January 7, 1931
[A47] *Queen Pawn Game*

1. d4 ♘f6 2. ♘f3 b6 3. e3 ♗b7 4. ♗d3 c5 5. 0-0 ♘c6 6. c3 e6 7. ♘e5 d6 8. ♘xc6 ♗xc6 9. ♕e2 ♗e7 10. ♗b5 ♕d7 11. ♗xc6 ♕xc6 12. ♘d2 0-0 13. dxc5 dxc5 14. e4 ♖ad8 15. e5 ♘d5 16. ♘f3 ♖d7 17. ♖d1 ♖fd8 18. ♗d2 b5 19. ♔f1 19. b3 19. ... ♘b6

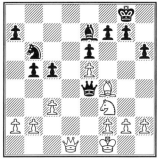

After 23. ... ♕e4

20. ♗f4 20. ♗g5 This move would free up her pieces or create structural issues for Black with the result of near equality **20. ... h6 21. ♖×d7** 21. ♖d2 ♖×d2 22. ♘×d2 ♕d7 23. ♘e4∓ **21. ... ♖×d7 22. ♖d1?** Menchik falls into the common trap—trade down when playing a stronger player. The result is she loses space and initiative. **22. ... ♖×d1+ 23. ♕×d1 ♕e4** *(see diagram)*

24. ♗g3 24. g3 or ♗e3 allow the bishop access to both sides of the board. The text ties up the pieces and prevents White from obtaining any counterplay. For a technician like Capablanca the game is now on autopilot **24. ... ♕c4+ 25. ♕e2 ♕×e2+ 26. ♔×e2 ♘a4 27. ♔d2 ♘×b2 28. ♔c2 ♘c4 29. ♘d2 ♘×d2 30. ♔×d2 c4 31. ♗f4 a6 32. ♗e3 ♔f8 33. ♗b6 ♔e8 34. ♔e3 ♔d7 35. ♔d4 ♔c6 36. ♗a7 f5 37. a4 g6 38. f4 h5 39. a×b5+ ♔×b5 40. g3 a5 41. ♔e3** *(see diagram)*

41. ... ♗c5+ 42. ♗×c5 ♔×c5 0–1 (Source: Wildhagen, *Capablanca*; notes by RT)

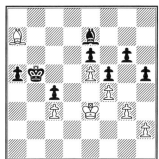

After 41. ♔e3

Antwerp 1931

(Match Tournament)
1931

Foreigners	6	7	8	9	10	11	Pts	Place
1 Rubinstein, Akiba	1	0	1	1	1	1	5	1–3
2 Yates, Frederick D.	0	1	1	1	1	1	5	1–3
3 Dake, Arthur	=	=	1	1	1	1	5	1–3
4 Winter, William	0	=	0	1	1	1	3½	5
5 Menchik, Vera	0	0	0	1	1	1	3	7
Belgium	**1**	**2**	**3**	**4**	**5**			
6 Sapira, Emanuel J.	0	1	=	1	1		3½	4
7 Koltanowski, George	1	0	=	=	1		3	6
8 Baert, Arthur	0	0	0	1	1		2	8
9 De Mey, Emiel	0	0	0	0	0		0	9–11
10 Perquin, Walter	0	0	0	0	0		0	9–11
11 Shernetsky, D.	0	0	0	0	0		0	9–11

Despite her 50 percent score, this event is definitely not one of Menchik's better. The Belgian team consisted of three solid masters and three second tier players. The foreign team was made up of five players returning home from the Prague Olympiad.

Worcester 1931

(24th B.C.F. Congress—Major Open)
August 10–22, 1931

	1	2	3	4	5	6	7	8	9	10	11	12	Points	Place
1 Menchik, Vera	•	1	=	1	1	1	1	=	=	=	1	1	9	1
2 Jackson, Edward M.	0	•	=	1	=	1	1	0	1	1	1	1	8	2
3 Seitz, Josef Adolf	=	=	•	0	1	=	1	0	1	1	1	=	7	3
4 Broadbent, Reginald	0	0	1	•	0	=	1	1	1	0	1	1	6½	4–5
5 Znosko-Borovsky, E.	0	=	0	1	•	0	=	1	1	1	=	1	6½	4–5
6 Golombek, Harry	0	0	=	=	1	•	=	1	=	=	0	1	5½	6–7
7 Reeve, H. T.	0	0	0	0	=	=	•	1	1	1	1	=	5½	6–7
8 Jacobs, Herbert	=	1	1	0	0	0	0	•	1	0	0	1	4½	8
9 Cross, Alfred Rupert	=	0	0	0	0	=	0	0	•	1	1	1	4	9–10
10 Watts, William H.	=	0	0	1	0	=	0	1	0	•	0	1	4	9–10
11 Stronach, Bernard H.	0	0	0	0	=	1	0	1	0	1	•	0	3½	11
12 Rhodes, H. G.	0	0	=	0	0	0	=	0	0	0	1	•	2	12

This has to rank among Menchik's greatest successes. Although not the strongest B.C.F. Major Open in which she played it was certainly a solid master event and her +7 =4 score says it all. High points include her victories against two of her most difficult opponents, Edward Jackson and the young Harry Golombek. This was Menchik's only serious victory against the latter player.

93 Menchik–Harry Golombek
Worcester (4), 1931

[E41] *Nimzo-Indian, Rubinstein Variation*

After 30. ... ♞d8

1. d4 ♞f6 2. c4 e6 3. ♞c3 ♝b4 4. e3 ♝×c3+ 5. b×c3 d6 6. ♝d3 e5 7. e4 c5 8. ♞e2 ♞c6 9. 0-0 ♛e7 10. f3 b6 11. ♝e3 0-0 12. d5 ♞a5 13. ♞g3 h6 14. ♛e2 ♚h7 15. ♖f2 g5 16. ♞f5 ♝×f5 17. e×f5 ♖ae8 18. ♝d2 ♖g8 19. ♖d1 ♛f8 20. ♝c2 ♛g7 21. g4 ♖h8 22. ♝a4 ♖e7 23. h4 ♚g8 24. ♝b5 ♚f8 25. ♖h2 g×h4 26. ♖×h4 ♞g8 27. ♚h2 f6 28. ♚f2 ♛h7 29. ♖h5 ♞b7 30. ♛h4 ♞d8 *(see diagram)*

31. g5?! [Objectively a bad move, it is a long hard battle to find a winning line despite White's unquestioned advantage. Strangely this move led to Black's disastrous (time trouble?) 34th move—RT] 31. ... ♛×f5 32. g×f6 ♛×f6 33. ♛×f6+ ♞×f6 34. ♖×h6 ♚g7?? 35. ♖g1+ 1-0 (Source: *BCM* #6744)

94 Eugene Znosko-Borovsky–Menchik
Worcester (8), 1931

[B19] *Caro-Kann, 3.Nc3*

1. e4 c6 2. d4 d5 3. ♞c3 d×e4 4. ♞×e4 ♝f5 5. ♞g3 ♝g6 6. ♞f3 e6 7. h4 h6 8. ♞e5

After 35. ♖×a4

♗h7 9. ♗d3 ♗×d3 10. ♕×d3 ♘d7 11. f4 ♗e7 12. 0-0 ♘gf6 13. ♘c4 ♘b6 14. ♘a5 ♕d7 15. f5 0-0-0 16. f×e6 f×e6 17. ♘b3 ♕d5 18. ♗f4 ♘c4 19. ♖ae1 g5 20. ♗e5 ♖hf8 21. ♗×f6 ♗×f6 22. c3 g×h4 23. ♘e4 ♗e7 24. ♖×f8 ♖×f8 25. ♘bc5 ♖g8 26. ♕h3 ♕f5 27. ♕×f5 e×f5 28. ♘f2 ♗×c5 29. d×c5 ♘×b2 30. ♖e6 ♘a4 31. ♖×h6 ♘c3 32. a3 ♘a4 33. ♘d3 ♖d8 34. ♖×h4 ♖×d3 35. ♖×a4 *(see diagram)*

35. ... ♖c3 36. ♖×a7 ♖×c5 37. ♔f2 ♔c7 38. ♔e3 ♖d5 39. ♖a8 c5 40. ♖h8 b5 41. ♔f4 c4 42. ♖h6 c3 43. ♖h1 ♔b6 44. ♔e3 ♔c5 45. ♖b1 ♖d4! 46. ♖b3 c2 **0–1** (Source: *Glasgow Herald* 5 September 1931)

95 Menchik–Reginald Broadbent
Worcester (9), 1931

[E43] *Nimzo-Indian, Rubinstein Variation*

1. d4 ♘f6 2. c4 e6 3. ♘c3 ♗b4 4. e3 ♗×c3+ 5. b×c3 b6 6. ♗d3 ♗b7 7. f3 e5 8. e4 d6 9. ♘e2 ♘bd7 10. 0-0 0-0 11. ♘g3 ♖e8 12. ♕c2 c5 13. ♘f5 ♘f8 14. ♗g5 h6 15. ♗×h6 g×h6 16. ♘×h6+ ♔g7 17. ♘f5+ ♔h8 18. ♕d2 ♘6h7 19. ♕h6 ♕f6 20. ♕×f6+ ♘×f6 21. ♘×d6 ♖e7 22. d×e5 ♘e8 23. ♘×b7 ♖×b7 24. ♗c2 ♖d7 25. ♗a4 ♖d3 26. ♗c6 ♖ad8 27. ♗d5 *(see diagram)*

White won in 60 moves. **1–0** (Source: *The Times*, August 21, 1931)

After 27. ♗d5

96 Menchik–H. T. Reeve
Worcester (11), 1931

[A56] *Benoni, Czech Variation*

After 14. 0-0-0

Following is a rather ugly game on the part of Reeve and a good example of technique on the part of Menchik.

1. d4 c5 2. d5 d6 3. c4 ♘f6 4. ♘c3 ♗f5 5. f3 e5 6. e4 ♗g6 7. ♗d3 ♗e7 8. ♘ge2 ♘fd7 9. ♗e3 0-0 10. g4 h5 11. ♕d2 h×g4 12. f×g4 ♗h4+ 13. ♘g3 ♘a6 14. 0-0-0 *(see diagram)*

14. ... ♗×g3? 15. h×g3 ♘b4 16. ♗f1 f6 17. g5 ♕a5 18. a3 ♘b6 19. ♕h2 ♔f7 20. ♕h3 ♖ae8 21. ♗e2 ♖h8 22. ♕g4 ♖×h1 23. ♖×h1 ♘a6 24. g×f6 g×f6 25. ♖h6 ♖g8 26. ♕e6+ ♔f8 27. ♕×f6+ ♗f7 28. ♖h7 **1–0** (Source: *BCM* #6745)

Hastings 1931-1932

December 28, 1931–January 6, 1932

		1	2	3	4	5	6	7	8	9	10	Points	Place
1	Flohr, Salo M.	•	=	=	1	1	1	1	1	1	1	8	1
2	Kashdan, Isaac I.	=	•	1	=	1	1	=	1	1	1	7½	2
3	Euwe, Machgielis	=	0	•	=	1	0	1	=	=	1	5	3
4	Sultan Khan, Mir	0	=	=	•	1	0	=	0	1	1	4½	4
5	Jackson, Edward M.	0	0	0	0	•	=	=	1	1	1	4	5–8
6	Menchik, Vera	0	0	1	1	=	•	0	0	1	=	4	5–8
7	Stoltz, Gösta	0	=	0	=	=	1	•	=	=	=	4	5–8
8	Yates, Frederick D.	0	0	=	1	0	1	=	•	1	0	4	5–8
9	Michell, Reginald P.	0	0	=	0	0	0	=	0	•	1	2	9–10
10	Thomas, George A.	0	0	0	0	0	=	=	1	0	•	2	9–10

Vera's sister, Olga, tied for first place in the "B Class" section.

97 Isaac Kashdan–Menchik
Hastings 1931-32 (1), December 28, 1931
[C14] *French, Classical*

1. e4 e6 2. d4 d5 3. ♘c3 ♘f6 4. ♗g5 ♗e7 5. e5 ♘fd7 6. ♗×e7 ♕×e7 7. ♕d2 0-0 8. f4 c5 9. ♘f3 ♘c6 10. ♖d1 A line of his own. [10. g3 is now the move most usually played; Capablanca (vs. Réti, New York 1924) played 10. d×c5 ♕×c5 11. ♗d3 f6 12. e×f6 ♕×f6 13. g3 and Dr. Alekhine pointed out in the tournament book that Black should have obtained a good game by 13. ... ♘×d3+ 14. c×d3 e5 15. 0–0 ♗h3 followed by ... ♖ae8—RT] **10. ... a6 11. a4** Unwilling to allow Black to get a strong queenside by ... b5. **11. ... f6 12. e×f6 ♘×f6 13. ♗e2 ♘e4** Aiming at temporary gain of a pawn, opening the center; White is secure of recovery of the pawn, and yields it to leave Black an isolated e-pawn. The

After 21. ♘×e4

eventual loss of this isolated pawn decides the game. **14. ♘×e4 d×e4 15. ♘g5 ♘×d4 16. 0–0 ♗d7** [16. ... e5 is untenable on account of 17. ♗c4+ and 18. f×e5; and 16. ... e3 on account of 17. ♕×e3! ♘×c2? 18. ♕e4!—RT] **17. a5 ♖ad8** [17. ... ♗c6 would be premature because of 18. ♗c4 ♗d5 19. ♗×d5 e×d5 20. c3!—RT] **18. ♕e3 ♘×e2+** White was now effectively threatening ♗c4 followed by ♕h3. **19. ♕×e2 ♗c6 20. ♖×d8 ♖×d8 21. ♘×e4** *(see diagram)*

21. ... ♗×e4 The turning point. Black's reason for getting rid of the knight was probably a realization of a weakness on the queenside black squares; nevertheless there are compensations, and the bishop here is a very strong piece. [21. ... ♖d4 22. ♘g5 ♗b5 23. ♕×e6+ ♕×e6 24. ♘×e6 ♖d2! 25. ♖c1 ♗c6 would be a variation in which Black would have the superior game—RT] **22. ♕×e4 ♖d4 23. ♕e3 ♕d7 24. ♖e1 ♖d1** [24. ... ♔f7 should come first—RT] **25. ♔f2 ♖×e1 26. ♕×e1 ♕d4+** [26. ... ♕d5 would be better—RT] **27. ♕e3 ♕d5 28. ♕d3 ♔f7 29. g4 ♕c6** This adventure decides the game; if the queen maintained its present position White would have a very strenuous task to win. [29. ... h6 would serve the present turn—RT] **30. ♕×h7 ♕b5 31. ♕h5+ ♔f8 32. ♕h8+ ♔f7 33. ♕h5+ ♔f8 34. ♕e5**

♛×a5 35. ♕b8+ ♔f7 36. ♕×b7+ ♔f8 37. ♕e4 ♛d2+ 38. ♔g3 ♛c1 [38. ... ♕b4 39. ♕×b4 c×b4 40. ♔f3! and the White king's march to the queenside, coupled with his kingside advantage, would be decisive—RT] **39. b3 ♛g1+ 40. ♔h3 ♛f1+ 41. ♔h4 ♛f2+ 42. ♔g5 ♛×h2 43. ♕×e6 ♛f2** [If 43. ... ♕×c2 44. ♕f5+ ♕×f5+ 45. ♔×f5 ♔e7 46. ♔e5 and wins—RT] **44. ♕f5+ ♔e8 45. ♔g6 1–0** (Source: *BCM* #6792 [additional notes by RT])

98 Menchik–Max Euwe
Hastings 1931-32 Hastings (2), December 29, 1931
[D17] Slav Defense

1. d4 d5 2. c4 c6 Probably no player had more experience with the Slav than Euwe who played both sides of it is no less than 19 world championship games. Despite being played by many top players it is rare for the second player to gain an advantage with it against strong competition. **3. ♘f3 ♘f6 4. ♘c3 d×c4 5. a4 ♗f5 6. e3 ♘a6** Within a few more years this move gave way to 6. e6. Not one of the games in the Euwe–Alekhine World Championships used ♘a6. **7. ♗×c4 ♘b4 8. 0–0 e6 9. ♘e5** (MCO gives 9. ♕e2 ♗e7 10. ♖d1 0–0 11. e4 ♗g4 12. ♗b3 ♕a5 13. a3 with advantage. This line looks more natural than the text which involves moving the same piece twice without necessity before White's development is complete.—WRM) **9. ... ♗d6 10. ♕e2 c5?** Probably more than any other world champion, Euwe was known for making inexplicable blunders. [Black can safely play 10. ... ♘bd5 [Not 10. ... 0–0 11. e4 ♗g6 12. ♘×g6 and e5—RT] and if 11. ♘×d5 (If 11. ♗×d5 c×d5) 11. ... e×d5—RT] (A rare blunder for a future world champion. He soon has to choose between submitting to a hot attack and losing a piece, and although he makes a hard fight with the two pawns he gets for it the result in inevitable.—WRM) **11. ♗b5+ ♔e7 12. e4** *(see diagram)*

After 12. e4

12. ... ♗g6?! [Black chooses to take the two pawns for the pieces with a strong center. The alternative is 12. ... c×d4 13. e×f5 d×c3 14. f×e6 f×e6 15. b×c3 ♘bd5 16. ♗b2 and after White wins the weak e-pawn Black has little counterplay—RT] **13. ♘×g6+ h×g6 14. e5 c×d4 15. ♖d1 ♗c7** [15. ... d×c3 16. ♖×d6 and Black melts away after 17.♗f4—RT] **16. e×f6+ g×f6 17. g3 a6 18. ♗e3!** *(see diagram)*

18. ... ♗b6 [If 18. ... a×b5 19. ♗×d4! (not 19. ♖×d4 ♘d5 20. ♘×d5+ e×d5 21. ♖×d5 ♕×d5 to stop ♗c5 mate. 22. ♗c5+ ♔d7 23. ♖d1 ♕×d1+ 24. ♕×d1+ ♔c6 25. ♕c2 b×a4 with play for both sides.) 19. ... ♗d6 20. ♗c5 ♗×c5 21. ♖×d8 ♖h×d8 22. ♕×b5 b6 23. ♘e4—RT] **19. ♗c4 ♔f8 20. ♘e4 ♔g7 21. ♖ac1 ♖h5 22. ♗f4 e5 23. g4 ♖h8 24. ♗g3 ♕e7** (Black has done very well to hold the game together and White still has to solve the problem of obtaining open lines for her pieces.—WRM) **25. ♘d2 ♖he8 26. ♕e4 ♕d7 27. ♘f3 ♕c6** (Otherwise g5 would be very difficult to meet—WRM) **28. ♕×c6 ♘×c6 29. ♗d5 ♖ac8 30. ♗e4 ♖c7 31. ♘e1** [31. ♗×c6 ♖×c6 (31. ... b×c6

After 18. ♗e3

32. ♘×d4 ♗×d4 33. ♖×d4 e×d4 34. ♗×c7 and White picks up the pawns after some jockeying.) 32. ♖×c6 otherwise ♖ec8—and Black's pawn phalanx can make White uncomfortable—RT] **31. ... ♖ec8 32. ♘d3 ♘e7** (He cannot allow White to play f4 rolling up his center pawns.—WRM) **33. ♖×c7 ♖×c7 34. ♔f1 ♖c4 35. ♗×b7 ♖×a4** Attempting to eliminate the queenside pawns. The win then becomes very difficult thanks to the wall of Black pawns that inhibit White's pieces. **36. ♖c1 g5** To again prevent g5 by White. **37. f3 ♖a2 38. ♗e1 a5 39. ♗d2 f5** Trying to maintain his pawns as a living organism. **40. g×f5 a4 41. ♔e1 a3 42. b4!** Showing the reason for not playing ♗×g5 earlier. In addition to the passed pawn, White has trapped Black's rook. **42. ... ♔f6 43. ♗a6 g4 44. ♗c4 ♖×d2 45. ♔×d2 g×f3 46. ♘c5?!** [More accurate is 46. ♘f2—RT] **46. ... ♔×f5** [An interesting line that White's 46th move allowed is 46. ... ♗×c5!? 47. b×c5 e4 48. ♖a1 e3+ 49. ♔d3 ♘c6 50. ♔e4 ♘a5 51. ♔×d4 e2 52. ♔e3 which falls a bit short—RT] **47. ♗×f7 ♗d8 48. ♗e6+ ♔f6 49. ♗g4 ♘d5 50. ♗×f3 ♘×b4 51. ♗e4 ♗e7 52. ♘d3 ♘a2 53. ♖c6+** (Not 53. ♖a1 ♘c3 54. ♖×P ♘b1+ etc.—WRM). **♔g5 54. ♖g6+ ♔h4 55. ♘×e5 ♘c3 56. ♔d3** Without the "a" pawn, which falls shortly, Black has no life and thus resigns. **1–0** (Source: *Chess*, August 1944, #1799; notes by WRM [additional notes by RT])

99 Reginald Michell–Menchik
Hastings 1931-32 (3), December 30, 1931
[D52] *Queen's Gambit Declined, Cambridge Springs Variation*

1. d4 ♘f6 2. c4 e6 3. ♘c3 d5 4. ♗g5 ♘bd7 5. e3 c6 6. ♘f3 ♕a5 7. ♘d2 ♗b4 8. ♕c2 0-0 9. ♗e2 e5 10. d×e5 ♘e4 11. ♘d×e4 d×e4 12. ♗f4 ♘×e5 13. ♖c1 ♘d3+ 14. ♗×d3 e×d3 15. ♕×d3 ♗f5 16. ♕d1 ♕×a2 17. 0-0 ♕×c4 *(see diagram)*

After 17. ... ♕×c4

BCM only published the first 17 moves of this game, noting that "The pieces were thinned down to rook and knight against rook and bishop, and the weight of Black's queenside pawns won in 55 moves." **0–1** (Source: *BCM* #6768)

(R44) Menchik–Edward M. Jackson
Hastings 1931-32 (4), December 31, 1931
1. d4 game score not available (43 moves) ½–½

100 Gösta Stoltz–Menchik
Hastings 1931-32 (5), January 2, 1932
[C00] *French*

1. e4 e6 2. ♕e2 c5 3. f4 ♘c6 4. ♘f3 ♗e7 5. g3 d5 6. d3 ♗d7 7. ♗g2 ♕c7 8. c3 d×e4 9. d×e4 ♘f6 10. ♘a3 a6 11. ♘c4 0-0 12. ♘ce5 ♖fd8 13. g4 ♘×e5 14. ♘×e5 ♗e8 15. g5 ♘d7 16. ♘g4 c4 17. 0-0 ♘c5 18. f5 e×f5 19. e×f5 ♘d3 20. f6 ♗c5+ 21. ♔h1 *(see diagram)*

21. ... g6?! (21. ... ♗d7?! 22. f×g7 ♗×g4 23. ♕×g4 ♘f2+ 24. ♖×f2 ♗×f2 25. ♗f4⩲; 21. ... ♗c6!? 22. f×g7 [22. ♗×c6 ♕×c6+ 23. ♕g2 {23. ♕f3!? ♕×f3+ 24. ♖×f3 ♗f8=}] 23. ... ♕×g2+ 24. ♔×g2 ♘×c1 25. ♖a×c1∓) **22. ♗e3 ♗c6? 23. ♗×c5**

After 21. ♔h1

♗×g2+ **24. ♕×g2** 24. ♔×g2!? ♕c6+ 25. ♔h3 ♕×c5± **24. ...
♕×c5 25. ♘h6+ ♔f8 26. b3?! c×b3 27. ♕×b7 ♕d5+** 27. ...
♖a7! 28. ♕×b3 ♖ad7 29. ♖ab1 (29. h4 ♕c6+ 30. ♔g1 ♘e4∓)
29. ... ♕×g5∓ **28. ♕×d5 ♖×d5 29. a×b3 ♖×g5 30. ♖f3
♖d8 31. h3 ♖c5?** 31. ... ♖d6 32. b4= **32. ♖×a6 ♖×c3
33. ♖a7 ♖c1+ 34. ♔h2 ♘e5 35. ♖e3 ♖e8 36. ♖e7 ♖×e7
37. f×e7+ ♔×e7 38. ♖×e5+ ♔f8 39. ♘g4 ♖c2+ 40. ♔g3
h5 41. ♘e3 ♖c3 42. b4 ♖b3 43. ♖e4 f5 44. ♖e5 ♖×b4
45. ♘d5 h4+ 46. ♔f3 ♖a4 47. ♖e6 ♖a3+ 48. ♔f4 ♖×h3
49. ♔g5 ♖a3 50. ♔f6 ♖a7 51. ♘e7 ♖a8 52. ♘×g6+ ♔g8
53. ♖e7 ♖a6+ 54. ♔g5** (*see diagram*)

Final position

There is no stopping White's ♔h6 followed by ♖g7 mate
short of sacrificing the exchange so Black resigned. **1–0** (Source: *www.Chessgames.com*; notes by RT)

101 Mir Sultan Khan–Menchik
Hastings 1931-32 (6), January 3, 1932
[D45] *Semi-Slav*

1. d4 ♘f6 2. c4 e6 3. ♘c3 d5 [Although regarded as less enterprising than the Nimzowitsch
Defense 3. ... ♗b4 this continuation has probably the merit of greater soundness. It is a wise
selection to make when paying Black against a player of White's reputation—RT] **4. c×d5**
This move is more usually played after 4. ♗g5 ♘bd7; but the transposition seems to be quite
unimportant. The idea of the exchange variation is, of course, to build up a kingside attack,
and he certainly can obtain considerable pressure. On the other hand Black has no difficulty
in obtaining good development for his pieces including the queen's bishop which, in the more
usual lines of the O.G.D. is a constant source of trouble to Black. On the whole 4. ♗g5 ♘bd7
5. e3, etc., seems still to hold priority of place as White's best line. **4. ... e×d5 5. ♘f3** The
omission of 5. ♗g5 and the subsequent shutting in of the queen's bishop by e3 only helps Black
to obtain a good position, but Sultan Khan never studied the openings very profoundly, preferring to rely on his natural gift for middle-game complications. **5. ... c6 6. ♕c2 ♗d6 7. e3**
[Now 7. ♗g5 was much better, for then if 7. ... ♘bd7 8. e3 0–0 9. ♗d3 h6 10. ♗h4 ♖e8 11. 0–0
would transpose into the game Marshall-Lasker, Moscow, 1925, with some advantage to
White—RT] **7. ... ♘bd7 8. ♗d3 0-0 9. ♗d2 ♖e8** After this Black stands quite satisfactorily.
There are no weaknesses in position and the open e-file guarantees freedom of movement.
10. h4 With this move White embarks upon a risky attempt to attack the Black king which
is strategically completely unjustifiable. Since the 32nd match game, Alekhine–Capablanca
1927, it has been assumed that White should castle on the queenside and follow with a violent
kingside advance. With the queen's bishop at g5 there might be some point in the idea, but
without it there can be none. [Strategically the correct plan is 10. 0–0 followed by the occupation of the c-file, the advance of the pawns to a3 and b4, and the maneuvering of the queen's
knight via a4 to c5. Black would counter with play for the square e4, and an involved positional
struggle would result—RT] **10. ... ♘f8** A good move making safe the kingside. White's attack
will hereafter have little prospect of success. **11. 0-0-0** He soon finds he has walked right into
it, but after his last move it was too late to draw back. **11. ... b5** Not only to attack the White
king but also to weaken White's hold on his e4. **12. ♘g5** White's attempt to open up the position only reacts to his own disadvantage. At least he should have tried to provide a defense for

Vera Menchik at the home of Sir Umar Hyat Khan for a dinner reception for Alexander Alekhine on 15 December 1931. Back row, left to right: Chas. Locock, R.H.S. Stevenson—her future husband), P.W. Sergeant, C. Relford-Brown, Sir Ernest Graham-Little, Col. Newab, Sir Umar Hyat Khan, R.C. Griffith, F.D. Yates, J. du Mont, A. Rutherford. Front row: unknown, Mrs. Latham, unknown, Vera Menchik, World Champion Alexander Alekhine, Agnes Stevenson, Dr. Jakob Seitz. On floor: unknown, unknown, Mir Sultan Khan (courtesy *British Chess Magazine* 1932).

his king's position, and the logical way to do so would be 12. ♔b1 followed by ♖c1 when White would still have a reasonable game. **12. ... a5 13. e4** [This simply leaves Black a second target in the weakened d-pawn, but it also allows an open diagonal against his king's position which Black can use with great effect. 13. ♔b1 still left him a defensible game. If then 13. ... b4 14. ♘a4 followed by ♖c1. If 13. ... a4 14. ♘e2!, and it will be difficult for Black to open the queenside by advancing the pawns—RT] **13. ... b4 14. ♘a4** There is little else to do. The pawns must be blockaded if possible. **14. ... d×e4 15. ♘×e4 ♘×e4 16. ♗×e4 ♗e6 17. ♔b1?** His last hope of staving off the attack on his king's position goes with this move. [For better or worse 17. b3 was necessary, although after 17. ... ♖c8 the threat of ... c5 is very nasty for if

18. ♘c5 ♗×c5 19. d×c5 (19. ♕×c5 ♗g4! 20. f3 ♖×e4 21. f×e4 *(21. f×g4 ♘e6)* 21. ... ♗×d1 22. ♖×d1 ♘e6) 19. ... ♗d5 20. ♗f5 (not 20. f3 ♗×e4 21. f×e4 ♕e7 and the weak e-pawn and c-pawn would prove fatal.) 20. ... ♖c7 Black has the better game because he can prepare an attack on the weak c-pawn—RT] **17. ... b3** A shock for White. The position is laid open and the Lady Champion can obtain an advantageous ending by the ensuing series of practically forced moves. **18. a×b3 ♖b8 19. ♘c5** Clearly there is nothing else against the threat of ♗×b3. **19. ... ♗×c5 20. ♕×c5 ♗×b3 21. ♖de1 ♘e6** *(see diagram)*

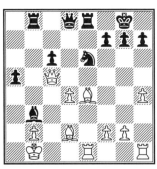

After 21. ... ♘e6

22. ♕c3 (If 22. ♕×a5 ♖×d4 23. ♗c3 [23. ♗×c6 ♕d3+ 24. ♔a1 ♘d4 25. ♖c1 *{not 25. ♖×e8+ ♖×e8 26. ♗×e8 ♘c2+ 27. ♔b1 ♘a3+ 28. ♔a1 ♕b1+ 29. ♖×b1 ♘c2 mate}* 25. ... ♘×c6 *{25. ... ♘c2+ 26. ♖×c2 ♕×c2 and wins, for if 27. ♗f3 or ♗h5 to stop 28. ... ♕d1+, then 27. ... ♖e1+ 28. ♗×e1 ♕c1 mate}* 26. ♖×c6 ♖a8 and wins.] 23. ... ♖a7 24. ♕a5 ♕×f2 25. ♗e3 (25. ♗×c6 ♖ed8 26. ♗c3 ♘c5! and there is no satisfactory defense to the threat of 27. ... ♕b2 28. ♔a1 ♗e6!, etc. [27. ♖hf1 ♕c2+ 28. ♔a1 ♗e6 29. ♕×c5 ♖a8+ 30. ♗×a8 ♖×a8+ 31. ♕a5 *{not 31. ♗a5 ♕×c5}* 31. ... ♖×a5+ 32. ♗×a5 ♕a4+ and wins.] The position is full of interesting complications, but White finds himself in great difficulties and he realizes his best chance is to remain a pawn behind and try to save the ending.) 25. ... ♕f6! 26. ♕c3 ♕×c3 27. b×c3 ♗d5+ and wins—RT) **22. ... ♕×d4 23. ♕×d4 ♘×d4 24. f3** Black threatened 24. ... ♖×e4 and ♗c7+. **24. ... a4 25. ♗f4 ♖bc8** Black now has a perfectly safe position, and it is a question of simple technique. Clearly a passed pawn must be established somewhere on the queenside, and this should win the ending automatically. **26. ♗d3** He wants to get his king's rook into play. Black avoids exchanging because the ending with bishop and knight vs. two bishops would present considerable technical difficulties. **26. ... ♘e6 27. ♗e5 c5 28. ♗b5 ♖ed8 29. ♖e4 ♘d4 30. ♗×d4** After this the passed pawn assures an easy win, but in any case the knight is a mighty piece now that it is securely centralized. The game was in fact lost in any case. **30. ... c×d4 31. ♗d3** Otherwise the passed pawn advances apace. **31. ... ♖b8** Now the weak b-pawn in to be "put on the spot." 32. ... a6 is threatened. **32. ♔a1** [32. ♔c1 would be similarly met—RT] **32. ... ♖b4 33. ♖he1 ♗e6 34. ♖e5** [No better was 34. ♖4e2 a3 35. b×a3 ♖a8 etc.—RT] **34. ... a3!** A neat blow. If now 35. b×a3 ♖a8 and mates; whilst if 35. ♖5e2 a×b2+ 36. ♖×b2 ♖a8+ 37. ♔b1 ♖×b2 38. ♔×b2 ♖a2+ followed by ♖×g2 with a simple win. **35. b3 ♖×b3 36. ♗c4 ♖b2 37. ♗×e6 f×e6 38. ♖a5** [If 38. ♖×e6 d3 39. ♖e8+ ♖×e8 40. ♖×e8+ ♔f7 41. ♖d8 d2 42. g3 ♖c2 43. ♔b1 a2+ and wins—RT] **38. ... d3! 39. ♖×a3 d2 40. ♖d1 ♖c2** If 40. ♔b1 ♖dc8 and wins. A masterly game. **0–1** (Source: *BCM* 1932, p. 53; *Chess* #1797; notes by WRM [additional notes by RT])

102 Menchik–Frederick D. Yates

Hastings 1931-32 (7), January 4, 1932

[A95] *Dutch, Stonewall*

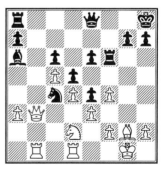

After 21. ♘d2

According to BCM, "A lively set-to between Miss Menchik and Yates, arising out of a Dutch Defense, found the lady champion short of time (as is unfortunately becoming her wont!) at a critical juncture, and this probably cost her a won game. Yates was running some risk to get a win."

1. d4 e6 2. ♘f3 f5 3. g3 ♘f6 4. ♗g2 ♗e7 5. 0–0 0–0 6. c4 d5 7. ♘c3 c6 8. a3 ♕e8 9. b4 ♘bd7 10. ♕b3 ♗d6 11. ♖b1 ♗c7 12. ♗d2 ♔h8 13. b5 ♘b6 14. c5 ♘c4 15. ♗f4 ♗×f4 16. g×f4 ♘e4 17. b×c6 b×c6 18. ♖fd1 ♗a6 19. e3 ♖f6 20. ♘×e4 f×e4 21. ♗d2 *(see diagram)*

21. ... g5 22. f×g5 ♕g6! 23. f4 23. g×f6?? ♖g8 **23. ... e×f3 24. ♘×f3 ♖×f3 25. ♗×f3 ♕×g5+ 26. ♔h1 ♖f8 27. ♖g1 ♕f5 28. e4 d×e4 29. ♗e2 e3** 29. ... ♘d2 30. ♕g3 **30. ♗×c4?** This was wrong. 30. ♖bf1 should have been played. If then 30. ... ♕e4+ 31. ♖g2 ♖×f1+ 32. ♗×f1 ♕f4! 33. ♗e2! (Not 33. ♗×c4 e2!) **30. ... ♗×c4 31. ♕×c4 ♕e4+ 32. ♖g2 ♕×b1+ 33. ♖g1 ♕e4+ 34. ♖g2 ♖f2!** **0–1** (Source: *BCM* January 1932, p. 52; notes by RT)

103 Salo Flohr–Menchik
Hastings 1931-32 (8), January 5, 1932
[D62] *Queen's Gambit Declined Classical Exchange*

This game is not an untypical loss for Menchik against a top caliber player. At times she seemed

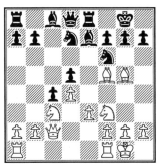

to lack a sense of danger. One could almost call it laziness except she was known for working very hard in her games—often getting into time trouble. In this case one oversight on move 11 and a simple game which is probably drawn is over. **1. d4 ♘f6 2. c4 e6 3. ♘c3 d5 4. ♗g5 ♘bd7 5. c×d5 e×d5 6. e3 ♗e7 7. ♗d3 0-0 8. ♕c2 c5 9. ♘f3 c4 10. ♗f5 ♖e8 11. 0-0** *(see diagram)*

After 11. 0-0

11. ... ♘f8? 11. ... ♘b6 12. ♗×f6 ♗×f5 13. ♕×f5 ♗×f6= 12. ♗×c8 ♖×c8 13. ♗×f6 ♗×f6 14. ♕f5 g6 15. ♕×d5 ♕e7 16. ♕a5 b6 17. ♕a6 ♖ed8 18. ♘d5 ♕d6 19. ♘×f6+ ♕×f6 20. ♖fe1 ♕e6 21. ♘d2 1-0 (Source: *BCM* #6766; notes by RT)

(R45) Menchik–George Thomas
Hastings 1931-32 (9), January 6, 1932
1. d4 Not available ½–½

London 1932

(International Tournament—Premier Division)
February 1–13, 1932

		1	2	3	4	5	6	7	8	9	10	11	12	Points	Place
1	Alekhine, Alexander	•	=	=	1	=	1	1	1	1	=	1	1	9	1
2	Flohr, Salomon M.	=	•	=	=	1	0	1	1	1	1	=	1	8	2
3	Kashdan, Isaac I.	=	=	•	=	0	=	1	1	1	1	1	=	7½	3–4
4	Sultan Khan, Mir	0	=	=	•	0	1	=	1	1	1	1	1	7½	3–4
5	Maróczy, Géza	=	0	1	1	•	=	=	=	=	=	=	=	6	5–6
6	Tartakower, Saviely	0	1	=	0	=	•	1	1	0	0	1	1	6	5–6
7	Koltanowski, George	0	0	0	=	=	0	•	=	1	1	=	1	5	7
8	Menchik, Vera	0	0	0	0	=	0	=	•	=	1	1	1	4½	8
9	Milner-Barry, Philip S.	0	0	0	0	=	1	0	=	•	=	=	=	3½	9–10
10	Thomas, George A.	=	0	0	0	=	1	0	0	=	•	=	=	3½	9–10
11	Berger, Victor	0	=	0	0	=	0	=	0	=	=	•	=	3	11
12	Winter, William	0	0	=	0	=	0	0	0	=	=	=	•	2½	12

London 1932 was hailed by the press as the greatest British tournament of the decade. Sponsored by the "Sunday Referee," the tournament was held for the first week in the central hall of Westminster Palace, the second week being held at Whitely's store in Bayswater. Scoring over 40 percent, this was one of Menchik's better events. She lost to the elite but scored 3½ of 5 against the native British contingent and also drew with Maróczy and Koltanowski.

Olga Menchik won a prize for her =3rd place finish in the women's section. A nice tournament book with text by J. du Mont and annotations by Alekhine was published by David McKay & Co.

104 Géza Maróczy–Menchik
London (1), February 1, 1932

[C01] *French Exchange*

1. e4 e6 2. d4 d5 3. ♘c3 ♘f6 4. ♗g5 ♗e7 5. e×d5 e×d5 6. ♗d3 ♘c6 7. ♘ge2 ♘b4 8. 0-0 [I would prefer here 8. ♘g3 at once in order to keep, after 8. ... ♘×d3+ 9. ♛×d3 the opportunity of castling on either wing—RT] **8. ... 0-0 9. ♘g3 ♘×d3 10. ♛×d3 h6 11. ♗f4 ♗d6 12. ♛d2 ♗×f4 13. ♛×f4 c6 14. ♖fe1 ♖e8 15. h3 ♗d7 16. ♖×e8+ ♛×e8 17. ♛d2 ♛f8 18. ♖e1 ♖e8 19. ♘b1 ♖×e1+ 20. ♛×e1 ♛e8 21. ♛d1** White has not the shadow of a winning chance and would have done better to exchange queens. After the text-move Black obtains a slight positional advantage. **21. ... ♘e4 22. ♘×e4 ♛×e4 23. c3** *(see diagram)*

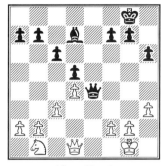

After 23. c3

23. ... ♛g6 The idea of putting the bishop in front of the queen is not good and leads in a few moves to a drawn position. [Correct and simple enough was 23. ... ♗f5 24. ♘d2 ♛d3 25. ♛e1 ♚h7, etc., and White would have to play very carefully to obtain a draw—RT] **24. ♚h1 ♗f5 25. ♘d2 ♗e4 26. ♘×e4 ♛×e4 27. f3 ♛e3 28. ♛b3 ♛c1+ 29. ♚h2 ♛f4+ 30. ♚g1 ♛e3+ 31. ♚h2 ♛f4+ 32. ♚h1 ♛c1+ 33. ♚h2 ½–½**

(Source: Alekhine, *66 Master Games Played in the London International Chess Tournament, 1932*; notes by AA [additional notes by RT])

105 Menchik–Alexander Alekhine
London International (2), February 2, 1932

[E14] *Queen's Indian Defense*

1. d4 ♘f6 2. c4 e6 3. ♘f3 b6 4. e3 A tame developing system but by no means a bad one. Black has thereby no opening difficulties, providing he does not over-estimate his position, and realizes that although he has sufficient forces to control e4, he is not yet developed enough for occupying it. **4. ... ♗b7 5. ♗d3 ♗b4+ 6. ♗d2 ♗×d2+ 7. ♘b×d2** This knight is not very happily placed at d2. More promising would be therefore, 7. ♛×d2, followed by ♘c3. **7. ... d6 8. 0-0 ♘bd7 9. ♛c2 ♛e7 10. ♖fd1 0-0 11. ♘e4 g6** A good move, the object of which is, as the continuation shows, to avoid the exchange of the queen's bishop. It is to Black's interest to keep as many pieces as possible on the board, his pawn position being much more elastic than his opponent's. **12. ♖d2 ♘×e4 13. ♗×e4 c6! 14. ♛a4** Probably hoping to provoke the answer 14. ... b5 which would be advantageously answered by 15. ♛b3! **14. ... ♖fc8 15. ♗d3 c5 16. ♛d1** None of the White pieces has a suitable square. But it will still be some time before Black will be able to obtain a serious initiative. **16. ... ♘f6 17. d×c5 b×c5** The right way to recapture, as the backward queen's pawn is very easy to protect in this kind of position. **18. ♛e2 ♘h5 19. ♖ad1 ♖f8!** Preparing the advance of the f and e pawns. **20. e4 ♘f4 21. ♛e3 e5 22. ♗f1 ♖ad8** Up to this point Black's tactics have been irreproachable, but here 22. ... ♖fd8 followed by ♘ to e6 and d4 would be more convincing as it would prevent White's next attempt. **23. b4! ♘e6** [White's pawn sacrifice was interesting in this difficult position, If 23. ... c×b4 24. ♛×a7 ♖a8 25. ♛b6 ♗×e4 26. ♛×d6 ♛×d6 27. ♖×d6 ♗×f3 28. g×f3 ♖×a2 29. ♖b6 with good drawing chances for White—RT] **24. ♖b2 ♗a8 25. b×c5 ♘×c5**

After 34. ... ♖e6

26. ♘d2 f5 27. e×f5 g×f5 With the opening of the g-file, Black gets at last the basis for a powerful king's attack. **28. f3 ♕g7** Threatening 29. ... f4 followed by e4. **29. ♖db1 ♔h8 30. ♘b3 ♘e6 31. ♖d2 ♘g5 32. ♔h1 ♖g8 33. ♖f2** The only defense against 33. ... ♘×f3. **33. ... ♖de8! 34. ♖d1 ♖e6** *(see diagram)*

35. f4 Desperation as Black was threatening 35. ... ♖h6 followed by 36. ... ♖×h2+; 37. ... ♕h6+; 38. ... ♘h6+, etc. And after 35. c5 d5, etc. he would win by the simple advance of his center pawns. **35. ... e×f4 36. ♕d4 ♖e5 37. c5 d×c5 38. ♘×c5 ♘h3 39. ♖b2 f3 40. g3 f2+** This is the longest bishop's check I ever gave in my life! **0–1** (Source: Alekhine, *66 Master Games Played in the London International Chess Tournament, 1932*; notes by AA, from *My Best Games of Chess 1924–37*, #50 [additional notes by RT])

106　Salo Flohr–Menchik
London International (3), February 3, 1932
[A34] *English, Symmetrical Variation*

1. c4 ♘f6 2. ♘c3 c5 3. g3 d5 4. c×d5 ♘×d5 5. ♗g2 ♘×c3 6. b×c3 e5 7. ♘f3 ♘c6 8. 0–0 ♗e7 9. ♘e1 [White has chosen rather a harmless opening, and obtained only an equal game, which is not improved by the unnatural knight maneuver in the text. The simple move 9. d3 was indicated here— RT] **9. ... 0–0 10. ♘c2 ♗e6 11. ♘e3 f5 12. c4 e4 13. ♖b1 ♖b8** Black has obtained the superior position with good attacking chances but begins to play inexactly. Stronger was 13. ... ♕d7 followed by ♖ad8. **14. ♗b2** *(see diagram)*

After 14. ♗b2

14. ... ♗f6? It is interesting that this, at first sight natural, exchange entirely spoils Black's strong position. Instead of it she could play either 14. ... f4, or 14. ... ♘d4, or even 14. ... g5 followed by f4, etc., always with better prospects. **15. ♗×f6 ♕×f6 16. f3! ♕d4 17. f×e4 f×e4** [And now Black does not exploit her relatively best chance, which consisted in playing 17. ... ♗×c4 18. e×f5 ♗×a2 19. ♖a1 ♗f7 with a complicated middle game position, giving slightly better prospects to White. The text move loses a pawn without compensation—RT] **18. ♖×f8+ ♖×f8 19. ♕c2!** The winning move. Of course the following endgame is still rather laborious and it is very instructive to follow the application by Flohr of the principles of Nimzowitsch's "Blockade" in this stage of the game. **19. ... ♘e5 20. ♕×e4 ♕×e4 21. ♗×e4 b6 22. d3 ♘d7 23. ♔g2 ♘f6 24. ♗f3 ♔f7 25. ♘d1 ♔e7 26. ♘c3 ♖f7 27. h3 ♔d8 28. a4 ♗d7 29. g4 h6 30. ♔g3 ♔c7 31. a5 ♗c6 32. a×b6+ a×b6 33. ♗×c6 ♔×c6 34. h4 ♘d7 35. ♘d5 ♖f8 36. h5 ♔d6** Menchik tries the impossible in order to save herself. If now 37. ♘×b6 then, of course, 37. ... ♖b8, etc. **37. ♘e3 ♖f7 38. ♖a1 ♘b8 39. ♖a8 ♘c6 40. ♘f5+ ♔c7 41. ♖g8 ♘e7 42. ♘×e7 ♖×e7 43. e4 ♔d6 44. ♔f4 ♖f7+ 45. ♔e3 ♖b7 46. ♖f8 ♔e7 47. ♖f5 ♖a7 48. g5 h×g5 49. ♖×g5 ♔f7 50. ♖g6 ♖b7 51. ♖c6 ♔e7 52. e5 ♔e8 53. ♔e4 b5 A** last hopeless attempt. **54. ♖×c5 b4 55. ♖a5 b3 56. ♖a1 b2 57. ♖b1 ♔e7 58. d4 ♖b3 59. d5 ♔d7 60. ♔d4 ♔e7 61. c5 1–0** (Source: Alekhine, *66 Master Games Played in the London International Chess Tournament, 1932*; notes by AA [additional notes by RT])

107 Menchik–George Thomas

London (4), February 4, 1932

[E85] *King's Indian Defense, Sämisch*

1. d4 ♘f6 2. c4 g6 3. ♘c3 ♗g7 4. e4 d6 5. f3 *(see diagram)*

After 5. f3

Arriving at the Sämisch variation of the King's Indian Defense. Depending on Black's response, White can either castle long and mount a ferocious attack on the g and h files or castle kingside and attempt to win through her spatial advantage on the queenside. **5. ... 0–0 6. ♗e3 e5 7. ♘ge2** [The most common replay is 7. d5 The text gives a quickly moving attack at the expense of the closed center—RT] **7. ... b6?** It must be remembered that the Sämisch variation was not considered a viable variation until 1925. As a result Thomas did not have the advantage of modern theory. The text move, 7. ... b6, is far too slow. Black's queen's bishop will usually land on e6 to counter White's expansion on the queenside. When it does go to b7 it is after the more assertive move of b5. In the above position 7. ... c6 is called for to contest the center and allow Black more mobility. The result is often an open c-file allowing

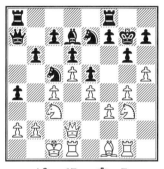

After 17. ... ♔×g7

Black's rooks counterplay. **8. ♕d2 ♘c6 9. d5** Black is forced to place his knight on e7 where it is basically impotent. It is now evident how bad b6 was. White can proceed with her attack on the kingside without fear of real counterattack in the center. **9. ... ♘e7 10. g4 ♘d7 11. ♖g1 a5 12. 0–0–0 ♘c5** [12. ... ♗a6 may offer a little more counterplay—RT] **13. ♘g3** White takes her time, putting each piece on its optimum square as Black is not going anywhere quickly. **13. ... ♗d7 14. h4 a4 15. h5 ♕b8** Black tries to mount a counterattack, but it's too slow. **16. ♗h6 ♕a7 17. ♗×g7 ♔×g7** *(see diagram)*

18. ♘f5+! ♘×f5?! [No better is 18. ... ♗×f5 19. g×f5 followed by ♘g8 or f6—RT] **19. g×f5 a3 20. f6+! ♔h8** The alternates end in mate in a few. **21. ♕h6 a×b2+ 22. ♔b1 ♖g8 23. h×g6 f×g6 24. ♕×h7+ 1–0** (Source: *Chess*, August 1944, #1800; Alekhine, *66 Master Games Played in the London International Chess Tournament, 1932*; notes by AA [additional notes by RT])

108 Mir Sultan Khan–Menchik

London International (5), February 5, 1932

[C01] *French, Exchange Variation*

1. e4 e6 2. d4 d5 3. e×d5 e×d5 4. ♗d3 ♗d6 5. ♘e2 ♘e7 6. ♘g3 0–0 7. 0–0 ♘g6 8. ♕h5 This breaks the symmetry as Black cannot play ♕h4 because of 9. ♗×g6, etc. But in Menchik's place I would simply play here 8. ... c6 9. ♗g5 ♕c7 in order to bring the queen's knight to f6 eventually. **8. ... ♘c6 9. c3 ♘ce7 10. ♗d2?** [10. f4 was necessary, followed, if 10. ... f5 by 11. ♗e3 and ♘bd2—RT] **10. ... f5 11. ♘e2 ♔h8?** [Why not 11. ... f4 ? If then 12. ♘f3 ♗f5 13. ♘g5 h6 14. ♘e6 ♗×e6 15. ♗×g6 ♘×g6 16. ♕×g6 ♕d7 with a clear positional superiority—RT] **12. f4 ♘g8 13. ♕h3** This good move maintains the balance of the position, as it prevents at this stage the entry of the Black knight via f6 at e4. **13. ... ♕h4 14. ♕×h4**

♘×h4 **15. g3 ♘g6 16. ♘f3 ♘f6 17. ♘e5 ♘e7 18. ♔g2 ♘e4 19. ♗e3 ♗e6 20. ♖fc1**
In spite of his inexact 10th move, Sultan Khan has succeeded in improving his position com-

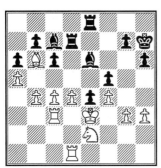

pared with the initial one, as he has gained the moves g3 and
♔g2, which are both useful for the coming endgame. In the
following stage he increases this small advantage in a very
instructive way. **20. ... ♘g8 21. ♗×e4 d×e4 22. c4 c6 23. a3
♘f6 24. h3 ♔g8 25. ♗d2 ♖fd8 26. ♗a5 ♖e8 27. ♗b4
♗c7 28. a4 ♖ac8 29. a5 ♗b8 30. ♖a3 ♘d7 31. ♘×d7
♗×d7 32. ♗c5 ♗e6 33. ♖b3 ♖c7 34. ♔f2 ♖f7 35. ♔e3
a6 36. ♖bc3 ♗c7 37. b4 h6 38. ♖f1 ♖d7 39. ♖d1 ♔h7
40. ♗b6** *(see diagram)*

　　　40. ... ♗×b6? Black's only pride was her two bishops,
and after having avoided for a long time the exchange of one
of them, she suddenly, without any appreciable reason, executes

After 40. ♗b6

it! After 40. ... ♗b8 followed eventually by g5, Sultan Khan would not find it at all easy to
bring his game to a happy end. **41. a×b6 ♖a8 42. ♖d2** He could of course, play at once
42. ♖a1 followed by ♖a5, etc. But his position is so strong now that he can without harm lose
a tempo. The final stage is easy to understand and does not need comment. **42. ... ♖dd8
43. ♖a2 ♖e8 44. ♖a5 ♖ad8 45. ♖e5 ♔g8 46. d5! c×d5 47. ♘d4 ♗f7 48. c5 ♖×e5
49. f×e5 ♗e8 50. ♘×f5 ♗b5 51. ♔d4 ♔f8 52. e6 ♔e8 53. ♘d6+ 1–0** (Source: Alekhine,
66 Master Games Played in the London International Chess Tournament, 1932; notes by AA [additional
notes by RT])

109　George Koltanowski–Menchik
London International (6), February 6, 1932

[D51] *Queen's Gambit Declined*

1. d4 ♘f6 2. c4 e6 3. ♘c3 d5 4. ♗g5 ♘bd7 5. e3 c6 6. a3 Introduced by Capablanca in
our (vs. Alekhine) 5th match game, this move is not worse than any other but hardly sufficient
to secure White any appreciable advantage. It has, however,
the advantage of having been less analyzed than the other continuations. **6. ... ♗e7 7. ♕c2 0–0 8. ♖d1 d×c4** In my opinion a little premature. [More chances of equalizing would lie
in 8. ... a6 followed by d×c4, b5, ♗b7 and finally c5—RT]
**9. ♗×c4 ♘d5 10. ♗×e7 ♕×e7 11. ♘f3 ♘×c3 12. ♕×c3
c5 13. 0–0** *(see diagram)*

　　　13. ... c×d4 14. e×d4? There was neither reason nor
necessity to isolate the pawn, inasmuch as after 14. ♕×d4
White would maintain without any weakness in his position
an appreciable advantage in development. After the text-move
Black has no difficulty in developing her queen's bishop, and

After 13. 0–0

the legitimate result should be a draw. **14. ... ♘b6 15. ♗a2 ♗d7 16. ♕c2 ♖ab8 17. ♕c5
♕f6 18. ♘e5 ♖fd8 19. ♖d3 ♗c6** The only saving move, but not difficult to find. **20. ♘×c6
b×c6 21. ♕×c6 ♖×d4 22. ♖f3 ♕e7 23. b4 ♖c8 24. ♕b5 ♘d5 25. ♗b3 ♕c7 26. ♖e1
♕c6** Some players would be tempted here or at the previous move by ♘c3, which however,

would not lead to a convincing advantage. But Menchik obviously is playing for the draw. **27. ♕×c6 ♖×c6 28. ♗×d5 ♖×d5 29. g3 g6 30. ♖ee3 a5 31. ♖c3 ♖×c3 32. ♖×c3 a×b4 33. a×b4 ♖d1+ 34. ♔g2 ♖b1 35. ♖c8+ ♔g7 36. ♖b8 e5 37. b5 e4 38. b6 g5 39. h3 h6 40. b7 ♔h7 41. f4 ♖b2+ 42. ♔f1 g×f4 43. g×f4** After 43. ... ♔g7 White, in view of the threat of ♔–f6–f5 etc. has quickly to exchange his b-pawn against Black's e-pawn. ½–½ (Source: Alekhine, *66 Master Games Played in the London International Chess Tournament, 1932*; notes by AA [additional notes by RT])

110 Menchik–William Winter
London International (7), February 8, 1932
[E43] *Nimzo-Indian, Rubinstein Variation*

1. d4 ♘f6 2. c4 e6 3. ♘c3 ♗b4 4. e3 b6 5. ♗d3 [A good system here is 5. ♘ge2 followed by 6. a3 etc.—RT] **5. ... ♗b7 6. f3** [And now the natural move 6. ♘f3 was to be preferred. The move chosen weakens the central position without any appreciable compensation—RT] **6. ... ♗×c3+** [Why not at once 6. ... d5 (7. ♕a4+ ♘c6 8. c×d5 e×d5 9. ♗b5 ♕d6 etc., with a good game)? Still, even after the unnecessary exchange, Black gets a satisfactory position—a proof that the sixth move of White is not to be recommended—RT] **7. b×c3 d5 8. ♘e2 c5 9. 0–0 0–0 10. ♘g3 c×d4 11. c×d4 ♘c6 12. ♗a3 ♖e8 13. ♕a4 a6 14. ♖ab1 ♘a5** [He could, instead, play 14. ... b5 15. c×b5 a×b5 16. ♕b3 ♗a6 etc., with some prospects. Still the text-move is perhaps even more effective—RT] **15. c5 b5 16. ♕c2 ♘c4 17. ♗c1 g6** Preparing the eventual advance of his king's pawn. **18. ♖d1 ♕e7 19. ♗×c4 d×c4 20. e4 e5!** The isolation of White's c-pawn is of appreciable importance in this position. After a couple of slight complications it will become apparent that Black has slightly the best of it. **21. ♗b2 e×d4 22. ♗×d4 ♘d7 23. ♕f2** A nice little trap; if now 23. ... ♖ac8, then 24. ♘f5, etc. [Black cannot play 24. ... g×f5 due to ♕g3 and mate in four—RT] winning. But after the next move of Black all White's hopes of an attack are practically over. **23. ... f6 24. a4 ♗c6 25. ♘e2 ♖ab8 26. a×b5 a×b5 27. ♘c3 ♖ec8** Preventing 28. ♘d5 and threatening again 28. ... b4. **28. ♖b4 ♘e5 29. ♘d5 ♗×d5 30. ♗×e5 f×e5 31. ♖×d5** *(see diagram)*

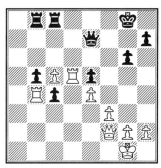

After 31. ♖×d5

31. ... ♖c6 After the (for White) practically compulsory exchange of the minor pieces, Black has succeeded in keeping the advantage of the two passed pawns against the one of his opponent. Still this advantage, in view of certain weaknesses in his king's position and in the center, seems not to be sufficient for a win. Consequently the simplest way for him was here 31. ... ♕a7, practically forcing the answer 32. c6 with the following exchange of the passed pawns and a draw in prospect. The text-move does not improve his position. **32. h3 ♕g5 33. ♕b2! ♕e3+ 34. ♔h2 ♕f4+?** [The decisive mistake. He could still save the game by 34. ... c3! 35. ♕b3 (or 35. ♕a2 ♔h8) Evidently Alekhine misses 36. ♖×b5 with a winning advantage—RT]) **35. ... ♔g7** etc. After the unfortunate check his position goes entirely to pieces—RT] **35. ♔h1 ♖a6 36. ♖d1! ♖ba8 37. ♖×b5 ♖a2 38. ♖b8+ ♖×b8 39. ♕×a2 ♖b3 40. c6 ♖×f3 41. ♖d8+ 1–0** (Source: Alekhine, *66 Master Games Played in the London International Chess Tournament, 1932*; notes by AA [additional notes by RT])

111 Philip S. Milner-Barry–Menchik
London (8), February 9, 1932
[C14] *French, Classical*

1. e4 e6 2. d4 d5 3. ♘c3 ♘f6 4. ♗g5 ♗e7 5. e5 ♘fd7 6. ♗×e7 ♕×e7 7. f4 0-0 8. ♗d3 The usual 8. ♘f3 is without doubt better, as White cannot know this moment which square— d3, e2 or even g2 (after g3) will be the most suitable for his bishop. **8. ... c5 9. ♘f3 f6 10. d×c5 ♘c6 11. ♕e2 ♘×c5 12. 0-0-0** [12. e×f6 The following opening of the f-file is distinctly favorable for Black. Relatively better was therefore 12. ... ♕×f6 13. g3 etc.—RT] **12. ... ♘×d3+ 13. ♖×d3 f×e5 14. f×e5 ♗d7 15. ♕d2 ♗e8** Black's positional advantage, owing to the two open files, is quite apparent, but she does not show at this stage enough energy to exploit it. Here, for instance, the natural move 15. ... ♘b4 and, if 16. ♖e3 b5, etc., would give her many more chances of a rapid success. **16. ♘e2 ♖c8 17. ♖c3 ♗g6 18. ♘ed4 ♘b4 19. ♔b1 a6 20. ♖e1 ♘c6 21. ♘×c6?** White's only strength was the knight's post at d4—and yet he annihilates this advantage by bringing a Black pawn on the c-file! From this moment his game is strategically lost, and the win for Black a matter of pure technique. He had to play a waiting game, e.g., 21. a3—although Menchik's chances in any case would be better. **21. ... b×c6! 22. ♕e2 ♕a7 23. ♖e3 ♖a8 24. ♕d2 c5 25. ♘g5 ♕e7 26. ♘f3 ♖fb8 27. ♕a5 h6 28. ♖b3**

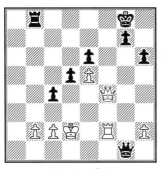

After 40. ♔d2

♖×b3 29. a×b3 ♖b8 30. ♕a4 ♖b4! 31. ♕×a6 ♖×b3 32. ♔c1 ♖b8 33. ♖e3 ♗e4! The exchange of the strong bishop against the apparently weaker knight shows a right conception of the positional necessities and is, in fact, the quickest way of winning. **34. ♕e2 ♗×f3 35. ♖×f3 c4 36. ♕d2** [If 36. ♖a3 ♕c5 and eventually d4, etc.—RT] **36. ... ♕a7 37. ♕f4 ♕g1+ 38. ♖f1 ♕×g2 39. ♖f2 ♕g1+ 40. ♔d2** *(see diagram)*

40. ... ♕g5? Menchik was obviously short of time, otherwise this mistake can hardly be explained. She could win very easily either by 40. ... ♖×b2 or by 40. ... ♖a8 etc. After the exchange of queens her material advantage becomes quite illusory, as the pawn end-game, owing to the favorable position of the White king is clearly drawn. **41. ♕×g5 h×g5 42. ♔c3 ♖f8 43. ♖×f8+ ♔×f8 44. ♔d4 ♔f7 45. ♔c5 g4 46. ♔d4 ♔g6 47. b3 c×b3 48. c×b3 ♔f7 49. ♔c5 ♔e7 50. ♔b5 ♔d7 51. ♔c5 ♔c7 52. ♔b5 ½-½** (Source: Alekhine, *66 Master Games Played in the London International Chess Tournament, 1932*; notes by AA [additional notes by RT])

112 Menchik–Victor Berger
London (9), February 10, 1932
[D63] *Queen's Gambit Declined, Classical*

1. d4 d5 2. c4 e6 3. ♘c3 ♘f6 4. ♗g5 ♗e7 5. e3 0-0 6. ♘f3 ♘bd7 7. ♖c1 c6 8. a3 ♘e4 A good way to answer the unusual 8th move of White. With a tempo more, the Stonewall Defense is playable. **9. ♗×e7 ♕×e7 10. ♕c2 f5 11. ♗d3 ♖f6 12. 0-0** As Black obviously will attack White's castled position, I would prefer not to castle at all, and prevent my opponent's aggressive plans by the move 12. h4! After the text-move Berger [*sic*; né Buerger] has an easy game, although Menchik in the following play defends herself very tenaciously. **12. ...** ♖h6 **13.** ♖fe1 g5 **14.** ♗×e4 f×e4 **15.** ♘d2 g4 **16.** ♘f1 ♕g5 [16. ... ♘f8 followed by ♘g6–h4 would probably more rapidly lead to a happy end—RT] **17.** ♘e2 ♘f8 **18.** ♘f4 ♗d7 **19. b4** One would hardly imagine at this stage that the harmless demonstration on the queenside would be finally successful. **19. ...** ♘g6 **20.** ♘×g6 ♖×g6 **21. a4 a6 22.** ♕a2 ♖f6 **23.** ♘g3 ♖af8 **24.** ♖c2 ♔h8 **25.** ♖b2 h5 **26. b5** a×b5 **27.** c×b5 h4 **28.** ♘f1 e5! Now the bishop will at last participate in the attack, which should in a few moves become irresistible. [According to Steinitz' theory we only make progress when we respond properly to inferior moves. Either the position is irresistible now or it is not—RT] **29. b6** Menchik shows in this desperate situation a remarkable coolness and self-control. **29. ...** e×d4 **30.** e×d4 *(see diagram)*

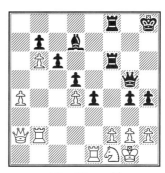

After 30. e×d4

30. ... g3 The winning combination. White is forced to take with the rook's pawn. After 31. f×g3 the answer 31. ... h3! would end the battle even more quickly than it should have happened in the actual game. **31.** h×g3 h×g3 **32.** ♘×g3 ♕h4 **33.** ♕a3 Still trying to set the opponent new little problems. **33. ...** ♖8f7 **34. a5** ♖h6 **35.** ♕e3 ♖hh7? [Why this loss of time? Immediately decisive was 35. ... ♗g4 36. f4 (forced) 36. ... ♕h2+ 37. ♔f2 (or ♔f1, ♗f3) 37. ... ♗f3 38. ♖g1 ♖g7 etc.—RT] **36. a6** ♗g4 **37. f4** b×a6 **38.** ♔f2 ♗c8 **39.** ♔e2 ♖×f4 **40.** ♖h1 In spite of his inexact 35th move, Black has still obtained a won game and has only to make the natural move 40. ... ♕g4+ followed, if 41. ♔e1 by ♖×a1+ and ♗b7, etc. The unfortunate text-move—obviously the consequence of time pressure—loses at once. **40. ...** ♕f6? **41.** ♖×h7+ ♔×h7 **42. b7** ♗g4+ **43.** ♔e1 **1–0** (Source: Alekhine, *66 Master Games Played in the London International Chess Tournament, 1932*; notes by AA [additional notes by RT])

113 Isaac Kashdan–Menchik
London International (10), February 11, 1932
[D37] *Queen's Gambit Declined*

After 6. ♗f4

1. d4 ♘f6 **2. c4 e6 3.** ♘f3 d5 **4.** ♘c3 ♘bd7 **5. a3** An irrelevant move, which could well be answered by c5. The next move of Black is distinctly not the best. **5. ...** ♗e7 **6.** ♗f4 *(see diagram)*

6. ... c5? [A terrible mistake, which loses at once. A playable variation here was 6. ... d×c4 7. e4 ♘b6 8. ♗×c4 ♘×c4 9. ♕a4+ ♗d7 10. ♕×c4 ♗c6 etc.—RT] **7.** ♘b5 0–0 **8.** ♗c7 ♕e8 **9.** ♘d6 ♗×d6 **10.** ♗×d6 c×d4 **11.** ♗×f8 ♔×f8 **12.** ♘×d4 After the win of the exchange the rest is only a matter of technique. In the following play Kashdan chooses one of the quickest ways to force capitulation. **12. ...** d×c4 **13. e3** ♘b6 **14. a4!** ♕e7 **15. a5** ♘bd5 **16.** ♘c2 ♘e4 **17.** ♕d4 f5 **18.** ♗×c4 ♘df6 **19. 0–0** ♗d7 **20.** ♖ad1 ♗c6 **21. f3 e5 22.** ♕d3 ♘c5 **23.** ♕×f5 **1–0** (Source: Alekhine, *66 Master Games Played in the London International Chess Tournament, 1932*; notes by AA [additional notes by RT])

114 Menchik–Saviely Tartakower
London International (11), February 12, 1932
[D40] *Queen's Gambit Declined Semi-Tarrasch Variation*

1. d4 d5 2. ♘f3 c5 3. c4 e6 4. e3 ♘f6 5. ♘c3 a6 6. ♗d3 Now Black obtains a variation of the Queen's Gambit Accepted with a tempo in his favor. Therefore 6. a3 was preferable. **6. ... d×c4 7. ♗×c4 b5 8. ♗d3 ♗b7 9. 0-0 ♘bd7 10. ♕e2 ♕c7 11. ♖d1 ♗e7 12. e4 c×d4 13. ♘×d4 0-0 14. a3 ♗c5** Black has slightly the better position but does not seen here and on the next move to make the most of his advantage. More natural, for instance, than the two bishop moves in the text was ♖fd8 with the intention of ♘e5, etc. **15. ♘b3 ♗d6 16. h3 ♖fd8 17. ♗e3 ♘e5 18. ♖ac1 ♘×d3 19. ♖×d3 ♗h2+ 20. ♔h1 ♖×d3 21. ♕×d3 ♕d6** [There was already nothing better, as 21. ... ♕b8 22. ♘c5 etc. did not look promising. After the exchange of queens, the end-game, in spite of the two Black bishops, should, of course, be drawn—RT] **22. ♕×d6 ♗×d6 23. f3 ♖c8 24. ♘e2 ♖×c1+ 25. ♘e×c1 ♘d7 26. ♘d3 f5 27. e×f5 e×f5 28. ♘bc5 ♘×c5 29. ♘×c5 ♗c8 30. f4 ♔f7 31. ♔g1 a5 32. b4 a×b4** If

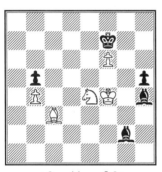

After 44. ... ♔f7

Black played for the win—as he obviously did—why did he not try the more complicated 32. ... a4? **33. a×b4 ♗e6 34. ♔f2 ♗c4 35. g3 ♗e7 36. ♗d4 g5 37. f×g5 ♗×g5 38. ♗c3 ♔e7 39. g4 ♗h4+ 40. ♔f3 ♗f1 41. g×f5 ♗×h3 42. ♔f4 h5 43. ♘e4 ♗g2 44. f6+ ♔f7** *(see diagram)*

45. ♘g5+? [In this dead drawn position White makes a truly inexplicable mistake. Either 45. ♘d6+ followed by ♘×b5 or 45. ♘g3 ♔g6 46. ♘×h5 ♔×h5 47. f7 ♗e7 48. ♗g7 etc. would force the draw. A lucky win for Dr. Tartakower—RT] **45. ... ♔g6 46. f7** [As it turns out a draw is still available with 46. ♘e6! ♗×f6 47. ♗×f6 ♔×f6 48. ♘c7 ♗f1 49. ♔g3 ♔g5 50. ♘e6+ ♔f5 51. ♘c7 ♗c4 52. ♔h4—RT] **46. ... ♗×g5+ 47. ♔g3 ♔×f7 48. ♔×g2 ♔e6 49. ♔h3 ♔d5 50. ♗e1 ♔c4 51. ♔g2 ♗e7 52. ♔h3 ♗×b4 53. ♗h4 ♗d6 54. ♗e1 ♗e7 55. ♗d2 ♗f6 56. ♗a5 ♗c3 57. ♗d8 0-1** (Source: Alekhine, *66 Master Games Played in the London International Chess Tournament, 1932*; notes by AA [additional notes by RT])

Cambridge 1932 (Easter Congress)
(Premier Division)
March 26–April 2, 1932

		1	2	3	4	5	6	7	8	Points	Place
1	Sultan Khan, Mir	•	1	1	=	1	=	=	1	5½	1
2	Alexander, C.H.O'D.	0	•	0	1	=	1	1	1	4½	2–3
3	Van den Bosch, J.	0	1	•	=	1	1	=	=	4½	2–3
4	Thomas, George	=	0	=	•	=	=	=	1	3½	4
5	Menchik, Vera	0	=	0	=	•	=	=	1	3	5–7
6	Tylor, Theodore	=	0	0	=	=	•	1	=	3	5–7
7	Yates, Frederick D.	=	0	=	=	=	0	•	1	3	5–7
8	Milner-Barry, Philip S.	0	0	=	0	0	=	=	•	1	8

(R46) **Theodore Tylor–Menchik**
Cambridge (1), March 26, 1932
1. e4 e6 ... 31 ½–½

(R47) **Menchik–Frederick D. Yates**
Cambridge (2), March 27, 1932
1. d4 e6 2. e4 d5 ... ½–½

115 Johannes Van den Bosch–Menchik
Cambridge (3), March 28, 1932
[C14] *French, Classical*

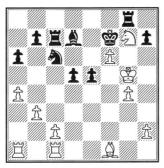

After 29. ♘g7

1. e4 e6 2. d4 d5 3. ♘c3 ♘f6 4. ♗g5 ♗e7 5. e5 ♘fd7 6. ♗×e7 ♕×e7 7. f4 0-0 8. ♘f3 c5 9. g3 ♘c6 10. ♗g2 c×d4 11. ♘×d4 ♕c5 12. ♘b3 ♕e3+ 13. ♕e2 ♕×e2+ 14. ♘×e2 ♖b8 15. ♘bd4 a6 16. a4 ♘b6 17. b3 ♗d7 18. ♔d2 ♘c8 19. ♔e3 ♘8e7 20. ♖hc1 ♖fc8 21. ♗f1 ♖c7 22. g4 g5 23. ♘×c6 ♘×c6 24. ♘g3 g×f4+ 25. ♔×f4 f6 26. e×f6 e5+ 27. ♔g5 ♔f7 28. ♘f5 ♖g8+ 29. ♘g7 *(see diagram)*

29. ... ♗×g4?! Patience to keep building on a good position is advised. 29. ... ♘d4! 30. ♗g2 ♘e6+ 31. ♔h6 ♘f4 32. c4 (32. ♗×d5+ ♘×d5 33. g5 ♖×g7 34. f×g7 ♖c6+ 35. ♔h5 ♘f4+ 36. ♔h4 ♖c3 37. g8♕+ ♔×g8 38. g6 h6 39. ♖g1 ♖h3 mate) 32. ... ♘×g2 **30. ♗g2 ♗e6 31. ♖f1 ♘d4 32. ♖f2 ♖c3?∓** 32. ... ♖×c2+ **33. ♖e1?** 33. ♖d1 holds the position **33. ... e4 34. ♖d1 ♘f3+?** 34. ... ♖×c2–+ **35. ♗×f3 ♖×f3 36. ♖×f3 e×f3** Time control has passed and so has Black's advantage! **37. ♖f1 ♗g4 38. h3 h6+?** 38. ... ♗×h3 39. ♖×f3 ♗g2 40. ♖c3 h6+ 41. ♔f5 (41. ♔×h6 ♔×f6 42. ♘h5+ ♔e5∓) 41. ... ♖c8 42. ♖×c8 ♗h3+ 43. ♔e5 ♗×c8= **39. ♔×h6 ♔×f6 40. ♘h5+ ♗×h5 41. ♔×h5 ♔e5 42. ♖×f3 ♖c8 43. ♖f2 ♖c3?! 44. ♔g4 d4 45. h4 d3 46. c×d3 ♖×d3 47. h5 ♖d1 48. ♖h2 ♖g1+ 49. ♔f3 ♖g7 50. h6 ♖h7 51. ♔e3 ♔f6 52. ♔d4 ♔e6 53. ♔e4 ♔f6 54. ♔d5 ♔f5 55. a5 ♖d7+ 56. ♔c5 ♖h7 57. ♔d6 ♔g5 58. ♔e6 ♔g6 59. ♖g2+ ♔h5 60. ♔f6 1-0** (Source: *www.Chessgames.com;* notes by RT)

116 Menchik–Mir Sultan Khan
Cambridge (4), March 29, 1932
[A82] *Dutch, Staunton Gambit*

The Times of March 31, 1932, indicated that Vera took a full hour for the first seven moves, which meant she was in time trouble for the rest of the game.

1. d4 f5 2. e4 f×e4 3. ♘c3 ♘f6 4. g4 h6 5. f3 d5 6. ♗f4 e6 7. ♕d2 ♗d6 8. 0-0-0 e×f3 9. ♗×d6 c×d6 10. ♘×f3 0-0 11. ♖g1 ♘e4 12. ♕g2 ♕f6 13. ♗e2 ♕f4+ 14. ♔b1 ♘c6 15. h4 g6 16. ♖df1 *(see diagram)*

16. ... ♘e7? Better is 16. ... ♘×c3+ 17. b×c3 ♕e3∓; but

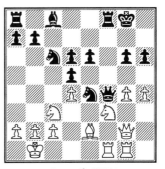

After 16. ♖df1

best is 16. ... ♘×d4 17. ♘×e4 ♘×e2 18. ♘fd2 ♕e3 19. ♖e1 ♘f4 20. ♖×e3 ♘×g2 21. ♖×g2–+ **17. ♔a1?** 17. ♘×e4 ♕×e4 18. ♗d3= **17. ... ♕e3?!** 17. ... ♘×c3 **18. ♗d3 ♗d7 19. ♕e2 ♕×e2 20. ♘×e2 ♖f7 21. c4 ♖af8 22. ♗×e4 d×e4 23. ♘d2 d5 24. ♔b1 ♖f2 25. ♖e1 ♘c6 26. ♘b3 ♗b4 27. ♘c5 ♗c8 28. ♘c3 b6 29. ♘b3 ♗a6 30. ♘c1 ♗×c4 0–1** (Source: *Mir Sultan Khan* by Coles #45; notes by RT)

117 Philip S. Milner-Barry–Menchik
Cambridge (5), March 1932

[E33] *Nimzo-Indian, Classical Variation*

Menchik's game against Milner-Barry was a tragedy of the time limits first for one, then for the other. Menchik took about an hour for her first eight moves and at one time had 16 moves to make in about half that number of minutes. Milner-Barry had much the best of the position, yet caught the same complaint, losing time and moving his pieces anyhow. He had three moves to make when his flag fell and so ended the game.[47]

Final position

1. d4 ♘f6 2. c4 e6 3. ♘c3 ♗b4 4. ♕c2 ♘c6 5. ♘f3 d6 6. a3 ♗×c3+ 7. ♕×c3 0–0 8. b4 e5 9. d×e5 ♘e4 10. ♕e3 f5 11. ♗b2 ♘×e5 12. ♘×e5 d×e5 13. ♖d1 ♕e7 14. g3 ♗e6 15. ♗g2 ♘d6 16. ♗×e5 ♘×c4 17. ♕c3 a5 18. b5? ♘×a3 19. ♕×c7 ♕×c7 20. ♗×c7 ♘×b5 21. ♗e5 ♗b3 22. ♖b1 a4 23. 0–0 ♘a3 24. ♖bc1 ♘c2 25. ♗×b7 ♖a5 26. f4 a3 27. ♖f3 ♗a4 28. ♖c3 ♖b5?? [28. ... a2—RT] **29. ♗c6 ♖×e5 30. f×e5 a2 31. ♗d5+ ♔h8** *(see diagram)* **0–1 Flag.** (Source: *www.Chessgames.com*)

118 C.H.O'D. Alexander–Menchik
Cambridge (6), April 1, 1932

[C14] *French, Classical Variation*

Alexander vs. Menchik was another short game where Menchik used far too much time in the first 10 moves. She had won a pawn by then, which Alexander later regained, but he disliked the complications to the extent of forcing a draw by repetition.[48]

1. e4 e6 2. d4 d5 3. ♘c3 ♘f6 4. ♗g5 ♗e7 5. e5 ♘fd7 6. h4 c5 7. ♗×e7 ♕×e7 8. ♕g4 ♘c6 9. ♘f3 c×d4 10. ♘b5 ♕a5+ 11. ♔d1 ♘d×e5 12. ♘×e5 ♘×e5 13. ♕×g7 ♗d7 14. ♘×d4 ♘c6 15. ♕g5+ ♔f8 16. ♕h6+ ♔e7 17. ♕g5+ ♔f8 18. ♕h6+ ♔e7 ½–½ *(see diagram)* (Source: *Best Games of C.H.O'D. Alexander*, p. 15)

Final position

(R48) Menchik–George Thomas
Cambridge (7), April 2, 1932
1. d4 ... 41 ½–½

London 1932

(25th B.C.F. Congress—Major Open)
August 15–27, 1932

		1	2	3	4	5	6	7	8	9	10	11	12	Points	Place
1	Koltanowski, George	●	1	1	=	=	1	1	=	1	1	1	1	9½	1
2	Menchik, Vera	0	●	1	1	0	1	1	1	1	1	1	1	9	2
3	Cross, Alfred R.	0	0	●	=	1	=	1	1	1	=	1	=	7	3
4	Seitz, Jakob A.	=	0	=	●	=	1	1	=	=	1	=	=	6½	4
5	Damant, C.A.S.	=	1	0	=	●	1	0	1	=	0	0	1	5½	5
6	Heath, Christopher	0	0	=	0	0	●	0	1	1	1	=	1	5	6–8
7	Stronach, Bernard	0	0	0	0	1	1	●	0	1	=	1	=	5	6–8
8	Wallis, Philip N.	=	0	0	=	0	0	1	●	1	0	1	1	5	6–8
9	Jacobs, Herbert	0	0	0	=	=	0	0	0	●	1	1	1	4	9–10
10	Watts, William H.	0	0	=	0	1	0	=	1	0	●	0	1	4	9–10
11	Reeve, H.T.	0	0	0	=	1	=	0	0	0	1	●	0	3	11
12	Israel, Harold	0	0	=	=	0	0	=	0	0	0	1	●	2½	12

A rule of this tournament was that no game could be drawn before move 30 (possibly that would be "without the arbiter's permission"). At any rate, in the game against Seitz, Menchik offered a draw in this game which was disallowed by the arbiter; following this, Seitz lost. Later in the tournament, a draw was offered to Menchik by Damant in an equal position, which was also disallowed by the arbiter; Menchik's play then deteriorated and she lost that game. Arbiters were obviously more respected in that era as many players have circumvented this type of rule over the last few decades. Most recently in Plovdiv 2012 the arbiters seem to be fighting back with double losses being awarded to guilty players.

119 Jakob Adolf Seitz–Menchik
London (1)—B.C.F. Major, August 1932

[D52] *Queen's Gambit Declined, Cambridge Springs Variation*

1. d4 ♘f6 2. c4 e6 3. ♘c3 d5 4. ♘f3 ♘bd7 5. ♗g5 c6 6. e3 ♕a5 7. ♗×f6 ♘×f6 8. ♗d3 ♗b4 9. ♕c2 0-0 10. 0-0 ♗×c3 11. b×c3 d×c4 12. ♗×c4 ♘d7 13. e4 e5 14. d×e5 ♘×e5 15. ♘×e5 ♕×e5 16. ♔h1 ♕f4 17. f3 ♗e6 18. g3 ♕f6 19. ♗×e6 ♕×e6 20. ♕b3 ♕e7 21. ♖ad1 ♖fd8 22. ♔g2 h6 23. ♕b4 ♕×b4 24. c×b4 ♔f8 25. ♖b1 ♖d4 26. ♖f2 ♖ad8 27. ♖e2 ♖c4 28. ♖b3 g5 29. h3 ♖dd4 30. a3 ♔e7 31. ♖be3 h5 32. f4 g4 33. e5 ♖d1 34. h×g4 h×g4 35. f5 ♖cc1 36. ♖e4 ♖g1+ 37. ♔f2?? [37. ♔h2=—RT] 37. … ♖cf1+ 38. ♔e3 ♖×g3+ 39. ♔d4 ♖d1+ 0-1 (Source: *www.365Chess.com*)

120 Menchik–William H. Watts
London (3)—B.C.F. Major, August 1932

[C10] *French*

1. d4 e6 2. e4 d5 3. ♘c3 d×e4 4. ♘×e4 ♘f6 5. ♘×f6+ g×f6 6. ♘f3 c5 7. ♗e3 c×d4 8. ♕×d4 ♕×d4 9. ♘×d4 a6 10. 0-0-0 ♗c5 11. ♗e2 ♘d7 12. ♖d2 e5 13. ♘f5! ♗×e3 14. f×e3! b5? *(see diagram)*

   15. ♗f3! ♖b8 16. ♗c6 ♖b6 17. ♘d6+ ♔e7? 18. ♘×c8+ ♖×c8 19. ♗×d7 1-0 (Source: *CS 1933*, v. 7 #878)

After 14. … b5

121   George Koltanowski–Menchik

London—B.C.F. Major (6), August 1932

[D95] *Grünfeld Defense*

In his book *Chess with the Masters*, Koltanowski lists this game as being played in Hastings 1931-32. Unfortunately Koltanowski was notorious for not checking his facts when writing up his anecdotes and they did not play in the same section that year. The game is actually #6869 in *British Chess Magazine* of 1932. Going into the game both players had perfect 5–0 scores.

After 29. c6

1. d4 ♘f6 2. ♘f3 d5 3. e3 g6 4. c4 ♗g7 5. ♘c3 0-0 6. ♕b3 c6 7. ♘e5 ♘bd7 8. f4 ♘xe5 9. fxe5 ♘e4 10. cxd5 ♘xc3 11. bxc3 cxd5 12. c4 ♗e6 13. ♗a3 dxc4 14. ♗xc4 ♗xc4 15. ♕xc4 ♕a5+ 16. ♗b4 ♕a4 17. ♕b3 ♕xb3 18. axb3 ♖fc8 19. ♔d2 e6 20. ♖hc1 a6 21. ♖c4 ♖xc4 22. bxc4 f6 23. exf6 ♗xf6 24. ♗a5 Although she is fighting an uphill battle, Menchik's last half dozen moves sped up the process through her typical time pressure. 24. ... ♖c8 25. ♔d3 b5 26. c5 ♔f7 27. ♗b6 ♖a8 28. e4 ♔e8 29. c6 *(see diagram)* 29. ... ♖c8 30. c7 ♖a8 31. ♖xa6 1-0 (Source: *BCM* #6869)

122   Harold Israel–Menchik

London—B.C.F. Major, August 1932

[C02] *French, Advance*

The following game entails an unusual variation of the Advance French where White never gets his pawns or pieces to coordinate—and Black wins in the main part by making rather self evident moves. **1. e4 e6 2. d4 d5 3. e5 c5 4. ♕g4** A move first appearing in MCO (5) in 1932 and which both then and now precedes 4. ... cxd4. **4. ... ♘c6 5. ♘f3** *(see diagram)*

After 5. ♘f3

5. ... ♘xd4 6. ♘xd4 cxd4 7. ♗d3 ♕c7 8. ♗f4 ♘e7 9. ♘d2 ♘g6 10. ♗xg6 hxg6 11. ♖c1 d3 12. ♕f3 dxc2 13. ♕b3 ♗d7 14. ♖xc2 ♕b6 15. ♕xb6 axb6 16. a3 f6 17. 0-0 g5 18. ♗g3 f5 19. f3 ♗c5+ 20. ♗f2 ♗xf2+ 21. ♖xf2 ♗c6 22. ♘f1 ♖a4 23. h3 ♔f7 24. ♘h2 b5 25. ♖fd2 ♖ha8 26. ♔f2 b4 27. axb4 ♖xb4 28. ♖c1 ♖a2 29. ♖b1 ♖b3 30. ♘f1 ♗b5 31. ♘e3 ♗d3 32. ♖c1 ♖bxb2 33. ♖xb2 ♖xb2+ 0-1 (Source: *BCM* #6911)

123   Menchik–C.A.S. Damant

London—B.C.F. Major, August 1932

[D19] *Semi-Slav*

1. d4 d5 2. c4 c6 3. ♘f3 ♘f6 4. ♘c3 dxc4 5. a4 ♗f5 6. e3 e6 7. ♗xc4 ♗b4 8. 0-0 0-0 9. ♕e2 ♘e4 10. ♘xe4 ♗xe4 11. ♖d1 ♘d7 12. ♘d2 ♗c2 13. ♖f1 ♗g6 14. f4 ♘f6 15. ♘f3 ♗e4 16. ♖d1 ♕a5 17. ♗d2 ♗d5 18. ♗d3 ♗e4 19. ♗xe4 ♘xe4 20. ♗xb4 ♕xb4 21. ♕c2 ♘f6 22. ♖ac1 ♕a5 23. ♖d3 ♕d5 24. ♖b3 ♖ab8 *(see diagram)*

After 24. ... ♖ab8

Somewhere in this range Bikova states that Damant offered a draw which was disallowed by the arbiter as they had not made 30 moves. For the next ten or so moves Menchik plays quite indecisively and lets her position deteriorate.
25. ♘e5 ♖fd8 26. ♕c4 ♘e4 27. ♕×d5 e×d5 28. a5 f6 29. ♘d3 ♘d2 30. ♖a3? 30. ♖bc3 **30. ... ♘c4 31. ♖a2 ♘×e3** More precise is 31. ... ♖e8 **32. a6 ♘f5 33. a×b7 ♘×d4 34. ♖d1 ♖×b7 35. ♘c5 ♘e2+ 36. ♔f1 ♖e7 37. g3 ♖de8 38. ♖a6 g5 39. f5 ♖e5 40. g4 ♖8e7 41. ♖×c6 h5 42. ♖×f6 h×g4 43. ♘d3 ♖e3 44. ♖g6+ ♔f7 45. ♖×g5 ♖f3+ 46. ♘f2 ♘f4 47. ♖d2 ♖c7 48. ♔e1 ♘g2+ 49. ♔d1 ♘e3+ 50. ♔e2 ♘c4 51. ♘×g4 ♘×d2 52. ♔×d2 ♔f8** *(see diagram)*

53. h4 An interesting try is 53. f6!? ♖b7 54. ♖×d5 ♖×b2+ 55. ♔c1 ♖e2 56. ♔d1 and Black still has some work ahead **53. ... ♖b3 54. ♘e3 ♖×b2+ 55. ♔d3 ♖b3+ 56. ♔d4 ♖b4+ 57. ♔×d5 ♖×h4 58. ♖g6 ♖hh7 59. ♘c4 ♖hg7 60. ♖h6 ♖h7 61. ♖g6 ♖h1 62. ♘d6 ♖d1+ 63. ♔e5 ♖e7+ 64. ♔f4 ♖f1+ 65. ♔g5 ♖g1+ 66. ♔f6 ♖×g6+ 67. f×g6 ♖c7 68. ♘f5 ♖c6+ 69. ♔g5 ♖b6 70. ♔h6 ♖b7 71. ♘d6 ♖d7 72. ♘e4 a5 73. ♘f6 ♖a7 74. ♘h5 ♔g8 0–1** (Source: *www.365Chess.com*; notes by RT)

After 52. ... ♔f8

Hastings 1932-1933

(Premier)
December 28, 1932–January 6, 1933

		1	2	3	4	5	6	7	8	9	10	Points	Place
1	Flohr, Salomon M.	●	=	1	1	=	1	=	1	1	=	7	1
2	Pirc, Vasja	=	●	=	1	1	=	1	1	0	1	6½	2
3	Steiner, Lajos	0	=	●	=	1	0	1	=	1	1	5½	3–4
4	Sultan Khan, Mir	0	0	=	●	0	1	1	1	1	1	5½	3–4
5	Michell, Reginald P.	=	0	0	1	●	1	=	=	=	=	4½	5
6	Thomas, George A.	0	=	1	0	0	●	=	=	=	=	3½	6–8
7	Alexander, C.H.O'D.	=	0	0	0	=	=	●	0	1	1	3½	6–8
8	Menchik, Vera	0	0	=	0	=	=	1	●	1	0	3½	6–8
9	Jackson, Edward M.	0	1	0	0	=	=	0	0	●	1	3	9
10	Tylor, Theodore H.	=	0	0	0	=	=	0	1	0	●	2½	10

124 Menchik–Lajos Steiner
Hastings 1932-33 (1), December 28, 1932

[D13] *Slav, Exchange*

1. d4 d5 2. c4 c6 3. c×d5 c×d5 4. ♘c3 ♘f6 5. ♘f3 e6 6. ♗f4 ♗d6 7. e3 ♗×f4 8. e×f4 ♕d6 9. g3 0–0 10. ♗d3 ♗d7 11. 0–0 ♖c8 12. ♖c1 ♘c6 13. ♗b1 ♕b4 14. ♕d2 ♘a5 15. b3 ♘c6 16. ♖fd1 ♘e7 17. ♘e5 ♗e8 18. ♘e2 ♕×d2 19. ♖×d2 ♖×c1+ 20. ♘×c1

After 46. ... a4

♖c8 21. ♖c2 g6 22. ♖×c8 ♘×c8 23. f3 ♘d6 24. ♔f2 ♔f8 25. ♘e2 ♘d7 26. ♘×d7+ ♗×d7 27. ♗d3 ♔e7 28. ♘c3 a5 29. g4 ♗c6 30. ♔e3 f6 31. ♗e2 ♔d7 32. ♗d3 ♔c7 33. ♗e2 ♔b6 34. ♗d3 ♗b5 35. ♗×b5 ♔×b5 36. ♔d3 ♘c7 37. a3 ♔c6 38. ♔e3 ♔d6 39. h3 ♔c6 40. ♔d3 ♔b6 41. ♘a4+ ♔b5 42. ♘c3+ ♔c6 43. ♔d2 ♘a6 44. ♔d3 ♘b8 45. ♘e2 ♘d7 46. ♔e3 a4 *(see diagram)*

    47. b×a4 ♘b6 48. ♘c3 ♘c4+ 49. ♔d3 ♘×a3 50. ♘d1 ♘c4 51. h4 ♔b6 52. f5 g×f5 53. g×f5 e×f5 54. ♘c3 ♔c6 55. f4 ♘b6 56. ♔c2 ♘c8 57. ♘e2 ♘e7 58. h5 ♘c8 59. ♘g3 ♘d6 60. ♔b3 b6 61. ♔b4 ♔d7 62. ♔b3 ♔e7 63. ♔b4 ♔f7 64. ♘f1 ♔e7 65. ♘g3 ♔e6 66. ♔b3 ♘e4 67. ♘f1 ♔d6 68. ♔b4 ♔c6 69. h6 ♘f2 70. ♘e3 ♘d3+ 71. ♔c3 ♘×f4 72. ♘×f5 ♔c7 73. ♔b4 ½-½ (Source: Cordingly, *Hasting 1932-1933*)

125   C.H.O'D. Alexander–Menchik

Hastings 1932-33 (2), December 29, 1932

[C00] *French*

1. e4 e6 2. b3 d5 3. ♗b2 ♘f6 4. e5 ♘fd7 5. c4 d×c4 6. ♗×c4 ♘b6 7. ♗e2 c5 8. ♘f3 ♘c6 9. 0-0 ♗e7 10. ♘c3 0-0 11. ♘e4 ♕d5 12. ♕c2 h6 13. ♖ac1?! ♖d8 13. ... ♘b4!? 14. ♘c3 (14. ♕b1 ♘×a2 15. ♘eg5 h×g5 16. ♕×a2∓) 14. ... ♘×c2 15. ♘×d5 e×d5 16. ♖×c2 ♗f5 14. ♕b1 ♘b4 15. ♘c3 ♕d7 16. ♗b5 ♘c6 17. ♘e4 a6 18. ♗×c6 ♕×c6 19. d4 ♘d5 20. ♘×c5 Better is 20. d×c5 20. ... ♘f4 21. ♔h1 ♕d5 22. ♕e4 ♕×e4 23. ♘×e4 ♘d3 24. ♖c7 ♖d7 25. ♖×d7 ♗×d7 26. ♗c3 ♖c8 27. ♔g1 ♗c6 28. ♘fd2 b5 29. a3? 29. ♘d6 ♗×d6 30. e×d6 ♖d8∓; 29. ♗a5 ♗d5 30. ♘c3 ♗a8= 29. ... ♗×a3 30. f3 ♗d5 31. ♖d1 ♘f4 32. ♔f1 ♗e7? 32. ... b4 33. ♗a1 ♖c2 34. g3 ♘d3-+ 33. b4?! 33. g3∓ 33. ... ♗×e4 *(see diagram)*

    34. ♘×e4 ♘d5 35. ♗d2 ♗×b4 36. ♗×b4 ♘×b4 37. ♖a1 ♖c4 38. ♘c5 ♖×d4 39. ♘×a6 ♘×a6 40. ♖×a6 g5 41. g3 ♖d5 42. f4 g×f4 43. g×f4 ♖d4 44. ♖b6 ♖×f4+ 45. ♔g2 ♖b4 46. ♔g3 ♔g7 47. h4 h5 48. ♖b8 ♖g4+ 49. ♔h3 b4 50. ♖b5 ♖d4 51. ♔g3 ♔g6 52. ♖b7 ♖g4+ 53. ♔h3 ♖e4 54. ♔g3 ♖e3+ 55. ♔f2 ♖×e5 56. ♖×b4 ♖a5 57. ♔f3 ♖a3+ 58. ♔f4 ♖h3 59. ♔e5 ♖g3 0-1 (Source: Cordingly, *Hastings 1932-1933*; notes by RT)

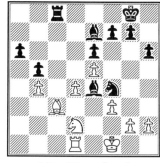

After 33. ... ♗×e4

126   Menchik–Theodore Tylor

Hastings 1932-33 (3), December 30, 1932

[D63] *Queen's Gambit Declined, Classical Variation*

1. d4 ♘f6 2. c4 e6 3. ♘f3 d5 4. ♗g5 ♘bd7 5. e3 ♗e7 6. ♘c3 0-0 7. ♖c1 a6 8. c5 c6 9. ♗f4 ♘h5 10. ♗d3 ♘×f4 11. e×f4 ♖e8 12. 0-0 ♗f6 13. ♖e1 ♘f8 14. ♖e3 ♗d7 15. ♘a4 ♕c7 16. g3 ♖e7 17. ♘b6 ♖d8 18. ♕d2 g6 19. ♖ce1 ♗g7 20. b4 ♗c8 21. a4 ♘d7 22. ♘×d7 ♗×d7 23. ♕b2 ♖a8 24. ♗f1 More solid would be 24. a5± while still retaining and practical winning chances; not good is 24. b5 c×b5 25. a×b5 ♕×c5! 24. ... ♗e8 24. ... b6 25. c×b6 ♕×b6± 25. ♖b3 ♕c8 26. ♖c1 ♖c7 *(see diagram)*

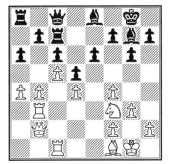

After 26. ... ♖c7

27. b5? 27. a5 **27. ... c×b5 28. a×b5 b6 29. ♖b1?** 29. ♖a1 ♖×c5 30. b×a6 b5 31. ♗×b5 ♗×b5 32. ♖×b5 ♖×b5 33. ♕×b5 ♕c3 and after all is said and done a draw is the expected result; 29. c6 a×b5 30. ♗×b5 ♖ca7= **29. ... b×c5 30. b6?** 30. b×a6 c4 31. ♖b7 ♖×a6 32. ♖b8 ♕d7 33. ♘e5 ♗×e5 (33. ... ♕e7?? 34. ♕b5+−) 34. f×e5 ♖c8 and Black should win, but with work **30. ... ♖b7 31. ♕a2 c4 32. ♖a3 ♖bb8 33. b7 ♖×b7 34. ♖×a6 ♖×b1 35. ♖×a8 ♖b8 36. ♖a3 ♕b7 37. ♕d2 ♗f8 38. ♖a2 ♕b3 39. ♘e5 c3 40. ♕c2 ♕×c2 41. ♖×c2 ♖c8 42. ♘d3 ♗g7 43. ♘e5 ♗a4 44. ♖c1 c2 0–1** (Source: Cordingly, *Hastings 1932-1933*; notes by RT)

127 Mir Sultan Khan–Menchik

Hastings 1932-33 (4), December 31, 1933

[D35] *Queen's Gambit Declined, Exchange*

Menchik plays a rather passive, but almost acceptable, game until she destructs in two (18 and 19) bizarre moves.

1. d4 ♘f6 2. c4 e6 3. ♘f3 d5 4. ♘c3 ♘bd7 5. c×d5 e×d5 6. g3 ♗d6 7. ♗g2 c6 8. 0–0 0–0 9. ♘h4 ♖e8 10. ♘f5 ♗f8?! 10. ... ♗c7 followed by ♘b6 seems to better maintain Black's options. **11. ♕c2 ♘b6 12. ♘h4 ♗e6 13. ♖d1 ♕d7 14. a4 ♖ad8?!** Black is engaging in too much slow maneuvering which allows White to build his position. **15. a5 ♘c8 16. ♘a4 ♗h3 17. ♗g5 ♗×g2 18. ♘×g2** *(see diagram)*

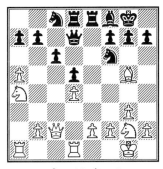

After 18. ♘×g2

18. ... ♕g4? 18. ... ♗e7 **19. ♗×f6 ♖×e2?** 19. ... g×f6‡ 20. e3 **20. ♕×e2 ♕×e2 21. ♗×d8 f6 22. ♗c7 g5 23. ♘e3 h5 24. a6 b×a6 25. ♖dc1 ♕b5 26. ♘c3 ♕×b2 27. ♖ab1 ♕d2 28. ♖c2 ♕d3 29. ♖b8 ♘e7 30. ♗d6 ♔f7 31. ♘cd1 a5 32. ♖cb2 a4 33. ♖2b7 a3 34. ♖×a7 a2 35. ♖×a2 f5 36. ♖aa8 ♗g7 37. ♖b7 ♗f6 38. ♗×e7 ♗×e7 39. ♖aa7 f4 40. ♖×e7+ 1–0** (Source: Cordingly, *Hastings 1932-1933*; notes by RT)

128 Menchik–Reginald Pryce Michell

Hastings 1932-33 (5), January 2, 1933

[D00] *Queen's Pawn Opening*

1. d4 ♘f6 2. e3 d5 3. ♗d3 e6 4. ♘d2 c5 5. c3 ♘bd7 6. f4 ♗d6 7. ♘h3 ♕e7 8. 0–0 b6 9. ♕f3 ♗b7 10. ♘f2 0–0–0 11. e4 d×e4 12. ♘d×e4 ♔b8 13. ♕e2 ♗c7 14. ♗a6 ♗×a6 15. ♕×a6 c×d4 16. c×d4 ♘×e4 17. ♘×e4 ♕b4 18. ♗e3 ♘f6 19. ♘c3 ♕e7 20. ♘b5 ♗d6 21. ♖ac1 ♘d5 22. ♗d2 ♕b7 23. ♕a4 g6 24. ♖c6 ♗e7 25. ♖fc1 ♖d7 26. a3 a6 27. ♘c3 ♖d6 28. ♖×d6 ♗×d6 29. ♘×d5 ♕×d5 30. ♗e3 ♕e4 31. ♕b3 ♕b7 32. d5 e×d5 33. ♗×b6 ♖c8 34. ♖×c8+ ♔×c8 35. ♕c3+ ♔d7 36. ♗e3 ♗e7 37. ♗d4 ♕c6 38. ♔f2 ♕c4 39. ♗e3 ♕f1 40. ♕c2 ♗d6 41. g3 ♕e1+ 42. ♔e2 ♕b1 43. ♕g2 ♕c1+ 44. ♕d2 ♕b1 ½–½ (Source: Cordingly, *Hasting 1932-1933*)

129 Salo Flohr–Menchik

Hastings 1932-33 (6), January 3, 1933

[B13] *Caro-Kann, Exchange Variation*

After 16. ... ♔g8

Flohr played a very elegant game, taking a slight edge and nursing it slowly until breaking the position open on move 17. This game was included in the book *Salo Flohr: Master of Tactics, Master of Technique*, 1985, from which the notes were based. **1. d4 ♘f6 2. ♘f3 d5 3. e3 c5 4. c3 c×d4 5. e×d4 ♗f5 6. ♕b3 ♕c7? 7. ♘a3!** [Not 7. ♗f4 ♕×f4 8. ♕×b7 ♕c1+ 9. ♔e2 e6 10. ♕×a8 ♘fd7 11. ♕b7 ♗×b1–+—RT] **7. ... ♘bd7** [Not 7. ... a6 8. ♗f4 as the c1 square is no longer available—RT] **8. ♘b5 ♕b8 9. g3 e5 10. d×e5 ♘×e5 11. ♘bd4 ♘×f3+** [If 11. ... ♘d3+ 12. ♗×d3 ♗×d3 13. ♗g5 followed by 0–0–0 or ♗×f6 threatening ♕b5+ and ♕×d5, with serious problems for Black. (13. ♗f4? ♗d6)—RT] **12. ♘×f3 ♗d6 13. ♗b5+ ♔f8 14. 0–0 a6 15. ♗e2 h6 16. ♗e3 ♔g8** *(see diagram)*

[16. ... ♕c7 maintains White's slight but tangible edge. The text allows White to increase the strength of his position—RT] **17. ♗d4!** Attacking Black's important defender. **17. ... ♔h7** The alternatives are little better. **18. ♗×f6 g×f6 19. ♕×d5 ♗g6 20. ♗d3 ♕c7 21. ♖fe1 ♖he8 22. ♖ad1 ♖×e1+ 23. ♖×e1 ♖d8 24. ♗×g6+ f×g6 25. ♕e6 ♔g7 26. ♘d4 ♗e5?** *(see diagram)*

After 26. ... ♗e5

27. ♕×e5 With a very pretty flourish at the end. **1–0**
(Source: Cordingly, *Hastings 1932-1933* [additional notes by RT])

130 Menchik–Vasja Pirc

Hastings 1932-33 (7), January 4, 1933

[D00] *Queen's Pawn Game*

1. d4 d5 2. e3 ♘f6 3. ♗d3 ♗g4 4. ♘e2 e6 5. ♘d2 c5 6. c3 ♘c6 7. 0–0 e5 8. f3 ♗d7 9. ♖e1 ♗e7 10. e4 c×d4 11. c×d4 e×d4 12. e×d5 ♘×d5 13. ♘c4 0–0 14. a3 b5 15. ♘d2 ♘e3 16. ♕b3 ♘a5 17. ♕a2 ♗c6 18. ♕b1 f5 19. ♗×b5 ♗d6 20. f4 ♗d5 21. ♘f3 ♘b3 22. ♘e×d4 ♘×d4 23. ♘×d4 ♘×g2 24. ♖f1 ♘×f4 and Black eventually won. **0–1** (Source: Cordingly, *Hasting 1932-1933*)

131 Edward M. Jackson–Menchik

Hastings 1932-33 (8), January 5, 1933

[C14] *French, Classical*

1. e4 e6 2. d4 d5 3. ♘c3 ♘f6 4. ♗g5 ♗e7 5. e5 ♘fd7 6. ♗×e7 ♕×e7 7. ♕d2 0–0 8. f4 c5 9. ♘f3 ♘c6 10. ♗e2 a6 11. 0–0 f6 12. ♖ad1 f5 13. ♔h1 ♔h8 14. ♕e3 b5 15. ♖d2 ♗b7 16. ♘d1 c×d4 17. ♘×d4 ♘c5 18. ♘f2 ♖ac8 19. ♘b3 ♘e4 20. ♖dd1 g5 *(see diagram)*

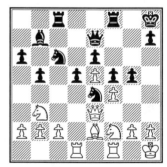

After 20. ... g5

21. ⌗×e4? Instead, White would be best to play 21. c3 b4 22. c×b4 ⌗×b4± **21. ... g×f4 22. ⌗×f4 d×e4 23. c4?! b×c4 24. ♗×c4 ⌗×e5 25. ♕d4 ⌗×c4** 25. ... ♕g7 26. ♗f1 ⌗g8 27. ⌗f2 ♘g4–+ **26. ♕×e5+ ♕g7 27. ♕×g7+ ♔×g7 28. ♘a5 ⌗c7 29. ♘×b7 ⌗×b7 30. g4?** Better is 30. ⌗f2 **30. ... ⌗×b2 31. ⌗d6 ⌗c8 32. ♔g1 ⌗c1+ 33. ⌗f1 ⌗cc2 34. ⌗e1 ⌗g2+ 35. ♔h1 ⌗×h2+ 36. ♔g1 ⌗bg2+ 37. ♔f1 ⌗×a2 0–1** (Source: Cordingly, *Hastings 1932-1933*; notes by RT)

132 Menchik–George Alan Thomas
Hastings 1932-33 (9), January 6, 1933

[D30] *Queen's Gambit Declined*

1. d4 ♘f6 2. c4 e6 3. ♘f3 d5 4. ♗g5 c6 5. ♗×f6 ♕×f6 6. e3 ♘d7 7. ♕b3 ♗d6 8. ♘bd2 ♕e7 9. ♗d3 0–0 10. 0–0 f5 11. a3 ♘f6 12. ♘e5 ♘e4 13. ♕c2 ♗×e5 14. d×e5 ♘×d2 15. ♕×d2 ⌗d8 16. ♕e2 ♗d7 17. f4 ♗e8 18. c×d5 c×d5 19. g4 g6 20. h3 ♕h4 21. ♔h2 f×g4 22. ♕×g4 ♕×g4 23. h×g4 ⌗ac8 24. ⌗ac1 *(see diagram)*
  24. ... ♗d7 25. ♔g3 ♔f7 26. g5 ⌗×c1 27. ⌗×c1 ⌗c8 28. ⌗×c8 ♗×c8 29. ♔f3 ♗d7 30. ♔e2 ♔e7 31. ♔d2 ♔d8 32. ♔c3 ♔c7 33. b4 ♔b6 34. ♗c2 ♔c7 35. ♗b3 ♔d8 36. ♔d4 ♔c7 37. a4 ♔c6 38. e4 d×e4 39. ♔×e4 b6 40. ♔d4 ♔c7 41. a5 ♔d8 42. a×b6 a×b6 43. ♗c4 ♔e7
½–½ (Source: Cordingly, *Hasting 1932-1933*)

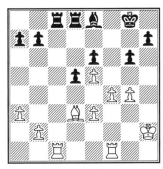

After 24. ⌗ac1

Mnichovo Hradiště 1933
(National Championship—Championship Section)
August 6–19, 1933

		1	2	3	4	5	6	7	8	9	10	11	12	Points	Place
1	Flohr, Salomon M.	●	0	1	1	=	=	1	0	=	1	1	=	7	1–2
2	Pokorný, Amos	1	●	0	=	1	1	=	0	1	=	=	1	7	1–2
3	Richter, Emil	0	1	●	=	0	1	1	1	=	1	0	=	6½	3
4	Treybal, Karel	0	=	=	●	1	1	=	1	=	0	1	0	6	4–5
5	Rejfíř, Josef	=	0	1	0	●	1	=	=	=	=	1	=	6	4–5
6	Opočenský, Karel	=	0	0	0	0	●	1	1	=	1	=	1	5½	6–7
7	Zinner, Emil	0	=	0	=	=	0	●	1	1	1	=	=	5½	6–7
8	Dobiáš, Josef	1	1	0	0	=	0	0	●	=	0	1	=	4½	8–12
9	Foltys, Jan	=	0	=	=	=	0	0	=	●	=	=	=	4½	8–12
10	May, Desider	0	=	0	1	=	0	0	1	=	●	=	=	4½	8–12
11	Menchik, Vera	0	=	1	0	0	=	=	0	=	=	●	1	4½	8–12
12	Roháček, Ivan V.	=	0	=	1	=	0	=	=	=	=	0	●	4½	8–12

This was the 13th Czechoslovakian National Chess Championship.

(R49) Emil Zinner–Menchik
Mnichovo Hradiště (1), August 7, 1933

½–½ (Source: Kalendovský, *XIII. Sjezd UJCS–Mnichovo Hradiště 1933*, 1989)

(R50) Menchik–Jan Foltys
Mnichovo Hradiště (2), August 8, 1933
½–½ (Source: Kalendovský, *XIII. Sjezd UJCS–Mnchovo Hradiště 1933*, 1989)

(R51) Karel Opočenský–Menchik
Mnichovo Hradiště (3), August 9, 1933
½–½ (Source: Kalendovský, *XIII. Sjezd UJCS–Mnchovo Hradiště 1933*, 1989)

133 Menchik–Josef Rejfíř
Mnichovo Hradiště (4), August 10, 1933
[A14] *English*

1. ♘f3 ♘f6 2. c4 e6 3. g3 d5 4. ♗g2 c5 5. 0-0 ♘c6 6. b3 ♗e7 7. ♗b2 d4 8. d3 e5 9. e4 ♗d7 10. ♘bd2 h5 11. ♕e2 ♘c8 12. ♖fb1 ♗g4 13. ♘f1 ♘h7 14. ♗c1 g5 15. a3 h4 16. ♕b2 ♗h3 17. ♗d2 ♕g4 18. ♗×h3 ♕×h3 19. b4 c×b4 20. ♗×b4 ♗×b4 21. a×b4 g4 22. ♘×h4 ♘g5 23. f4 e×f4 24. g×f4 ♖×h4 25. f×g5 ♘e5 26. ♕g2 ♕×d3 27. ♖d1 ♘f3+ 28. ♔h1 ♕c3 29. ♖ac1 ♕×b4 30. ♕g3 ♕c5 31. ♖d3 ♕×g5 32. ♖×f3 ♕×c1 33. ♕×h4 g×f3 34. ♕h8+ ♔d7 35. ♕×d4+ ♔e6 36. ♕d5+ ♔f6 37. ♕d6+ ♔g7 38. ♕g3+ ♔h7 39. ♕h3+ ♔h6 40. ♕×f3 ♔g6 41. ♘g3 ♖d8 42. ♘f5 ♕g5 43. ♘e3 ♔g8 44. ♘d5 ♖d6 45. ♕a3 ♖a6 46. ♘e7+ ♔f8 47. ♕b2 ♖b6 0-1 (Source: Kalendovský, *XIII. Sjezd UJCS–Mnchovo Hradiště 1933*, 1989)

134 Josef Dobiáš–Menchik
Mnichovo Hradiště (5), August 11, 1933
[D53] *Queen's Gambit Declined*

CS 1933 v. 7 shows this game as by Boleslav pp. 172–74 (game) & 127 (crosstable) whereas in Di Felice's *Chess Results 1931–1935* the game is listed as against Josef Dobias.

1. d4 ♘f6 2. c4 e6 3. ♘c3 d5 4. ♗g5 ♘bd7 5. e3 ♗e7 6. ♘f3 ♘e4 7. ♗×e7 ♕×e7 8. c×d5 ♘×c3 9. b×c3 e×d5 10. ♗d3 0-0 11. 0-0 ♘f6 12. c4 ♗e6 13. ♕b3 d×c4 14. ♗×c4 ♗×c4 15. ♕×c4 ♖ac8 16. ♖fc1 ♖fd8 17. ♖ab1 b6 18. ♕c6 ♘d5 19. ♖c4 f6 20. ♖bc1 ♕d7 21. ♔f1 ♕×c6 22. ♖×c6 ♖d7 23. a3 ♔f7 24. ♘e1 ♘e7 25. ♖6c4 c6 26. ♔e2 ♔e8 27. ♘d3 ♖cd8 28. ♖4c3 a5 29. ♖b3 b5 30. ♘c5 ♖d5 31. ♘e6 ♖8d7 32. e4 ♖5d6 33. ♘c5 ♖a7 34. ♔e3 f5 35. f3 ♖h6 36. h3 ♖g6 37. ♔f2 f×e4 38. f×e4 ♘c8 39. e5 a4 40. ♖d3 ♘b6 41. ♘e4 ♘c4 42. ♖e1 ♖f7+ 43. ♔g1 ♖d7 44. ♖f1 ♖f7 45. ♖e1 ♖d7 46. ♘c5 ♖f7 47. ♖b1 ♘b6 48. ♘e4 ♖f4 49. ♘c3 ♖f5 50. ♖e1 ♖fg5 51. g4 ♖f5 52. d5 ♘×d5 53. ♘×d5 c×d5 54. ♖×d5 ♖gg5 55. ♖×b5 h5 56. ♖e4 h×g4 57. h×g4 ♖f3 58. ♖×a4 ♖g3+ 59. ♔f2 ♖5×g4 60. ♖×g4 ♖×g4 61. ♖b4 ♖g5 62. ♖b5 ♖g4 63. ♖a5 ♔e7 64. ♔f3 ♖h4 65. ♖a6 g5 66. a4 ♖b4 67. a5 ♖a4 68. ♖a8 g4+ 69. ♔g3 ♔e6 70. a6 ♔f5 71. a7 ♖a3+ 72. ♔f2 ♖a2+ 73. ♔e3 ♖a3+ 74. ♔d4 ♖a4+ 75. ♔d5 ♖a5+ 76. ♔d4 ♖a4+ 77. ♔c5 ♔×e5 78. ♖e8+ ♔f4 79. a8♕ ♖×a8 80. ♖×a8 ♔e3 81. ♖g8 *(see diagram)*

Final position

1-0 (Source: Kalendovský, *XIII. Sjezd UJCS–Mnchovo Hradiště 1933*, 1989)

135 Menchik–Ivan Roháček
Mnichovo Hradiště (6), August 12, 1933

[A13] *English*

1. ♘f3 ♞f6 2. c4 e6 3. g3 d5 4. ♗g2 c6 5. 0–0 ♞bd7 6. d3 ♝e7 7. ♘c3 0–0 8. ♕c2 ♖e8 9. b3 b6 10. ♗b2 ♝b7 11. ♖ad1 ♛c7 12. d4 ♜ad8 13. a3 ♛b8 14. ♖d2 ♛a8 15. ♘e5 c5 16. ♘×d7 ♖×d7 17. c×d5 ♞×d5 18. d×c5 ♝×c5 19. ♘×d5 ♝×d5 20. e4 ♝c6 21. ♖×d7 ♝×d7 22. b4 ♝e7 23. ♕c3 e5 24. f4 ♝c6 25. f×e5 ♝×e4 26. ♕c4 ♝×g2 27. ♕×f7+ ♚h8 28. e6 ♞g8 29. ♖f2 ♛f8 30. ♚×g2 1–0 (Source: Kalendovský, *XIII. Sjezd UJCS–Mnchovo Hradiště 1933*, 1989)

(R52) Desider May–Menchik
Mnichovo Hradiště (7), August 14, 1933

½–½ (Source: Kalendovský, *XIII. Sjezd UJCS–Mnchovo Hradiště 1933*, 1989)

136 Menchik–Emil Richter
Mnichovo Hradiště (8), August 15, 1933

[A30] *English, Symmetrical Variation*

1. ♘f3 ♞f6 2. c4 b6 3. g3 ♝b7 4. ♗g2 e6 5. 0–0 c5 6. ♘c3 ♝e7 7. d4 d6 8. a3 0–0 9. ♕d3 ♞a6 10. e4 ♜c8 11. b3 ♛c7 12. ♗b2 ♛b8 13. ♖ad1 ♛a8 14. d5 ♞c7 15. ♘d2 ♜cd8 16. f4 e×d5 17. e×d5 ♝c8 18. ♖de1 ♜de8 19. ♘f3 h6 20. ♘h4 ♝d8 21. ♘e4 ♞×e4 22. ♗×e4 ♝×h4 23. g×h4 f5 24. ♕g3 ♜f7 25. ♗f3 ♝a6 26. ♗h5 ♜×e1 27. ♗×f7+ 1–0 (Source: Kalendovský, *XIII. Sjezd UJCS–Mnchovo Hradiště 1933*, 1989)

137 Karel Treybal–Menchik
Mnichovo Hradiště (9), August 16, 1933

[C14] *French, Classical*

1. e4 e6 2. d4 d5 3. ♘c3 ♞f6 4. ♗g5 ♝e7 5. e5 ♞fd7 6. ♗×e7 ♛×e7 7. ♕d2 0–0 8. f4 c5 9. ♘f3 ♞c6 10. g3 a6 11. ♗g2 ♞b6 12. b3 ♝d7 13. ♘e2 c×d4 14. ♘e×d4 ♞×d4 15. ♘×d4 ♞c8 16. 0–0 ♛c5 17. ♚h1 ♞e7 18. ♖ac1 ♞c6 19. ♘×c6 ♝×c6 20. c4 d×c4 21. ♖×c4 ♝×g2+ 22. ♚×g2 ♛b6 23. ♕f2 ♛b5 24. ♖fc1 ♜ad8 25. ♖c5 ♛b4 26. ♖1c4 ♛d2 27. ♖c2 ♛b4?! [Not all rook and pawn endings are drawn, but ... there is certainly an element of truth to that aphorism. 27. ... ♛×f2+ 28. ♚×f2 f6 and while White has a pull it will be tough to see it to fruition—RT] **28. ♖5c4 ♛a5 29. ♖c7 ♜d3 30. ♚h3 ♛d5 31. ♚g2 ♜f3 32. ♛e2 ♜d3 33. ♖2c5 ♜d2 34. ♖×d5 ♜×e2 35. ♖dd7 b5 36. ♖a7** *(see diagram)*

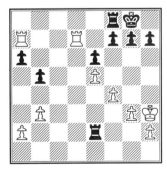

After 36. ♖a7

36. ... **h5** From here Black's position deteriorates rapidly. But he still gets one more chance. [36. ... ♜×a2 Black needs to pick up the pawn while it is available. It is a fair assumption that the clock is now taking its toll on the players—RT] **37. b4** *(see diagram)*

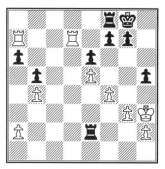

After 37. b4

A lot of calculation (should have) went into this move. A sampling is as follows. It certainly seems like Black had one last chance to score the draw. [37. a4 ℤb2 38. ℤd3 ℤc8 39. ℤ×a6 g5 40. f×g5 (40. g4 ℤcc2 41. f×g5 ℤ×h2+ 42. ♔g3 ℤhg2+ 43. ♔f3 ℤbf2+ 44. ♔e3 ℤe2+ 45. ♔f3 with a draw. **a**—But if 45. ♔f4 ℤ×g4+ 46. ♔f3 ℤ×e5 with a strong Black edge; **b**— and if 45. ♔d4 ℤ×g4+ 46. ♔c5 *(not 46. ♔c3 b4 mate)* 46. ... b×a4 47. b×a4 ℤ×e5+ and Black wins) 40. ... ℤcc2 41. g4 ℤ×h2+ 42. ♔g3 ℤbg2+ 43. ♔f3 ℤ×g4 with a drawn position; 37. ℤ×a6 ℤc8 38. ℤd1 g5 39. f×g5 ℤcc2 40. ℤh1 ℤ×e5 41. a4 b×a4 42. b×a4 ♔g7 43. ℤa7 ♔g6 and another drawn position—RT] **37. ... g6?** [37. ... ℤ×a2 38. f5 definitely best here. 38. ... e×f5 39. e6 ℤe2 40. e×f7+ ♔h7 41. ℤ×a6 ℤe4 42. ℤd5 ℤ×b4 43. ℤ×f5 g6 44. ℤg5 ℤ×f7 45. ℤa×g6 ℤf5! 46. ℤg7+ ♔h8 and drawn—RT] **38. ℤ×a6 ℤb2** [Black needs to fight back and to do that requires both rooks. 38. ... ℤc8—RT] **39. a3 ℤa2 40. ℤb7 ♔g7 41. ℤ×e6 ♔h6 42. ℤf6 ℤ×a3 43. e6 ♔g7 44. ℤf×f7+ ℤ×f7 45. ℤ×f7+ ♔g8 46. ℤb7 ℤe3 47. ℤ×b5 ℤ×e6 48. ♔h4 1–0** (Source: Kalendovský, *XIII. Sjezd UJCS–Mnchovo Hradiště 1933*, 1989 [additional notes by RT])

(R53) Menchik–Amos Pokorný
Mnichovo Hradiště (10), August 17, 1933

½–½ (Source: Kalendovský, *XIII. Sjezd UJCS–Mnchovo Hradiště 1933*, 1989)

138 Salo Flohr–Menchik
Mnichovo Hradiště (11), August 19, 1933

[D00] Queen's Pawn Game

1. d4 ♘f6 2. e3 d5 3. ♗d3 ♗g4 4. ♘e2 e6 5. 0–0 c5 6. c3 ♘c6 7. f4 ♗d6 8. ♘d2 ♕c7 9. ♘f3 ♘e4 10. ♗×e4 d×e4 11. ♘g5 c×d4 12. e×d4 f5 13. ♘×e6 ♕d7 14. ♘g5 h6 15. ♘h3 0–0–0 16. ♘f2 ♗h5 17. ♕c2 g5 18. ♘g3 ♗f7 19. ♘h3 g4 20. ♘f2 h5 21. ♗e3 h4 22. ♘e2 g3 23. ♘h3 ♗c4 24. ℤfd1 ♕g7 25. d5 g×h2+ 26. ♔h1 ℤhg8 27. ♘g5 ♘e7 28. ♘d4 ♘×d5 29. ♕f2 ♘×e3 30. ♕×e3 ♗×f4 31. ♕×f4 ♕×g5 32. ♕×f5+ ♕×f5 33. ♘×f5 ℤ×d1+ 34. ℤ×d1 ♔c7 35. b3 ♗d3 36. ♔×h2 ℤf8 37. ♘×h4 ℤf2 38. ℤa1 ♗d6 39. ♔g3 ℤc2 40. ♔f4 ℤ×c3 41. g4 ♔e7 42. ♘f5+ ♔f8 43. ℤh1 ♔g8 44. ℤh2 a5 45. ♘e7+ ♔g7 46. ♘d5 ℤc1 47. ♘e3 b5 48. ♘f5+ ♔f8 48. ... ♔g8 49. ♕e5?! 49. ℤh8+ ♔f7 50. ℤa8 ♔e6 51. ℤa6+ ♔d5 52. ♘e3+ ♔d4 53. ℤ×a5 **49. ... b4 50. ♘e3** *(see diagram)*

50. ... a4? A better shot at the draw is 50. ... ♗b1 51. g5 ♔f7 52. ♔f4 ℤe1 53. ℤh7+ ♔g6 54. ℤh6+ ♔f7 55. ℤa6 ♗×a2 56. g6+ ♔e8 57. ℤ×a5 ♗×b3 **51. b×a4 ℤc5+ 52. ♔f4 ℤa5 53. g5 ℤ×a4 54. g6 ♔g7 55. ♔g5 ℤa5+ 56. ♘f5+ ℤ×f5+ 57. ♔×f5 e3+ 58. ♔g5! e2 59. ℤh7+ ♔f8 60. ♔f6 ♗c4 61. ℤh8+ ♗g8 62. g7+ 1–0** (Source: *Mnchovo Hradiště 1933*, 1989; notes by RT)

After 50. ♘e3

Hastings 1933-1934
(Premier)
December 27, 1933–January 5, 1934

		1	2	3	4	5	6	7	8	9	10	Points	Place
1	Flohr, Salo	•	=	=	1	1	=	1	=	1	1	7	1–3
2	Alekhine, Alexander	=	•	1	=	=	=	1	=	1	1	6½	2–3
3	Lilienthal, Andor	=	0	•	=	=	1	1	1	1	1	6½	2–3
4	Alexander, C.H.O'D.	0	=	=	•	=	=	0	1	1	1	5	4–5
5	Eliskases, Erich	0	=	=	=	•	=	1	1	=	=	5	4–5
6	Thomas, Sir George	=	=	0	=	=	•	1	0	=	1	4½	6
7	Menchik, Vera	0	0	0	1	0	0	•	1	=	=	3	7–8
8	Tylor, Theodore H.	=	=	0	0	0	1	0	•	0	1	3	7–8
9	Michell, Reginald P.	0	0	0	0	=	=	=	1	•	0	2½	9
10	Milner-Berry, Philip S.	0	0	0	0	=	0	=	0	1	•	2	10

139 Menchik–Philip S. Milner-Barry
Hastings 1933-34 (1), December 27, 1933

[E11] *Bogo-Indian Defense*

**1. d4 ♘f6 2. c4 e6 3. ♘f3 ♗b4+ 4. ♗d2 ♕e7 5. g3 ♗×d2+
6. ♕×d2 d6 7. ♘c3 0-0 8. ♗g2 ♘bd7 9. 0-0 ♘b6 10. b3 e5
11. ♖ad1 ♖e8 12. d×e5 d×e5 13. h3 ♗d7 14. e4 ♖ad8
15. ♕e3 ♗c8 16. ♘d5 ♘f×d5 17. e×d5 ♕a3 18. ♖fe1 f6
19. ♘d2 f5 20. ♘f3 ♘d7 21. ♕c3 ♕d6 22. b4 b6 23. a3 h6
24. ♘d2 e4 25. ♘b3** *(see diagram)*

After 25. ♘b3

25. ... **♘e5 26. ♖e3 c5 27. b5 ♖e7 28. ♘c1 ♖f8 29. ♖de1
♖fe8 30. a4 ♕f6 31. ♔h1 ♔f8 32. ♗f1 ♔g8 33. a5 ♗d7
34. a×b6 a×b6 35. ♘e2 ♘d3 36. ♕×f6 g×f6 37. ♖a1 ♘×f2+
38. ♔g1 ♘d3 39. ♖a6 ♖g7 40. ♔h2 ♖b8 41. ♘f4 ♘×f4
42. g×f4 ½–½** (Source: Cordingly, *Hastings 1933-1934*)

140 Menchik–Alexander Alekhine
Hastings 1933-34 (2), December 28, 1933

[A43] *Old Benoni*

After 11. ... ♗e6

Given how close the game was after move 20 it is a testament to Alekhine's abilities and Menchik's weak last half dozen moves that this game ends as almost a miniature.

1. d4 c5 2. ♘f3 c×d4 3. ♘×d4 d5 4. c4 e5 5. ♘c2
[More common is 5. ♘f3 where most position end up even or rather unbalanced—RT] **5. ... d4 6. e3 ♘c6 7. e×d4 e×d4**
Tarrasch would certainly feel comfortable! **8. ♗d3 ♘f6
9. 0-0 ♗e7 10. ♖e1 ♗g4! 11. f3 ♗e6** *(see diagram)*

This is another Menchik game which made it into ECO (A43 note #1) with an evaluation of –/+. **12. b3 0-0 13. ♗b2**

♕c7 14. ♘d2 ♖ad8 15. ♘f1 ♘h5 16. g3 ♘f6 17. f4 ♗g4 18. ♕d2 a5 19. ♗a3 ♗×a3 20. ♘×a3 ♘b4 21. ♘b5 ♕d7 22. a3 ♘×d3 23. ♕×d3 ♗f5 24. ♕d2 b6 *(see diagram)*

25. ♖e5? [Much better, if not fully satisfactory is 25. ♕g2∓—RT] **25. ... ♗e4? 26. ♕e1** [26. ♖e1∓—RT] **26. ... ♗a8 27. ♖a2 ♕b7 0–1** (Source: Cordingly, *Hastings 1933-1934*; *The Times*, December 29, 1933, p. 8 [additional notes by RT])

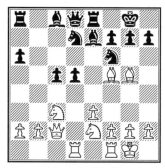

After 24. ... b6

141 Erich Eliskases–Menchik
Hastings 1933-34 (3), December 29, 1933
[A02] *Bird's Opening*

1. f4 ♘f6 2. ♘f3 c5 3. e3 g6 4. b3 ♗g7 5. ♗b2 0–0 6. ♗e2 ♘c6 7. 0–0 ♕c7 8. c4 d6 9. ♕c1 e5 10. f×e5 d×e5 11. d3 ♗g4 12. ♘c3 ♖ad8 13. h3 ♗c8 14. e4 ♘d4 15. ♖f2 ♕d6 16. ♘d5 ♘×d5 17. c×d5 f5 18. ♕d2 b6 19. ♖af1 h6 20. ♗c1 ♗×e2+ 21. ♕×e2 ♗a6 22. ♘d2 f×e4 23. ♖×f8+ ♖×f8 24. ♖×f8+ ♔×f8 25. ♕f2+ ♕f6 26. d×e4 ♕×f2+ 27. ♔×f2 ♗d3 28. ♗b2 ♗f6 29. ♔e3 ♗a6 30. ♘f3 ♗c8 31. ♗×e5 ♗g5+ 32. ♘×g5 h×g5 33. ♗b8 b5 34. ♗d6+ ♔e8 35. ♗×c5 a6 36. g3 ♗×h3 37. e5 ♔f7 38. b4 ♗f5 39. ♔d4 and White won after a few more moves ... unfortunately not recorded. **1–0** (Source: Cordingly, *Hastings 1933-1934*)

142 Andor Lilienthal–Menchik
Hastings 1933-34 (4), December 30, 1933
[D35] *Queen's Gambit Declined, Exchange Variation*

1. d4 ♘f6 2. c4 e6 3. ♘c3 d5 4. ♗g5 ♘bd7 5. c×d5 e×d5 6. e3 ♗e7 7. ♗d3 0–0 8. ♕c2 c5 9. ♘ge2 a6?! [Best is 9. ... c4 10. ♗f5 ♖e8—RT] **10. ♗f5 ♖e8 11. 0–0 b6 12. d×c5 b×c5 13. ♖ad1** *(see diagram)*

13. ... ♕a5? [13. ... ♘b6∓—RT] **14. ♘×d5 ♘×d5 15. ♗×h7+ ♔h8 16. ♖×d5 ♘b6 17. ♖e5 f6 18. ♗×f6 g×f6 19. ♖h5 ♗g4 20. ♗g8+ 1–0** (Source: Cordingly, *Hastings 1933-1934*)

After 13. ♖ad1

143 Menchik–Salo Flohr
Hastings 1933-34 (5), January 1, 1933
[A83] *Dutch, Staunton Gambit*

1. d4 f5 2. e4 f×e4 3. ♘c3 ♘f6 4. ♗g5 e6 5. ♘×e4 ♗e7 6. ♗×f6 ♗×f6 7. ♘f3 ♕e7 8. ♗d3 ♘c6 9. c3 b6 10. ♕e2 ♗b7 11. 0–0–0 0–0–0 12. ♖he1 ♔b8 13. ♔b1 ♕f7 14. ♘×f6 ♕×f6 15. ♘d2 ♖hf8 16. f3 ♘e7 17. ♘e4 ♕f4 18. ♕d2 ♘d5 19. ♕×f4 ♘×f4 20. ♗f1 h6 21. g3 ♘h5 22. f4 g5 23. f×g5 ♖×f1 24. ♖×f1 ♗×e4+ 25. ♔c1 h×g5 26. ♖f7 ♗g6 27. ♖e7 c6 28. ♖f1 g4 29. c4 ♔c7 30. c5 ♖g8 and with no way to avoid losing the exchange, White resigns.

0–1 (Source: Cordingly, *Hastings 1933-1934*)

144 Menchik–George Thomas

Hastings 1933-34 (6), January 2, 1933

[E16] *Queen's Indian*

Chess is an amazing game: For some there are the swashbuckling games of Andersson and Morphy, others the subtle wins and draws of Petrosian and Karpov. This particular game is of special interest. Throughout Menchik seems to be on the verge of defeat—even the computers take a substantial time to find that White's position is not as bad as it certainly looks most of the time. Sadly for Vera, on move 35 she makes a wrong step on the high wire she has been walking and falls to her doom.

1. d4 ♘f6 2. c4 e6 3. ♘f3 ♗b4+ 4. ♗d2 ♕e7 5. g3 b6 6. ♗g2 ♗b7 7. 0–0 ♗×d2 8. ♕×d2 d6 9. ♘c3 ♘e4 10. ♕d3 ♘×c3 11. ♕×c3 ♘d7 12. ♖ad1 0–0 13. ♖fe1 f5 14. b4 a5 15. a3 ♘f6 16. ♘d2 If 16. b5 ♘e4 17. ♕c2 ♖ac8 18. e3 c6= **16. ... ♗×g2 17. ♔×g2 ♕f7 18. f4 ♕d7 19. b5 c6 20. b×c6** Alternatively 20. ♕d3 c×b5 21. c×b5 ♘d5 22. ♖c1 and the game likely coasts into a draw; a result these two seemed to avoid when facing one another **20. ... ♕×c6+** (*see diagram*)

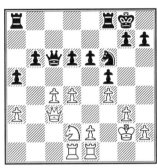

After 20. ... ♕×c6+

21. ♕f3 ♖ac8 22. ♕×c6 ♖×c6 23. ♖b1?! Alternatives include 23. e4 f×e4 24. ♘×e4 ♘×e4 25. ♖×e4 ♖×c4 (25. ... d5 26. c×d5 e×d5 27. ♖e5=) 26. ♖×e6= **23. ... d5 24. c×d5 ♘×d5 25. e4 f×e4 26. ♘×e4 h6 27. ♘f2?** 27. ♖bc1 ♖fc8 28. ♖×c6 ♖×c6 29. ♔f3 **27. ... g5 28. ♖bc1 ♖×c1 29. ♖×c1 g×f4 30. g4** Another major line is 30. ♘g4 h5 31. ♘e5 f×g3 32. h×g3 ♘e3+ (32. ... a4 33. ♖c6 b5 34. ♖×e6 ♘e3+ 35. ♔h3 ♘c2 36. ♔h4 ♘×d4 (*36. ... ♘×a3 37. ♔×h5=*) 37. ♖g6+ ♔h7 38. ♖b6 ♘f5 39. ♘d7 ♔g7 40. g4 ♖f3 41. g×h5 ♖×a3 42. h6+ ♔h7 43. ♘f8+ ♔g8 44. h7+ ♔h8 45. ♖b7 ♘f5+ 46. ♔g5 ♘g7 47. ♖×b5=) 33. ♔h3 ♘f5 34. ♘d7 ♖f7 35. ♘×b6 ♖b7 36. ♘a4 ♖g7 37. ♖c3 ♘×d4 38. ♖d3 ♘f5 39. ♘c5 ♔f7 40. ♖d7+ ♔f6 41. ♖×g7 ♘×g7 42. a4 e5 43. ♘b7= **30. ... f3+ 31. ♔g3 ♘f4 32. ♔h4 ♘e2 33. ♖c6 ♘×d4** Also not succeeding is 33. ... b5 34. ♖×e6 ♘×d4 35. ♖×h6 ♘c2 36. a4 b×a4 37. ♖a6 a3 38. ♖×a5‡ **34. ♖×b6** (*see diagram*)

After 34. ♖×b6

34. ... ♔g7 No better are 34. ... ♖c8 35. ♖a6 ♖c5 36. ♔g3 ♔g7 37. ♖a7+=; 34. ... ♖d8 35. ♖b7 ♖d5 36. ♘e4 ♔f8 37. ♔g3 ♖b5 38. ♖a7 ♖b1 39. ♖×a5 ♖e1=; 34. ... ♘c2 35. ♖×e6 ♘×a3 36. ♖×h6 ♘c4 (36. ... ♖a8 37. ♔g5 ♖a7 38. ♖g6+ ♖g7) 37. ♖a6 ♔g7 38. ♔g3± **35. ♖d6?** 35. ♖a6! ♘b3 36. ♖×e6= **35. ... ♖f4 36. ♔h5** 36. ♖a6 a4 37. ♔h5 (Not 37. ♖×a4 ♘f5+–+) 37. ... ♘b5 38. ♖×e6 ♘×a3 39. ♖g6+ ♔f8 40. ♖×h6 ♘b5 41. ♖a6 a3 42. ♔g6 ♘d4 43. ♖a8+ ♔e7 44. h4 ♖d2 45. ♘e4 ♖c2 46. ♘g3 f2 47. ♖a5 ♖c3 48. ♘f1 ♖c1–+ **36. ... e5 37. ♖d7+ ♔f6 38. ♔×h6 ♘f5+ 39. ♔h5 e4 40. g×f5 e3 41. ♖d1 e×f2 42. ♖f1 ♔×f5 43. ♖×f2 ♔e4 0–1** (Source: Cordingly, *Hastings 1933-1934*; notes by RT)

145 Reginald Michell–Menchik
Hastings 1933-34 (7), January 3, 1934

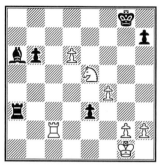

After 33. ... e3

Although the full game score has been lost, we do have this fragment of the 64 move Michell vs. Menchik game.

33. ... e3 *(see diagram)*
34. Rc1 Kf8 35. d7 Ke7 36. Rd1 Bd3 *(see diagram)*

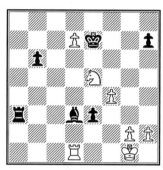

After 36. ... Bd3

If 37. R×d3? Ra1 and mate. If 37. N×d3?! e2 38. Re1 R×d3 etc. However 37. d8(Q)+! K×d8 wins for White. In the game Michell played 37. Nd3 and drew in 64 moves. **37. N×d3? e2 38. Re1?** [Still winning is 38. d8Q+ K×d8 39. Rd2—RT] **38. ... R×d3 ½–½** (Source: Cordingly, *Hastings 1933-1934*)

146 C.H.O'D. Alexander–Menchik
Hastings 1933-34 (8), January 4, 1934
[A34] English, Symmetrical

1. c4 Nf6 2. Nc3 d5 3. c×d5 N×d5 4. Nf3 c5 5. e4 N×c3 6. b×c3 e6 7. Bb5+ Bd7 8. B×d7+ N×d7 9. 0-0 Be7 10. d4 0-0 11. Bf4 Nf6 12. Qe2 Qa5 13. Rab1 b6 14. Ne5 Over the next five moves Black makes a series of second best moves culminating in

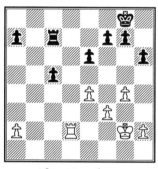

After 32. ... b×c5

19. Qe2. **14. ... Rac8 15. Rbc1 Qa4 16. Qd3 h6 17. f3 Rfd8 18. Be3 Bf8 19. Qe2?!** [Better is 19. Rfd1 ∓—RT] **19. ... c×d4 20. c×d4 R×c1 21. R×c1 R×d4 22. Kh1 Rd8 23. Bf2 Ba3 24. Rc2 Qb4 25. g4 Qd6 26. Bg3 Qd1+ 27. Q×d1 R×d1+ 28. Kg2 Bc5 29. Bf2 Nd7 30. N×d7 R×d7 31. B×c5 Rc7 32. Rd2 b×c5** *(see diagram)*

33. Rd8+ Kh7 34. f4 Kg6 35. Kf3 Kf6 36. Rd3 Ke7 37. e5 g5 38. f5?! e×f5 39. g×f5 c4 40. Rc3 h5 41. Ke4 f6 42. Kd5 f×e5 43. K×e5 Rc5+ 44. Kd4 R×f5 45. K×c4 Rf2 46. h3 h4 47. a3 Kf6 48. Kd4 Kf5 49. Ke3 Rh2 0-1 (Source: Cordingly, *Hastings 1933-1934*)

147 Theodore Tylor–Menchik
Hastings 1933-34 (9), January 5, 1934
[C01] French, Exchange Variation

Often the most enjoyable games are not the "best" games. Certainly this game would have been a rollercoaster to watch: material imbalances, extremely imbalanced pawn structures, both players fighting for wins, time pressure and more.

1. e4 e6 2. d4 d5 3. e×d5 e×d5 4. Bd3 Nc6 5. c3 Bd6 6. Nf3 Bg4 7. 0-0 Qd7 8. Re1+ Nce7 9. Nbd2 f6 10. Qb3 0-0-0 11. c4 Nh6 12. c5 Bf4 13. Qa3 Qb8 14. Nb3 g5

15. c6 ᘒ×c6 16. ♗×f4 g×f4 17. ᘒc5 ♕d6 18. ♖ac1 ♔a8
If 18. ... ♗×f3 19. ♖e6 ♖hg8 20. ♖×d6 ♖×g2+ 21. ♔f1 c×d6
22. ᘒa6+ ♔a8 (22. ... ♔c8 23. ♗×h7+–) 23. ᘒc7+ ♔b8
24. ᘒa6+= **19. ♗b5 ᘒb8 20. ♖c3?!** 20. h3 ♗f5 21. ♕b4=
20. ... c6 21. ♗f1 ᘒd7 22. ♕a4 ᘒ×c5 23. d×c5 ♕b8
24. ᘒd4 ♗d7 25. ♖b3 *(see diagram)*

25. ... ♖he8 26. ♖c1 ᘒf5 27. ♗a6 ᘒ×d4 28. ♗×b7+
♕×b7 29. ♖×b7 ᘒe2+ 30. ♔f1 ♔×b7 31. ♖e1 f3
32. ♕b3+ ♔c8?! 32. ... ♔a8!? 33. ♕×f3 ♗c8 34. ♕a3 ᘒf4∓
33. ♕×f3 ᘒd4 34. ♕×f6 ♖×e1+ 35. ♔×e1 ♖e8+ 36. ♔d2
ᘒe6 37. b4 ♔b7? 37. ... ♖f8 38. ♕h4 ♖f4 **38. f4 ♖g8**

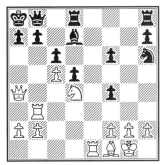

After 25. ♖b3

39. g3 ♔c8 40. ♕e7 ♖g7 41. ♕d6 ♖f7 42. h3 Better
is 42. b5 ᘒd8 43. b6 ♗e6 44. a4 **42. ... a6 43. a4 ᘒc7**
44. g4 ♔d8 45. f5 ᘒe8 46. ♕b8+ ♗c8 47. ♕b6+
♖c7 48. ♔d3 ᘒf6 49. ♔d4 h6 50. ♕a5 ᘒe4 *(see diagram)*

51. ♔e5?? A sad blunder at the time control. White
needs to play 51. b5 which appears to be the only easily winning move. Followed by 51. ... a×b5 52. a×b5 c×b5 53. c6 ᘒd6
54. ♔×d5 ᘒf7+– and White wins with relative ease **51. ... ᘒd2**
52. ♔d6 ᘒc4 mate 0–1 (Source: Cordingly, *Hastings 1933-1934*;
notes by RT)

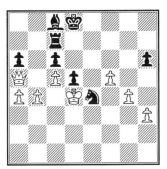

After 50. ... ᘒe4

Groningen 1934

	1	2	3	4	5	Pts.	Place
1 Menchik, Vera	•	=	1	1	1	3½	1
2 Wolthuis, J.A.	=	•	1	=	1	3	2
3 Schlotens, C.	0	0	•	1	1	2	3
4 Braam	0	=	0	•	1	1½	4
5 Groenevelt, J.	0	0	0	0	•	0	5

Sonja Graf vs. Menchik Match

(Rotterdam, Netherlands)
March 22–25, 1934

	1	2	3	4	Pts
Menchik, Vera	0	1	1	1	3
Graf, Sonja	1	0	0	0	1

Although prior to this short match, Vera and Sonja Graf had never played one another,
Sonja had been building a reputation within Germany and Austria as a strong player in the
local clubs and taverns. A product of a dysfunctional family, she was very much the bohemian
and was a pupil of Siegbert Tarrasch's at the end of his life. Stylistically she was the antithesis
of Vera—she took chances and was known as a tactician as opposed to Menchik's positional
emphasis and striving for a good endgame.

Contrary to many sources this was not a match for the world title. Eales goes so far as to state that this match (and that of 1937) was proof that it was questionable as to whether FIDE could control the women's title.[49] This overlooks the fact that this event was not for the title and that the 1937 match was sanctioned by FIDE and directed by its president. It is obvious that for many encyclopedias and articles, a very few sources have been consulted and copied without adequate verification.

148　Menchik–Sonja Graf
Match, Rotterdam (1), March 21, 1934

[D40] *Queen's Gambit Declined, Semi-Tarrasch Variation*

1. d4 d5 2. c4 e6 3. ♘c3 c5 4. e3 ♘f6 5. ♘f3 ♘c6 6. a3 ♗d6 7. ♗d3 0-0 8. 0-0 b6 9. ♕e2 ♗b7 10. c×d5 e×d5 11. d×c5 b×c5 12. ♖d1 ♘e5 13. ♗a6 ♘×f3+ 14. g×f3 ♗×h2+ 15. ♔×h2 ♕d6+ 16. f4 ♗×a6 17. ♕f3 ♗b7 18. ♗d2 ♕d7 19. ♕h3 ♕×h3+ 20. ♔×h3 d4 21. e×d4 c×d4 22. ♘b5 d3 23. ♗e3 ♖fd8 24. ♘d4 ♗a6 25. b4 ♘d5 26. b5 ♘×f4+ 27. ♔g4 ♘e2 28. ♖×d3 ♗×b5 29. ♘×b5 ♖×d3 30. ♔f3 ♘c3 0-1 (Source: *www.Chessgames.com*)

149　Sonja Graf–Menchik
Match, Rotterdam (2), March 22, 1934

[D36] *Queen's Gambit Declined, Exchange Variation*

1. d4 ♘f6 2. ♘f3 e6 3. c4 d5 4. ♗g5 ♘bd7 5. ♘c3 c6 6. c×d5 e×d5 7. e3 ♗e7 8. ♗d3 0-0 9. ♕c2 ♖e8 10. 0-0-0 ♘f8 11. h3 a5 12. ♘e5 ♘6d7 13. ♗f4 ♘×e5 14. d×e5 ♗d7 15. g4 b5 16. ♗f5 ♕b6 17. ♘e2 ♗e6 18. h4 b4 19. ♗g5 a4 20. ♗×e7 ♖×e7 21. ♕d3 a3 22. b3 ♕c7 23. f4 c5 24. ♗×e6 f×e6 25. ♖d2 c4 26. b×c4 d×c4 27. ♕e4 ♕b7 28. ♕×b7 ♖×b7 29. ♔b1 ♘d7 30. ♖hd1 ♘b6 31. e4 ♔f7 32. f5 c3 33. ♖d6 ♘c4 34. f×e6+ ♔e7 35. ♖d7+ ♖×d7 36. ♖×d7+ ♔×e6 37. ♖×g7 ♘e3 38. ♖b7 ♔×e5 39. ♖×b4 ♖f8 40. ♖b5+ ♔×e4 41. ♘g3+ ♔d3 42. ♘f5 ♖×f5 43. g×f5 ♔d2 44. ♖c5 c2+ 45. ♖×c2+ ♘×c2 46. f6 ♘d4 47. h5 h6 48. f7 ♘e6 49. ♔a1 ♔e3 0-1

(R54)　Menchik–Sonja Graf
Match, Rotterdam (3), March 23, 1934
1-0

(R55)　Sonja Graf–Menchik
Match, Rotterdam (4), March 24, 1934
0-1

Amsterdam 1934

(Section 1)
April 1–2, 1934

	1	2	3	4	Pts.	Place
1 Mulder, Emile A.J.M.	•	=	=	1	2	1
2 Felderhof, H. William	=	•	1	0	1½	2–3
3 Menchik, Vera	=	0	•	1	1½	2–3
4 Veerkamp, J.	0	1	0	•	1	4

This event was an Easter Tournament played in two quadrangular sections. Section two was won by Nicholaas Cortlever with a score of 2½–½ ahead of Sonja Graf who finished with a score of +1 =2 (2–1) in second place. Sonja and Vera had played their first match one week earlier.

Maribor 1934
August 5–15, 1934

	1	2	3	4	5	6	7	8	9	Points	Place
1 Pirc, Vasja	●	1	=	=	1	1	1	1	=	6½	1–2
2 Steiner, Lajos	0	●	1	1	=	1	1	1	1	6½	1–2
3 Menchik, V.	=	0	●	1	=	=	=	1	1	5	3
4 Rejfíř, Josef	=	0	0	●	1	=	=	1	1	4½	4–5
5 Spielmann, Rudolf	0	=	=	0	●	1	=	1	1	4½	4–5
6 Asztalos, Lajos	0	0	=	=	0	●	1	=	=	3	6
7 Vidmar, Milan, Jr.	0	0	=	=	=	0	●	=	=	2½	7
8 Stupan, Bogumir	0	0	0	0	0	=	=	●	1	2	8
9 Drezga, Tihomil	=	0	0	0	0	=	=	0	●	1½	9

This event is frequently listed as one of Menchik's best results, coming in as she did ahead of five strong internationally recognized masters.

150 Menchik–Milan Vidmar, Jr.
Maribor (1), August 5, 1934
[A09] *Réti's Opening*

1. ♘f3 d5 2. c4 d4 3. e4 ♘c6 4. d3 e5 5. g3 ♗b4+ 6. ♗d2 a5 7. ♗g2 ♗e6 8. 0-0 ♕d7 9. ♘g5 ♗g4 10. f3 ♗h5 11. a3 ♗×d2 12. ♘×d2 ♕e7 13. ♕b3 ♖a7 14. f4 ♘f6 15. h3 ♘d7 16. ♕c2 ♘c5 17. ♘gf3 f6 18. ♖f2 a4 19. f×e5 ♘×e5 20. ♘×e5 f×e5 21. ♔h2 ♗f7 22. ♖af1 0-0 23. ♘f3 ♖aa8 24. ♕d2 ♖ad8 25. ♘h4 g6 26. ♘f3 *(see diagram)*

After 26. ♘f3

26. ... ♗e8? 26. ... ♗×c4 27. ♘×e5 ♖×f2 28. ♕×f2 (28. ♖×f2 ♕×e5 29. d×c4 ♘×e4∓) 28. ... ♗×d3 29. ♕f7+ ♔×f7 30. ♖×f7∓ **27. ♘×e5 ♖×f2 28. ♕×f2 b5 29. ♕f3 b×c4 30. ♘×c4 ♗b5 31. ♕e2 ♗×c4 32. d×c4 ♕e5 33. ♕f3 d3 34. ♕f4** Somewhat better seems 34. ♕f7+ ♔h8 35. ♖d1 c6 36. ♖d2 ♕g5 (Certainly not 36. ... ♘b3 37. ♖×d3! losing for Black) **34. ... ♕×f4 35. g×f4 ♖d4 36. e5 ♔f8 37. ♔g3 ♖×c4 38. f5 g×f5 39. ♖×f5+ ♔e7 40. ♖f4 d2** No better is 40. ... ♖×f4 41. ♔×f4 d2 42. ♗f3 ♘d3+ 43. ♔e3 ♘×e5 44. ♗h5 ♘c4+ 45. ♔e2 **41. ♖×c4 d1♕ 42. ♖×c5** *(see diagram)*

After 42. ♖×c5

42. ... ♕d4?! A better try may be 42. ... ♕e1+ with one line going 43. ♔f3 ♔d7 44. ♖d5+ ♔e6 45. ♖d3 ♕c1 46. ♖e3 ♕×b2 47. ♗f1 ♕d4 48. ♗a6 h5 49. ♗c8+ ♔f7 50. ♗a6 h4 51. ♗c8 c5 52. ♗f5 c4 and Black should win **43. ♖×c7+ ♔e6**

After 72. ♖b4+

44. ♖b7 ♛×e5+ 45. ♔f3 ♔f5 46. ♖b4 the game is clearly drawn. 46. … h5 47. h4 ♛d5+ 48. ♔g3 ♛d6+ 49. ♔h3 ♛d1 50. ♗e4+ ♔e5 51. ♖b7 ♛d2 52. ♗f3 ♛e3 53. ♔g2 ♛d2+ 54. ♔f1 ♛c2 55. ♗×h5 ♛c1+ 56. ♔e2 ♛c2+ 57. ♔e3 ♛d6 58. ♗g6 ♛c1+ 59. ♔e2 ♔e5 60. ♗d3 ♛d5 61. ♔f2 ♔e5 62. ♗e2 ♔d5 63. ♗b5 ♔e5 64. h5 ♛d2+ 65. ♔f3 ♛d1+ 66. ♔e3 ♛c1+ 67. ♔f2 ♛d2+ 68. ♗e2 ♛c1 69. ♖b5+ ♔f4 70. ♖b4+ ♔e5 71. ♖b5+ ♔f4 72. ♖b4+ (see diagram)

72. … ♔e5 ½–½ (Source: Lachaga, *Maribor 1934*; notes by RT)

151   Menchik–Lajos Steiner
Maribor (2), August 6, 1934

[A03] *Bird's Opening*

1. e3 d5 2. f4 g6 3. ♘f3 ♗g7 4. c4 c6 5. ♘c3 ♘f6 6. d4 0-0 7. ♛b3 b6 8. c×d5 c×d5 9. ♗d2 ♘c6 10. ♛a4 ♗d7 11. ♗b5 ♛e8 12. ♖c1 a6 13. ♗e2 e5? [13. … b5—RT] 14. f×e5 ♘×e5 15. ♛b3 ♘c4? [15. … ♘eg4 16. 0-0 b5±— RT] 16. ♘×d5 ♘×d2 17. ♘×f6+ ♗×f6 18. ♘×d2 ♗a4 19. ♛d3 ♗b5 20. ♘c4 ♗h4+ 21. g3 ♗g5 22. ♔f2 ♛e6 23. h4 ♗h6 24. d5 ♛f6+ 25. ♗f3 ♖fe8 *(see diagram)*

26. ♛d4?? [26. ♛c3—RT] 26. … ♛×d4? Ironically beginning with a weak move, Steiner's position increasingly becomes insurmountable [26. … ♗×e3+ 27. ♛×e3 ♖×e3 28. ♘×e3 ♗d3 29. ♖c3 ♗e4 30. ♘d1 ♗×d5–+—RT] 27. e×d4 ♗×c1 28. ♖×c1

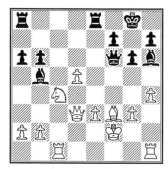

After 25. … ♖fe8

♖ac8 29. b3 ♖ed8 30. a4 ♗×a4 31. b×a4 b5 32. a×b5 a×b5 33. ♗e2 b×c4 34. ♖×c4 ♖×c4 35. ♗×c4 ♔f8 36. ♔f3 ♔e7 37. ♔f4 ♔d6 38. g4 ♖b8 39. ♔g5 ♖b4 40. ♗e2 ♖×d4 41. ♔f6 ♖e4 42. ♗d1 ♖e1 43. ♗c2 ♖h1 44. ♔×f7 ♖×h4 45. g5 ♔×d5 46. ♔f6 ♖h2 0-1 (Source: Lachaga, *Maribor 1934* [additional notes by RT])

152   Bogumir Stupan–Menchik
Maribor (3), August 7, 1934

[D35] *Queen's Gambit Declined Exchange Variation*

1. d4 ♘f6 2. ♘f3 e6 3. c4 d5 4. ♘c3 ♘bd7 5. c×d5 e×d5 6. ♗f4 c6 7. e3 ♗b4 8. ♗d3 0-0 9. 0-0 ♖e8 10. ♛c2 ♘f8 11. h3 ♗d6 12. ♘e5 ♘g6 13. ♘×g6 h×g6 14. ♗g5 ♗e6 15. e4 d×e4 16. ♘×e4 ♗e7 17. ♘c5 ♗c8 18. ♛b3 ♛d4 19. ♗×g6? ♛d5 20. ♗×f6 g×f6 21. ♛g3 ♛g5 22. ♗h7+ ♔×h7 23. ♛b3 ♖g8 0-1 (Source: Lachaga, *Maribor 1934*)

153   Menchik–Vasja Pirc
Maribor (4), August 8, 1934

[D13] *Slav, Exchange*

Neither player seemed inclined to put much on the line in this round. Pirc, the tournament winner, seemed content to have an easy day, while Menchik found it quite acceptable to be at 50 percent after four rounds—including her two strongest opponents.

1. ♘f3 d5 2. d4 ♘f6 3. c4 c6 4. c×d5 c×d5 5. ♘c3 ♘c6
6. ♗f4 a6 7. e3 ♗f5 8. ♗d3 ♗×d3 9. ♕×d3 e6 10. 0-0
♗e7 11. ♖ac1 0-0 12. ♘e5 ♖c8 13. h3 ♘×e5 14. ♗×e5
♘d7 15. e4 ♘b6?! 16. e×d5 ♘×d5 17. ♕e4 ♘×c3 18. ♖×c3
♖×c3 19. b×c3 ♕d5 20. ♕×d5 e×d5 21. a4 f6 22. ♗f4
g5 23. ♗g3 ♗d8 24. ♖b1 ♖f7 25. ♔f1 ♗a5 26. ♖b3 ♖e7
27. ♗d6 ♖d7 28. ♗b4 ♗×b4 29. ♖×b4 ♖c7 30. ♖b3 ♖e7
(see diagram)

    31. ♖b6 ½–½ (Source: Lachaga, *Maribor 1934*)

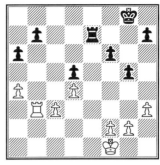

After 30. ... ♖e7

154 Josef Rejfíř–Menchik
Maribor (5), August 10, 1934

[D32] *Queen's Gambit Declined, Tarrasch Defense*

After 12. ... 0-0

1. c4 e6 2. ♘c3 d5 3. d4 c5 4. c×d5 c×d4 5. ♕×d4
♘c6 6. ♕a4 e×d5 7. ♘f3 ♗c5 8. ♕b5 ♕d6 9. g3 ♘f6
10. ♗g5 ♘e4 11. ♘×e4 d×e4 12. ♘d2 0-0 *(see diagram)*

    13. ♘×e4? 13. ♖c1 ♗b4 14. a3= **13. ... ♗b4+ 14. ♗d2
♗×d2+ 15. ♘×d2 ♘d4 16. ♕c4?** Best is 16. ♕d3 ♘c6
17. ♕×d4 ♕×h1–+ **16. ... ♗e6 17. ♘e4 ♕b6 18. ♕d3?**
♖ac8 Better is 18. ... ♕×b2 **19. ♘c3 ♕×b2 20. ♖b1 ♕×c3+
0–1** (Source: Lachaga, *Maribor 1934*)

Menchik received the bye in round 6.

155 Lajos Asztalos–Menchik
Maribor (7), August 12, 1934

[C14] *French, Classical*

    Unlike Menchik's draw in round 2 against Steiner, the
players gave everything they had in this game and played until
there was no play left at all.

1. e4 e6 2. d4 d5 3. ♘c3 ♘f6 4. ♗g5 ♗e7 5. e5 ♘fd7
6. ♗×e7 ♕×e7 7. ♕d2 0-0 8. f4 c5 9. ♘f3 ♘c6 10. g3
♘b6 11. ♗e2 ♗d7 12. ♖d1 ♖fd8 13. ♘b5 c×d4
14. ♘b×d4 ♘×d4 15. ♘×d4 ♘c4 16. ♗×c4 d×c4 17. ♕f2
c3 18. b×c3 ♕a3 19. 0-0 ♕×a2 20. g4 ♕a5 21. ♕e3 ♖ac8
22. ♖d3 ♗b5 23. ♘×b5 ♕×b5 *(see diagram)*

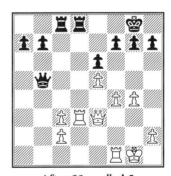

After 23. ... ♕×b5

    24. ♖×d8+ ♖×d8 25. ♕×a7 g6 26. ♕e3 ♖d5 27. h3
♕c5 28. ♕×c5 ♖×c5 29. ♖f3 g5 30. f×g5 ♖×e5 31. ♔f2 ♖×g5 32. ♔e3 b5 33. ♖f4 ♖c5
34. ♔d3 ♔f8 35. c4 b×c4+ 36. ♖×c4 ♖×c4 37. ♔×c4 ♔e7 38. g5 f6 39. g×f6+ ♔×f6
40. ♔d4 e5+ 41. ♔e4 ♔e6 42. h4 h5 43. c3 ♔d6 ½–½ (Source: Lachaga, *Maribor 1934*)

156 Menchik–Tihomil Drezga
Maribor (8), August 13, 1934

[A35] *English, Symmetrical*

1. ♘f3 ♘f6 2. c4 c5 3. d4 c×d4 4. ♘×d4 ♘c6 5. ♘c3 g6 6. e4 ♗g7 7. ♘b3 0-0 8. ♗e3

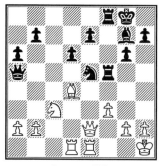

After 20. ♖fe1

d6 9. f3 ♗e6 10. ♖c1 ♘d7 11. ♗e2 f5 12. ♕d2 ♘de5 13. ♘d4 ♗xc4 14. exf5 ♘xd4 15. ♗xd4 ♗xe2 16. ♕xe2 ♖xf5 17. ♖d1 ♕a5 18. 0–0 ♖af8 19. ♔h1 a6 20. ♖fe1 (*see diagram*)

20. ... **h5?!** The price of stopping White's g4 is too great in terms of long term weaknesses and initiative. [20. ... e6!?— RT] **21. b4 ♕d8 22. ♘d5 ♖5f7 23. ♗b6 ♕d7 24. f4 ♘c6 25. a4 e5 26. b5 axb5 27. axb5 ♘e7 28. ♘xe7+ ♕xe7 29. ♕d3 ♖xf4 30. ♕xg6 ♖4f6 31. ♕xh5 ♖h6** [A little better seems 31. ... d5 32. ♗g1 ♖f5 33. ♕e2 ♕e6=—RT] **32. ♕e2 ♕h4 33. ♗g1 ♖f7 34. b6 ♕e7 35. ♖c1 d5 36. ♖c8+ ♔h7 37. ♕d3+ ♖g6 38. ♕xd5 ♕g5?** [Better resistance is from 38. ... ♕e6 39. ♕xe6 ♖xe6—RT] **39. ♖e3 ♖f1 40. ♕g8+ 1–0** (Source: Lachaga, *Maribor 1934* [additional notes by RT])

157 Rudolf Spielmann–Menchik
Maribor (9), August 14, 1934

[C02] *French, Advance*

1. e4 e6 2. d4 d5 3. e5 c5 4. ♕g4 ♘c6 5. ♘f3 ♘xd4 6. ♘xd4 cxd4 7. ♕xd4 ♘e7 8. ♕g4 ♕c7 9. ♗b5+ ♗d7 10. ♗xd7+ ♕xd7 11. 0–0 ♖c8 12. c3 ♘g6 13. ♕g3 ♗c5 14. ♗e3 ♕b5 15. b4 ♗xe3 16. ♕xe3 0–0 17. ♘d2 a6 18. a4 ♕c6 19. ♖a3 ♖fd8 20. ♘f3 ♕c4 21. ♘d4 ♘e7 22. ♖d1 (*see diagram*)

22. ... **♘f5?!** This seems like a troublesome way to make the draw, but the result is never in question. **23. ♘xf5 exf5 24. ♖d4 ♕c6 25. f4 ♕b6 26. a5 ♕e6 27. ♖a1 g6 28. ♖ad1 b5 29. ♖1d3** [29. axb6 ♕xb6 30. ♕f3 a5 31. bxa5 ♕xa5=; 29. ♕f3 ♖d7 30. ♖xd5 ♖xc3=—RT] **29. ... ♖d7 30. ♕d2**

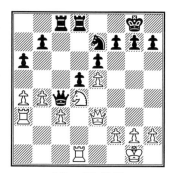

After 22. ♖d1

♖cd8 Now that the fortress is complete the players make a few more moves to achieve the time control and make peace. **31. ♕f2 ♔g7 32. ♕h4 h6 33. ♖h3 ♖h8 34. ♖hd3 ♖hd8 ½–½** (Source: Lachaga, *Maribor 1934*)

Semily 1934
August 20–25, 1934

	1	2	3	4	5	6	7	8	Points	Place
1 Hadač, Pavel	•	=	=	1	1	1	1	1	6	1
2 Menchik, Vera	=	•	0	1	1	1	1	1	5½	2–3
3 Paroulek, Vít	=	1	•	1	0	1	1	1	5½	2–3
4 Matejka	0	0	0	•	1	=	1	1	3½	4
5 Skrbek	0	0	1	0	•	0	1	1	3	5
6 Rada, Josef	0	0	0	=	1	•	0	=	2	6
7 Kovarik	0	0	0	0	0	1	•	=	1½	7
8 Blažej	*0	0	0	0	0	=	=	•	1	8

Gino Di Felice, in his *Chess Results 1921–1930*, lists this Czechoslovakian event as being played by Olga Menchik. Based on the following published game, the listings of Menchik's events posthumously, the final results (and C.S.1934 vol. 8, as well as SCQ p. 445) it is evident that Di Felice was in error and that it was Vera rather than her sister who played in this event.

Prior to the tournament Vera and Karel Opočenský played a tandem simultaneous exhibition where they scored +19 −4 =2.

158 Menchik–Josef Rada
Semily, 1934
[A03] *Bird's Opening*

After 28. Rg3

It seems sufficient to let the game speak for itself. Black seemed set on auto pilot and often seemed uninterested in what White's responses would be to his moves. **1. f4 d5 2. ♘f3 c5 3. e3 ♘c6 4. ♗b5 ♗d7 5. 0-0 e6 6. b3 ♘f6 7. ♗b2 ♗e7 8. ♗×c6 ♗×c6 9. ♘e5 ♕c7 10. d3 0-0 11. ♘d2 b5 12. ♖f3 ♖ad8 13. ♖h3 ♗a8 14. ♘df3 h6 15. ♕e1 d4 16. e4 ♘h7 17. ♕g3 ♔h8 18. ♖f1 ♗f6 19. ♗c1 a5 20. f5 ♕e7 21. ♘g4 e×f5 22. ♘×f6 ♕×f6 23. ♘h4 ♗b7? 24. ♘×f5 ♕g6 25. ♕e5 ♖de8 26. ♕×c5 ♖c8 27. ♕×d4 ♖×c2 28. ♖g3** *(see diagram)*
28. ... ♘g5 29. ♗×g5 1-0 (Source: *Československý Šach* 1934, v. 8)

Hastings 1934-1935
(Premier)
December 27, 1934–January 5, 1935

		1	2	3	4	5	6	7	8	9	10	Points	Place
1	Thomas, Sir George	●	0	=	1	1	1	0	1	1	1	6½	1–3
2	Euwe, Dr. Max	1	●	=	=	1	=	1	=	1	=	6½	1–3
3	Flohr, Salo	=	=	●	=	=	1	1	1	1	1	6½	1–3
4	Capablanca, José R.	0	=	=	●	=	0	1	1	1	1	5½	4
5	Botvinnik, Mikhail M.	0	0	=	=	●	=	=	1	1	1	5	5–6
6	Lilienthal, Andres	0	=	=	1	=	●	1	=	=	=	5	5–6
7	Michell, Reginald P.	1	0	0	0	=	0	●	=	1	1	4	7
8	Menchik, Vera	0	=	0	0	0	=	=	●	1	=	3	8
9	Milner-Berry, Philip S.	0	0	0	0	0	=	0	0	●	1	1½	9–10
10	Norman, George M.	0	=	0	0	0	=	0	=	0	●	1½	9–10

159 Menchik–Reginald Michell
Hastings 1934-35 (1), December 27, 1934
[A12] *English*

1. ♘f3 d5 2. c4 c6 3. b3 ♗f5 4. ♗b2 e6 5. g3 ♘f6 6. ♗g2 ♘bd7 7. 0-0 ♗d6 8. d3 ♕e7 9. ♘bd2 0-0 10. ♕c2 h6 11. ♖ad1 ♗h7 12. e4 d×e4 13. d×e4 ♖fd8 14. ♖fe1 ♗b4 15. ♘d4 ♘c5 16. a3 ♗×d2 17. ♖×d2 e5 18. ♘f5 ♗×f5 19. e×f5 ♖×d2 20. ♕×d2 ♖d8 21. ♕b4 a5 22. ♕×a5 ♘×b3 *(see diagram)*

23. ♕b4?! [23. ♕×e5 ♕×e5 24. ♗×e5± —RT] **23. ...**

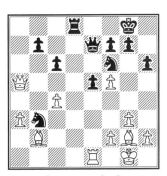

After 22. ... ♘×b3

♕×b4 24. a×b4 ♘d2 25. c5 ♘c4 26. ♗×e5 ♘×e5 27. ♖×e5 ♖d1+ 28. ♗f1 ♔f8 29. ♖e3 ♖b1 30. b5 c×b5 31. ♖a3 ♘e4 32. ♔g2 ♖b2 33. ♔f3 ♘d2+ 34. ♔g2 ♘×f1 35. ♔×f1 ♖c2 36. ♖a8+ ♔e7 37. ♖b8 ♖×c5 38. ♖×b7+ ♔f6 39. g4 h5 40. h3 h×g4 41. h×g4 ½–½ (Source: Cordingly, *Hastings 1934-1935*)

160 George M. Norman–Menchik
Hastings 1934-35 (2), December 28, 1934
[D51] *Queen's Gambit Declined*

This is a modestly interesting game for a draw with both players poking and prodding, yet without any great risks taken.

1. d4 ♘f6 2. c4 e6 3. ♘c3 d5 4. ♗g5 ♘bd7 5. e3 c6 6. a3 ♗e7 7. ♘f3 ♘e4 8. ♘×e4 d×e4 9. ♗×e7 ♕×e7 10. ♘d2 f5 11. ♗e2 c5 12. d×c5 ♕×c5 13. 0-0 0-0 14. b4 ♕e7 15. c5 ♘f6 16. ♘c4 ♗d7 17. ♘e5 ♗c6 [17. ... ♘d5!? 18. ♕b3 ♖fd8—RT] 18. ♘×c6 b×c6 19. ♕b3 ♘d5 20. ♗c4 ♖f6!? 21. ♖fd1 ♖b8 22. ♗×d5?! e×d5 23. ♕c3 f4 24. e×f4 Any

After 47. ... ♔e6

other "reasonable" move would be met by 24. ... f3 and will never be able to bring enough power to the queenside to accomplish anything. 24. ... ♖×f4 25. ♖a2 ♕e6 26. ♖ad2 a6 27. ♖e1 ♕f6 28. ♕×f6 ♖×f6 29. h3 h6 30. ♖e3 ♖f7 31. ♖b3 ♖fb7 32. ♖db2 [No better is 32. f3 e×f3 33. ♖×f3 a5 34. b×a5 ♖a8 35. ♖e2 ♖×a5 36. ♖e8+ ♔h7 37. ♖c3 ♖ba7 38. ♖e6=—RT] 32. ... ♔f7 33. f3 ♖e8 34. ♖e2 ♖be7 35. ♖be3 e×f3 36. ♖×f3+ ♔g8 37. ♖×e7 ♖×e7 38. ♔f2 ♖f7 39. ♖×f7 ♔×f7 40. ♔e3 ♔e6 41. ♔d4 ♔f6 42. g3 g6 43. g4 g5 44. a4 ♔e6 45. ♔e3 ♔e5 46. ♔d3 ♔f6 47. ♔d4 ♔e6 (*see diagram*)
48. ♔c3 ½–½ (Source: Cordingly, *Hastings 1934-1935*)

161 Menchik–José Raúl Capablanca
Hastings 1934-35 (3), December 29, 1934
[A45] *Queen's Pawn Game*

According to *BCM* 1935, p. 52, this game went seven hours.

1. d4 ♘f6 2. c4 e6 3. ♘f3 b6 4. g3 ♗b7 5. ♗g2 ♗b4+ 6. ♗d2 ♗×d2+ 7. ♕×d2 d6 8. ♘c3 ♘e4 9. ♘×e4 ♗×e4 10. 0-0 ♘d7 11. ♕e3 ♘f6 12. ♘d2 ♗×g2 13. ♔×g2 0-0 14. ♕d3 e5 15. ♘e4 ♘d7 16. ♘c3 f5 17. d×e5 ♘×e5 18. ♕d5+ ♔h8 19. e3 ♕e8 20. ♘e2 c6 21. ♕d4 [White cannot hold the pawn without being subjected to a massive attack as in: 21. ♕×d6 c5 22. ♕d5 ♖d8 23. ♕b7 ♖d7 24. ♕a6 ♕a8+ 25. f3 ♖d2 26. ♖ae1 ♖e8 27. ♖f2 ♘×f3 28. ♖×f3 ♖×e3–+—RT] 21. ... ♕h5 22. ♘g1 ♘f6 23. ♖ac1 ♖e8 24. ♕d1 ♕f7 25. ♕b3 g5 26. ♕c3 f4 27. e×f4 g×f4 28. ♖fe1 f×g3 29. f×g3 ♖f2+ 30. ♔h1 ♕h5 31. h3 ♖ef8 32. g4 ♕f7 33. ♘e4 ♖f1 34. ♖×f1 ♕×f1 35. b3 ♘f3 36. ♖e3 ♖f2 37. ♖g3 ♖×a2 38. ♕d4 ♕f2 39. ♕×f2 ♖×f2 40. ♖g2 ♖f1 41. ♖g3 ♖f2 42. ♖g2 ♖×g2 43. ♔×g2 a5 44. ♘e2 a4 45. b×a4 ♘×c4 46. ♔f3 d5 47. ♘d4 c5 48. ♘e6 ♔g8 49. ♘f4 d4 50. ♘d3 ♔f7 51. h4 ♔e6 52. ♔f4 ♘e3 53. h5 ♘d5+ 54. ♔e4 ♘c3+ 55. ♔f3 ♘×a4 0-1 (Source: Cordingly, *Hastings 1934-1935*)

162 Mikhail M. Botvinnik–Menchik
Hastings 1934-35 (4), December 31, 1934

[D37] *Queen's Gambit Declined*

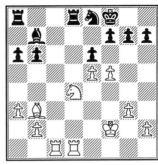

After 23. f5

1. d4 ♘f6 2. c4 e6 3. ♘c3 d5 4. ♘f3 ♘bd7 5. ♗f4 d×c4 6. e3 ♘d5 7. ♗×c4 ♘×f4 8. e×f4 ♗d6 9. g3 0-0 10. 0-0 ♘f6 11. ♕e2 b6 12. ♖fd1 ♗b7 13. ♖ac1 ♕e7 14. a3 ♖fd8 15. ♘e5 c5 16. ♘b5 c×d4 17. ♘×d4 ♗×e5 18. ♕×e5 ♕d6 19. ♗b3 ♕×e5 20. f×e5 ♘e8? Where does the knight go? [20. ... ♘g4—RT] **21. f4 a6 22. ♔f2 ♔f8 23. f5** *(see diagram)*

23. ... ♗d5? [23. ... e×f5—RT] **24. f×e6 ♗×b3 25. e7+ 1-0** (Source: Cordingly, *Hastings 1934-1935*)

163 Menchik–Max Euwe
Hastings 1934-35 (5), January 1, 1935

[D36] *Queen's Gambit Declined, Exchange Variation*

In this, the final of their four games, Menchik gets a solid advantage early only to let her opponent complicate the position on move 34 and find himself with three minors versus a pair of rooks. After Euwe builds a fortress both side jockey around until agreeing to a draw on move 55. Later in the year Dr. Euwe won his match for the World Championship against Alexander Alekhine—a player Menchik in eight tries could never best.

After 21. ♘e5

1. d4 d5 2. c4 c6 The move that was used 11 times in the first Alekhine–Euwe world championship later in the year. **3. ♘f3 ♘f6 4. ♘c3 e6 5. c×d5 e×d5 6. ♗g5 ♗e7 7. ♕c2 ♗g4 8. e3 ♘bd7 9. ♗d3 ♖c8 10. h3 ♗h5 11. ♗f4 ♗g6 12. 0-0 ♗×d3 13. ♕×d3 0-0 14. ♖ac1 ♘e8 15. e4** Having completed her development, White is virtually compelled to attack and accept the isolani, else her position is condemned to passivity. **15. ... d×e4 16. ♘×e4 ♘df6 17. ♘g3 ♘d5 18. ♗d2 ♕b6 19. ♘f5 ♗f6 20. ♕a3 ♘ec7 21. ♘e5** *(see diagram)*

21. ... ♖cd8?! [21. ... ♘b5 22. ♕g3 ♕c7=—RT] **22. ♗a5 ♕a6 23. ♕g3! ♕×a5?!** [Better may be 23. ... g6 where none of White's three best choices: ♗×c7; ♘×c6; and ♘h6+ lead to much of any advantage—RT] **24. ♘h6+ ♔h8 25. ♘h×f7+ ♖×f7 26. ♘×f7+ ♔g8 27. ♘×d8 ♗×d8 28. ♕d6 ♘b5?** [28. ... ♗f6—RT] **29. ♕d7** [Slightly stronger is 29. ♕e6+ ♔f8 30. ♖fe1—RT] **29. ... ♘f6 30. ♕×b7 ♘×d4 31. ♖fe1 ♕b6 32. ♕c8 ♔f7 33. ♖cd1 c5** *(see diagram)*

34. b3?! [34. b4! ♗c7 (Not 34. ... c×b4? 35. ♕c4++−) 35. b×c5 ♕×c5 36. ♕b7 (36. ♖×d4?? ♗h2+ 37. ♔×h2 ♕×c8 and losing) 36. ... ♕b6 37. ♕×b6 and although it may be long, White has a substantial advantage—RT] **34. ... ♗c7 35. ♖d3**

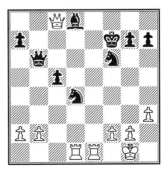

After 33. ... c5

Final position

♕c6 36. g3 ♗a5 37. ♕×c6 ♘×c6 38. ♖c1 ♗b6 39. ♔g2 ♘d4 40. ♖cd1 ♔e6 41. ♖c1 ♔d6 42. a3 ♔d5 43. f3 ♘d7 44. ♖e3 ♘e5 45. f4 ♘ec6 46. ♖d1 ♗d8 47. ♖e8 ♗f6 48. g4 h6 49. ♔g3 ♘e7 50. h4 ♔c6 51. ♖d3 ♘d5 52. g5 An interesting case of the threat being greater than the execution. Here chess program Fritz likes the three adjacent pawns, but as soon as g5 was played the rating drops because of a reduction in opportunities and White holes. **52. ... ♗e7 53. ♖c8+ ♔d7 54. ♖a8 ♘e2+ 55. ♔f3 ♘e×f4** (see diagram)

Here Black offered a draw which was accepted by Menchik. Any win that may exist is problematic and would consume a lot of time. ½–½ (Source: Cordingly, *Hastings 1934-1935* [additional notes by RT])

164   George Thomas–Menchik
Hastings 1934-35 (6), January 2, 1935

[E74] *King's Indian, Averbach Variation*

White gets a cramped and disjointed position early on and never gets any substantial play.

1. d4 ♘f6 2. c4 c5 3. d5 e5 4. ♘c3 d6 5. e4 g6 6. ♗e2 ♗g7 7. ♗g5 0-0 8. ♕d2 ♘a6 9. h4 ♘c7 10. ♘h3 ♗d7 11. f3 a6 12. ♘f2 b5 13. g4 b×c4 Better is 13. ... b4 **14. a4** Called for is 14. ♗×c4 **14. ... ♕b8 15. ♗×c4 ♕b4 16. b3 ♖ab8 17. ♘d3 ♕a5 18. ♖c1 ♖b7 19. h5 ♖fb8 20. h×g6 h×g6 21. ♗h6 ♘ce8 22. ♕h2 ♔f8 23. ♕d2** (see diagram)

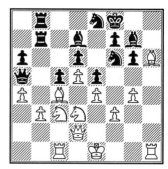

After 23. ♕d2

23. ... ♘g8 24. ♗×g7+ ♔×g7 25. ♖h2 ♘ef6 26. ♘e2 ♕×d2+ 27. ♔×d2 ♘e7 28. ♖ch1 ♘c8 29. ♘dc1 ♖a7 30. ♘g3 ♘b6 31. ♗e2 ♘g8 32. g5 ♗e8 33. ♖h8 ♗d7 34. ♘f1 ♗e8 35. ♘e3 ♗d7 36. a5 ♘c8 37. ♗c4 ♖aa8 38. ♘d3 ♔f8 39. ♘f2 ♘a7 40. ♘fg4 ♗×g4 41. ♘×g4 ♘b5 42. ♗×b5 a×b5 43. a6 ♖d8 44. a7 ♖dc8? The final nail in the coffin. 44. ... b4 **45. ♘f6 ♔e7 46. ♖a1 1-0** (Source: Cordingly, *Hastings 1934-1935*; notes by RT)

165   Menchik–Salo Flohr
Hastings 1934-35 (7), January 3, 1935

[E16] *Queen's Indian Defense*

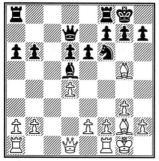

After 13. ... ♗×d5

A sad game for Menchik as she had a win, only to miss it; then she let the draw also slip away.

1. d4 ♘f6 2. c4 e6 3. ♘f3 b6 4. g3 ♗b7 5. ♗g2 d5 6. 0-0 ♗d6 7. ♘c3 0-0 8. ♘e5 ♘bd7 9. ♗g5 ♕e7 10. ♘b5 a6 11. ♘×d7 ♕×d7 12. ♘×d6 c×d6 13. c×d5 ♗×d5 (see diagram)

14. ♕d3? Winning is 14. ♗×f6 ♗×g2 15. ♗×g7 ♔×g7 (15. ... ♗×f1 16. ♗×f8 ♗×e2 17. ♕×e2±) 16. ♔×g2± **14. ... ♗×g2 15. ♔×g2 ♘d5 16. ♗d2 f5 17. e3 ♖fc8 18. ♖fc1 ♕a4 19. b3 ♕d7 20. f3 ♕b7 21. ♖×c8+ ♖×c8 22. ♖c1 ♖×c1**

23. ♗×c1 b5 24. ♗d2 ♕c6 25. ♔f2 h6 26. h4 ♔f7 27. ♕b1
♔e7 28. ♔e2 ♔d7 29. ♕c1 29. e4 ♘c3+ 30. ♗×c3 ♕×c3
31. ♕d3 ♕b2+ 32. ♕d2 and we can call it a draw 29. ... ♕b7
30. ♕c2 ♘f6 31. ♗e1? 31. ♔f2 holds the game easily 31. ... g5
32. h×g5 h×g5 33. a4 g4 34. f×g4 ♘×g4 *(see diagram)*
    35. ♗f2?? White should play 35. ♕d3 and there is at least
a chance of holding the position. The text is an embarrassing
oversight. Not a game to be proud of by either player! 35. ...
♕g2 0–1 (Source: Cordingly, *Hastings 1934-1935*; notes by RT)

After 34. ... ♘×g4

166 Menchik–Philip S. Milner-Barry
Hastings 1934-35 (8), January 4, 1935
[D12] *Slav Defense*

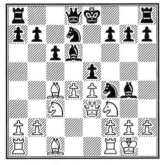

After 11. ... e5

1. d4 ♘f6 2. ♘f3 d5 3. c4 c6 4. ♘c3 ♗f5 5. c×d5 ♘×d5
6. e3 e6 7. ♗c4 ♘d7 8. 0-0 ♗d6 9. ♕e2 ♗g4 10. e4 ♘f4
11. ♕e3 e5?! *(see diagram)*
    Overlooking White's response of [11. ... ♗c7] 12. ♗×f7+!
Although not winning by force, this move is surprising and forces
Black to solve various problems; none of which are completely
satisfactory for Black. [Not 12. d×e5 ♘×e5 13. ♘×e5 ♗×e5
14. h3 ♗h5 15. ♕c5 ♕g5 16. ♗×f4 ♕×f4 17. g3 ♕f6 where
Black retains the bishop pair and greater long term options at
the expense of having to find a decent placement for his king—
RT] 12. ... ♔e7?? [12. ... ♔×f7 13. d×e5 ♘×g2 14. ♔×g2 ♗×e5
15. ♘g5+ ♔e8 16. f3 Leaving White with a small but definite advantage—RT] 13. ♘×e5 ♘×e5
14. d×e5 ♗×e5 15. ♗b3 Regrouping to take her pawn advantage and a slightly cramped position. [Better seems to be 15. ♕c5+ ♔×f7 16. ♕×e5 ♘d3 17. ♕g3 ♕d7 18. f4—RT] 15. ... g5?
This finishes the game off in short order. [Delaying matters is 15. ... ♕d6 but it is doubtful that
the draw can be found—RT] 16. ♕c5+ ♔f6 17. ♗e3 ♘d3 18. ♕c4 ♕d7 19. f3 ♗e6
20. ♘d5+ c×d5 21. ♕×d3 ♖ad8 22. f4 g×f4 23. ♗×f4 ♗×f4 24. ♖×f4+ ♔e7 25. e×d5
1–0 (Source: Cordingly, *Hastings 1934-1935* [additional notes by RT])

167 Andor Lilienthal–Menchik
Hastings 1934-35 (9), January 5, 1935
[D36] *Queen's Gambit Declined, Exchange Variation*

1. d4 ♘f6 2. c4 e6 3. ♘c3 d5 4. ♗g5 ♘bd7 5. c×d5 e×d5
6. e3 ♗e7 7. ♗d3 0-0 8. ♘ge2 c6 9. ♕c2 ♖e8 10. 0-0-0
♘f8 11. ♘g3 b5 12. ♘f5 ♗×f5 13. ♗×f5 a5 14. ♔b1 a4
15. ♘e2 ♖a6 16. ♘c1 ♘e4 17. ♗×e7 ♖×e7 18. ♗×e4
d×e4 19. ♘e2 ♕a8 20. ♘g3 b4 21. ♕c5 ♖e8 22. d5 ♘d7
23. ♕c4 c×d5 24. ♕×d5 ♘f6 25. ♕×a8 ♖a×a8 26. ♖d4
b3 27. ♖c1 g6 28. ♖cc4 ♔g7 29. ♖×a4 b×a2+ 30. ♔×a2
♖×a4+ 31. ♖×a4 h5 32. h3 h4 33. ♘e2 ♖e5 34. ♘c3 ♖g5
35. ♘×e4 ♘×e4 36. ♖×e4 ♖×g2 37. ♖×h4 ♖×f2 38. ♖f4
♖h2 39. ♖f3 f5 ½–½ *(see diagram)*

Final position

A few months later these two played a rather bizarre game in the Moscow tournament.
½–½ (Source: Cordingly, *Hastings 1934-1935*)

Moscow 1935

February 15–March 14, 1935

		1	2	3	4	5	6	7	8	9	10	11	12	13	14	15	16	17	18	19	20	Pts	Place
1	Botvinnik, Mikhail M.	•	=	=	=	1	0	1	=	1	1	=	1	=	1	=	0	1	=	1	1	13	1–2
2	Flohr, Salomon M.	=	•	=	=	=	=	=	=	=	1	=	1	1	=	1	1	1	1	=	=	13	1–2
3	Lasker, Emanuel	=	=	•	1	=	1	=	=	=	=	=	1	=	=	=	=	=	1	1	1	12½	3
4	Capablanca, José R.	=	=	0	•	=	1	1	=	1	=	1	=	=	0	1	=	=	=	1	1	12	4
5	Spielmann, Rudolf	0	=	=	=	•	=	=	=	=	0	1	1	=	0	=	=	=	1	1	1	11	5
6	Kan, Ilia A.	1	=	0	0	=	•	=	0	1	0	=	=	1	1	0	1	1	=	=	1	10½	6–7
7	Levenfish, Grigory Y.	0	=	=	0	=	=	•	=	=	=	1	=	0	1	1	1	1	=	0	1	10½	6–7
8	Lilienthal, Andor	=	=	=	=	=	=	1	•	0	=	=	=	0	1	=	=	0	1	1	=	10	8–10
9	Ragozin, Vyachslav	0	=	=	0	1	0	=	1	•	0	0	=	=	1	=	=	1	1	=	1	10	8–10
10	Romanovsky, Pyotr	0	0	=	=	0	1	=	=	1	•	=	=	1	0	=	1	0	1	1	1	10	8–10
11	Alatortsev, Vladimir	=	=	=	0	0	=	0	=	1	=	•	0	0	1	1	=	=	=	1	1	9½	11–14
12	Goglidze, Viktor A.	0	0	0	=	=	=	=	=	=	=	1	•	=	=	=	=	0	1	1	1	9½	11–14
13	Rabinovich, Ilya L.	=	0	=	=	1	0	1	1	=	0	1	=	•	0	0	=	0	=	1	1	9½	11–14
14	Riumin, Nikolay N.	0	=	=	1	=	0	0	0	0	1	0	=	1	•	0	1	1	1	=	1	9½	11–14
15	Lisitsin, Georgy M.	=	0	=	0	=	1	0	=	=	=	0	=	1	1	•	0	=	=	=	1	9	15
16	Bohatirchuk, Fyodor	1	0	=	=	=	0	0	=	=	=	=	=	0	1	•	=	=	0	=		8	16–17
17	Ståhlberg, Anders G.	0	0	=	=	0	0	0	1	0	0	=	1	1	0	=	=	•	=	1	1	8	16–17
18	Pirc, Vasja	=	0	0	=	0	=	=	0	0	1	=	0	=	0	=	=	=	•	1	1	7½	18
19	Chekhover, Vitaly	0	=	0	0	0	=	1	0	=	0	0	0	0	=	=	1	0	0	•	1	5½	19
20	Menchik, Vera	0	=	0	0	0	0	0	=	0	0	0	0	0	0	0	=	0	0	0	•	1½	20

Moscow 1935, along with Carlsbad 1929, was one of the two truly great tournaments in which Menchik played. In addition to three World Champions and an official challenger, the entire cream of Russian chess played. At present the best information on Vera and her participation comes from Bikova's book. One should take her comments with a grain of salt given the circumstances under which she wrote.

Many foreign masters declared that they wished to come. Among them was Vera Menchik. She doubtless wanted both to play against the strong competition and to visit her native city. When the candidates were discussed the opinion was expressed that Menchik was too weak to play at such a tournament. But one remembered that she was a world champion and had enough experience in playing at the men's competitions. The Soviet functionaries expected that her participation would improve the Soviet chess movement among women; so Menchik received the invitation.

The tournament book, edited by Krylenko and annotated by many of the players, is one of the best of all time. One often learns the player's thoughts since they annotated many of their own games, although the analysis in those precomputer days does have errors. There is also a detailed commentary on how the tournament was analyzed as well as good indices and an openings analysis section.

The tournament was held at the Museum of Fine Arts. According to Nicolai Zubarev in the tournament book neither the Hall of Columns nor the Hotel Metropol could accommodate the four to five thousand (!) spectators expected daily. As it was, the two tournament halls used in round one were adequate in size and a third had to be pressed into service before round two. Lighting and ventilation were also problems, but, according to the book, eventually remedied.

At the opening banquet, held in the "National" Hotel on February 14, Vera joked that she is not fully satisfied with her victories and she looked forward, "to drinking some men's blood." She was ready for combat.

For Menchik the competition began unsuccessfully. She lost one game after another. Later she bitterly wrote, "First time in my life I felt helpless and to be a weak woman who has nothing with which to oppose my adversaries. It's my first time I have had such an unsuccessful start."

Until the eighth round she played only against the Soviet chess players. The beginning of her third round, against Botvinnik, was played quite well, and Menchik had a better position, but then in time trouble she made a mistake. The position became worse and a pawn was lost. The game was adjourned and in the break Menchik resigned.

In the fifth round, her game against Goglidze ended very soon and later she wrote, "All my games were played badly and that is not my style. I've made errors that are absolutely unusual for me."

In the eighth round Menchik got a good game out of the opening against Pirc, but then she began to play worse and lost. The first meeting with ex–World Champion Lasker was conducted quite well but she made some mistakes and suffered defeat.

She no doubt was upset, but she did not show it to anybody. She thought that her sightseeing in Moscow played a bad role in her efforts at the competition. During her free time she visited the museums and theaters. She said, "It is a great joy to be here watching perfect performances with great actors and to remember how in 1919 I sat here in my *valenki*" (a kind of felt boots).

She always stated to the press that she was fond of the Soviet reality. She underlined great achievements of the country since 1921 when she left and she was enthusiastic about the women's equality and so on. She hoped all this should improve the development of women's chess here. The first game which ended in a draw was that in the 11th round. Then the game against Lilienthal in the 13th round was also drawn. They traded queens early and the game became closed in nature.

Menchik played well in the 14th game against Flohr. She conducted it well and stubbornly. For Flohr this game could be the decisive one in his struggle for first place, but he could not win, and after an equal middle game it became a four rook endgame and was drawn on the 57th move. Vera played a wider variety of openings in this tournament than in most "male" events. Possibly this was because her results were so poor that she was looking for a way to mix things up. Despite this suggestion by Jennifer Shahade in *Chess Bitch*, it did not work, possibly because she was already demoralized.

The spectators of the match gave Menchik an ovation. She was congratulated by many people. She soon won the sympathy of many chess fans and often was supported in case of her failures and congratulated for her victories. She was really affected by such attention.[50]

With 1½ points Menchik took last place. The first two places were shared by Botvinnik and Flohr (13 points each), Lasker was third with 12½ points and fourth was Capablanca with 12.

During the tournament two multiboard simultaneous exhibitions were held by the Women's World Champion against ten Soviet players. In each Menchik won nine games and ended one with a draw.

Menchik always remembered this trip with warmth. She hoped to visit Moscow again but never did.

168　Grigory Levenfish–Menchik

Moscow 1935 (1), February 15, 1935

[C14] *French, Classical*

1. e4 e6 2. d4 d5 3. ♘c3 ♘f6 4. ♗g5 ♗e7 5. e5 ♘fd7 6. h4 c5 6. ... c5 being Breyer's line ... currently listed in ECO as +/= At the time 6. ... h6 was often recommended. [Less solid is 6. ... f6—RT] **7. ♗×e7 ♔×e7** [In the tournament book Levenfish claims that the following loses the exchange. 7. ... ♕×e7 8. ♘b5 However after 8. ... ♔d8± the position, although unpleasant, does not lose material—RT] **8. f4 c×d4 9. ♕×d4 ♘c6 10. ♕d2 ♕a5** [More in the modern vein would be 10. ... ♕b6 11. 0–0–0 ♘c5±—RT] **11. ♘f3 ♖d8 12. ♖h3?! ♔f8 13. ♗d3 ♘b6 14. ♘b5** [A major mistake would be 14. ♗×h7 ♘c4 15. ♕e2 (not 15. ♕c1? d4∓) 15. ... ♘×b2 leading to a comfortable position for Black—RT] **14. ... ♘b4 15. ♘fd4** *(see diagram)*

After 15. ♘fd4

15. ... a6? [15. ... ♘×d3+—RT] **16. ♘d6 ♕c5 17. c3 ♘×d3+ 18. ♕×d3 f5??** [Providing much better resistance is 18. ... ♔g8—RT] **19. 0–0–0?** [19. e×f6 g6 with an overwhelming advantage; no better is 19. ... ♔g8 20. ♖g3 ♖d7 21. f7+ ♖×f7 22. ♘×f7 ♔×f7 23. ♕×h7] **19. ... ♘c4** [19. ... ♖×d6 20. e×d6+–—RT] **20. ♘4×f5 ♘×b2 21. ♔×b2 e×f5 22. ♕×d5 ♕×d5 23. ♖×d5 ♗e6 24. ♖d4 ♖d7 25. ♖g3** Although Black could legitimately play on a bit, Menchik may have decided to cut her losses and call it a night. **1–0** (Source: Krylenko, *Moscow 1935*, translated by J. Adams, 1998; Cordingly, *Moscow 1935* [additional notes by RT])

169　Menchik–Nikolay Riumin

Moscow 1935 (2), February 16, 1935

[A21] *English Defense*

1. ♘f3 f5 2. g3 ♘f6 3. ♗g2 d6 4. 0–0 e5 5. d3 ♗e7 6. c4 0–0 7. ♘c3 ♕e8 8. b4 ♕h5 9. ♕b3 ♔h8 10. ♖e1?! Preparing for 11. e4 which is very weak. White's 10th move, in and of itself, does not lose though if it were followed up with moves such as d4, a3, Bb2 etc. as allowed. [Yudovich suggests 10. ♘d5 ♗d8 11. ♗b2 with a follow-up of ♖ac1 and c4 with equality; an alternate try is 10. d4 where Black has a plethora of choices that lead to differing but reasonable options including e4, ♘bd7, a5 or e×d4—RT] **10. ... ♘bd7** *(see diagram)*

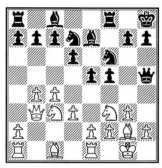

After 10. ... ♘bd7

11. e4? a5! 12. ♗g5 a×b4 13. ♗×f6 ♗×f6 14. ♕×b4

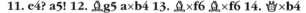

♘c5 15. ♕b1 f4 16. ♔h1 ♗g4 17. ♘g1 ♗g5 18. ♕c2 f3 19. ♗f1 ♖f6 20. h3 ♖h6 21. ♘d5 ♘e6 22. ♕b2 b6 23. a4 ♖f8 24. a5 b×a5 25. ♖×a5 ♗d8! Threatening, as appropriate, both ♘g5 and c6. **26. ♘e3 ♗×h3** If 27. ♘×h3 (or 27. ♗×h3) ♘g5 and all ends quickly. **0–1** (Source: Krylenko, *Moscow 1935*, translated by J. Adams, 1998; Cordingly, *Moscow 1935* [additional notes by RT])

170 Mikhail M. Botvinnik–Menchik
Moscow 1935 (3), February 17, 1935
[A34] *English, Symmetrical*

1. c4 ♘f6 2. ♘c3 c5 3. ♘f3 d5 4. c×d5 ♘×d5 5. e4 ♘b4 6. ♗c4 e6 7. 0-0 ♘8c6 8. d3 ♗e7 9. a3 ♘a6 10. ♗e3 ♘ab8 11. ♖c1 0-0 *(see diagram)*

After 11. ... 0-0

12. ♕d2 [Rabinovitch, in the tournament book, felt the following to be better, given White's development: 12. d4 c×d4 13. ♘×d4 ♘×d4 14. ♗×d4 ♘c6 15. ♗e3 ♕×d1 16. ♖f×d1— RT] **12. ... ♘d4!** [Freeing Black's position and impeding the benefits of White's better development—RT] **13. ♗×d4 c×d4 14. ♘e2 ♘c6 15. b4 a6 16. ♗b3 ♕d6!** [If 16. ... e5 Rabinovitch claims that 17. ♗d5 wins a pawn, but after 17. ... ♕d6 the pawn is elusive. Having said that, White does have to deal with a fragmented pawn structure and a problematic c file, as well as how best to use or dispose of his bishop pair—RT] **17. ♘e1 ♔h8 18. f4 f6 19. ♘f3 ♗d7 20. ♘g3 ♖ac8 21. ♖fe1 a5?** Doing nothing to prevent White's next move. [Better is 21. ... ♕b8 in order to meet e5 with ... f5, or alternatively f5 with ... e5. If 21. ... ♕b8! and later ... ♕a7 Black can simplify her position and develop a counterattack on the queen's flank. (If 22. e5 f5; better is 22. ... f×e5 23. f×e5 b5 and we have a very wild game with chances for all) 23. ♕f2 ♗d8 24. ♘e2 and White has a very nice position—RT] **22. e5! ♕b8** [22. ... f×e5!?—RT] **23. e×f6 ♖×f6 24. b5 ♘d8 25. ♖×c8 ♗×c8 26. ♘e5!** *(see diagram)*

After 26. ♘e5

[Rabinovitch notes here that White's advantage is obvious. However while acknowledging that, it should be noted that there is still a lot of work to be done—unfortunately Menchik is getting into time pressure (Bikova) and too often now she picks second rate moves—RT] **26. ... b6 27. ♕c1** [It is necessary to defend the a3 pawn, since on 27. ♘e4 could follow 27. ... ♗×a3 28. ♘×f6 g×f6 with the threats 29. ... f×e5 and 29. ... ♗b4—RT] **27. ... ♖f8 28. ♘e4 ♗b7 29. ♕d1!** A clever move. Black cannot take either of the offered pawns a3 and f4 in view of 30. ♕h5. **29. ... ♗f6** [29. ... ♗×a3 30. ♕h5 ♔g8 31. ♘g5 h6 32. ♘×e6 ♗×e6 33. ♗×e6+ winning at least the exchange; 29. ... ♖×f4 30. ♕h5 ♔g8 31. ♘c6 ♕c7 32. ♕e8+ ♗f8 33. ♘×d4 winning the pawn—RT] **30. ♕h5 ♗×e5 31. f×e5 h6 32. ♗c4 ♕c7 33. ♘g5** *(see diagram)*

After 33. ♘g5

33. ... ♘c5? [After move 31 Rabinovitch declared Black's position "helpless" but with 33. ... ♕e7 the game is far from over. Fritz calls it even 34. ♘f3 (the only move) ♕×a3 and it is still a game—RT] **34. ♘f3 ♖d8? 35. ♕g4 ♕d7 36. ♘h4 ♔g8?** [36. ... ♕e8 37. ♖f1 ♔h7 Keeps the game going for awhile, but is no fun being Black in this position—RT] **37. ♘f5 ♗b7** another bad move, but the game is hopeless. **38. ♘×h6+** Here the game was adjourned. Menchik resigned before the resumption. **1–0** (Source: Krylenko, *Moscow 1935*, translated by J. Adams, 1997; notes based on those of Ilya Rabinovitch [additional notes by RT]; Cordingly, *Moscow 1935*)

171 Menchik–Vladimir Alatortsev
Moscow 1935 (4), February 18, 1935
[D13] *Slav, Exchange*

The Slav Defense was coming into its own at this time. It was a major component of the soon to come Alekhine–Euwe matches. Despite its reputation as a drawing weapon, Alatortsev shows how to use it for a win when White does not play with energy. **1. ♘f3 d5 2. d4 ♘f6 3. c4 c6 4. c×d5 c×d5 5. ♘c3 ♘c6 6. ♗f4 a6 7. e3 ♗f5 8. ♖c1 ♖c8 9. ♗d3 ♗×d3 10. ♕×d3 e6 11. 0-0 ♗e7 12. h3 0-0 13. ♖fd1?!** Both Alatortsev and Fritz agree that 13. a3 is preferable to the text. In reality this may be more in showing Menchik to have no ambition in the game rather than in any objective weakness of 13. ♖fd1. It is evident that she was striving for the draw and to get on the scoreboard. The text, however, does not limit Black's position in any significant way. **13. ... ♘a5** Black's plan consists of occupying the c4 square and playing ... b5 which allows his to start play on the queenside. **14. ♘e5 ♘c4 15. ♕e2** It is clearly bad to capture the knight as, after 15. ♘×c4 d×c4 followed by b5, as Black gets an extra pawn on the queenside. However, she should retreat the queen to b1 where it would defend the somewhat weakened a and b pawns. **15. ... ♕a5 16. ♘d3 b5! 17. ♘c5!** [Fritz is not as convinced as Alatortsev about the merits of White's last move and finds the following to give White solid equality: 17. b3 ♘b6 18. ♘b1—RT] **17. ... ♗×c5 18. d×c5 ♖×c5!** Tempting here was 18. ... b4, but then follows 19. b3! with apparently sufficient defense in all variations: {1.} [18. ... b4 19. b3 b×c3 20. b×c4 ♖×c5 (if 20. ... ♕×c5 21. ♖×c3 indirectly defending the c4 pawn and intending 22. ♗e5 as well as 22. ♖dc1) 21. ♗d6 ♖×c4 22. ♗×f8 ♔×f8 23. ♖c2 In this variation Black has two pawns for the exchange, the result of the game is far from clear since the c3 pawn is in need of defense; {2.} (19. ... ♘a3 20. ♘a4 ♘e4 21. f3! ♘×c5 22. ♘×c5 (22. ♗d6? ♘×a4 23. ♗×f8 ♘c3 *and Black wins*) 22. ... ♖×c5 23. ♗d6 ♖×c1 24. ♖×c1 ♖e8 25. ♕d2 and White wins back the pawn with good position.) Ironically the computer finds this line preferable to that actually played by Black ... of course they did not have computers in the 1930s—RT] **19. b3 ♖fc8?** [Stronger was 19. ... ♘b6! 20. b4! ♕×b4 21. ♗d6 ♘c4! Giving up the exchange but obtaining in return two pawns and a solid pawn structure. In this variation Black retains serious chances of a win—RT] **20. b×c4! ♖×c4** *(see diagram)*

21. e4?? The decisive mistake. White apparently did not notice Black's 22nd move. [She should have played 21. ♗e5 ♘d7 22. ♗d4 e5 23. ♘×d5 ♖×c1 24. ♘e7+ ♔f8 25. ♘×c8 ♖×c8 26. ♗b2 and Black cannot hold onto his material advantage—RT] **21. ... ♖×c3 22. ♗d2 ♕×a2 23. ♖×c3 ♖×c3 24. e×d5**

After 20. ... ♖×c4

♘×d5 **25. ♕g4 ♖c5 26. ♕g3 ♖c8 27. ♗e3 ♕b3 0–1** (Source: Krylenko, *Moscow 1935*, translated by J. Adams, 1998; notes based on those by Alatortsev [additional notes by RT]; Cordingly, *Moscow 1935*)

172 Victor Goglidze–Menchik
Moscow (5), February 21, 1935

[D63] *Queen's Gambit Declined, Classical Variation*

This was one of the two shortest losses by Vera in her career.

1. d4 ♘f6 2. c4 e6 3. ♘c3 d5 4. ♗g5 ♘bd7 5. e3 ♗e7 6. ♘f3 0–0 7. ♖c1 b6 8. c×d5 e×d5 9. ♕a4 ♗b7 10. ♗a6 ♗×a6 11. ♕×a6 c5 12. 0–0 h6 13. ♗h4 ♕c8 14. ♕×c8 ♖a×c8 15. ♘e5 *(see diagram)*

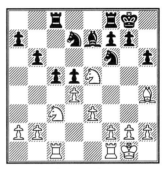

After 15. ♘e5

15. ... g5? It almost appears that at this time Vera took a nap as she certainly was not paying attention. [15. ... ♖fd8 16. ♖fd1 c4= and we still have a game—RT] **16. ♘×d7 ♘×d7 17. ♘×d5 ♗d6? 18. ♗g3 ♖c6? 19. ♘b4 1–0** (Source: Krylenko, *Moscow 1935*, translated by J. Adams, 1998; Cordingly, *Moscow 1935*)

173 Menchik–Georgy Lisitsin
Moscow (6), February 22, 1935

[A30] *English, Symmetrical*

1. ♘f3 ♘f6 2. c4 e6 3. g3 One of the solid methods of development, allowing White to successfully fight for the center. **3. ... b6 4. ♗g2 ♗b7 5. 0–0** [After 5. d4 a well known variation of the Queen's Indian Defense would have been reached—RT] **5. ... c5 6. ♘c3 ♗e7 7. d4 c×d4 8. ♘×d4 ♗×g2 9. ♔×g2 ♕c8 10. ♕d3 0–0 11. e4?** This is a positional mistake giving Black the rather better game. White strives to prevent the break ... d7–d5, not noticing Black's 14th move. Simpler and better here is 11. b3 followed by ♗b2 and ♖ad1. **11. ... ♘c6 12. ♘×c6** Perhaps even here she should prefer 12. b3 since the exchange only plays into Black's hands as he is preparing the break d7–d5. **12. ... ♕×c6 13. f3 ♖fd8!** As will be seen, the move d7–d5 is realized as a consequence of the bad position of the queen on d3. **14. b3?** *(see diagram)*

After 14. b3

[Now this natural move is a mistake. She should, of course make the break more difficult by means of 14. ♖d1—RT] **14. ... d5!** After this move Black's game already is preferable, since White has spent a great deal of time on mot very useful pawn moves e4, f3 etc. and allowed her opponent to outstrip her in development. **15. c×d5 e×d5 16. e5 d4!** This is the point of Black's whole idea. White cannot reply 17. e×f6? because of 17. ... d×c3 18. ♕e2 ♗×f6. **17. ♘d1?** This interferes with the freedom of the rooks as well as taking the eye off of the passed pawn [17. ♘e2 ♘d7 18. ♘×d4 ♕d5 19. ♗b2 seems to hold—RT] **17. ... ♘d7 18. ♗f4?** [If now 18. ♕×d4 then 18. ... ♘×e5! 19. ♕×e5 (Better is 19. ♕e4∓)—RT] **19. ... ♗f6** winning the exchange; better than the text (since she loses a pawn) was 18. 罝e1 罝ac8 with the advantage to Black—RT] **18. ... g5!** leading to the win of a pawn; the weakening of the king's flank plays a specific role here because of the poor placement of the White pieces. **19. 罝c1 豐e6 20. 鉬d2 幻×e5 21. 豐e4 f5!** Black endeavors to create a strong post for his knight, which is necessary for the final attack. **22. 豐e2 豐d5 23. 當g1 鉬c5 24. 豐g2 g4 25. f×g4 f×g4 26. 豐×d5+ 罝×d5 27. 當g2 幻f3 28. 鉬f4 罝e8 29. h3 h5 30. h×g4 h×g4 31. 幻f2 罝e2 32. b4 罝h5 0–1** (Source: Krylenko, *Moscow 1935*, translated by J. Adams, 1998; notes by G. Lisitsin; Cordingly, *Moscow 1935* [additional notes by RT])

174 Vyacheslav Ragozin–Menchik
Moscow (7), February 23, 1935
[A56] *Benoni Defense*

After 5. ... b5

1. d4 幻f6 2. c4 c5 3. d5 d6 4. 幻c3 g6 5. e4 b5? *(see diagram)*

After this move the game is for all intents over; Black never gets near equality. [5. ... 鉬g7—RT] **6. c×b5 鉬g7 7. 幻f3 0–0 8. 鉬e2 鉬b7 9. 0–0 幻bd7 10. 幻d2 豐c7 11. a4 a6 12. 幻c4 罝fb8 13. 豐c2 豐d8 14. 鉬d2 幻e8 15. 罝a3 e6 16. 幻e3 幻c7 17. 鉬c4 當h8 18. 豐b3 幻b6 19. d×e6 幻×c4 20. 豐×c4 a×b5?!** [20. ... 幻×e6 gives more resistance—RT] **21. 幻×b5 f×e6 22. 鉬c3 鉬c6?** This is merely the last nail in the coffin. **23. 鉬×g7+ 當×g7 24. 幻×c7 豐×c7 25. 豐×e6 罝e8 26. 幻f5+ 當f8 27. 豐f6+ 1–0** (Source: Krylenko, *Moscow 1935*, translated by J. Adams, 1998; Cordingly, *Moscow 1935*)

175 Menchik–Vasja Pirc
Moscow (8), February 24, 1935
[D35] *Queen's Gambit Declined, Exchange Variation*

1. d4 d5 2. c4 c6 3. 幻f3 幻f6 4. 幻c3 e6 5. c×d5 e×d5 6. 豐c2 鉬e7 7. 鉬f4 0–0 8. h3 罝e8 9. e3 幻bd7 10. 鉬d3 幻f8 11. 0–0–0!? Committing to the attack when 11. 0–0 would have been much safer. **11. ... b5 12. 幻e5 鉬b7 13. 當b1 豐b6 14. 罝c1** White finally goes over to the defense, building her game on prevention of c6–c5. However since this advance cannot be held back, all her maneuvers prove to be very weak. She should play for an attack on the Black king: 14. g4! a6 15. g5 幻h5 16. 鉬×h7+ 幻×h7 17. g6 f×g6 18. 豐×g6 and White's attack would guarantee at least a draw. This continuation, in any event, would have been the logical consequence of White's sharp 11th move 0–0–0—Yudovich in the tournament book. **14. ... 幻e6 15. 鉬h2 a6 16. 幻g4 h6 17. 罝hd1?!** [17. 幻×f6+ 鉬×f6 18. 幻e2 seems more in the spirit of the position—RT] **17. ... 罝ac8 18. 幻×f6+ 鉬×f6** *(see diagram)*

19. 鉬f5? This takes the bishop off the perfect d3 square and the defense of the queenside. [19. 豐b3 and everything holds. Best seems to be 19. ... 鉬h4 (For example 19. ... c5 will not work here due to 20. 幻×d5 鉬×d5 21. 豐×d5 c×d4 22. 罝×c8 罝×c8=) 20. g3 鉬f6 and White has a choice between g4 and

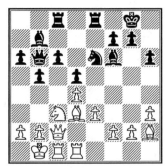
After 18. ... 鉬×f6

♘a4—RT] **19. ... c5 20. d×c5 ♖×c5 21. ♗×e6? ♛×e6 22. ♛d2 ♖ec8 23. ♗f4 b4 24. ♘e2 ♛e4+ 25. ♛d3 ♖×c1+ 26. ♘×c1 ♛×g2 0–1** (Source: Krylenko, *Moscow 1935*, translated by J. Adams, 1998; Cordingly, *Moscow 1935*)

176 Ilia Kan–Menchik

Moscow (9), February 27, 1935

[C07] *French, Tarrasch*

In this game Menchik found herself outplayed from early on to the very end of the game. It would seem she had no real plan and moved her pieces fairly aimlessly.

1. e4 e6 2. d4 d5 3. ♘d2 c5 4. d×c5 ♘c6 [Better is 4. ... ♗×c5—RT] **5. e×d5 e×d5 6. ♘b3 ♗×c5 7. ♘×c5 ♛a5+ 8. c3 ♛×c5** Already Black is in hot water due to White having the two bishops on an open board. **9. ♗e3 ♛a5 10. ♘f3 ♘ge7 11. ♗e2 0–0 12. 0–0 ♖d8 13. ♗d3 ♗f5 14. ♖e1 ♖ac8 15. ♘d4 ♗×d3 16. ♛×d3 ♘×d4 17. ♛×d4 ♘c6 18. ♛g4 ♘e5 19. ♛g3 f6 20. ♗d4** (see diagram)

20. ... ♘g6 21. h4 ♛b5 22. h5 ♘e5 23. f4 ♘c6 24. ♗×f6 ♖d7 25. ♛g4 1–0 (Source: Cordingly, *Moscow 1935*; Krylenko, *Moscow 1935*, translated by J. Adams, 1998)

After 20. ♗d4

177 Menchik–Emanuel Lasker

Moscow (10), February 28, 1935

[D52] *Queen's Gambit Declined, Cambridge Springs Variation*

This was Menchik's one game against the legendary Emanuel Lasker. Despite Ilya Rabinovitch's notes in the official tournament book, Vera obtained a decent opening. Lasker's advantages were the complicated nature of the position (his forte) and the bishop pair. His undefeated third place finish, only ½ point out of first, at age 63 is still considered an outstanding achievement.

1. d4 ♘f6 2. ♘f3 d5 3. c4 e6 4. ♗g5 ♘bd7 5. e3 c6 6. ♘c3 ♛a5 7. ♗×f6 Making it more difficult for Black to play c5 or e5 given the displacement of the knight on d7. **7. ... ♘×f6 8. ♗d3 d×c4** [More solid is 8. ... ♗b4 followed by c5. In this line however, Black will have to exchange on c3, simplifying the game, which does not fit into Lasker's plan—RT] **9. ♗×c4 a6 10. 0–0 ♗e7 11. a3** [According to Rabinovitch there is no better continuation. White is attempting to prevent ... c6–c5 by playing b4, but apparently does not take into account that after b4 Black can counterattack with a6–a5! Stronger is 11. ♛e2 followed by Rfd1 and e4. A bit of a dichotomy if as we are told there is nothing better than a3! Lastly Fritz shows only ⅛ point difference in the top 12 moves—all quite even—RT] **11. ... 0–0 12. b4 ♛c7 13. e4** [Better still is 13. ♛e2, so if 13. ... a5 14. b5; and if Black plays a preliminary 13. ... b5, then 14. ♗d3, and if 14. ... a5, then 15. ♖ab1 followed by a siege of the c6 pawn—RT] **13. ... a5!** The riskiness of the advances b2–b4 and e3–e4 already is evident: White cannot reply 14. b5 in view of 14. ... c×b5 winning a piece. **14. ♛b3 ♖d8 15. ♖fc1** [Better, apparently, was 15. b×a5 ♖×a5 16. a4! followed by ♖fe1 and ♖ad1—RT] **15. ... ♛f4** Already it is obvious that Lasker's risky experiment (8. ... d×c4, 9. ... a6 and 10. ♗e7 instead of the more solid 8. ... ♗b4) has succeeded: Black retains the two bishops as well as a solid position; however his white-squared bishop is still blocked in, while White's pawn center is still intact. [What this says is enigmatic, at least in terms of who is winning. Computer analysis shows White to be holding her own although with plenty of opportunities to go wrong; this is the type of position Dr. Lasker would have thrived in—RT] **16. e5** With this and particularly the next move White spoils her position. [More to the point would have been 16. ♗d3 on which Black would probably replied 16. ... a×b4 17. a×b4 ♗d7 with a difficult maneuvering struggle for both sides—RT] **16. ... ♘d5 17. ♗×d5?** A hard move to understand; which frees the bishop on c8. Apparently White feared an imaginary attack on the weakened d4 pawn. It is possible, however,

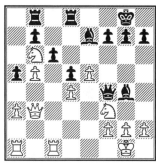

After 20. ... ♗g4

that she overlooked Black's 20th move. [Correct was 17. b5, still retaining a good game—RT] **17. ... e×d5 18. b5 ♗d7** [Not 18. ... ♗g4 19. ♘e2 ♕e4 20. ♘g3 ♕f4 21. ♘e2 forcing a draw—RT] **19. ♘a4 ♖ab8 20. ♘b6** [Better is 20. ♘c3 with a slight pull for Black—RT] **20. ... ♗g4!** *(see diagram)*

21. b×c6? [Also after 21. ♖d1 f6 White's position is unenviable. (Significantly better than either of the above choices was 21. ♕e3 ♕×e3 22. f×e3 where Black's bishop pair and experience may well win, but there is still a lot of play left)— RT] **21. ... b×c6 22. ♖×c6 ♗×f3 23. ♕×f3** [Not 23. g×f3 ♕×d4 24. ♖e1 in view of 24. ... ♗c5—RT] **23. ... ♕×d4 24. ♖d1 ♕×e5** White cannot take on d5 due to the mate threat. **25. g3 d4 26. ♕d3 ♗f6 27. ♖dc1 ♕e8 28. ♕f3 d3 29. ♖×f6** Desperation. [If for example 29. ♖d1 d2 30. ♘c4 (or 30. ♘d5 ♖×d5) 30. ... ♕e1+ 31. ♔g2 ♖b1! 32. ♖×b1 ♕×b1 33. ♘×d2 ♖×d2 34. ♖c8+ ♖d8 and wins—RT] **29. ... d2! 30. ♖d1 g×f6 31. ♘d5 ♖×d5 0–1** (Source: Cordingly, *Moscow 1935*; Krylenko, *Moscow 1935*, translated by J. Adams, 1998; notes based on those of Ilya Rabinovitch [additional notes by RT])

178 Fyodor Bohatirchuk–Menchik
Moscow (11), March 1, 1935
[E87] *King's Indian, Sämisch Variation*

A very interesting game which resulted in Menchik's first drawing of blood with a draw. Bohatirchuk vacillates in his play and in the book tries to justify this. It seems obvious that he was very afraid of losing when the position became unclear and the goal became do not lose rather than aim for the win with some risk.

1. d4 ♘f6 2. c4 c5 3. d5 e5 4. ♘c3 d6 5. e4 g6 6. f3 ♗g7 7. ♗e3 0–0 8. ♗d3 ♘e8 9. ♘ge2 ♘d7 10. ♕d2 a6 11. 0–0–0? White puts his king in the line of fire. **11. ... ♘c7 12. ♔b1 ♘f6 13. h4 ♗d7 14. a4?!** 14. h5!? b5 15. h×g6 f×g6 After all is said and done this is at least as good as if not better than 14. a4 **14. ... b5! 15. a×b5 a×b5 16. ♘×b5** *(see diagram)*

16. ... ♘a6 16. ... ♘×b5 17. c×b5∓ **17. ♘ec3** Bohatirchuk awards the following a question mark due to the loss of the exchange—Fritz finds it the best continuation with an edge to White. 17. ♘×d6 ♗a4 with the computer suggesting 18. ♘b5

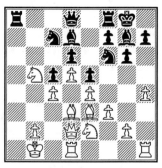

After 16. ♘×b5

♗×d1 19. ♖×d1 ♕b6 20. g4 ♘c7± **17. ... ♗×b5 18. ♘×b5 ♘b4 19. ♕c3 ♘e8 20. ♕b3 ♘c7 21. ♗d2 ♘×b5 22. c×b5 ♕a5 23. ♗×b4 c×b4 24. g4 f5 25. ♖hf1 ♖fc8 26. ♗c4 f4 27. ♖c1 ♗f6 28. h5 g5 29. ♕a2 ♕b6 30. ♕b3 ♕a5 31. ♕a2 ½–½** (Source: Krylenko, *Moscow 1935*, translated by J. Adams, 1998; Cordingly, *Moscow 1935*; notes by RT)

179 Menchik–Vitaly Chekhover

Moscow (12), March 2, 1935

[E38] *Nimzo-Indian, Classical Variation*

An interesting game where Vera held a modest advantage for the first third, Checkhover for the second third, and in the last third the position deteriorated for Menchik.

1. d4 ♘f6 2. c4 e6 3. ♘c3 ♗b4 4. ♕c2 c5 5. d×c5 ♘c6 6. ♘f3 ♗×c5 7. ♗g5 h6 8. ♗h4 0–0 9. ♖d1 ♗e7 10. e3 b6 11. ♗e2 ♗b7 12. 0–0 ♖c8 13. ♕a4! a6 14. ♗g3 From here the White advantage dissipates and Black slowly takes over. [Better is 14. ♖d2—RT] **14. ... ♘a5 15. ♘e5 d6 16. b4 ♘c6 17. ♗f3 ♕c7 18. ♘d3 ♘b8 19. ♗×b7 ♕×b7 20. ♕b3 ♕c6 21. ♘a4? b5! 22. c×b5 a×b5 23. ♘ab2 ♘e4 24. ♖c1 ♕b7 25. ♖×c8 ♖×c8 26. ♖c1 ♖×c1+ 27. ♘×c1 h5!** Provoking White to create weaknesses on her kingside. **28. f3 ♘×g3 29. h×g3 d5 30. ♘e2 ♘c6 31. ♘d3?** ***(see diagram)***

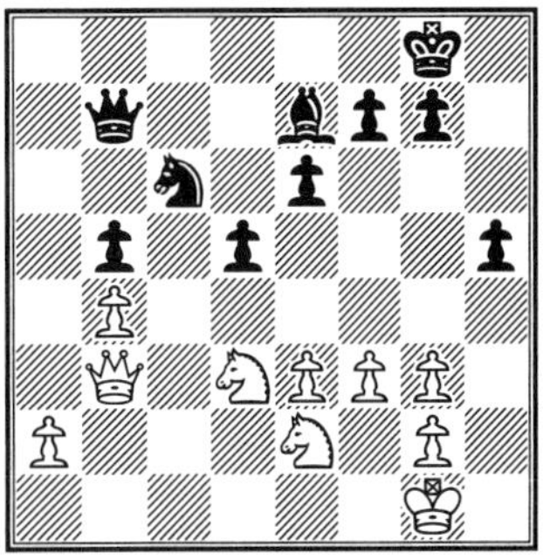
After 31. ♘d3

Despite the relative simplicity of the position the game is virtually over—too many weaknesses. [31. a3—RT] **31. ... ♕a7 32. ♔f2 d4 33. e×d4 ♘×d4 34. ♘×d4 ♕×d4+ 35. ♔e2 ♗d6 36. f4 g5 37. ♔f3 h4 38. f×g5 h×g3 39. g6 ♕f6+ 40. ♔e3 ♕×g6 41. ♕c3 ♕g5+ 42. ♔e2 ♕d5 0–1** (Source: Krylenko, *Moscow 1935*, translated by J. Adams, 1998; Cordingly, *Moscow 1935*)

180 Andor Lilienthal–Menchik

Moscow (13), March 5, 1935

[C14] *French, Classical*

A frustrating game. After a solid drawn game we get into the moves of the 30s where both sides seem determined not to see promising ideas and in the last 30 moves or so White consistently misses opportunities to virtually put the game away—only some of which I have pointed out. An endgame ensues that is hard to believe at this level.

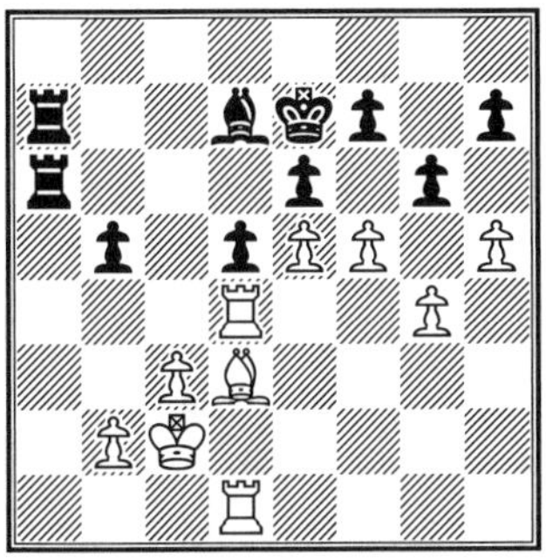
After 34. h5

1. e4 e6 2. d4 d5 3. ♘c3 ♘f6 4. ♗g5 ♗e7 5. e5 ♘fd7 6. h4 c5 7. ♕g4? ♘c6 8. ♗×e7 ♔×e7 9. ♕g5+ ♔f8 10. ♕×d8+ ♘×d8 11. f4 ♘c6 12. ♘f3 a6 13. 0–0–0 b5 14. g3 ♘×d4 15. ♘×d4 c×d4 16. ♖×d4 ♔e7 17. ♗h3 ♖d8 18. ♖f1 ♗b7 19. ♘d1 ♖e8 20. ♘e3 ♔d8 21. ♖fd1 ♖c8 22. ♔b1 ♖c7 23. a4 ♔e7 24. a×b5 a×b5 25. ♗f1 ♗c6 26. c3 ♖a8 27. ♘c2 ♘c5 28. ♗d3 g6 29. g4 ♖b7 30. ♘b4 ♗d7 31. ♔c2 ♘a6 32. ♘×a6 ♖×a6 33. f5 ♖ba7 34. h5 ***(see diagram)***

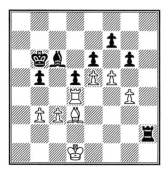

After 49. ... ♖h2

34. ... ♖a1 34. ... e×f5 35. g×f5= **35. ♖×a1?** Winning looks to be 35. h×g6! h×g6 36. f×g6 f×g6 37. ♗×g6+– **35. ... ♖×a1 36. h×g6 h×g6 37. ♔b3 ♖a8?!** Better being 37. ... e×f5 38. g×f5 g×f5 39. ♔b4 ♔e6 Where the chances, such as they may be reside with Black **38. ♔b4?!** 38. f×g6 f×g6 39. ♗×g6 ♖a1 40. ♗d3 ♖e1± **38. ... ♔d8 39. ♔c5? ♖c8+ 40. ♔b4 ♔c7 41. ♗f1 ♔b6 42. ♖d2 ♖h8 43. b3? ♖h4 44. ♖d4 ♖h1 45. ♗d3 ♗c6 46. ♔a3 ♖d1 47. ♔b2 ♖d2+ 48. ♔c1 ♖f2 49. ♔d1 ♖h2** (*see diagram*)

50. ♗e2 Again with 50. f×g6 f×g6 51. ♗×g6 and little doubt of the win **50. ... ♔c5 51. b4+ ♔b6 52. ♔d2 ♖h3 53. ♖d3 ♖×d3+ 54. ♔×d3 ♗d7 55. ♔d4 ♗c6 56. ♗f3 ♗d7 57. ♔e3 ♔c6 58. ♔f2 ♗c8 ½–½** (Source: Krylenko, *Moscow 1935*, translated by J. Adams, 1998; Cordingly, *Moscow 1935*; *Chess*, August 1944, #1804; notes by RT)

181 Menchik–Salo Flohr
Moscow (14), March 6, 1935
[D00] *Queen's Pawn Game*

This game turned out to be one of Menchik's most important; see the full story in Part I. The notes were compiled for a posthumous tribute in *Chess Magazine* in November 1944 and are a composite of those by Menchik and those in *L'Echequier* magazine.

1. d4 d5 2. ♘c3 This opening has received scant attention from the analysts, and if only for this reason it appears deserving of a lease on life. Combine with the idea of forcing an early e4 it appears to have quite a lot in its favor. **2. ... ♗f5 3. ♗f4** [Menchik: I did not adopt the system 3. f3 and e4 in this game, considering that after ... ♘f6 ... e6 and ... c5 complications would occur.] **3. ... e6 4. e3 ♗d6** Flohr also desires to avoid complications, preferring to aim for a simple game where he can make use of his magnificent technique; but this time he meets his match. **5. ♗d3 ♗g6** [This looks like a bit of wood shifting. Why not get on with the development by 5. ... ♘f6. It is not much use having a technique if you do not give it a chance to get going—RT] **6. ♘f3 ♘e7 7. ♘e5** With the idea of exchanging so as to be left with bishop against knight. Black's fifth move is having awkward repercussions. **7. ... a6** To prevent ♘b5 with further exchanging. Tarrasch would doubtless have been quite explosive in his observations on all this play. **8. ♕d2 c5 9. ♘×g6 h×g6** (*see diagram*)

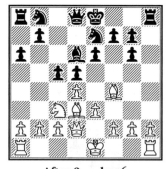

After 9. ... h×g6

Note how Flohr's technique has steered into a simple type of game with bold strategic features. He now hopes to make something of the open file plus the fact that White cannot very well castle on either wing. **10. ♗×d6** [Well played. If 10. 0-0-0 c4 11. ♗e2 b5 with an attack; and if 10. d×c5 ♗×c5 11. 0-0-0 ♗b4 with complications. Castling on the queenside entered into my plans; but by castling at once I was in danger of ... c5 with an ensuing advance of the queenside pawns, and thus I considered it necessary to exchange. The capture of the Black bishop had to precede the exchange on c5 for this bishop might have displayed the activity of the queenside—RT] **10. ... ♕×d6 11. d×c5 ♕×c5 12. ♘e2 ♕d6** Probably by this move Flohr wished to parry the threat of the exchange of queens after 13. ♕c3. **13. f4** With this move I control e5 and prepare a place d'armes for the ♘ at d4. **13. ... ♕b6** White's e3 is a weakness which must be put under pressure. **14. 0-0-0 ♘bc6 15. c3 0-0-0 16. ♔b1 ♔b8 17. ♘d4 ♔a8** Flohr's move is difficult to understand; probably he intended to await my mistakes! **18. h3 ♘c8 19. ♖he1 ♘d6 20. ♘×c6** Necessary exchange as ♘a5 and threatening occupation of c4. **20. ... ♕×c6** [20. ... b×c6 followed by ... ♖b8; looks more promising for attacking purposes, but Flohr has his eye on ... ♘c4 with positional pressure—RT] **21. ♕e2 ♖he8 22. ♗c2** [White cannot play 22. e4 ♘×e4 23. ♗×e4 d×e4 24. ♖×d8+ ♖×d8 25. ♕×e4 ♖d1+ 26. ♔c2 ♖×e1 27. ♕×e1 ♕×g2+ etc.—RT] **22. ... f5** Black has now fixed the weakness and threatens ... e5 to expose it. **23. ♕d2 ♕b6** [There was nothing in 23. ... ♘e4 24. ♗×e4 d×e4 25. ♕×d8+ ♖×d8 26. ♖×d8+ ♔a7 27. ♖d4 followed by ♖ed1—RT] **24. ♕d4 ♕c7 25. g4!** Having made herself safe against ... e5 White can now endeavor to open the g-file so as to get pressure on the weak g-pawn, thus setting up a state of equilibrium from which the draw comes naturally. **25. ... ♖h8 26. g×f5 ♘b5 27. ♕d2 g×f5 28. ♖g1 ♖×h3 29. ♖g6** *(see diagram)*

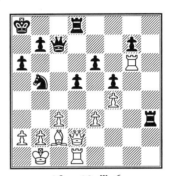

After 29. ♖g6

29. ... ♕b6 [Better than going on the defensive by 29. ... ♕d7 30. ♖dg1 ♖h7 31. ♕g2 ♖g8 32. ♕g5 and Black is completely tied up (Crafty feels that Black is still with a strong position.)—RT] **30. ♗×f5 ♖×e3 31. ♗d3 ♖f3 32. ♗×b5 a×b5 33. ♖×g7 ♖f8 34. ♖g4** [Capablanca considered that here the stronger move was 34. ♖g6 but unfortunately a great lack of time gave me no chance to calculate all the variations (Note after 34. ... Qe3 the position is still drawn)—RT] **34. ... ♖f2 35. ♕d4 ♔a7 36. ♕×b6+ ♔×b6 37. ♖d4 ♔c5 38. a3 ♖f6 39. ♖b4 ♔c6 40. ♔a2 ♖e2 41. ♖h4 ♖e4** The position is drawn and Flohr's further attempts lead to nothing. **42. ♔b3 ♖c4 43. ♖g4 ♔c5 44. ♖h4 ♖×b4+ 45. a×b4+ ♔d6 46. ♔c2 b6 47. ♔d3 ♖g6 48. ♖h7 ♖g3+ 49. ♔e2 d4 50. ♖b7 ♔c6 51. ♖e7 d×c3 52. b×c3 ♔d5 53. ♔d2 ♖f3 54. ♖d7+ ♔c4 55. ♖d6 ♖×f4 56. ♖×e6 ♖f2+ 57. ♔e3** ½-½ (Source: Krylenko, *Moscow 1935*, translated by J. Adams, 1998; Cordingly, *Moscow 1935*; *Chess* Nov. 1944 #1829; notes by V.M. and B.H. Wood [additional notes by RT])

Menchik's result in the above Flohr game was immensely popular with the Muscovites. One of many messages (this in the form of a telegram) was, "Moscow tournament to Vera Menchik draw with Flohr—brilliant victory. Warmly congratulate and firmly shake hand—Engineers of Rutchenkovsky factory No. 2."[51] The fact that her draw prevented the Czech from moving ahead of the Soviet Botvinnik might have had something to do with the public frenzy!

182 Ilya Rabinovitch–Menchik
Moscow (15), March 7, 1935
[E72] *King's Indian Defense*

One of the frequent criticisms leveled at Menchik by the annotators (players) of the tournament book was her passivity. This game could have been the standard for that behavior. It is also a bear for an annotator as it is a game of lots of maneuvering without too many grand

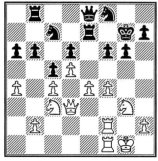

After 23. ♖af1

tactics—at least for the first 25 to 30 moves. Throw away your computer. Still there is no question that with a little more dynamic play early on she might have saved this game. **1. d4 ♘f6 2. c4 g6 3. g3 c5 4. d5 d6 5. ♘c3 ♗g7 6. ♗g2 0-0 7. e4 e5 8. ♘ge2 ♘bd7 9. 0-0 ♘e8 10. ♗e3 ♖b8 11. ♕d2 a6 12. a4 b6 13. ♗g5 f6 14. ♗h6 ♘c7 15. ♗×g7 ♔×g7 16. ♕d3 ♖f7 17. f4 ♕e8 18. ♗h3 e×f4 19. g×f4 ♖e7 20. ♘g3 ♘f8 21. ♗×c8 ♖×c8 22. ♖f2 ♖b8 23. ♖af1** (*see diagram*)

23. ... ♘d7 24. h4 ♔g8 25. ♖g2 ♖g7 26. ♔h2 ♕d8 27. ♖h1 ♖b7 28. h5 ♘f8 29. ♔g1 b5 30. c×b5 a×b5 31. a×b5 ♘×b5 32. ♘×b5 ♕b6 33. ♕c3 ♕×b5 34. ♕×f6 g×h5 35. ♖×h5 ♕a6 36. ♖f5 ♖bf7 37. ♕c3 ♖×f5? But the game is virtually over anyway. **38. ♘×f5 ♖×g2+ 39. ♔×g2 1-0** (Source: Krylenko, *Moscow 1935*, translated by J. Adams, 1998; Cordingly, *Moscow 1935*)

183 Menchik–Rudolf Spielmann
Moscow (16), March 8, 1935
[A45] Bird's Opening

1. e3 ♘f6 2. f4 g6 3. ♘f3 ♗g7 4. d4 c5 5. c3 b6 6. ♗d3 ♗b7 7. 0-0 0-0 8. ♕e2 ♘e4 9. b3 d5 10. ♗b2 ♘d7 11. ♘bd2 ♘df6 12. ♖ac1 a6 13. ♖fd1 b5 14. c4 ♘×d2 15. ♖×d2 d×c4 16. b×c4 b×c4 17. ♖×c4 c×d4 18. ♗×d4 ♖c8 19. ♖dc2 ♖×c4 20. ♗×c4 ♘d5 21. ♗×g7 ♔×g7 22. ♖d2 ♕a5 23. ♖d3 ♖c8 24. ♕b2+ ♘f6 25. ♕×b7 ♖×c4 26. ♕b2 ♕c5 27. ♘d4?? [27. h3 ♖c2 28. ♕b3 and White can still put up a struggle—RT] **27. ... ♖c1+ 28. ♔f2 ♕h6 29. h3 ♘e4+ 30. ♔e2 ♖g1 0-1** (Source: Krylenko, *Moscow 1935*, translated by J. Adams, 1998; Cordingly, *Moscow 1935*)

184 José Raúl Capablanca–Menchik
Moscow (17), March 11, 1935
[E85] King's Indian, Sämisch Variation

This is an interesting game, in which Capablanca jumps to a quick spatial advantage. He then maneuvers until he feels it time to press the attack. Menchik makes a few errors in the ending, but there was little doubt as to who the ultimate winner would be.

1. d4 ♘f6 2. c4 g6 3. ♘c3 ♗g7 4. e4 d6 5. f3 0-0 6. ♗e3 e5 7. ♘ge2 a6 8. ♕d2 ♗d7 9. d5 ♘e8 10. g4 h6 11. h4 ♔h7 12. ♘g3 c5 13. ♗d3 ♕a5 14. ♕e2 ♖h8 15. a3 ♕d8 16. b4 b6 17. ♕b2 ♗c8 18. ♔e2 ♘d7 19. ♖ag1 ♖b8 20. b5 a5 21. ♔d1 ♔g8 22. ♕d2 ♘f8 23. ♔c2 f6 24. g5 f×g5 25. h×g5 h5 (*see diagram*)

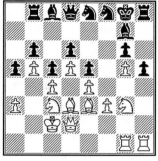

After 25. ... h5

26. ♘f5!? ♔f7? [26. ... g×f5 27. e×f5—RT] **27. ♘h4** [Somewhat better would have been 27. ♘h6+ ♔e7 28. ♖f1 ♘d7 best 29. f4 e×f4 30. ♖×f4 ♘e5 (30. ... ♗×h6 31. g×h6 ♘e5 32. ♖ff1 ♔d7 33. ♗g5 ♕c7 34. ♖×h5 ♗b7 (*34. ... g×h5 35. ♕f4 ♕d8 36. ♕f7+ ♘×f7 37. ♖×f7+ ♔e7 38. ♖×e7+ ♔d8 39. ♖h7+*)) 31. ♖hf1+—RT] **27. ... ♕e7 28. ♔h2 ♘c7 29. ♖f1 ♔e8??**

30. f4 e×f4 31. B×f4 Qd7?? 32. B×d6 1–0 (Source: Krylenko, *Moscow 1935*, translated by J. Adams, 1998; Cordingly, *Moscow 1935*)

185 Gideon Ståhlberg–Menchik
Moscow (18), March 12, 1935
[D37] Queen's Gambit Declined

1. Nf3 d5 2. d4 Nf6 3. c4 e6 4. Nc3 Nbd7 5. Bf4 d×c4 6. e3 Nb6 7. B×c4 N×c4 8. Qa4+ c6 9. Q×c4 Be7 10. 0-0 0-0 11. Rad1 Qa5 12. e4 b5 13. Q×c6 Bd7 14. Qb7 b4 15. Bc7 Qh5 16. e5 b×c3 17. e×f6 B×f6 18. b×c3 Bb5 19. Rfe1 Bc4 20. Qb2 Qd5 21. Ra1 Rfc8 22. Bg3 a5 23. Nd2 Bd3 24. Rac1 a4 25. Nf1 a3 26. Qd2 B×f1 27. R×f1 Bg5 28. f4 Bd8 29. Rb1 Rab8 30. Qc2 Ba5 31. f5 R×b1 32. R×b1 e×f5 33. Rb3 h6 34. Qd3 Bc7 [Much better is 34. ... Qb3 35. a×b3 a2 36. Qf1 B×c3—RT] **35. c4 Qd7 36. B×c7 Q×c7 37. c5 Re8 38. Rb1 Qa5 39. Kf2 f4 40. c6 f3 41. d5 f×g2 42. K×g2 Qc5 43. Kh1 g6 44. Rd1 Rb8 45. Qf3 Qd6 46. Qg3 Qb4 47. c7 Re8 48. d6 Qb2 49. Kg1 Re2 50. d7 1–0** (Source: Krylenko, *Moscow 1935*, translated by J. Adams, 1998; Cordingly, *Moscow 1935*)

186 Menchik–Pyotr Romanovski
Moscow (19), March 14, 1935
[A02] Irregular

1. e3 d6 2. b3 Nf6 3. Bb2 g6 4. f4 Bg7 5. Nf3 0-0 6. Be2 Nc6 7. Qc1 e5 8. 0-0 e×f4 9. e×f4 Re8 10. Nc3 d5 11. Bb5 Bd7 12. B×c6 B×c6 13. Ne5 d4 14. Ne2 Ng4 15. B×d4 Qd5 16. Rf3 N×e5 17. f×e5 B×e5 18. B×e5 R×e5 19. Rf2 Rae8 20. Nf4 Qd7 21. Qf1 Re4 22. Rd1 Bb5 23. d3 Re3 24. c4 Bc6 25. d4 Be4 26. d5 Qd6 27. Rfd2 Bf3 28. g×f3 Q×f4 29. Rf2 b6 30. Kh1 R8e5 31. Qh3 f5 32. Qg3 Re1+ 33. R×e1 R×e1+ 34. Kg2 Qc1 35. Q×c7 Rg1+ 0–1 (Source: Krylenko, *Moscow 1935*, translated by J. Adams, 1998; Cordingly, *Moscow 1935*)

Margate 1935
April 24–May 3, 1935

		1	2	3	4	5	6	7	8	9	10	Points	Place
1	Reshevsky, Samuel	•	1	=	=	1	1	1	=	1	1	7½	1
2	Capablanca, José R.	0	•	1	=	1	1	=	1	1	1	7	2
3	Thomas, George	=	0	•	=	=	1	=	1	=	=	5	3
4	Klein, Ernst Ludwig	=	=	=	•	0	=	1	0	1	=	4½	4–6
5	Reilly, Brian P.	0	0	=	1	•	=	1	=	0	1	4½	4–6
6	Sergeant, Edward G.	0	0	0	=	=	•	=	1	1	1	4½	4–6
7	Fairhurst, William A.	0	=	=	0	0	=	•	=	1	1	4	7
8	Milner-Barry, Philip S.	=	0	0	1	=	0	=	•	0	1	3½	8
9	Menchik, Vera	0	0	=	0	1	0	0	1	•	0	2½	9
10	Mieses, Jacques	0	0	=	=	0	0	0	0	1	•	2	10

The Margate tournaments were created along the same lines as the Hastings tournaments with multiple round robin sections, each with about 10 players. In the premier event 120 players competed. Held at Easter time, one of the major organizers and fundraisers was Vera's future husband, Rufus H.S. (Henry) Stevenson.

187 Ernst Klein–Menchik

Margate (1), April 24, 1935

[D00] *Irregular Opening*

After 10. ... 罝×e5

1. d4 ♘f6 2. ♘f3 g6 3. ♘c3 This move (whereby White refrains from any dogmatic attempt to obtain the advantage and is content to post his pieces on good squares) is not the best objectively, but it leads to interesting play. **3. ... d5 4. ♗g5 ♗g7 5. e3 0-0 6. ♗d3 ♘bd7 7. ♘e2 罝e8** Since ... c5 can now be answered by c3, Black plays for the advance of the e-pawn. **8. 0-0 e5 9. d×e5 ♘×e5 10. ♘×e5 罝×e5** *(see diagram)*

11. ♗f4 [Klein believed that he could now have refuted Black's opening with 11. f4 罝×e3 12. f5, etc. White would obtain a dangerous attack, to be sure, but only a close analysis could justify a positive statement as to its outcome. Fritz is not sanguine about White's chances and gives the following sample line: 12. ... 罝e8 13. f×g6 f×g6 14. 豐d2 豐d6 15. ♗×f6 ♗×f6∓ — RT] **11. ... 罝e8 12. ♘g3 ♘d7 13. c3!** ♘c5 The text seems to force some such move as ♘e2 to create a retreat for the bishop, but Klein has a clever resource available. [On 13. ... g5 White would save his pieces with 14. ♘h5 not 14. ... g×f4? 15. 豐g4—RT] **14. ♗c2 g5?** This attractive move is a mistake. [With 14. ... ♘e6 Menchik would have had an excellent game—RT] **15. ♘h5! g×f4** [Although Reinfeld is right that the Black's 14th move was an error, the bigger mistake is on move 15. Black still has a game after 15. ... ♗h8 16. ♗g3 ♘e4—RT] **16. ♘×g7 豐×g7 17. 豐d4+ 豐f6 18. 豐×c5 f3 19. 豐×d5 f×g2 20. 罝fe1** [Better than 20. 豐×g2+ ♔h8 21. ♔h1 ♗d7! with a dangerous attack—RT] **20. ... 罝e5 21. 豐d1!** Another fine defensive move, which prevents ... 罝h5 and threatens to force the exchange of queens with f4 and 豐d4. **21. ... ♗e6 22. f4 罝d5 23. 豐e2 罝ad8 24. 罝ad1 罝×d1 25. 罝×d1 罝×d1+ 26. 豐×d1 豐h6** [Not 26. ... ♗×a2 27. 豐d3 followed by b3 etc.—RT] **27. 豐d4+** [27. a3 at once was simpler; but White was in time-pressure (Klein)—RT] **27. ... f6 28. a3 豐h4** Since the g-pawn cannot live very long, Black must seek compensation in tactical threats. **29. 豐d2 ♔h8 30. ♗e4 c6 31. ♗×g2 f5 32. h3 ♔g8 33. ♔h2 ♔f7 34. 豐e2** The best chance. **34. ... ♗d5! 35. ♗×d5+ c×d5 36. 豐g2 ♔f6 37. 豐×d5 豐f2+ 38. 豐g2 豐×e3 39. 豐g5+ ♔e6 40. 豐g8+** *(see diagram)*

After 40. 豐g8+

40. ... ♔d6? [40. ... ♔f6 would very likely have drawn. The unfortunate text allows Klein to force a clever win—RT] **41. 豐f8+! ♔c7 42. 豐g7+ ♔b8 43. 豐g8+ ♔c7 44. 豐×h7+ ♔c6 45. 豐g6+ ♔c7 46. 豐g1 豐e2+ 47. 豐g2 豐e3 48. 豐g7+ ♔c8 49. 豐h8+ 1-0** (Source: Reinfeld, *Margate 1935* [additional notes by RT])

188 Menchik–José Raúl Capablanca

Margate (2), April 25, 1935

[A48] *Irregular Opening*

1. e3 g6 2. d4 ♗g7 3. ♗d3 c5 4. c3 ♘f6 5. ♘f3 b6 6. 0-0 ♗b7 7. 豐e2 0-0 8. 罝e1

♘e4 9. b3 f5 10. ♗b2 e6 11. ♘fd2 d5 12. f3 ♘d6 13. ♘a3 e5 14. d×e5 ♗×e5 15. ♘f1 ♕f6 16. ♖ac1 ♕g7 17. ♖c2 ♖e8 18. ♔h1 a6 19. c4 ♗×b2 20. ♖×b2 d4 21. ♕f2 ♘c6 22. ♖d2 d×e3 23. ♘×e3 ♘d4 24. ♘ac2 f4 25. ♘d5 ♖×e1+ 26. ♕×e1 ♖e8 *(see diagram)*

27. ♗e4?? Best is 27. ♕d1 ♗×d5 28. c×d5 b5 29. ♘×d4 c×d4 30. ♗c2 and all is even **27. ... ♘×e4 28. f×e4 ♘×c2 29. ♖×c2 ♗×d5 30. c×d5 ♖×e4 31. ♕f1 ♕e5 32. ♖c1 f3 33. g×f3 ♖e2 34. ♕h3 ♕×d5 35. b4 ♕d2 0–1** (Source: Reinfeld, *Margate 1935*; note by RT)

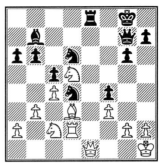

After 26. ... ♖e8

189 William Fairhurst–Menchik
Margate (3), April 26, 1935

[E72] *King's Indian Defense*

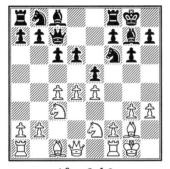

After 9. h3

1. d4 ♘f6 2. c4 g6 3. g3 ♗g7 4. ♗g2 0–0 5. e4 d6 6. ♘e2 c6 7. ♘bc3 ♕c7 8. 0–0 e5 9. h3 *(see diagram)*

9. ... h6?! Much of Black's play over the next few moves is lackadaisical, allowing White to place his pieces well and ultimately gain a passed d pawn that essentially decides the game. White needs to pre-empt this play and place her own pieces in commanding positions. [9. ... e×d4 10. ♘×d4 ♖e8=— RT] **10. ♗e3 ♘bd7** [Black's last chance to get in 10. ... e×d4 11. ♘×d4 ♖e8 12. ♕d2 ♔h7 although the benefits are somewhat diminished with White's bishop on e3—RT] **11. ♖c1 ♖d8 12. ♕d2 ♔h7 13. f4 a6 14. f×e5 d×e5 15. d5 c5 16. ♖f2 ♕d6 17. ♖cf1 ♖b8 18. a4 b6 19. ♘c1 ♖f8 20. ♘d3 ♕e7 21. a5! b5** [If 21. ... b×a5 22. ♘a4—RT] **22. ♘×c5 ♘×c5 23. d6 ♕e6 24. ♗×c5 ♕×c4 25. ♕e3 ♘d7** [Better is 25. ... b4—RT] **26. ♗a7 ♖b7 27. ♘d5 ♘b8 28. ♗×b8 ♖×b8 29. ♖×f7 ♖×f7 30. ♖×f7 ♗e6** *(see diagram)*

31. ♘f6+ ♔h8 32. ♕×h6+ 1–0 (Source: Reinfeld, *Margate 1935* [additional notes by RT])

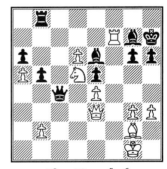

After 30. ... ♗e6

190 George Thomas–Menchik
Margate (4), April 27, 1935

[A09] *Réti's Opening*

This has to be one of the most fiendishly outlandish chess games between two masters ever. Menchik starts with a bizarre gambit that appears to leave Sir George so rattled he cannot win any of the numerous opportunities he is granted. Punctuation marks lose their meaning or impact.

1. ♘f3 d5 2. c4 ♗f5 3. ♕b3 d×c4 4. ♕×b7 ♘d7 5. ♘c3 e5 6. ♘×e5 ♖b8 7. ♕f3 [7. ♕c6 ♕f6 8. f4+——RT] **7. ... ♘×e5 8. ♕×f5 ♗d6 9. g3** [9. f4! With the idea of 9. ... ♕d7

After 12. ... ♘g4

10. ♕xd7+ ♘xd7 11. e3 ♘b6 12. b3 cxb3 13. axb3—RT]
9. ... ♘e7 10. ♕c2 0-0 11. ♗g2 f5? Maybe the point is "in for a penny in for a dollar." **12. f4 ♘g4 (see diagram)**

13. 0-0? [13. ♘b5! seems decisive. 13. ... ♕d7 14. ♕xc4+ ♔h8 15. ♘xd6 cxd6 16. b3—RT] **13. ... ♗c5+ 14. e3 ♕d3 15. ♕xd3 cxd3 16. b3 ♘c8 17. ♖d1 ♘d6 18. ♘d5 ♘e4 19. ♘xc7 ♖f6 20. ♘d5?!** [Better is 20. h3—RT] **20. ... ♖c6?** [20. ... ♖h6 21. ♗xe4 fxe4—RT] **21. ♗xe4?** [21. ♗b2—RT] **21. ... fxe4 22. ♗b2 ♖d8 23. ♘c3 ♘xe3? 24. dxe3 ♗xe3+ 25. ♔g2 ♗d4 26. ♖ac1 ♖dc8 27. ♘xe4 ♖c2+ 28. ♖d2?! ♗xb2 29. ♖cd1 ♗c1 (see**

diagram)

30. ♖xc2 ♖xc2+ 31. ♔f3 d2 32. ♘e2 ♖xa2 33. ♘xd2 ♗a3 34. ♔d3 ♗b4 35. ♘f3 a5 36. ♖c1?! [36. ♔d4 with the idea of ♖d3—RT] **36. ... h6** [36. ... ♖b2 37. ♖c8+ ♔f7 ± —RT] **37. ♖c8+ ♔f7 38. ♖c2 ♖a1** A matter of confidence no doubt. Which way is more (if at all) or more readily likely to bring about the draw. To trade rooks or not—that was her question. **39. ♔e4 ♖b1 40. ♘e5+ ♔e7 41. ♘c6+ ♔f6**

After 29. ... ♗c1

42. ♘d4 ♖e1+ 43. ♔d5 ♔g6 44. f5+ ♔f6 45. ♖c6+ ♔f7 46. ♖c2 ♖e3 47. ♖e2 ♖d3 48. ♔e4 ♖c3 49. ♖c2 (see diagram)

49. ... ♖xc2 50. ♘xc2 Clearly White feels the odds favor him with no rooks. **50. ... ♗c5 51. ♘e3 ♔f6 52. ♘g4+ ♔g5 53. ♘e5 ♗b4 54. h4+ ♔f6 55. g4 ♗d2 56. ♘f3 ♗c1 57. ♘e5 ♗d2 58. ♘c4 ♗e1 59. ♔f4 ♗xh4 60. ♘xa5 g6 61. fxg6 ♔xg6 62. ♘c6 ♗g5+ 63. ♔e4 ♗d2 64. ♘e5+ ♔f6 65. ♘f3 ♗b4 66. ♔d5 ♔g6 67. ♔e5 h5 68. g5 ½-½** (Source: Reinfeld, *Margate 1935* [additional notes by RT])

After 49. ♖c2

191 Menchik–Jacques Mieses
Margate (5), April 28, 1935
[D15] Slav

An interesting game. Menchik incorrectly sacrificed a pawn early in the game and tied up Mieses' pieces. After missing a shot at equality and also a probable win following Mieses' errors, she embarks on an unsound sacrifice on move 22 which results in her resignation on move 29.

1. d4 d5 2. c4 c6 3. ♘f3 ♘f6 4. ♘c3 dxc4 5. e3 ♗f5 6. ♗xc4 e6 7. 0-0 ♗e7 8. ♕e2 ♘bd7 9. e4 ♗g4 10. h3 White should have increased her advantage by ♖d1 and ♗f4; instead she plays for complications. **10. ... ♗xf3 11. ♕xf3 ♘b6 12. ♗b3** [12. ♕d3 would now save the pawn, but White prefers to sacrifice in order to gain time. As will be seen this latter course is incorrect—RT] **12. ... ♕xd4 13. ♖d1 ♕c5 14. ♗e3 ♕a5 15. ♕g3 (see diagram)**

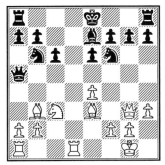

After 15. ♕g3

15. ... ♘bd7 [15. ... 0–0 seems simpler since 16. ♕c7 can be answered by 16. ... ♗b4 17. ♕xb7? ♖fc8 and the queen cannot be extricated. After the text White should recover the pawn with 16. ♕xg7 ♖g8 17. ♕h6 since Black's attack is not to be feared overmuch—RT] **16. ♗d2? ♕c5 17. ♖ac1 ♗d6 18. ♕d3** [18. ♕xg7 ♖g8 19. ♕h6 ♕e5 20. g3 ♖g6–+ —RT] **18. ... ♕e5 19. g3 ♘c5 20. ♕c2 ♕h5 21. ♗e3 ♗e7** *(see diagram)*

Black is already out of his difficulties. Now comes an unsound combination which is easily refuted. **22. ♘b5? cxb5 23. ♗xc5 ♖c8 24. ♕d3 ♖xc5 25. g4 ♕e5 26. f4 ♕xe4 27. ♕xb5+ ♖xb5 28. ♖c8+ ♗d8 0–1** (Source: Reinfeld, *Margate 1935* [additional notes by RT])

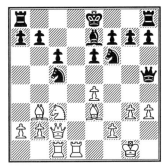

After 21. ... ♗e7

192 Samuel Reshevsky–Menchik
Margate (6), April 30, 1935
[D35] *Queen's Gambit Declined, Exchange Variation*

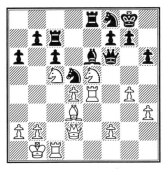

After 22. ♖e4

1. d4 ♘f6 2. c4 e6 3. ♘c3 d5 4. ♗g5 ♘bd7 5. cxd5 exd5 6. e3 ♗e7 7. ♕c2 0–0 8. ♗d3 ♖e8 9. ♘f3 ♘f8 10. h3 ♗e6 11. 0–0–0 ♘6d7 12. ♗xe7 ♕xe7 13. ♔b1 a6 14. ♖c1 ♖ac8 15. e4 c6 16. ♖he1 dxe4 17. ♘xe4 h6 18. g4 ♘f6 19. ♘c5 ♘d5 20. ♕d2 ♕f6 21. ♘e5 ♖c7 22. ♖e4 *(see diagram)*

22. ... g5 It is important for Black to maintain counterplay opportunities as well as to keep the structural integrity of her pawns. 22. ... ♕h4 better accomplishes this **23. h4 ♘f4** 23. ... gxh4!? is an unforgiving line that may hold, but has plenty of opportunities for Black to go awry. 24. f4 ♕g7 (24. ... ♖ce7 25. ♖h1 b6 26. g5 ♕g7 (26. ... hxg5 27. fxg5 ♕g7 28. ♖exh4+–) 27. ♘xe6 ♘xe6±) 25. ♖h1 ♗c8 26. ♖xh4= **24. hxg5 hxg5 25. ♖ee1 ♖d8 26. ♗c2 ♕g7** 26. ... b6!? 27. ♘e4 ♕g7= **27. ♕c3 ♗c8 28. ♖cd1 ♘8e6 29. ♘xe6 ♗xe6 30. ♖h1 ♗d5?!** 30. ... f6 **31. ♗h7+ ♔f8 32. ♖h2 c5 33. ♗f5** *(see diagram)*

33. ... ♘e2?? 33. ... b6 and White is coming out of her problems with a slight edge. In the two Reshevsky vs. Menchik games the clock played a decisive role. Almost certainly Vera lost this game because of time pressure, while a few months later Reshevsky lost on time **34. ♕a5 f6 35. ♖h7 1–0** (Source: Reinfeld, *Margate 1935*; Gordon, *Samuel Reshevsky*, 1997; notes by RT)

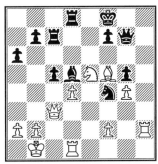

After 33. ♗f5

193 Menchik–Brian Reilly
Margate (7), May 1, 1935
[D37] *Queen's Gambit Declined*

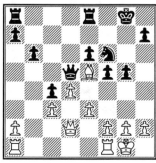

1. c4 ♘f6 2. ♘c3 d5 3. d4 e6 4. ♘f3 ♘bd7 5. ♗f4 ♗b4 6. ♕b3 ♗×c3+ 7. b×c3 0-0 8. e3 b6 9. ♗d3 ♗a6 10. 0-0 c5 11. ♗d6 ♖e8 12. ♕a4 ♗×c4 13. ♗×c4 d×c4 14. ♕×c4 ♘e4 15. ♗f4 g5 16. ♕d3 f5 17. ♗g3 c4 18. ♕c2 ♘df6 19. ♘d2 ♕d5 20. ♗e5 ♘×d2 21. ♕×d2 *(see diagram)*

    21. ... ♘d7?? [Probably the best try is 21. ... ♘e4 but White is struggling anyway—RT] **22. e4 1-0** (Source: Reinfeld, *Margate 1935*)

After 21. ♕×d2

194 Edward G. Sergeant–Menchik
Margate (8), May 2, 1935
[E61] *King's Indian Defense*

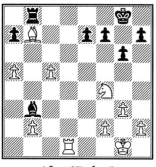

After 27. d×c5

1. d4 ♘f6 2. c4 g6 3. ♘c3 ♗g7 4. ♘f3 0-0 5. g3 d5 6. c×d5 ♘×d5 7. ♗g2 c5 8. ♘×d5 ♕×d5 9. 0-0 c×d4 10. ♗e3 d3 11. ♘e1 ♕h5 12. ♘×d3 ♘c6 13. a4 ♕f5 14. ♖c1 ♖d8 15. ♖c5 ♕e6 16. ♕c2 ♘d4 17. ♗×d4 ♗×d4 18. ♘f4 ♕a6 19. ♖c7 ♗f5 20. ♕b3 ♕d6 21. ♖×b7 ♖ab8 22. a5 ♖×b7 23. ♗×b7 ♖b8 24. ♖d1 ♕c5 25. e3 ♗c2 26. e×d4 ♗×b3 27. d×c5 *(see diagram)*

    27. ... ♖×b7? [27. ... ♗×d1 ∓ —RT] **28. c6 ♖c7 29. ♖c1 e5 30. ♘d3 f6 31. ♖c3 ♗a4 32. ♘b4 ♔f7 33. b3 ♗b5 34. ♖c5 a6 35. f4 e×f4 36. g×f4 ♔e6 37. ♔f2 ♖c8 38. ♔e3 ♖e8 39. c7 ♖c8 40. ♘d5 ♔d6 41. ♘b6 ♖×c7 42. ♖×c7 ♔×c7 43. ♘d5+ ♔d6 44. ♘×f6 h5 45. ♘e4+ ♔d5 46. ♘c3+ ♔c5 47. ♘×b5 ♔×b5 48. ♔d4 ♔×a5 49. ♔c5 h4 50. h3 g5 51. b4+**
1-0 (Source: Reinfeld, *Margate 1935*)

195 Menchik–Philip S. Milner-Barry
Margate (9), May 3, 1935
[A15] *English*

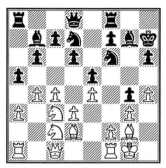

    1. ♘f3 ♘f6 2. c4 b6 3. g3 ♗b7 4. ♗g2 e5 5. 0-0 d6 6. ♘c3 ♘bd7 7. d3 g6 8. ♗d2 ♗g7 9. ♕c1 h6 10. b4 g5 Creating a weakness at f5 which is cleverly exploited by Menchik later on. **11. e4 0-0 12. h4! g4 13. ♘e1 ♔h7 14. ♘c2** Heading for f5. **14. ... a5 15. a3** *(see diagram)*

    15. ... a×b4 Out of place; Black will be so busy defending his weak points that he can hardly expect to have time to dispute the "a" file. **16. a×b4 ♕e7 17. ♘e3 ♖×a1 18. ♕×a1**

After 15. a3

🜚a8 19. 🜛d1 🜛e6 20. ♘cd5 🜚c8 21. ♘f5 c6 22. ♘de7!
The winning move. 22. ... 🜚h8 [If 22. ... 🜚e8 23. ♘×g7 wins
easily—RT] 23. ♘×g7 🜛×g7 24. ♘f5+ 🜛g6 25. 🜛e2 d5
26. 🜚a1 d×c4 27. d×c4 c5 28. 🜚a7 ♗a8 29. 🜛e3 ♗×e4
[Reinfeld sees this as a move of desperation, or maybe overlooking White's 32nd move, but Fritz sees nothing better—
RT] 30. ♗×e4 ♘×e4 31. 🜛×e4 ♘f6 *(see diagram)*
    32. h5+! 🜛h7 33. 🜛b7 ♘×h5 34. ♘×h6 🜛g6
35. ♘×f7 An excellent game by Menchik. **1–0** (Source: Reinfeld, *Margate 1935* [additional notes by RT])

After 31. ... ♘f6

Yarmouth 1935

(28th B.C.F. Congress—Major Open)
July 8–20, 1935

		1	2	3	4	5	6	7	8	9	10	11	12	Points	Place
1	Reshevsky, Samuel	•	1	0	1	1	1	1	1	1	1	1	1	10	1
2	Seitz, Jakob A.	0	•	1	=	1	=	=	1	1	1	1	1	8½	2
3	Menchik, Vera	1	0	•	=	=	1	1	1	1	0	1	0	7	3
4	Conde, Adrian G.	0	=	=	•	0	0	1	1	=	1	1	1	6½	4–5
5	Fajarowicz, Sammi	0	0	=	1	•	1	=	1	0	=	1	1	6½	4–5
6	Klein, Ernst L.	0	=	0	1	0	•	0	0	1	1	1	1	5½	6
7	Graf, Sonja	0	=	0	0	=	1	•	0	1	1	=	=	5	7–8
8	Wood, Baruch H.	0	0	0	0	0	1	1	•	0	1	1	1	5	7–8
9	Butcher, A.J.G.	0	0	0	=	1	0	0	1	•	=	0	1	4	9–10
10	Prins, Lodewijk	0	0	1	0	=	0	0	0	=	•	1	1	4	9–10
11	Ivanoff, V.	0	0	0	0	0	0	=	0	1	0	•	1	2½	11
12	Kitto, Francis E.	0	0	1	0	0	0	=	0	0	0	0	•	1½	12

The two notable events of Yarmouth 1935 are Menchik's win against Reshevsky and the only time that Vera played against Sonja Graf in a mixed gender event. Yarmouth being the British Championship, the championship section was closed to Menchik until she gained her British citizenship in 1937. In addition to the British Championship a number of other sections would be held including the British Women's Championship and a number of groups based upon ability which were open to players of all nationalities. Often the "Major Open" would have mostly non–British players and be the strongest section of the event. Some of these events were among Menchik's better results. In 1931 she took first place in Worcester, second in London 1932 and third here at Yarmouth. Prizes were £16, £12, £8, £4 with 10 shillings per win to non-prize winners.[52]

196 Menchik–Sonja Graf
Yarmouth—B.C.F. Cong., July 1935

[A09] *Réti's Opening*

In this game Menchik methodically makes slightly better moves than her opponent—never rushing the position. The key seems being more consistent in making medium term plans.
    1. ♘f3 d5 2. c4 d4 3. b4 c5 4. ♗b2 ♘c6 5. b5 ♘b8 6. e3 g6 7. e×d4 ♗g7 8. d3 c×d4

Sonja Graf at Hastings 1935-1936 (Premier Reserve) (courtesy Hastings Chess Club).

9. ♘bd2 ♘h6 10. g3 0-0 11. ♗g2 e5 12. 0-0 ♗g4 13. h3 ♗e6?! *(see diagram)*

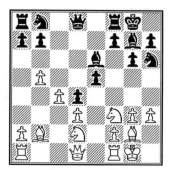

After 13. ... ♗e6

14. ♖e1 [14. ♘xe5?! ♗xe5 15. ♗xb7 ♘d7 16. ♗xa8 ♕xa8 and White's open king and extra pawn should not be adequate for the bishop pair and the vulnerable king—RT] 14. ... ♘d7 15. ♗a3 ♖e8 16. ♘e4 ♕a5 17. ♕b3 ♗f8 18. ♗xf8 ♖xf8 19. a4 f6 20. ♕a3 ♘f5 21. ♘fd2 ♖ac8 22. ♘b3 ♕c7 23. ♖ac1 b6 24. c5 bxc5 25. ♘bxc5 ♘xc5 26. ♖xc5 ♕e7 27. ♖ec1 ♘g7 28. ♖1c2 f5 29. ♘d2 ♗f7 30. ♕c1 ♖xc5 31. ♖xc5 f4 32. ♘e4 fxg3 33. fxg3 ♘f5 34. ♖c7 ♕b4 35. ♖xa7 ♘e3 36. ♔h2 ♘xg2 37. ♕h6 with mate in three. 1-0 (Source: *www.Chessgames.com* [additional notes by RT])

197　Samuel Reshevsky–Menchik
Yarmouth—B.C.F. Cong. (5), July 12, 1935
[D51] *Queen's Gambit Declined*

Elizaveta Bikova in her book indicates that Reshevsky had only a few seconds left for his last five or six moves (the time control was 36 moves in two hours); surprising that he should lose when considering the relative simplicity of the position. Although down a pawn, Menchik defends magnificently which may account for Reshevsky taking so much time—trying to find the win.

1. d4 ♘f6 2. c4 e6 3. ♘c3 d5 4. ♗g5 ♘bd7 5. cxd5 exd5 6. e3 ♗b4 7. ♗d3 c5 8. ♘ge2 c4 9. ♗c2 h6 10. ♗h4 ♗e7 11. 0-0 b5 12. ♘xb5 ♕b6 13. ♘bc3 0-0 14. b3 ♗a6 15. ♖b1 ♕a5 16. bxc4 ♗xc4 17. ♗d3 ♖ac8 18. ♗xc4 ♖xc4 19. ♖b5 ♕a6 20. ♕b3 ♖fc8 21. ♗xf6 ♘xf6 22. ♖b8 ♗d6 23. ♖xc8+ ♕xc8 24. ♘b5 ♗f8 25. ♘bc3 ♗d6 26. a3 ♕e6 27. h3 ♖c6 28. ♖c1 ♖b6 29. ♕a2 ♕d7 30. ♖b1 ♖xb1+ 31. ♘xb1 ♕b7 32. ♘ec3 g6 33. ♕c2 ♔g7 34. ♕a2 ♗e7 35. ♔f1 ♗d6 *(see diagram)*

White's flag fell. 0-1 (Source: Gordon, *Reshevsky*, 1997)

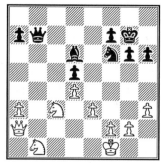

Final position

Margate 1936

(Premier Division)
April 15–24, 1936

	1	2	3	4	5	6	7	8	9	10	Points	Place
1 Flohr, Salomon	•	=	=	1	1	1	=	1	1	1	7½	1
2 Capablanca, José R.	=	•	=	=	1	=	1	1	1	1	7	2
3 Ståhlberg, Gideon	=	=	•	0	=	=	1	1	=	1	5½	3
4 Lundin, Erik R.	0	=	1	•	=	=	1	0	=	1	5	4
5 Milner-Barry, Philip S.	0	0	=	=	•	0	1	=	1	1	4½	5–6
6 Tylor, Theodore H.	0	=	=	=	1	•	=	=	0	1	4½	5–6
7 Menchik, Vera	=	0	0	0	0	=	•	1	=	1	3½	7
8 Sergeant, Edward G.	0	0	0	1	=	=	0	•	=	=	3	8–9
9 Thomas, George A.	0	0	=	=	0	1	=	=	•	0	3	8–9
10 Reilly, Brian P.	0	0	0	0	0	0	0	=	1	•	1½	10

Considering that the other four Margate tournaments are represented by all of their games, it is disappointing that only 31 of the games (including four of Vera's) have been found for this iteration of the Margate series. Flohr demonstrated his excellence in this era; having tied for first with Botvinnik in Moscow 1935, placing ahead of Capablanca here and later in the year surpassing Alekhine in Poděbrady. Prizes to the top four were awarded of £12, £8, £4, and £2.[53]

198 Edward G. Sergeant–Menchik
Margate (1), April 15, 1936
[C11] *French, Advance*

This is one of those games that belongs in an anthology of arbiter errors. After Sergeant misplays his kingside attack he adjourns in a worse position on move 34. Upon resumption, Menchik wins the game only to have it discovered that they had resumed from an incorrect position. The arbiter had them go back to the adjourned position and replay the last part of the game, which Menchik won more quickly than the first time.[54]

1. e4 e6 2. d4 d5 3. ♘c3 ♘f6 4. e5 ♘fd7 5. ♘f3 c5 6. d×c5 ♘c6 7. ♗f4 ♗×c5 8. ♗d3 a6 9. 0–0 ♗e7 10. ♖e1 b5 11. ♘e2 ♗b7 12. ♘ed4 ♘c5 13. c3 ♘×d3 14. ♘×c6 ♗×c6 15. ♕×d3 0–0 16. ♘d4 ♗d7 17. ♖e3 b4 18. ♖h3 g6 19. ♗h6 ♖e8 20. c×b4 ♗×b4 21. ♗d2 ♗f8 22. ♘f3 ♗g7 23. ♘g5 h6 24. ♘×f7 ♔×f7 25. ♖f3+ ♔g8 26. ♕×g6 ♖e7 27. ♗×h6 ♕b8 28. ♗g5 ♗e8 29. ♕d3 ♖f7 30. ♖×f7 ♗×f7 31. ♗f6 ♗×f6 32. e×f6 ♕f4 33. ♕c3 ♖d8 34. h3 (following is the correct adjourned position) *(see diagram)*

After 34. h3

34. ... ♕f5 35. ♖e1 d4 36. ♕d2 ♗g6 37. f4 ♕×f6 38. ♖e5 d3 39. b4 ♖d4 40. ♖g5 ♔f7 0–1 (Source: *www. 365Chess.com*)

199 Menchik–Brian Reilly

Margate (2), April 16, 1936

[A30] *English, Symmetrical Variation*

After 50 moves of maneuvering in which both players do their best to get something going, the game finally begins. Menchik shows a very nice technique in the later part of the game.

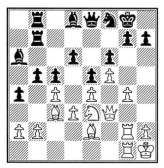

After 30. Rdg1

1. ♘f3 ♘f6 2. c4 e6 3. g3 b6 4. ♗g2 ♗b7 5. 0–0 c5 6. ♘c3 ♘c6 7. e4 e5 8. d3 ♗e7 9. ♘e1 d6 10. f4 ♕d7 11. ♘d5 0–0 12. ♘e3 ♘d4 13. ♗d2 ♘e8 14. ♘f3 ♘c7 15. f5 b5 16. ♘g4 ♘×f3+ 17. ♕×f3 f6 18. ♘f2 a5 19. g4 a4 20. ♘d1 ♗a6 21. ♘e3 ♖ab8 22. ♖ab1 ♖b7 23. ♗c3 ♖fb8 24. ♖f2 ♘a8 25. ♗f1 ♘b6 26. ♖d1 ♗d8 27. ♖g2 ♕e8 28. ♔h1 ♘d7 29. ♗e2 ♘f8 30. ♖dg1 *(see diagram)*

30. ... g5 31. f×g6 h×g6 32. ♘d5 ♕e6 33. ♖f1 ♘h7 34. ♕f2 ♖f7 35. h4 ♖bb7 36. ♕e1 b4 37. ♗d2 ♘f8 38. ♗d1 ♕e8 39. ♕g3 ♖a7 40. ♖gf2 ♘h7 41. ♘e3 ♗c8 42. ♖g1 ♗e6 43. ♘f1 ♕c6 44. ♕e3 ♘f8 45. ♘g3 ♖h7 46. ♖h2 ♕e8 47. h5 g5 48. ♖f1 ♕d7 49. ♕f3 a3 50. b×a3 ♖×a3 51. ♗c1 ♖a7 52. ♗×g5 ♗×g4 53. ♕×g4 ♕×g4 54. ♗×g4 f×g5 55. ♖hf2 ♖hf7 56. ♗f5 ♖f6 57. ♔g2 ♖a3 58. ♖d1 ♔g7 59. ♘f1 ♘e6 60. ♗×e6 ♖×e6 61. ♘e3 ♖f6 62. ♘f5+ ♔h7 63. ♖dd2 ♗a5 64. ♖d1 b3? [64. ... ♗d8± —RT] 65. a×b3 ♗c3?! [65. ... ♖×b3± —RT] 66. ♔h3 *(see diagram)*

66. ... ♗d4 One has to question putting one's bishop in a place where it cannot even begin to help in the struggle against his kingside. 67. ♖g2 ♖×b3 68. ♖×g5 ♖b2 69. ♖g7+ ♔h8 70. ♖g2 ♖b3 71. ♖a2 ♖×f5 72. e×f5 e4 73. ♔g4 e3 74. ♔f3 ♖b7 75. ♖e2 ♖f7 76. ♔f4 ♗e5+ 77. ♔e4 ♗d4 78. ♖h1 ♔h7 79. ♖h3 ♔h6 80. ♖g3 ♖e7+ 81. ♔f4 ♖e5 82. ♖g6+ ♔h7 83. ♔g5 1–0 (Source: *www.365Chess.com* [additional notes by RT])

After 66. ♔h3

(R56) George Alan Thomas–Menchik

Margate (3), April 17, 1936

[C??] *French Defense*

1. e4 e6 2. d4 d5 ½–½ (Source: *The Times*, April 18, 1936)

(R57) Menchik–Erik Lundin

Margate (4), April 19, 1936

Réti Opening

0–1 (Source: *The Times*, April 20,1936)

200 Salo Flohr–Menchik

Margate (5), April 20, 1936

[A90] *Dutch*

Before the resumption of the adjournment of this game, Flohr had to play Ståhlberg; he

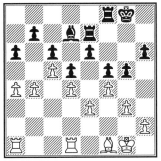

After 24. ... a6

agreed to a draw in that game, believing that he could win his adjournment against Vera…. Had he forgotten about Moscow? Needless to say, he only drew, which allowed Capablanca to catch up to him at 4½ for the moment.

1. d4 e6 2. c4 f5 3. g3 ♘f6 4. ♗g2 ♗b4+ 5. ♗d2 ♗×d2+ 6. ♕×d2 0–0 7. ♘c3 d5 8. ♘f3 c6 9. 0–0 ♘bd7 10. ♕c2 ♕e8 11. e3 ♕h5 12. ♘e2 g5 13. b4 ♘b6 14. c5 ♘c4 15. ♘c1 ♗d7 16. ♘d3 ♖ae8 17. ♕d1 ♖e7 18. ♘fe5 ♕×d1 19. ♖f×d1 ♘×e5 20. ♘×e5 ♗e8 21. a4 ♘d7 22. ♘×d7 ♗×d7 23. f4 h6 24. ♗f1 a6 *(see diagram)* **25. b5 c×b5 26. a×b5 ♗×b5 27. ♗×b5 a×b5 28. ♖db1 g4 29. ♖×b5 ♖c8 30. ♖a7 ♖cc7 31. ♖a8+ ♔f7 32. ♖b8 ♖cd7 33. ♔f2 ♖c7 34. ♔e2 ♖cd7 35. ♔d2 ♖c7 36. ♔c3 h5 37. ♔b4 ♔f6 38. ♖b6 ♔g7 39. ♔b5 ♔f7 40. ♖d6 ♔g6 41. ♔b6 h4 42. ♖a8 h×g3 43. h×g3 ♔f6 44. ♖a7 ♖f7 45. c6 ♖×c6+ 46. ♖×c6 b×c6 47. ♖×f7+ ♔×f7 48. ♔×c6 ♔g6 49. ♔c7 ♔g7 50. ♔c8** *(see diagram)*

50. … ♔g8 51. ♔c7 ♔g7 52. ♔c8 ♔g8 ½–½ (Source: www.365Chess.com)

201 José Raúl Capablanca–Menchik
Margate (6), April 21, 1936
[D06] *Queen's Gambit, Symmetrical Variation*

After 50. ♔c8

1. d4 d5 2. ♘f3 ♘f6 3. c4 c5 4. c×d5 c×d4 5. ♘×d4 ♘×d5 6. e4 ♘b4 Threatening ♕×d4 and ♘c2+ **7. ♗e3 a6** [Here it was also possible to try 7. … e5 and if 8. ♘b5 a6 9. ♕a4? a×b5 10. ♕×a8 ♘c2+ 11. ♔e2 ♘c6 etc.; if 7. … ♘8c6 8. ♗b5 ♗d7 9. ♘c3 is good for White—RT] **8. ♕a4+ ♘4c6** [Now 8. … ♘8c6 would be definitely bad on account of 9. a3 e5 10. ♘f3 ♘d3+ (10. … b5 11. ♗×b5 a×b5 12. ♕×a8 ♘c2+ 13. ♔e2 etc.) 11. ♗×d3 ♕×d3 12. ♘×e5 etc.—RT] **9. ♘c3 e6** Black dare not try e5 as then White settles a knight on d5 **10. ♘db5** [Possibly 10. ♖d1 first was stronger; now White threatens ♖d1 as well as ♗f4—RT] **10. … ♘d7 11. ♖d1** [Now 11. ♗f4 was no good because of 11. … ♘c5 12. ♕a3 ♘d3+ winning the queen; also Black could have met ♗f4 with e5—RT] **11. … ♖b8 12. ♘d4 ♘×d4 13. ♕×d4 ♕f6 14. ♕c4 ♗e7 15. f4** [If 15. ♕c7 then 15. … ♗d8 (but not of course 15. … ♕e5 on account of 16. ♖×d7)—RT] **15. … ♗d8 16. e5 ♕h4+** Possibly an error as the opening of the long diagonal turns out to be in White's favor. **17. g3 ♕e7 18. ♘e4 ♗a5+ 19. ♔f2 0–0 20. ♘d6 ♗b6 21. ♗×b6 ♘×b6 22. ♕d4 ♘d5 23. ♗g2 ♗d7 24. ♗×d5 e×d5 25. ♖he1 ♗c6 26. ♘f5 ♕e6 27. g4 ♖bc8** [27. … h5 at once was better (Fritz disagrees)—RT] **28. h3 ♖c7 29. ♕b6 ♖cc8 30. ♔g3** *(see diagram)*

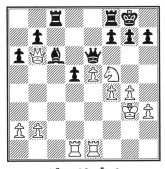

After 30. ♔g3

30. … d4?? Overlooking, in time pressure, that after ♕×a2 White will be able to win the exchange with ♘e7+; now White has an easily won game. [30. … ♖fd8± (F)—RT] **31. ♖×d4 ♖ce8 32. b3 h5 33. ♖d6 ♕c8 34. ♕d4** Threatening 35. e6 f6 36. e7 ♖f7 37. ♖d8 etc. **34. … ♖e6 35. ♖×e6**

♛×e6 36. ♕d6 h×g4 37. ♘e7+ ♔h7 38. ♕×e6 f×e6 39. h×g4 ♖d8 40. ♔h4 [Or 40. ♘×c6 b×c6 41. ♖c1 ♖c8 42. ♖d1 and ♖d6 wins easily—RT] 40. ... ♗f3 41. ♔g5 ♖d7 42. ♘g6 ♖d2 43. ♖c1 Threatening ♖c8 and ♖h8 mate against which there is no adequate defense. 43. ... ♗c6 44. ♘f8+ ♔g8 45. ♘×e6 ♖×a2 46. ♘d4 ♗b5 47. ♖c8+ ♔h7 48. ♘e6 1–0 (Source: *Chess* June 1936, #181; notes by VM [additional notes by RT])

(R58) Menchik–Gideon Ståhlberg
Margate (7), April 22, 1936
Réti Opening
0–1 (Source: *The Times*, April 23, 1936)

(R59) Philip S. Milner-Barry–Menchik
Margate (8), April 23, 1936
[C??] *French*
1. e4 e6 2. d4 d5 and Milner-Barry won in 50 moves **1–0** (Source: *BCM*, 1936; *The Times*, April 24, 1936)

(R60) Theodore Tylor–Menchik
Margate (9), April 24, 1936
½–½ (Source: *The Times*, April 25, 1936)

Poděbrady 1936
(International Tournament)
July 5–26, 1936

		1	2	3	4	5	6	7	8	9	10	11	12	13	14	15	16	17	18	Pts.	Place
1	Flohr, Salomon M.	•	=	=	1	=	0	1	1	=	1	1	=	=	1	1	1	1	1	13	1
2	Alekhine, Alexander	=	•	1	=	=	1	1	=	=	=	1	=	1	1	=	1	1	=	12½	2
3	Foltys, Jan	=	0	•	=	=	1	0	1	0	=	1	=	1	=	1	1	1	1	11	3
4	Pirc, Vasja	0	=	=	•	=	=	=	=	=	=	=	1	1	1	1	1	0	1	10½	4–5
5	Ståhlberg, Anders G.	=	=	=	=	•	0	=	1	0	1	1	=	1	1	1	0	1	=	10½	4–5
6	Eliskases, Erich	1	0	0	=	1	•	=	1	=	1	=	=	=	0	0	1	1	=	9½	6–7
7	Frydman, Paulin	0	0	1	=	=	=	•	1	=	0	1	0	0	1	1	1	1	1	9½	6–7
8	Pelikan, Jiří	0	=	0	=	0	0	0	•	1	1	0	1	1	=	1	=	1	1	9	8–9
9	Richter, Kurt	=	=	1	=	1	=	0	0	•	=	0	1	0	=	0	1	1	1	9	8–9
10	Petrovs, Vladimirs	0	=	=	=	0	0	1	0	=	•	1	=	1	1	0	=	1	=	8½	10–11
11	Steiner, Lajos	0	0	0	=	0	=	=	1	1	0	•	1	0	1	1	=	=	1	8½	10–11
12	Opočenský, Karel	=	=	=	0	=	=	0	0	×	=	0	•	0	=	1	1	1	1	8	12
13	Menchik, Vera	=	0	0	0	0	=	1	0	0	0	1	1	•	0	1	1	0	1	7	13
14	Zinner, Emil	0	0	d	0	0	1	1	=	1	0	0	=	1	•	0	0	0	1	6½	14
15	Skalicka, Carlos	0	=	0	0	0	=	0	1	0	0	0	1	0	=	•	=	1	=	6	15–16
16	Treybal, Karel	0	0	0	0	1	0	0	=	1	=	=	0	0	1	=	•	=	=	6	15–16
17	Fazekas, Stefan	0	0	0	1	0	0	0	0	0	=	0	1	1	0	=	=	•	0	4	17–18
18	Thomas, George A.	0	=	0	0	=	=	0	0	0	=	0	0	0	0	=	=	1	•	4	17–18

The Poděbrady tournament was the 14th Czechoslovakian Championship; the national title going to the top Czech player. In at least some sources Vera was recognized as the Czech

Women's Champion as a result of her results. Her sister Olga, playing in one of the subsidiary preliminary groups, scored 3–4.

202 Menchik–Karel Treybal
Poděbrady (1), July 5, 1936
[E01] *Catalan Opening*

1. d4 d5 2. ♘f3 ♘f6 3. c4 e6 4. ♘c3 c6 5. g3 ♘e4 6. ♗g2 ♗b4 7. ♕b3 ♕a5 8. ♗d2 ♗×c3 9. ♗×c3 ♕a6 10. 0-0 d×c4 11. ♕c2 ♘×c3 12. ♕×c3 0-0 13. ♘e5 ♘d7 13. ... b5?! 14. a4 b×a4 15. ♘×c4± **14. ♘×c4 ♘b6 15. ♖fc1 ♖d8 16. e3 ♘×c4 17. ♕×c4 ♕b6 18. b4 ♗d7 19. ♖ab1 ♗e8 20. f4 ♖d6 21. a4 ♕d8 22. b5 c×b5 23. a×b5 ♖b8** 23. ... a6!? 24. b×a6 b5 25. ♕c5 ♖a×a6 **24. ♕c5 ♕b6 25. ♗f1 g6?** 25. ... ♖a8 **26. ♖a1 ♖d5** *(see diagram)*

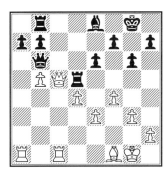
After 26. ... ♖d5

　　　27. ♕×b6 a×b6 28. ♖a7 ♕f8 29. g4 h5 30. g5 ♔e7 31. ♔f2 ♗×b5 If 31. ... f5 32. ♖c7+ ♔d8 33. ♖a×b7 ♗×b5 34. ♖d7+ ♗×d7 35. ♖×b8+ ♔c7 36. ♖g8 ♗a5 37. ♖×g6 ♖a2+ 38. ♔g3 ♔d6 39. ♖g8 ♖a3 40. g6 ♖×e3+ 41. ♔g2 ♗c6+ 42. ♔g1 ♔e7 43. g7 ♔f7 44. ♖c8 ♔×g7 45. ♖×c6 and the rest (as was the last) is, as they say, a matter of technique. **32. e4 ♗×f1 33. e×d5 ♗a6 34. ♖c6 ♖d8 35. ♖×b6 ♖d6** If 35. ... ♖×d5? 36. ♖b×a6 **36. ♖×d6 ♔×d6 37. d×e6 ♔×e6 38. ♔e3 ♔d5 39. h4 ♔e6 40. ♔e4 ♗c4 41. ♖a5 b6 42. ♖e5+ ♔d6 43. f5 ♗b3 44. f6 ♗c4 45. ♔e3 ♗d5 46. ♔d3 ♔c6 47. ♔c3 ♗g2 48. ♔c4 ♗f1+ 49. ♔b4 ♗g2 50. ♖e7 ♗d5 51. ♖e2 ♔c7 52. ♖c2+** *(see diagram)*

Final position

1–0 (Source: *www.Chessgames.com*; notes by RT)

203 Menchik–Vladimirs Petrovs
Poděbrady (2), July 6, 1936
[D13] *Slav, Exchange*

1. ♘f3 d5 2. c4 c6 3. c×d5 c×d5 4. d4 ♘f6 5. ♘c3 e6 6. ♗f4 ♘c6 7. e3 ♗e7 8. ♗d3 0-0 9. ♖c1 ♘h5 10. ♗e5 f6 11. ♘g5 ♕e8 12. ♘×h7 f×e5 13. ♘×f8 ♗×f8 14. ♘b5 ♗b4+ 15. ♔f1 ♕f7 16. g4 ♘f6 17. g5 ♘e4 18. ♗×e4 d×e4 *(see diagram)*

After 18. ... d×e4

　　　19. ♖g1?! Better is 19. d×e5= **19. ... g6?** 19. ... e×d4 20. g6 ♕f3 21. e×d4 e5 22. ♕×f3 e×f3 23. ♖g3 e×d4∓ **20. a3 ♗f8 21. ♖g3 e×d4 22. e×d4 e5? 23. d×e5** Regaining at least equality is 23. d5 ♘d8 24. ♕e1 **23. ... ♘×e5 24. ♘d6 ♗×d6 25. ♕×d6 ♘c6 26. b4?!** More hope is offered by 26. ♕f6 **26. ... ♗e6 27. ♖gc3 ♖f8 28. ♕g3 ♘d4 29. ♕e3 ♗h3+ 30. ♔g1 ♘f3+ 31. ♔h1 ♕e6 32. ♖c7 ♕e5 0–1**
(Source: *www.Chessgames.com*; notes by RT)

204 Salo Flohr–Menchik
Poděbrady (3), July 7, 1936
[D06] *Queen's Gambit, Symmetrical Variation*

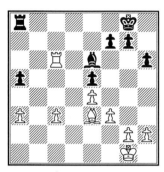

After 21. ... a5

1. ♘f3 ♘f6 2. d4 d5 3. c4 c5 4. c×d5 c×d4 5. ♘×d4 ♘×d5 6. e4 ♘b4 7. ♕a4+ ♘8c6 8. ♘×c6 ♘×c6 9. ♘c3 e6 10. ♗e3 ♗b4 11. ♗b5 0-0 12. 0-0 ♕a5 13. ♖fd1 ♗×c3 14. b×c3 ♕×a4 15. ♗×a4 e5 16. ♖ab1 h6 17. f3 ♖d8 18. a3 ♖×d1+ 19. ♖×d1 ♗e6 20. ♗×c6 b×c6 21. ♖d6 a5 *(see diagram)*

22. ♖×c6 ♖c8 23. ♖×c8+ ♗×c8 24. ♗b6 a4 25. c4 ♔f8 26. ♔f2 h5 27. ♔e3 ♔e7 28. ♔d3 ♗d7 29. ♗c5+ ♔e6 30. ♔c3 ♗c6 31. ♔b4 g6 32. ♗f8 f5 33. ♔c5 ♔d7 34. e×f5 g×f5 35. ♗g7 e4 36. f4 e3 37. g3 e2 38. ♗c3 ♗g2 39. ♗e1 ♔c7 40. ♔d4 ♔c6 41. ♗b4 ♗f1 42. ♔e5 ♗h3 43. ♔f6 e1♕ 44. ♗×e1 ♔c5 45. ♔g5 ♗g4 46. ♔h4 ♗e2 47. h3 ♗f1 48. g4 h×g4 49. h×g4 f×g4 50. ♗f2+ ♔×c4 51. f5 ♗d3 52. ♔×g4 ♗×f5+ ½-½ (Source: *www.Chessgames.com*)

205 Menchik–Erich Eliskases
Poděbrady (4), July 9, 1936
[E67] *King's Indian Defense*

Despite the structural imbalances and the flurry at the end neither side ever had a winning advantage in this intriguing game. **1. ♘f3 ♘f6 2. c4 d6 3. d4 g6 4. g3 ♗g7 5. ♗g2 0-0 6. 0-0 ♘bd7 7. ♘c3 ♖e8 8. h3 c6 9. ♕b3 ♕c7 10. ♗e3 b6 11. ♖ac1 ♗b7 12. ♖fd1 ♖ad8 13. ♔h2 ♕b8 14. ♕c2 c5 15. d5 ♘f8 16. ♗d2 h6 17. e4 e6 18. ♘g1 e×d5 19. ♘×d5 ♘×d5 20. c×d5 ♗c8 21. ♘e2 ♕b7 22. ♘f4 f5 23. ♘e6 ♘×e6 24. d×e6 f×e4 25. ♗×e4 d5 26. ♗×g6 ♖×e6 27. ♖e1 ♕c6 28. ♗h5** *(see diagram)*

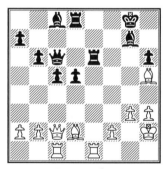

After 28. ♗h5

28. ... ♖×e1 29. ♖×e1 ♕f6 30. ♗c1 d4 31. ♗f4 d3 32. ♕a4 ♗e6 33. ♕c6 ♗f7 34. ♗×f7+ ♕×f7 35. b3 ♔h7 36. ♕e4+ ♕g6 37. ♕c4 ♖d4 38. ♕c1 ♖e4 39. ♔g2 b5 40. ♗d2 c4 41. b×c4 b×c4 42. f3 ♗e5 43. g4 ♖×e1 44. ♕×e1 ♗g7 45. ♗c3 ♗×c3 46. ♕×c3 ♕e6 47. ♕d4 ♕e2+ 48. ♔g3 ♕e7 49. ♕×c4 ♕e5+ 50. ♔f2 ♕e2+ 51. ♔g3 ½-½ (Source: *Wiener Schach-Zeitung*, August 36 #111)

206 Emil Zinner–Menchik
Poděbrady (5), July 10, 1936
[C11] *French, Advance*

1. e4 e6 2. d4 d5 3. ♘c3 ♘f6 4. e5 ♘fd7 5. ♘f3 c5 6. d×c5 ♘c6 7. ♗f4 ♘×c5 8. ♗d3 ♗e7 9. ♕d2 a6 10. 0-0 0-0 11. ♖fe1 b5 12. ♖ad1 ♗d7 13. g4 b4 14. ♘e2 f5 15. g×f5 ♘×d3 16. c×d3 ♖×f5 *(see diagram)*

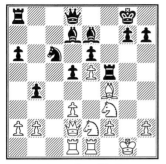

After 16. ... ☐×f5

17. ♘ed4? Required is 17. ♘fd4 **17. ... ♘×d4?** 17. ...
♛f8! 18. ♘×f5 ♛×f5 19. h3 ☐f8 and Black picks up a second
minor and a nice position in return for her rook **18. ♘×d4
☐f8 19. ☐c1 ☐c8 20. ☐×c8 ♛×c8 21. ☐c1 ♛b7 22. ♗g5
♗×g5 23. ♛×g5 ♛b6 24. ♘e3 ☐c8 25. ☐×c8+ ♗×c8
26. ♚f1 ♗d7 27. ♚e2 a5 28. f4 g6 29. ♘b3 ♛c6?** Best is
29. ... ♛a6 **30. ♛c5 a4 31. ♛×c6 ♗×c6 32. ♘d4 ♗d7
33. b3 ♚f7 34. ♘c2 a×b3 35. a×b3 g5 36. f×g5 ♚g6
37. ♘×b4 ♚×g5 38. ♚f3 ♗b5 39. d4 ♚h4 40. ♘a2 ♚h3
41. ♘c3 ♗f1 42. b4 ♚×h2 43. b5 ♚g1 44. b6 ♗a6
45. ♘a4 h5 46. ♚g3 h4+ 47. ♚×h4 ♚f2 48. ♘c5 ♗c8**
49. ♘×e6 1–0 (Source: *www.Chessgames.com*; notes by RT)

207 Menchik–Kurt Richter

Poděbrady (6), July 11, 1936

[D26] *Queen's Gambit Accepted*

**1. d4 ♘f6 2. ♘f3 d5 3. c4 d×c4 4. e3 c5 5. ♗×c4 e6 6. 0-0
♗e7 7. ♛e2 0-0 8. ☐d1 ♘c6 9. d×c5 ♛c7 10. a3 ♗×c5
11. b4 ♗d6 12. ♗b2 e5 13. e4 ♗g4 14. ♘bd2 ♘h5
15. ☐ac1 ♘f4 16. ♛e3 ♛e7 17. ♗f1 ☐ad8 18. h3 ♗×f3
19. ♘×f3 ♗c7 20. ♛c3 ♗b6 21. g3 ♘g6 22. ♛c4 ♘d4
23. ♘×d4 e×d4 24. ♗g2 ♘e5 25. ♛b3 h5** *(see diagram)*

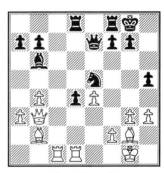

After 25. ... h5

26. ♚h2? Giving away what she has so laboriously fought
to get after a difficult opening. [26. a4± —RT] **26. ... h4
27. a4 d3 28. ♗×e5 ♛×e5 29. f4 h×g3+ 30. ♚×g3 ♛d4
31. ♚h2?!** [31. ☐f1—RT] **31. ... ♛f6 32. ☐f1 ♗e3
33. ☐cd1 ♗×f4+ 34. ♚h1 d2 35. ♛f3 g5 36. e5 ♛×e5 37. ♛×b7 ☐d3 38. ♛×a7 ♛c3
39. ☐×f4 g×f4 40. ♛f2 ☐e8 41. ♛×f4 ☐e1+ 42. ♗f1 ☐×h3+ 43. ♚g2 ☐×d1 0–1** (Source:
www.Chessgames.com [additional note by RT])

208 Lajos Steiner–Menchik

Poděbrady (7), July 12, 1936

[C14] *French, Classical*

**1. e4 e6 2. d4 d5 3. ♘c3 ♘f6 4. ♗g5 ♗e7 5. e5 ♘fd7 6. ♗×e7 ♛×e7 7. ♘b5 ♘b6
8. c3 a6 9. ♘a3 0-0 10. f4 f5 11. ♘f3 ♗d7 12. ♛d2 c5
13. ♗d3 ♘a4 14. 0-0 ♘c6 15. ☐ae1 c×d4 16. c×d4 ♛b4**
(see diagram)

After 16. ... ♛b4

17. ♛e3? Required if White wants to maintain an unbalanced position. White would have been better advised to accept
the better ☐f2. **17. ... ♛×b2 18. ♗c2 ♘c3 19. ♛b1 ♘b5
20. ☐f2 ♛b×d4 21. ♗b3 ♘×f3+ 22. ♛×f3 ♛d4 23. g4
f×g4 24. ♛×g4 ♘e7 25. ♘d2 ♘g6 26. ♛g3 ☐×f4 27. ♘f3
♛c3 28. ☐ee2 ☐af8 29. ☐c2 ♛a1+ 30. ♚g2 ♘×e5
31. ♘×e5** White resigns without waiting for Black's answer.
0–1 (Source: *www.Chessgames.com*; notes by RT)

209 Menchik–George Thomas

Poděbrady (8), July 14, 1936

[D30] *Queen's Gambit Declined*

1. ♘f3 d5 **2.** d4 c6 **3.** c4 e6 **4.** g3 ♘d7 **5.** ♗g2 ♗d6 **6.** 0–0 f5 **7.** ♗f4 ♗×f4 **8.** g×f4 ♘h6 **9.** c×d5 e×d5 **10.** ♘c3 0–0 **11.** ♖c1 ♘f6 **12.** e3 ♘e4 **13.** ♘e5 ♕h4 **14.** f3 ♘d6 **15.** ♕e1

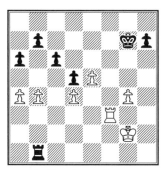

After 45. ... ♔g7

♕×e1 **16.** ♖f×e1 ♗e6 **17.** ♘a4 ♖fe8 **18.** ♗f1 ♘hf7 **19.** b3 ♖e7 **20.** ♖c2 ♘e8 **21.** ♖ec1 ♘×e5 **22.** f×e5 f4 **23.** ♘c5 f×e3 **24.** ♖c3 g6 **25.** ♘×e6 ♖×e6 **26.** ♗h3 ♖e7 **27.** ♖×e3 ♘g7 **28.** ♗g4 ♖f8 **29.** b4 a6 **30.** a4 ♖f4 **31.** ♖d3 ♘e6 **32.** ♗×e6+ ♖×e6 **33.** ♔f2 ♖h4 **34.** ♔g2 g5 **35.** ♖c2 ♖eh6 **36.** ♔g1 ♖h3 **37.** ♖g2 ♔f7 **38.** ♖c3 ♖6h4 **39.** ♖d3 g4 **40.** ♖g3 ♖×h2 **41.** f×g4 ♖h1+ **42.** ♔f2 ♖4h2+ **43.** ♖g2 ♖×g2+ **44.** ♔×g2 ♖b1 **45.** ♗f3+ ♔g7? *(see diagram)*

With this last move Sir George gives up his initiative and starts his self-destruction. **46. b5?** [46. e6—RT] **46. ... a×b5?** [46. ... c×b5! 47. a×b5 ♖×b5∓ —RT] **47.** a×b5 ♖×b5 **48.** e6 ♖b2+ **49.** ♔f1 ♖a2?! [49. ... ♖b1+ 50. ♔e2 ♖b2+ 51. ♔e1 and a quick draw ensues—RT] **50.** ♖f7+ ♔g6?? This move would have been just before time control. [50. ... ♔g8 51. ♖×b7 ♖a8 52. ♖c7 ♖e8 53. ♖×c6 ♔g7 54. ♖d6 ♔f6 55. ♔f2 ♖a8 56. ♖×d5 ♔×e6 and we have arrived at a drawn position—RT] **51.** ♖f8 **1–0** (Source: *Xxxxxxx Xxxxxxxx*; notes by Xxxxxxx Xxxxxx [additional notes by RT])

210 Stefan Fazekas–Menchik

Poděbrady (9), July 15, 1936

[A15] *English Opening*

1. ♘f3 ♘f6 **2.** c4 g6 **3.** b4 ♗g7 **4.** ♗b2 0–0 **5.** ♕b3 c6 **6.** g3 d6 **7.** ♗g2 e5 **8.** d3 h6 **9.** 0–0 ♗e6 **10.** a4 ♕c8 **11.** ♖d1 a5 **12.** ♘c3 a×b4 **13.** ♕×b4 ♖d8 **14.** ♗a3 ♘a6 **15.** ♕b3 ♖b8 **16.** ♖ab1 ♕c7 **17.** d4 ♘d7 **18.** e3 ♗g4 **19.** ♖d2 e×d4 **20.** e×d4 ♘f6 **21.** h3 ♗f5 **22.** ♖e1 ♖e8 **23.** ♖de2 *(see diagram)*

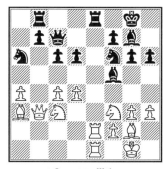

After 23. ♖de2

23. ... g5?! Rather than overextend her kingside and create targets, Black would have been better to challenge on the e file and bring her knight on a6 into the game. 23. ... ♖×e2 24. ♖×e2 ♖e8= **24.** ♗c1 ♖×e2 **25.** ♖×e2 ♕d7 **26.** h4 g4 **27.** ♘h2 ♘c7 **28.** a5 ♘e6? 28. ... d5 29. c×d5 ♘f×d5= **29.** ♗e3 ♕d8 **30.** ♖a2 ♘d7?! **31.** ♕d1 ♕f6? 31. ... h5± **32.** ♘×g4 ♕g6 **33.** ♘h2 ♘f6 **34.** ♖b2 ♖a8 **35.** ♖×b7 ♖×a5 **36.** ♗×c6 ♗c2 **37.** ♕e1 ♔h7 **38.** ♗g2 ♖a3 **39.** ♖b6 ♗d3 **40.** ♖×d6 ♗f8 **41.** ♖b6 ♗×c4 **42.** d5 ♘g7 **43.** ♗e4 ♘f5 **44.** g4 ♖×c3 **45.** ♗×f5 **1–0** (Source: *www.Chessgames.com*; notes by RT)

211 Menchik–Jan Foltys

Poděbrady (10), July 16, 1936

[D02] *Réti Opening*

This was the event in which Foltys first made his reputation. One of the top Czechoslovakian players from 1935 to 1952, he died in that same year. In this particular contest Menchik turns over the initiative to Black very early in the game.

1. ♘f3 ♘f6 2. g3 d5 3. ♗g2 c5 4. 0-0 ♘c6 5. d4 e6 6. c3 ♛b6 7. h3 ♗d7 8. ♕d3 ♖c8 9. ♘bd2 c×d4 10. ♘×d4 ♘×d4 11. c×d4 ♗b5 12. ♕e3 ♗e7 13. ♘b1 0-0 14. ♘c3 ♗c6 15. ♖b1 ♖fd8 16. ♖d1 ♘e8 *(see diagram)*

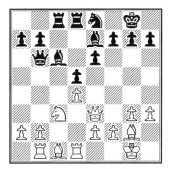

After 16. ... ♘e8

17. ♗d2?? 17. ♕f3= Gaining breathing room and counterplay 17. ... ♗f6 18. ♗e1 e5 19. d×e5 d4 20. ♕f4?–+ 20. ♖×d4!? ♖×d4 21. e×f6 ♘×f6 22. f3∓ 20. ... d×c3 21. b×c3 ♖×d1 22. ♖×b6 ♖×e1+ 23. ♔h2 a×b6 24. e×f6 ♘×f6 25. ♗×c6 b×c6 26. ♕d2 ♖b1 27. g4 h6 28. c4 ♖a8 29. ♕d6 ♖b2 30. ♕×c6 ♖a×a2 31. ♕c8+ ♔h7 32. ♕f5+ ♔h8 33. ♔g3 ♖×e2 34. f3 ♖a3 0-1 (Source: *CS* 1936 #86; Podgorný, *J Foltys*; *WSZ 1936 Yearbook*, game 112; notes by RT)

212 Carlos Skalicka–Menchik
Poděbrady (11), July 18, 1936
[A05] Réti Opening

1. ♘f3 ♘f6 2. b4 g6 3. ♗b2 ♗g7 4. e3 0-0 5. ♗e2 d6 6. d4 ♘fd7 7. ♘bd2 e5 8. d×e5 d×e5 9. 0-0 ♕e7 10. e4 ♖e8 11. a3 b6 12. ♗c4 ♗b7 13. ♖e1 a6 14. ♕e2 ♘f8 15. ♕e3

After 27. ... ♕e7

h6 16. ♕b3 ♘bd7 17. ♖ad1 ♖ab8 18. ♘b1 b5 19. ♗f1 c5 20. c4 b×c4 21. ♗×c4 c×b4 22. a×b4 ♗c6 23. ♕a2 ♘e6 24. ♗d5 24. ♕×a6!? ♖ec8± 24. ... ♗×d5 25. e×d5 ♘f4 26. ♕×a6 ♕×b4 26. ... ♘×g2! if 27. ♔×g2 ♕×b4 winning back the material either at b2, by ♕g4+, or via the counter sacrifice at e5. 28. ♗×e5 ♘×e5 29. ♖d4 ♕c5∓ **27. ♗c3 ♕e7** *(see diagram)*

28. ♕f1? 28. g3 ♘h3+ other lines are worse for Black. 29. ♔g2 ♘g5 30. ♘×g5 ♕×g5± **28. ... ♕c5 29. d6 ♖×b1 30. ♗d4 Possibly a better alternate is 30. ♖×b1 30. ... ♕c8 31. ♖×b1 e×d4 32. g3 ♖×e1 33. ♖×e1 ♘e6 34. ♕b5 ♗f6 35. ♘d2 ♘ef8 36. ♘b3 ♔g7 37. ♖c1 ♕e8 38. ♖d1 ♘e6 39. ♘a5 ♘g5 40. ♕f1 ♕e6 41. ♕c6 ♘e5 42. ♕g2 ♘gf3 43. ♕h1 ♕×d6 44. ♔g2 ♕d5 45. ♔h3 ♕×a5 0-1** (Source: *www.Chessgames.com*; notes by RT)

213 Menchik–Paulin Frydman
Poděbrady (12), July 19, 1936
[A13] English Opening

1. ♘f3 ♘f6 2. c4 e6 3. g3 d5 4. ♗g2 d4 5. d3 c5 6. 0-0 ♘c6 7. e4 e5 8. ♘e1 ♗d6 9. f4 ♕c7 10. ♘a3 a6 11. f5 ♘g8 12. ♗d2 f6 13. ♘ac2 ♕f7 14. ♖b1 b5 15. b3 ♘ge7 16. ♕e2 g6 17. f×g6 h×g6 18. ♕f2 ♘g8 19. ♘f3 b4 20. a3 ♖a7 21. a×b4 c×b4 22. ♘ce1 g5 23. h4 g×h4 24. ♘×h4 ♕h7 25. ♘ef3 ♖g7 26. ♗e1 ♘h6 27. ♔h2 ♗e7 28. ♕a2 ♘g4 29. ♘×g4 ♖×g4 30. ♕a4 *(see diagram)*

After 30. ♕a4

30. ... ♗d7? 30. ... ♗b7 31. ♖f3 ♕g8∓ 31. ♔×a6 ♘d8 32. ♕a8?! 32. ♖f3 32. ... f5 33. ♖×f5 ♗×h4 34. g×h4 ♗×f5 35. e×f5 ×f5 36. ♗×b4 36. ♖b2 36. ... ♖hg8 37. ♖b2 ♕g6? 37. ... ♖×h4∓ 38. ♖e2 *(see diagram)*

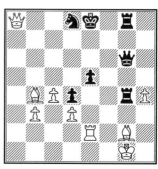

After 38. ♖e2

38. ... ♕c6 39. ♕×c6+ ♘×c6 40. ♗e1 ♗d7 41. ♔h2 ♔d6 42. b4 ♖4g7 43. c5+ ♔c7 44. b5 ♘e7 45. ♖a2 ♘f5 46. b6+ ♔d7 47. ♗d5 ♖b8 48. ♖a7+ ♔d8 49. ♖×g7 ♘×g7 50. ♗g3 1–0 (Source: *www.365Chess.com*; notes by RT)

214 Jiří (Jorge) Pelikan–Menchik
Poděbrady (13), July 20, 1936
[A03] *Bird's Opening*

1. f4 d5 2. ♘f3 g6 3. e3 ♗g7 4. ♗e2 ♘f6 5. 0–0 0–0 6. ♕e1 c5 7. d3 ♘c6 8. ♕h4 ♕c7 9. ♘c3 d4 10. ♘d1 d×e3 11. ♘×e3 ♘d4 12. ♗d1 ♘f5 13. ♘×f5 g×f5?! 13. ... ♗×f5= 14. ♗d2 ♘d5 15. c4 ♘b4 16. ♗c3 ♘c6 16. ... ♕d6!? 17. ♗b3 ♘c6± 17. ♗×g7 ♔×g7 18. ♕g5+ ♔h8 19. ♕h6 ♕d8 20. d4 ♖g8 21. d5 ♘d4 22. ♘×d4 c×d4 23. ♗h5 ♖g7 24. ♖fe1 ♗d7 24. ... b5!? 25. b3 e6 26. ♗f3 ♕c7 27. ♖ad1 ♖g6 28. ♕h4 e×d5 29. ♖e7 ♕d8 30. ♗×d5 ♗c6 31. ♗×c6 b×c6 32. ♕e1 ♕d6 33. ♕e5+ ♕×e5 34. ♖×e5 ♖d6 35. ♖×f5 ♔g7 36. ♖d3 ♖e8 37. ♔f2 ♖e4 38. g3 f6 39. ♖a5 ♖e7 40. ♔f3 ♔g6

After 63. ... ♖c1

41. g4 h6 42. h4 ♔g7 43. f5 ♖dd7 44. ♖a6 c5 45. g5 h×g5 46. h×g5 ♖f7 47. ♖c6 f×g5 48. ♖×c5 ♔f6 49. ♔g4 ♖fe7 50. ♖c6+ ♔e5 51. ♖d1 d3 52. ♖e1+ ♔d4 53. ♖×e7 ♖×e7 54. ♖d6+ ♔c3 55. f6 ♖e1 56. c5 d2 57. ♔×g5 ♖g1+ 58. ♔h6 ♖h1+ 59. ♔g7 ♖g1+ 60. ♔f8 d1♕ 61. ♖×d1 ♖×d1 62. f7 ♔b4 63. c6 ♖c1 *(see diagram)*

64. a3+!! 64. ♔e7 ♖e1+ 65. ♔d6 ♖d1+ 66. ♔e5 (66. ♔c7 ♖f1 67. ♔b8=) 66. ... ♖e1+ 67. ♔d4 ♖d1+ 68. ♔e3 ♖d8 69. ♔e4 ♔c5 70. ♔e5 ♔×c6 71. ♔e6 a5= 64. ... ♔b5 65. ♔e7 ♖e1+ 66. ♔d8 ♖d1+ 67. ♔c8 ♖f1 68. c7 ♖×f7 69. ♔b8 ♖f8+ 70. c8♕ ♖×c8+ 71. ♔×c8 ♔c6 72. ♔b8 ♔b6 73. ♔a8 a5 74. ♔b8 a4 75. b4 ♔b5 76. ♔b7 ♔c4 77. ♔c6 ♔b3 78. b5 ♔×a3 79. b6 ♔b2 80. b7 a3 81. b8♕+ ♔a1 82. ♕f4 ♔b2 83. ♕b4+ 1–0 (Source: *www.Chessgames.com*; notes by RT)

215 Menchik–Vasja Pirc
Poděbrady (14), July 22, 1936
[E07] *Catalan Opening*

1. ♘f3 d5 2. d4 e6 3. c4 ♘d7 4. g3 ♘gf6 5. ♗g2 ♗e7 6. 0–0 0–0 7. ♘c3 d×c4 8. e4 c6 9. ♕e2? 9. a4 is generally the accepted move here which leads to a complicated game. The text here dropped a pawn and Menchik never found a way to extract herself from the bind 9. ... b5 10. ♖d1 ♗b7 11. ♘e1 ♖e8 12. ♘c2 ♕b6 13. ♗e3 c5 14. e5 ♘d5 15. ♘×d5 e×d5 16. f4? 16. d×c5 ♘×c5∓ 16. ... c×d4 17. ♘×d4 ♗c5 18. ♕f2?! 18. ♕d2!? 18. ... f6 19. ♗h3 f×e5 20. ♗×d7 e×d4 21. ♗×d4 ♗d4 22. ♖×d4 ♖e7 23. ♗g4 ♖ae8 24. ♖ad1 b4 25. ♗h5? g6 26. ♗f3 a6 27. ♔g2 a5 28. g4 a4 29. ♖1d2 ♖e3 30. ♗×d5+ Ending the game quickly. 30. ... ♗×d5+ 31. ♖×d5 c3 0–1 (Source: *www.Chessgames.com*; notes by RT)

216 Karel Opočenský–Menchik
Poděbrady (15), July 23, 1936

[A16] *English Opening*

1. c4 ♘f6 2. ♘c3 d5 3. c×d5 ♘×d5 4. e4 ♘b4 5. ♗c4 ♘d3+ Gaining the bishop pair, which is probably adequate reason to be suspicious of White's opening plan. **6. ♗×d3 ♕×d3 7. ♕e2 ♕×e2+ 8. ♘g×e2 e5 9. d4 e×d4 10. ♘×d4 c6 11. ♗g5 f6 12. ♗e3 ♘a6 13. 0-0 ♗e7 14. ♖ad1 0-0 15. f3 ♖d8 16. g4 ♘c7 17. ♔g2 ♗d7 18. ♗f2 ♘e6 19. ♘×e6 ♗×e6 20. ♖×d8+ ♖×d8 21. ♗×a7 ♗c4 22. ♖d1 ♖×d1 23. ♘×d1 ♗×a2 24. ♘c3 ♗b3 25. ♗b6 ♗d6 26. h4 ♗b4 27. ♘e2 ♗d2 28. ♔f2 ♔f7 29. ♗e3 ♗a5 30. ♘c3 ♗c7 31. f4 ♗d6 32. g5 ♗c2 33. ♔e2 ♗b4 34. g×f6 g×f6 35. ♔f3 ♔e6 36. f5+ ♔e5 37. ♗f4+ ♔d4 38. ♗e3+** [38. ♗c7—RT] **38. ... ♔d3 39. ♗h6 ♗d6** [39. ... ♗c5 40. ♗g7 ♗d4‡—RT] **40. ♗f4 ♗e7** Black wishes of course to retain the bishop pair as well as to avoid opposite colored bishops. **41. e5 ♔d4 42. ♘e2+ ♔c4 43. ♘g3 f×e5 44. ♗×e5 ♔d5 45. f6 ♗f8 46. ♗c3 c5 47. ♔g4 ♔e6** *(see diagram)*

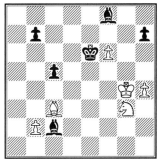

After 47. ... ♔e6

48. ♔g5?! White seems to not have realized just how easily he will be booted out of the northeast corner of the board and how much time it will lose. [48. ♘f1‡—RT] **48. ... b5 49. ♘h5 h6+ 50. ♔f4 ♗d6+ 51. ♔e3 b4 52. ♗e1 ♗e5 53. ♘f4+ ♔×f6 54. ♘d3 ♗×d3 55. ♔×d3 ♗×b2 56. ♔c4 h5 57. ♗d2** [If 57. ♔×c5 ♗c3—RT] **57. ... ♗d4 58. ♗h6 ♔f5 59. ♗d2 ♔e4 60. ♗g5 ♗e3 61. ♗e7 ♔f3 62. ♗f6 ♔e2 63. ♗e7 ♔d2 0-1** (Source: *www.Chessgames.com* [additional notes by RT])

217 Menchik–Alexander Alekhine
Poděbrady (16), July 24, 1936

[A46] *Queen's Pawn Game*

1. d4 ♘f6 2. ♘f3 b5 3. g3 [At such early stages it is a sound principle not to give the opponent an objective, such as this: the enterprise may succeed, as it does here, but only if the adversary continues to develop the pieces without trying to avail oneself of the unusual situation. Instead of the fianchetto development as selected by the Ladies' World Champion a good method would have been for instance, 3. ♗f4 ♗b7 4. e3 a6 5. a4 b4 6. c4, and whether Black takes en passant or not, his position remains slightly inferior—RT] **3. ... ♗b7 4. ♗g2 e6 5. 0-0 ♗e7 6. ♘bd2** [Because of her pointless mobilization plan, White has obtained no advantage from the opening. The text move, which prepares for the exchange of Black's exposed b-pawn is not worse than 6. a4 a6; and certainly better than 6. b3 b4! etc.—RT] **6. ... ♕c8!** Protecting the bishop in order to answer 7. ♖e1 by 7. ... ♘e4; and after 7. c4 the queen will obviously find a large field of action on the queenside. **7. c4 b×c4 8. ♘×c4 0-0 9. b3** [As so often in the Queen's Indian Defense, White cannot find a suitable square for the queen's bishop. Comparatively better than the text move, which weakens the queenside, is 9. ♘fe5 in order to clear as soon as possible the situation on the diagonal—RT] **9. ... a5!** Not only preventing once and for all ♘a5 (which on the previous move would be met by ♗d5) but also threatening eventually ... a4. **10. a3?** A decisive strategical error in an already delicate position. [White should profit from the fact that the threat mentioned was not of an immediate character by proposing an exchange of bishops with 10. ♗a3 ♗×a3 11. ♘×a3 ♘c6 followed by … ♘b4, Black's position, although superior, would not be anything like so easy to improve decisively as after the text move, which creates an incurable weakness on c3—RT] **10. … ♗d5 11. ♕c2 ♕b7 12. ♗b2**

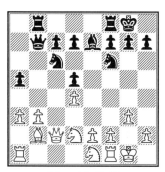

After 15. ♘d2

[White has only the choice between a few evils; for instance, after 12. ♗d2 ♘c6 Black would already threaten 13. … ♘×d4—RT] **12. … ♘c6 13. ♘e1 ♖ab8 14. ♗×d5** The only move that temporarily saves the pawn. **14. … e×d5!** [Much stronger than 14. … ♘×d5—the point is Black's next move—RT] **15. ♘d2** *(see diagram)*

15. … ♘e4! Thus Black becomes the master of the central sector. The b-pawn is not lost immediately but cannot long escape its fate. This purely positional battle is, in my opinion, noteworthy chiefly because of the methods adopted by Black in order to exploit his opening advantage: these methods, unusual at first sight, were in fact quite simple. **16. ♘ef3** [If 16. ♘×e4 then 16. … ♕×b3! etc., winning material—RT] **16. … f5 17. ♖fb1 ♕b5! 18. ♘×e4** [If now 18. e3 (which was comparatively the best), then 18. … ♕e2 19. ♖f1 g5! 20. ♖ae1 ♕b5 21. ♘×e4 d×e4 22. ♘d2 d5 23. ♖c1 ♖b6 and White would finally be executed on the king's flank; but Menchik prefers to succumb in open fight—RT] **18. … f×e4 19. ♘e5 ♘×e5** Simplest [19. … ♕×b3 would probably have won also, but after 20. ♕c1 more resistance would have been possible than in the endgame forced by the text maneuver—RT] **20. d×e5 ♕c5!** Rough, but extremely sound. **21. ♕×c5 ♗×c5 22. e3 ♖×b3 23. ♗d4 ♗×d4 24. e×d4 ♖ff3** Wins perforce a second pawn. **25. ♖×b3 ♖×b3 26. ♖c1 c6 27. e6 d×e6 28. ♖×c6 ♔f7 29. ♖c7+ ♔f6 30. g4 h6 31. h4 ♖×a3 0–1** (Source: Alekhine, *Best Games 1924–1937*—Game 83; notes by AA [additional notes by RT])

218 Gideon Ståhlberg–Menchik

Poděbrady (17), July 26, 1936

[D66] *Queen's Gambit Declined, Classical Variation*

1. d4 d5 2. c4 e6 3. ♘c3 ♘f6 4. ♘f3 ♘bd7 5. ♗g5 ♗e7 6. ♖c1 h6 7. ♗h4 0–0 8. e3 c6 9. ♗d3 d×c4 10. ♗×c4 ♘d5 11. ♗g3 ♘×c3 12. b×c3 ♖e8 13. 0–0 ♕a5 14. e4 b5 15. ♗b3 ♗b7 16. c4 b×c4 17. ♗×c4 c5 18. d5 e×d5 19. ♗×d5 ♗×d5 20. ♕×d5 ♘b6 21. ♕b3 c4 22. ♕c2 ♗a3 23. ♖cd1 ♖ac8 24. ♘d4 c3 25. ♘b3 ♕b5 26. ♗f4 *(see diagram)*

After 26. ♗f4

The next half dozen moves are of very erratic quality on the part of both players (time pressure?) with Menchik in a lost position after the time control is met. **26. … ♗b4** [26. … ♗b2!? 27. ♖fe1 ♘c4 28. ♘d4 ♕a6∓—RT] **27. ♗c1 ♘c4 28. ♖d5 ♕b7 29. ♕d3 ♖c6?** [Better is 29. … ♕a6—RT] **30. ♘d4 ♖cc8 31. ♕g3?!** [31. ♘b3—RT] **31. … ♘d2? 32. ♘f5 g6 33. ♘×h6+ ♔f8??+—** [33. … ♔g7±—RT] **34. ♖f5 ♖e7 35. ♕×g6 ♔e8 36. ♕g8+ ♔d7 37. ♕g4 ♕×e4 38. ♖f4+ ♕e6 39. ♖×b4 ♕×g4 40. ♘×g4 ♖e2 41. ♗×d2 ♖×d2 42. ♘e3 ♖×a2 43. h4 ♖b2 44. ♖d4+ ♔e8 45. ♖c1 c2 46. ♔h2 1–0**

(Source: *www.365Chess.com* [additional notes by RT])

Nottingham 1936

Major Open B
August 10–28, 1936

	1	2	3	4	5	6	7	8	9	10	11	12	Points	Place
1 Tsukerman, Iosif	•	0	0	1	=	1	1	1	1	1	1	1	8½	1–2
2 Reynolds, Arthur	1	•	1	1	1	1	0	0	1	=	1	1	8½	1–2
3 Abrahams, Gerald	1	0	•	=	1	=	1	0	1	=	=	1	7	3–4
4 Opočenský, Karel	0	0	=	•	1	1	1	=	1	1	=	=	7	3–4
5 Mallison, Harold V.	=	0	0	0	•	1	1	=	=	1	1	=	6	5
6 Lenton, Alfred	0	0	=	0	0	•	1	1	0	1	1	1	5½	6
7 Wood, Baruch H.	0	1	0	0	0	0	•	1	1	0	1	1	5	7
8 Menchik, Vera	0	1	1	=	=	0	0	•	0	=	1	0	4½	8
9 Watts, William H.	0	0	0	0	=	1	0	1	•	1	0	=	4	9
10 Craddock, James M.	0	=	=	0	0	0	1	=	0	•	0	1	3½	10–11
11 Collins, F.G.T.	0	0	=	=	0	0	0	0	1	1	•	=	3½	10–11
12 Coggan, S.S.	0	0	0	=	=	0	0	1	=	0	=	•	3	12

The *British Chess Magazine* (1936, p. 514) commented that Menchik, despite scoring 2½ out 4 against the prize winners seemed quite out of form against the tail-enders, and indeed her score might have been worse had Mallison not missed a win in their game. An interesting note is that her female rival, Sonja Graf in the comparable Major Open A Section outscored her with 5 out of 10 as opposed to Vera's 4½ out of 11.

Group Shot from the 1936 Nottingham Congress. Sonja Graf, J.H. Blake, J.N. Derbyshire, F.J. Hingley, Vera Menchik, Mrs. Derbyshire, E. Montague-Jones (courtesy *British Chess Magazine*, 1936).

219 Menchik–F.G.T. Collins
Nottingham—Major B Nottingham, August 1936
[A14] *English Opening*

After 23. ... ♗a8

1. ♘f3 ♘f6 2. c4 e6 3. g3 d5 4. ♗g2 c5 5. 0-0 ♘c6 6. b3 ♗e7 7. ♗b2 0-0 8. d3 ♕c7 9. ♘c3 d4 10. ♘b5 ♕d7 11. ♕d2 a6 12. ♘a3 ♖b8 13. e4 ♗d6 14. ♘h4 e5 15. ♘f5 ♗e7 16. ♘×d6 ♕×d6 17. ♘c2 ♘g6 18. ♗a3 b6 19. b4 ♘d7 20. ♖ab1 ♗b7 21. ♗h3 ♖fd8 22. ♖b2 ♘gf8 23. ♖fb1 ♗a8 *(see diagram)*

24. b×c5 b×c5 25. ♘a1 g6 26. ♖×b8 ♖×b8 27. ♖×b8 ♕×b8 28. ♘b3 ♕c7 29. ♕a5 ♕×a5 30. ♘×a5 ♘e6 31. ♗×e6 f×e6 32. ♘b3 ♔f7 33. ♗×c5 ♘b8 34. ♘a5 ♘c6 35. ♘×c6 ♗×c6 36. f4 ♗a4 37. ♔f2 ♔f6 38. ♗d6 e×f4 39. g×f4 ♗c2 40. ♔e2 h5 41. ♔d2 ♗a4 42. ♗e5+ ♔e7 43. ♗×d4 ♔d6 44. ♗e5+ ♔c5 45. ♔c3 ♗e8 46. d4+ ♔c6 47. d5+ e×d5 48. e×d5+ ♔c5 49. ♗g7 ♗f7 50. ♗f8+ ♔b6 51. ♔d4

1–0 (Source: *BCM* #7826)

Hastings 1936-1937
December 28, 1936–January 6, 1937

		1	2	3	4	5	6	7	8	9	10	Points	Place
1	Alekhine, Alexander	•	1	=	1	1	1	1	=	1	1	8	1
2	Fine, Reuben	0	•	1	1	=	1	1	1	1	1	7½	2
3	Eliskases, Erich	=	0	•	=	=	1	1	=	=	1	5½	3
4	Feigin, Movsa	0	0	=	•	1	0	1	1	=	=	4½	4–5
5	Vidmar, Milan, Sr.	0	=	=	0	•	=	=	1	=	1	4½	4–5
6	Tylor, Theodore H.	0	0	0	0	=	•	=	1	1	=	4½	6–7
7	Winter, William	0	0	0	0	=	=	•	1	1	=	3½	6–7
8	Koltanowski, George	=	0	=	0	0	1	0	•	=	=	3½	8
9	Menchik, Vera	0	0	=	=	=	0	=	•	0		2½	9
10	Thomas, Sir George	0	0	0	=	0	0	=	=	1	•	2½	10

After failing to compete in Hastings 1935-36, Vera returned to the lists in 1936. This was her last appearance at the Christmas Congresses. She accepted her invitation to compete in the 1937-38 tournament, but had to withdraw due to health issues plaguing her new husband, R.H.S. Stevenson. An interesting sidebar to this event was the participation of Alekhine's wife in the third part of the "A" section. A dispute arose between the former world champion's wife and an opponent over castling. The dispute was resolved in favor of Mrs. Alekhine by her husband![55] Also participating, in the Premier Reserves—Section 1, was Menchik's rival Sonja Graf who scored 3½ of 9 to place equal 7th in the section.

220 Menchik–George Thomas
Hastings 1936-37 (1), December 28, 1936
[D46] *Queen's Gambit Declined*

1. d4 d5 2. c4 e6 3. ♘f3 ♘f6 4. e3 c6 5. ♗d3 ♘bd7 6. 0-0 ♗d6 7. ♘c3 0-0 8. e4

d×e4 9. ♘×e4 ♘×e4 10. ♗×e4 ♘f6 11. ♗c2 ♕c7 12. ♗g5
♘e8 13. ♕d3 g6 14. ♖ad1 ♘g7 15. ♖fe1 f6 16. ♗d2 b6
17. ♗c3 a5 *(see diagram)*

18. a3 ♗a6 19. g3 ♖ad8 20. ♕f1 c5 21. d×c5 ♕×c5
22. ♗d3 ♗b7 23. ♗e4 ♗×e4 24. ♖×e4 ♕c6 25. ♕e2 e5
26. ♘d2 ♘e6 27. ♖e3? [27. ♘f3 a4 28. ♖e3=—RT] 27. ...
♗c5 28. ♖d3 ♘g5 29. g4 e4 30. ♖g3 ♗d6 31. ♖e3 ♗f4
32. h4 ♗×e3 33. ♕×e3 ♘f3+ 34. ♔g2 ♘×h4+ 0–1 (Source:
Chess, October 1937, #411; Cordingly, *Hastings 1936-37*)

After 17. ... a5

221 Theodore Tylor–Menchik

Hastings 1936-37 (2), December 29, 1936

[C14] *French, Classical Variation*

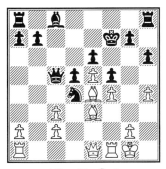

After 21. ♗e3

1. e4 e6 2. d4 d5 3. ♘c3 ♘f6 4. ♗g5 ♗e7 5. e5 ♘fd7
6. h4 h6 7. ♗e3 c5 8. ♕g4 ♔f8 9. f4 c×d4 10. ♗×d4 ♘c6
11. ♘f3 ♗b4 12. ♗e3 f5 13. ♕g3 ♗×c3+ 14. b×c3 ♕a5
15. ♗d2 ♕a3 16. ♗d3 ♘c5 17. 0-0 ♘e4 18. ♕e1 ♔f7
19. ♘d4 ♕c5 20. ♗×e4 ♘×d4 21. ♗e3 *(see diagram)*

21. ... d×e4 this avoids the problem of playing against
the two bishops at the cost of a pawn won. Menchik seemed
to naturally gravitate towards the safer lines. [21. ... ♕×c3!?
22. ♗d3 ♕×e1 23. ♖f×e1 ♘c6∓—RT] **22. c×d4 ♕d5 23. c4**
White chooses to sacrifice a
pawn, relying on his quick
development and the opposite
colored bishops to provide compensation and the means to a
draw. **23. ... ♕×c4** *(see diagram)*

24. ♖c1 ♕a4 Menchik signals her willingness to the
draw by immediately returning the pawn while strengthening
her defensive structure. [The question is what happens if Black
chooses to hold onto his pawn? 24. ... ♕d5 25. ♖c7+ (25. ♖c5
♕d8 26. ♕g3 b6 27. ♖c3 g6 28. ♖fc1∞) 25. ... ♗d7 26. ♕b4
b6—RT] **25. ♖c7+ ♗d7 26. ♖×b7 ♖ab8 27. ♕b1 ♖×b7
28. ♕×b7 ♕c6 29. ♕×c6 ♗×c6 30. ♖c1 ♖c8 ½-½**

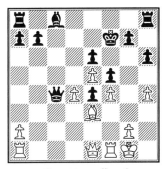

After 23. ... ♕×c4

(Source: Cordingly, *Hastings 1936-37* [additional notes by RT])

222 Menchik–Reuben Fine

Hastings 1936-37 (3), December 30, 1936

[D40] *Queen's Gambit Declined, Semi-Tarrasch Variation*

According to *Chess* magazine, Reuben Fine considered this the best game he played at
Hastings. The annotations are by Fine.

1. d4 ♘f6 2. ♘f3 d5 3. c4 e6 4. e3 The Queen's Gambit is an opening that requires very
precise play and this move does not answer the needs of the position. If White wishes to play
the gambit without developing his QB for some time, he should first play ♘c3, thereby forcing

Black to disturb the symmetry of the position. **4. ... c5** The difference between this defense and the Tarrasch Defense (c5 on the second or third move) is that White no longer has the powerful Rubinstein-Schlecter attack 5. c×d5 c×d4 6. g3 at his disposal. **5. ♘c3 a6** [With 5. ... ♘c6 Black by simply imitating his opponent's moves, can obtain an even game. But the text move is likewise quite promising since it disturbs the symmetry—RT] **6. d×c5** [To avoid moral disgrace. After 6. ♗d3 d×c4 7. ♗×c4 b5 8. ♗d3 c×d4 etc., Black would be playing a Queen's Gambit Accepted with colors reversed without having lost a tempo with his king's bishop—RT] **6. ... ♗×c5 7. ♗e2 0–0 8. 0–0 ♘c6 9. a3** Imitation it has been said (though by someone who may not have been a chess player) is the sincerest form of flattery. **9. ... ♗d6** Losing a tempo to avoid simplification. The text move it should be noted prevents White from playing the logical 10. b4 as after d×c4 11. ♗×c4 ♕c7 wins a pawn. **10. ♖e1** [Preparing the later advance of the e-pawn. More logical was 10. c×d5 e×d5 when a normal Queen's Gambit with colors reversed ensued—RT] **10. ... d×c4 11. ♗×c4 b5 12. ♗a2 ♗b7** Black is now most promisingly developed. **13. e4 ♘g4** A centralization maneuver. The square e5 is to be used as a pivot for the Black forces. The first step is to occupy the square with a knight which will keep an eye on the squares c4, d3 and f3. **14. h3** [Repelling the dangerous beast, but driving him where he wants to go. White need not have been in such a hurry, in fact the reply 14. ♗g5 would have been far better; for 14. ... ♗×h2+ is unsound because of the reply 15. ♘×h2 (14. ... ♕c7 15. h3 ♘ge5 16. ♖c1 with a fair position)—RT] **14. ... ♘ge5 15. ♗e3 ♖c8** Threatening to win a pawn by 16. ... ♘×f3+ 17. ♕×f3 ♘e5 followed by ♗×a3. **16. ♖c1** Defending herself against the immediate threat and setting an ingenious trap, but allowing the ruin of her pawn position. [If 16. ♘×e5 ♘×e5 17. ♖c1 ♘c4 with a great positional advantage—RT] **16. ... ♘×f3+** *(see diagram)*

After 16. ... ♘×f3

Avoiding the trap. [16. ... ♘d3 apparently wins the exchange for nothing, for if then 17. ♕×d3! ♗h2+ 18. ♔×h2 ♕×d3 but here White replies 19. ♖ed1 and the Black queen is beyond good and evil—RT] **17. g×f3** [Unfortunately this unwanted weakness cannot be avoided. If 17. ♕×f3 ♘e5 does win the exchange although Black's knight must go through some tortuous movements. The main variations are now: 18. ♕e2 (18. ♕d1 ♘d3 19. ♖c2 ♘×e1 20. ♖e2 ♘c2 21. ♗a7 ♘×a3 with a winning advantage.) 18. ... ♘d3 19. ♖cd1 (or 19. ♕×d3 ♗h2+ 20. ♔×h2 ♕×d3 21. ♖ed1 ♖×c3! and wins.) 19. ... ♘×e1 20. ♗f4 (or 20. e5 ♘×g2!) 20. ... ♖c6 21. e5 ♘×g2! and wins—RT] **17. ... ♘e5 18. ♔g2** [A better defense was 18. f4 ♘g6 19. ♕g4 with some attacking chances on the g-file. Now the White pawns are completely blockaded—RT] **18. ... ♘g6 19. ♖h1 ♕e7 20. ♖c2 ♖fd8 21. ♖d2 ♘f4+ 22. ♔f1** [The alternative is equally cheerless: 22. ♗×f4 ♗×f4 23. ♖×d8+ ♖×d8 24. ♕e1 ♕g5+ followed by ♖d2 with a crushing position—RT] **22. ... ♗e5 23. ♗b6** Both players were already in time trouble, but White's position suffers chiefly from the fact that the blockade of her kingside pawns has immobilized her king and king's rook, which makes it certain that a pawn will fall on the queenside. With the text move White at any rate deprives Black of the queen's file. **23. ... ♖×d2 24. ♕×d2 g6** [Black cannot undertake any directly decisive action but must quietly build up his position, certain that eventually the f-pawn will fall. Mating attacks such as 24. ... ♕g5 are refuted by simply 25. ♖g1 threatening, among other things ♕d7—RT] **25. ♗b3** [An inaccuracy which further cramps her game. But even after 25. ♗e3 ♖d8 followed by ♘d3; or 25. ♗a5 ♕c5 26. ♗b4 ♕b6, White's difficulties are for practical purposes insurmountable—RT] **25. ... b4** Because of her last move, the pawn cannot be captured by White for then 26. ... ♕×b3 wins at once. **26. ♘b1 ♕d6** [An inconsistency which does not, however, spoil the position effectively. Correct was the energetic 26. ... a5 when against the threat of ♗a6+ followed by ♕g5+ or ♘d6+ the White player has no defense—RT] **27. ♕×d6 ♗×d6** [Not attempting 27. ... ♖c1+ 28. ♕d1 and wins. But now the check is threatened—RT] **28. ♗e3 a5 29. ♗a4** In bad time pressure, both players were swimming; but White is practically stalemated. **29. ... ♗e5 30. a×b4 a×b4 31. b3** Thus saving the b-pawn but her bishop is now out of play and Black gains absolute control of the seventh rank. **31. ... ♖c2 32. ♔e1** [The only chance was 32. ♗b5 but then 32. ... ♖b2 wins at least a pawn—RT] **32. ... ♘g2+ 33. ♔d1 ♘×e3+ 34. f×e3** If now 35. f4 B×e4 **34. ... ♖f2 35. ♘d2 ♗c3** Resigns. For after 36. ♘c4 ♖×f3 37. ♘d6 ♗a6 38. ♘c4 ♖f2 (to choose the simplest line) White's position is so weakened that further resistance is obviously useless. **0–1** (Source: Cordingly, *Hastings 1936-37*; *Chess*, January 1937 #353; notes by R. Fine [additional notes by RT])

223 George Koltanowski–Menchik
Hastings 1936-37 (4), December 31, 1936
[D04] *Colle System*

1. d4 ♘f6 2. ♘f3 d5 3. e3 a6 4. ♗d3 ♗g4 5. c4 e6 6. ♕b3 ♘c6 7. c5 ♕c8 8. ♘c3 ♗e7 9. h3 ♗h5 10. ♘d2 0–0 11. f4 b6 12. c×b6 c×b6 13. 0–0 b5 14. ♘f3 ♖a5 15. ♕c2 ♗g6 16. ♘e5 ♗×d3 17. ♕×d3 ♕c7 18. b3 ♖fc8 19. ♗b2 ♘b7 20. ♖fc1 ♕b6 21. ♖c2 ♖c7 22. ♖ac1 ♖ac8 23. a3 ♘d6 24. ♘d1 ♘de4 25. ♘f3 ♘e8 26. ♘d2 ♘×d2 27. ♕×d2 ♘f6 28. ♖×c7 ♖×c7 29. ♖×c7 ♕×c7 30. ♕c3 ♕×c3 31. ♘×c3 ♕f8 32. ♔f1 ♔e8 33. ♔e2 ♔d7 34. ♔d3 *(see diagram)* Menchik turned down a draw offer here by Koltanowski as her bishop had more freedom of action, but the game was drawn anyway.[56]

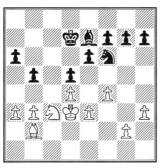
After 34. ♔d3

34. ... ♔c6 35. ♗c1 h5 36. ♘b1 ♘e4 37. ♘d2 ♘×d2 38. ♔×d2 ♗h4 39. ♔e2 a5 40. a4 b×a4 41. b×a4 ♗e7 42. g4 h×g4 43. h×g4 ½–½ (Source: Cordingly, *Hastings 1936-37*)

224 Menchik–Alexander Alekhine
Hastings 1936-37 (5), January 2, 1936
[D40] *Queen's Gambit Declined, Semi-Tarrasch Variation*

1. d4 d5 2. ♘f3 c5 3. c4 e6 4. e3 ♘f6 5. ♘c3 ♘c6 6. a3 ♘e4 7. ♕c2 ♕a5 8. ♗d2 ♘×d2 9. ♕×d2 c×d4 10. ♘×d4 d×c4 11. ♘×c6 b×c6 12. ♗×c4 ♗e7 13. 0–0 0–0 14. ♔e2 ♖b8 15. ♖fd1 ♗f6 16. ♖ac1 c5 17. ♗d3 ♗b7 18. ♕c2! g6 19. ♘b5 ♗d5 20. ♕×c5 ♗×b2 *(see diagram)*

21. ♘c7? [21. ♖b1 ♗×a3 22. ♕×a3 ♖×b5 23. ♕×f8+ ♔×f8 24. ♖×b5 and real drawing chances exist. V. Ragozin, *Shakhmaty v SSSR*, 1937, p. 40—RT] **21. ... ♕×c5! 22. ♖×c5**

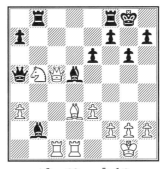
After 20. ... ♗×b2

♗b3 23. ♖b1 ♗a2 24. ♖d1 ♖fd8 25. ♘b5 a6 26. ♘d4 ♗×d4 27. e×d4 ♖×d4 28. ♔f1 ♖b3 29. ♔e2 ♖×a3 30. ♔e3 ♖d5 31. ♖c8+ ♔g7 32. ♔e2 ♗b3 33. ♖d2 ♖e5+ 34. ♔f3 ♗d5+ 35. ♔f4 ♖h5 0–1 (Source: Cordingly, *Hastings 1936-37*)

225 Milan Vidmar, Sr.–Menchik
Hastings 1936-37 (6), January 3, 1937
[E10] *Blumenfeld Variation*

After 17. ♗×e5

Within half a dozen moves Menchik is struggling with mobility and initiative issues. Vidmar builds up an overwhelming position several times only to lose the thread of the position. When considering the number of times Vera messed up better positions it is interesting to see stronger masters doing likewise. Consistency was not the name of the game in the 1930s.

1. d4 ♘f6 2. c4 e6 3. ♘f3 c5 4. d5 e×d5 5. c×d5 d6 6. e4 ♗e7 7. ♗d3 0–0 8. h3 b5 9. 0–0 ♗a6 10. ♖e1 b4 11. ♗×a6 ♘×a6 12. ♕d3 ♘c7 13. ♘bd2 ♘d7 14. ♘c4 ♘e8 15. ♗f4 a5 16. e5 d×e5 17. ♗×e5 *(see diagram)*
   17. ... ♗f6 18. d6 g6

19. ♖ad1 ♖c8 20. g4 ♘g7 21. ♗×f6 ♘×f6 22. ♘fe5 ♘e6 23. ♕f3 ♔g7 24. ♕e3?! 24. ♘×f7! ♖×f7 25. ♖×e6 24. ... ♘d4 25. ♖×d4?± c×d4 26. ♕×d4 ♕g8 27. g5 ♘d7 28. ♘×d7 ♕×d7 29. ♘e5 ♕f5? Better resistance is gained from 29. ... ♕e6 30. ♘g4 ♕×g5 *(see diagram)*
   31. f4? Winning is 31. h4 31. ... ♕h4 32. ♖e3 ♖c1+ 33. ♔g2 ♖c2+ 34. ♔f1 ♖c1+ 34. ... ♖fc8 If Black attempts to grab the whole point we would see 35. d7 ♖c1+ 36. ♔g2 ♖8c2+ 37. ♔f3 and White's king escapes 35. ♔g2 ♖c2+ 36. ♔h1 ½–½ (Source: Cordingly, *Hastings 1936-37*; notes by RT)

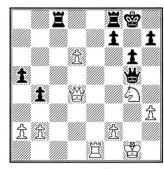

After 30. ... ♕×g5

226 Menchik–Erich Eliskases
Hastings 1936-37 (7), January 4, 1937
[D52] *Queen's Gambit Declined, Cambridge Springs Variation*

After 28. ... ♔×e7

1. d4 ♘f6 2. c4 e6 3. ♘f3 d5 4. ♘c3 ♘bd7 5. ♗g5 c6 6. e3 ♕a5 7. c×d5 ♘×d5 8. ♕d2 ♘7b6 9. ♘×d5 ♕×d2+ 10. ♘×d2 e×d5 11. ♗d3 ♗d6 12. 0–0 0–0 13. ♖fc1 ♗d7 14. ♖ab1 ♖ae8 15. ♘b3 h6 16. ♗f4 ♗×f4 17. e×f4 ♖e7 18. ♘c5 ♗c8 19. b4 ♘d7 20. ♘×d7 ♗×d7 21. ♔f1 a6 22. ♖e1 ♖fe8 23. ♖e5 f6 24. ♖×e7 ♖×e7 25. f5 ♕f8 26. h3 ♔e8 27. ♖e1 ♔d8 28. ♖×e7 ♔×e7 *(see diagram)*
   29. ♔e2 ♔d6 30. ♔d2 b6 31. g4 a5 32. a3 a×b4 33. a×b4 c5 34. b×c5+ b×c5 35. ♔c3 ♗a4 36. ♗e2 ♔c6 37. h4 ♗b5 38. ♗f3 ♗f1 39. h5 ♗a6 40. ♗d1 ♗b5 41. ♗f3 ♗f1 42. ♗d1 ½–½ (Source: Cordingly, *Hastings 1936-37*; *Chess*, August 1944, #1803)

227 William Winter–Menchik
Hastings 1936-37 (8), January 5, 1937
[A32] *English, Symmetrical Variation*

1. d4 e6 2. ♘f3 c5 3. c4 c×d4 4. ♘×d4 ♘f6 5. g3 ♕b6 6. ♗g2 ♗c5 7. e3 ♘c6 8. ♘b3 ♗b4+ 9. ♘c3 d5 10. c×d5 ♘×d5 11. 0-0 ♘×c3 12. b×c3 ♗×c3 13. ♖b1 0-0 14. ♕c2 ♗b4 15. a3 ♗e7 16. ♗d2 ♘d8 17. ♖fd1 e5 18. ♗a5 ♕f6 19. ♘c5 ♗g4 20. ♖d2?! ♘c6 21. ♗c7 b6? [The time has come to return the pawn and maintain at least some activity. 21. ... ♖ac8 22. ♘e4 ♕f5 23. ♖×b7 ♘d8—RT] 22. ♘d7 ♗×d7 23. ♖×d7 ♗c5?? [At least with 23. ... ♘b8 24. ♖dd1 ♘a6 25. ♗×a8 ♖×a8 we have a struggle, but the move as played ends everything—RT] 24. ♕a4 ♕f5 25. ♖bd1 ♘e7 26. ♗×a8 ♖×a8 27. ♖d8+ 1–0 (Source: *Chess*, January 1937, #363; Cordingly, *Hastings 1936-37*)

228 Menchik–Movsa Feigin
Hastings 1936-37 (9), January 6, 1937
[D78] *Neo-Grünfeld*

1. ♘f3 ♘f6 2. c4 c6 3. g3 d5 4. ♗g2 g6 5. 0-0 ♗g7 6. d4 0-0 7. ♗f4 d×c4 8. ♕c1 ♗e6 9. ♘bd2 ♘d5 10. ♗×b8 ♖×b8 11. ♘×c4 ♘b6 12. ♘ce5 ♕d6 13. ♖d1 ♖fd8 14. e3 ♖bc8 15. ♘d3 ♘d7 16. b4 ♗g4 17. h3 ♗×f3 18. ♗×f3 e5 19. d×e5 ♘×e5 20. ♘×e5 ♕×e5 21. ♖b1 ♖×d1+ 22. ♕×d1 ♕e6 23. ♕e2 ♖d8 24. ♔g2 ♕e7 25. ♕c2 h5 26. h4 ♕c7 27. a4 ♖d7 28. ♖d1 ♗f8 29. b5 ♖×d1 30. ♗×d1 ♕d7 31. b×c6 ♕×c6+ 32. ♕×c6 b×c6 33. ♗f3 c5 34. ♗d5 ♗g7 35. f4 ♗c3 36. e4 ♔f8 37. ♔f3 f6 38. ♗c4 ♔e7 39. ♗b5 a5 40. ♔f2 ♔f7 41. ♗c4+ ♔g7 42. ♗e6 ♔h7 43. ♔f3 ♗d4 *(see diagram)*

½–½ (Source: Cordingly, *Hastings 1936-37*)

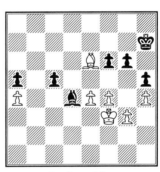

Final position

London 1937

		1	2	3	4	5	6	Pts.	Place
1	Golombek, Harry	•	0	1	1	1	1	4	1
2	Wheatcroft, George S.	1	•	0	0	1	1	3	2
3	Craddock, James M.	0	1	•	1	=	x	2½	3–4
4	Parr, Frank	0	1	0	•	1	=	2½	3–4
5	Menchik, Vera	0	0	=	0	•	1	1½	5
6	Berger, Victor	0	0	x	=	0	•	½	6

This event was held to determine the fifth spot for the British Olympiad team in Stockholm. Harry Golombek who was already a part of the team, and Menchik who was to play in the Women's World Championship there, were playing "*hors concours*." As a result the spot was won by George Wheatcroft. Bikova mentions this event as being part of Menchik's preparation for her upcoming title defense with Sonja Graf.

229 Harry Golombek–Menchik
London, 1937
[D22] *Queen's Gambit Accepted*

After 19. ... ♗×b4

1. d4 d5 2. c4 d×c4 3. ♘f3 a6 4. e3 ♗g4 5. ♗×c4 e6 6. ♕b3 ♖a7 7. ♘e5 ♗h5 8. 0-0 ♘d7 9. f4 ♘×e5 10. f×e5 b5 11. ♗d3 c5 12. ♗e4 ♖c7 13. ♗d2 c4 14. ♕c2 ♕d7 15. ♗a5 ♖c8 16. ♘d2 ♘e7 17. ♘f3 ♘c6 18. ♗e1 ♘b4 19. ♗×b4 ♗×b4 *(see diagram)*

20. a4 Tempting is 20. ♗×h7 but after 20. ... c3 (Not 20. ... g6 21. ♘g5 ♖f8 22. ♕f2 ♕b7 23. ♕h4 c3 24. b×c3 ♖×c3 25. g4+−) 21. ♖ac1 ♗×f3 22. ♖×f3 g6 23. ♗×g6 f×g6 24. ♕×g6+ ♔d8 25. ♖f7 ♗e7 26. ♖×c3 ♖×c3 27. b×c3 and it is a courageous player who would be willing to risk this position seven moves out! **20. ... ♗e7** 20. ... ♗g6!? 21. ♗×g6 h×g6 22. a×b5 a×b5 and the chances favor White, but only slightly **21. a×b5 a×b5 22. d5 ♗g6 23. d6 ♗×e4 24. ♕×e4 ♗d8 25. ♘d4 0-0 26. ♖a6 c3 27. b3 ♖c5** 27. ... ♗g5!? 28. ♖fa1 f5 29. ♕f3 (Not 29. e×f6 ♗×f6∓ 30. ♕×e6+ ♕×e6 31. ♘×e6) 29. ... c2 30. ♖c1= **28. ♖fa1 ♖d5?** 28. ... f5 29. ♕f4± **29. b4 c2? 30. ♘×c2 f6 31. ♖a7 ♕e8 32. ♕g4 g6 33. ♕h4 ♗f7 34. ♖×f7 ♕×f7 35. ♖a8 ♕d7 36. ♕×f6 1-0** (Source: Tartakower, *500 Master Games* #361; notes by RT)

Menchik vs. Eugene Znosko-Borovsky
Match 1937 (London)

This event is mentioned by Bikova as having been part of Menchik's preparation for the 1937 Sonja Graf match and is alluded to in other sources. No original sources, games or individual results are available. Menchik scored +0 −2 =2.[57]

Margate 1937
(Major Tournament)
March 31–April 9, 1937

		1	2	3	4	5	6	7	8	9	10	Points	Place
1	Fine, Reuben	•	=	1	1	1	1	=	=	1	1	7½	1–2
2	Keres, Paul	=	•	1	=	=	1	1	1	1	1	7½	1–2
3	Alekhine, Alexander	0	0	•	1	1	1	1	1	0	1	6	3
4	Foltys, Jan	0	=	0	•	1	1	=	1	1	=	5½	4
5	Milner-Barry, Philip S.	0	=	0	0	•	=	1	1	1	1	5	5
6	Menchik, Vera	0	0	0	0	=	•	=	1	1	1	4	6–7
7	Alexander, C.H.O'D.	=	0	0	=	0	=	•	=	1	1	4	6–7
8	Thomas, George	=	0	0	0	0	0	=	•	1	1	3	8
9	Berger, Victor	0	0	1	0	0	0	0	0	•	1	2	9
10	Tylor, Theodore H.	0	0	0	=	0	0	0	0	0	•	½	10

230 Paul Keres–Menchik
Margate (1), March 31, 1937
[D75] Grünfeld

1. ♘f3 ♘f6 2. c4 g6 3. ♘c3 ♗g7 4. d4 0-0 5. g3 d5 6. c×d5 ♘×d5 7. ♗g2 ♘×c3 8. b×c3 c5 9. 0-0 c×d4 10. c×d4 ♘c6 11. e3 ♖b8 12. ♘d2 ♘a5 13. ♗a3 b6 14. ♗b4 ♗b7 15. ♗×b7 [If 15. ♗×a5 ♗×g2 16. ♔×g2 ♕d5+= The same sequence applies if White plays 16. ♗×b6—RT] **15. ... ♘×b7 16. ♖c1 ♕d7 17. ♕b3 a5?!** [Better is 17. ... ♖fc8—RT] **18. ♗a3 b5 19. ♗c5 a4 20. ♕b4 ♘×c5 21. ♖×c5 ♖fc8 22. ♖fc1 ♖×c5 23. d×c5! ♖c8 24. ♘b1** *(see diagram)*

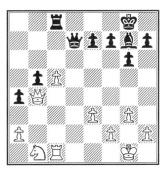

After 24. ♘b1

24. ... ♕d5 This is the start of a slide by Black; it can be argued that the push of the Black a and b pawns merely weakened Black's structure. [At this point 24. ... ♕d3 gives Black better chances to retain equality. An example being 25. ♘d2 h6 26. ♘f3 ♕d5 27. ♘d4 ♕×a2 28. ♕×b5 ♗×d4 29. e×d4 ♕d2∓; 24. ... e6 25. ♘a3 ♗f8 26. ♕×b5 (26. ♘×b5±) 26. ... ♕×b5 27. ♘×b5 ♖×c5 28. ♖×c5 ♗×c5 29. ♘c3 a3 30. ♔f1 and White picks up a pawn—RT] **25. ♕×b5 ♕×a2 26. ♕b7 ♖e8?!** [The text is too passive in this situation; the only viable option is to counterattack. 26. ... ♖d8!? 27. c6 (27. ♕×e7? ♖b8! 28. ♕e4 ♕b2 29. ♖d1 a3 30. ♘×a3 ♕×a3∓) 27. ... ♕b2 28. ♕×b2 ♗×b2∓—RT] **27. c6 ♕b2 28. ♖c4 ♖b8 29. ♕×b2 ♗×b2 30. ♖×a4 ♖c8 31. ♖c4 ♔f8 32. f4 e6 33. ♖c2 ♗g7 34. ♘a3 ♔e7 35. ♘b5 e5 36. ♔f2 f5 37. ♖c4 e×f4 38. g×f4 ♔e6 39. ♔e2 ♗f6 40. ♔d3 h6 41. ♖c2 g5 42. c7 ♔d7 43. ♖c5 g×f4 44. e×f4 ♗e7 45. ♖×f5 1–0** (Source: Reinfeld, *Keres' Best Games of Chess 1931–1948*, Printed Arts, 1949 and Dover, 1960 [additional notes by RT])

231 Reuben Fine–Menchik
Margate (2), April 1, 1937
[D45] Semi-Slav

1. d4 ♘f6 2. c4 e6 3. ♘c3 d5 4. ♘f3 ♘bd7 5. e3 a6 6. c5 c6 7. ♗d2 e5 [Black of course gets the pawn back, but possibly 7. ... ♕7 first would have led to an easier game.] **8. d×e5 ♘g4 9. ♘a4 ♘×c5** [If 9. ... ♘g×e5 10. ♘×e5 ♘×e5 11. ♗c3 ♘d7 12. b4 and Black's game is difficult. If 12. ... ♘f6 13. ♘b6 followed by ♗e5 and ♕d4—RT] **10. ♘×c5 ♗×c5 11. h3 ♘h6 12. ♗d3 ♕e7** [Evidently not 12. ... ♗f5 at once as then 13. ♗×f5 ♘×f5 14. ♕c2; 12. ...

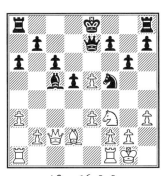

After 16. 0-0

f5 13. e×f6 ♕×f6 14. ♕c2 ♗d6 15. ♗×h7 ♖×h7 16. ♕×h7 ♗f5 17. ♕h8+ ♗f8 18. ♘c3 ♕e7 and Black castles queenside and gets some attack for the exchange; but unfortunately the simple move 15. ♗c3 first wins the pawn without trouble (Note: 15. ♗c3, according to Fritz, is not as good as ♗×h7 which leads to a winning advantage)—RT] **13. a3** An important move, not only preventing the exchange of bishops, but threatening the line of play ♕c2, ♖c1 and ♗b4. **13. ... ♗f5 14. ♗×f5 ♘×f5 15. ♕c2 g6** This leaves a permanent weakness. 15. ... ♘h6 is better, though Black's game is very trying. **16. 0-0** *(see diagram)*

16. ... ♘g7 [An alternative is 16. ... ♗a7 if then 17. e4 d×e4 18. ♗g5 Black could play 18. ... ♘d4 with some improvement in position. White however could play 19. ♕×e4 with a much superior game. Possibly 16. ... 0-0-0 is Black's best chance, if then 17. e4 ♘d4—RT] **17. e4 d×e4** [17. ... ♘e6 is no worse—RT] **18. ♗g5 ♕c7** [18. ... ♕f8 would hold out a good deal longer; but there is not much hope of anything beyond delay—RT] **19. ♕×c5 e×f3 20. ♗f6 f×g2 21. ♖fe1 ♘e6 22. ♕e3 ♖g8** [Evidently 22. ... 0-0 would be useless against 23. ♕h6 and ♖e4—RT] **23. ♖ad1 g5 24. ♖d3 ♘f4 25. ♗×g5 ♖×g5** [Not 25. ... ♘×h3+ 26. ♕×h3 ♖×g5 27. ♕×h7 ♕e7 28. ♖ed1+-—RT] **26. ♕×f4 ♕e7 27. e6 f6 28. ♖d7 ♕c5 29. ♖×h7 ♕a5 30. b4 1-0** (Source: *BCM* 1937, p. 274; notes by H.E. Aitkins [additional notes by RT])

232 Menchik–Philip S. Milner-Barry
Margate (3), April 2, 1937
[A11] *English Opening*

1. ♘f3 d5 2. g3 ♘f6 3. ♗g2 ♗f5 4. 0-0 ♘bd7 5. d3 c6 6. c4 e6 7. h3 h6 8. ♘c3 ♕c7 9. c×d5 e×d5 10. ♘d4 ♗h7 11. e4 d×e4 12. d×e4 0-0-0 13. ♕c2 ♗b4 14. ♘de2 ♖he8

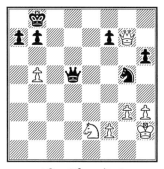

After 36. ... ♘g5

15. ♗f4 ♗d6 16. ♖ac1 ♗×f4 17. ♘×f4 ♕b8 18. b4 ♘b6 19. ♖fe1 ♖d7 20. ♘d3 ♖de7 21. ♘c5 ♘fd5 22. ♘×d5 ♘×d5 23. ♕b2 ♘f6 24. b5 ♕b6 25. a4 c×b5 26. a×b5 ♖c7 27. ♘d3 ♖×c1 28. ♘×c1 ♗e4 29. ♕b4 ♗×g2 30. ♖×e8+ ♘×e8 31. ♔×g2 ♕d6 32. ♕b3 ♕e6 33. ♕b2 ♕d5+ 34. ♔h2 ♘f6 35. ♘e2 ♘e4 36. ♕×g7 ♘g5 (*see diagram*)

37. ♕h8+ ♔c7 38. ♕c3+ ♔b6 39. ♕f6+ ♕e6 40. ♕d8+ ♔c5 41. ♕c7+ ♔b4 42. ♕c3+ ♔a4 43. ♕a1+ and the game was drawn by perpetual check. ½–½ (Source: *BCM* #7985)

233 C.H.O'D. Alexander–Menchik
Margate (4), April 3, 1937
[C14] *French, Classical*

1. e4 e6 2. d4 d5 3. ♘c3 ♘f6 4. ♗g5 ♗e7 5. e5 ♘fd7 6. ♗×e7 ♕×e7 7. f4 0-0 8. ♘f3 c5 9. ♗d3 Threatening ♗×h7+, but a doubtful move. **9. ... f6** [Black should reply 9. ... c×d4 10. ♗×h7+ (10. ♘b5 f6! 11. e×f6! *(11. ♘c7? f×e5 12. f×e5 ♘×e5 13. ♘×a8 ♘×f3+ 14. g×f3 ♕h4+ 15. ♔e2—other king moves are no better—15. ... e5 with a winning game.)* 11. ... ♘×f6 12. 0-0, a difficult game for both sides. Chances are about equal. As played by Black, White is able to avoid exchanging his e-pawn which remains as a permanent wedge in the Black position.) 10. ... ♔×h7 11. ♘g5+ ♔g5! 12. f×g5 d×c3 and Black probably has the better game with his strong center pawns—RT] **10. d×c5 ♘×c5** [10. ... ♕×c5 is more natural, keeping up pressure on the White e-pawn—RT] **11. 0-0 f5 12. ♘b5 ♗d7 13. ♘d6 ♘c6 14. ♕d2 ♗e8 15. b4 ♘×d3 16. c×d3 a6 17. ♕c3 ♕c7 18. ♕c5 b6 19. ♕c3 ♕b8 20. ♘d4 ♘×d4 21. ♕×d4 ♗a4 22. ♖ac1 ♖a7 23. ♕e3 ♖d8 24. ♖c3 ♖c7 25. ♖fc1 ♖dd7 26. ♕d4 h6 27. h3 ♔h7 28. ♔h2 ♖e7 29. ♕e3 ♗b5 30. ♘×b5**

a×b5 31. 罝c6 豐a7 32. 豐f2 罝×c6 33. 罝×c6 豐a4 34. 豐d2
豐a7 35. 豐f2 豐a3 36. 豐d2 豐a7 37. d4 豐g8 38. 豐c2
豐f7 39. 豐b3 豐a6 40. a3 罝a7 41. 豐g3 豐×a3 42. 罝c7+
豐e8 43. 豐g6+ 豐d8 44. 罝×a7 豐×a7 45. 豐×e6 豐d7 (*see
diagram*)

46. 豐×d7+? [46. 豐×b6+ 豐e7 47. 豐g6 豐d8 48. e6 豐c7
49. 豐×f5 and a perfunctory win follows—RT] 46. ... 豐×d7
47. g4 f×g4 48. h×g4 g5! ½–½ (Source: *BCM* #7993 [additional notes by RT])

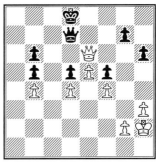

After 45. ... 豐d7

234 Menchik–Victor Berger

Margate (5), April 4, 1937

[A08] King's Indian Attack

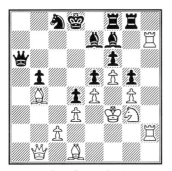

After 40. ... 彐c8

1. 彐f3 d5 2. g3 c5 3. 彐g2 彐c6 4. 0-0 e5 5. d3 彐ge7
6. e4 f6 7. 彐fd2 彐e6 8. 彐c3 d4 9. 彐e2 豐d7 10. f4 0-0-0
11. f5 彐f7 12. 彐b3 豐d6 13. 彐d2 g6 14. g4 豐b8 15. 彐g3
g5 16. 彐f3 彐c8 17. 彐a5 豐c7 18. 彐×c6+ 豐×c6 19. b3
h6 20. 豐g2 彐e7 21. 罝h1 彐d6 22. a4 b6 23. h4 a6
24. 豐e2 豐b7 25. 罝h2 罝dg8 26. 罝ah1 豐e8 27. 豐d1 罝f8
28. 罝h3 罝hg8 29. 罝1h2 b5 30. a×b5 a×b5 31. 豐b1 豐a8
32. h×g5 h×g5 33. 彐e2 豐a3 34. b4 豐a7 35. b×c5 豐×c5
36. 彐b4 豐b6 37. 罝h7 豐c8 38. 彐g3 豐d8 39. 彐d1 豐a6
40. 豐f3 彐c8 (*see diagram*)

41. c3 d×c3 42. 彐b3 彐×b3 43. 豐×b3 彐×b4 44. 豐×b4
豐a4 45. 豐×c3 豐d1+ 46. 彐e2 彐e7 47. 罝×e7! 豐f1+ 48. 豐e3 1–0 (Source: *BCM* #8007)

235 Theodore Tylor–Menchik

Margate (6), April 6, 1937

[C14] *French, Classical*

1. e4 e6 2. d4 d5 3. 彐c3 彐f6 4. 彐g5 彐e7 5. e5 彐fd7 6. 彐×e7 豐×e7 7. 豐d2 0-0 8. f4
c5 9. 彐f3 彐c6 10. g3 彐b6 11. b3 c×d4 12. 彐b5 [This line was Black's intent after her 10th
move. 12. 彐×d4 豐c5 13. 彐ce2 彐×d4 14. 彐×d4 彐d7 15. 彐e2 Intending to bring the second
knight to c6 via c8 and e7—RT] 12. ... 彐d7 13. 彐b×d4 f6
14. e×f6? A mistake which gives Black the better game. [White
should have tried here 彐g2 or 彐h3, when in reply to 14. ... f×e5
White would have to choose between 15. d×e5 or 15. 彐×c6
followed by 16. 彐×e5 with prospect of developing an attack
against Black's backward e-pawn. 14. 彐g2—RT] 14. ... g×f6
15. 0-0-0 e5 16. 彐×c6 [Not 16. 彐b5 on account of 16. ... d4
and then a6—RT] 16. ... b×c6 17. 罝g1? 彐g4 [Stronger was
at once 17. ... 豐a3+ 18. 豐b1 彐a4 19. c3 (or c4) 19. ... 罝ab8
threatening 彐f5+, also 罝×b3+—RT] 18. 彐e2 彐×f3 19. 彐×f3
豐h8 20. f×e5? f×e5 21. 罝df1 豐a3+ (*see diagram*)

After 21. ... 豐a3+

22. ♔d1 [If 22. ♔b1 ♘a4 23. c3 ♕c5 24. b×a4 ♖×f3 etc.—RT] **22. ...** ♕×a2 **23.** ♕c3 [If 23. ♕h6 threatening 24. ♗e4, then simply 23. ... ♘d7—RT] **23. ...** d4 **24.** ♕c5 [Better at once 24. ♕×c6 whereas if 24. ♕b4 then c5, etc.—RT] **24. ...** ♘d7 **25.** ♕×c6 ♖ac8 **26.** ♕e4 ♘f6 **27.** ♕f5 d3 **28.** c×d3 ♖c2 If now 29. ♔e1 ♕a1+ 30.Bd1 ♕c3 mate **0–1** (Source: *BCM* #8011; notes by VM [additional notes by RT])

236   Menchik–George Thomas
Margate (7), April 7, 1937

[A14] *English*

1. c4 ♘f6 2. ♘f3 e6 3. g3 d5 4. ♗g2 c5 5. 0-0 ♘c6 6. b3 ♗e7 7. ♗b2 0-0 8. d3 ♕c7 9. ♘a3 d4 10. ♘c2 e5 11. e3 ♖b8 12. e×d4 e×d4 13. b4 b6 14. b5 ♘d8 15. a4 ♘e6 16. ♗c1 ♗b7 17. ♗d2 a5 18. b×a6 ♗×a6 19. ♘a3 ♘d7 20. ♖e1 ♗f6 21. ♖a2 ♖fe8 22. ♘b5 ♗×b5 23. a×b5 ♘ef8 24. ♕a1 ♖×e1+ 25. ♕×e1 ♘g6 26. ♕a1 h6 27. ♖a7 ♖b7 28. ♖a8+ ♖b8 29. ♕a7 ♕d6 30. ♖×b8+ ♘×b8 31. ♗h3 ♗d8 32. ♗f5 ♕c7 33. ♕a8 *(see diagram)*

33. ... ♗e7?? **34.** ♗×g6 **1-0** (Source: *www.Chessgames.com*)

After 33. ♕a8

237   Alexander Alekhine–Menchik
Margate (8), April 8, 1937

[D60] *Queen's Gambit Declined, Classical Variation*

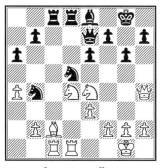

After 21. ... ♕×e7

1. d4 ♘f6 2. c4 e6 3. ♘c3 d5 4. ♗g5 ♘bd7 5. e3 ♗e7 6. ♗d3 d×c4 7. ♗×c4 c5 8. ♘f3 0-0 9. 0-0 a6 10. a4 c×d4 11. ♘×d4 ♘e5 12. ♗b3 ♗d7 13. ♕e2 ♘c6 14. ♖fd1 ♕c7 15. ♖ac1 ♖fd8 16. ♕f3 ♖ac8 17. ♗c2 ♗e8 18. ♕h3 g6 19. ♕h4 ♘d5 20. ♘e4 ♘cb4 21. ♗×e7 ♕×e7 *(see diagram)*

22. ♘g5 h5 23. ♗b3 ♖×c1 24. ♖×c1 e5? White's positional deterioration is possibly due to trying to keep life in the position; at any rate this move returns the advantage Menchik had accumulated. [24. ... ♘d3 25. ♗b1 ♘c5∓ —RT] **25. ♘df3 ♔g7 26. e4 ♘f6 27. h3 ♘c6 28. g4 ♕b4 29. ♖c3 ♘d4 30. ♘×d4 ♖×d4 31. ♖f3 ♕d6** *(see diagram)*

32. ♘e6+ f×e6 33. ♕×f6+ ♔h7 34. g×h5 ♖d3? 35. ♖×d3 1-0 (Source: *BCM* #8019 [additional note by RT])

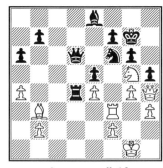

After 31. ... ♕d6

238 Menchik–Jan Foltys
Margate (9), April 9, 1937

[A25] *English*

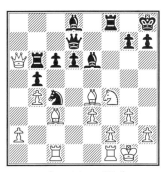

1. c4 e5 2. ♘c3 ♘c6 3. g3 f5 4. ♗g2 ♘f6 5. e3 d6 6. ♘ge2 ♗e7 7. 0-0 0-0 8. ♘d5 ♗e6 9. ♕b3 ♖b8 10. ♘ec3 ♔h8 11. d3 ♕d7 12. ♗d2 ♖d8 13. ♕a4 a6 14. b4 b5 15. ♕xa6 e4 16. dxe4 fxe4 17. ♖ac1 ♘e5 18. ♘xe4 ♘xe4 19. ♗xe4 ♘xc4 20. ♗c3 c6 21. ♘f4 ♖b6 (see diagram)
    22. ♗xh7!? ♖xf4! [If in reply 22. … ♖xa6 23. ♘g6+ is effective—RT] **23. ♕xb6 ♘xb6 0-1** (Source: *BCM* #8023)

After 21. … ♖b6

Bournemouth 1938

The only records of this event are in the listing of Menchik's events in her *Chess* obituary and Di Felice's crosstable which references her participation and score without a specific date or the rest of the participants. According to these sources, Vera scored one out of three and tied for 3rd–4th places.

Łódź 1938
March 20–April 5, 1938

		1	2	3	4	5	6	7	8	9	10	11	12	13	14	15	16	Points	Place
1	Pirc, Vasja	•	=	1	=	=	1	=	=	1	=	=	1	1	1	1	1	11½	1
2	Tartakower, Saviely	=	•	=	=	=	0	1	1	1	1	1	=	=	=	=	1	10	2
3	Petrovs, Vladimirs	0	=	•	=	1	1	1	=	=	=	0	=	1	1	1	=	9½	3–5
4	Eliskases, Erich	=	=	=	•	=	=	1	=	=	=	=	=	1	1	=	1	9½	3–5
5	Ståhlberg, Anders G.	=	=	0	=	•	1	=	=	=	0	1	=	1	1	1	1	9½	3–5
6	Gerstenfeld, Eduard	0	1	0	d	0	•	1	1	0	=	1	1	0	=	1	1	8½	6
7	Frydman, Paulin	=	0	0	0	=	0	•	=	=	1	=	=	1	1	1	1	8	7
8	Steiner, Lajos	=	0	=	=	=	0	=	•	1	=	1	0	=	1	0	1	7½	8–9
9	Appel, Izaak	0	0	=	=	=	1	=	0	•	1	=	=	=	0	1	1	7½	8–9
10	Najdorf, Miguel	=	0	=	=	1	=	0	=	0	•	0	=	1	=	=	1	7	10–12
11	Foltys, Jan	=	0	1	=	0	0	=	0	=	1	•	=	=	=	1	=	7	10–12
12	Kolski, Josek	0	=	=	=	=	0	=	1	=	=	=	•	0	=	=	1	7	10–12
13	Regedziński, Teodor	0	=	0	0	0	1	0	=	=	0	=	1	•	1	=	1	6½	13
14	Sulik, Franciszek	0	=	0	0	0	=	0	0	1	=	=	=	0	•	1	=	5	14
15	Menchik, Vera	0	=	0	=	0	0	0	1	0	=	0	=	=	0	•	0	3½	15
16	Seitz, Jakob A.	0	0	=	0	0	0	0	0	0	0	=	0	0	=	1	•	2½	16

239 Menchik–Jakob Adolf Seitz
Łódź (1), March 20, 1938

[D40] *Queen's Gambit Declined, Semi-Tarrasch Variation*

1. d4 d5 2. c4 e6 3. ♘c3 ♘f6 4. ♘f3 ♗e7 5. e3 c5 6. ♗d3 ♘c6 7. 0-0 0-0 8. ♖e1 b6 9. b3 ♗b7 10. ♗b2 cxd4 11. exd4 ♔h8 12. ♖c1 dxc4 13. ♗xc4 ♘b4 14. ♘e5 ♖c8 15. ♗f1 ♘bd5 16. ♘xd5 ♗xd5 17. ♕d3 ♗b7 18. ♕h3 ♗e4 19. ♗a6 ♖xc1 20. ♖xc1 ♕d6 21. ♕e3 ♔g8 22. ♗b5 ♗f5 23. ♘c6 ♘d5 24. ♕e5 ♗xe5 25. ♘xe7+ ♘xe7

26. d×e5 ♖d8 27. f3 h5 28. a4 ♖d2 29. ♗c3 ♖a2 30. ♗d4 ♘d5 31. g3 g5 32. ♖c8+
♔g7 33. ♗c4 ♖d2 34. ♗f2 ♗h3 35. ♗e1 ♖g2+ 36. ♔h1 ♖c2 37. ♗a6 ♖b2 38. ♖c1
♗g2+ 39. ♔g1 ♗×f3 40. ♗c4 ♖g2+ 0–1 (Source: Lachaga, *Łódź 1938*)

240   Eduard Gerstenfeld–Menchik
Łódź (2), March 21, 1938

[A95] *Dutch, Stonewall*

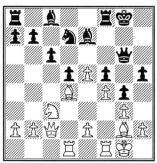

After 18. ♗d4

1. c4 f5 2. ♘c3 ♘f6 3. g3 e6 4. ♗g2 ♗e7 5. d4 0–0 6. ♘f3
d5 7. 0–0 c6 8. ♗f4 ♕e8 9. ♘e5 ♕h5 10. f3 g5 11. ♗c1
♘bd7 12. ♕c2 ♘×e5 13. d×e5 ♘d7 14. c×d5 e×d5 15. f4
g4 16. ♗e3 ♕g6 17. ♖ad1 h5 18. ♗d4 *(see diagram)*
     18. ... ♖d8? [18. ... ♕h7 Allowing the bishop coverage
by the queen holds the position. 19. ♗×d5+ c×d5 20. ♘×d5
♘b6=—RT] 19. ♗×d5+ c×d5 20. ♘×d5 ♗f8 21. e6 ♕×e6
22. ♘c7 ♕c6 23. ♕×f5 ♘f6 24. ♕g5+ ♔f7 25. ♕×f6+
♕×f6 26. ♗×f6 ♗c5+ 27. ♔g2 ♗d7 28. ♗×d8 ♗c6+
29. ♘d5 ♖×d8 30. e4 1–0 (Source: Lachaga, *Łódź 1938*; *BCM*
#8253)

241   Menchik–Vasja Pirc
Łódź (3), March 22, 1938

[D52] *Queen's Gambit Declined, Cambridge Springs Variation*

1. d4 ♘f6 2. ♘f3 d5 3. c4 e6 4. ♘c3 ♘bd7 5. ♗g5 c6 6. e3 ♕a5 7. c×d5 e×d5 8. ♗d3
♘e4 9. 0–0 ♘×g5 10. ♘×g5 ♘f6 11. e4 The isolani was often embraced during this era;
after all, Tarrasch had only recently died. Games with Menchik on either side of the formation
are common. [11. ♖e1 or 11. ♕c2 were called for at this stage—
RT] 11. ... h6 12. ♘f3 d×e4 13. ♘×e4 ♘×e4 14. ♗×e4
♗d6 15. d5! c5 16. ♗c2 0–0 17. ♕d3 f5 18. ♖fe1 ♕c7
19. ♕c3 b5 20. ♖ad1 b4 21. ♕c4 ♗d7 22. a4 b×a3
23. b×a3 ♕a5 *(see diagram)*
     24. ♖e6? This is no *Fingerfehler*, but a deliberate sacrifice;
but for what? [A more logical idea might be 24. ♘e5 ♖fe8
25. f4 ♖e7 26. ♖e3 ♕c7 27. ♖f3±—RT] 24. ... ♗×e6 25. d×e6
♗e7 26. ♖d7 ♕×a3 27. h3 ♕a1+ 28. ♔h2 ♕f6 Was this
what Menchik had failed to see on move 24? 29. g3 ♖ad8
30. ♖×a7 ♔h8 31. ♖×e7 ♕×e7 32. ♘e5 ♕f6 33. ♘d7 [If
33. e7 ♕×e5 34. ♕h4 ♖c8 35. e×f8♕+ ♖×f8–+—RT] 33. ...

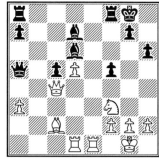

After 23. ... ♕a5

♖×d7 34. e×d7 ♕d6 35. h4 g6 36. h5 g×h5 37. ♕d3 ♕×d3 38. ♗×d3 ♔g7 39. ♗×f5
♔f6 40. g4 h×g4 41. ♗×g4 c4 42. ♔g3 c3 43. ♗d1 ♔e7 44. ♗a4 ♖a8 45. ♗b3 ♖a3
0–1 (Source: Lachaga, *Łódź 1938* [additional notes by RT])

242   Lajos Steiner–Menchik
Łódź (4), March 23, 1938

[C14] *French, Classical*

     A fascinating game with errors on both sides. The game starts off with a fairly standard

Classical French which Menchik builds on to gain a solid advantage. After blocking her own rook and then taking it out of play it looks like she will be "praying" for a draw—only to find a poisoned rook sacrifice to gain the perpetual. Steiner refuses to accept this and after some jockeying around he has a brief moment of blindness, allowing Vera to bring her queen in for a decisive finish. Di Felice in his crosstable book incorrectly lists this as a result by Herman Steiner (the Hungarian American IM), but all other evidence including the tournament book make it clear that Menchik's opponent was Lajos.

1. e4 e6 2. d4 d5 3. ♘c3 ♘f6 4. ♗g5 ♗e7 5. e5 ♘fd7 6. ♗×e7 ♕×e7 7. ♕d2 0-0 8. f4 c5 9. ♘f3 ♘c6 10. g3 a6 11. ♗g2 b5 12. 0-0 ♘b6 13. ♕f2 ♗b7 14. f5 b4 15. ♘e2 e×f5 16. ♘h4 g6 17. c3 c×d4 18. c×d4 ♘d8 19. ♗h3 ♗c8 20. ♘g2 ♘e6 21. ♘e3 ♘g5 22. ♗g2 ♗e6 23. ♕f4 ♖ac8 24. ♔h1 ♘e4 25. g4 f×g4 26. b3 f5 27. ♕h6 ♖c6 28. ♖ac1 ♖fc8 29. ♖×c6 ♖×c6 30. ♗×e4 d×e4 31. ♘f4 *(see diagram)*

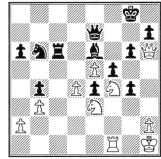

After 31. ♘f4

31. ... ♖c3? [31. ... ♗d7 Maximizing the mobility of her pieces—the c file is not going to go anywhere in the meantime—RT] **32. ♘×g4 f×g4 33. ♘×g6 h×g6 34. ♕×g6+ ♔h8 35. ♕h6+ ♔g8 36. ♖f6 ♖h3 37. ♕g6+ ♔h8 38. ♖×e6** *(see diagram)*

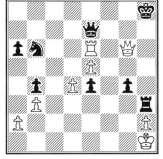

After 38. ♖×e6

38. ... ♖×h2+ 39. ♔g1 ♖h1+ 40. ♔g2 ♖h2+ 41. ♔f1 ♖h1+ 42. ♔e2 ♖h2+? [42. ... ♘d5! 43. ♖×e7 ♘f4+ and wins—RT] **43. ♔f1 ♖h1+ 44. ♔g2 ♖h2+ 45. ♔g1 ♖h1+ 46. ♔f2?? ♕h4+ 47. ♔e3** *(see diagram)*

47. ... ♘d5+? [47. ... ♕g3+ and mate in one—RT] **48. ♔×e4 ♘c3+ 49. ♔d3 ♕h3+ 50. ♔c4 ♕f1+ 51. ♔×b4 ♘×a2+ 52. ♔c5 ♕b5+ 53. ♔d6 ♕b4+ 54. ♔d5 ♕×b3+ 55. ♔d6 ♕b4+ 56. ♔d5 ♘c3+ 57. ♔c6 ♕b5+ 58. ♔d6 ♕b8+ 59. ♔d7 ♕b7+ 60. ♔e8 ♕a8+** To have been in the audience for the finish! **0-1** (Source: Lachaga, *Łódź 1938* [additional notes by RT])

After 47. ♔e3

243 Menchik–Vladimirs Petrovs

Łódź (5), March 24, 1938

[D40] *Queen's Gambit Declined, Semi-Tarrasch Variation*

1. d4 ♘f6 2. ♘f3 d5 3. c4 e6 4. ♘c3 ♗e7 5. e3 ♘bd7 6. ♗d3 d×c4 7. ♗×c4 c5 8. 0-0 c×d4 9. e×d4 ♘b6 10. ♗b3 0-0 11. ♕e2 ♘bd5 12. ♘e5 ♗d7 13. ♖e1 ♗b4 14. ♗d2 ♖c8 15. ♖ac1 ♗d6 16. ♗g5 ♗e7 17. ♗×f6?! Giving up the bishop pair. [An alternate line might be 17. ♘×d5 ♘×d5 18. ♗×e7 ♕×e7± —RT] **17. ... ♘×c3 18. ♖×c3 ♗×f6 19. ♖h3 g6 20. ♕d2 ♗g7 21. ♕f4 ♖c7** *(see diagram)*

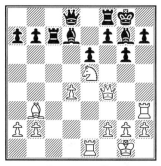

After 21. ... ♖c7

22. g4 signaling that the game will not be a draw—although with her weaknesses a little discretion might have been appropriate. **22. ... h6 23. d5** Having decided that the isolani no longer fits in with the plan it is time to trade it before it is lost. **23. ... e×d5 24. ♗×d5 ♗c6 25. ♘×c6 b×c6 26. ♗b3 ♖d7 27. ♖he3 ♔h7 28. ♕e4?!** Providing Black a nice spot for his rook with the gain of tempo [28. ♖3e2—RT] **28. ... c5 29. ♖3e2 ♖d4 30. ♕f3** [Better would be 30. ♕g2—RT] **30. ... ♕g5 31. h3 h5 32. ♕e3 ♖f4 33. ♕e7?** [White's position is becoming untenable, but 33. ♖c2 gives it a little dynamic life—RT] **33. ... ♕×e7 34. ♖×e7 c4 35. ♗d1 ♗×b2 36. g×h5 g×h5 37. ♖1e4 ♖×e4 38. ♖×e4 ♖c8 39. ♗c2 ♔g7 40. ♖e7 ♗d4 41. ♖d7 ♗b6 42. ♔g2 ♖c5 43. ♖b7 ♖b5 44. ♗e4 ♖b2 45. ♗d5 ♖×f2+ 46. ♔g3 c3 0–1** (Source: Lachaga, *Łódź 1938* [additional notes by RT])

244 Miguel Najdorf–Menchik
Łódź (6), March 25, 1938

[D61] *Queen's Gambit Declined, Classical Variation*

White maintains a slight pull throughout the game that never becomes adequate. **1. d4 ♘f6 2. c4 e6 3. ♘c3 d5 4. ♘f3 ♘bd7 5. ♗g5 ♗e7 6. e3 0–0 7. ♕c2 c5 8. d×c5 ♘×c5 9. c×d5 e×d5 10. ♗e2 ♘ce4 11. 0–0 ♘×g5 12. ♘×g5 d4 13. e×d4 ♕×d4 14. ♗f3 ♕f4 15. ♘d5 ♕×g5 16. ♘×e7+ ♔h8 17. ♕b3 ♘e4 18. ♕b4 ♘c5 19. ♖fc1 ♕×e7 20. ♕×c5 ♖e8 21. ♕c7 g6 22. h3 ♔g7 23. ♖c3 ♕f6** (*see diagram*)

After 23. ... ♕f6

24. ♗×b7 ♗×b7 25. ♕×b7 ♖ab8 26. ♕d5 ♖×b2 27. ♖f3 ♖d2 ½–½ (Source: Lachaga, *Łódź 1938*; BCM #8333)

245 Menchik–Jan Foltys
Łódź (7), March 26, 1938

[D37] *Queen's Gambit Declined*

For the first 20 moves or so Menchik plays well and even has an edge; then, within five moves, she is completely lost. Still, she drags it out for another 30 moves. Foltys was one of the top Czech players from 1936 (Poděbrady) until his early death in 1950. **1. d4 ♘f6 2. c4 e6 3. ♘f3 d5 4. ♘c3 c5 5. e3 ♘c6 6. ♗d3 d×c4 7. ♗×c4 a6 8. a4 ♗e7 9. 0–0 0–0 10. ♘e5 c×d4 11. ♘×c6 b×c6 12. e×d4 ♗b7 13. ♗e3 ♘d5 14. ♘×d5 c×d5 15. ♗d3 ♗d6 16. b4 f5 17. ♖b1 f4 18. ♗d2 ♕f6 19. ♕f3 g6 20. ♖fe1 ♖fe8** (*see diagram*)

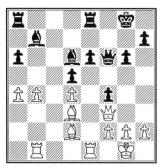

After 20. ... ♖fe8

21. b5? 21. ♗c3 maintains the advantage **21. ... ♕×d4 22. b×a6** Better would be 22. ♖ed1 e5 23. ♗b4 e4 24. ♗×e4 ♕×e4 25. ♕×e4 ♖×e4 26. ♗×d6 ♖×a4∓ **22. ... ♗×a6**

23. ♗×a6 ♖×a6 **24.** ♗c3 ♕×a4 **25.** ♖b7 ♖a7 **26.** ♖b6 ♖a6 **27.** ♖b7 ♖a7 **28.** ♖b6 ♕d7
29. ♕d3 ♗c5 **30.** ♖b5 ♗f8 **31.** ♗e5 ♖a3 **32.** ♔b1 ♖a7 **33.** ♗×f4 ♗g7 **34.** ♕b3 ♕f7
35. ♖b8 ♖ae7 **36.** ♗d6 ♖×b8 **37.** ♕×b8+ ♖e8 **38.** ♕b6 ♕d7 **39.** g3 d4 **40.** f4 ♖d8
41. ♗e5 ♗×e5 **42.** ♖×e5 d3 **43.** ♖e1 ♕f7 **44.** ♕f2 ♕d5 Not 44. ... ♕d4+? 45. ♔×d4 ♖×d4
46. ♔e3 d5 47. ♖d1 with a draw in the making **45.** ♕a7+ ♖d7 **46.** ♕e3 d2 **47.** ♖d1 ♕h5
48. ♕f3 Even worse is 48. ♖×d2 ♖×d2+ 49. ♕×d2 ♕×h2+ 50. ♔e3 ♕×d2+ 51. ♔×d2 **48. ...**
♕×h2+ **49.** ♔e3 h5 **50.** ♔e4 ♕h3 **51.** ♔e3 ♕f5 **52.** ♖×d2 ♕c5+ **53.** ♔e2 ♖×d2+
54. ♔×d2 ♕d5+ **55.** ♔e2 ♕f3+ **56.** ♔×f3 ♕f6 **57.** g4 h4 **58.** ♔e4 g5 **59.** ♔f3 g×f4
60. ♔×f4 e5+ **0–1** (Source: Lachaga, *Łódź 1938*; Podgorný, *J. Foltys*, p. 83, 1956; notes by RT)

246 Menchik–Teodor Regedziński
Łódź (8), March 27, 1938
[D13] Slav, Exchange

In this game with lots of maneuvering, White gets a nice spatial and mobility advantage, but
never provokes enough weaknesses in Black's position to collect the point. **1. d4 d5 2.** ♘f3
♘f6 **3. c4 c6 4. c×d5 c×d5 5.** ♘c3 ♘c6 **6.** ♗f4 e6 **7. e3 a6 8.** ♗d3 ♗e7 **9.** ♘e5 0-0
10. 0-0 ♗d7 **11.** ♖c1 ♕a5 **12.** ♗g5 ♕d8 **13. f4** ♘e8 **14.** ♗×e7 ♕×e7 **15.** ♘×d7 ♕×d7
16. ♘a4 ♕e7 **17.** ♘b6 ♖b8 **18. a3** ♘f6 **19.** ♕c2 ♕c7 **20.** ♕c5 ♖fd8 **21. b4** ♖d6 **22. a4**
♕d8 **23. a5** ♘e8 **24.** ♕c3 ♘a7 **25.** ♕c2 g6 **26.** ♕a4 ♘c8
27. ♘×c8 ♖×c8 **28.** ♖c5 ♖×c5 **29. b×c5** ♖c6 **30.** ♖b1 ♕c8
31. ♕b4 ♖c7 **32. h3** ♘f6 **33.** ♗c2 ♔g7 **34.** ♗a4 ♘d7
35. ♕c3 ♔g8 **36.** ♖b4 h6 **37.** ♕b2 ♔h7 **38.** ♔h2 ♔g8
39. g4 ♔h7 **40.** ♕b1 ♔g7 **41.** ♖b2 ♘f6 *(see diagram)*

After 41. ... ♘f6

　　　42. ♗c2 h5 **43. g5** ♘g8 **44. e4** ♘e7 **45. f5** e×f5
46. e×f5 ♘×f5 **47.** ♗×f5 g×f5 **48.** ♕e1 ♖c6 **49.** ♕e5+ ♔g6
50. ♖b6 ♕d7 **51. h4** ♔h7 **52.** ♔g3 ♖×b6 **53. a×b6 a5**
54. ♔f4 a4 **55.** ♕d6 ♕e8 **56.** ♕×d5 a3 **57.** ♕×f5+ No better is 57. ♕b7 a2 58. g6+ ♔×g6 59. ♕g2+ and a draw will
ensue **57. ...** ♔g7 **58.** ♕f6+ ♔g8 **59. c6 a2 60. d5 b×c6**
61. d×c6 ♕e1 **62.** ♕d8+ With 62. b7 ♕b4+ 63. ♔f3 White
can torture Black a bit, but should not get the win **62. ...** ♔g7 **63.** ♕f6+ ♔g8 **64.** ♕d8+
♔h7 **65.** ♕d3+ ♔g7 **66.** ♕d4+ ♔h7 ½–½ (Source: Lachaga, *Łódź 1938*; notes by RT)

247 Saviely Tartakower–Menchik
Łódź (9), March 28, 1938
[C00] French

An intriguing game in which Tartakower played one of his idiosyncratic openings and in which
Menchik missed a win **1. e4 e6 2. g3** Proof that there are few opening moves that are flat out
losing! Of course Tartakower was known for playing "strange" lines as in 1. b4 in New York.
2. ... d5 3. ♗g2 d×e4 **4.** ♘c3 ♘f6 [The question is, what would the materialistic line of
4. ... f5 provide, given its weak dark squares and, at least for the moment, loose king position?—RT] **5.** ♘×e4 ♘×e4 Menchik chooses to return the pawn and liquidate to force equality. **6.** ♗×e4 c5 **7.** ♘e2 ♗e7 **8. 0-0** ♘c6 **9. c3 0-0 10.** ♕c2 g6 **11. d3** ♗d7 **12. f4** ♕c8
13. ♗e3 ♖d8 **14.** ♖ad1 ♘a5 **15. g4 f5 16.** ♗f3 ♗c6 **17. g5** ♗×f3 **18.** ♖×f3 ♕c6 **19.** ♖ff1

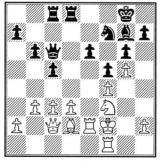

After 26. ♗d2

♗f8 20. b3 ♖ac8 21. ♔f2 b6 22. ♖d2 ♘b7 23. ♘g1 ♘d6 24. ♘f3 ♗g7 25. ♖e2 ♘f7 26. ♗d2 *(see diagram)*

26. ... ♕d6 27. ♖fe1 ♕×d3 28. ♕×d3 ♖×d3 29. ♖×e6 It is almost difficult to find a losing plan. 29. ... ♖dd8 30. ♖e7 ♘d6 31. ♖1e6 [If 31. ♖×a7? ♘e4+ 32. ♔e2 ♘×d2 33. ♖×g7+ ♔×g7 34. ♘×d2∓—RT] 31. ... ♘e4+ 32. ♔e3 c4 33. b×c4 ♘c5 34. ♖×g7+ ♔×g7 35. ♖e7+ ♔g8 36. ♘e5 *(see diagram)* 36. ... a5?! [Better is 36. ... ♖a8 37. h4 ♖e8 38. ♖c7 ♖ad8 39. ♖×a7 ♘d3 and Black wins—RT] 37. ♔e2! Ultimately saving the game if the alternative scenario just above came up again. 37. ... ♖e8 38. ♖a7 ♖a8 39. ♖c7 ♖ac8 40. ♖a7 ♖a8 [40. ... ♖cd8 41. ♗e3—RT] 41. ♖c7 ♖ac8 42. ♖a7 ♖a8 Drawn by repetition. ½–½ (Source: Lachaga, *Łódź 1938* [additional notes by RT])

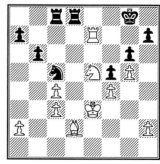

After 36. ♘e5

248　Josek Kolski–Menchik
Łódź (10), March 29, 1938

[E11] *Bogo-Indian Defense*

Mostly this game drifted pretty close to equality although at the end White's bishop for knight and better placed king left him with some chances when the players agreed to split the point.

Final position

1. d4 ♘f6 2. c4 e6 3. ♘f3 ♗b4+ 4. ♗d2 ♗×d2+ 5. ♘b×d2 d6 6. e3 ♕e7 7. ♗e2 0-0 8. 0-0 e5 9. d×e5 d×e5 10. ♕c2 h6 11. ♖fd1 e4 12. ♘d4 a6 13. c5 ♗d7 14. b4 ♘c6 15. ♘×c6 ♗×c6 16. a4 ♕e5 17. ♘c4 ♕f5 18. f4 ♕e6 19. ♖d4 ♗d5 20. ♘e5 c6 21. ♘c4 ♗×c4 22. ♗×c4 ♕e7 23. ♖ad1 ♖fd8 24. ♕b3 ♖×d4 25. ♖×d4 ♔f8 26. h3 ♖c8 27. a5 ♖c7 28. ♕d1 ♖d7 29. ♖×d7 ♕×d7 30. ♕×d7 ♘×d7 31. g4 ♔e7 32. ♔f2 ♘f6 33. ♔e2 ♘d5 34. ♔d2 ♔d7 35. h4 f6 *(see diagram)*

Although not an easy task, White still has real winning chances—no guarantee (based on numerous computer generated variations)—both in lines where Black gets in ♘×b4 and where White plays ♗×d5. Of course the players have just made time control and no doubt felt exhausted. ½–½ (Source: Lachaga, *Łódź 1938*; notes by RT)

249　Izaak Appel–Menchik
Łódź (11), March 30, 1938

[D78] *Neo-Grünfeld*

1. ♘f3 ♘f6 2. c4 g6 3. d4 ♗g7 4. g3 0-0 5. ♗g2 c6 6. 0-0 d5 7. ♘e5 ♗e6 8. ♘c3 d×c4 9. e4 ♘fd7 10. ♘f3 ♘b6 11. ♗e3 ♗g4 12. a4 ♘a6 13. a5 ♘d7 [Better would have been 13. ... ♘c8—RT] 14. ♕a4 ♗×f3?! There appears to be no good reason to part with

the bishop pair yet. [Better seems 14. ... c5 15. ♖fd1 (or 15. d×c5 ♘d×c5 16. ♕×c4 ♕d6) 15. ... ♘b4 16. d×c5 ♘d3—RT] **15. ♗×f3 e6 16. ♕×c4 ♕e7 17. ♗e2 c5 18. d5 ♘b4 19. ♖ad1 e×d5 20. ♘×d5 ♘×d5 21. ♖×d5 b6 22. ♗g5 ♕e6 23. ♕d3?** = [23. ♖fd1 ♘f6 24. ♗×f6 ♕×f6 25. e5 ♕e7 26. f4—RT] **23. ... ♗d4 24. ♔g2** [24. ♖d1—RT] **24. ... ♘e5 25. ♕c2 ♘c6 26. ♗c4 ♘b4** [26. ... b5 leads to a solid Black advantage. 27. ♖×d4 ♘×d4 28. ♗×e6 ♘×c2—RT] **27. ♕e2 ♘×d5 28. ♗×d5 ♕e8 29. f4? ♖b8 30. a6 ♔g7 31. e5 f5 32. ♖e1 h6 33. ♗f6+ ♔h7 34. g4 ♕d7 35. ♗f3** *(see diagram)*

After 35. ♗f3

35. ... ♕e6? [35. ... f×g4 36. ♗×g4 ♕d5+ 37. ♗f3 ♕b3 38. h4 ♕×b2 39. ♕×b2 ♗×b2 40. h5 with realistic chances for the win—RT] **36. h4** [36. g5!?—RT] **36. ... ♖be8 37. g5 ♕b3 38. h5 g×h5** It's hard to comprehend how fast Black goes from an almost certain win to a loss. One has to suspect a 40 move time control, with Vera in her frequent time pressure. **39. ♗×h5 ♕×b2?? ** [39. ... ♖e6 holds the position—RT] **40. ♕×b2 ♗×b2 41. ♗×e8 ♖×e8 42. ♖h1 ♔g8 43. g6 ♖f8 44. ♗×h6 ♖×f6 45. e×f6 ♗×f6 46. ♖h7 ♗g7 47. ♔f3 b5 48. ♖h5 b4 49. ♖×f5 ♗d4 50. ♔e4 ♔g7 51. ♖f7+ ♔×g6 52. ♖×a7 c4 53. ♔×d4 1–0** (Source: Lachaga, *Łódź 1938* [additional notes by RT])

250 Menchik–Paulin Frydman

Łódź (12), March 31, 1938

[E01] *Catalan*

1. d4 ♘f6 2. c4 e6 3. g3 d5 4. ♗g2 b6 5. c×d5 e×d5 6. ♘h3 ♗e7 7. ♘c3 0-0 8. 0-0 ♗f5 9. ♘f4 c6 10. ♕a4 ♕c8 11. b4 b5 12. ♕b3 a5 13. b×a5 ♖×a5 14. ♗d2 ♖a3 15. ♕b2 ♘bd7 16. ♖fc1 ♕a8 17. g4 ♗×g4 18. f3 ♗e6 19. e4 ♘b6 20. ♗e1 ♘c4 21. ♕f2 d×e4 22. f×e4 b4 23. ♘×e6 f×e6 24. ♕e2 ♘b6 25. ♘b1 ♖a5 26. ♗h3 ♖g5+ 27. ♔h1 c5 28. ♘d2 c×d4 29. ♗h4 ♘e5 30. ♗g2 ♘fd5 31. ♗×e7 ♘×e7 32. ♕d3 ♖a5 33. ♕b3 ♔h8 34. ♕×e6 ♘bc8 35. ♖f1 ♖g8 36. ♘c4 ♕a6 37. ♕f7 ♖c5 38. ♘d2 ♕g6 39. ♕f2 ♘c6 40. ♘b3 ♖c4 41. ♖ac1 ♖×c1 42. ♖×c1 ♘8e7 43. ♘×d4 ♕g5 44. ♖c2 ♘×d4 45. ♕×d4 ♕g4 46. h3 ♕h4 47. ♕×b4 ♘d5 48. ♕d2 ♘f4 49. ♕f2 ♘×g2 50. ♕×g2 ♕d8 51. ♕f3 h6 52. ♔g2 ♕g5+ 53. ♕g3 ♕b5 54. ♕f4 ♕d3 55. ♖b2 ♖e8 56. ♖b8 ♕e2+ 57. ♔g3 ♕e1+ 58. ♔g4?? 58. ♔h2= **58. ... ♕g1+?** 58. ... ♕d1+ 59. ♔g3 ♕g1+ 60. ♔f3 ♕f1+ **59. ♔h5??** 59. ♔f5= **59. ... ♔h7 60. ♖×e8 g6+ 61. ♔h4 g5+ 62. ♔h5 g×f4 63. ♖e7+ ♔g8 0–1** (Source: Lachaga, *Łódź 1938*; notes by RT)

251 Gideon Ståhlberg–Menchik

Łódź (13), April 1, 1938

[D68] *Queen's Gambit Declined, Classical*

1. d4 ♘f6 2. c4 e6 3. ♘c3 d5 4. ♗g5 ♘bd7 5. e3 ♗e7 6. ♘f3 0-0 7. ♖c1 c6 8. ♗d3 d×c4 9. ♗×c4 ♘d5 10. ♗×e7 ♕×e7 11. 0-0 ♘×c3 12. ♖×c3 e5 13. ♕c2 e×d4 14. e×d4 ♘f6 15. ♖e1 ♕d6 16. ♘g5 ♕f4?? 17. ♘×f7 ♖×f7 18. ♖f3 ♕c7 19. ♖fe3 ♔f8 20. ♕×h7 ♗g4 21. ♕h8+ ♘g8 22. a3 ♗f5 23. ♗×f7 ♔×f7 24. ♖f3 1–0 (Source: Lachaga, *Łódź 1938*)

252 Menchik–Erich Eliskases
Łódź (14), April 4, 1938
[D48] *Semi-Slav, Meran*

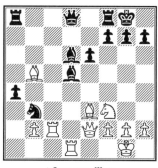

After 22. ♖c2

1. d4 ♘f6 2. c4 e6 3. ♘f3 d5 4. ♘c3 c6 5. e3 ♘bd7 6. ♗d3 d×c4 7. ♗×c4 b5 8. ♗d3 a6 9. 0-0 c5 10. ♕e2 ♗b7 11. ♖d1 ♕c7 12. ♗d2 c×d4 13. e×d4 ♗e7 14. ♖ac1 ♕d8 15. d5 ♘×d5 16. a4 b×a4 17. ♘×d5 ♗×d5 18. ♗×a6 0-0 Also of interest is 18. ... ♗×f3 19. g×f3 a3 20. b×a3 ♗×a3–+ **19. ♗f4 ♘c5 20. ♗b5 ♗d6 21. ♗e3?** A better move, still with problems, would be 21. ♗×d6 ♕×d6 22. ♘e5 **21. ... ♘b3 22. ♖c2** *(see diagram)*

      22. ... ♕f6?! More solid and maintaining more pressure is 22. ... ♗×f3 23. g×f3 ♖a5 **23. ♗c6 ♗×c6 24. ♖×c6 ♗f4 25. ♗×f4 ♕×f4 26. ♖c4 ♕f6 27. ♕e4 ♖ad8 28. ♖×d8 ♖×d8 29. g3 g6 30. ♖×a4 ♘d2 31. ♘×d2 ♖×d2 32. ♕a8+ ♔g7 33. ♖f4 ♕e7** The stronger, but irrelevant, alternative was 33. ... ♕×b2 34. ♕f3 ♕c1+ 35. ♔g2 ♖d7 leading to a book draw—a result that was foreordained after Menchik gave up her a pawn **34. ♕a3 ♖d1+ 35. ♔g2 ♕b7+ 36. ♕f3 ♕×f3+ 37. ♖×f3 g5 38. h3 h5 ½-½** (Source: Lachaga, *Łódź 1938*; notes by RT)

253 Franciszek Sulik–Menchik
Łódź (15), April 5, 1938
[C14] *French, Classical*

1. e4 e6 2. d4 d5 3. ♘c3 ♘f6 4. ♗g5 ♗e7 5. e5 ♘fd7 6. ♗×e7 ♕×e7 7. ♕d2 0-0 8. ♘b5 ♘b6 9. f4 a6 10. ♘a3 f5 11. ♘f3 ♗d7 12. ♗e2 ♘a4 13. c3 c5 14. 0-0 b5 15. ♖ab1 c×d4 16. c×d4 ♖c8 17. ♖fc1 ♘c6 18. ♘c2 ♗e8 19. b3 ♘b6 20. ♘ce1 b4 21. ♘d3 a5 22. ♖c5 ♘×d4 23. ♘×d4 ♖×c5 24. ♘×c5 ♕×c5 25. ♖c1 ♕e7 26. ♗f3 g6 27. ♕e3 ♖c8 28. ♖×c8 ♘×c8 29. g3 ♕c7 30. ♔f2 ♗d7 31. g4 ♕c5 32. ♗e2 f×g4 33. ♗×g4 ♕f7?! 34. f5 g×f5?? [34. ... e×f5 35. e6+ ♗×e6 36. ♕×e6+ ♔g7± —RT] **35. ♗h5+ ♔g8 36. ♕g5+ ♔f8 37. ♕f6+ ♔g8 38. ♗f7+ 1-0** (Source: Lachaga, *Łódź 1938*)

Margate 1938
April 20–28, 1938

		1	2	3	4	5	6	7	8	9	10	Points	Place
1	Alekhine, Alexander	•	=	0	1	1	1	=	1	1	1	7	1
2	Spielmann, Rudolf	=	•	1	=	=	=	1	=	1	=	6	2
3	Petrovs, Vladimirs	1	0	•	0	1	1	0	1	=	1	5½	3
4	Böök, Eero Einar	0	=	1	•	=	=	1	=	0	1	5	4–5
5	Milner-Barry, Philip S.	0	=	0	=	•	=	=	1	1	1	5	4–5
6	Golombek, Harry	0	=	0	=	=	•	1	=	1	=	4½	6
7	Alexander, C.H.O'D.	=	0	1	0	=	0	•	=	=	1	4	7
8	Sergeant, Edward G.	0	=	0	=	0	=	=	•	1	=	3½	8
9	Menchik, Vera	0	0	=	1	0	0	=	0	•	1	3	9
10	Thomas, George	0	=	0	0	0	=	0	=	0	•	1½	10

254 Rudolf Spielmann–Menchik
Margate (1), April 20, 1938
[C11] *French, Advance*

1. e4 e6 2. d4 d5 3. ♘c3 ♘f6 4. e5 ♘fd7 5. ♘ce2 This move was played a good deal in offhand games by the late Mr. [Amos] Burn. White prepares to play c3 and f4 to support his center against Black's attack by c5, etc. He has, however, difficulty in developing his kingside. **5. … c5 6. c3 ♘c6 7. f4 ♕b6 8. ♘f3 f6 9. a3** An old move of which is to prevent a subsequent ♗b4+ [9. g3 cxd4 10. cxd4 fxe5 11. fxe5 ♗b4+ 12. ♘c3 0–0 13. ♗f4 ♗e7 14. ♕d2 g5 with advantage to Black. A game Alapin vs. Maróczy (Vienna 1908) continued as follows: 15. ♘xg5 ♗xg5 16. ♗xg5 ♘xd4 17. 0–0–0 ♘f3 18. ♗e3 ♘xd2 19. ♗xb6 axb6 20. ♖xd2 ♘xe5 and Black eventually won—RT] **9. … fxe5** [Black exchanges pawns prematurely and so allows White to get a splendid post at c4 for his queen's knight. Much better is 9. … ♗e7 10. ♘g3 0–0 11. ♗d3 fxe5 12. fxe5 ♘xd4 13. cxd4 and Black has a good game—RT] **10. fxe5 cxd4**

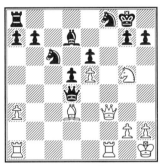

After 19. ♕f3

11. cxd4 ♗e7 12. ♘f4 0–0 13. ♗d3 [Not 13. ♘xe6 because of 13. … ♖xf3 followed if 14. ♕xf3 (or, if 14. gxf3 ♗h4+ and Ndxe5 with a fine attack) by 14. … ♘dxe5. Note that this fails to 15. ♕xd5, missed by annotator Smith—RT] **13. … ♖xf4** Already Black is in difficulties. If ♘d8 or ♘a5 then ♕c2. Unfortunately she does not get sufficient compensation for the exchange she now sacrifices. **14. ♗xf4 ♕xb2 15. 0–0 ♘f8 16. ♗g5 ♗xg5 17. ♘xg5 ♕xd4+ 18. ♔h1 ♗d7 19. ♕f3** *(see diagram)*

19. … ♘xe5 [19. … ♕c5 to prevent the mating combination that follows the text move, then 20. ♕f7+ ♔h8 21. ♕h5 h6 (21. … g6 22. ♖xf8+ ♔g7 23. ♖f7+ and mate the next move) 22. ♖xf8+ ♕xf8 23. ♕g6 ♕g8 24. ♘f7+ ♕xf7 25. ♕h7 mate—RT] **20. ♕xf8+** After 20. … ♖xf8 21. ♗h7+ ♔h8 22. ♖xf8 mate **1–0** (Source: Lachaga, *Margate 1938*; *Chess*, July 1938, #644; notes by G.E. Smith from *The Field* [additional notes by RT])

255 Vladimirs Petrovs–Menchik
Margate (2), April 21, 1938
[A11] *English*

Although Menchik had a slight edge throughout the game, the symmetrical material and pawns prevented a decisive result.

1. c4 ♘f6 2. g3 c6 3. b3 d5 4. ♗b2 g6 5. ♗g2 ♗g7 6. ♘f3 0–0 7. 0–0 ♘bd7 8. ♕c2 ♖e8 9. d4 ♘f8 10. ♘bd2 ♗f5 11. ♕d1 ♕a5 12. a3 ♖ad8 13. b4 ♕c7 14. ♕b3 ♘e4 15. ♖fd1 ♘xd2 16. ♖xd2 ♗e4 17. ♖c1 dxc4 18. ♕xc4 ♕d6 19. ♖cd1 ♗h6 20. e3 ♕d5 21. ♕xd5 cxd5 22. ♖c1 ♖c8 23. ♖dd1 ♘d7 24. ♗h3 e6 25. ♘e5 ♘b6 26. ♔f1 ♗c2 27. ♖d2 ♗a4 28. ♖c5 ♗f8 29. ♖xc8 ♖xc8 30. ♗g4 ♗d6 31. ♗e2 f6 32. ♘f3 ♘c4 33. ♗xc4 ♖xc4 34. ♘e1 b6 35. f3 ♔f7 36. ♔f2 ♔e7 37. ♘d3 ♔d7 38. e4 ♖c2 39. ♔e3 ♖xd2 40. ♔xd2 *(see diagram)*

After 40. ♔xd2

40. ... ♗b5 41. e5 ♗×d3 42. ♕×d3 f×e5 43. d×e5 ♗f8 44. b5 ♗c5 45. a4 ♗g1 46. h3 ♗h2 47. g4 ♗f4 48. ♔d4 ♔c7 49. ♔d3 ♔b7 50. ♗d4 a5 51. ♔e2 ♔c7 52. ♔f2 ♔b7 53. h4 h5 54. ♗c3 ♔c7 55. ♗b2 ♔b7 56. ♗a1 ½–½ (Source: Lachaga, *Margate 1938*)

256 Menchik–C.H.O'D. Alexander
Margate (3), April 22, 1938
[D40] *Queen's Gambit Declined, Semi-Tarrasch Variation*

1. ♘f3 d5 2. d4 ♘f6 3. c4 e6 4. ♘c3 c5 5. e3 ♘c6 6. ♗d3 a6 7. 0-0 d×c4 8. ♗×c4 b5 9. ♗d3 ♗b7 10. a4 ♕a5 11. a×b5 ♕×a1 12. b×c6 ♗×c6 13. ♘e5 ♗d7 14. ♕f3 ♖b8 15. ♘c4 ♗b5 16. ♗d2 ♗×c4 17. ♖×a1 ♗×d3 18. e4 ♗c4 19. ♗g5 ♘d7 20. d5?! [20. ♖d1—RT] 20. ... e5? [20. ... ♖×b2—RT] 21. ♗c1 f6 22. ♘d1 ♗b5 23. b3 ♗e7 24. ♘e3 ♗d3 25. ♘f5 ♖×b3 26. ♘×g7+ ♔d8 *(see diagram)*

After 26. ... ♔d8

27. ♖×a6?! [27. ♕d1—RT] 27. ... ♖b1 28. ♕×d3?? Time pressure? After this, White must be quite happy to get a draw. [28. ♘e6+ ♔c8 29. ♖c6+ ♔b8 30. ♕e3 ♗×e4 31. ♖c7 ♘b6 32. ♕a3 ♘c8 33. ♖d7+—RT] 28. ... ♖×c1+ 29. ♕f1 ♖×f1+ 30. ♔×f1 ♔c8 31. ♖c6+ ♔b7 32. ♘f5 ♗f8 33. ♔e2 ♖g8 34. g3 ♖g6 35. h4 h5 36. f4 e×f4 37. g×f4 ♖g2+ 38. ♔f3 ♖b2 39. ♘g3 ♖b3+ 40. ♔f2 ♖b2+ 41. ♔f3 ½–½ (Source: Lachaga, *Margate 1938* [additional notes by RT])

257 Philip S. Milner-Barry–Menchik
Margate (4), April 23, 1938
[C14] *French Classical*

Menchik quickly gets into trouble until on moves 29 and 30 the players blunder away with Milner-Barry coming out on top in the end.

1. e4 e6 2. d4 d5 3. ♘c3 ♘f6 4. ♗g5 ♗e7 5. e5 ♘fd7 6. h4 c5 7. ♗×e7 ♕×e7 8. f4 c×d4 9. ♕×d4 ♘c6 10. ♕d2 ♕a5 11. ♘f3 a6 12. 0-0-0 ♔f8 13. ♖h3 b5 14. ♘d4 ♘×d4 15. ♕×d4 b4 16. ♘e2 ♕c5 17. ♕d2 a5 18. ♘d4 ♗a6 19. f5 e×f5 20. ♗×a6 ♖×a6 21. ♘×f5 ♖c6 22. ♘d4 ♖g6? [22. ... ♖c8—RT] 23. h5 ♖g4 24. ♘b3 ♕c7 25. ♕×d5 ♔e7 26. ♖f3 ♘×e5 27. ♖e1 f6 28. ♘d4 ♖e8 *(see diagram)*

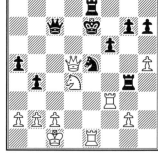
After 28. ... ♖e8

29. ♕e6+? ♔f8 30. ♖×e5? ♖×e6?? [30. ... ♕×e5!!–+—RT] 31. ♘×e6+ ♔e7 32. ♘×c7+ f×e5 33. ♘d5+ 1–0 (Source: Lachaga, *Margate 1938*)

258 Menchik–George Thomas
Margate (5), April 24, 1938
[D74] *Neo-Grünfeld*

1. ♘f3 d5 2. d4 ♘f6 3. c4 g6 4. c×d5 ♘×d5 5. g3 ♗g7 6. ♗g2 0-0 7. 0-0 c6 8. ♖e1

Final position

♕b6 9. ♘a3 a5 10. e4 ♘f6 11. ♘c4 ♕d8 12. ♗g5 h6 13. ♗d2 b5 14. ♘ce5 ♘bd7? [14. ... ♘g4—RT] 15. ♘×d7? Vera almost gave away a half point with this move. [15. ♘×c6 ♕e8 16. ♘×a5+-—RT] 15. ... ♕×d7 16. ♕c1 ♔h7 17. a3 ♖d8 18. ♗c3 ♕c7 19. ♕e3 ♘d7 20. d5 c×d5 21. ♗×g7 ♔×g7 22. e×d5 ♘f6 23. ♖ac1 ♕a7 24. ♕×a7 ♖×a7 25. ♘d4 ♖ad7 26. ♘c6 ♖e8 27. ♖c5 ♗a6 28. ♘×a5 b4? 29. a×b4 e6 30. b5 ♗b7 31. d×e6 ♗×g2 32. ♔×g2 f×e6 33. ♖c6 ♖d5 34. ♖c7+ ♔f8 35. ♘c4 ♖e7 36. ♖×e7 ♔×e7 37. b6 ♖b5 38. ♖a1 ♘d7 39. ♖a7 e5 40. b7 ♔e6 41. ♖a6+ ♔e7 42. ♖b6 *(see diagram)*

1–0 (Source: Lachaga, *Margate 1938* [additional notes by RT])

259 Harry Golombek–Menchik
Margate (6), April 25, 1938
[D95] *Grünfeld*

1. d4 ♘f6 2. c4 c6 3. ♘f3 d5 4. e3 g6 5. ♘c3 ♗g7 6. ♕b3 0-0 7. ♗d2 e6 This variation of the Grünfeld Defense is not a very satisfactory line for Black. The move c6 is out of place in the Grünfeld, where one of the main chances of counterattack lies in the undermining of White's center by c5. [An alternative to the text move is 7. ... d×c4 8. ♗×c4 b5 9. ♗e2 ♗e6 10. ♕c2 and Black has succeeded in developing his queen's bishop but only at the cost of seriously weakening his queenside pawns—RT] **8. ♖c1 ♘bd7 9. ♗d3 a6 10. 0-0 d×c4** This vain attempt to develop the queenside anticipates 11. ♗×c4 b5 followed by ♗b7 and c5. But it fails against White's reply, which prevents any liberation of the queen's wing and obtains the superior position in the center. In any case, Black has little to do but watch White build up an overwhelming position by ♖fd1 and ♘e5. **11. ♕×c4 ♘d5 12. ♖fd1 ♘5b6 13. ♕b3 e5 14. ♘e4 ♘d5** White threatened ♗a5 or ♗b4. An alternative and slightly better way of meeting this threat was 14. ... a5. **15. ♗c4 e×d4 16. e×d4 ♘7f6 17. ♗g5 h6** White was threatening to win a pawn by 18. ♗×d5; the text move leads to a catastrophe on the kingside. **18. ♘×f6+ ♘×f6 19. ♘e5!** *(see diagram)*

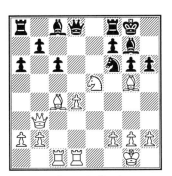

After 19. ♘e5

19. ... h×g5 Black must accept this temporary sacrifice, for if the queen protects the bishop's pawn, e.g., ♕c7 or ♕e8, White simply plays ♗×f6 followed by ♘×g6. **20. ♗×f7+ ♖×f7** Forced; if 20. ... ♔h8 21. ♖c3 g4 22. ♖dd3 and the threat of ♖h3+ cannot be averted. **21. ♕×f7+ ♔h8 22. ♕×g6 ♕d5 23. ♕×g5 ♔g8 24. ♖d3 ♘h7** Black must prevent White doubling on the g-file. **25. ♕g6 ♕e6 26. ♕g3 ♕h6 27. ♖e1 ♗f5 28. ♖f3 ♕d2 29. ♖f1 ♖f8 30. ♘c4?!** [Both sides get a bit sloppy in the ending. Golombek missing faster wins as here 30. ♖×f5 ♖×f5 31. ♕b3+ ♔h8 32. ♘g6 mate and Menchik missing better albeit futile lines of resistance—RT] **30. ... ♕g5** If ♕×d4, then 31. ♘e3 bishop on f5 moves, 32. ♖d1 followed by h4, with a decisive attack on the Black king. **31. ♕c7 ♗e6 32. ♖g3 ♕f6 33. ♘e5 ♘g5 34. h4 ♘e4 35. ♖g6 1–0** (Source:

Lachaga, *Margate 1938*; *BCM* #8326 including notes by Harry Golombek in *BCM* [additional notes by RT])

260   Menchik–Edward G. Sergeant
Margate (7), April 26, 1938
[A13] *English*

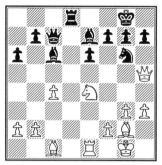

After 21. ... ℤ×d8

1. ♘f3 ♘f6 2. c4 e6 3. g3 d5 4. ♗g2 d4 5. 0-0 c5 6. e3 ♘c6 7. e×d4 ♘×d4 8. ♘c3 ♘×f3+ 9. ♕×f3 ♗e7 10. d3 0-0 11. ♗f4 a6 12. h3 ♘d7 13. ♕e2 ℤe8 14. ℤad1 ♘f8 15. ℤfe1 ♘g6 16. ♗c1 ♕c7 17. d4 c×d4 18. ℤ×d4 ♗d7 19. ♘e4 ♗c6 20. ♕h5 ℤad8 21. ℤ×d8 ℤ×d8 *(see diagram)*
22. ♘g5? [Something like 22. b3 with the idea of simply strengthening her position incrementally would better serve here—RT] 22. ... ♗×g5 23. ♕×g5 ♗×g2 24. ♔×g2 ♕c6+ 25. ♔h2 f6 26. ♕e3? [26. ♕g4 Allows some resistance, although White's prospects are bleak—RT] 26. ... ♘e5 0-1
(Source: Lachaga, *Margate 1938*; *BCM* #8277)

261   Alexander Alekhine–Menchik
Margate (8), April 28, 1938
[D54] *Queen's Gambit Declined*

Although far from a perfect game, there is a lot of instruction as to how a strong master often beats a lower rated master. In the first half of the game the players jockey around with Alekhine making many second rate moves that seem designed to keep the position out of balance. For much of that portion of the game he might even be considered slightly worse, although never so much as to endanger the game. After Miss Menchik makes a substantial error on move 32 his moves tighten up to where each move is generally the "best" move available—an exception being where he misses a coup de grâce on move 40.

1. d4 ♘f6 2. c4 e6 3. ♘c3 d5 4. ♗g5 ♗e7 5. e3 0-0 6. ℤc1 ♘e4 7. ♗×e7 ♕×e7 8. c×d5 ♘×c3 9. ℤ×c3 e×d5 10. ♗d3 c6 11. ♕h5 f5 Black has freed her game by exchanges, but Alekhine is a past master in creating problems—or of convincing his opponent that problems exist! The alternative ... h6 or ... g6 would create a target for White to open the g or h file respectively. 12. ♘e2 ♘d7 13. 0-0 ♘f6 14. ♕h4 ℤf7 15. ℤb3 ♘e8 16. ♕×e7 ℤ×e7 17. ♘f4 g5 18. ♘h5 ♗e6 19. f4 g4 20. ♔f2 ♘d6 21. ℤh1 ♗f7 22. ♘g3 ♗g6 23. h3 h5 24. h×g4 h×g4 25. ℤc3 ♔f7 26. b4 a6 27. a4 ♔f6 White has taken his cue from Black's 11th move, and has fixed all the Black pawns on white squares. The result is that Black is limited to purely defensive play, and that White has maneuvering facilities on the c and h files plus a breakthrough possibility at b5 (hence his last two moves). 28. ℤc5 ℤe6 29. ℤa5 ℤee8 30. ℤc1 ℤec8 31. ℤac5 ♗e8 32. ℤ5c2 *(see diagram)*

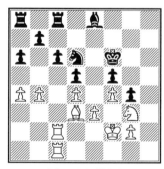

After 32. ℤ5c2

32. ... b5? The break with b5 was not so formidable as to necessitate the drastic deterioration of Black's pawn position which now ensues. [32. ... a5 seems better in all variations. 33. ♖b2 (33. b5 c×b5 34. ♖×c8 ♖×c8 35. ♖×c8 ♘×c8 36. a×b5 ♘d6 37. b6 a4; 33. b×a5 ♖×a5 34. ♖a2 ♖ca8 35. ♗c2) 33. ... a×b4 34. ♖×b4 b5 35. a×b5 c×b5 36. ♖×c8 ♖×c8; A solid alternative is 32. ... ♗d7 33. ♖h1 ♖h8=—RT] **33. ♖a2 ♗d7?** Missing an important defensive finesse. Necessary was 33. ... ♖a7 34. ♖ca1 ♖ca8 35. a×b5 c×b5 with far better defensive chances than after the text. Having been given his opportunity, Alekhine now makes decisive inroads into the hostile position. As will be seen, the utilization of the a file is of vital importance. **34. ♖ca1 ♖ab8 35. a×b5 a×b5 36. ♖a7 ♗e8 37. ♖h1 ♗g6 38. ♖h6 ♖g8 39. ♖d7!** White's last move was decisive. If 39. ... ♖bd8 40. ♘h5+ ♔e6 41. ♖×d8 wins a piece, and on any knight move but the text, 40. ♗×f5 wins. **♘f7** Seemingly driving back the enemy ... **40. ♘×f5!! g3+** A meaningless interpolation. However, if 40. ... ♘×h6; 41. ♖d6+ ♔f7 42. ♘×h6 winning easily. **41. ♔f3 ♖bd8** This looks good, for if 42. ♖×d8 ♖×d8 and White must lose some material. White has a simple but effective reply. **42. ♖c7!** ♘g5+ Permitting White a decisive simplification. But if 42. ... ♘×h6 43. ♖×c6+ etc. **43. f×g5+ ♔×g5 44. ♖h3 ♗×f5 45. ♖×g3+ ♔f6 46. ♖×g8 ♖×g8 47. ♗×f5 ♔×f5 48. ♖×c6 1–0** (Source: Lachaga, *Margate 1938*; Skinner, *A. Alekhine's Chess Games 1902–1946*; *Chess Review*, June 1938, p. 144; notes by Fred Reinfeld in *CR* [additional notes by RT])

262 Menchik–Eero Böök
Margate (9), April 28, 1938
[D51] *Queen's Gambit Declined*

1. ♘f3 ♘f6 2. c4 e6 3. ♘c3 d5 4. d4 c6 5. c×d5 c×d5 6. ♗g5 ♗e7 7. e3 0-0 8. ♗d3 ♘bd7 9. 0-0 a6 10. a4 b6 11. ♕b1 h6 12. ♗h4 ♗b7 13. ♗g3?! [Maintaining the pressure is 13. ♖c1—RT] **13. ... ♘h5 14. ♗e2 ♘×g3 15. h×g3 ♗d6 16. ♖d1 ♕e7 17. ♕c2 ♖fc8 18. ♕b3 ♖c7 19. ♖ac1 ♖ac8 20. ♖×c7 ♖×c7 21. ♗b1 f5 22. ♘f4 ♗c6 23. ♗d3 ♗b7? 24. ♘e2?!** [24. ♗b1!—RT] **24. ... ♕d8 25. ♘h2 ♖c8 26. e4 f×e4 27. ♗×e4 ♕c7 28. ♗d3 e5 29. ♘f3?** [29. ♖c1 ♕b8 30. ♖×c8+ ♕×c8 31. ♗f5=—RT] **29. ... e×d4 30. ♗f5 ♘c5 31. ♕a2 ♖e8 32. ♘e×d4 ♕f7 33. ♘h4 ♘e4** *(see diagram)*

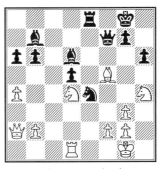

After 33. ... ♘e4

34. b3!? setting a trap with her opponent in severe time pressure. **♘c3?** [Maintaining his slight advantage is 34. ... ♗c5 35. ♕b2∓—RT] **35. ♕c2 ♘×d1 36. ♗h7+ ♔h8 37. ♘g6+ ♔×h7 38. ♘e5+ ♔g8 39. ♘×f7 ♖e1+ 40. ♔h2 ♔×f7 41. ♕d2 ♖e4 42. ♕×d1 ♗e5 43. ♘f5 ♗b8 44. ♕h5+ ♔f6 45. ♘×h6 g×h6 46. ♕×h6+** and facing the loss of another piece, Black resigned. **1–0** (Source: Lachaga, *Margate 1938* [additional notes by RT])

Britain vs. Holland Match 1938

June 5–6, 1938

Bd		Round 1	Round 2		Round 1	Round 2
1	Fairhurst, William	0	=	Euwe, Max	1	=
2	Alexander, C.H.O'D.	0	=	Landau, Salo	1	=
3	Milner-Barry, Philip S.	=	1	Fontein, George S.	=	0
4	Thomas, George A.	=	=	De Groot, Adrianus	=	=
5	Tylor, Theodore H.	1	1	Prins, Lodewijk	0	0
6	Golombek, Harry	0	0	Van Scheltinga, Tjeerd	1	1
7	Broadbent, Reginald	1	1	Van Doesburgh, Gerrit	0	0
8	Menchik, Vera	=	=	Mühring, Willem J.	=	=
9	Sergeant, Edward G.	=	0	Mulder van Leens Dijkstra, K.D.	=	1
10	Lenton, Alfred	1	=	Vlagsma, Chris	0	=
		5	5½		5	4½

263 Menchik–Willem Jan Mühring
England vs. Holland, London (1), June 5, 1938
[A84] *Dutch Defense*

1. ♘f3 d5 2. d4 e6 3. c4 c6 4. e3 ♗d6 5. ♗d3 f5 6. 0-0 ♘f6 7. ♕b3 0-0 8. ♗d2 a5 9. ♘e5 ♗×e5 10. d×e5 ♘fd7 11. f4 ♘c5 12. ♕c2 ♘×d3 13. ♕×d3 ♘a6 14. c×d5 e×d5 15. ♕a3 b6 16. ♖d1 ♗e6 17. ♗e1 ♘c5 18. ♘d2 ♕c8 19. ♗h4 ♖f7 20. ♘f3 ♘e4 21. ♖ac1 c5 22. ♕a4 ♕b7 23. ♕b5 ♖b8 24. h3 ♕d7 25. ♕e2 h6 26. ♘d2 ♘×d2 27. ♖×d2 ♕a4 28. b3 ♕e4 29. ♗f2 g5 30. ♕h5 g×f4 31. ♕×h6 f×e3 32. ♗×e3 f4 33. ♗f2 ♕f5 34. ♗h4 ♖h7 35. ♕g5+ ♖g7 36. ♕×f5 ♗×f5 37. ♗f6 ♖g6 38. ♖f1 c4 39. b×c4 d×c4 40. ♖×f4 c3 41. ♖df2 ♖c8 42. ♖h4 ♖×f6 43. e×f6 c2 44. f7+ ♔×f7 45. ♖×f5+ ♔g6 46. ♖f1 c1♕ 47. ♖g4+ ♔h5 48. ♖×c1 ♖×c1+ 49. ♔h2 ♖c2 50. a4 b5 51. a×b5 ♖b2 52. ♔g3 ♖×b5 53. ♔f3 ♖b3+ 54. ♔e2 ♖b2+ 55. ♔d3 a4 56. ♔c3 a3 57. ♖g8 ♖f2 ½–½ (Source: *www.Chessgames.com*)

264 Willem Jan Mühring–Menchik
England vs. Netherlands, London (2), June 6, 1938
[E72] *Kings Indian*

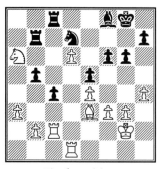

Final position

1. d4 ♘f6 2. c4 g6 3. g3 ♗g7 4. ♗g2 0-0 5. ♘c3 d6 6. e4 e5 7. ♘ge2 ♗d7 8. 0-0 ♕c8 9. d×e5 d×e5 10. ♘d5 ♖e8 11. ♗g5 ♘×d5 12. c×d5 ♘a6 13. ♖c1 c6 14. ♕d2 f6 15. ♗e3 ♕d8 16. ♖fd1 ♕e7 17. ♘c3 ♖ed8 18. ♗f1 ♗g4 19. ♗e2 ♗×e2 20. ♕×e2 c5 21. ♘a4 ♖ac8 22. ♖d2 ♕c7 23. ♕b5 ♗f8 24. ♖dc2 ♕d7 25. ♕×d7 ♖×d7 26. a3 ♖dc7 27. ♘c3 b6 28. ♘b5 ♖d7 29. ♔g2 ♖e8 30. f3 ♘b8 31. h4 ♖b7 32. ♖d1 a6 33. ♘c3 b5 34. d6 ♘d7 35. ♘d5 c4 36. ♘c7 ♖c8 37. ♘×a6 (see diagram)

[37. ... ♖c6 38. ♘c7 ♖×d6 39. ♘d5 and any progress is problematical—RT] ½–½ (Source: *www.Chessgames.com*)

Brighton 1938—31st B.C.F. Championship

August 8–19, 1938

		1	2	3	4	5	6	7	8	9	10	11	12	Pts.	Place
1	Alexander, C.H.O'D.	•	1	=	1	=	0	=	1	=	1	1	1	8	1
2	Golombek, Harry	0	•	=	1	=	=	1	1	1	=	=	1	7½	2–3
3	Sergeant, Edward G.	=	=	•	0	1	=	=	1	1	1	1	=	7½	2–3
4	Milner-Barry, Philip	0	0	1	•	=	1	=	0	=	1	1	1	6½	4
5	Thomas, George	=	=	0	=	•	0	=	1	1	1	=	=	6	5–6
6	Tylor, Theodore H.	1	=	=	0	1	•	=	=	0	1	=	=	6	5–6
7	Menchik, Vera	=	0	=	=	=	=	•	=	0	=	1	1	5½	7
8	Aitken, James M.	0	0	0	1	0	=	=	•	1	1	0	1	5	8
9	Reynolds, Arthur	=	0	0	=	0	1	1	0	•	0	=	1	4½	9
10	Lenton, Alfred	0	=	0	0	0	0	=	0	1	•	1	=	3½	10–11
11	Parr, Frank	0	=	0	0	=	=	0	1	=	0	•	=	3½	10–11
12	Mallison, Harold V.	0	0	=	0	=	=	0	0	0	=	=	•	2½	12

Until her marriage to Rufus Stevenson, Vera was not a British subject and therefore not eligible to play for the British Championship. Thus this was her first, and only, attempt at the title. The next year the Buenos Aires world title tournament intervened and then World War II put a stop to the tournament.

265　Arthur Reynolds–Menchik

Brighton B.C.F. Cong. (10), August 18, 1938

[D73] *Neo-Grünfeld*

In this game Menchik loses due to a steady diet of weak but not individually disastrous moves. Reynolds plays with great steadiness. **1. d4 ♘f6 2. c4 g6 3. g3 ♗g7 4. ♗g2 d5 5. ♘c3 c6 6. ♕b3 d×c4 7. ♕×c4 0-0 8. ♘f3 ♕a5 9. b4 ♕h5 10. h3 ♕f5 11. ♗g5 ♕d7 12. 0-0 ♘e8 13. ♖d1 ♘d6 14. ♕b3 h6 15. ♘f3 ♕e6 16. d5 c×d5 17. ♘d4 ♕d7 18. ♘×d5 ♘c6?! 19. ♗b2 ♖b8? 20. ♖ac1 ♘×d4 21. ♗×d4 ♗×d4 22. ♖×d4 ♕e6 23. ♖d3 ♕×e2 24. ♖e3 ♕h5 25. ♖×e7 ♗e6 26. ♘f6+ ♔h8 27. ♕×e6 ♕g5 28. ♖c5 ♕×c5 29. b×c5 f×e6 30. ♖h7 mate 1-0** (Source: *BCM* #8362)

Plymouth 1938—Jubilee Congress

(Premier)

September 5–10, 1938

		1	2	3	4	5	6	7	8	Points	Place
1	Alekhine, Alexander	•	=	=	1	1	1	1	1	6	1–2
2	Thomas, George A.	=	•	1	1	=	1	1	1	6	1–2
3	List, Paul M.	=	0	•	0	1	=	=	1	3½	3–4
4	Milner-Barry, Philip S.	0	0	1	•	0	1	1	=	3½	3–4
5	Menchik, Vera	0	=	0	1	•	0	=	1	3	5
6	Mallison, Harold V.	0	0	=	0	1	•	=	=	2½	6–7
7	Wheatcroft, George	0	0	=	0	=	=	•	1	2½	6–7
8	Bruce, Ronald M.	0	0	0	=	0	=	0	•	1	8

In addition to the following two games there are a couple of side notes regarding Menchik. Harold Mallison offered her a draw which she accepted, following which it was discovered that she was out of time. For whatever reason, Mallison was awarded a win; certainly not the procedure today. Ronald Bruce had to play Alekhine and Menchik on the same day; a story which he told for the rest of his lifetime. In fairness to Bruce it is worth noting that he was active on the organizing committee which cannot have helped his performance.

266 Menchik–Alexander Alekhine

Plymouth (4), September 7, 1938

[D90] *Grünfeld*

After 20. ... ♗d7

1. ♘f3 d5 2. d4 c6 3. c4 ♘f6 4. c×d5 c×d5 5. ♘c3 g6 6. ♗f4 ♗g7 7. ♗e5 0-0 8. ♕b3 ♘c6 9. e3 ♘×e5 10. ♘×e5 ♕c7 11. ♘d3 ♖d8 12. ♖c1 ♕b8 13. ♗e2 ♗f5 14. ♘e5 ♗e6 15. 0-0 a6 16. a4 ♖d6 17. ♘d3 ♘e4 18. ♖fd1 ♕d8 19. ♘f4 ♘×c3 20. ♕×c3 ♗d7 *(see diagram)*

Note that the Skinner book transposes White's 21st and 22nd moves **21. ♕c7?** Needed here is 21. ♕a3 with at least equality **21. ... ♗×a4 22. ♖d2 ♗c6 23. ♕×d8+ ♖d×d8 24. ♘d3 e6 25. ♘c5 a5 26. f4 ♗f8 27. ♗d1 ♗d6 28. ♗b3 ♔f8 29. ♖dc2 ♔e7 30. ♗a4 ♗×a4 31. ♘×a4 ♖a6 32. ♔f2 b5 33. ♘c5 ♖b6** *(see diagram)*

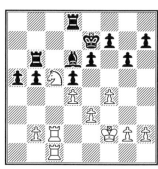

After 33. ... ♖b6

34. b4?! Better is 34. ♘b3 a4 35. ♘a5∓ ♖a8 ...36. ♘c6+ **34. ... a4 35. ♔e2 f6 36. g3 ♖c8 37. ♔d3 ♖bc6 38. ♖f2 ♖a8 39. ♔c3 ♖cc8 40. ♔b2 h6 41. ♖cf1 ♖f8 42. ♔a3 g5 43. f5 e5 44. ♖d2 ♖ac8 45. ♖c1 e4 46. ♖g2?** Better is 46. ♖dc2 **46. ... g4 47. ♖h1 ♖h8 48. ♔b2 ♖cg8** *(see diagram)*

After 48. ... ♖cg8

49. ♔c3? 49. ♖c1 **49. ... ♖g5 50. ♖f1 h5 51. ♘b7 ♗b8 52. ♔d2 h4 53. ♘c5 h×g3 54. h×g3 ♗d6 55. ♔e2 ♖gh5 56. ♘e6 ♖h2 57. ♖ff2 ♖×g2 58. ♖×g2 ♖h1 59. ♘f4 ♗×f4 60. g×f4 a3** If 61. ♖×g4 ♔f7 62. ♔f2 a2 **0–1**

(Source: Skinner, *A. Alekhine Games 1902–1946*; *Chess Stars: Alexander Alekhine III*, Bulgaria, 2002; notes by RT)

267 Menchik–George Thomas

Plymouth (6), September 9, 1938

[D57] *Queen's Gambit Declined, Lasker Defense*

In this, the penultimate round, Menchik got an inferior position in the beginning, but Thomas forced the pace too rapidly and by the 44th move Vera appeared to have an easy win.

Unfortunately in time pressure she traded off queens and Sir George was able to draw the resulting position. The game was important as it determined the final tie for first place between Thomas and World Champion Alekhine. The reality is that in time pressure, and given the status of the White pawns, it is no easy matter to determine the best course of play.

1. ♘f3 ♘f6 2. c4 e6 3. ♘c3 d5 4. d4 ♗e7 5. ♗g5 h6 6. ♗h4 0–0 7. e3 ♘e4 8. ♗×e7 ♕×e7 9. c×d5 ♘×c3 10. b×c3 e×d5 11. ♕b3 ♕d6 12. c4 d×c4 13. ♗×c4 ♘c6 14. 0–0? 14. ♗e2 **14. ... ♘a5 15. ♕c3 ♘×c4 16. ♕×c4 ♗e6 17. ♕c3 ♖ac8 18. ♖fc1 b6 19. ♖c2 ♕d5 20. ♕a3 ♗f5 21. ♖d2 ♗e4 22. ♘e1 ♕d6 23. ♕c3 c5?!** 23. ... ♖fd8 **24. d5? ♖fe8 25. f3 ♗g6 26. g4 h5 27. g×h5 ♗×h5 28. e4 ♖c7 29. ♘g2 f5 30. e×f5 ♖ce7 31. ♖f1 b5 32. ♕b2 a6 33. a4 c4?** 33. ... b×a4 34. ♕c2 (34. ♕a2 ♖e5 35. f6 g×f6 36. ♕×a4±) 34. ... ♖e5 35. ♘f4 ♗f7 36. ♖g2 a3+– **34. a×b5 ♖b8 35. b6 ♖×b6 36. ♕d4 ♖b4 37. ♖c2 ♖c7 38. ♖c3 ♖c5 39. ♘f4 ♖b2 40. ♖f2 ♖b1+ 41. ♔g2 ♗f7 42. ♖×c4 ♖×c4 43. ♕×c4 ♕f6 44. ♘e6 ♖d1 45. ♕×a6 ♗×e6 46. ♕×e6+ ♔h7** *(see diagram)*

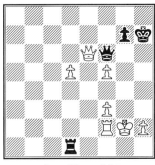

After 46. ... ♔h7

47. ♕×f6 g×f6 48. ♔g3

Final position

♖×d5 **49. ♔f4 ♖d4+ 50. ♔e3 ♖a4 51. ♖d2 ♔h6 52. ♖d4 ♖a2 53. h4 ♖a5 54. ♔f4 ♖a7 55. ♖c4 ♖a2 56. ♖c6 ♔g7 57. h5 ♖a7 58. h6+ ♔×h6 59. ♖×f6+ ♔g7 60. ♖d6 ♖a1 61. ♖b6 ♔f7 62. ♖b3 ♔f6 63. ♖b6+ ♔f7 64. ♔g3 ♖g1+ 65. ♔f2 ♖a1 66. f4 ♖a5 67. f6 ♖f5 68. ♔f3 ♖×f6 69. ♖b7+ ♔g6 70. ♔g4 ♖a6** *(see diagram)*

½–½ (Source: *BCM* #8358; notes by RT)

Margate 1939

(Premier Division)
April 12–24, 1939

		1	2	3	4	5	6	7	8	9	10	Points	Place
1	Keres, Paul	•	=	=	1	=	1	1	1	1	1	7½	1
2	Capablanca, José R.	=	•	=	1	=	=	1	=	1	1	6½	2–3
3	Flohr, Salomon M.	=	=	•	0	=	1	1	1	1	1	6½	2–3
4	Thomas, George	0	0	1	•	=	1	=	=	=	1	5	4
5	Milner-Barry, Philip S.	=	=	=	=	•	0	1	=	=	=	4½	5
6	Najdorf, Miguel	0	=	0	0	1	•	0	1	=	1	4	6
7	Golombek, Harry	0	0	0	=	0	1	•	=	=	1	3½	7
8	Sergeant, Edward G.	0	=	0	=	=	0	=	•	1	0	3	8
9	Menchik Vera	0	0	0	=	=	=	=	0	•	=	2½	9
10	Wheatcroft, George	0	0	0	0	=	0	0	1	=	•	2	10

Vera's husband R.H.S. Stevenson, as organizer, had the unenviable task of finding an alternative site when the Grand Hotel with its beautiful ballroom was unavailable. The tournament was finally moved to the Norfolk Hotel where play was distributed among five or six rooms.[58]

This was also the last of the Margate tournament series, as by the following year the war was in full force. One has to wonder if the lack of fighting spirit in some of Menchik's games was the result of working with her husband as well as her well known activities as a hostess at a number of the clubs and tournaments. This was also Vera's last tournament before leaving for the Women's World Championship in Buenos Aires.

268 Menchik–Miguel Najdorf

Margate (1), April 12, 1939

[E68] *King's Indian Fianchetto*

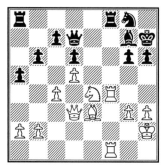

After 22. ... ♛d7

1. ♘f3 ♘f6 2. c4 g6 3. g3 ♗g7 4. ♗g2 0-0 5. 0-0 d6 6. d4 ♘bd7 7. ♘c3 e5 8. h3 ♖e8 9. d5 a5 10. e4 ♘c5 11. ♘e1 ♖f8 12. ♗g5 h6 13. ♗e3 b6 14. ♘d3 ♔h7 15. ♔h2 ♘g8 16. f4 ♘×d3 17. ♛×d3 e×f4 18. ♖×f4 f5 19. ♖af1 ♗d7 20. e×f5 ♗×f5 21. ♗e4 ♗×e4 22. ♘×e4 ♛d7 *(see diagram)*

23. ♖×f8?! [Possibly a better route for White is to play 23. ♖h4 where after 23. ... ♖×f1 24. ♛×f1 ♖f8 25. ♘g5+ ♔h8 26. ♛g2 ♖f5 27. ♘e6 b5 she has a little more pull to try concoct something—RT] 23. ... ♖×f8 24. ♖×f8 ♗×f8 25. ♗d4 ½-½ (Source: *www.Chessgames.com*)

269 Edward G. Sergeant–Menchik

Margate (2), April 13, 1939

[D73] *Neo-Grünfeld*

1. d4 ♘f6 2. c4 g6 3. g3 ♗g7 4. ♘f3 0-0 5. ♘c3 d5 6. ♛b3 c6 7. ♗g2 ♘a6 8. c×d5 ♘×d5 9. ♘×d5 ♛×d5 10. ♛×d5 c×d5 11. ♗g5 ♖e8 12. ♗d2 ♗f5 13. 0-0 ♗e4 14. ♘e5 ♗×g2 15. ♔×g2 f6 16. ♘f3 e5 17. ♖fc1 e4 18. ♘g1 ♗f8 19. a3 ♖ac8 20. e3 ♘c7 21. ♘e2 ♔f7 22. ♗a5 From here on life was not good for Black. Pieces became cramped and did not coordinate well. 22. ... b6 23. ♗b4 ♘e6 24. ♘c3 ♖ed8 25. ♘b5 a6 26. ♘a7 *(see diagram)*

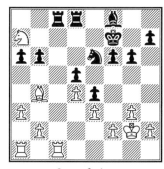

After 26. ♘a7

26. ... ♖×c1?! [26. ... ♖a8 27. ♘c6 ♖d7 28. ♗×f8 ♖×f8=—RT] 27. ♖×c1 ♗×b4 28. a×b4 ♖d7 29. ♘c8 b5 30. ♖c6 ♘c7 31. ♘d6+ ♔e7 32. ♘b7 ♔f7 33. ♘c5 ♖e7 34. ♘×a6 ♘×a6 35. ♖×a6 ♖d7 36. ♖b6 ♔e7 37. ♖×b5 f5 38. ♔f1 ♔d6 39. ♖b6+ ♔e7 40. b5 ♖c7 41. ♖a6 ♖b7 42. b6 ♔e6 43. ♖a7 ♖×b6 44. ♖×h7 ♔f6 45. h4 *(see diagram)*

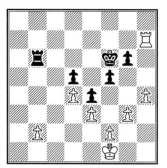

Final position

Here we have a mystery. White has an advantage, but it is certainly premature for Black to resign. We would appear to have about seven or so moves until time control and the previous moves do not seem to have been excessively difficult to find. Maybe someday we will find the answer. **1–0** (Source: *www.Chessgames.com* [additional note by RT])

270 Menchik–Harry Golombek
Margate (3), April 14, 1939

[D14] *Slav, Exchange Variation*

When Black plays the Slav and White chooses the Exchange Variation the result is often that of this game ... a draw. Both players poked and prodded with Golombek making a brief breakthrough, but the game ended as could be expected.

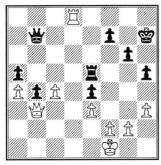

After 40. ... ♔h7

1. ♘f3 d5 2. c4 c6 3. d4 ♘f6 4. c×d5 c×d5 5. ♘c3 ♘c6 6. ♗f4 ♗f5 7. ♕b3 ♘a5 8. ♕a4+ ♗d7 9. ♕c2 ♖c8 10. e3 g6 11. ♗d3 ♗g7 12. 0–0 0–0 13. ♕e2 a6 14. ♖ac1 b5 15. h3 ♗c6 16. ♘e5 ♗b7 17. ♘b1 ♕b6 18. ♘d2 ♖fd8 19. ♘df3 ♘c4 20. b3 ♘d6 21. a3 ♘de4 22. ♕b2 b4 23. a4 ♘c3 24. ♘d2 a5 25. ♘b1 ♘×b1 26. ♗×b1 ♘e4 27. ♗×e4 d×e4 28. ♘c4 ♕a6 29. ♕e2 ♗d5 30. ♖c2 ♖c6 31. ♖fc1 ♖dc8 32. ♔f1 ♗×c4 33. ♖×c4 ♖×c4 34. b×c4 e5 35. d×e5 ♖c5 36. ♕c2 ♕b7 37. ♖d1 h5 38. ♕b3 ♗×e5 39. ♗×e5 ♖×e5 40. ♖d8+ ♔h7 *(see diagram)*

41. ♖d4 ½–½ (Source: *www.Chessgames.com*)

271 Menchik–Philip S. Milner-Barry
Margate (4), April 15, 1939

[E54] *Nimzo-Indian, Rubinstein Variation*

1. ♘f3 d5 2. d4 ♘f6 3. c4 e6 4. e3 c5 5. ♗d3 c×d4 6. e×d4 d×c4 7. ♗×c4 ♗b4+ 8. ♘c3 0–0 9. 0–0 b6 10. ♕e2 ♗b7 11. ♗g5 ♘bd7 12. ♖fc1 ♖c8 13. ♘e5 ♗e7 14. ♗a6 ♗×a6 15. ♕×a6 ♘×e5 16. d×e5 ♘g4 17. ♖d1 ♗×g5 18. ♖×d8 ♖f×d8 *(see diagram)*

19. ♖f1 ♖c7. ½–½ (Source: *www.Chessgames.com*)

After 18. ... ♖f×d8

272 José Raúl Capablanca–Menchik
Margate (5), April 16, 1939

[D34] *Tarrasch Defense*

As was the case more than once, Menchik played a solid game against Capablanca and had a shot at a draw. As usual, the former World Champion generally maintained a small but definite advantage and she would finally make a large enough error for him to put her away.

1. d4 d5 2. c4 e6 3. ♘c3 c5 4. c×d5 e×d5 5. ♘f3 ♘c6 6. g3 ♘f6 7. ♗g2 ♗e7 8. 0–0 0–0 9. d×c5 ♗×c5 10. ♘a4 ♗e7 11. ♗e3 ♘e4 12. ♖c1 ♗e6 13. a3 ♕d7 14. ♘c5 ♘×c5 15. ♗×c5 ♖fc8 16. ♕d2 ♗×c5 17. ♖×c5 ♘e7 18. ♖×c8+ ♖×c8 19. ♘d4 ♗h3 20. ♖d1 ♗×g2 21. ♔×g2 h6 22. ♕f4 a6 23. ♖d3 ♖c4 24. b3 ♖c8 25. ♖e3 ♔f8 26. h4 ♔g8 27. h5 ♖d8 28. ♖f3 ♖f8 29. b4 ♔h7?! [Possibly better is 29. ... ♘c6 30. ♘f5 ♘e7—RT]

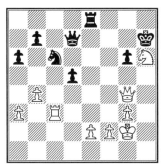

After 34. ♘×h6

30. ♖c3 ♘c6 31. ♘f5 ♖e8? Opening up the position and leading to the trade of queens which is rarely beneficial to the player with the isolani. Better may be 31. ... ♖d8 or even 31. ... d4. **32. ♕g4 g6 33. h×g6+?!** [Worse is 33. ♘×h6 ♕×g4 34. ♘×g4 ♖×e2 35. ♘f6+ ♔g7 36. ♘×d5 g×h5 37. ♘f4 ♖e5± —RT] **33. ... f×g6 34. ♘×h6** *(see diagram)*

34. ... ♕×g4? [A very interesting line with drawing chances is 34. ... ♕g7!? 35. ♖c1 ♘e4 36. ♕g5 ♖e5 37. ♕f4 ♕×h6 38. ♖×c6 ♕×f4 39. g×f4 ♖×e2—RT] **35. ♘×g4 ♖×e2 36. ♘f6+ ♔h6 37. ♘×d5 ♖b2 38. ♘e3 a5 39. b×a5 ♘×a5 40. ♘g4+ ♔g5 41. ♔h3 b6 42. ♖f3 ♖b1 43. ♖f7 ♖h1+ 44. ♔g2 ♖c1 45. ♘e5 ♘c4 46. f4+ ♔h6 47. ♘g4+ 1–0** (Source: Wildhagen, *Capablanca*, 1963 [additional notes by RT])

273 Menchik–George Thomas

Margate (6), April 17, 1939

[D46] Semi-Slav

1. ♘f3 d5 2. d4 ♘f6 3. c4 e6 4. ♘c3 c6 5. e3 ♘bd7 6. ♗d3 ♗d6 7. 0-0 0-0 8. e4 d×e4 9. ♘×e4 ♘×e4 10. ♗×e4 f5 11. ♗c2 e5 12. c5 ♗e7 13. ♘×e5 ♘×e5 14. d×e5 ♗e6 15. ♗b3 ♕c8 16. ♕c2 f4 17. f3 ♔h8 18. ♗d2 ♗×b3 19. a×b3 ♕d7 20. ♕c3 ♗×c5+ 21. ♕×c5 ♕×d2 22. ♖×a7 ♕×b2 23. ♖×b7 ♖fe8 24. ♕×c6 ♕×e5 25. h3 ♖a2 26. ♕d7 ♖e2 27. ♔h2?! [27. b4 ♖a8 28. ♖c7 h5 29. ♔h1 ♕g5 30. ♖g1 ♖d8—RT] **27. ... h6** *(see diagram)*

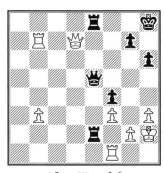

After 27. ... h6

28. ♖d1? Time pressure or just a lack of a sense of danger? [28. ♕g4—RT] **28. ... ♖×g2+ ½–½** (Source: *www.Chessgames.com* [additional notes by RT])

274 Salo Flohr–Menchik

Margate (7), April 19, 1939

[D36] Queen's Gambit Declined, Exchange Variation

1. d4 d5 2. c4 e6 3. ♘c3 ♘f6 4. ♗g5 ♘bd7 5. e3 c6 6. c×d5 e×d5 7. ♗d3 ♗e7 8. ♕c2 0-0 9. h3 ♖e8 10. ♘f3 ♘f8 11. 0-0 ♗e6 12. a3 ♘6d7 13. ♗×e7 ♕×e7 14. ♘a4 f6?! Menchik starts building a wall that only creates a lot of holes and weaknesses. Still it seems that the biggest problem may have been finding the right moves during the assault as it appears that the game was lost on time. **15. b4 b5 16. ♘c5 ♘b6 17. a4 a6 18. ♖a2 g6 19. ♖fa1 ♔f7 20. ♘d2 ♘fd7 21. ♘db3 ♘×c5 22. ♘×c5 ♖ec8 23. a×b5 a×b5 24. ♘×e6 ♖×a2 25. ♖×a2 ♔×e6 26. ♖a6 ♘c4 27. ♕b1 f5 28. ♗×c4 d×c4 29. ♕b2 ♔d5 30. ♕a2?** ♖c7 [30. ... ♕×b4—RT] **31. ♖a8 ♖d7** [31. ... ♕×b4—RT] **32. ♕a6 ♕×b4 33. ♖e8** *(see diagram)*

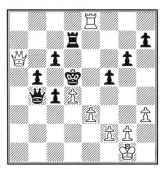

Final position

A reasonable assumption is that Vera lost the game on time as her position is far from resignable. **1–0** (Source: *www. Chessgames.com* [additional notes by RT])

275 Menchik–G.S.A. Wheatcroft
Margate (8), April 20, 1939
[D37] *Queen's Gambit Declined*

1. ♘f3 d5 2. d4 ♘f6 3. c4 e6 4. e3 ♗e7 5. ♘c3 0-0 6. ♗d3 d×c4 7. ♗×c4 c5 8. 0-0 a6 9. ♗d3 ♘bd7 10. ♕e2 b6 11. ♖d1 ♕c7 12. ♗d2 ♗b7 13. ♖ac1 ♖fd8 14. a4 e5 15. ♘×e5 ♘×e5 16. d×e5 ♕×e5 17. e4 ♖d7 18. f3 g6 19. ♗e3 ♕c7 20. ♗c4 ♗d6 21. g3 ♗e5 22. ♖×d7 ♕×d7 23. ♖d1 ♕e8 24. ♕c2 ♖d8 25. ♖×d8 ♕×d8 26. ♕d3 ♕×d3 27. ♗×d3 ♘d7 28. ♘d1 f5 29. ♗c4+ ♔g7 30. f4 ♗d4 31. e5 ♘f3 32. ♗×d4 c×d4 33. ♘f2 ♘c5 34. b3 ♗c6 35. ♘d3 ½-½ (Source: *www.Chessgames.com*)

276 Paul Keres–Menchik
Margate (9), April 21, 1939
[C06] *French, Tarrasch*

A sad game which shows the dangers one can walk in the French if one makes a single error. **1. e4 e6 2. d4 d5 3. ♘d2 ♘f6 4. ♗d3 c5 5. e5 ♘fd7 6. c3 c×d4 7. c×d4 ♘c6 8. ♘e2 f6 9. ♘f4** *(see diagram)*

After 9. ♘f4

9. ... ♕b6?? Evidently Menchik transposed lines. if ♕b6 was desired it should have been played on move 8, and after (or if) White plays 9. ♘f3 then we can play 9. ... f6. The text shows Menchik to be playing on autopilot. **10. ♕h5+ ♔d8 11. ♘×e6+ ♔e7 12. ♘f4 ♕×d4 13. ♘f3 ♕b4+ 14. ♗d2 ♕×b2 15. 0-0 ♔d8** [No better is 15. ... ♘d×e5 16. ♘×e5 f×e5 17. ♘×d5+ ♔d6 18. ♗c3+– where we see the full devastation of the open king and lack of development—RT] **16. ♘e6+ ♔e7 17. ♘c7 ♔d8 18. ♖fb1 ♕×b1+ 19. ♖×b1 ♕×c7 20. e6 ♘de5 21. ♘×e5 f×e5 22. ♕e8 ♖b8 23. ♗b5 ♘e7 24. ♗b4 ♘g6 25. ♖c1+ ♔b6 26. ♕d8+ 1-0** (Source: *www.Chessgames.com* [additional notes by RT])

Montevideo 1939—
Millington Drake International Tournament
April September 21–29, 1939

		1	2	3	4	5	6	7	8	Points	Place
1	Alekhine, Alexander	●	1	1	1	1	1	1	1	7	1
2	Golombek, Harry	0	●	=	1	1	1	1	1	5½	2
3	Menchik, Vera	0	=	●	1	1	1	=	1	5	3
4	Hounié Fleurquin, Carlos	0	0	0	●	=	1	=	1	3	4
5	Oliviera, Alfredo	0	0	0	=	●	=	=	1	2½	5–7
6	Roux Cabral, Luis	0	0	0	0	=	●	1	1	2½	5–7
7	Wood, Baruch H.	0	0	=	=	=	0	●	1	2½	5–7
8	Gulla, Luis Alberto	0	0	0	0	0	0	0	●	0	8

This Uruguayan tournament was put together as a fundraiser for the Red Cross and held shortly after the Olympiad and Women's World Championship in Buenos Aires.

277 Menchik–Harry Golombek

Montevideo, Uruguay, September 1939

[D78] *Neo-Grünfeld*

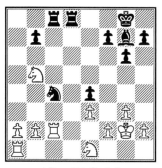

After 27. ♘×b5

1. ♘f3 ♘f6 2. c4 g6 3. g3 ♗g7 4. ♗g2 0-0 5. 0-0 d5 6. d4 c6 7. ♕b3 d×c4 8. ♕×c4 ♗e6 9. ♕c2 ♗f5 10. ♕b3 ♕b6 11. ♘bd2 ♘a6 12. ♕×b6 a×b6 13. ♘c4 b5 14. ♘e3 ♗e4 15. ♗d2 ♘c7 16. ♖fc1 ♖fd8 17. ♘c2 ♘fe8 18. e3 ♘d6 19. ♗b4 ♘d5 20. ♘fe1 ♗×g2 21. ♔×g2 ♘×b4 22. ♘×b4 e5 23. d5 c×d5 24. ♘×d5 e4 25. ♖c2 ♘c4 26. ♘c7 ♖ac8 27. ♘×b5 *(see diagram)*

27. ... ♘×b2 [Black could have won here by 27. ... ♗×b2 28. ♖b1 ♘e3+! 29. f×e3 ♖×c2+ 30. ♘×c2 ♖d2+ etc.; or even by 27. ... ♘e3+ at once—RT] Instead he played 28. ♖×c8 ♖×c8 29. ♖b1 ♖a8 30. a3 ♖a5 31. ♘d4 ♗×d4 32. e×d4 ♘c4 33. ♘c2 ♘×a3 34. ♘×a3 ♖×a3 35. ♖×b7 ♖d3 36. ♖b4 ½–½ (Source: *Chess*, December 1939, #960)

278 A. Oliviera–Menchik

Montevideo, Uruguay, September 1939

[C14] *French, Classical*

[For those who think of the French as a dull opening leading to dull games, look at this game which is wild beyond belief—RT]

1. e4 e6 2. d4 d5 3. ♘c3 ♘f6 4. ♗g5 ♗e7 5. e5 ♘fd7 6. ♗×e7 ♕×e7 7. ♘b5 Orthodox so far. 7. ... ♘b6 8. c3 a6 9. ♘a3 0-0 [Lasker–Lilienthal, Moscow 1936, played 9. ... c5 10. ♘c2 ♘c6 11. f4 ♘a4 12. ♖b1 b5 13. ♘f3 ♗d7 14. ♕d2 ♖c8 etc.—RT] 10. ♗d3 f5 11. f4 ♗d7 12. ♘f3 ♘a4 13. ♖b1 ♘×c3 14. b×c3 ♕×a3 15. ♖b3 ♕a5 16. ♘g5 h6 17. h4 ♕×a2 18. ♖×b7 h×g5 19. h×g5 ♕×g2 20. ♕h5 ♕g3+ 21. ♔d2 ♕×f4+ 22. ♔c2 ♕g4 23. ♕h7+ ♔f7 24. ♖h6 ♕×g5 25. ♖f6+ ♔e8 26. ♖g6 ♕e3 27. ♖×g7 *(see diagram)*

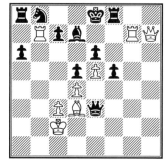

After 27. ♖×g7

White has sacrificed a lot of material but has a ferocious attack with the threat of 28. ♖×b8+ and if 28. ... ♖×b8 29. ♖e7 with repeated checks till Black is mated. 27. ... ♕f2+! 28. ♔b3 ♔d8 For now 29. ♖×b8+ is answered by 29. ... ♖×b8 with check. [Dr. Alekhine here walked across from his own game, gave the position a casual glance and quietly mentioned to B.H. Wood that 29. ♗b5 would win. Both players overlooked this fine move. The main variation is 29. ♗b5 ♗×b5 30. ♖g×c7 ♗c4+ 31. ♖×c4 d×c4+ 32. ♔a3 avoiding further checks—RT] 29. ♔a3 ♔c8 30. ♖×b8+ ♖×b8 31. ♗×a6+ ♖b7 32. ♖×d7 ♕b2+ 0–1 (Source: *Chess*, December 1939, #961; notes by VM [additional notes by RT])

279 Alexander Alekhine–Menchik

Montevideo, Uruguay (4), September 24, 1939

[D36] *Queen's Gambit Declined, Exchange Variation*

Alekhine quickly gains a winning position only to dither so much in the middlegame that Menchik almost gained the draw. Certainly not a game for the World Champion to be proud of.

1. d4 d5 2. c4 e6 3. ♘c3 ♘f6 4. ♗g5 ♘bd7 5. e3 ♗e7 6. c×d5 e×d5 7. ♗d3 0–0 8. ♕c2 ♖e8 9. ♘ge2 c6 10. h3 ♘f8 *(see diagram)*

11. g4!? ♕a5 12. ♘g3 c5 12. ... h6 appears to give Black some pull via the two bishops **13. 0–0 c×d4 14. e×d4 ♘e6 15. ♗e3 ♗d7 16. ♕b3 ♗c6 17. g5 ♘e4?? ** 17. ... ♘d7 **18. ♗×e4 d×e4 19. d5 ♗d7 20. d×e6 ♗×e6 21. ♕b5 ♕c7 22. ♘d5 ♗×d5 23. ♕×d5 ♖ad8 24. ♕b3 ♗×g5 25. ♗×g5**

After 10. ... ♘f8

♖d3 26. ♖ac1 ♕e5 27. ♖c3 ♖×c3 28. ♕×c3 ♕×g5 29. ♖e1 g6 30. ♕b3 ♕e7 31. ♕c4 h5 32. h4 ♕×h4 33. ♖×e4 ♖×e4 34. ♕×e4 ♕g5 35. ♔h2 ♕b5 36. ♕d4 f5 37. a4 ♕a6 38. b3 ♔f7 39. ♕g1 ♔e6 40. ♕g7 ♔d5 41. ♘f1 ♕c6 42. ♘d2 b6 43. ♘f3 ♕c1+ 44. ♔g2 ♕f4 45. ♕×a7 ♔c6 46. a5 b×a5 47. ♕×a5 ♕g4+ 48. ♔f1 ♕b7 49. ♕d5+ ♔b6 50. ♘d4 *(see diagram)*

After 50. ♘d4

50. ... ♕h3+ 50. ... ♕d1+ 51. ♔g2 ♕g4+ 52. ♔h2 ♕h4+ 53. ♔g1 ♕g4+ 54. ♔g2 ♕×d4 55. ♕×g6+ ♔c7 56. ♕×f5 ♕d1+ 57. ♔g2 ♕×b3 58. ♕×h5 **51. ♔e2 g5 52. b4** Better was 52. ♕c6+ ♔a7 53. ♘b5+ ♔b8 54. ♕c7+ ♔a8 55. ♕a7 mate but why quibble after the World Champion played such a poor middlegame as to almost allow Black to escape? **1–0** (Source: Skinner, *Alexander Alekhine Chess Game 1902–1946*, 1998; notes by RT)

London 1939—Hampstead Invitation Tournament
December 4–16, 1939

		1	2	3	4	5	6	7	8	9	10	11	12	Pts	Place
1	König, Imre R.	•	1	=	=	1	1	=	=	0	=	1	1	7½	1–2
2	Milner-Barry, Philip S.	0	•	1	0	1	1	0	1	1	=	1	1	7½	1–2
3	Thomas, George A.	=	0	•	1	1	=	=	=	=	1	1	=	7	3
4	List, Paul M.	=	1	0	•	=	0	1	=	1	1	0	1	6½	4
5	Blum, Martin	0	0	0	=	•	0	1	=	1	1	1	1	6	5–7
6	Fazekas, Stefan	0	0	=	1	1	•	0	0	=	1	1	1	6	5–7
7	Menchik, Vera	=	1	=	0	0	1	•	0	1	0	1	1	6	5–7
8	Golombek, Harry	=	0	=	=	=	1	1	•	0	=	=	=	5½	8
9	Schenk, Holger S.	1	0	=	0	0	=	0	1	•	1	1	0	5	9
10	Mieses, Jacques	=	=	0	0	0	0	1	=	0	•	=	1	4	10
11	Morry, William Ritson	0	0	0	1	0	0	=	=	0	=	•	=	2½	11–12
12	Solomon, J.D.	0	0	=	0	0	0	0	=	1	0	=	•	2½	11–12

This tournament was initiated by the Hampstead Chess Club and held at the National Chess Center, which was run by Vera Menchik. The tournament included five foreign players who lived in London as well as all the top Londoners. One can suspect only that the atmosphere was unique with the war and London blitz having started. Menchik, not unusually, found herself holding her own against the players above her in the standings, but having only mediocre results below that level. Sadly no games have come to light.

London Easter Congress 1940

March 19–28, 1940

		1	2	3	4	5	6	7	8	9	10	Points	Place
1	Golombek, Harry	•	=	=	1	1	1	1	=	1	1	7½	1–2
2	List, Paul M.	=	•	1	0	1	1	1	1	1	1	7½	1–2
3	Menchik, Vera	=	0	•	=	=	=	1	1	1	1	6	3
4	Thomas, George A.	0	1	=	•	0	1	1	0	1	1	5½	4
5	Morry, William Ritson	0	0	=	1	1	1	0	1	=	0	4	5–6
6	Podhorzer, David	0	0	=	0	0	•	1	1	1	=	4	5–6
7	Collins, F.G.T.	0	0	0	0	1	0	•	0	1	1	3	7–8
8	Mieses, Jacques	=	0	0	1	0	0	1	•	0	=	3	7–8
9	Fazekas, Stefan	0	0	0	0	=	0	0	1	•	1	2½	9
10	Schenk, Holger S.	0	0	0	0	1	=	0	=	0	•	2	10

Because of the war Margate had to cancel their annual Easter Congress. The National Chess Center picked up the slack and held a comparable tournament at the restaurant hall in the London building of the N.C.C. Six sections of 10 players played from 19 to 28 March. Menchik's score of +4 −1 =4 was a solid result. Less than six months later the Center was destroyed in a German bombing. The tournament was supervised by Vera's husband, R.H.S. Stevenson, and prizes were £5, £3, £2, and £1.[59]

280 Menchik–Stefan Fazekas
London Easter Congress (1), March 19, 1940
[A35] *English, Symmetrical Variation*

1. ♘f3 c5 2. c4 ♘c6 3. ♘c3 g6 4. d4 c×d4 5. ♘×d4 ♗g7 6. ♘b3 b6 7. e4 ♗a6 8. ♗e3 ♖c8 9. f4 d6 10. ♗e2 ♗×c3+ 11. b×c3 ♘f6 12. ♗d3 0-0 13. 0-0 ♕d7 14. ♕e2 ♖c7 15. ♖ad1 ♕e6 16. ♘d2 ♖fc8 *(see diagram)*

17. e5 d×e5 18. f5 ♕d6 19. ♘e4 ♘×e4 20. ♗×e4 ♕a3 21. f×g6 h×g6 22. ♗h6 ♕c5+ 23. ♗e3 ♕×c4 24. ♗d3 ♕×c3 25. ♗×a6 ♖f8 26. ♗h6 ♖b8 27. ♕f2 f5 28. ♖c1 ♕d4 29. ♗c4+ e6 30. ♗×e6+ ♔h8 31. ♗e3 ♕e4 32. ♖c4 ♕d3 33. ♕h4+ ♔g7 34. ♗h6+ ♔h8 35. ♗f8+ 1-0 (Source: *BCM* #8673)

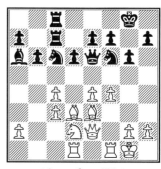

After 16. ... ♖fc8

Black to make move 32

281 Jacques Mieses–Menchik
London Easter Congress (6), March 1940

Although the first 31 moves are missing the following ending is quite attractive. 32. ... ♗×f4 33. ♔g2 ♗e3 34. ♖he1 ♕f2+ 35. ♔h3 ♗×d4 36. ♖f1 ♕b2 37. ♖c1 ♖h4+ 1-0 (Source: *BCM*, 1940, p. 153)

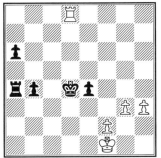

After [1.] Rd8+

(R61) Holger S. Schenk–Menchik
London Easter Congress London (6), March 1940

The full score to this game is not available. The following is from the *BCM*. White has just played Rd8+? **1. ... Kc3 2. Rc8+ Kb3 3. Re8 Ra1+ 4. Ke2 a5 5. R×e4 Rc1 6. f4 Rc2+ 7. Kf3 a4 8. f5 a3 9. f6 a2 10. Re1 Rc6 11. g4 R×f6+ 12. Kg3 Ra6 13. g5 a1Q 14. R×a1 R×a1 15. h4 Kc4 16. h5 b3 0–1** (Source: *BCM*, 1940, p. 153)

282 Menchik–Paul List
London Easter Congress (9), March 1940
[E10] English, Symmetrical

1. Nf3 Nf6 2. c4 c5 3. d4 e6 4. e3 c×d4 5. e×d4 Bb4+ 6. Bd2 Qe7 7. Bd3 B×d2+ 8. Nb×d2 0–0 9. 0–0 b6 10. Re1 Bb7 11. Rc1 d6 12. Rc3 Qd8 13. b4 a5 14. b5 Nbd7 15. Nf1 Rc8 16. Bb1 Nd5 17. Qd3 N5f6 18. Ng3 Re8 19. Ng5 g6 20. f4 d5 21. Rec1 d×c4 22. R×c4 R×c4 23. Q×c4 Nd5 24. Be4 Qf6 25. Ne2 Rc8 *(see diagram)*
26. Q×c8+ B×c8 27. R×c8+ Kg7 28. B×d5 e×d5 29. Nf3 Qe6 30. Kf2 Nf6 31. Rc6 Ng4+ 32. Ke1 Qe4 33. h3 Qb1+ 34. Rc1 Qb4+ 35. Nc3 Ne3 0–1 (Source: *BCM* #8672)

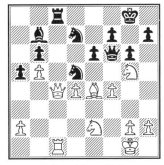

After 25. ... Rc8

London National Chess Center Championships 1940

		1	2	3	4	5	6	7	8	9	10	11	12	Points	Place
1	Golombek, Harry	•	1	=	=	=	1	=	=	1	=	1	1	8	1
2	Brown, E.	0	•	=	1	1	=	=	=	1	=	1	1	7½	2
3	Booth, A.N.	=	=	•	1	0	0	1	1	1	=	1	=	7	3
4	Craddock, James M.	=	0	0	•	1	1	=	=	1	0	1	1	6½	4–5
5	Thomas, George A.	=	0	1	0	•	=	=	1	1	1	1	0	6½	4–5
6	Sergeant, Edward G.	0	=	1	0	=	•	1	0	=	1	1	=	6	6
7	Menchik, Vera	=	=	0	=	=	0	•	0	1	=	1	1	5½	7–8
8	Fazekas, Stefan	=	=	0	=	0	1	1	•	0	1	0	1	5½	7–8
9	Alexander, Frederick	0	0	0	0	0	=	0	1	•	1	1	1	4½	9
10	Brierley, W.L.	=	=	=	1	0	0	=	0	0	•	0	1	4	10
11	Heath, Christopher	0	0	0	0	0	0	0	1	0	1	•	1	3	11
12	Spitz, R.	0	0	=	0	1	=	0	0	0	0	0	•	2	12

283 Edward G. Sergeant–Menchik
National Chess Center—Preliminary B Section, London, 1940
[C14] French, Classical

1. e4 e6 2. d4 d5 3. Nc3 Nf6 4. Bg5 Be7 5. e5 Nfd7 6. B×e7 Q×e7 7. Nb5 Nb6

8. c3 a6 9. ♘a3 0-0 10. f4 f5 11. ♘f3 ♗d7 12. ♗d3 ♘a4 13. ♕d2 c5 14. ♖b1 ♘c6 15. ♘c2 ♖fc8 16. 0-0 b5 17. a3 ♘a5 18. d×c5 ♘c4 19. ♗×c4 b×c4 20. c6 ♖×c6 21. ♘fd4 ♖b6 22. ♘×f5 ♕c5+ 23. ♘fd4 ♖ab8 24. ♔h1 ♘×b2 25. f5 e×f5 26. ♘×f5 ♗×f5 27. ♖×f5 ♘d3 28. ♖×b6 ♕×b6 29. h3 ♕g6 30. ♖g5 ♕e4 31. ♘d4 ♖b2 32. ♖×g7+ ♔×g7 33. ♕g5+ ♕g6 34. ♘f5+ ♔h8?? [34. ... ♔f8=—RT] 35. ♕d8+ 0-1

(Source: Elizaveta Bykova, *Vera Menchik*, 1957, game 84)

284 A.N. Booth–Menchik
NCC London, 1940
[C14] *French, Classical*

Menchik misses two opportunities to win in this game. It seems like she viewed the game as a casual offhand game and did not put too much effort into it. Such games were not uncommon in the last few years of her career when she was playing in minor events against relatively minor players. **1. e4 e6 2. d4 d5 3. ♘c3 ♘f6 4. ♗g5 ♗e7!?** Objectively a poor move as it gives

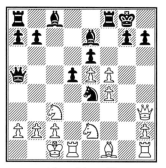

up the bishop pair—the benefit of course is that we leave the book behind. Menchik pushed too hard and really did not pay adequate attention to White's attack. **5. ♗×f6 ♗×f6 6. e5 ♗e7 7. ♕g4 0-0 8. 0-0-0 c5 9. d×c5 ♘d7 10. f4 f5?!** [f5 only speeds up White's threats by allowing White to open key lines more quickly. Better is 10. ... ♘×c5 to get her own threats on the queenside and the center moving—RT] **11. ♕h3 ♘×c5 12. g4? ♕a5?** [12. ... f×g4 13. ♕×g4 ♖×f4! and if 14. ♕×f4 ♗g5–+—RT] **13. ♘ge2 ♘e4 14. g×f5** *(see diagram)*

After 14. g×f5

14. ... ♖×f5?? [14. ... ♘f2 15. ♕g2 ♗c5 (Not 15. ... ♘×h1 16. f6 ♗×f6 17. e×f6 ♖×f6 18. ♕×h1) 16. ♖g1 ♖f7 17. ♖d2 ♗e3 with a nice advantage to Black—RT] **15. ♘×e4 d×e4 16. ♔b1 g6 17. ♕e3 ♖b8 18. ♘g3 ♖f8 19. ♘×e4 ♕b6 20. ♕g3 ♕b4 21. ♗d3 ♗d7 22. h4 ♔h8 23. h5 g×h5 24. ♖×h5 ♖f7 25. ♖dh1 1-0** (Source: *BCM* #8698 [additional notes by RT])

Menchik vs. Jacques Mieses
June 1942

	1	2	3	4	5	6	7	8	9	10	Points
Menchik, Vera	1	=	=	1	1	0	=	1	=	=	6½
Mieses, Jacques	0	=	=	0	0	1	=	0	=	=	3½

In 1942 a match was arranged between Vera and the 77 year old grandmaster Jacques Mieses in London. Although certainly past his prime he was still a forceful player. A refugee from Germany, he later gained his British citizenship and was named Britain's first official grandmaster in 1950. Never an advocate of the positional concepts of Steinitz and Tarrasch, he was famous for his attacking style which won him many brilliancy prizes at the turn of the century. This was the first ever serious match between a woman and a strong master.

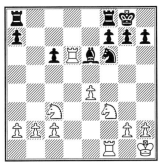

Final position

285 Menchik–Jacques Mieses
Match (1), 1942
[B00] *Nimzowitsch Defense*

**1. d4 d6 2. e4 ᐧc6 3. f4 e5 4. d×e5 ᐧe7 5. ᐧc3 d×e5
6. ᐧf3 ᐧf6 7. ᐧb5 e×f4 8. 0-0 ᐧd7 9. ᐧ×f4 ᐧc5+
10. ᐧh1 ᐧ×d1 11. ᐧa×d1 0-0 12. ᐧ×c7 ᐧe6 13. ᐧ×c6
b×c6 14. ᐧd6 ᐧ×d6 15. ᐧ×d6** *(see diagram)*

On page 170 of the July-August 1942 issue of *Chess*, Menchik states that, "after a hard struggle the extra pawn decided matters in White's favor." **1–0** (Source: *Chess*, July-Aug. 1942, p. 170)

(R62) Jacques Mieses–Menchik
Match (2), 1942
No score available
½–½

286 Menchik–Jacques Mieses
Match (3), 1942
[C30] *Irregular King's Pawn*

**1. d4 d6 2. e4 ᐧc6 3. f4 e5 4. ᐧf3 e×d4 5. ᐧb5 ᐧd7
6. 0-0 ᐧf6 7. ᐧe1 ᐧe7 8. ᐧ×c6 ᐧ×c6 9. ᐧ×d4 0-0
10. ᐧc3 ᐧe8 11. ᐧd2 d5 12. e×d5 ᐧ×d5 13. ᐧ×d5
ᐧ×d5 14. ᐧ×d5 ᐧ×d5 15. ᐧd4 ᐧc5 16. c3 ᐧ×e1+
17. ᐧ×e1 ᐧe8 18. ᐧf2 ᐧ×d4 19. c×d4 ᐧe2 20. ᐧe1
ᐧ×e1+ 21. ᐧ×e1 ᐧ×a2** *(see diagram)*

Drawn eventually by reason of the bishops of opposite colors. ½–½ (Source: *BCM* 1942, p. 209)

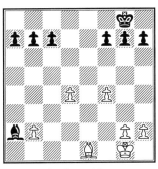

Final position

287 Jacques Mieses–Menchik
Match (4), May 29, 1942
[C01] *French, Exchange*

1. e4 e6 2. d4 d5 3. e×d5 e×d5 4. ᐧd3 {In the remaining three games where the French Defense was adopted, Mieses played here 4. ᐧc3, which is probably slightly stronger than the text move. The advantage, if any, is very slight indeed and lies mainly in the fact that the attack on the d-pawn forces Black to make up his mind which way he will defend the pawn. If he means to play … ᐧd6, [he would] thus give White (who knows by then what to expect) a greater choice of continuations—VM} **ᐧc6 5. c3 ᐧd6 6. ᐧc2 ᐧge7 7. ᐧe2 ᐧg4!** The best move. **8. ᐧe3 ᐧd7 9. ᐧd2 ᐧf5 10. ᐧg3 ᐧ×d3 11. ᐧ×d3 0-0-0 12. b4** This is not the right way of initiating a storming attack. Castling short followed by ᐧfc1 with a view to pushing the c-pawn at the proper moment would be a sound line of play, although Black would have good chances of a counterattack on the kingside. **12. … h5! 13. ᐧb3 h4 14. ᐧe2 ᐧde8** Very well played. **15. ᐧc5** [15. h3 is better—RT] **15. … ᐧg4 16. ᐧb5?** White is underestimating the imminent danger. Castling long, instead, is compulsory. After the weak text move

After 18. ♕d3

White's position collapses surprisingly quickly. **16. ... ♗×c5 17. d×c5** As shown by the further course of the game taking with the b-pawn would have been better, although even then, after 17. ... ♘f5 18. ♕d3 ♘×e3 19. f×e3 White's position soon becomes untenable. **17. ... ♘f5 18. ♕d3** *(see diagram)*

    18. ... d4! A powerful move leading to a neat finish. **19. h3 ♕g6! 20. c×d4** [To 20. ♘f4 Black has the winning reply 20. ... ♕g5!; If 20. ♘×d4 then 20. ... ♘×e3 21. ♕×g6 ♘c2+ etc.—RT] **20. ... ♘×b4** The fatal stroke. **21. ♕b1 ♘×e3 22. ♕×g6 f×g6 23. ♖b1 ♘ed5 0–1** (Source: *BCM* #9013; *Chess* #1432; notes by J. Mieses in *BCM* [additional notes by RT])

288 Menchik–Jacques Mieses
Match (5), London, June 1942
[A41] *Queen's Pawn Game*

1. d4 d6 This defense is quite a favorite of Mieses and was adopted by him in all the games where he had Black. **2. ♘f3** [In the first game White played 2. e4 when followed 2. ... ♘c6 3. f4 e5 4. d×e5 (In the third game the sequence was 4. ♘f3 e×d4 5. ♗b5 ♗d7 6. 0–0 ♘f6 7. ♖e1 ♗e7 8. ♗×c6 ♗×c6 9. ♕×d4 0–0 10. ♘c3 the game has developed on the lines similar to the Steinitz Defense in the Ruy Lopez, but White has no advantage having wasted a move with f4. 10. ... ♖e8 11. ♗d2 d5! 12. e×d5 ♘×d5 13. ♘×d5 ♕×d5 14. ♕×d5 ♗×d5 15. ♘d4 ♗c5 16. c3 ♖×e1+ 17. ♗×e1 ♖e8 18. ♗f2 ♗×d4 19. c×d4 ♖e2 20. ♖e1! ♖×e1+ 21. ♗×e1 ♗×a2 and because of the different-colored bishops the game was eventually drawn) 4. ... ♕e7 (trying to bring a close player into the open!) 5. ♘c3 d×e5 6. ♘f3 ♘f6 7. ♗b5 e×f4 (presumably hoping for 8. ♗×c6+, when Black could obtain some counterplay with ... ♗a6 and ... ♖d8) 8. 0–0 ♕d7 (The natural looking 8. ... ♗d7 would have been answered by 9. ♘d5) 9. ♗×f4 ♗c5+ 10. ♔h1 ♕×d1 11. ♖a×d1 0–0 12. ♗×c7 ♗e6 13. ♗×c6 b×c6 14. ♗d6 ♗×d6 15. ♖×d6 and after a hard struggle the extra pawn decided the issue in White's favor—RT] **2. ... ♘c6 3. ♗f4 ♘f6 4. h3 ♗f5** [A stronger continuation here is 4. ... g6 transposing the opening into the King's Indian Defense—RT] **5. e3 ♗e4 6. ♘bd2 ♕d7 7. ♘×e4 ♘×e4 8. ♗d3 ♘f6 9. 0–0 h6 10. ♗b5** Well aware of what was coming, White hastened to start a counter offensive on the queenside. **10. ... a6 11. ♗a4 b5 12. ♗b3 g5 13. ♗g3 ♖g8** *(see diagram)*

    [It was necessary first of all to eliminate the "white bishop menace" by 13. ... ♘a5—RT] **14. a4! b4** [If now 14. ... ♘a5 then 15. a×b5 ♘×b3 16. ♖×a6! ♖×a6 17. b×a6 ♘a5 18. a7 ♕c8 19. ♕a1 etc.—RT] **15. a5 ♘a7 16. ♗a4 c6 17. ♕d3 ♕b7** [If 17. ... ♘b5 18. c4 b×c3 19. b×c3 threatening ... c4 and then ... d5—RT] **18. d5 ♘d7 19. d×c6** [At once 19. ♗×d6 was perhaps even stronger, as in reply to 19. ... c×d5 White could play (If after 19. ... e×d6 20. d×c6 then 20. ... ♘×c6 21. ♕e4+ regaining the material with a winning position) 20. ♗×d7+ ♕×d7 (20. ... ♔×d7 21. ♗×b4 ♕×b4 22. ♕d5+ etc.) 21. ♗×b4 and Black cannot play 21. ... g4 on account of 22. ♘e5 etc.—RT] **19. ... ♘×c6 20. ♗×d6**

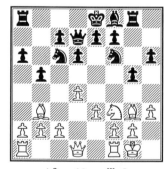

After 13. ... ♖g8

♖g6 21. ♗×c6 ♕×c6 22. ♗×b4 g4 23. h×g4 ♖×g4 24. e4 Forced, as Black is threatening not only ... ♖×b4 but also ... ♕×f3. To avoid this counterattack White could have played 22. ♗g3, which was a safer continuation than the one chosen. 24. ... ♗g7 [24. ... f5 looks promising but does not lead anywhere: e.g. 25. ♘d4 ♕g6 (25. ... ♕b7 26. c3 f×e4 27. ♕h3 etc.) 26. e×f5 ♖×g2+ 27. ♔h1 ♕g4 28. ♕f3 attacking the two rooks—RT] 25. ♖ad1 ♖×e4 26. c3 *(see diagram)*

After 26. c3

26. ... ♘e5 [Black has no really good continuation; the most promising seems to be 26. ... 0–0–0 with a view to ... ♖g8, but then simply 27. ♘d2 and if the Black rook retires to 27. ... ♖e5 (Whilst if 27. ... ♖g4 28. f3 ♘f6 29. ♕e2 ♖g6 30. ♕c4 ♕×c4 31. ♘×c4 with a won endgame; 27. ... ♘c5 28. ♕×d8+ ♔×d8 29. ♘×e4+ ♘d7 30. ♘c5 etc.) 28. ♘c4 threatening 29. ♘b6+—RT] 27. ♘×e5 ♖×e5 28. ♖fe1 ♖×e1+ 29. ♖×e1 ♗f8 30. ♕e4 ♕×e4 31. ♖×e4 ♖c8 32. ♖g4 f5 33. ♖g6 ♖a8 34. f4 ♔f7 35. ♖b6 ♖a7 36. ♗c5 ♗g7 37. c4 [If 37. ♖×h6 ♗×h6 38. ♗×a7 ♗×f4 39. b4 ♔e6 with (minimal—Fritz) defensive chances (now not 39. ... ♗d2 40. b5!)—RT] 37. ... h5 38. b4 ♗c3 39. ♔f2 h4 40. ♔e2 e6 41. ♔d3 ♗b2 42. ♗d6 ♔e8 43. c5 ♔d7 44. ♗b8 ♖a8 45. c6+ ♔c8 46. c7 e5 47. ♖g6 1–0 (Source: *Chess* #1433; *BCM* #90; notes by VM [additional notes by RT])

289 Jacques Mieses–Menchik
Match (6), June 3, 1942
[C01] *French, Exchange*

1. e4 e6 2. d4 d5 3. e×d5 e×d5 4. ♘c3 c6 5. ♗f4 ♘f6 6. ♕f3 ♗b4 7. ♗e5 ♘bd7 8. a3 ♕a5 9. ♗×f6 ♘×f6 10. ♘ge2 0–0 11. 0–0–0 ♗g4 An enterprising life of play, but hardly sound. Black, it is true, gets two pawns for a bishop and a rather promising looking attack, the refutation of which needs a very careful defense. 12. a×b4 ♕a1+ 13. ♔d2 ♕×b2 14. ♕d3 ♕×b4 15. f3 ♗h5 16. ♘f4 ♘e4+ With a sound judgment of position Black realizes that this second sacrifice is her only chance. 17. f×e4 ♗×d1 18. ♔×d1 d×e4 19. ♕c4 ♕a5 20. ♘fe2 b5 21. ♕c5 ♖ad8 22. g3 ♕a1+ 23. ♔d2 b4 24. ♕×b4 c5! A position like this must be treated in a desperate style, of course. From this point of view Black's last moves are justified. 25. ♕b1 Accepting the second pawn sacrifice looks more risky than it is, since 25. ♕×c5 ♖c8 would be refuted by ♗g2. 25. ... e3+ 26. ♔×e3 c×d4+ 27. ♔f2 ♕a3 28. ♘d1 ♕c5 29. ♔e1 ♕a5+ 30. ♔f2 ♕c5 31. ♔g2 ♖fe8 32. ♘f2 a5! A very ingenious conception of the position. Attacks directed against White's king would now be frustrated, but the passed rook's pawn is still an appreciable weapon in Black's hands. 33. ♘f4 ♕c6+ 34. ♔g1 ♕c3 35. ♕b3 ♕a1 36. ♘4d3 a4! 37. ♕c4 [If 37. ♕b2? then 37. ... ♕×b2 38. ♘×b2 a3 and White loses a piece—RT] 37. ... a3 38. ♘b4 ♖c8 39. ♕d5 [To 39. ♕b3 Black has the strong reply 39. ... ♖e1 40. ♔g2! ♖b8! etc.—RT] 39. ... ♖b8 40. ♔g2! Threatening ♗c4. 40. ... ♕b2 41. ♘c6! By this move White obtains a clear advantage. 41. ... a2 Black has no better continuation. 42. ♗c4 a1♕ 43. ♖×a1 ♕×a1 44. ♘×b8 ♖×b8 45. ♕×f7+ ♔h8 46. ♗d3! Threatening ♕h5, etc. 46. ... ♕a8+ 47. ♔h3 ♖b6 48. ♘g4 ♕c8 49. ♔g2 ♕a8+ 50. ♕f3 ♕×f3+ 51. ♔×f3 ♖e6 *(see diagram)*

After 51. ... ⌶e6

To win an endgame like this needs a faultless technique. The finish of the game deserves to be appreciated as an instructive specimen of how to treat the encounter of two minor pieces against a rook. **52. ♔f4 g6 53. ♘e5 ♔g7 54. ♘f3 ♔f6 55. ♘×d4 ⌶e7 56. h4 h5 57. ♘f3 ⌶e8 58. ♘g5 ⌶e1 59. ♘e4+ ♔f7 60. ♔e5 ♔e7 61. ♗d5 ⌶g1 62. c4! ⌶g2 63. c5 ⌶g1 64. ♔e5 ⌶d1 65. ♗c4 ⌶c1 66. ♗d5 ⌶f1 67. c6 ⌶d1 68. ♘d6 ⌶e1+ 69. ♗e4 ⌶c1 70. ♗d5 ⌶e1+ 71. ♘e4 ⌶d1 72. ♘f6!** The decisive maneuver. **72. ... ⌶e1+ 73. ♗e4 ⌶c1 74. ♘d5+ 1–0** (Source: *BCM* #9012; *Chess* #1434; notes by J. Mieses in *BCM* [additional notes by RT])

290 Menchik–Jacques Mieses
Match (7), June 1942
[A41] *Queen's Pawn Opening*

1. d4 d6 2. ♘f3 ♘c6 3. ♗f4 g6 4. h3 ♗g7 5. e4 ♘×d4 6. ♘×d4 e5 7. ♗e3 e×d4 8. ♗×d4 ♘f6 9. ♘c3 0-0 10. ♕f3! ♗d7 11. 0-0-0 ⌶e8 12. ♗c4 ♗c6 13. ⌶he1 ♕e7 14. g4! A strong attacking move. It is not an easy task for Black to discover the only right counter-action. **14. ... ♗h6+! 15. ♗e3** [If 15. ♔b1? then 15. ... ♘×e4 {Mieses here overlooks 16. ♘×e4 ♗×e4 17. ⌶×e4 and if the queen recaptures then ♕×f7 is mate. He apologized for the oversight on p. 182 of the August 1942 *BCM*}—RT] **15. ... ♗×e3+ 16. ⌶×e3 ♔g7 17. ⌶de1 ♘d7 18. ♕g3 ♘e5 19. ♗d5 g5** compulsory **20. ♘e2 ♗×d5 21. e×d5 ♕d7! 22. ♘d4** *(see diagram)*

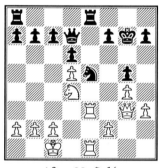

After 22. ♘d4

[22. f4 should lead to a win. 22. ... ♘g6 23. f×g5 ⌶×e3 24. ♕×e3 etc.—RT] **22. ... ♕a4!** This is the key move of Black's defensive system. Black has how obtained a safe position with even some counter chances. **23. ♘f5+ ♔f8 24. a3 ♕a5 25. ♕g2!** [This is better than 25. ⌶d1 ♘c4 26. ⌶×e8+ ⌶×e8 27. ♕d3 b5 with a slight advantage in position for Black—RT] **25. ... ♘c4 26. ⌶×e8+ ⌶×e8 27. ⌶×e8+ ♔×e8 28. ♕e4+ ♘e5 29. c3 ♕b5 30. ♔c2 ♕f1 31. ♕e3 ♕c4 32. ♕×g5 ♕d3+ 33. ♔b3 ♕×d5+ 34. ♔c2 ♕d3+ 35. ♔b3 ♕d5+ ½–½** (Source: *BCM* #9000; notes by J. Mieses [additional notes by RT])

(R63) Jacques Mieses–Menchik
Match (8), London, June 1942
No score available
0–1

291 Menchik–Jacques Mieses
Match (9), June 11, 1942
[A41] *Queen's Pawn Opening*

1. d4 d6 2. ♘f3 ♘c6 3. c4 e5 4. ♘c3 e×d4 5. ♘×d4 g6 6. ♘×c6 b×c6 7. ♕d4 ♕f6 8. ♕×f6 ♘×f6 9. g3 ♗e6 10. ♗g2 ♔d7 11. b3 ♗g7 12. ♗b2 ⌶he8 13. 0-0 ⌶ab8

14. ♘a4 [The alternative would be 14. ♖ab1 since Black threatened ♗×c4—RT] **14. ... ♗×c4** An enterprising reply producing interesting complications, the final result of which was difficult to foresee. **15. b×c4 ♖b4 16. ♘c5+ d×c5 17. ♖fd1+** [Here 17. ♗h3+ instead was to be taken into consideration; there might have followed 17. ... ♔e7 18. ♗a3 ♖×c4 19. ♖ac1 ♖×c1 20. ♖×c1 ♘e4 21. ♗g2 ♘d6 22. ♗×c5 and the endgame resulting is not easy to adjudicate—RT] **17. ...** **♔c8 18. ♗a3 ♘e4 19. ♗×b4 ♗×a1 20. ♗a3 ♗g7 21. e3 f5 22. ♖d3 ♖e6 23. f3 ♘d6 24. ♗×c5 ♘×c4 25. ♗×a7 ♖d6 26. ♖×d6 c×d6 27. ♗f1 ♘d2 28. ♗e2 ♔c7 29. ♗d4 ♗×d4 30. e×d4 ♘b1 31. ♗c4 ♘d2 32. ♗e2 ♘b1 33. ♗c4 d5 34. ♗b3 ♔b6 35. ♔f2 ♔b5 36. ♔e3 ♔b4** *(see diagram)*

37. h4! An exciting endgame with chances on both sides. Black had to be aware of the danger of White's getting an opportunity of sacrificing her bishop in order to break through with a pawn. **37. ... ♘c3 38. h5 ♘a3 39. ♗c2 ♔×a2 40. h6 ♔b2 41. ♗d3 ♘b5** Compulsory, since White threatened ♗×f5 followed by g4. **42. g4 ♘d6 43. g×f5 g×f5 44. ♔f4 ♔c3 45. ♗×f5 ♘×f5** [If 45. ... ♔×d4 46. ♗×h7 ♘f7 47. ♔f5 ♘×h6+ 48. ♔g6 c5 49. ♔×h6 c4 50. f4 and Black cannot get more than a draw—RT] **46. ♔×f5 ♔×d4 47. f4 c5 48. ♔e6** A draw was agreed. A lively and interesting game throughout. ½–½ (Source: *BCM* #9014; notes by J. Mieses [additional notes by RT])

After 36. ... ♔b4

(R64) Jacques Mieses–Menchik
Match (10), London, June 1942
No score available
½–½

Sidcup 1942—Kent County Congress
August 10–15, 1942

	1	2	3	4	5	6	Points	Place
1 Bruce, R.M.	•	1	=	1	1	1	4½	1
2 Menchik, Vera	0	•	=	1	1	1	3½	2–3
3 Farkas, Private V.	=	=	•	=	1	1	3½	2–3
4 Chauvet, Lt. M.	0	0	=	•	=	1	2	4
5 Podger, C.V.	0	0	0	=	•	1	1½	5
6 Brierley, W.L.	0	0	0	0	0	•	0	6

As the war ran its course, the number of available players diminished. Going into the final round Vera and R.M. Bruce were tied at 3½ points. The two players played a hard and well-fought game, but Menchik entered a line which led to a Bruce breakthrough without noticing an attractive saving maneuver on move 33. At the end of the tournament a match of eight boards was held between members of the Armed Forces and other Congress participants. On Board One Menchik won against Lt. A.C. Bloom, but the match was won by the Armed Forces by a score of 5–3.[60]

292 Menchik–V. Farkas
Kent County at Sidcup, 1942
[D37] *Queen's Gambit Declined*

1. d4 d5 2. c4 e6 3. ♘c3 ♘f6 4. ♘f3 ♗e7 5. e3 a6 6. a3 d×c4 7. ♗×c4 c5 8. 0-0 0-0 9. ♕e2 b5 10. ♗a2 ♗b7? [10. ... ♘bd7 so as to meet 11. d×c5 with 11. ... ♘×c5 would have been better—RT] **11. d×c5 ♗×c5 12. e4 ♕c7** For the next few moves Black of course has to be on his guard against e5. On the next move it could have been safely met by 13. ... ♘fd7; and on the following move by ... ♗×f3. **13. ♗g5 ♘bd7 14. ♖ac1 ♕b8** [14. ... ♕b6 would have been inferior on account of 15. b4 and if 15. ... ♗e7 16. e5; and if 15. ... ♗d6 16. ♗×f6—RT] **15. ♔h1** White commits herself to a kingside attack. As the plan nearly succeeds, it is difficult to criticize it, but there are good positional alternatives in 15. b4 or 15. ♖fd1. **15. ... ♖c8** Presumably Black foresees White's plans and wishes to react in the correct way with ... ♗c6 and ... ♕b7. No doubt however he does not like 15. ... ♗c6 on account of such variations as 16. ♗×f6 and if 16. ... ♘×f6 17. ♘e5 [*sic*; source shows 17. ♘d5, which cannot be correct—

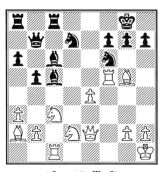

After 19. ♖×f5

RT] and if 16. ... g×f6 17. b4. In the light of the continuation of the actual game, it is arguable that 15. ... ♖e8 would have been better than the text move. White might, of course have countered with a different continuation. **16. ♘d2 ♗c6 17. f4 ♕b7 18. f5** The right way to continue as 18. e5 would have led nowhere. **18. ... e×f5 19. ♖×f5 (see diagram)**

19. ... ♗d6? [19. ... ♗d4 would have been better for in answer to the text move, White misses the strong 20. ♗×f6 and if 20. ... ♘×f6 21. e5 ♖e8 22. ♖×f6 with ♕g4+ and e×d6 to follow, while if 20. ... g×f6 21. ♘d5. Instead, White delays coming to grips for a move which gives Black an opportunity for a most intrepid defense—RT] **20. ♖cf1 ♖e8 21. ♗×f6 ♘×f6 22. ♖×f6** It is now difficult to suggest anything better although, as his two bishops remain, Black is really left with all the play. **22. ... g×f6 23. ♖×f6 ♗e5 24. ♖×f7 ♕×f7 25. ♗×f7+ ♔×f7 26. ♘d1** White must defend even as she has not got enough to defend with. **26. ... ♖ad8 27. b4 ♗f6 28. ♘f2 ♖d6 29. ♘f3 ♖de6 30. ♕a2 ♔g7 31. h4 ♗×e4** Black cannot force a decision with his two bishops because of White's pawn majority. **32. ♘×e4 ♖×e4 33. ♕d5 ♗×h4 34. ♘×h4 ♖×h4+ 35. ♔g1 ♖h6 ½–½** (Source: *BCM* #9035; notes by R. Cross [additional notes by RT])

293 M. Chauvet–Menchik
Kent County at Sidcup, 1942
[C02] *French, Advance*

1. e4 e6 2. d4 d5 3. e5 c5 4. ♘f3 ♕b6 5. c3 ♘c6 6. ♗e2 c×d4 7. c×d4 ♘ge7 8. ♘a3 ♘f5 9. ♘c2 ♗b4+ 10. ♔f1 ♗e7 11. b3 h5 12. g3 ♗d7 13. ♗b2 0-0-0 14. ♘e3 ♕b8 15. ♘×f5 e×f5 16. ♕d2 ♖dg8 17. h4 ♘d8 18. ♗c1 ♘e6 19. ♕b2 ♗b5 20. ♗×b5 ♕×b5+ 21. ♔g2 ♕d3 22. ♕b1! ♕×b1 [If 22. ... ♕e4 23. ♖e1 ♕g4 24. ♘h2! ♕g6 25. ♘f3 etc.—RT] **23. ♖×b1 ♖c8 24. ♗b2 ♖c2 25. ♖hc1 ♖hc8 26. ♖×c2 ♖×c2 27. ♘e1! ♖c6 28. f4 ♖a6 29. ♖a1 ♖c6 30. ♔f3 a5 31. ♔e3 ♗b4 32. ♔d3 ♘c7 33. a3 ♗e7 34. ♘c2?** *(see diagram)*

34. ... ♖g6! 35. ♖g1 ♗×h4 36. ♘e3 ♖×g3 37. ♖×g3 ♗×g3 38. ♘×f5 ♗×f4 39. ♘×g7 h4 40. ♔e2 h3! 41. ♔f2 ♘e6 42. ♔f5 [Or 42. ♘h5 h2 43. ♔g2 ♗e3 44. ♘f6 ♗×d4 45. ♗×d4 ♘×d4 46. b4 a×b4 47. a×b4 ♘c6 etc.—RT] 42. ... ♘g5! 43. ♘g3 Black threatened 43. ... ♘e4+ 44. ♔g1 h2+ 45. ♔g2 ♘f2+! 43. ... ♘e4+ 44. ♘×e4 d×e4 45. ♗c3 b6 46. d5 e3+ 47. ♔f3 h2 48. ♔g2 ♗g3! 49. e6 f×e6 50. d×e6 ♔c7 51. a4 e2 52. b4 e1♕ 53. ♗×e1 ♗×e1 54. b×a5 ♗×a5 55. ♔×h2 ♔d6 56. ♔g3 ♔×e6 0–1 (Source: *Chess*, Oct. 1942, #1464)

After 34. ♘c2

294 Menchik–R. Bruce
Kent County at Sidcup (5), 1942
[E32] *Nimzo-Indian Defense*

1. d4 ♘f6 2. c4 e6 3. ♘c3 ♗b4 4. ♕c2 d6 Although they have to some extent been superseded by 4. ... d5; and 4. ... ♘c6; the text move and 4. ... 0–0; are not easy to meet. Against the text move, in addition to the line chosen by White, 5. e4, 5. ♗g5, and 5. e3, have all been tried. There is also of course the possibility of 5. g3. 5. e4, has as an advantage over the moves mentioned above and 5. ♘f3, the fact that it takes immediate action in the center, and reserves the opportunity of the elastic development of the knight at e2. If e4 is played in conjunction with ♘f3, in positions of this sort, the king's knight almost always has to withdraw so as to allow for f3, and an eventual f4. This game is no exception, see White's tenth move, but the line chosen by White is very solid. **5. ♘f3 ♗×c3+ 6. b×c3 ♘bd7** [6. ... ♕e7 would have reserved more options—RT] **7. e4 e5 8. ♗d3 0–0 9. 0–0 ♖e8 10. ♘e1 ♕e7 11. f3 b6** Black has succeeded in preventing White from playing f4 for the time being. The result is a positional struggle in which both players maneuver behind their own lines, in the case of White for a favorable opportunity of playing f4, and in the case of Black in order to be ready for this move when it comes. It is arguable, however, that the text move is slightly inaccurate as Black wants to get in ... c5 so as to increase his freedom of maneuvering on his second rank, and White could have prevented this with 12. d5 meeting 12. ... ♘c5 with 13. ♗e2 and 14. ♘d3. **12. ♕f2 c5 13. d5 ♘f8 14. ♘c2 ♘g6 15. g3 ♘f8 16. ♗g5 h6 17. ♗d2 ♔h7** Recognizing that ... g6 will sooner or later be necessary. **18. ♕g2** [18. f4 could have been answered by 18. ... e×f4 19. ♕×f4 ♕e5 and White presumably did not like the possibility of ... ♗a6 as an immediate or eventual reply to other moves. Black's reply looks like a waste of time, and 18. ... ♕c7 would probably have been better—RT] **18. ... ♕d7 19. ♘e3 g6 20. a4 ♖e7 21. ♗c2 ♕c7 22. f4 ♘g8 23. ♖f2** [23. f5 was well worth considering as after 23. ... g5 White could arrange to play h4 at a time when ... g5 could not be played. After the text move, White still has a slight pull, and there is no reason as yet why she should have lost, but Black defends himself very well, and never appears to be in great danger—RT] **23. ... f6 24. f×e5 ♖×e5 25. ♖af1 ♗d7 26. g4 ♖ae8 27. h3** [27. h4 would have been better if she were playing for a win—RT] **27. ... ♗c8 28. ♕f3** The knight must be brought into the attack, but Black can also bring a knight into the game, and 28. ♘d1 with the idea of ♘b2–d3 might have been better than the text move. **28. ... ♘d7 29. ♘g2 ♖5e7** *(see diagram)*

30. e5? Overlooking Black's 33rd move. 30. ♘f4 would have been better, although Black's defensive resources would have remained fully adequate. **30. ... ♘×e5 31. ♕e4 ♖g7 32. ♖×f6**

After 29. ... ♖5e7

Still overlooking Black's 33rd move, which is decisive. 32. ♘f4 with the idea of ♘h5 would still have been better, although it would have been difficult to continue the attack after 32. ♔h8. **32. ... ♘×f6 33. ♖×f6 ♘×g4! 34. ♕×e8 ♘×f6 35. ♕e3 ♘g8 36. ♘f4 ♕e7 37. ♘e6 ♖f7 38. ♗×g6+** Black's material advantage will be decisive, however White plays. **38. ... ♔×g6 39. ♕e4+ ♖f5 40. ♕g2+ ♔f6 41. ♕×g8 ♗×e6 42. d×e6 ♕g7+ 43. ♕×g7+ ♔×g7 44. e7 ♖e5 45. ♗f4 ♖×e7 46. ♗×d6 ♖e1+ 47. ♔f2 ♖a1 48. ♔e3 ♖×a4 49. ♔d3 ♔g6 50. h4 ♔f5 51. ♗c7 h5 52. ♗d8 ♖a2 53. ♗c7 ♖b2 0–1** (Source: *BCM* #9036; notes by R. Cross [additional notes by RT])

West London Summer Tournament 1943

The Summer Tournament at the West London C.C. resulted in a victory for Paul M. List with 7½ points out of nine, followed by George Thomas (7) and Vera Menchik (6½). The final placing depended entirely on the individual games between the three leaders: List was lucky to score a win against Menchik, whilst Sir George Thomas, having won a pawn against her, simplified prematurely and could only draw instead of winning.[61] The notes below are probably by B.H. Wood.

295 Paul List–Menchik
West London C.C. Tournament London, 1943
[D12] *Slav Defense*

1. d4 ♘f6 2. ♘f3 d5 3. e3 ♗f5 4. ♗d3 ♗g6 5. 0–0 e6 6. ♕e2 ♘bd7 7. c4 c6 8. ♘c3 ♗b4 9. a3 ♗×c3 10. b×c3 ♕c7 11. a4 d×c4 12. ♗×c4 0–0 13. ♘d2 e5 14. f3 ♘d5 15. e4 ♘×c3 16. ♕d3 e×d4 17. ♕×d4 ♕b6 18. ♕f2 ♕×f2+ 19. ♔×f2 b5 20. a×b5 c×b5 21. ♗b3 ♘c5 22. ♗a3 b4 23. ♗c1 ♖fd8 24. ♗c4 a5 25. ♔e3 ♔f8 26. ♘b1 ♘×b1 27. ♖×b1 *(see diagram)*

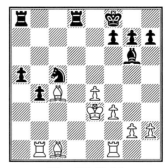

After 27. ♖×b1

27. ... **f5 28. ♗b2 ♗f7 29. ♗×f7 ♖d3+??** [29. ... ♔×f7–+ —RT] **30. ♔e2 ♔×f7 31. ♖fc1! ♖b3 32. ♖×c5 f×e4?!** [32. ... a4—RT] **33. f×e4 a4 34. ♖f1+ ♔e6 35. ♗×g7 ♖g8 36. ♖f6+ ♔d7 37. ♖f7+ ♔e6 38. ♖cc7 ♖×g7 39. ♖×g7 a3 40. ♖ge7+ ♔d6 41. ♖ed7+ ♔e5 42. ♖d2 ♖b1 43. ♖e7+ ♔f6 44. ♖a7 ♖a1 45. ♖d6+ ♔e5 46. ♖b6 1–0**
(Source: *Chess*, November 1943, #1654)

296 Edward G. Sergeant–Menchik
West London C.C. Tournament London, 1943
[B08] *Pirc Defense*

1. e4 d6 2. d4 ♘f6 3. ♘c3 g6 4. ♘f3 4. f4 is more enterprising **4. ... ♗g7 5. ♗f4 0–0 6. ♕d2 ♖e8 7. 0–0–0 c6 8. e5 d×e5 9. ♘×e5 ♘bd7 10. h3 ♘b6 11. g4 ♗e6 12. ♗g2 ♘bd5 13. ♘d3 ♘×c3 14. ♕×c3 ♘d5 15. ♗×d5 ♗×d5 16. ♖he1 ♗f3 17. ♖d2 ♕×d4**

18. ♕a3 18. ♕xd4 ♗xd4 19. ♘e5 ♗xe5 20. ♗xe5 ♗d5 probable would have led to a draw **18. ... ♕c4 19. ♖e3 ♗d5 20. ♗e5** If 20. b3 ♕c3 etc. **20. ... ♗xe5 21. ♖xe5 a5 22. ♖xe7 ♖xe7 23. ♕xe7 ♕xa2 24. ♖e2 a4** *(see diagram)*

25. ♕xb7 c5 26. ♕d7 ♗e6 27. ♕b7 ♖d8 28. ♕b6 ♖c8 29. ♔d2 Not 29. ♘xc5 ♕c4 30. ♘d3 ♕xd3 etc. **29. ... c4 30. ♘b4** If 30. ♖xe6 c3+ etc. **30. ... c3+ 31. bxc3 ♕c4 32. ♕d4 ♕c7 33. ♕e5 ♖d8+ 34. ♔c1 ♕b6 35. ♕b2 a3+ 36. ♔xa3 ♕a7+ 37. ♔b2 ♖d1**

0–1 (Source: *Chess*, November 1943, #1656; notes by RT)

After 24. ... a4

297 Menchik–George Alan Thomas
West London C.C. Tournament London, 1943

[A85] *Dutch Defense*

1. d4 d5 2. c4 e6 3. ♘c3 ♘f6 4. ♘f3 c6 5. e3 ♘e4 6. ♗d3 f5 7. ♘e5 ♕h4 8. 0-0 ♘d7 9. f4 ♗d6 10. cxd5 exd5 11. ♗xe4 fxe4 12. ♗d2 0-0 13. ♘xd7 ♗xd7 14. ♕b3 ♕e7 15. ♕xb7 ♖ab8 16. ♕a6 ♖xb2 17. ♕e2 ♗e6 18. ♘a4 ♖b5 19. ♖ac1 ♗d7 20. ♖c2 ♖fb8 21. ♗c1 ♖a5 22. ♘c3 ♗c8 23. ♖b2 ♖xb2 24. ♕xb2 ♗a6 25. ♖f2 ♗c4 26. ♕b1 ♗d3 27. ♕b3 ♗c4 28. ♕d1 ♗a3 29. ♗d2 ♖a6 30. ♕g4 ♕b6 31. f5 ♕f6 32. ♕h5 ♖b8 33. ♕d1 ♗b4 34. ♕c1 ♗d3 35. h3 ♗d6 36. ♗e1 *(see diagram)*

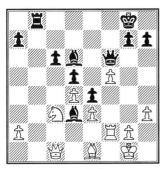

After 36. ♗e1

36. ... ♗g3 37. ♖d2 ♗xe1 38. ♕xe1 ♕xf5 39. ♖f2 ♕g5 40. ♔h2 ♕e7 41. ♕c1 ♕d6+ 42. ♔g1 h6 42. ... ♕b4 was much better and probably would have led to a win **43. ♖b2 ♖f8 44. ♖f2 ♖xf2 45. ♔xf2 c5 46. dxc5** If 46. ♕a3 ♕f6+ etc. **46. ... ♕xc5 47. ♕d2** If 47. ♕b2? d4 48. ♘d1 ♕f5+ 49. ♔g3 ♕g5+ 50. ♔f2 dxe3+ 51. ♘xe3 ♕f4+ etc. **47. ... d4 48. ♘d1 ♕c2 49. ♔e1 ♕xd2+ 50. ♔xd2 ♗f1 51. exd4 ♗xg2 52. h4 ♔f7 53. ♔e3 ♔f6 54. ♔f4 g5+ 55. hxg5+ hxg5+ 56. ♔e3 ♔f5 57. ♘c3 a6 58. ♘e2 a5** 58. ... ♔g4 59. d5 ♔f5 60. ♔d4 g4 61. ♘g3+ ♔f6 62. ♘xe4+ etc. **59. ♘g3+ ♔e6 60. ♘xe4 ♗xe4 61. ♔xe4 a4 62. a3 ½–½** (Source: *Chess*, November 1943, #1653; notes by RT)

West London C.C. Championship 1944

Besides the players listed below, other competitors included Saviely Tartakower (playing under the pseudonym Lt. Cartier) and Albert Simonson of the United States. Final results included: equal first: Edward Sergeant and Albert Simonson, third: Saviely Tartakower, sixth Vera Menchik.[62]

298 Menchik–A. Lightfoot
West London C.C. Championship—Section B, 1944

[D00] *Stonewall*

1. d4 d5 2. e3 e6 This is a perfectly good move of course, though one must admit that in the art of "timing" one's moves in the opening it is an undoubted advantage to keep the opponent in suspense as long as possible with regard to the line of play one actually intends to adopt. In this case Black discloses his intentions unnecessarily early; had he but waited and played the noncommittal 2. ... ♘f6 he would have been able to render the Stonewall Variation ineffective by replaying to 3. ♗d3 with 3. ... ♗g4 and later challenging the white bishop with ♗g6; or had White played 3. ♘d2 then 3. ... ♗f5. **3. ♗d3 ♘f6 4. ♘d2** This is a very important preparatory move, as it is essential for the success of a kingside attack, which is the prime aim of this variation, to keep the diagonal b1–h7 unobstructed, hence it would be upsetting to one's plans to allow the Black knight to come to e4 and then be supported by ... ♗f4. **4. ... ♗e7** A more enterprising alternative is at once 4. ... c5 while in days gone by 4. ... ♘c6 used to be tried, and if 5. f4 then 5. ... ♘b4 either dislodging or exchanging the harmful bishop. **5. f4 ♘bd7 6. ♕e2** A preparatory move to 7. ♘gf3 which, if played at once, could be met by 6. ... ♘g4 attacking the unguarded e-pawn and thus gaining the necessary time to play ♗f5. White could also play 6. ... ♘h3 followed by 0–0; ♘f2 ♕e3 and later ♗g4 or ♗e4 according to Black's play. **6. ... c5 7. c3 c4** There are two good reasons against advancing f4 in this type of position: firstly White can get rid of the only handicap in her position, the weak QB by freeing it with e4; and secondly, this blocking of the center makes White's position all the safer for the advance of the kingside pawns when the time is finally ripe for it. With regard to the first point it is interesting to note that so long as Black keeps a pawn at c5 White hardly dare advance e4, since a double exchange in the center would leave Black in control of the center files and will probably also result in his occupying the long White diagonal with his QB; now however, he will have to think twice

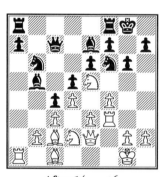

After 14. ... g6

before he captures the e-pawn, lest he lose his weakling at c4! **8. ♗c2 b5 9. a4** The weakness of 7. ... c4 is now evident, for if Black captures the a-pawn then 10. e4 threatening 11. e5. **9. ... ♗a6 10. a×b5 ♗×b5 11. ♘gf3 ♕c7 12. 0–0 0–0 13. ♘e5 ♘b6 14. ♖f3 g6** (see diagram)

[Black could not move the ♘ in order to play f5 because of 14. ... ♘fd7 15. ♗×h7+ ♔×h7 16. ♖h3+ ♔g8 17. ♕h5 etc., winning—RT] **15. ♖h3 ♘e8 16. e4 f5 17. e×d5 e×d5** [Not 17. ... ♘×d5? 18. ♘×g6 h×g6 19. ♕×e6+ and 20. ♕×d5—RT] **18. ♘df3 ♘g7** [18. ... ♘d6 19. ♘g5 ♗×g5 20. f×g5 ♘e4 21. ♗f4 ♕g7 22. ♖h6 (threat 23. ♘×g6 h×g6 24. ♗e5 etc.) 22. ... ♖fe8 23. h4 with a dangerous attack—RT] **19. ♗d2 ♖fe8 20. ♕f2** ♘c8 **21. ♕g3 ♗f8 22. ♖×h7 ♗d6** [This is fatal, and so would have been 22. ... ♔×h7 23. ♕×g6+ ♔g8 (23. ... ♔h8 24. ♘f7+ ♔g8 25. ♘3g5 wins) 24. ♘g5 winning; Black's only defense was in 22. ... ♖×e5! but, even then, after 23. ♖×g7+ ♔×g7 24. f×e5 White is a pawn up and still has the attack—RT] **23. ♕×g6 ♗×e5 24. ♘×e5 ♖e7 25. ♘g4** Black resigned because if 25 f×g4 ♖h8+ 26 ♔×h8 ♕h7 mate **1–0** (Source: *Chess*, March 1944, #1719; notes by VM [additional notes by RT])

299　Menchik–E.A. Beamish
West London C.C. Championship—Section B, 1944
[D05] *Colle System*

1. d4 ♘f6 2. e3 d5 3. ♗d3 b6 4. ♘d2 ♗b7 5. ♘gf3 ♘bd7 6. 0–0 e6 7. c4 ♗d6 8. c×d5 e×d5 9. ♘h4 g6 10. f4 ♘e4 11. ♘hf3 0–0 12. ♘e5 f6 13. ♘×e4 d×e4 14. ♗c4+ ♔g7

15. ♘g4 ♕e7 16. ♗d2 ♖ac8 17. ♗c3 h5 18. ♘f2 c6 19. a4 ♔h7 20. f5 c5 21. ♗e6 c×d4 22. e×d4 ♖cd8 23. ♖e1 ♘c5 24. d×c5 ♗×h2+ 25. ♔×h2 ♖×d1 26. ♖a×d1 ♕×c5 27. ♖d7+ ♔h6 28. ♗d4 ♕b4 29. ♗e3+ g5 30. ♖c1 [Better is 30. ♘g4+ h×g4 31. ♖h1; or 30. ♖h1 ♕e1 31. ♖×e1 ♗c8 32. ♗e7—RT] 30. ... ♗c8 31. ♖d4 ♕e7 32. ♗×c8 ♕e5+ 33. ♔g1 ♕b8 34. ♗e6 ♕g3 35. ♖c3 h4 36. ♗d2 ♕b8 37. ♖d7 b5 38. ♖cc7 1–0 (Source: *Chess*, October 1944, #1825)

300 Menchik–Edward G. Sergeant
West London C.C. Championship, London, 1944
[E14] *Queen's Indian Defense*

This is one of a series of games that Menchik wrote as educational essays and could easily have been put in Part III: The Writings of Vera Menchik. Despite its length I have chosen to include it, unedited and altered only in move notation, with all of its notes, herewith.

1. d4 ♘f6 2. ♘f3 d5 3. c4 e6 4. ♘c3 We have stressed on many occasions the importance of keeping the opponent in suspense about an opening variation one may hope to adopt. Sometimes, as pointed out in a note in game No. 1718, the course of action may not be decided upon when the game begins. One starts by merely trying to keep the opening phase as elastic and dynamic as possible, waiting for an injudicious or over-cautious looking move on the part of the opponent, when one suddenly makes up one's mind. This process of "foxing" in the opening is a weapon freely used by masters, though a reader when playing a game over from a book, may be ignorant of the fact, since to all intents and purposes the moves made often appear to be quite straightforward, and one is naturally unaware of what was going on in the mind of the players. May I be forgiven, therefore, for quoting a game of my own. Here, too, the move just made seems a common-sense move that a master and a novice alike might have played without undue reflection. And yet there is a considerable difference between playing 4. e3 or 4. ♘c3 at this stage, though the two taken together lead to exactly the same play. What is this difference? Of the two moves 4. e3 is the more passive one, since it discloses more and hides less, without compelling Black to divulge any immediate information. For example, by playing 4. e3 White plainly informs his opponent that he will probably develop his queen's bishop at either d2 or b2; that having already made an outlet for his king's bishop, he will not attempt to play the Catalan Variation, viz., g3 and ♗g2; but leaves Black uncertain as to where he will developed his queen's knight. Now with regard to 4. ♘c3 the situation is rather different: White has made a very non-committal yet not a passive move, and challenges Black to show his hand, that is to give some indication whether he means to play ... c5 early or late or not at all. Black has a number of perfectly satisfactory replies at his disposal, and it is possible that in the end nothing may come of White's "foxing," but the fact that a player is in a position to "fox" is an undoubted asset to him, and here is an instance where White might possibly reap the benefit of his low cunning, or shall we say, of correct "timing" in the opening. Let us suppose that when the game began White had toyed with the idea of playing the old-fashioned variation of the Queen's Gambit, shutting in his queen's bishop by e3, and later developing it at b2. It is well known however, that the variation 1. d4 d5 2. c4 e6 3. e3, if played in this order, is not in any way dangerous for Black, and Tarrasch even went so far as to recommend that Black should copy White's development, claiming equality for him in the symmetrical position. It stands to reason, therefore, that should White's plan be to adopt this old-fashioned line of play, he should "time" his moves in such a way as to avoid the symmetrical play and simplifications arising from it. This is exactly what White might hope to achieve by playing the opening as shown above, for should Black now reply with 4. ... ♗e7 then 5. e3 and though Black can still play 5. ... c5 he has committed his king's bishop to a passive role, and would have to waste a move with it if he were to try and obtain what Tarrasch called the "Normal Defense." Incidentally, here is another minor point in favor of 4. ♘c3: in answer to either 4. ... ♗e7 or 4. ... ♘bd7, White could play 5. ♗f4 much more efficiently than were he to do so a move earlier, since to oppose it now with 5. ... ♗d6 would either cost Black a move or result in the doubling of his d-pawn. **4. ... ♗e7 5. e3** White is now pre-supposing that Black will either take the c-pawn, and thus turn the game into a variation of the Queen's Gambit Accepted, or else will himself play ... c5, when White would hope to obtain some positional advantage from Black's inactively developed bishop at e7, occupying the square to which the queen usually migrates for safety when hostile rooks come to occupy the d and c files. **5. ... 0–0 6. ♗d3 b6** The merits of this move are threefold: it prepares: (1) to vacate c8 for occupation by the queen's rook should Black play ... c5; (2) to play ... d×c4 clearing the long diagonal for the queen's bishop; (3) to help to advance ... ♘e5, and thus exercise a firmer grip on the center. These three eventualities, each treated from different angles may lead to three (possibly more) totally different lines of action, and it is interesting to note here that Black, who as yet is in no way harassed, is delaying the straightforward ... c5, and is, for his part, keeping White guessing as to his ultimate intentions. **7. 0–0 ♗b7 8. ♕e2** Making room for ♖d1; 8. ♘e5 was also worth consideration here. **8. ... ♘bd7 9. b3 ♘e4** White's last move has determined Black's course of action: the attack on the unguarded knight gives Black time to strengthen his command of e4. **10. ♗b2 a6** Hindering ♘b5 and preparing for ... ♗d6 or possibly for ... c5 and ... ♕c7. **11. ♖fd1** It is not always easy to decide in a position of this kind how best to use one's rooks. Anticipating

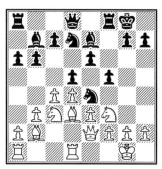

After 11. ... f5

... c5 White means to play ♖ac1, taking the most obvious course. The alternative would have been to play 25. ♖ad1 and ♖fe1, with a view to dislodging the Black knight on e5 by ♘d2 and f6 and later advancing e4. **11. ... f5** *(see diagram)*

This advance will not combine very well with ... c5, so at last it is becoming clear that Black means to keep ... c5 back, and to try for a direct kingside attack instead. **12. ♖ac1 ♗d6** Threatening to play 13. ... ♖f6 then 14. ... ♖h6 with a view to 15. ... ♗×h2+ 16. ♘×h2 ♕h4, etc. **13. c×d5** Clearing the c-file which is important to the key move to White's counterattack which follows. **13. ... e×d5 14. ♘e5!** Best. White is just in time to close the dangerous diagonal of the Black king's bishop without suffering material loss. **14. ... ♘×e5 15. d×e5 ♗×e5 16. ♘×e4 ♗×b2 17. ♕×b2 f×e4 18. ♗×e4 c6!** [Not 18. ... ♕g5 19. ♖×c7 etc.; nor 18. ... c5 because of 19. ♕e5; whilst 18. ... ♕d6 could have been met by 19. ♕c2 attacking the c and h pawns—RT] **19. ♗b1** [19. ♗d3 was probably safer, but naturally not 19. ♕e5 on account of 19. ... ♖e8—RT] **19. ... ♕h4** [If 19. ... c5 20. b4 ♕e7 21. b×c5 b×c5 22. ♕c2 g6 (The text move given by Menchik does not match the analysis she gives. Down a pawn in her line, Black appears in a bad state. The only viable move is 22. ... ♕h4—RT) 23. ♕×c5 it is difficult to say which side has the better game here: Black exercises some pressure on the open f-file, but is at a disadvantage on the queenside, where for the time being his bishop is tied to the defense of the d-pawn—RT]

After 24. ... 🜚a6

20. 🜚d4 🜚f6 21. 🜚c2 g6 22. b4 Preventing ... c5 which would liberate the Black bishop and create unpleasant threats on the long diagonal. **22. ... a5!** [If 22. ... c5 23. b×c5 b×c5 24. 🜚f4 (24. 🜚×c5? 🜚×f2+) 24. ... 🜚e5 25. 🜚×c5 etc.—RT] **23. a3 a×b4 24. a×b4 🜚a6** *(see diagram)*

Tempting White to play 25. 🜚f4 🜚d6! 26. 🜚×c6? when would follow 🜚fc8!! winning. **25. h4** [25. 🜚f4 🜚d6 26. 🜚×f8+ 🜚×f8 27. 🜚×c6 🜚c8 28. 🜚×c8+ 🜚×c8 29. 🜚×c8+ 🜚g7—RT] **25. ... 🜚b5 26. h5 🜚f5** [Or 26. ... 🜚a4 27. 🜚e2 🜚b5 etc. —RT] **27. h×g6 h×g6 28. e4** [28. 🜚×f5 g×f5 29. 🜚f4? 🜚a1 etc.—RT] **28. ... d×e4** [28. ... 🜚f4 or ... 🜚f6 could also have been tried and if 29. e5 🜚f5 (Not 29. ... 🜚×e5? 30. 🜚×g6+ 🜚g7 31. 🜚e6+ 🜚f7 32. 🜚g4+) 30. 🜚d2 🜚h5 winning—RT] **29. 🜚×e4** [29. 🜚d2 was stronger, with the combined threats of 🜚×e4 followed by 🜚h6 or 🜚d7, and in this case Black were to play 29. ... 🜚d3 the probably 30. 🜚a2+ 🜚g7 31. 🜚×c6 etc.—RT] **29. ... 🜚a7 30. 🜚a2+ 🜚g7 31. 🜚e6 🜚f6 32. 🜚b3** Overlooking that Black also has a nasty threat up his sleeve; 32. 🜚c4 was a safe move and would have led to a draw. **32. ... 🜚d3!! 33. 🜚×d3 🜚×f2+ 34. 🜚h2 🜚h8+ 35. 🜚h3 🜚×h3+ 36. 🜚×h3 🜚b2 1–0** (Source: *Chess*, May 1944, #1748; notes by VM [additional notes by RT])

Menchik's last serious event was the Southern Counties Chess Union Championship. With a score of 3–0 she had qualified for the semifinals, but would not live to play them. The only game available (versus G.W. Rutland) can be found in chapter 8, Supplemental Games (mostly club and team).

Women's World Chess Championships

London 1927
(Women's World Championship)
July 18–30, 1927

		1	2	3	4	5	6	7	8	9	10	11	12	Pts.	Place
1	Menchik, Vera	•	1	1	1	=	1	1	1	1	1	1	1	10½	1
2	Beskow, Katarina	0	•	0	1	1	1	1	1	1	1	1	1	9	2
3	Wolf-Kalmar, Paulina	0	1	•	1	1	1	0	=	0	1	=	1	7	3
4	Holloway, Edith M.	0	0	0	•	=	1	=	1	=	1	1	=	6	4–5
5	Michell, Edith	=	0	0	=	•	0	1	0	1	1	1	1	6	4–5
6	Price, Edith	0	0	0	0	1	•	1	1	1	0	=	1	5½	6
7	Harum, Gisela	0	0	1	=	0	0	•	0	1	0	1	1	4½	7
8	Stirling, F.H.	0	0	=	0	1	0	1	•	0	1	0	=	4	8
9	Frigard, Marie Jeanne	0	0	1	=	0	0	0	1	•	0	1	0	3½	9–11
10	Stevenson, Agnes	0	0	0	0	0	1	1	0	1	•	=	0	3½	9–11
11	Synnevaag, S.	0	0	=	0	0	=	0	1	0	=	•	1	3½	9–11
12	Daunke, M.	0	0	0	=	0	0	0	=	1	1	0	•	3	12

Vera Menchik won 10 straight games before conceding a draw to Edith Michell in the last round. In the final position both players had a queen, knight and five pawns.[63] The tournament was declared a world championship after the fact, with Vera receiving the title retroactively. Paulina Wolf-Kalmar was a student of Richard Réti. This is the one world championship where Menchik played as a Russian. Bikova speculates that since she could not speak English when she arrived in Hastings she was assumed to be Russian and was thus recorded that way in the tournament. From then through 1937 she competed as a Czech.

Although the present author has been unable to track down the games we do have some information about how the event progressed thanks to Bikova. In the sixth round Menchik won a long game against Synnevaag who had been hoping for a perpetual check and offered a rook for a pawn. Vera sidestepped the threat and advanced to 6–0. In her last game Menchik was unable to gain an advantage against Edith Michell and a draw was agreed.

Later, at the Hastings 1929-30 tournament she was awarded a cup from FIDE along with a gold medal. The medal currently resides in the Hastings Chess Club and has had bars attached to the ribbon that commemorate her further championships.

No scores are available.

Hamburg 1930
(Women's World Championship)
July 1930

		1		2		3		4		5		Points	Place
1	Menchik, Vera	●	●	=	1	0	1	1	1	1	1	6½	1
2	Wolf-Kalmar, Paulina	=	0	●	●	1	0	1	1	1	1	5½	2
3	Henschel, Wally	1	0	0	1	●	●	1	1	0	=	4½	3
4	Beskow, Katarina	0	0	0	0	0	0	●	●	1	1	2	4
5	Stevenson, Agnes	0	0	0	0	1	=	0	0	●	●	1½	5

This event was possibly Vera's closest call in the world championship. Losing as White to Wally Henschel and drawing against Paulina Wolf-Kalmar in the first half of the event left her down a point. To her good fortune Wolf-Kalmar made a mistake in the opening and lost her second game. Shortly thereafter Paulina also lost to Wally and Menchik won her second title.

301 Agnes Stevenson–Menchik
Hamburg—Women's World Championship, 1930
[C77] *Ruy Lopez*

The only game in which Menchik played 1. ... e5 allowing the Ruy Lopez. Agnes Stevenson plays this game with extreme passivity—trying to set up a fortress as her only goal. How Vera would have finished the game is anyone's guess, but it was a moot point when Mrs. Stevenson went out of her way to lose the exchange.

1. e4 e5 2. ♘f3 ♘c6 3. ♗b5 a6 4. ♗a4 ♘f6 5. d3 d6 6. ♗g5 ♗e7 7. ♘bd2 0–0 8. h3 b5 9. ♗b3 ♘a5 10. ♕e2 c5 11. c3 ♕c7 12. ♗c2 ♘c6 13. a4 ♗e6 14. 0–0 b4 15. c4 ♘e8 16. ♗×e7 ♕×e7 17. b3 f5 18. ♔h2 f4 19. ♖h1 ♘f6 20. ♔g1 h6 21. ♖h2 ♘h5 *(see diagram)*

After 21. ... ♘h5

22. ♔h1?? This is almost the worst move on the board; among the ones that do not drop material they are virtually the same in impact! **22. ... ♘g3+ 23. f×g3 f×g3 24. ♕e1 g×h2 25. ♔×h2 ♕f6 26. ♕g3 ♕f4 27. ♕×f4 ♖×f4 28. ♖f1 ♖af8 29. ♗d1 ♗d7 30. ♔g3 ♘d8 31. ♔h2 g6 32. ♔g3 ♔g7 33. ♖f2 g5 34. ♖f1 h5 35. ♖e1 ♘e6 36. ♔h2 ♖4f6 37. ♔g3 a5 38. ♔h2 g4 39. h×g4 h×g4 40. ♘h4 ♘f4 0–1** (Source: Toth, *Schacholympiade von Hamburg*)

302 Wally Henschel–Menchik
Hamburg—Women's World Championship, 1930
[E94] *King's Indian Defense*

1. d4 ♘f6 2. c4 g6 3. ♘c3 ♗g7 4. ♘f3 0–0 5. e4 d6 6. ♗e2 ♘bd7 7. 0–0 e5 8. ♗g5

h6 9. d×e5 d×e5 10. ♗h4 c6 11. ♕d2 ♖e8 12. ♖fd1 ♕b6 13. ♗f1 ♘h5 14. b3 ♘f4 15. ♘a4 ♕c7 16. ♖ac1 ♘e6 17. ♘c3 ♘d4 18. ♘e1 ♘f8 19. f3 ♗e6 20. ♘c2 ♔h7 21. ♘×d4 e×d4 22. ♘e2 c5 23. ♘f4 ♗e5 24. ♗g3 ♕d6 25. ♗d3 b6 26. ♘e2? Losing space and time. [26. ♘d5! ♗×g3 27. ♘f6+ ♔g7 28. ♘×e8+ ♖×e8 29. h×g3 ♕×g3=—RT] 26. ... ♗×g3 27. ♘×g3 a5 28. a4 ♗c8 29. ♖f1 ♖a7 30. ♖ce1 ♖ae7 31. f4 ♗b7? Apparently Menchik, not realizing how precarious her position is, decided to go on the attack. She looks to build up on the e4 square while also looking to control the a8–h1 diagonal—in reality the bishop is desperately needed to hit f5. [31. ... ♕e6 —RT] 32. e5! ♕b8 *(see diagram)*

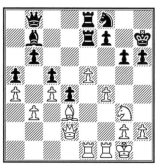

After 32. ... ♕b8

33. ♘h5?! [33. f5 ♖×e5 34. f×g6+ f×g6 35. ♖×e5 ♖×e5 36. ♕f4+—RT] 33. ... ♘d7 34. f5 ♘f8 [Better is 34. ... ♘×e5 35. ♘f6+ ♔g7 36. ♘×e8+ ♖×e8+—RT] 35. f×g6+ f×g6 36. e6? ♘e5?? 37. ♖×f8 ♕×f8 38. ♖×e5 ♗c8 39. ♘f4 ♕f6 40. ♘×g6 ♖g7 41. ♖h5 1–0 (Source: Toth, *Schacholympiade von Hamburg*; notes by L. Toth [additional notes by RT])

Prague 1931
(Women's World Championship)

		1		2		3		4		5		Pts.	Place
1	Menchik, Vera	●	●	1	1	1	1	1	1	1	1	8	1
2	Wolf-Kalmar, Paulina	0	0	●	●	0	1	0	1	1	1	4	2
3	Stevenson, Agnes	0	0	1	0	●	●	1	=	1	0	3½	3
4	Beskow, Katarina	0	0	1	0	0	=	●	●	1	0	2½	4
5	Henschel, Wally	0	0	0	0	0	1	0	1	●	●	2	5

It was no doubt events like this that caused Alexander Alekhine to bemoan Vera's fate at having to defend her title in events with no competition. The competition here is identical to that in Hamburg. Wolf-Kalmar still captured second, but with only half as many points as Menchik. Health may have played a role in this as she died shortly after the tournament.

303 Katarina Beskow–Menchik
Prague—Women's World Championship (1), 1931
[E21] *Nimzo-Indian Defense*

This game is a long grind where Beskow appears to be afraid of her opponent and plays far too passively. Vera on the other hand gives an appearance of just waiting for her opponent to make enough mistakes for her to win. The errors are small but adequate to achieve the goal.

1. d4 ♘f6 2. ♘f3 e6 3. c4 b6 4. g3 ♗b7 5. ♗g2 ♗b4+ 6. ♘c3 0-0 7. 0-0 ♗×c3 8. b×c3 d6 9. ♕c2 ♘bd7 10. ♗b2? c5 11. ♖ad1 ♕c7 12. ♖fe1 ♗e4 13. ♕d2 ♖fd8 14. ♖c1 ♖ac8 15. e3 ♗b7 16. ♕c2 ♘e4 17. ♖e2 ♘df6 18. ♘e1 d5 19. c×d5 e×d5 20. ♗h3 ♖b8 21. ♘f3 ♗c8 22. ♗×c8 ♖b×c8 23. ♔g2 c4 24. ♘e5 ♘d7 25. f3? Better is 25. ♘×d7 ♕×d7 which at least maintains some equilibrium in the position—cramped up as it is **25. ...**

After 39. ... ♕c6

♘×e5 26. d×e5 ♘c5 27. f4 ♕c6 28. ♔g1 f6 29. e×f6 ♕×f6 30. ♖d1 ♘d3 31. ♖×d3 c×d3 32. ♕×d3 ♕c6 33. ♖d2 ♕c4 34. ♕b1 ♕e4 35. ♕d1 ♖e8 36. ♔f2 ♖c4 37. a3 ♕e6 38. ♖d3 ♖e4 39. ♗c1 ♕c6?! *(see diagram)*

39. ... ♖d8 40. ♕d2 40. ♖×d5 ♕×c3 41. ♖d7 40. ... b5 41. ♕d1 ♖c4 42. ♗b2 ♕e6 43. ♕h5 a5 44. ♕×d5 ♕×d5 45. ♖×d5 b4 46. a×b4 a×b4 47. ♖d3 ♖ec8 48. ♔e2 b×c3 49. ♗c1 ♖a4 50. h4 ♖a2+ 51. ♔f3 ♖a1 52. ♖d1 c2 53. ♖e1 ♖d8 54. ♔e2 h5 55. ♖f1 g6 56. ♖e1 ♔f7 57. ♖f1 ♖d7 58. ♖e1 ♔e6 59. ♖f1 ♔f5 60. ♖e1 ♔g4 61. ♖g1 ♖b1 62. e4 ♖b4 63. ♗e3 ♖×e4 64. ♖c1 ♖de7 65. ♖×c2 ♖×e3+ 66. ♔f2 ♖f3+ 67. ♔g2 ♖×g3+ 68. ♔h2 ♖ee3 0–1 (Source: Prague 1931; notes by RT)

304 Menchik–Wally Henschel

Prague—Women's World Championship (2), 1931

[A50] *Queen's Fianchetto Defense*

1. d4 ♘f6 2. c4 e6 3. ♘c3 b6 4. e4 ♗b4 5. ♗d3 ♗b7 6. f3 d5 7. ♕a4+ ♘c6 8. c×d5 ♗×c3+ 9. b×c3 e×d5 10. e5 ♘d7 11. ♘e2 ♘e7 12. 0-0 c6 13. f4 ♕c7 14. f5 *(see diagram)*

14. ... c5? Better was 14. ... 0–0 **15. e6 ♗c6 16. e×d7+ ♕×d7 17. ♕d1 0-0-0 18. d×c5 b×c5 19. ♖b1 ♗b7 20. ♗b5 ♘c6 21. ♕a4 ♖he8 22. ♗a6 ♖×e2 23. ♖×b7 ♕×b7 24. ♗×b7+** More precise was 24. ♕×c6+ ♔b8 25. ♕×b7 mate **24. ... ♔×b7 25. ♕b5+ 1-0** (Source: Prague 1931; notes by RT)

After 14. f5

305 Paulina Wolf-Kalmar–Menchik

Prague—Women's World Championship (3), 1931

[E60] *King's Indian Defense*

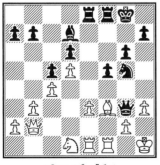

After 26. ♔h1

1. ♘f3 ♘f6 2. b3 g6 3. ♗b2 ♗g7 4. e3 0-0 5. c4 d6 6. d4 ♘fd7 7. ♘c3 e5 8. ♗e2 f5 9. ♕c2 c6 10. ♖d1 e4 11. ♘d2 ♘f6 12. d5 c5 13. 0-0 ♘bd7 14. f4 e×f3 15. ♘×f3 ♕e7 16. ♖d3 ♘g4 17. ♗c1 ♘df6 18. h3 ♘e5 19. ♘×e5 ♕×e5 20. ♗f3 ♗d7 21. ♖dd1? ♖ae8 21. ... ♘g4! 22. h×g4 f×g4 **22. ♖de1 ♘e4 23. ♘d1 ♕g3 24. ♗b2 ♗×b2 25. ♕×b2 ♘g5 26. ♔h1** *(see diagram)*

26. ... f4?! Best is 26. ... ♘×f3 27. g×f3 f4 28. ♕h2 ♗×h3–+ **27. ♕f2 ♕×f2 28. ♖×f2 f×e3 29. ♖×e3 ♖×e3 30. ♘×e3 ♘×f3 31. g×f3 ♗×h3 32. ♔h2 ♗f5 33. ♔g3 ♗d7** This makes the 32nd move look a bit sloppy! **34. ♖e2 ♖e8 35. ♔f4 ♔g7 36. ♖g2 h6 37. ♖e2 g5+ 38. ♔g3 ♔g6 39. ♔f2 h5 40. ♖e1 a6 41. a3 b5 42. ♖g1 ♖b8 43. ♖b1 ♗f5 44. ♖b2 ♗d3 45. c×b5 ♖×b5 46. b4 a5 47. ♖d2 c4**

48. b×a5 ♖×a5 49. ♖b2 ♖×a3 50. ♖b6 ♖a2+ 51. ♔g3 h4+ 52. ♔g4 ♖g2+ 53. ♔h3
53. ♘×g2 ♗f5 mate **53. ... ♖g3+ 54. ♔h2 ♖×f3 55. ♖×d6+ ♖f6** Better is 55. ... ♔h5 56. ♖e6
c3 **56. ♖d8 ♖f2+ 57. ♔g1 ♖e2 58. ♖d6+ ♔f7 59. ♘g4 c3 60. ♖c6 c2 61. ♖c7+ ♔g6**
62. d6 ♗f5 63. ♘e5+ ♖×e5 64. d7 ♗×d7 0–1 (Source: Prague 1931; notes by RT)

306 Menchik–Agnes Stevenson
Prague—Women's World Championship (4), 1931

[D15] *Slav*

1. d4 d5 2. c4 c6 3. ♘f3 ♘f6 4. ♘c3 ♗f5 5. c×d5 ♘×d5
6. e3 ♘×c3 7. b×c3 e6 8. ♗c4 h6 9. ♕e2 ♗e4 10. 0–0
♘d7 11. ♘d2 ♗g6 12. e4 ♘b6 13. ♗b3 ♗e7 14. f4 0–0
15. ♘f3 ♗h5 16. ♗e3 ♗f6 17. ♗c2 ♗g6 18. g4 ♗h7
19. ♔h1 ♗e7 20. f5 e×f5 21. g×f5 *(see diagram)*

21. ... f6? 22. ♖g1 ♔h8 23. ♕g2 ♖g8 24. ♗b3 ♕d6
25. ♘h4 g5 26. f×g6 f5 27. ♘×f5?! 27. g7+ ♖×g7 28. ♕×g7
mate **27. ... ♖×g6 28. ♘×d6 ♖×g2 29. ♘f7+ ♔g7 30. ♖×g2+**
1–0 (Source: Prague 1931; note by RT)

After 21. g×f5

307 Menchik–Katarina Beskow
Prague—Women's World Championship (5), 1931

[E43] *Nimzo-Indian, Rubinstein Variation*

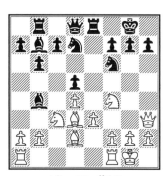

After 12. ♕h3

Menchik obviously was out for a quick win in this game, but
the way her opponent obliges makes one wonder about the
length of their first game. **1. d4 ♘f6 2. c4 e6 3. ♘c3 ♗b4**
4. e3 b6 5. ♕f3 d5 6. ♗d3 ♗b7 7. ♗d2 ♘bd7 8. ♘h3
♖b8 9. c×d5 e×d5 10. 0–0 0–0 11. ♘f4 ♖e8 12. ♕h3 *(see
diagram)*

12. ... ♕e7?? Black's choices of moves to keep equality
are abundant—this was not one of them! **13. ♘c×d5 ♘×d5**
[Best is 13. ... ♗×d5 14. ♘×d5 ♕d6 15. ♘×b4 and the game
will be over anyway—RT] **14. ♕×h7+ 1–0** (Source: Prague
1931 [additional note by RT])

308 Wally Henschel–Menchik
Prague—Women's World Championship (6), 1931

[A46] *Queen Pawn Opening*

The first 25 or so moves of this game may have been the best of all Menchik's games in
this event. Black gained a small advantage and nursed it along without any major errors on
either side until White started collapsing in the late twenties. One possible reason being time
pressure as move 34 was a common first time control in this era.

1. d4 ♘f6 2. ♘f3 e6 3. ♗g5 h6 4. ♗h4 c5 5. e3 ♕b6 6. ♕c1 ♘c6 7. ♗×f6 g×f6 8. c3
d5 9. ♗e2 ♗d7 10. 0–0 ♗d6 11. ♘bd2 0–0 12. ♖d1 f5 13. ♘b3 c4 14. ♘bd2 ♕c7
15. ♘f1 ♔h7 16. ♕c2 ♘e7 17. ♖d2 b5 18. ♘e1 ♘g8 19. f4 ♘f6 20. ♘g3 ♘e4

21. ♘×e4 f×e4 22. ♘f3 f6 23. ♘h4 ♖g8 24. ♔f2 ♖ab8 25. g3 f5 (*see diagram*)

   26. ♖f1?! b4 27. ♖dd1 ♕a5 28. ♖a1 b×c3 29. b×c3 ♗a4 30. ♕c1 ♖b7 31. ♔g1? [Marginally better may be 31. ♖b1 ♖×b1 32. ♕×b1 ♗a3—RT] **31. ... ♖gb8 32. ♖f2 ♗e8 33. ♗d1 ♗a3 34. ♕c2?** Finishing the game quickly. [34. ♕d2—RT] **34. ... ♖b2 0–1** (Source: Prague 1931 [additional notes by RT])

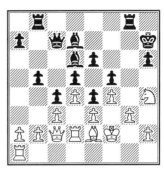

After 25. ... f5

309 Menchik–Paulina Wolf-Kalmar
Prague—Women's World Championship (7), 1931
[C10] *French*

After 23. ... ♕g5

1. d4 e6 2. e4 d5 3. ♘c3 d×e4 4. ♘×e4 ♘f6 5. ♘×f6+ ♕×f6 6. ♘f3 h6 7. ♗d3 ♗d6 8. 0–0 0–0 9. ♕e2 ♘d7 10. ♖e1 ♖e8 11. ♘e5 ♘f8 12. ♕h5 ♗×e5 13. d×e5 ♕e7 14. ♖e3 ♕g5 15. ♕e2 ♘g6 16. ♖e4 ♕e7 17. ♖g4 ♗d7 18. ♗×g6 f×g6 19. ♖×g6 ♕f7 20. ♖g3 ♔h8 21. ♖f3 ♕g6 22. ♗×h6 g×h6 23. ♖f6 ♕g5 (*see diagram*)

   24. f4? [24. h4! ♕×h4 (worse is 24. ... ♕g7 25. ♕h5) 25. ♕d2—RT] **24. ... ♕h4 25. g3 ♕h3 26. ♖d1 ♖e7 27. ♖d4 ♗c6 28. f5 ♖g8 29. f×e6 ♖eg7 30. ♖d3 ♖g4** (*see diagram*)

   This move and Black's response to it were missed in Menchik's notes in the tournament book. **31. ♕d2??** [Troubling, but the best try may be 31. e7—RT] **31. ... ♖4g5??** [31. ... ♖×g3+ 32. h×g3 ♖×g3+ 33. ♖×g3 ♕×g3+ 34. ♔f1 ♗b5+—RT] **32. e7?** [Required is 32. b3—RT] **32. ... ♕g7? 33. ♖d8** [33. ♖×c6—RT] **33. ... ♖×g3+ 34. h×g3 ♕h1+ 35. ♔f2 ♕g2+ 36. ♔e1 ♕×g3+ 37. ♖f2 ♗e8 38. ♕d3 ♕×e5+ 39. ♖e2 ♕g5 40. ♕d4+ ♔h7 41. ♕e4+ ♔h8 42. ♕e5+ ♕×e5 43. ♖×e5 ♔h7**

After 30. ... ♖g4

44. ♖f5 ♔g7 45. ♔f2 ♖h8 46. ♔g3 ♖g8 47. ♔h4 ♖h8 48. ♖f2 h5 49. b4 b5 50. ♖f1 c6 51. ♖f2 1–0 (Source: Prague 1931 [additional notes by RT])

After 14. ... h5

310 Agnes Stevenson–Menchik
Prague—Women's World Championship (8), 1931
[B12] *Caro-Kann, Advanced Variation*

   Mrs. Stevenson essayed the advance variation against Menchik's Caro-Kann, but within 10 moves found herself falling behind, never to recover.

1. e4 c6 2. d4 d5 3. e5 ♗f5 4. ♗d3 ♗×d3 5. ♕×d3 e6 6. f4 ♘h6 7. ♘f3 ♕b6 8. c3 c5 9. 0–0 ♘c6 10. b3 ♖c8 11. ♗e3 c×d4 12. ♗×d4 ♘×d4 13. c×d4 ♘f5 14. ♔h1 h5 (*see diagram*)

15. a3? 15. ♘c3 Development first **15. ... ♗e7 16. ♘bd2 0-0 17. b4 a5 18. b5 ♖c7 19. ♘b3 a4 20. ♘c1 ♖c4 21. ♘e2 ♛×b5 22. ♖ab1 ♛d7 23. ♘d2 ♖c7 24. h3 h4 25. g4 h×g3 26. ♘×g3 ♖fc8 27. ♘e2 ♖c2 28. ♖bc1 ♛c7 29. ♔h2 ♗h4 30. ♖cd1 ♛a5 31. ♔g2 ♘g3 32. ♖f3 ♘×e2 33. ♛×e2 ♖8c3 34. ♖d3 ♖×d3** Missing 34. ... ♛b5 **35. ♛×d3 ♖c3 36. ♛b1 ♛a6 37. ♘f1 ♛e2+ 0-1** (Source: Prague 1931; notes by RT)

Folkstone 1933

(Women's World Championship)

	1	2	3	4	5	6	7	8	Pts.	Place
1 Menchik, Vera (Czech)	• •	1 1	1 1	1 1	1 1	1 1	1 1	1 1	14	1
2 Price, Edith (England)	0 0	• •	1 =	0 =	1 1	0 1	1 1	1 1	9	2
3 Gilchrist, M. (Scotland)	0 0	0 =	• •	1 1	1 =	= =	1 =	1 1	8½	3
4 Michell, Edith (England)	0 0	1 =	0 0	• •	= 1	1 1	0 1	1 1	8	4
5 Benini, Clarice (Italy)	0 0	0 0	0 =	= 0	• •	1 1	0 1	1 1	6	5
6 Schwartzmann, P. (Ger.)	0 0	1 0	= =	0 0	0 0	• •	1 =	1 1	5½	6
7 d'Autrement (France)	0 0	0 0	0 =	1 0	1 0	0 =	• •	1 1	5	7
8 Harum, Gisela (Austria)	0 0	0 0	0 0	0 0	0 0	0 0	0 0	• •	0	8

BOROUGH OF
STAINER

FOLKESTONE.
MAYOR.

THE BRITISH CHESS FEDERATION CONGRESS. 1933.
including
THE INTERNATIONAL TEAM TOURNAMENT, F.I.D.E.

The Mayor and Mayoress of Folkestone

(Alderman and Mrs J. W. Stainer)

on behalf of the Corporation

request the pleasure of the company of

Miss Vera Menchik

at a Reception at the Leas Cliff Hall, Folkestone, on Tuesday, the 13th June, 1933.

RECEPTION 3.30 TO 6.30 P.M.
MUNICIPAL ORCHESTRA.
MADAME SOFI SCHONNING. VOCALIST.

An invitation inscribed to Miss Vera Menchik for a reception held for the participants in the Folkstone 1933 Women's World Championship and Olympiad. Such receptions/dinners and cards were commonplace at the major events of the day (author's collection).

With a larger entry the event grew in prestige, but not much in strength as Vera again swept the field. As a side comment, Bikova indicates that Harum did not compete because of financial problems and was declared lost in all games. This was the last double round event as the event kept growing.

311 Edith Price–Menchik
Folkstone—Women's World Championship, 1933
[A45] *Queen Pawn Opening*

1. d4 ♘f6 2. e3 g6 3. ♗d3 ♗g7 4. ♘e2 0-0 5. ♘d2 d6 6. ♘g3 [6. e4 was better here; White's move is too defensive—RT] **6. ... e5 7. c3 ♘c6 8. ♘b3 ♕e7 9. ♗d2** [Now if 9. e4 e×d4 10. ♘×d4 ♘×d4 11. c×d4 ♘×e4 12. ♗×e4 f5 13. 0-0 f×e4 14. ♖e1 d5 15. f3 ♕b4 etc. —RT] **9. ... d5** [Not so good would be 9. ... e4 which blocks the center and allows White in greater safety to castle on the queenside—RT] **10. ♕c2 b6 11. 0-0-0** [Possibly 11. 0-0 was less dangerous—RT] **11. ... a5 12. h4 a4 13. ♘a1 ♗a6 14. ♗×a6 ♖×a6 15. ♕d3 ♖a7 16. ♘c2 ♘a5 17. ♘a3 c6 18. ♘e2** [This is purely defensive; White should try for some counterattack with 18. h5—RT] **18. ... b5 19. d×e5 ♕×e5 20. ♘d4 ♖c8 21. ♕e2** [If 21. ♘f3 ♕b8 followed by ♘c4—RT] **21. ... ♘c4 22. ♘×c4 b×c4 23. a3 ♖b7 24. ♔b1 c5 25. ♘f3 ♕f5+ 26. ♔a1 ♖cb8 27. ♖b1** [Not 27. ♗c1 ♘e4 and ♘×c3—RT] **27. ... ♘e4 28. ♖hc1 ♖b3** *(see diagram)*

After 28. ... ♖b3

... Still threatening 29. ... ♘×c3; 30. ♗×c3 ♗×c3; 31. ♖×c3 ♖×c3 32. b×c3 ♕×b1 mate **29. ♔e1 ♘d6** [Better was here 29. ... ♕g4 and if 30. ♕f1 then 30. ... d4 with a strong attack—RT] **30. ♕d1 ♘b5 31. ♔a2 d4** [Or 31. ... ♕g4 32. g3 d4 33. c×d4 c×d4 34. ♖×c4 etc. (or 34. ♘×d4 ♕×d1 35. ♖×d1 ♘×d4 36. e×d4 ♗×d4 with a won ending) 34. ... ♘×a3—RT] **32. c×d4 c×d4 33. ♘×d4 ♘×d4 34. e×d4 ♗×d4?** A serious mistake which makes Black's winning chances very doubtful [The right line of play here was 34. ... ♕×f2! attacking three pawns and allowing the bishop only one move; 35. ♗c3 (If however 35. ♖×c4 ♖d3! 36. ♖c2 ♕×d4 threatening ♕d5+ and ♖×a3 mate)—RT] **35. ♗b4 ♕×f2 36. ♖c2 ♕f6 37. ♖d2 ♗e5 38. ♖c2 ♕×h4 39. ♕e2 ♕g3 40. ♕×c4** [If 40. ♖×c4? ♖3×b4 41. ♖×b4 ♖×b4 42. a×b4 ♕b3+ 43. ♔a1 ♕a3 mate —RT] **40. ... ♕d3 41. ♕×d3 ♖×d3 42. ♖bc1** In view of Black's reply this loses a tempo. [Better was 42. ♖e1 f6 43. ♖e4 with excellent drawing chances—RT] **42. ... ♖g3 43. ♖e2 f6 44. ♖c4 h5 45. ♖c6** [Here again 45. ♗e1 ♖g4 46. ♖×g4 h×g4 47. ♗b4 ♖c8 48. b3 etc. is better than the continuation chosen—RT] **45. ... ♖a8 46. ♗e1 ♖g4 47. ♖b6 ♔g7 48. ♗d2 g5 49. ♗b4 h4 50. ♔b1 ♖g3 51. ♗e1 ♖g4 52. ♖c6 ♖f4 53. ♔a2 ♖g4 54. ♔b1 ♖f4 55. ♔c2 ♖f1 56. ♖c4 ♔g6 57. ♗d2 ♔h5 58. ♗e1 ♖a7 59. ♗c3 ♗×c3 60. ♖×c3 ♖a5 61. ♖c4 g4 62. ♖c8 g3 63. ♖h8+ ♔g5 64. ♖e4** [If 64. ♖g8+ ♔f4 65. ♖h8 ♖c5+ 66. ♔d2 ♖c4 etc.—RT] **64. ... ♖f2+ 65. ♔c3 ♖×g2 66. ♖e×h4 f5 67. ♖8h5+ ♔f6 68. ♖h8 ♖a7 69. ♖h1 ♖c7+ 70. ♔d4 ♖×b2 71. ♖g8 ♖d7+ 72. ♔c5 f4 73. ♖h4 ♖f2 74. ♖hg4 ♔f5**

0-1 (Source: Kashdan, *Folkstone International Team Tournament*; notes by VM [additional notes by RT])

Mrs. R.P. (Edith) Michell (*British Chess Magazine* and John G. White Chess Collection, Cleveland Public Library).

312 Menchik–Edith Michell
Folkstone—Women's World Championship, 1933

[B02] *Alekhine's Defense*

1. e4 ♘f6 2. ♘c3 d5 3. e5 ♘fd7 4. e6 f×e6 5. d4 c5 6. ♘f3 c×d4 7. ♘×d4 ♘f6 8. ♗f4 e5? This move not only returns the pawn, but grants White both space and development (8. ... ♘c6=) **9. ♗×e5 a6 10. ♗×f6 e×f6 11. ♕h5+ g6 12. ♕×d5 ♕e7+ 13. ♗e2 ♗g7 14. 0-0-0 f5 15. ♖he1 ♗×d4 16. ♗c4** *(see diagram)*

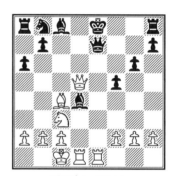

Final position

1–0 (Source: Kalendovský, *Program XI Ročníku Šachoveho Turnaje*, 1986, game 42; notes by RT)

313 Paulette Schwartzmann–Menchik
Folkstone—Women's World Championship, 1933

[A45] *Queen Pawn Opening*

1. d4 ♘f6 2. e3 g6 3. f4 ♗g7 4. ♗d3 0-0 5. ♘d2 d6 6. ♕e2 ♘c6 7. c3 e5 8. f×e5 d×e5 9. d×e5 ♘×e5 10. ♗c2 ♖e8 11. h3? *(see diagram)*

11. ♘gf3∓ **11. ... ♘d5** Better is 11. ... ♗f5! 12. ♗×f5 (12. e4 ♘×e4 13. ♘×e4 ♗×e4 14. ♗×e4–+) 12. ... g×f5 13. ♔d1 ♘c4 14. ♕×c4 ♘d5 15. ♔e2 ♘×e3∓ **12. ♘f1 ♗f5 13. ♗×f5 g×f5 14. ♗d2 ♘f4 15. ♕b5 c6 16. ♕a4 ♘ed3+**

0–1 (Source: Kalendovský, *Program XI Ročníku Šachoveho Turnaje*, 1986, game 41; notes by RT)

After 11. h3

Warsaw 1935

(Women's World Championship)
August 22–September 1935

	1	2	3	4	5	6	7	8	9	10	Points	Place
1 Menchik Vera	•	1	1	1	1	1	1	1	1	1	9	1
2 Gerlecka, Regina	0	•	=	=	1	1	1	=	1	1	6½	2
3 Harum, Gisela	0	=	•	=	1	1	1	1	0	1	6	3
4 Menchik, Olga	0	=	=	•	=	=	=	1	1	1	5½	4
5 Thierry, Helene	0	0	0	=	•	1	1	=	1	1	5	5
6 Hermanowa, Dr. R.	0	0	0	=	0	•	0	1	1	1	3½	6–7
7 Holloway, Edith	0	0	0	=	0	1	•	0	1	1	3½	6–7
8 Skjonsberg, Catherina	0	=	0	0	=	0	1	•	1	0	3	8
9 Kowalska, N.	0	0	1	0	0	0	0	0	•	=	1½	9
10 Shannon, A.M.S.	0	0	0	0	0	0	0	1	=	•	1½	10

Despite a batch of new players Menchik swept the field for a third straight year. The tragedy and irony of the event was that Agnes Stevenson, one of the English players, was killed at the Poznan airport when she walked into a moving propeller. Agnes was the wife of prominent English organizer R.H.S. Stevenson, who two years later married Vera. The tournament was played in a "roomy" and separate apartment from the rest of the Olympiad according to the *British Chess Magazine*.

314 Menchik–Regina Gerlecka
Warsaw—Women's World Championship, 1935
[C01] *Dutch Defense*

It is quite obvious that we have here a game fragment. White, while having more play certainly is not in a position to have had her opponent resign.

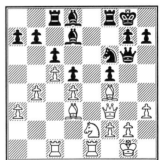

1. d4 e6 2. e4 f5 3. e×f5 e×f5 4. ♗d3 d5 5. ♘c3 ♘f6 6. ♗g5 ♗b4 7. ♕e2+ ♔f7 8. ♕f3 ♕e8+ 9. ♘ge2 ♘e4 10. ♗e3 ♖f8 11. 0-0 c6 12. a3 ♗a5? 13. ♗f4? 13. ♘×e4 d×e4 14. ♗c4+ ♔e7 15. ♕g3+– **13. ... ♔g8 14. ♖fe1 ♕g6 15. b4 ♗d8 16. ♘d1 ♘d7 17. c4 ♘df6 18. h3 ♗d7 19. ♘dc3 ♖c8 20. ♖ac1 ♗e6?!** **21. c5** 21. ♗d6!? ♖e8 22. ♘f4 **21. ... ♗d7 22. ♗e5 ♘h5 23. ♘f4 ♘×f4 24. ♗×f4 ♘f6 25. ♘e2** *(see diagram)*

1–0 (Source: Gawlikowski, *Olimpiady Szachowe*; notes by RT)

Final position

Menchik vs. Sonja Graf—Semmering, 1937

(Women's World Championship Match)
June 26–July 17, 1937

	1	2	3	4	5	6	7	8	9	10	11	12	13	14	15	16	Points
Menchik, Vera	=	1	=	1	1	1	0	1	=	1	0	1	1	1	=	=	11½
Graf, Sonja	=	0	=	0	0	0	1	0	=	0	1	0	0	0	=	=	4½

By 1937 Sonja Graf had increased her reputation and again challenged Vera to a match—this time for the Women's World Championship. Bikova indicates that George Koltanowski assisted Graf. The chief arbiter was FIDE President Alexander Rueb. Details of this event are included in the biographical section of the present work; suffice it to say that the match was recognized by FIDE as being for the title. Sadly the present author has been able to track down only five of the 16 games. The fourteenth game is particularly attractive and culminates with a beautiful sacrifice.

(R65) Sonja Graf–Menchik
Semmering Women's World Championship Match (1), June 26, 1937
½–½

315 Menchik–Sonja Graf
Semmering Women's World Championship Match (2), June 27, 1937
[A30] *English, Symmetrical Variation*

1. c4 e6 2. g3 d5 3. ♗g2 ♘f6 4. ♘f3 c5 5. 0-0 ♘c6 6. d3 ♗e7 7. a3 0-0 8. b3 d4 9. e4 e5 10. ♘e1 h6 11. f4 ♘g4 12. f5 ♘e3 13. ♗×e3 d×e3 14. ♘c3 ♘d4 15. ♗f3 ♕a5 16. ♘d5 ♗g5 17. h4 ♗d8 18. ♘×e3 ♕b6 19. ♖b1 ♗d7 20. ♘d5 ♕a5? [20. ... ♕d6—RT] 21. ♕c1 ♕h7 22. ♘c2 ♗c6?? 23. b4 c×b4 24. a×b4 ♕a4 25. ♘×d4 ♗×d5 26. ♘c2 ♗c6 27. ♖a1 ♕b3 *(see diagram)*

Sonja Graf with Vera Menchik signing the accords for their 1937 world championship match (*Chess Magazine*, 14 August 1937).

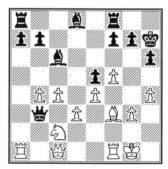

After 27. ... ♕b3

28. ♖a3 1-0 (Source: Olihroniade, *Campionii de Șah Al Lumii*)

(R66) Sonja Graf–Menchik
Semmering Women's World Championship Match (3), June 28, 1937
½–½

316 Menchik–Sonja Graf
Semmering Women's World Championship Match (4), June 29, 1937

[D38] *Queen's Gambit Declined, Ragozin Variation*

1. d4 d5 2. ♘f3 e6 3. c4 ♘f6 4. ♘c3 ♘bd7 5. ♗g5 ♗b4 6. c×d5 e×d5 7. e3 c5 8. ♗d3 ♕a5 9. 0-0 c4 10. ♗f5 ♗×c3 11. b×c3 ♕×c3 12. ♕b1 ♕a5 13. e4 d×e4 14. ♗×d7+ ♗×d7 15. ♗×f6 g×f6 16. ♕×b7 ♖c8 17. ♕×e4+ ♔d8 18. d5 ♕a3 19. ♕d4 ♖g8 20. ♕×f6+ ♕e7 21. ♕c3 ♗h3 22. ♘e1 ♗f5 23. ♘c2 ♖g6 24. ♘d4 ♕g5 25. ♕f3 ♗d3 26. ♘c6+ ♖c×c6 27. d×c6 ♗×f1 28. ♖×f1 ♔c7 29. ♕×f7+ ♔×c6 30. ♕×c4+ ♔c5 31. ♖c1 ♕×c4 32. ♖×c4+ ♔b6 33. f4 h5 34. ♔f2 ♔b5 35. ♖e4 h4 36. ♔f3 ♖a6 37. a4+ ♔c5 38. f5 1-0 (Source: *www.Chessgames.com*)

(R67) Sonja Graf–Menchik
Semmering Women's World Championship Match (5), June 30, 1937
0-1

(R68) Menchik–Sonja Graf
Semmering Women's World Championship Match (6), July 3, 1937
1-0

317 Sonja Graf–Menchik
Semmering Women's World Championship Match (7), July 4, 1937

[D00] *Queen Pawn Opening*

1. d4 d5 2. ♗f4 c5 3. c3 c×d4 4. ♕×d4 ♘c6 5. ♕a4 ♗d7 6. ♘d2 e5 7. ♗g3 ♗d6? 8. ♕b3 ♘ge7 9. ♘gf3 0-0 10. e4! d×e4 11. ♘×e4 ♗c7 12. 0-0-0! ♕b6 13. ♗×e5 ♔h8 14. ♗g3 ♘f5 15. ♘eg5 ♕e7 16. ♗d3 ♖ac8 17. ♗×f5 ♗×f5 18. ♗d6 ♕f6 19. ♗×f8 ♖×f8 20. ♕a3 ♖e8 21. ♖he1 ♗e6 22. ♘×e6 f×e6 23. ♖e2 ♗c7 24. ♕a4 (see diagram)

After 24. ♕a4

and Black loses after a dozen or so more moves. **1-0** (Source: *www.Chessgames.com*)

318 Menchik–Sonja Graf
Semmering Women's World Championship Match (8), July 5, 1937

[D01] *Queen Pawn Opening, Richter Variation*

1. d4 d5 2. ♘c3 ♘f6 3. ♗g5 c6 4. ♘f3 ♘e4 5. ♗f4 f6 6. ♘×e4 d×e4 7. ♘g1 ♕b6 8. ♗c1 ♗f5 9. e3 g5 10. ♘e2 ♘d7 11. ♘g3 0-0-0 12. ♘×f5 ♕a5+ 13. ♗d2 ♕×f5 14. ♗e2 ♕e6 15. c4 c5 16. ♗a5 b6 17. ♗c3 c×d4 18. e×d4 ♕d6 19. 0-0 ♗g7 20. a4 f5 21. a5 ♔b7 22. ♕a4 ♗×d4 23. ♗×d4 ♕×d4 24. ♖fd1 ♘c5 25. ♖×d4 ♘×a4 26. ♖×d8 ♖×d8 27. ♖×a4 and White wins after an unknown number of moves. **1-0** (Source: *www.Chessgames.com*)

(R69) Sonja Graf–Menchik
Semmering Women's World Championship Match (9), July 6, 1937
½-½

(R70) Menchik–Sonja Graf
Semmering Women's World Championship Match (10), July 7, 1937
1–0

(R71) Sonja Graf–Menchik
Semmering Women's World Championship Match (11), July 10, 1937
1–0

(R72) Menchik–Sonja Graf
Semmering Women's World Championship Match (12), July 11, 1937
1–0

(R73) Sonja Graf–Menchik
Semmering Women's World Championship Match (13), July 12, 1937
0–1

319 Menchik–Sonja Graf
Semmering Women's World Championship Match (14), July 13, 1937
[D46] *Semi-Slav*

1. c4 e6 2. ♘c3 d5 3. d4 ♘f6 4. ♘f3 ♘bd7 5. e3 c6 6. ♗d3 ♗e7 This move has been criticized by many commentators as being overly passive, but in fairness it has been used by Levenfish, Robatasch, Prins, and Petrosian. [Certainly more common, even in 1937, was 6. ... d×c4 going into the Meran Variation. The continuation being 7. ♗×c4 b5 8. ♗d3 a6—RT] **7. 0–0 0–0 8. e4!?** The text is a very tactical response to the position. The fact that Alekhine used similar means in his match with Bogoljubow may have influenced Menchik. A safer and more positional approach would have been to play b3, maintaining more direct control on the center and controlling the queenside at the expense of the attack on the Black king. **8. ... d×e4 9. ♘×e4 ♘×e4?** *(see diagram)*

After 9. ... ♘×e4

[Stronger is 9. ... b6 binging the queen's bishop into play more quickly and allowing the queen's rook to join in. Further plans should include putting the king's rook on e8, fianchettoing the dark square bishop, and planning a break with c5. White will focus at h7 with both knights, bishop and queen. Black's play is precarious, but play still exists if great care is shown—RT] **10. ♗×e4 ♘f6 11. ♗c2 c5** Necessary to free Black's cramped pieces. **12. d×c5 ♕a5** Black weighs the options of trading queens, which gives White a very good endgame as opposed to keeping the wood on the board and submitting to the indignities of the kingside attack. Hindsight is always best! **13. ♗e3** A nice finesse to divert Black's dark square bishop from the kingside and keeping the queen out of play even while optimizing the position of her own cleric. **13. ... ♗×c5 14. ♗d2 ♕c7** [If 14. ... ♗b4 15. a3 ♗×d2 16. ♕×d2 and White is somewhat better—RT] **15. ♗c3 ♗e7 16. ♕e2 b6?** [Better is 16. ... ♖d8 or a number of other alternatives!—RT] **17. ♘g5** [Not 17. ♗×f6? ♗×f6 18. ♕e4 g6 19. ♕×a8 ♗b7 20. ♕×a7 ♖a8 21. ♕×a8+ ♗×a8 and Black has real counterplay thanks to the bishop pair. The text maintains White's positional advantage—RT] **17. ... g6?!** [17. ... ♗a6—RT] **18. ♕f3 ♗b7 19. ♕h3 h5** [19. ... ♘h5?? 20. ♕×h5! (20. g4 ♕c6 21. ♗e4)

20. ... ♗×g5 21. ♕×g5 and it is all over—RT] **20. ♖ad1** (*see diagram*)

The threat is 21. ♘×e6 f×e6 22. ♕×e6 and 23. ♖e7. **20. ... ♘g4 21. ♖d7!!** The point is 21. ♕×h5 fails due to 21. ... ♕×h2+ and the material evaporates. In the game, if 21. ... ♕×d7 22. ♕×h5! with mate on h7 or h8 using the bishop or queen as necessary. If 21. ... ♕c6 White plays 22. ♖×e7 and threatens 23. ♖×b7, renewing the threat. In the face of one of the prettiest combinations ever, Black resigned. **1–0** (Source: *www. Chessgames.com* [additional notes by RT])

After 20. ♖ad1

(R74) Sonja Graf–Menchik
Semmering Women's World Championship Match (15), July 14, 1937
½–½

(R75) Menchik–Sonja Graf
Semmering Women's World Championship Match (16), July 17, 1937
½–½

Stockholm 1937
(Women's World Championship)
July 31–August 14, 1937

Given the large number of players—26—the Women's World Championship was played on the Monrad pairing system. Games were played on the second floor of the Hotel Royale while the games of the concurrent Olympiad were played on the first floor. The first session of play took place in the evenings with adjournments the following mornings. This was the first year of participation for the United States, which was represented by future U.S. Champion Mary Bain. Menchik scored a crushing 14–0 result with second going to Clarice Benini (Italy—10 points) and 3rd–4th shared between Sonja Graf of Austria and Milda Lauberte (Latvia) with nine points each.

As with previous championships this tournament was held concurrently with the Olympiad. The Stockholm Olympiad is often given the sobriquet "The Lost Olympiad" as there were no bulletins and publicity was minimal. Sadly this carried over to the women's tournament.

Mary Bain gave an interview to Edith Lucy Weart, with her impressions of the event:

"...Everything was very well arranged and the accommodations were very good. It was a most successful tournament." She stated that Miss Menchik is a very friendly person, charming to her. Miss Sonja Graf dresses mannishly and walks, hands in pockets, with a masculine stride.

"We (ELW) had been told that at Warsaw, the women contestants were more interested in having a good time than in playing chess, but Mrs. Bain said this was certainly not true in Stockholm. The women, she said, all took their games very seriously; indeed, were often under a severe nervous strain. 'I was the most calm person there,' she said, but admits that when she began forging to the top she felt the strain, herself. 'The weakness of all the girls is that they have no experience,' she told us. One thing which impresses Mrs. Bain particularly is the fact that most of the European women are under the instruction of some chess master...."[64]

Following are Vera's opponents for each round—color is often not known—as listed in *The Times* (London) between August 9 and 16, 1937:

1. Elisabeth Mellbye
2. Mona Karff—Palestine
3. Ingrid Larsen
4. Sonja Graf—Germany
5. Gisela Harum

6. Mary Bain—USA
7. Clarice Benini—Italy
8. Clara Faragó
9. Milda Lauberte—Poland
10. Ingeborg Anderssen

11. F. Thomson
12. Barbara Fleröw-Bulhak
13. Catharina Roodzant—Holland
14. Mary Gilchrist—Scotland

320 Ingrid Larsen–Menchik
Stockholm—Women's World Championship (3), 1937

[D05] *Colle System*

After 25. ... ♘g4

1. d4 ♘f6 2. ♘f3 d5 3. e3 ♗g4 4. ♗d3 e6 5. ♘bd2 c5 6. c3 ♘c6 7. 0-0 ♕c7 8. ♕e1 0-0-0 9. d×c5 ♗×c5 10. ♘d4 ♘×d4 11. e×d4 ♗d6 12. h3 ♗h5 13. ♗e2 g5 14. ♕d1 ♗g6 15. ♘f3 h6 16. ♖e1 g4 17. ♘e5? g×h3 18. ♘×g6 ♗h2+ 19. ♔h1 h×g2+ 20. ♔×g2 ♖hg8 21. ♖h1 ♖×g6+ 22. ♔f1 ♖dg8 23. ♔e1 ♖g1+ 24. ♖×g1 ♖×g1+ 25. ♗f1 ♘g4 *(see diagram)*

26. ♕f3?? A suggestion if the game is to continue: 26. ♕d3 **26. ... ♗g3** Much better is 26. ... ♗d6 27. ♕d3 ♘h2 Maybe Menchik could not resist showing that she could play anything or maybe we have an error in the notation **27. ♗×h6?** 27. f×g3 and Menchik still wins, but they would have played a lot longer **27. ... ♖×f1+ 28. ♔e2 ♖×f2+ 0–1** (Source: *www.365Chess.com*; notes by RT)

321 Sonja Graf–Menchik
Stockholm—Women's World Championship (4), 1937

[D02] *Queen Pawn Opening*

1. d4 d5 2. ♘f3 ♘f6 3. c3 c5 4. d×c5 e6 5. ♗g5 ♗×c5 6. e3 ♕b6 7. ♕c2 ♘e4 8. ♗f4 ♗d6 9. ♗×d6 ♘×d6 10. ♘bd2 ♘c6 11. ♗e2 ♗d7 12. 0-0 0-0-0 13. e4 ♖ac8 14. ♖ad1 ♖fd8 15. e5 ♘f5 16. ♕d3 a6 17. ♖fe1 ♘a5 18. ♕b1 ♗b5 19. ♗×b5 ♕×b5 20. g4 ♘e7 21. ♘d4 ♕b6 22. ♘2f3 ♘ac6 23. ♘g5 *(see diagram)*

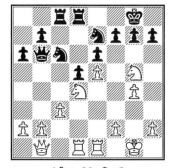
After 23. ♘g5

23. ... g6?! 23. ... ♘g6 24. ♕d3 h6 25. ♘×f7 ♔×f7 26. ♕f3+ ♔g8 27. ♘×e6 ♖f8 28. ♘×f8 ♖×f8 29. ♕g3?! **29. ♕e3=** 29. ... ♕×b2 30. ♖b1 ♕d2 31. ♖ed1 ♕c2? **31. ... ♕×a2** 32. ♖dc1 ♕d2 33. ♖d1 ♕×a2 34. ♖×b7 ♕e2 35. ♖f1 ♘×e5 36. f4 ♘5c6 37. ♖e1 ♕c4 38. ♖e×e7 ♘×e7 39. ♖×e7 ♖×f4 40. ♕e1 ♖×g4+ 41. ♔f2 ♖e4 42. ♖×e4 ♕×e4 43. ♕×e4 d×e4 0–1 (Source: *www.Chessgames.com*)

322 Menchik–Mary Bain
Stockholm—Women's World Championship (6), 1937

[D64] *Queen's Gambit Declined, Classical Variation*

1. d4 ♘f6 2. c4 e6 3. ♘c3 d5 4. ♘f3 ♘bd7 5. ♗g5 ♗e7 6. e3 0-0 7. ♖c1 c6 8. a3 ♖e8 9. ♕c2 h6 10. ♗h4 ♘h5 11. ♗×e7 ♕×e7 12. ♘e5 f5 13. ♗d3 ♘hf6 14. f4 ♘×e5

Rond: .... Bord: ....

Vit: miss Vera menchik   Svart: Mary Bain

1	P - Q4	N - KB3	26	N - R2	B - R3
2	P - QB4	P - K3	27	QR X R	R X R
3	N - QB3	P - Q4	28	R - R	K - R2
4	N - B3	QN - Q2	29	R - Q4	R - B2
5	B - N5	B - K2	30	N - N4	B - R4
6	P - N3	O - O	31	K - B2	P - QR4
7	R - B	P - B3	32	N - B2	B - B3
8	P - QR3	R - K	33	R - Q5	P - N4
9	Q - B2	P - KR3	34	R - R4	P - R5
10	B - R4	N - R4	35	R - R3	R - R5
11	B X B	Q X B	36		
12	N - K5	P - KB4	37		
13	P - B4	KN - B3	38		
14	B - Q3	N X N	39		
15	QN X N	N - Q5	40	Mary Bain	
16	O - O	P - QN3	41		
17	P X P	BP X P	42		
18	B X N	QP X B	43		
19	K R B	B - R3	44		
20	Q R4	B - Q6	45		
21	N - N5	Q - Q2	46		
22	N - B3	Q X Q	47		
23	N X Q	QR B	48		
24	N - B3	K R - Q	49		
25	R - B2	K B	50		

Scoresheet of Mary Bain (USA) vs. Vera Menchik in the Stockholm 1937 World Championship. Scoresheet by Ms. Bain (author's collection).

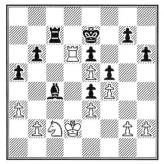

After 33. ☖d6

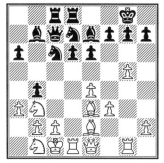

After 17. ♘b1

15. d×e5 ♘e4 16. 0-0 b6 17. c×d5 c×d5 18. ♗×e4 d×e4
19. ♖fd1 ♗a6 20. ♕a4 ♗d3 21. ♘b5 ♕d7 22. ♘c3 ♕×a4
23. ♘×a4 ♖ac8 24. ♘c3 ♖ed8 25. ♔f2 ♔f8 26. ♘a2 ♗a6
27. ♖×c8 ♖×c8 28. ♔e1 ♔e7 29. ♖d4 ♖c7 29. ... ♖c2!?
Pretty much forces a draw if desired 30. ♘b4 ♗b5 31. ♔d2
a5 32. ♘c2 ♗c4 33. ♖d6 *(see diagram)*
     33. ... b5?! 33. ... ♖d7= 34. ♘d4 a4 35. ♖b6 ♗d3? 35. ...
♖d7 36. h4 ♔d8 37. ♔c3 ♔c7± 36. ♖×e6+ ♔f7 37. ♖c6
♖×c6 38. ♘×c6 1-0 (Source: *www.365Chess.com*; notes by RT)

323 Barbara Fleröw-Bulhak–Menchik
Stockholm—Women's World Championship (12), 1937
[B84] *Sicilian, Scheviningen Variation*

1. e4 c5 2. ♘f3 e6 3. d4 c×d4 4. ♘×d4 ♘f6 5. ♘c3 d6
6. ♗e2 a6 7. ♗e3 ♕c7 8. f3 ♘c6 9. ♘b3 b5 10. ♕d2
♗e7 11. 0-0-0 ♗b7 12. g4 0-0 13. g5 ♘d7 14. ♖hg1
♖fd8 15. ♕e1 ♖ac8 16. a3? b4 17. ♘b1?? *(see diagram)*
     [After 17. a×b4 ♘×b4 Menchik will still have to convert
the advantage into a win. As played, the game is essentially
over—RT] 17. ... ♘a5 18. ♘a1 ♕×c2+ 19. ♘×c2 ♘b3
mate 0-1 (Source: Gawlikowski, *Olimpiady Szachowe 1924–1970*)

Buenos Aires 1939
(Women's World Championship)
August 24–September 18, 1939

		1	2	3	4	5	6	7	8	9	10	11	12	13	14	15	16	17	18	19	20	Pts.	Place
1	Menchik, Vera	•	1	1	1	1	=	1	1	1	1	=	1	1	1	1	1	1	1	1	1	18	1
2	Graf, Sonja	0	•	0	1	0	1	1	1	1	1	1	1	1	1	1	1	1	1	1	1	16	2
3	Carrasco Araya, B.	0	1	•	0	1	1	1	1	1	1	1	0	1	=	1	1	1	1	1	1	15½	3
4	Rinder, Friedl	0	0	1	•	1	d	1	1	1	1	1	1	=	1	1	1	0	1	1	1	15	4
5	Karff, Mona May	0	1	0	0	•	1	1	=	=	1	1	1	1	1	0	1	1	1	1	1	14	5
6	Lauberte, Milda	=	0	0	=	0	•	1	=	1	=	=	1	=	1	1	1	=	1	1	=	12	6
7	Mora, María Teresa	0	0	0	0	0	0	•	1	0	=	1	1	1	1	1	=	1	1	1	1	11	7–8
8	Roodzant, Catharina	0	0	0	0	=	=	0	•	1	=	=	1	1	=	1	1	1	1	1	1	11	7–8
9	Janečková, Blažena	0	0	0	0	=	0	1	0	•	=	=	1	1	1	=	0	1	1	0	1	9	9–10
10	Schwartzmann, Paulette	=	0	0	0	0	=	=	=	=	•	=	1	=	=	=	=	0	1	1	1	9	9–10
11	Larsen, Ingrid	0	0	0	0	0	=	0	=	=	=	•	=	1	1	1	0	1	1	1	1	8½	11
12	Trepat de Navarro, Dora	0	0	1	=	0	0	0	0	0	0	=	•	=	1	=	0	1	1	1	1	7½	12–13
13	Anderssen, Ingeborg	0	0	0	0	0	=	0	0	0	=	0	=	•	=	=	1	1	1	1	1	7½	12–13
14	Reischer, Salome	0	0	=	0	0	0	0	=	0	=	0	0	=	•	1	1	1	0	1	1	7	14–15
15	Berea de Montero, M.	0	0	0	0	1	0	0	0	=	=	0	=	=	0	•	1	=	1	=	1	7	14–15
16	Stoffels, M.	0	0	0	0	0	0	=	=	1	=	1	0	0	0	0	•	1	1	=	=	6½	16
17	DeVigil, M.	0	0	0	1	0	=	0	0	0	1	1	=	0	0	=	0	•	0	=	1	6	17
18	Raclauskiene, Elena	0	0	0	0	0	0	0	0	0	0	0	0	0	1	0	0	1	•	=	1	3½	18
19	Nakkerud, Ruth	0	0	0	0	0	0	0	0	1	0	0	0	0	0	=	=	=	=	•	0	3	19
20	Lougheed, Anabelle	0	0	0	0	0	=	0	0	0	0	0	0	0	0	0	=	0	0	1	•	2	20

The Argentine and Uruguayan chess federations agreed to cover all expenses of travel and hospitality for participants in the 1939 Olympiad. As a result a number of countries decided to charter a ship for the 17 day trip from Europe to Buenos Aires.[65] For the first time Menchik was able to represent England in an Olympiad as she had gained citizenship upon marrying R.H.S. Stevenson. Sonja Graf, on the other hand, was stripped of her right to represent Germany by the Nazis and played under the flag of "Liberty."

324 Milda Lauberte–Menchik
Buenos Aires—Women's World Championship (11), 1939
[D13] Slav, Exchange Variation

Milda Lauberte (age 21 of Latvia), without being excessively passive, plays the Exchange Slav and slowly builds a fortress which leaves Menchik without any real play. Neither player was able to gain any substantial advantage and Vera gives up her first draw in women's tournament play since 1930.

1. d4 d5 2. ♘f3 ♘f6 3. c4 c6 4. c×d5 c×d5 5. ♘c3 ♘c6 6. e3 g6 7. ♗d3 ♗g7 8. 0-0 0-0 9. b3 a6 10. ♗b2 ♘b4 11. ♗b1 ♕c7 12. a3 ♘c6 13. b4 ♖d8 14. ♕e2 ♗g4 15. h3 ♗×f3 16. ♕×f3 e5 17. ♖d1 e×d4 18. e×d4 b5 19. ♗a2 ♘e7 20. ♘e2 ♕d6 21. ♘f4 ♘e8 22. ♘d3 ♕f6 23. ♕×f6 ♗×f6 24. ♘c5 ♘d6 25. ♗c3 ♘c4 26. ♗b3 ♘c6 27. a4 ♖a7 28. a5 ♔f8 29. ♔f1 ♖e8 30. ♖a2 ♖ee7 31. ♖e2 ♘b8 32. ♖×e7 ♖×e7 33. ♖e1 ♖×e1+ *(see diagram)*

½–½ (Source: *www.Chessgames.com*)

Final position

325 Menchik–Sonja Graf
Buenos Aires—Women's World Championship (12), 1939
[E53] Nimzo-Indian, Rubinstein Variation

A tie for the title would have resulted if this game, in which the champion had a rocky voyage, had gone the other way. In her book, Sonja Graf indicated this game was one of the great disappointments of her life.

1. d4 d5 2. c4 e6 3. ♘f3 ♘f6 4. ♘c3 ♘bd7 5. e3 ♗b4 6. ♗d3 c5 7. 0-0 0-0 8. ♗d2 a6 9. c×d5 e×d5 10. ♖c1 c4 11. ♗b1 ♖e8 12. ♘e2 ♗d6 13. ♗c3 b5 14. ♘g3 g6 15. ♖e1

After 60. ♕e2

♗b7 16. ♖e2 b4 17. ♗e1 a5 18. ♘g5 ♘g4 19. ♘h3 f5 20. ♘f1 ♕c7 21. f4 ♘df6 22. ♗h4 a4 23. ♘g5 ♕e7 24. ♖e1 a3 25. b3 c3 26. ♘f3 ♕g7 27. h3 ♘h6 28. ♗×f6 ♕×f6 29. ♘e5 ♕e7 30. ♘h2 ♖ec8 31. ♘hf3 ♘f7 32. ♗d3 ♖c7 33. ♕e2 ♕d8 34. ♗c2 ♕c8 35. ♘×f7 ♖×f7 36. ♗b5 ♖c7 37. ♗d3 ♗f8 38. ♘e5 ♗g7 39. ♔h2 ♗f6 40. ♖g1 ♔f8 41. g4 ♗×e5 42. f×e5 f×g4 43. ♖f1+ ♖f7 44. ♖×f7+ ♔×f7 45. h×g4 ♕d8 46. ♔g3 ♔g7 47. ♕f1 ♕e7 48. ♖f2 ♖f8 49. ♖f4 ♗c8 50. ♗c2 ♗e6 51. ♖×f8 ♕×f8 52. ♕a6 ♕e7 53. ♗d1 ♔f7 54. ♔f4 h6 55. ♕f1 ♔g7 56. ♔g3 h5 57. g×h5 ♕g5+ 58. ♔f2 ♕f5+ 59. ♗f3 ♕c2+ 60. ♕e2 *(see diagram)*

60. ... ♛×e2+? Here 60. ... ♛b2 wins almost at once **61. ♚×e2 ♝f5?** 61. ... g5 would have won, since White cannot possibly cope with the two widely separated passed pawns, and Black soon picks up the h-pawn by ♚h6 and g4 etc. Examine the play: 62. e4 (62. ♚d3 g4 63. ♝g2 *(63. ♝e2 ♝f5+)* 63. ... ♚h6 64. ♚c2 *(64. e4 d×e4+ and ♝×b3)* 64. ... ♚×h5 65. e4 d×e4 66. ♝×e4 ♚g5 67. d5 ♝f5! and wins with ease) 62. ... d×e4 63. ♝×e4 ♝×b3! and wins **62. h×g6 ♚×g6 63. ♝×d5 ♝b1 64. ♚d1 ♝d3 65. ♝c6 ♚f7 66. d5 ♚e7 67. e4 ♚f7 68. e6+ ♚f6 69. e5+ ♚e7 70. ♝b7 ♝g6 71. ♝a6 ♝e4 72. ♝c4 ♝g6 73. d6+ ♚d8 74. ♝b5 1–0** (Source: *Chess*, October 1939, #938; notes by RT)

326 Menchik–Paulette Schwartzmann
Buenos Aires—Women's World Championship, 1939
[D13] Slav, Exchange Variation

As in Menchik's previous draw against Lauberte we have an Exchange French—although with colors reversed. In this case Vera probably committed too strongly to the kingside attack and when it was repulsed Schwartzmann picked up the initiative and was able to liquidate any pieces needed to continue.

Final position

1. d4 d5 2. c4 c6 3. ♘f3 ♘f6 4. ♘c3 ♘bd7 5. c×d5 c×d5 6. ♗f4 a6 7. e3 e6 8. ♗d3 ♗e7 9. 0–0 ♘h5 10. ♖c1 ♘×f4 11. e×f4 ♘f6 12. ♖e1 0–0 13. ♘e5 ♗d7 14. ♖e3 g6 15. g4 ♚g7 16. ♖h3 ♖h8 17. ♛d2 ♘g8 18. ♘e2 ♗e8 19. ♚h1 f6 20. ♘f3 ♖c8 21. ♖g3 ♖×c1+ 22. ♛×c1 ♗d6 23. ♖g1 ♗f7 24. ♗b1 ♘e7 25. ♘e1 ♛c7 26. ♛×c7 ♗×c7 27. ♘d3 ♗d6 28. ♖c1 ♖c8 29. ♖×c8 ♘×c8 30. ♚g2 ♗e8 31. ♘c3 ♗c6 32. ♚f1 ♘b6 33. b3 ♘d7 34. ♚e2 ♚f7 35. ♚e3 ♘b8 36. ♗c2 a5 37. ♗d1 ♘a6 38. ♗e2 ♘c7 *(see diagram)*

½–½ (Source: *www.Chessgames.com*)

327 B. Carrasco Araya–Menchik
Buenos Aires—Women's World Championship, 1939
[D52] Queen's Gambit Declined, Cambridge Springs Variation

1. d4 ♘f6 2. c4 e6 3. ♘c3 d5 4. ♘f3 ♘bd7 5. ♗g5 c6 6. e3 ♛a5 7. ♘d2 ♗b4 8. ♛c2 0–0 9. ♗e2 e5 10. d×e5 ♘e4 11. ♘d×e4 d×e4 12. ♖c1? ♘×e5! **13. ♗f4 ♘d3+ 14. ♗×d3 e×d3 15. ♛×d3** If 15. ♛d2 ♗e6 16. b3 b5–+ **15. ... ♗f5 16. ♛e2 ♖ad8 17. a3 ♗×c3+ 18. ♖×c3 ♗d3 19. ♛g4** *(see diagram)*

After 19. ♛g4

If 19. b4 ♗×e2 20. b×a5 ♖d1+ **19. ... f5!** Not 19. ... ♗×c4 20. ♘c7 (More to the point 20. ♗h6 ♛e5 21. ♖×c4) **20. ♛g3 ♗×c4 21. ♗e5 ♖d7 22. b4** Better is 22. ♗d4∓ **22. ... ♛d5 23. ♗d4 ♖e8** 23. ... f4 24. ♛f3 ♛e6 25. ♛h3 threatening ♖×c4 **24. f4?** If 24. ♚d2 ♖e4 and ♖×d4 wins **24. ... ♛×d4 0–1** (Source: *Chess*, October 1939, #945; notes by RT)

328 Mona Karff–Menchik
Buenos Aires—Women's World Championship, 1939

[E60] *King's Indian Defense*

This was a tough game for Menchik against a seven-time United States Women's Champion. As early as move six she blunders the exchange and the middle of the game is more than a little rough for her too. At any rate it will not go into either players' lists of best games.

1. d4 ♘f6 2. c4 g6 3. g3 ♗g7 4. ♗g2 0-0 5. e4 d6 6. ♘e2 White had a plethora of choices, including: **6. ... ♗g4?** [6. ... c5; 6. ... e5; 6. ... ♘bd7 were all valid options. What made her choose the move she did is a mystery—RT] **7. e5 ♘e8 8. ♗×b7 ♘d7 9. ♗×a8 ♕×a8 10. ♖g1 d×e5 11. d5 ♘d6 12. ♘a3?!** [12. ♘d2—RT] **12. ... e4 13. h3 ♗f3 14. ♕c2 ♘e5**

After 22. ... ♗d4

15. g4? This loses much of her advantage. [15. ♔f1—RT] **15. ... ♕d8?** Returning the favor. [15. ... c6 16. ♘f4= with lots of opportunities for complications—RT] **16. ♔f1 e6 17. ♖g3 ♗×e2+ 18. ♕×e2 e×d5 19. c×d5 f5 20. ♗f4 f×g4** [20. ... ♘d3!?—RT] **21. ♗×e5 ♗×e5 22. ♖×g4 ♗d4 (see diagram) 23. f4 ♘f5 24. ♕d2?** Turning the game over to Menchik. [24. ♘c4 at least holds basic equality—RT] **24. ... ♕×d5 25. ♔e2?!** [Putting up more resistance is 25. ♖e1 and developing her last piece—RT] **25. ... c5 26. ♖g5 ♕e6 27. ♘c2 ♕c4+ 28. ♔d1 ♖d8** [More accurate is 28. ... ♗×b2 29. ♖×f5 ♖×f5 30. ♘e3 ♕a4+—RT] **29. ♔e1 ♗f6 30. ♕e2 ♕×e2+ 31. ♔×e2 ♗×g5 32. f×g5 ♘d4+ 33. ♘×d4 c×d4 34. ♖d1 ♔f7 35. b3 ♔e6 36. ♖d2 ♔f5 37. h4 ♔g4 38. ♖d1 ♖d7 39. ♖h1 ♖c7 40. ♔d2 ♔f4 41. ♖f1+ ♔e5 42. ♖f8 e3+ 43. ♔d1 ♔e4 44. ♖e8+ ♔d3 45. h5 e2+ 0-1** (Source: *www.Chessgames.com*; Karff Scoresheet [additional notes by RT])

329 Menchik–Frield Rinder
Buenos Aires—Women's World Championship, 1939

[A46] *Queen's Pawn Game*

1. d4 ♘f6 2. ♘f3 e6 3. ♗f4 c5 4. e3 ♘c6 5. ♗e2 b6 6. c4 c×d4 7. e×d4 d5 8. 0-0 d×c4 9. ♗×c4 ♘a5 10. ♗b5+ ♗d7 11. ♗×d7+ ♕×d7 12. ♘e5 (see diagram)

After 12. ♘e5

12. ... ♕b7? [12. ... ♕b5=—RT] **13. ♕a4+ ♔d8 14. b4 ♘d5 15. ♗d2 f6 16. b×a5 f×e5 17. d×e5 ♖c8 18. a×b6 a×b6 19. ♖d1 b5 20. ♕g4 ♔f7 21. ♘c3 ♗c5? 22. ♘e4 ♖f8 23. ♗g5+?!** [23. ♘×c5 ♖×c5 24. ♗b4—RT] **23. ... ♔e8? 24. ♖×d5 ♗×f2+ 25. ♔h1 ♗c5 26. ♖dd1 ♕g6 27. ♘×c5 ♖×c5 28. ♖d8+ 1-0** (Source: *www.Chessgames.com*)

330 Menchik–Ingrid Larsen
Buenos Aires—Women's World Championship, 1939

[A52] *Budapest Gambit*

1. d4 ♘f6 2. c4 e5 3. d×e5 ♘g4 4. ♘f3 ♘c6 5. e3 ♘g×e5 6. ♗e2 d6 7. 0-0 ♗e6 8. ♕c2

g6 9. ♘d4 ♗g7 10. ♘xe6 f×e6 11. ♘c3 0-0 12. ♖e1 ♕h4 13. h3 ♘f3+?? [13. ... ♕xf2+ 14. ♔h1 ♕xe1+ 15. ♔h2 ♘g4+ 16. h×g4 ♗e5+ 17. g3 ♕×g3+ 18. ♔h1 ♕h2 mate—RT] **14. g×f3 ♕×h3 15. ♕e4 ♘e5 16. f4 ♖f5 17. ♕h1 ♕×h1+ 18. ♔×h1 ♘c6 19. ♗g4 ♖a5 20. ♗×e6+ ♔h8 21. ♗d2 ♖h5+ 22. ♔g2 ♘e7 23. ♖h1 ♖×h1 24. ♖×h1 a6 25. ♘d5 ♘×d5 26. c×d5 1-0** (Source: *www.Chessgames.com*)

331 Menchik–Teresa Mora
Buenos Aires—Women's World Championship, 1939
[D37] *Queen's Gambit Declined*

1. d4 d5 2. c4 e6 3. ♘c3 ♘f6 4. ♘f3 ♘bd7 5. e3 ♗e7 6. ♗d3 d×c4 7. ♗×c4 c5 8. 0-0 a6 9. a4 Boldly preventing Black's counter-action by ... b5. The weakening of White's own b4 square is not to be feared as there is no Black knight available for the maneuver ♘–c6–b4 and eventually d5. **9. ... c×d4 10. e×d4** An isolated pawn, but one in the center. **10. ... ♘b6**

After 14. ... ♗c6

[Blocking White's d5, but it would be better to centralize by 0-0-0 followed by ... ♖e8; ... ♘f8; ♗d7; etc.—RT] **11. ♗b3 0-0 12. ♕e2 ♗d7 13. ♘e5 ♖c8** In order to go on with ... ♗c6 without the fear of weakening the pawns. **14. ♗g5 ♗c6** *(see diagram)*

Now the bishop is fully developed, but the critical square, e6, is thereby weakened. Black hopes to hold up White's attack momentarily by the threat to the d-pawn, and to simplify the position by **15. ♖fe1** A masterly decision. [15. ♖ad1 ♗d5 —RT] **15. ... ♗d5** Still trying—unwisely—to simplify the position. [15. ... ♕×d4 16. ♖ad1 (16. ♘×f7 ♖×f7 17. ♕×e6 ♖cf8 18. ♕×e7 ♕g4) 16. ... ♕b4 17. ♗a2 and White dominates all the avenues—RT] **16. ♘×d5 ♘b×d5** [Less damaging is 16. ... ♘f×d5—RT] **17. ♖ad1 h6 18. ♗×d5 h×g5 19. ♘×f7 ♖×f7 20. ♗×e6 1-0** (Source: Tartakower, *100 Best Games of Modern Chess*; notes by S. Tartakower [additional notes by RT])

332 Catharina Roodzant–Menchik
Buenos Aires—Women's World Championship, 1939
[A84] *Dutch Defense*

1. d4 f5 2. ♘f3 e6 3. g3 b6 4. ♗g2 ♗b7 5. 0-0 ♘f6 6. c4 ♗e7 7. d5 ♕c8 8. d×e6 d×e6 9. ♘c3 0-0 10. b3 ♖d8 11. ♕c2 ♘a6 12. a3 ♘c5 13. ♗b2 ♘ce4 14. ♖ad1 ♖×d1 15. ♖×d1 a5 16. ♘d4 ♘×f2 17. ♗×b7 ♕×b7 18. e4 [18. ♔×f2 ♘g4+ 19. ♔e1 ♕h1+ 20. ♔d2 ♗g5+ 21. e3 ♕×h2+ If not pretty, is a lot better than the text. Sometimes the simple ideas are the best—RT] **18. ... ♘×d1 0-1** (Source: *www.Chessgames.com*)

333 M. DeVigil–Menchik
Buenos Aires—Women's World Championship, 1939
[A05] *Réti Opening*

1. ♘f3 d5 2. b3 ♘f6 3. ♗b2 g6 4. e3 ♗g7 5. ♗e2 0-0 6. 0-0 c5 7. ♘e5 ♘fd7 8. f4 ♘×e5 9. ♗×e5 f6 10. ♗b2 ♘c6 11. ♕c1 e5 12. f×e5 f×e5 *(see diagram)*

After 12. ... f×e5

13. d3? [13. 罝×f8+ 曾×f8 14. c4 d4 15. ⓵f3=—RT] **13. ...
⓵h6 14. 曾d2? ⓵d4?** A strange move. Did she do it because
she could? Was it a case of blindness where she forgot that
White did not have to exchange the minors? [14. ... d4–+
—RT] **15. ⓵×d4??** [15. 罝×f8+ 曾×f8 16. ⓵c3 and Black has
only the thinnest of edges—RT] **15. ... c×d4 16. 曾d1 ⓵×e3+
17. 曾h1 罝×f1+ 18. 曾×f1 ⓵e6 19. 曾e1 曾g5 20. ⓵a3
曾e7 21. ⓵b1 罝c8 22. ⓵d1 罝f8 23. ⓵e2 曾g5 24. ⓵a3
⓵d2 25. 曾d1 a6 26. ⓵f3 ⓵c3 27. 罝c1 ⓵b2? 28. 罝b1
⓵×a3 29. b4 b5 30. 罝b3 ⓵c1 31. 罝b1 ⓵e3 32. 曾e2 曾h4
33. g3 曾f6 34. 曾g2 ⓵h3+ 35. 曾×h3 曾×f3 36. 曾×f3
罝×f3 37. 罝b2 罝f2 38. a3 e4 39. d×e4 d×e4 40. 罝b3 罝×c2**

0–1 (Source: *www.Chessgames.com* [additional notes by RT])

334 Blażena Janečjová–Menchik
Buenos Aires—Women's World Championship, 1939
[D52] *Queen's Gambit Declined, Cambridge Springs Variation*

**1. d4 d5 2. ⓵f3 ⓵f6 3. c4 c6 4. ⓵c3 e6 5. ⓵g5 ⓵bd7
6. e3 曾a5 7. ⓵d2 ⓵b4 8. 曾c1 ⓵e4 9. ⓵c×e4 d×e4** *(see
diagram)*

10. a3?? [10. ⓵h4 would have left White in a good position—RT] **10. ... ⓵×d2+ 11. 曾×d2 曾×g5**

0–1 (Source: *www.Chessgames.com*)

After 9. ... d×e4

335 Anabelle Lougheed–Menchik
Buenos Aires—Women's World Championship, 1939
[D02] *Queen Pawn Game*

**1. d4 d5 2. ⓵f3 ⓵f6 3. ⓵f4 c5 4. e3 曾b6 5. ⓵d3? c4 6. ⓵e2 曾×b2 7. 0–0?? 曾×a1
8. ⓵bd2 曾×d1 9. 罝×d1 ⓵c6 10. c3 ⓵f5 11. ⓵e5 ⓵×e5 12. ⓵×e5 e6 13. ⓵f1 ⓵e4
14. 罝b1 ⓵×c3 0–1** (Source: *www.Chessgames.com*)

336 Menchik–Ingeborg Anderssen
Buenos Aires—Women's World Championship, 1939
[D55] *Queen's Gambit Declined*

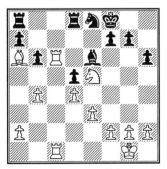

After 21. ... 曾f8

**1. d4 ⓵f6 2. c4 e6 3. ⓵c3 d5 4. ⓵g5 ⓵e7 5. e3 0–0 6. ⓵f3
⓵e4 7. ⓵×e7 曾×e7 8. 曾c2 ⓵×c3 9. 曾×c3 c6 10. ⓵d3
⓵d7 11. 0–0 罝e8 12. c×d5 e×d5 13. b4 曾d6 14. 罝fc1
b6?? 15. 曾×c6 曾×c6 16. 罝×c6 ⓵f6 17. 罝c7 ⓵e6 18. ⓵a6
罝ed8 19. 罝ac1 ⓵e8 20. 罝7c6 h6 21. ⓵e5 曾f8** *(see diagram)*

22. ⓵b7?! It's not often that one's opponent resigns after
you make a rather pointless second rate move. On the other
hand White is up a pawn and Black must just sit and wait to
be slowly crushed. **1–0** (Source: *www.Chessgames.com*)

Vera (left) vs. Ingeborg Anderssen in Buenos Aires 1939.

Final position

337   Menchik–M. Berea de Montero
Buenos Aires—Women's World Championship, 1939
[D40] *Queen's Gambit Declined, Semi-Tarrasch Variation*

1. c4 e6 2. ♘c3 d5 3. d4 ♘f6 4. ♘f3 c5 5. e3 b6 6. c×d5 c×d4? [6. ... e×d5—RT] **7. ♗b5+ ♗d7 8. d×e6 ♗×b5?** [8. ... d×c3 9. e×d7+ ♘b×d7 10. b×c3∓—RT] **9. e×f7+ ♔×f7 10. ♕b3+ ♔e8 11. ♕×b5+ ♘bd7 12. ♘×d4 a6 13. ♕c6 ♖c8 14. ♕e6+ ♕e7 15. 0-0 ♕×e6 16. ♘×e6 ♔f7 17. ♘×f8 ♖h×f8 18. e4 ♖fe8 19. f3 ♘c5 20. ♖d1 h6 21. ♗e3 ♔f8 22. ♖d6 ♖b8 23. ♖ad1 ♘cd7 24. ♖×d7 ♘×d7 25. ♖×d7 ♖e7 26. ♖×e7 ♔×e7 27. ♗×b6 ♔f7 28. ♘d5 ♖c8 29. ♗c7 ♔e6 30. ♔f2** *(see diagram)*
     1–0 (Source: *www.Chessgames.com*)

338   Menchik–Ruth Nakkerud
Buenos Aires—Women's World Championship, 1939
[D37] *Queen's Gambit Declined*

1. d4 d5 2. c4 e6 3. ♘c3 ♘f6 4. ♘f3 ♗e7 5. e3 0-0 6. ♗d3 d×c4 7. ♗×c4 ♘d5 8. 0-0 b6 9. ♕e2 ♗b7 10. e4 ♘×c3 11. b×c3 c5 12. ♗f4 ♘d7 13. ♖ad1 ♕c8 14. ♘d2 a6 15. a4 ♗c6 16. ♗b3 *(see diagram)*

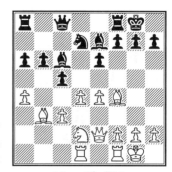

After 16. ♗b3

16. ... ♕**b7??** [16. ... c×d4 17. c×d4 e5 18. ♗×e5 ♘×e5 19. d×e5± —RT] **17. d5 e×d5 18. e×d5 ♗×d5 19. ♗×d5 ♕×d5 20. ♕×e7 ♖fe8 21. ♕d6 ♕×d6 22. ♗×d6 ♖e2 23. ♖fe1 ♖ae8 24. ♖×e2 ♖×e2 25. ♗f4 b5 26. a×b5 a×b5 27. ♗e3 ♘b6 28. ♔f1 ♖×e3 29. f×e3 ♘d5 30. ♘c4 ♘×e3+ 31. ♘×e3 h5 32. ♖d5 1–0** (Source: *www.Chess games.com*)

339 Menchik–Salome Reischer
Buenos Aires—Women's World Championship, 1939
[E16] *Queen's Indian Defense*

1. d4 ♘f6 2. ♘f3 e6 3. g3 b6 4. ♗g2 ♗b7 5. 0–0 ♕c8 6. c4 ♗e7 7. ♘c3 d5 8. c×d5 ♘×d5 9. ♖e1 0–0 10. e4 ♘×c3 11. b×c3 ♘d7 12. ♗b2 ♖d8 13. ♖c1 b5 14. ♘d2 ♖b8 15. ♖c2 ♘b6 16. ♕h5 ♘c4 17. ♘×c4 b×c4 18. ♗c1 ♗c6 19. ♕e2 ♗a4 20. ♖b2 ♕a6 21. ♗f4 ♖×b2 22. ♕×b2 ♕b6 23. ♕×b6 c×b6 24. ♗f1 b5 25. ♗c7 ♖d7 26. ♗a5 ♗c2 27. e5 ♗g6 28. ♗g2 (*see diagram*)

28. ... a6? [28. ... ♗d8 (the only move)=—RT] **29. ♗c6 ♗d8 30. ♗×d7 ♗×a5 31. ♖c1 1–0** (Source: *www.Chessgames.com*)

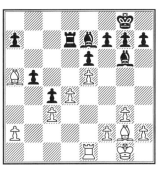

After 28. ♗g2

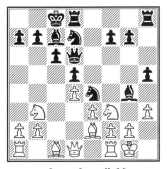

After 16. ... ♕d6

340 Elena Raclauskiene–Menchik
Buenos Aires—Women's World Championship, 1939
[D04] *ColleSystem*

1. d4 d5 2. e3 ♘f6 3. ♗d3 ♗g4 4. ♗e2 ♗f5 5. ♘f3 e6 6. ♘bd2 ♗d6 7. 0–0 ♘bd7 8. c3 ♕e7 9. ♘b3 ♘e4 10. ♗d3 0–0–0 11. c4 c6 12. c×d5 e×d5 13. ♘a5 ♗c7 14. ♘b3 ♗g4 15. ♗e2 h5 16. h3 ♕d6 (*see diagram*)

17. ♘e5 ♗×e2 18. ♕×e2 f6 19. ♘f3 g5 20. g3 g4 21. ♘h4 ♘×g3 22. f×g3 ♕×g3+ 0–1 (Source: *www.Chess-games.com*)

341 M. Stoffels–Menchik
Buenos Aires—Women's World Championship, 1939
[B40] *Sicilian*

1. e4 c5 2. ♗c4 e6 3. ♘f3 a6 4. a3 d5 5. e×d5 e×d5 6. ♗e2 ♘c6 7. c3 ♗d6 8. d3 ♘ge7 9. ♗g5 0–0 10. 0–0 ♖e8 11. ♗h4 ♕c7 12. ♗g3 ♘g6 13. ♔h1 ♘f4 14. ♘g1 ♗f5 15. b3 ♖ad8 16. ♖e1 ♘×d3 17. ♗×d3 ♖×e1 18. ♕×e1 ♗×d3 19. ♘d2 ♗×g3 20. h×g3 ♕e5 21. ♕×e5 ♘×e5 22. ♖e1 f6 23. ♘gf3 ♘c6 24. b4 d4 25. c×d4 c×b4 26. ♖e3 ♗f5 (*see diagram*)

0–1 (Source: *www.Chessgames.com*)

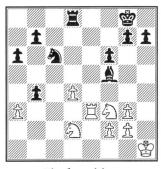

Final position

342 Dora Trepat de Navarro–Menchik

Buenos Aires—Women's World Championship, 1939

[D52] *Queen's Gambit Declined, Cambridge Springs Variation*

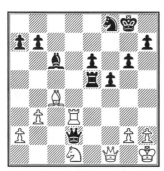

After 31. ♖d3

1. d4 ♘f6 2. c4 e6 3. ♘c3 d5 4. ♗g5 ♘bd7 5. e3 c6 6. ♘f3 ♕a5 7. ♗×f6 ♘×f6 8. ♕c2 ♗e7 9. ♗d3 0–0 10. 0–0 ♗d7 11. ♘e5 ♖fd8 12. b3 ♗e8 13. f4 g6 14. ♖f3?! ♘d7 15. ♖af1 ♘f8 16. ♖g3 f6 17. ♘f3 f5 18. ♖h3 c5 19. ♘d1? [19. ♖d1—RT] 19. ... ♖ac8 20. ♕e2 ♗f6 21. ♘e5? [Better is 21. d×c5 ♕×c5 22. ♘f2∓—RT] 21. ... c×d4 22. c×d5 ♗×e5 23. f×e5 ♕×d5 24. e×d4 ♕×d4+ 25. ♔h1 ♖c5 26. ♖e1 ♖dd5 27. ♕f3 ♖×e5 28. ♖×e5 ♖×e5 29. ♕f1 ♗c6 30. ♗c4 ♕d2 31. ♖d3 *(see diagram)*

31. ... ♕×g2+! Resigns because of 32. ♕×g2 ♖e1 mate 0–1 (Source: *www.Chessgames.com*; notes by RT)

Supplemental Games

343 J.H. Illot–Menchik
MacArthur Cup Hastings, February 2, 1924
[C02] *French, Advance Variation*

1. e4 e6 2. d4 d5 3. e5 c5 4. c3 ♘c6 5. ♘f3 ♕b6 6. ♗e2 c×d4 7. c×d4 ♗b4+ 8. ♘c3 ♘ge7 9. a3 ♗×c3+ 10. b×c3 0-0 11. ♕c2 ♗d7 12. ♗d3 ♘g6 13. h4 ♖fc8 14. h5 ♘f8 15. ♗g5 ♕a5 16. ♕c1 b5 17. ♗d2 ♕b6 18. ♖h4 ♘e7 19. g4 ♖ab8 20. g5 a5 21. g6 f×g6 22. h×g6 ♘e×g6 23. ♗×g6 ♘×g6 24. ♖h3 b4 25. a×b4 a×b4 26. ♖b1 b3 27. ♔f1 ♗b5+ 28. ♔g2 ♗d3 29. ♕h1 ♗×b1 30. ♕×b1 ♘f8 31. ♘g5 h6 32. ♘f3 b2 33. ♖g3 ♖a8 34. ♗×h6 ♖c7 35. ♗c1 ♖b7 36. ♗×b2 ♕×b2 0-1 (Source: *H&StLO*, February 9, 1924, p. 10)

344 Menchik–George M. Norman
Albany Cup Hastings, June 1924
[C14] *French, Classical*

1. e4 e6 2. d4 d5 3. ♘c3 ♘f6 4. ♗g5 ♗e7 5. e5 ♘fd7 6. h4 a6 7. ♕g4 ♗×g5 8. h×g5 c5 9. g6 h6 10. g×f7+ ♔×f7 11. 0-0-0 ♘c6 12. ♘×d5 c×d4 13. ♘f3 ♖e8 14. ♘f4 ♘f8 15. ♘h5 g6 16. ♕f4+ ♔e7 17. ♘f6 ♕a5 18. ♘×e8 ♔×e8 19. a3 b5 20. ♘×d4 ♗b7 21. ♘×c6 ♗×c6 22. ♖×h6 ♕b6 23. ♖h8 ♕c5 24. ♗d3 ♗d5 25. ♗×g6+ ♔d7 26. ♕f7+ ♔c6 1-0 (Source: *HSLO*, June 28, 1924, p. 2)

345 Menchik–T.J. Camon
Middlesex vs. Sussex Hastings, 1924
[D53] *Queen's Gambit Declined*

1. d4 d5 2. c4 e6 3. ♘c3 ♘f6 4. ♗g5 ♗e7 5. e3 ♘e4 6. ♗×e7 ♕×e7 7. c×d5 ♘×c3 8. b×c3 e×d5 9. ♕b3 c6 10. ♘f3 ♘d7 11. ♗d3 0-0 12. 0-0 ♖d8 13. a4 ♘f6 14. a5 ♖b8 15. c4 d×c4 16. ♗×c4 b5 17. a×b6 ♖×b6 18. ♕a2 ♘d5 19. ♕×a7 ♖b7 20. ♕a3 ♕f6 21. ♘e5 ♗f5 22. ♕c5 ♗e4 23. f3 ♕g5 24. f×e4 ♘×e3 25. ♖f2 ♖db8 26. ♗×f7+ ♔h8 27. ♗e8 1-0 (Source: *Sussex Daily News*, November 3, 1924)

346 Menchik–A.E. Smith

Hastings vs. Rest of Sussex Bd. 9 Hastings, 1925

[E22] Nimzo-Indian Defense

1. d4 ♘f6 2. c4 e6 3. ♘c3 ♗b4 4. ♕b3 ♗×c3+ 5. b×c3 d6 6. ♘f3 0-0 7. ♗g5 ♘bd7 8. e3 b6 9. ♗e2 ♗b7 10. a4 ♕e7 11. 0-0 h6 12. ♗h4 ♖fe8 13. a5 ♘f8 14. a×b6 a×b6 15. ♕b5 ♘g6 16. ♗×f6 ♕×f6 17. ♕b2 ♘h4 18. ♘×h4 ♕×h4 19. ♖fd1 ♕g5 20. ♗f1 ♗c6 21. ♖×a8 ♖×a8 22. ♖a1 ♖×a1 23. ♕×a1 ♕a5 24. ♕b2 ½–½ (Source: *QCH* #14, p. 341)

347 W. Winser–Menchik

Hastings Club Tournament, 1931

[E23] Nimzo-Indian

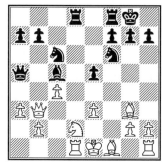

Nothing is available on this event except the following game.

1. d4 ♘f6 2. c4 e6 3. ♘c3 ♗b4 4. ♕b3 c5 5. d×c5 ♘c6 6. ♘f3 ♗×c5 7. ♗f4 0-0 8. e3 d5 9. ♖d1 ♕a5 10. ♘d2 d4 11. ♘cb1 e5 12. ♗g3 d×e3 13. f×e3 ♗f5 14. a3 ♗×b1 15. ♖×b1 ♖ad8 16. ♖d1 *(see diagram)*

16. ... ♘g4 17. ♕×b7 ♗×e3 18. b4 ♕×a3 19. ♕×c6 ♗×d2+ 20. ♔e2 ♕e3 mate 0-1 (*CS* 1931, v. 5, #702)

After 16. ♖d1

348 Menchik–Verveort

Simul Antwerp

[D11] Slav Defense

In this Antwerp tandem simultaneous, Menchik along with Karel Opočenský +12 –5 =3. The paper indicated that she competed in a tournament at this time, but all that is evident is the simultaneous exhibition.

1. ♘f3 d5 2. d4 ♘f6 3. c4 c6 4. e3 ♗g4 5. ♘bd2 ♘e4 6. ♕b3 ♕c7 7. c×d5 ♗×f3 8. g×f3 ♘×d2 9. ♗×d2 a6 10. ♖c1 ♕d7 11. ♗c4 c×d5 12. ♗×d5 ♘c6 13. ♕×b7 ♕×b7 14. ♗×c6+ 1-0 (Source: *HSLO*, November 17, 1928)

Blitz Games and Events

Like most players Menchik played and enjoyed many blitz games and tournaments. Her first recorded event was listed in the September 1940 issue of *Chess* as being held at the National Center. First place was captured by P.M. List (7 points) with second going to Saviely Tartakower (5 points). Menchik tied for third–fourth places with Imre König at 4 points. Rounding out the field were H. Israel, E. Brown, J. Strachstein and Dr. Stefan Fazekas. Vera lost the three games to those tying or exceeding her score while defeating the four others.

Many of the events were held at the Hastings Chess Club and West London Chess Club. Regarding the latter, her first recorded event was on 25 April 1942 where she placed fourth (4 points out of 7) behind Thomas, Klugman and Mieses. In the next event she was first (+6 –1). In the spring 1943 event she was again fourth with six points. In the summer of 1943 the club lightning tournament was won by Tartakower with seven; Vera took second place with five points.

As was the custom of that era the games were played at a rate of 10 seconds per move.[66]

349 Menchik–Edward G. Sergeant
West London Chess Club Lightning Tournament, London, November 28, 1942

[C14] *French, Classical Variation*

This is Menchik's only known surviving speed chess game.

1. d4 ♘f6 2. ♘c3 d5 3. ♗g5 e6 4. e4 ♗e7 5. e5 ♘fd7 6. h4 f6 7. ♕h5+ ♔f8 8. e×f6 ♘×f6 9. ♕f3 c5 10. d×c5 ♘c6 11. 0-0-0 *(see diagram)*
11. ... ♘e5 12. ♕e3 ♘fg4 13. ♕f4+ ♔e8 14. ♘h3 ♖f8 15. ♕a4+ ♗d7 16. ♕b4 ♕c7 17. ♗×e7 ♔×e7 18. ♖×d5 ♘c6 19. ♕×g4 e×d5 20. ♘×d5+ ♔d8 21. ♕g5+ 1-0 (Source: *WLCC Gazettte* #14, December 1942)

After 11. 0-0-0

350 Edward G. Sergeant–Menchik
Ladies vs. Gentlemen West London Chess Club, 1943

[C11] *French*

According to *Chess*, July 1943, this game was played in the Ladies vs. Gentlemen Match at the West London Chess Club.

1. e4 e6 2. d4 d5 3. ♘c3 ♘f6 4. ♗d3 c5 5. ♘f3 c×d4 6. ♘×d4 d×e4 [6. ... ♘c6 was better, and if 7. ♘×c6 b×c6 8. e5 ♘d7 9. ♗f4 ♕a5 10. 0-0 ♗a6 forcing the exchange of a useless bishop—RT] **7. ♘×e4 ♘c6** [Not 7. ... ♕×d4?? 8. ♗b5+—RT] **8. ♘×c6 b×c6 9. ♗g5 ♗e7 10. 0-0 ♘d5** [Here 10. ... ♘×e4 11. ♗×e7 ♔×e7! 12. ♗×e4 ♕×d1 13. ♖f×d1 ♗d7 might have been tried—RT] **11. ♗×e7 ♕×e7 12. c4 ♘b4** [12. ... ♘f4 was better since actually it does not pay Black to exchange the knight for the bishop—RT] **13. c5 0-0 14. a3** [If at once 14. ♘d6 then 14. ... ♗a6 15. ♗×a6 ♘×a6 16. ♕c1 ♖fd8 threatening 17. ... ♘×c5—RT] **14. ... ♘×d3?** This exchange allows the White knight to become a permanent fixture at d6, which has a very cramping effect on Black's game. **15. ♕×d3 ♖d8** [Black did not like 15. ... a5 because of 16. ♖fd1 and 17. ♕d6—RT] **16. ♘d6 a5** [16. ... e5 is not very promising because of 17. ♖fe1 and f4—RT] **17. ♕c3 ♗a6 18. ♖fd1 a4 19. ♖d4 ♗e2 20. f3 ♕f6 21. ♖e1 ♗b5 22. ♖ed1 h5** *(see diagram)*

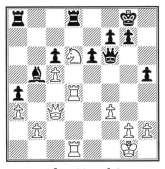

After 22. ... h5

23. ♘×b5 c×b5 24. ♖×d8+ ♖×d8 25. ♖×d8+ ♕×d8 26. c6! ♕b6+ 27. ♔f1 ♕a6 28. ♔e1 ♔f8 29. c7 ♔e8 30. ♕c5+ 1-0 (Source: *Chess*, July 1943, #1590; notes by VM [additional notes by RT])

* * *

The Southern Counties Chess Union Championship was the very last tournament for Menchik. With a 3–0 score she had qualified for the semifinals and was due to play her next game the day after her death. Her results included wins against A. Camperown (Middlesex), G.W. Rutland (Middlesex), and J.J. Moore (Essex).[67]

351 G. Rutland–Menchik
Southern Counties Chess Union (3), 1944
[C11] *French*

1. e4 e6 2. d4 d5 3. ♘c3 ♘f6 4. e5 ♘fd7 5. ♘ce2 c5 6. c3 ♘c6 7. f4 ♕b6 8. ♘f3 f6 9. a3 ♗e7 10. g3 cxd4 11. cxd4 0-0 12. ♗h3 fxe5 13. ♗xe6+ ♔h8 14. ♗xd5 ♘xd4 15. ♘fxd4 ♕a5+ 16. ♘c3 exd4 17. b4 ♗xb4 18. axb4 ♕xa1 19. ♘b5 ♘f6 20. ♗f3 ♗d7 21. ♘xd4 ♗a4 22. ♕d2 ♖ad8 23. ♕b2 ♕xb2 24. ♗xb2 ♖fe8+ 25. ♔f2 ♘e4+ 26. ♔g2 ♘d6 27. ♖a1 b5 28. ♘c6 ♖c8 29. ♗e5 ♘c4 30. ♘xa7 ♘xe5 31. fxe5 ♖c2+ 32. ♔h3 ♖xe5 33. ♗c6 g6 34. ♗xb5 ♗xb5 35. ♖a5 ♗d7+ 0-1 (Source: Polihroniade, *Campionii de Şah Al Lumii*)

* * *

352 Menchik–L. Kent
Simul London, 1944
[B24] *Sicilian, Closed Variation*

In this simultaneous, Vera's score was +22 =2.

1. e4 c5 2. ♘c3 ♘c6 3. g3 g6 4. ♗g2 ♗g7 5. ♘ge2 e6 6. 0-0 ♘ge7 7. d3 0-0 8. ♗e3 b6 9. ♕d2 ♖e8 10. ♗h6 ♗h8 11. ♘d1 d5 12. exd5 exd5 13. ♘f4 ♗b7 14. ♗g5 ♘b4 15. c3 f6 16. ♗h6 ♘f5 17. cxb4 ♘xh6 18. ♘xg6 ♗g7 19. ♘f4 ♖b8 20. bxc5 bxc5 21. ♘c3 d4 22. ♗xb7 dxc3 23. ♕xc3 ♖xb7 24. ♕xc5 ♖xb2 25. ♕c4+ ♔h8 26. ♘e6 ♕b6 27. ♘xg7 ♔xg7 28. ♖ac1 ♖ee2 29. ♕c7+ ♕xc7 30. ♖xc7+ ♔g6 31. ♖xa7 ♘g4 32. h4 ♖xa2 33. ♖xa2 ♖xa2 34. f3 ♘e5 35. d4 ♘c4 36. ♖c1 ♘e3 37. g4 h5 38. ♖e1 ♘d5 39. ♖e6 ♖g2+ 40. ♔xg2 ♘f4+ 41. ♔g3 ♘xe6 42. d5 ♘d8 43. gxh5+ ♔xh5 44. ♔f4 ½-½ (Source: *Times* [London], July 7, 1944)

353 Menchik–Elaine Saunders
Casual Game London
[D00] *Queen Pawn Opening*

This game was published in *BCM* (1625). Its origins are unknown, but it shows Menchik in a rare loss to another woman. Her opponent (born 7 January 1926, died 7 January 2012) later became a women's international master (WIM) and was a four time British Ladies' Champion as well as the two time Women's Junior World Champion.

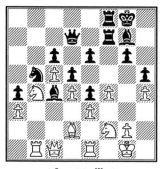

After 32. ♖e1

1. d4 d5 2. e3 c6 3. ♘d2 e6 4. ♗d3 f5 5. ♘h3 ♗d6 6. 0-0 ♕c7 7. f4 ♘f6 8. c4 ♘e4 9. ♗xe4 fxe4 10. ♕h5+ g6 11. ♕e2 ♘a6 12. c5 ♗f8 13. a3 ♗g7 14. b4 b6 15. ♖b1 bxc5 16. bxc5 ♕e7 17. ♕d1 ♘c7 18. ♘b3 ♗a6 19. ♖e1 ♗d3 20. ♖b2 a5 21. ♗d2? [21. a4 followed by 22. ♗d2 and the right continuation, should give White the better game—RT] 21. ... a4! 22. ♘c1 ♗b5 23. ♘a2 ♗c4 24. ♘f2 ♗b3 25. ♕c1 0-0 26. ♘b4 ♕d7 27. ♖b1 ♘b5 28. ♘g4 ♖f7 29. ♗f1 ♖af8 30. h4 h5 31. ♘f2 ♗c4 32. ♖e1 *(see diagram)*

32. ... e5!! 33. d×e5 ♗×e5 34. ♘×e4 d×e4 35. f×e5 ♗d3 [If at once 35. ... ♖f1+ then 36. ♔h2 Now Black threatens ... ♖f1+—RT] **36. ♘×d3 ♕×d3 37. ♗a5?** [37. ♗b4 was the only chance, but White has a bad game in any case—RT] **37. ... ♘×a3 38. ♖a1 ♘c2 39. ♖d1 ♕×e3+** [A still simpler way of winning was by 39. ... ♘a1! 40. ♖×d3 ♖f1+ 41. ♕×f1 ♖×f1+ 42. ♔×f1 e×d3 43. ♔e1 ♘b3 44. ♗c3 a3 etc.—RT] **40. ♕×e3 ♘×e3 41. ♖d6 ♖f1+ 42. ♖×f1 ♖×f1+ 43. ♔h2 ♘g4+ 44. ♔g3 ♘×e5 45. ♗c3 ♘d3 46. ♖×c6 e3 47. ♖×g6+ ♔f7 48. ♖g7+ ♔e6 49. ♖g6+ ♔d5 50. ♖d6+ ♔c4 51. c6 ♖f8 52. ♗a5 ♖c8 53. c7 a3 54. ♖d8 a2** Good enough, though it is interesting to point out here the following variation which is a favorite theme of so many endgame composers: 54. ... ♖×c7 55. ♗×c7 a2 56. ♖a8 e7 wins. **55. ♖×c8 a1♕ 56. ♖d8** *(see diagram)*

After 56. ♖d8

[It turns out that as late as her last move Menchik had a win with 56. ♖e8!! and there is no way to stop the promotion!—RT] **56. ... ♕e5+ 0–1** (Source: *Chess* #1625 [additional notes by RT])

354 Philip S. Milner-Barry–Menchik
Friendly Match Game
[C11] *French, Classical Variation*

1. e4 e6 2. d4 d5 3. ♘c3 ♘f6 4. ♗g5 ♗e7 5. e5 ♘fd7 6. h4 This is a promising variation for an attacking player, since even if it is not theoretically sound, White preserves tactical possibilities for a long period. **6. ... h6** [Russian analysts have recently revived the claims of 6. ... f6 7. ♗d3 f5 Other moves are 6. ... a6 and 6. ... c5—RT] **7. ♗e3 c5 8. ♕g4 ♔f8 9. ♖h3 c×d4 10. ♗×d4 ♘c6 11. ♖g3 ♖g8 12. ♘f3 ♘×d4 13. ♕×d4 ♕b6 14. ♕d2** Offering the b2 pawn to avoid the exchange of queens, which would leave only an equal position. **14. ... ♘c5** [But Black would have done best to accept the bait since White gets a strong attack in any case. After 14. ... ♕×b2 15. ♖b1 ♕a3 There does not seem to be any way of taking advantage of the unsatisfactory position of the Black queen—RT] **15. 0–0–0 ♕a5 16. ♘d4 a6 17. ♕f4 ♗d7 18. ♖f3 ♗e8 19. ♗d3 g5** This weakening move is forced for White threatens 20. ♗g6, and if 19. ... ♘×d3+ 20. ♖d×d3 (threatening 21. ♘×e6 mate) wins at once (21. ... ♕b6 22. ♘a4). **20. ♕e3 b5 21. ♔b1 b4 22. ♘×d5!?** A very interesting speculative sacrifice, which may have been analytically sound, but was uncalled for: since after 22. ♘be2 the knight can be rapidly transferred to the kingside by g3 and h5, before Black's counterattack (... ♕b6 ... a5–a4 etc.) becomes dangerous. [Fritz on the other hand finds 22. ♘ce2 and the text move to be a major error—RT] **22. ... e×d5 23. e6 f6 24. ♕e5** *(see diagram)*

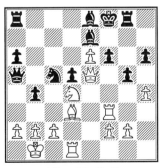

After 24. ♕e5

24. ... ♗h5? Rather a desperate measure. Black can try to hold the position by ... ♔g7 or ... ♕d8. [24. ... ♕d8 25. h×g5 (Milner-Barry suggests 25. ♕h2 but his 25. ... ♗d6 fails in light of *(25. ... ♕b8 26. g3 g4)*) 25. ... ♖×g5 26. ♕h2 h5 and despite the tension in the game, Black is in by far the preferable position—RT] **25. ♖×f6+ ♗×f6 26. ♕×f6+ ♔e8 27. g4** [Better and faster is 27. ♗h7 —RT] **27. ... ♘×d3 28. g×h5 ♕c7** [Not 28. ... ♖f8 29. ♕g6+ followed by ♘c6+—RT] **29. ♘f5 ♘e5** If the knight goes anywhere else, 30. ♘d6+ ♔×d6 31. ♕f7+. **30. ♖×d5 g×h4 31. c3** The game was broken off here, but Black resigned without resumption. White threatens 32. ♘d6+, if 31. ... ♖d8 32. e7 ♖×d5 33. ♘g7+ ♖×g7 (... ♔d7 34. ♕e6 mate) 34. ♕f8+ ♔d7 35. e8/♕ mate. If 31. ... ♘g4 32. ♘d6+ ♕×d6 33. ♕f7+. **1–0** (Source: *BCM* #8110; notes by Milner-Barry [additional notes by RT])

Epilogue

Some chess players react in shock or with great commiseration when a friend loses a game to a woman. Mostly this is expressed at the scholastic level. It is also still a given that girls and women are a minority in the chess community. In the United States about 20 percent of the scholastic tournament players are female and when one looks at the adult population it is not much more than 2 percent female. But the numbers are growing. Certainly there are more top female players, chess administrators, arbiters and coaches than ever before. It would be a rare active chess player nowadays who can state, "I've never lost to a woman!"

The Vacancy and Custodianship

After Menchik died the Women's World Champion title remained vacant for over five years. The Fédération Internationale des Échecs was occupied with getting a new (overall) world champion and qualifying cycle in place. This was achieved in 1948 when Mikhail Botvinnik won the Hague-Moscow tournament. The next order of business for both FIDE and the Soviet federation was the Women's title. The Soviets had of course been working very hard at building their program into a world power. One of the reasons for inviting Vera to the Moscow 1935 tournament was to expose their female players to a good role model and inspire them. She had after all been raised in Russia and represented the U.S.S.R. in her first win of the world title.

Elizaveta Ivanova Bikova upon winning the World Women's Championship in 1953. Miss Bikova wrote a Russian biography of Vera in 1957 (John G. White Chess Collection, Cleveland Public Library).

253

A 16 player round robin tournament was held in the Central Soviet Army Hall in Moscow from 19 December 1949 through 18 January 1950. First prize was 10,000 rubles (about $1,100) with fifth through seventh places receiving 2,000 rubles; of course the ruble was not a desirable currency to most of the world.

Moscow 1949-1950 Women's World Chess Championship

	1	2	3	4	5	6	7	8	9	10	11	12	13	14	15	16	Pts.	Place
1 Rudenko, Liudmila (USSR)	•	1	1	d	d	d	d	1	1	1	1	1	1	0	d	1	12	1
2 Rubtsova, Olga (USSR)	0	•	1	1	d	d	d	0	d	1	1	1	1	1	1	d	11	2
3 Bikova, Elizaveta (USSR)	0	0	•	d	1	1	1	1	0	1	d	1	d	1	d	1	10	3–4
4 Belova, Valentina (USSR)	d	0	d	•	1	1	1	0	0	0	1	1	1	1	1	1	10	3–4
5 Tranmer, Eileen (G. Britain)	1	1	0	0	•	1	0	1	1	d	d	1	1	1	d	1	9½	5–7
6 Chaudé de Silans, C. (France)	d	d	0	0	0	•	1	1	0	d	1	1	1	1	1	1	9½	5–7
7 Keller, Edith (Germany)	d	d	0	0	1	0	•	1	1	d	1	1	0	1	1	1	9½	5–7
8 Heemskerk, Fenny (Holland)	0	1	0	1	0	0	0	•	1	d	d	d	1	1	1	d	8	8
9 Benini, Clarice (Italy)	0	d	1	1	0	1	0	0	•	0	0	1	d	0	1	1	7	9
10 Langos, Józsa (Hungary)	0	0	0	1	d	d	d	d	1	•	d	0	0	0	1	0	6	10–11
11 Mora, María Teresa (Cuba)	0	0	d	0	d	0	0	d	1	d	•	1	1	1	0	0	6	10–11
12 Karff, Mona May (USA)	0	0	0	0	0	0	0	d	0	1	0	•	d	1	1	1	5	12–14
13 Hrušková-Bělská, Nina (Pol.)	0	0	d	0	0	0	1	0	d	1	0	d	•	0	1	d	5	12–14
14 Gresser, Gisela (USA)	1	0	0	0	0	0	0	0	1	1	0	0	1	•	0	1	5	12–14
15 Larsen, Ingrid (Denmark)	d	0	d	0	d	0	0	0	0	0	1	0	0	1	•	1	4½	15
16 Hermanowa, Róża (Poland)	0	d	0	0	0	0	0	d	0	d	1	0	d	0	0	•	3	16

Gerald Abrahams attended as a journalist and observed that "This tournament produced no Menchik." On the other hand he had the highest praise for the organization and direction of the tournament.[68]

Starting in 1952, FIDE organized Candidates tournaments to determine the challenger. The winner of the first Candidates was Elizaveta Bikova, who went on to capture the title. After Olga Rubtsova won the 1955 Candidates; a three way match of Bikova, Rubtsova and Rudenko was held with Olga coming out on top. Bikova then won a rematch and, for the first time since Menchik, successfully defended her title in 1959 against Kira Zvorikina.

Although the consensus is that the three Russians were not on Vera's level, there is some argument on the subject. Certainly when comparing their results with Menchik's against players of both eras, such as Graf, Gresser, Karff and others, they exhibited dominance. Unfortunately they never played against the top men to any degree so it is difficult to determine. At any rate they were very active in many areas of chess. Rubtsova in her 60s became the Women's World Correspondence Champion as well as an International Arbiter. Kira Zvorikina was also an IA. Bikova wrote a number of books, including the first biography of Menchik and books about the Women's World Championship and chess in the Soviet Union.

The Georgian Dominance

In 1961 Nona Gaprindashvili of Georgian S.S.R. burst onto the scene by winning the Vrnjacka Banja Candidates with two points to spare. A year later she beat Bikova by a score of 9–2 (+7 −0 =4) to capture the world title; the start of a 16 year reign. Nona won three matches against the Russian Alla Kushnir and in 1975 beat fellow Georgian Nana Alexandria. In 1980 Nona was the first woman to be awarded the (non-gendered) Grandmaster (GM) title. The title was based in part on her first place result at the Lone Pine tournament in 1977. Some controversy arose as Nona had not fully met (some recently altered) FIDE regulations, and this has allowed Zsuzsa (later Susan) Polgar to correctly state that she was the first person to "earn" the GM title.[69]

Next up was Maia Chiburdanidze, also of Georgia, who defeated Nona by a score of 8½–6½. Although only drawing in her first title defense, against Nana Alexandria (1981), it was enough to retain her title. She then won matches against Irina Levitina (1984), Elena Akhmilovskaya (1986), and Nana Ioseliani (1988). Maia was the second woman to achieve the GM title.

The Modern Era

Towards the end of the reign of Georgian women a new phenomenon was making itself felt—the Polgars. Unlike the previous top women they had little or no interest in playing in women's events. Gaprindashvili and Chiburdanidze certainly played in open (men's) events and had accumulated a number of male scalps, but they were still thought of as "less" than the men. The Polgars, as is well known, were part of an experiment by their father to determine whether excellence/genius in a field was based on nature or nurture. The nature and results of that experiment are beyond the scope of this book, but the impact is not.

Judit became the eighth highest ranked player in the world and, after marriage and motherhood, is still in the top 20. As a child she won several age-based world championships (not female world championships one should note) and as an adult plays almost exclusively in super elite "men's" events. Virtually her only concession to women's chess was in 1988 when she played on Board Two for the Hungarian women's team, scoring 12½ points out of 13. Thereafter she played for the "men's" team. Without any question she is the strongest female chess player of all time.

Susan (born Zsuzsa), the eldest sister, became the third woman to receive the GM title (and the first to earn it by strict FIDE standards). Like her sisters she played mostly males—defeating numerous grandmasters in the process. In 1992, however, she decided to go for the Women's title. After winning the Candidates tournament decisively she only draw her qualifying match against Ioseliani and, on tie-breaks, lost her chance for a title match. Three years later she again won the Candidates tournament and this time demolished Chiburdanidze in the playoff match to earn a shot at Xie Jun, the titleholder. After winning the title by a score of 8½–4½ she gave every expectation of defending the title, but in a mass of charges, counter-charges, and controversy regarding the organizing of the match she ended up forfeiting the title.

Susan determined that her goals included promoting women in chess in her adopted country, the United States, and to that end she decided to play in the 2004 Women's Olympiad in Calvia. Garry Kasparov was brought in to work with Susan, Irina Krush, Anna Zatonskih and Jennifer Shahade. At the Olympiad they won the silver team medal behind the Chinese, with Susan taking the Board One gold medal.

In 2016 Susan was working as a collegiate chess coach and an organizer of women's chess tournaments.

Sofia, the youngest sister had one of the highest rated performances ever in Rome 1989 and has attained the IM title. Although there is little doubt she could have earned the GM title, she has chosen to largely give up competitive chess.

Since 1999 when Susan Polgar stepped down as Women's World Champion the title has become quite mobile—going to no fewer than seven players (See Appendix 2 for a complete listing) with the Chinese providing four of the champions. All of these players have the Grandmaster title and are a legitimate threat to any player.

Certainly no player can sneer at women's chess anymore. There were in 2016 more than 20 female GMs from at least 10 countries. Prominent chess politicians include FIDE Vice President WIM Beatriz Marinello, Estonian Chess Federation President Carmen Kass, former United States Chess Federation President Susan Polgar and former U.S.C.F. Secretary Rachel Lieberman.

International Arbiter Carol Jarecki was the Chief Arbiter in the Kasparov vs. Anand match. Dr. and WGM Jana Bellin of England is the chair of the FIDE Medical Commission, which oversees the Fédération's compliance with the International Olympic Committee's anti-doping regulations. Chess authors include WGM Jennifer Shahade (U.S.C.F. website editor, *Chess Bitch*, *Play Like a Girl*) and GM Susan Polgar. Prominent female chess coaches of strong scholastic teams abound in numerous countries.

If we could get the number of "serious" girls up to even 75 percent of the boys we would obviously have a renaissance of chess worldwide. Certainly we are not there yet, but progress is being made and as we produce more role models, like Vera Menchik, the number of new female players and promoters will grow.

PART III.
THE WRITINGS
OF VERA MENCHIK

–1–

"The Max Lange Attack"

From the *Social Chess Quarterly*—October 1932—Vol. 3: pp. 212–214

• • • •

To make the last lesson more complete, we will look now at some examples of the Max Lange Attack.

This very complicated offshoot of the Giuoco Piano differs greatly from its parent opening in this, that when the other often leads to a rather quiet game, hence the name Giuoco Piano—Max Lange is exceedingly tricky and gives a game full of surprises. White's sacrifice of a pawn offers him limitless possibilities for combinative play. So difficult is Black's game, that, since Marshall defeated Tarrasch in 1910. no modern master is willing to give White a chance to play it.

After the usual moves—**1. e4 e5 2. ♘f3 ♘c6 3. ♗c4 ♗c5 4. 0-0 ♘f6 5. d4 e×d4 6. e5**—we reach the turning point in the opening. If Black accepts the challenge, he answers here with **6. ... d5** [Steinitz recommended 6. ... ♘g4—RT] We must try now to find out what compensation White gets for his pawn. To say that he gave it up with a view of obtaining superior development, would not be quite correct—the chief point of the sacrifice is the clearing of the e-file, which at once becomes for Black a source of great worry. White continues therefore: **7. e×f6 d×c4 8. ♖e1+!** Here we must note that had White delayed taking advantage of the open-file and tried first 7. ♗b3 or ♗d3, Black would have obtained a satisfactory game with ♘e4 followed by ♗g4; also it must be remembered that from now on White should conduct the attack very energetically, because if Black is allowed to come out of the middle game unscratched, in the end game his advanced pawns become distinctly unpleasant. So after **8. ... ♗e6** (in reply to 8. ♖e1+), White makes a double threat, **9. ♘g5** *(see diagram)*

He attacks the g5 bishop and at the same time threatens to win the other bishop by 10. ♘×e6 f×e6 11. ♕h5+ and ♕×c5. To meet both threats Black has only one move, **9. ... ♕d5**

After 9. ♘g5

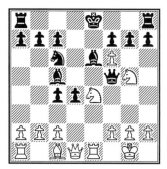

After 11. ♘ce4

[9. ... ♕×f6 of course does not defend the c5 bishop, and 9. ... ♕d6 loses on account of 10. ♘e4 ♕d5 11. f×g7 ♖g8 12. ♘f6+—RT] Now the open position of the Black queen gives White further opportunity to gain time and bring another piece into the game: **10. ♘c3 ♕f5** The knight cannot be taken because of 11. ♕×d5, [Also if 10. ... ♕d7 11. f×g7 ♖g8 12. ♖×e6+ f×e6 13. ♕h5+ ♔d8 14. ♘ce4 ♗e7 15. ♕f7 and wins—RT] **11. ♘ce4** *(see diagram)*

In this position Black has four possible moves at his disposal: 0–0–0, ♗b6, ♗d6 or ♗f8. Since castling seems natural and safest, we will consider it first.

As soon as Black castles, his e6 bishop becomes unpinned, and so, White, having no further use for the knight at g5, takes it off: **11. ... 0–0–0 12. ♘×e6 f×e6 13. g4** This is a very interesting move; the idea here is not merely to drive the Black queen away from the defense of the bishop, but it is a far reaching plan to gain time, and prepare for f×g6 which he afterwards intends to support with the bishop at h6, and in turn to be able to support the bishop, when necessary, with g5. **13. ... ♕e5 14. f×g7 ♖hg8 15. ♗h6 d3** [15. ... ♗e7 16. ♕f3 etc.—RT] **16. c3 d2 17. ♖e2** [Not 17. ♘×d2 ♕f6 attacking the bishop and the f2–pawn—RT] **17. ... ♗b6 18. ♕f1 ♖d3 19. ♖d1 ♘d8 20. g5** just in time to meet ♘f7, to which he can reply with ♘g3 threatening the d-pawn, and also the knight is in an excellent position from which he may later get to f6 via h5.

As there is no space to treat this line of play in any detail, we will turn back to Diagram II, and see what comes out of Black's 1. ... ♗b6 or ♗f8 instead of 11. ... 0–0–0.

For continuation to Black's 11. ... ♗b6 we will refer to game No. 54, Where White answers it with 12. ♘g3 ♕×f6 (better 12. ... ♕g6) 13. ♘h5 ♕g6 *(see diagram)*

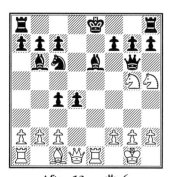

After 13. ... ♕g6

14. ♘×e6 f×e6 15. ♖×e6+ ♕×e6 16. ♘×g7+ and ♘×e6 winning easily.

After 18. ♖×e6

Had Black played 12. ... ♕g6 there might have followed: 13. ♘×e6 f×e6 14. ♖×e6+ ♔d7 15. ♘h5! ♖hg8! 16. ♘f4 ♕f7 and Black is in no immediate danger; White can improve on his 12th move, however and play 12. f×g7 instead Then of course, 12. ... ♖g8 13. g4 ♕g6 14. ♘×e6 f×e6 15. ♗g5 ♖×g7 16. ♕f3 now we see the point of White's 13th move. 16. ... ♔d7 17. ♘f6+ ♔c8 18. ♖×e6 *(see diagram)*

This interesting offer of a bishop is the quickest way to victory.; 18. ... ♕×g5 19. h4 ♕g6 (if 19. ... ♕×h4 20. ♖e8+ ♘d8 21. ♕f5+ wins.) 20. h5 ♕g5 21. ♖ae1 (threat 22. ♖e8+ Nd8 23. ♖×d8+ ♔×d8 24. Re8 mate) 21. ... ♘d8 22. ♖6e5 ♕h4 23. ♕f5+ ♔b8 24. ♘d7+ ♖×d7 25. ♕×d7 c6 26. ♖e8 ♕g5 27. ♖1e7 and wins. Black does best to play 19. ... ♕h5, but this only prolongs the game, eventually losing more or less in the same way.)

Had Black played 12. ... ♕g6 there might have followed: 13. ♘×e6 f×e6 14. ♖×e6+ ♔d7

15. ♘h5! ♖hg8! 16. ♘f4 ♕f7 and Black is in no immediate danger; White can improve on his 12th move, however and play.)

The third possibility, Black's 11. ... ♗f8 Rubinstein's Defense, protects the king's side, but here also Black never gets a chance of castling, because White immediately stops it by 12. ♘×f7 The knight must be taken, so 12. ... ♔×f7 (12. ... ♗×f7? 13. ♘d6+) 13. ♘g5+ ♔g8 (or ♔g6) 14. g4 ♕d5 (the intention of White's last move was to force the Black queen to such a square where White can play ♘×e6 with a threat; of course if (14. ... ♕×g4+ 15. ♕×g4 ♗×g4 16. f7 mate; 14. ... ♕g6 15. f×g7 ♗×g7 16. ♖×e6 etc.) 15. ♘×e6 ♖c8 16. ♘f4 ♕f7 17. f×g7 ♗×g7 18. ♘h5 h6 19. f4 ♔h7 20. ♕f3 ♖he8 21. ♗d2 etc., is decidedly in White's favor. This is an analysis by Dr. Tartakower; for fuller notes see the Modern Chess Openings or Wiener Schachzeitung, 1924.

Now just a few general remarks before we finish.

Although the Max Lange Attack is rather difficult to play for a beginner, and our analysis of it has been very brief and incomplete, these examples are really instructive. They teach us that a rook can be just as useful in the middle game, as it is in the end game. For Black's benefit, in order to avoid the more complicated forms of this attack, we suggest 6. ... ♘g4 (instead of 6. ... d5) but even then after 7. ♗f4 d6 8. e×d6 ♗×d6 9. ♖e1 ♗e7 10. ♗b5 0–0 11. ♗c6. White still has the better game. Little help, however, would Black get out of 5. ... ♗×d4 (instead of e×d4), because White plays 6. ♘×d4 ♘×d4 7. f4 with a strong attack—RT]

–2–

"Studies in Pawn Play"

From the *Social Chess Quarterly*—January 1933—vol. 3: pp. 242–245

• • • •

Study of the end-game, like that of any other subject, should first of all begin on broad general lines and not with the analysis of single positions. To be able to get a clear idea of it, we must above all try to remember that the end-game is not a separate isolate part of the game, but is something, which is the natural outcome of all our preceding plans and maneuvers. There are three important questions which must not be overlooked: (1) How do we distinguish the end-game from the middle-game? (2) What is the most important factor of the end-game? (3) What influence and connection has the opening with the end-game? To these we shall turn our immediate attention, and since all three questions are closely bound together, I shall not attempt to answer each separately, but will try to draw a rough picture of the end-game as a whole.

Usually we distinguish the end-game from the middle-game by a greatly reduced number of pieces, particularly by the absence of queens; queen endings are comparatively rare. The exchanges which in the course of time take place alter the general aspect of the game, though still leaving plenty of play in it. For example, in the middle-game the attack often centers around the king, sometimes ending in an overwhelming victory—in the end-game this is hardly ever possible because we are left with too little material even to contemplate such an attack. From this we see, and experience confirms it, that in the end-game the king is comparatively free from danger. There is no need for him, therefore, to hide away in a distant corner, he CAN and SHOULD comes out towards the center and take an active part in the game. In fact when the pieces are finally reduced to a bare minimum, the king undoubtedly becomes an attacking piece, but in the early stages of the end-game, he can serve most usefully for purposes of defense, for example a king at f2 (or f7 for Black) guards e1, e2 and e3 and so prevents an opponents rook from entering there. This is a point of vital importance, but few beginners realize it, and lose their game even in very promising positions, simply because they will not use their king, which means, of course, that the battle is being fought a piece down.

Bearing in mind what has been said before, it is not difficult to guess what we are really striving for in the end-game. The end-game is a game of pawns. If we want to win, but see no means of doing so with only a couple of minor pieces at our disposal, then we must try to add to our forces, that is we hope to do so by forcing a pawn through and making it into a queen. A pawn therefore, is a most important factor in the end-game; and we also soon convince ourselves that it is a factor which really influences the whole game. It is through the pawn-skeleton (the general pawn arrangement) that the opening is connected with the end-game, for any weakening of the pawn-formation in the early part of the game, affects our chances of winning later on. Again it is the pawn-skeleton which gives the game its characteristics and differences of structure, which we notice, for example, between a king pawn and queen pawn game, and last but not least, we curiously observe that it is not the pawns that adapt themselves to the play of the pieces, but the pieces adapt themselves to the position of pawns.

It is natural, of course, to expect that certain pawn-positions will be more favorable than others, and so I give a diagram illustrating three types, and all commonly occurring in the end-game.

Beginning with a White pawn in the middle of the board, we come across an isolated pawn. Usually such a pawn is considered rather weak, because it has no pawn support, so that when attacked it must be defended with a piece. On the left-hand side we see another isolated pawn—a Black pawn. The difference between the two is that the first is a passed pawn, it will meet no opposition as it goes on to queen and the second is not. For attacking purposes, the first is, of course, more useful, but in this position it is the least valuable since it is securely stopped, and the Black pawn is acting as an excellent defensive piece in blocking the two White pawns. Let us now look at these White pawns; are they strong attacking pawns? No, they are not; and here we have an example of a very unsatisfactory pawn position. When two pawns are opposed by one, we naturally expect to get a passed pawn; in this case it is not possible (without the loss of a pawn) since the would be passed pawn (the pawn at a2) is blocked which leaves White with a backward pawn instead; this is a truly bad pawn, it has no pawn support, and no pawn by its side to help it on. Turning now to the Black pawns on the right, we see two united passed pawns. This is the strongest combinations that we can ever hope to get, because they are self supporting, that is if the king were actually to attack and capture the supporting pawn the other goes on, and the king is just one move too late to prevent it queening. The fact that Black has these two pawns with no compensating factor on White's side, leaves him here with a very easy win, which I trust even a beginner to find. A very interesting situation arises if we alter the position slightly by putting a White pawn at b2 instead of b3. In the position on Diagram I it makes no difference who moves first, Black wins in either case; no however, White has counter chances on the queen's side, and wins if allowed to take the first move, but draws if Black moves first. The play will be:

1. a4	b×a3		1.	h5
2. b×a3	h5		2. a4	b×a3
3. a4	h4		3. b×a3	h4
4. a5	h3		4. a4	h3
5. ♔f3! (a)			5. ♔f3	♔×e5
			6. ♔g3 (b)	

Notes—(a) Wins, because Black cannot stop both pawns. (b) Draw; if we allowed Black one more moves last time he would have won with g5 , and if then .♔g3, g4 and the two pawns are self supporting, so that the king can leave them alone, go across to the queen's side, capture the remaining pawn, and then return to help one of the pawns to queen.

Now I give a position where White is a pawn up, but has to go a long ways before we can definitely say that it is a win for White; the question is how should we try to win, and how should we value the position.

First of all we notice that White has three pawns to two on the king's side, which should, of course, give him a passed pawn there. By the position of these pawns we can even tell that it will be the f-pawn, because it has no pawns facing it—that is we advance our pawns to f5 and g5 then play f6, and we have a passed pawn. The next question is has Black got a counter chance on the queen's side? Here we observe that the pawns in this side are not symmetrically placed, which might lead to both sides ob-taining passed pawns (it should be the a-pawn for Black and the c-pawn for White). If Black is allowed to pass his a-pawn he will get a distinct counterattacking possibility, because the White king must hasten to stop it, allowing Black full liberty to attack the king's side.

This could happen in the following way (diagram above), and White actually has no means of saving the game: **1. ... a4 2. b×a4** [2. b4 ♚e6 3. ♚c3 ♚f5 4. ♚b2 ♚e4 5. c4 b×c4 6. ♚a3 c3 7. b5 c2 8. ♚b2 ♚d3 9. ♚c1 a3 wins—RT] **2. ... b×a4 3. ♚c3 ♚c5! 4. ♚b2 ♚b4 5. c3+ ♚c4 6. ♚a3 ♚×c3 7. ♚×a4 ♚d3 8. ♚b4 ♚e3 9. ♚c4 ♚f3 10. ♚d4 ♚×g3 11. ♚e5 ♚g4!** [11. ... ♚×h4? 12. ♚f6 ♚g4 13. ♚×g6 draws—RT] **12. ♚f6 ♚×f4! 13. ♚×g6 ♚g4 14. ♚f6 ♚×h4 15. ♚f5 ♚g3** and wins. All this arose through White playing his pawns badly early on; a block on the king's side is quite unpardonable, nor is it at all necessary to allow Black a passed pawn on the queen's side. let us see how it should be correctly treated.

1. ♚e2 (The king is now an attacking piece) **1. ... ♚e6 2. ♚e3 ♚d5 3. f4 h5 4. g3** (preparing h3 and g4; if h3 at once then h4 and the pawns are blocked) **4. ... a5 5. ♚d3** [Of course not 5. b3 b5 and a4 and Black obtains a passed pawn—RT] **5. ... b5 6. h3 a4 7. c3** (had Black played 6. ... b4, then of course 7. b3) **7. ... ♚c5 8. g4 h×g4 9. h×g4 ♚d5 10. f5 ♚e5 11. ♚e3 ♚d5 12. g5 ♚e5 13. f6 g×f6 14. g×f6 ♚×f6 15. ♚d4** and wins as Black cannot save his pawns. Let us suppose that this time Black refuses to move any of his at all, how do we proceed to win then? The method is just the same, we try to push back the opponent's king as far as possible, eventually attacking on the side on which he is not; the game may continue **1. ♔e2 ♚e6 2. ♔e3 ♚d5 3. f4 ♚c5 4. ♔e4! ♚d6 5. g4 ♚e6 6. f5+ ♚f6 7. ♔f4 h6 8. h4 ♚f7 9. g5 h×g5+ 10. h×g5 ♚e7 11. ♔e5 ♚f7 12. ♔d6** and wins easily.

These examples have shown us how important pawns are, and I hope that some players have learnt their lesson and realize now that a game of chess can be won by other means than a direct attack on the king. In fact my advice to all who wish to get a deeper insight in the game is, "Study the end-game, and do not be afraid of exchanging pieces when you are a pawn up, provided there is no marked weakness in your pawn-position. Remember, it is easier to learn to play accurately when the board is fairly clear, than when it is crowded."

–3–

"How to Meet an Attack"

From the *Social Chess Quarterly*—January 1935—Vol. 5: pp. 479–482

• • • •

"Counter-attack is the soul of the game," said Blackburne, and all the authorities agree that counter-attack is the best possible defense.

It is useful, therefore to remember that in the times of need when we are faced with a very cramped or even a lost game, our best chance of recovering the balance is to introduce complications. Often through energetic handling alone, games which appeared to be hopelessly lost, have been pulled out of the fire and saved. In such cases had the tactics adopted by the defensive side been merely passive, the loss would have been inevitable even if slow.

To know anything about the remedy we must first of all know something about the disease, and so to begin with let us settle what sort of an attack we will try to meet. For convenience sake we will divide these into three groups: (1) Attack in the center; (2) Attack on the king's side; and (3) Attack on the queen's side.

Our choice this time will be a king's side Attack arising from White's 6. h4 in the French Defense, a move at one time greatly favored by Dr. Alekhine. As will be seen from the variations below 6. h4 leads to a very keen fight indeed, but in analyzing and judging the lines of play given, the student must remember the following:—That we are not analyzing an Opening, but studying an Attack, therefore there may be plenty of lines of play not mentioned. That everybody's play is more or less influenced by the individual's temperament so that different players may adopt different methods in their attempt to exploit an opponent's weakness, eventually arriving perhaps at the same result; both players however will be guided by the same considerations and principles, which are automatically decided for all of us be the nature of the position. Thus we know that to be successful with our attack against the king (or any given spot) we must be able to bring to that place a greater number of pieces than our opponent has available for the defense, which shows that a counter-attack usually takes place on a different side of the board. For example if A is attacking on the queen's side, B's best policy would be to threaten A in the Center or on the king's side—adopting aggressive tactics; on the Q's side; B cannot hope to establish a Counter-Attack, because we know already that A has there a greater number of pieces than B: Should B, however, busy himself on the queen's side it would probably consist of purely defensive tactics.

Alekhine's Attack in the French Defense is a very good example of what has been said, and the study of the following variations will illustrate the argument more clearly.

After the conventional moves: **1. e4 e6 2. d4 d5 3. ♘c3 ♘f6 4. ♗g5 ♗e7 5. e5 ♘fd7 6. h4**

Diagram 1
After 6. h4

we arrive at the following position (see diagram 1). Here White has very good possibilities on the king's side, since he was able to advance the center-pawn to e5 driving away Black's king's knight from the protection of that side. White's last move 6. h4 was expressly made with the view of sustaining the tension on the king's wing in order to attack it immediately. Had he continued, however, 6. ♗×e7, then ♛×e7 and the exchange of bishops would have developed Black's game, bringing on another piece to the king's side and so hindering a direct attack. The only question is how should Black reply to 6. h4? This we can only answer after some further analysis, but we do notice that if White were allowed to make another move he would play ♛g4 threatening ♗×e7 and ♛×g7. And so Black must find a line of play that will meet (make ineffective) ♛g4. New we will see that threats can be parried either be neutral, defensive play, or by a direct counter-threat on a different side of the board which calls for immediate attention.

(A)

6. ... ♗×g5 7. h×g5 ♛×g5 8. ♘h3! ♛e7 9. ♘f4 a6 10. ♛g4 g6 11. 0-0-0 c5 12. ♛g3 ♘b6 (threat 13. ♘c×d5) **13. d×c5 ♛×c5 14. ♗d3 ♛f8 15. ♗e4 d×e4 16. ♘×e4 ♘8d7 17. ♛c3** *(see diagram 2)*

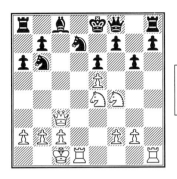

Diagram 2
After 17. ♕c3

(B)

6. ... f6 7. ♗d3 f×g5 8. ♕h5+ ♔f8 9. h×g5 ♗×g5 10. ♖h3 *(see diagram 3)*

Diagram 3
After 10. ♖h3

(C)

6. ... h6 7. ♗×e7 ♕×e7 8. ♕d2 0-0 9. 0-0-0 c5 10. f4 c×d4 11. ♘b5 ♘c6 12. g4 *(see diagram 4)*

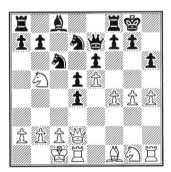

Diagram 4
After 12. g4

(D)

6. ... 0-0 7. ♗d3 c5 8. ♘h3 ♖e8 or ♕a4 (the move in the text threatens **9. ♗×e7** followed by **♗×h7+**) **9. ♘b5 f5 10. ♘d6 c×d4 11. ♘×e8 ♕×e8 12. ♗b5** *(see diagram 5)*

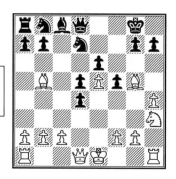

Diagram 5
After 12. ♗b5

Although we are not able to analyze each variation thoroughly, a brief comment on each might help the reader to get a better insight of the position. In the column (A), White obtains a decisive attack, as Black's gain of a pawn entailed a considerable loss of time. White is even able to sacrifice a piece to press his attack, and careful analysis will show that at move 12. Nc×d5 followed by N×d5[70] and e6 was threatened, and a little later a sacrifice on g6. Column (B), does not promise Black any more that does the first one, for the piece he has gained will have to be given back when White plays Rf6, whereupon White will castle on the Q's side leaving Black with a badly compromised position. Column (C) is much more interesting to us theoretically, for here White can simply exchange the bishops, transposing the game into an ordinary classical variation, which would be unsatisfactory for him should he castle on the kings side, but rather more advantageous than the normal variation after he castles on the queen's side, because Black's pawn at h6 is then a source of weakness. There is more however to be said of this variation than for the two previous, and the column by no means exhausts all the possibilities. In the Column D, White again seems to have it all his own way; and if this is the best Black can do the variation would appear to drive the French Defense out completely. That is not the case, however, the trouble so far was because Black has failed to spot White's weak points and has met 6. h4 too passively.

If we were to look for the solution in our early generalizations, we would be able to apply them here as follows: White is intending to follow 6. h4 with Qg4 making a direct attack on the king's wing, but will, through this, leave his own queen's wing protected by one piece, the knight. White has a strong pawn in the center which has passed the middle line, and unless we succeed in weakening it, he will always have the better game. How can we weaken this advanced pawn? Well, naturally by removing its support, and so we strike a blow in the center and play 6. ... c5. It is not a move that is going to defeat White immediately, but it is a move which will give Black a sporting chance as it not only attacks the center, but also opens up a road by which his pieces will be able to reach the Q's side to start a counter-attack against the White king.

Let us see now how Black should continue if White still tries 7. Qg4, also what he should do in reply to 7. Nb5 which threatens to dislodge the Black king with Nd6+. The variations which will follow may puzzle a careful player, for Black readily moves his king, giving up the privilege of castling, and does not seem to suffer for it any great hardships. That of course is entirely a matter of circumstances, and the compensating factor in this case is no doubt the fact that through this Black gains in development and is able to quickly to start a counter-attack against the White king, sometimes succeeding in compelling him also to give up castling.

(E)

6. ... c5 7. ♕g4 ♘c6 8. ♗×e7 ♚×e7 9. ♕×g7 ♖g8 10. ♕×h7 ♘×d4 11. f4 ♘b6 Threatening ♘c4. (not 11. ... ♘f5? 12. ♘×d5+)—RT] **7. h×g5 ♕×g5 8. ♘h3! ♕e7 9. ♘f4 a6 10. ♕g4 g6**

(F)

6. ... c5 7. ♕g4 ♘c6 8. ♗×e7 ♚×e7 9. ♘f3 c×d4 10. ♘b5 ♕a5+ 11. ♔d1 ♘d×e5 12. ♕×g7 ♗d7 13. ♘×e5 ♘×e5 14. ♘×d4 ♘c6

(G)

6. ... c5 7. ♘b5 c×d4 8. ♘d6+ ♔f8 9. ♗×e7+ ♕×e7 10. ♘×c8 ♕b4+ 11. ♔d2 ♕×b2 12. ♖d1 ♘c6 13. ♘d6 ♘d×e5 14. ♘b5 ♖c8

In the column (E) White clearly gets the worst of it since the capture of the king's pawn assists Black's development who can easily recover his pawns and threatens with Nc5 to trap the queen. Black can also be quite certain of a draw if he plays 10. ... c×d4 [*sic*] instead of Rg8. White then has nothing better that to draw the game by perpetual checks, because if he tries 11. Nb5 Qg8 the exchange of queens leaves Black with quite a satisfactory endgame. In the next column White certainly has a little the better of it, but hardly enough to frighten Black from adopting this line of defense. White can also obtain a slightly better end-game if he plays 9. Qg5+ Kf8 10. Q×d8+ N×d8 11. f4 c×d4 12. Nb5 etc. ... last but not least, column (G) is an example where pawns should triumph over a piece (analysis by Breyer and Réti, who say that Black is left with the better game). And so once more we repeat: Counter attack is the soul of the game, and is the best defense; strength of players can be estimated by their ability and depth of analysis, and though over and again we may fail in our judgment, we must remember that a strong player is usually a lucky as well as a plucky player.

–4–

"A Strong Center"

From the *Social Chess Quarterly*—July 1935—pp. 442–546

• • • •

From the early days when the game of chess first became invaded by analysts there arose this vexed question about the fight for the center of the board. Fashions have changed, old truths have been replaced by new ones, but the importance of establishing control of the center and the debate as to how this can best be effected continues still.

New methods have been suggested and tried and if we take the trouble to look through the history of the development and treatment of the opening play, we will be able to follow its progress step by step until we come to the modern times and encounter Réti's ideas.

Réti was a great exponent of the close game, and after considerable study and research proved to the chess world that control of the center can be effected not only by advancing a middle pawn to the fourth rank and supporting it with another pawn, but also by commanding the center squares with a bishop placed on a long diagonal, or in other words, that the center can be controlled by means of pieces as well as pawns.

We will not argue which of the methods is the better one, but will simply note the fact that whichever we adopt, the center must be taken care of, for if neglected our game will suffer in consequence not only in the opening, but even throughout its later stages.

To acquaint the reader with the modern ideas we have chosen one of the popular defenses to the Queen's Pawn Opening, favored by Réti, and know as the King's Indian (or Fianchetto) Defense.

The usual opening moves lead to the position in Diagram 1 **1. d4 ♘f6 2. c4 g6 3. ♘c3 ♗g7 4. e4 d6** *(see diagram 1)*

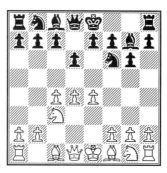

Diagram 1
After 4. ... d6

We must notice that at move three Black was forced to face the threatening advance of e4 and had to decide whether he should try to prevent it or will allow the king's pawn to come on, with the hope of later on creating a weakness in White's strong array of pawns. He could have contested the center immediately with Grünfeld's move: 3. ... d5; but he preferred not to, and so now we will watch with interest the struggle that ensues.

It is easily seen that White is not yet prepared to advance his e-pawn still further to e5 (for after 5. e5 d×e5 6. d×e5 ♛×d1+ 7. ♘×d1 ♘g4 Black has nothing to fear and has disposed of White's center). Yet a move like e5 is a very tempting one and is worth preparing for. A pawn which passes the middle line, if well supported, is usually very strong and becomes a thorn in the opponent's flesh. And so, with Alekhine and others, we prepare this advance and play here **5. f4**.

Now we have the so-called "Four Pawns Game." It held the sway for some time, and put fear into Black, until a way was discovered by which Black successfully attacked these formidable pawns. In reply to 5. f4, Black can quietly castle **5. ... 0-0** since 6. e5 is still premature on account of 6. ... d×e5 7. f×e5 ♘g4 with a threat of c5 breaking up the pawn chain.

It is instructive to notice that c5 is once again the key move to White's usual continuation **6. ♘f3 c5!** *(see diagram 2)*

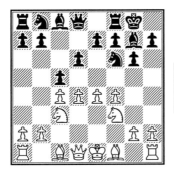

Diagram 2
After 6. ... c5!

after which White has the choice of three distinct continuations; he can capture the c-pawn; he can allow his own pawn to be captured or else he can advance the pawn to d5.

This example is instructive because it illustrates a definite and comprehensive method of attacking and breaking up advanced but insufficiently well-supported pawns. If we grasp the principles, it will be useful to us in similar positions. The strength of the move c5 will become more apparent when we work through the variations given below, but before we play them over the following considerations are worth bearing in mind: In the case of the first continuations mentioned, the object gained by Black is not difficult to follow; he gets rid of one of White's valuable center pawns for a side pawn of his own, making the possible advance of the e-pawn more uncertain; in the latter event (if White plays d5) he hopes that this early advance will enable him to start an immediate attack by opening a file in the center, and will sufficiently compensate him for a temporary inactivity of his queen's side.

The first possibility might easily lead to very disastrous results for White if he tries to be greedy, but at best leads only to equality, for example: **7. d×c5 ♕a5! 8. c×d6? ♘×e4! 9. d×e7 ♖e8** *(see diagram 3)*

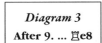

Diagram 3
After 9. ... ♖e8

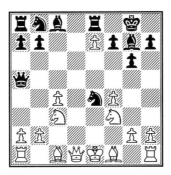

Owing to a strong attack on the c3-knight and a well developed king's rook, Black easily gets the better game.

White's fault, of course, lay in capturing the second pawn, but even if he tries 8. ♗d2 ♕×c5; and White has to lose more time when he brings ♗e3 in order to castle on the king's side, and at e3 the bishop has to be further protected against the possible attack of ♘g4. If, on the other hand, White decides to castle on the queen's side, the game might continue 9. ♕e2 (9. ♗d3 ♘c6 10. ♘a4 ♕h5 etc.) 9. ... ♘c6 10. 0–0–0 ♗g4 11. ♕e3 ♘d7 12. ♘a4 ♕×e3 13. ♗×e3 ♗×f3 etc., as in the game Wahltuch-Vidmar, Hastings 1926. In both these cases a very strong asset in Black's favor is the open c-file, which presently becomes a most useful means of attack against the c-pawn.

It might be argued perhaps, that after all, White still has three strong pawns in the center and Black has none. On careful examination, however, we see that White's squares d3 and d4 have gone weak—they are no longer no longer protected by a pawn, particularly his d4, which Black can no command with his knight at c6 and the bishop. The bishop here is extremely strong on the long diagonal, and should not be exchanged without good reason. The bishop at g7, the knight at c6 and the pawn at d6, all three together, put strong pressure on the black squares, the e5 and d4. This is exactly what Réti meant be controlling the center by means of pieces instead of pawns, only unfortunately it requires rather more than just a hasty analysis of a position like this for his ideas to be properly understood.

We have another similar example in the second possible continuation to 6. ... c5 (see diagram 2). A quiet move like 7. ♗e2 or ♗e3, allowing Black to capture the d-pawn, leads pretty well to the same type of game as in the variations just seen (we mean that the similarity will arise through pawn-skeleton remaining the same), for example: 7. ♗e2 cxd4 8. ♘xd4 ♘c6 9. ♗e3 (9. 0–0 ♘xe4) 9. ... ♕b6 10. ♘a4 ♕a5+ 11. ♗d2 ♕c7 etc. This variation is also interesting because it is analogous (though unfavorable for White) to the Dragon Variation in the Sicilian Defense; careful comparison and study of both will be found helpful.

Much more promising is the third possibility—advancing the pawn to d5, as by so doing White takes the best square from Black's queen's knight and so hampers his development. Black should deal with this rapidly and energetically, as any delay will leave him with a cramped game. He is recommended here to contest the center at once with e6.

Here the variation sub-divides again; White can allow his d-pawn to be taken, retaking either with the e-pawn or the c-pawn; or he himself can capture the pawn.

Retaking with the e-pawn is quite harmless and leads to play which is easy to understand without additional analysis. Black immediately obtains excellent counter chances, and even the better game, through his attack along the open e-file.

Retaking with the c-pawn leads to some interesting play, but still appears to be in Black's favor (see diagram 2).

A.

7. d5 e6 8. ♗e2 exd5 9. cxd5 a6 10. a4 ♖e8 11. ♕c2 ♕e7 12. ♘d2 ♗g4, etc. (see diagram 4)

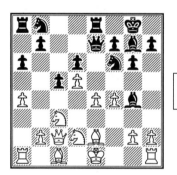

Diagram 4

B.

7. d5 e6 8. ♗d3 exd5 9. cxd5 ♕b6 (preventing 0–0 by threat of c4+, etc.) 10. ♘d2 ♘g4 11. ♘c4 ♕d8 12. ♗e2 (threatening if 12. 0–0 ♗d4+ 13. ♔h1 ♘xh2) 12. ... h5 13. ♗xg4 ♗xg4 14. ♕c2 ♕h4+ 15. g3 ♕e7 16. 0–0 h4 (see diagram 5)

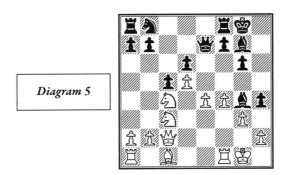

Diagram 5

And finally we try (see diagram 2) 7. d5 e6; 8. d×e6. This move, 8. d×e6 if only supported by a better development on White's part, would promise good chances of attack along the open d-file, putting strong pressure upon Black's weakened d-pawn. Obviously Black plays 8. ... f×e6 and not 8. ... ♗×e6, as in that case the d-pawn will remain permanently backward. The game might continue: 9. ♗e2 ♘c6 10. 0–0 ♕e7 (see diagram 6) with about equal chances.

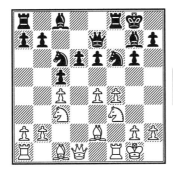

Diagram 6

Although the opening stage is now over, we notice that the struggle for the center, the struggle for space, and the attempt to place the pieces into more aggressive and dominating positions, still continues. White still hopes to advance (when ready for it) his e-pawn in order to strengthen his command on the square d6, where he may eventually try to establish his knight, bringing it there via b5 or e4. Black on the other hand may be successful in advancing d5 supported by a rook behind it, or her may adopt a different line of play with e5 establishing his knight at d4. How this game will end we do not know, but we do know that in the early stages White's center looked very formidable, and one felt uneasy for Black. However, he managed to attack it successfully, and so once more we repeat: The four middle pawns if advanced to the fourth rank are immensely strong, but their advance must be accurately timed; a pawn which passes the middle line is strong if well supported, otherwise it becomes a source of weakness.

–5–

A Political Dialog Between Menchik and B.H. Wood

Chess politicians and chess players have been battling amongst one another and each other since before the first pawn was pushed. In 19th century Britain, there were the Hoffer vs. Steinitz feuds as well as the battles between Staunton and everyone. Today it seems little better.

The following is a commentary on the state of the British Chess Federation during World War II by Baruch H. Wood (the editor of "*Chess*" Sutton Coldfield) and Menchik's response in that same journal three months later. There were a number of additional well thought out responses in the interval. It should be noted that Vera's husband, R.H.S. Stevenson, had died just before the initial report. At the time of his death, he was the Hon. Secretary of the British Chess Federation.

"A Disgraceful Report"

Baruch H. Wood
Chess Sutton Coldfield—February 1943

Throughout Britain at war, football matches draw their millions of spectators weekly. Cinemas draw their millions nightly. Dog-racing, skating, music, plays, billiards, dancing, continue to provide recreation and refreshment for thousand of jaded war-workers. The Soviet Union, fighting for its life, revels in the respite of chess tournaments, to which contestants come a thousand miles or more.

What of the British Chess Federation, whose members are elected to further the interests of British chess. We have their latest "Annual Report" before us, and a sorry document it is. Having already ceased practically all activity for several years, the Federation has now decided not even to hold an Annual Meeting.

Surely, if the B.C.F. has a legitimate mission in wartime, it is the fostering of chess in the Forces? The B.C.F. has not done one iota of work in this field. Worse—though Owen Dixson receives a word of appreciation in the "Annual Report," the work of such as Ashley Vernieux and J. Du Mont, who have rescued Services' chess from oblivion—doing the B.C.F.'s own shamefully shirked work—is ignored.

Of these, one fought for, and conducted in the Services organ "Blighty," a chess feature which ran for many months, whilst the second, as is well known, secured official collaboration in organizing an Army Championship, inaugurated Allied vs. Home Forces matches, and won mentions on the radio. If the insult to them is unintentional as we hope, how blind the B.C.F. must be to what is happening in chess around them!

The B.C.F. is beginning to revolve round two or three rich and influential men, whose love of, and enthusiasm for chess, nobody could doubt. But if these few energetic minds are distracted for a moment, the barrenness of the back-benches becomes blatantly apparent. This disgraceful report reveals once again, in a blinding light, how far behind the times the Federation is falling: nine-tenths of it needs replacing by new blood.

[Response by Vera Menchik]

Chess—May 1943

Dear Mr. Wood,

As one ponders over your recent attack on the B.C.F. one cannot help wondering what useful purpose has this outburst served? Surely the answer is in the negative. Such an attitude could not result in goodwill and co-operation, and it most probably has resulted in prejudicing a number of your readers who, not having had personal acquaintance of chess organizers may have taken you at your word and decided that the B.C.F. Committee is as lethargic as you say. Anyway this impression must have been still further strengthened when you took the trouble of publishing, and publishing uncommented, such remarks as: "That the backwardness and the standard of play are due to people seeking and retaining office who really do nothing beyond carrying on normal activities in a normal manner. But they feel important, and that is about all that matters in most cases."

However, what I chiefly want to say is how it amazes me that a man of your international chess experience should attempt to draw a comparison between chess-life in U.S.S.R. and in Britain?

If the Soviet Union can boast the strongest team of players in the world and the largest rank and file, it is not merely because of their superior chess organization, but because of social conditions under which the whole nation lives and works. Millions of spectators do not go (in Russia) to football matches in the winter months; nor do they go to dog-racing or indulge in any shape of gambling; nor, I think have they access to the world's literature in the same way we have to the excellent series of Penguin Books, etc.; and if the theatres and cinemas of Moscow are crowded every night, they are not nearly as numerous as the places of amusement in big cities in England, and few people have either the time or the means to frequent them as regularly as so many do here.

If, today, people in Russia continue to play chess in very strenuous and difficult conditions, it is because they are used to hard life and value comfort far less than we do. In the few years before the war the Soviet nation was fortunate to enjoy considerable prosperity, but the many years succeeding the 1917 revolution had been very hard and trying, and few people could have forgotten them. For example, during the winter of 1919-20 the school I attended was for some time without water, heating or electric light, yet the classes went on and the students, clad in their fur-lined coats and hats, read by the light of a few flickering candles or an oil lamp, and then perhaps had an hours walk home through the snow, for all traffic stopped after working hours. People also played chess in the same conditions, and they most likely still do, though we here prefer to forego our game of chess because of inconvenience of the black-out. How understandable it all is, but can you really blame the B.C.F. that such vast differences exist? There are many other important points which make comparison impossible, such as the average age of players here and in Russia—a difference of perhaps of 20 years! Then again the actual attitude to chess: in Russia—serious and studious; here—often very light hearted. Have you not met players who pride themselves on never having read a chess book in their lives; who regard all theory as the invention of the Evil One specially devised to spoil the leisure hours? Have you never heard them say that they play chess just for pleasure? In Russia they would be officially and severely reprimanded, but do you think the B.C.F. can alter their outlook?

To finish up I should like to relate an experience I had regarding Army chess. A year ago I was working at a soldiers' canteen run by the W.V.S. I volunteered to organize a chess section and to give lectures and displays. This suggestion was received quite enthusiastically and I was even asked to contribute a chess article for the weekly Gazette. I wrote an article of a very elementary kind, explaining how to read and record a game, accompanied by a short brilliancy to serve as an example. It had two diagrams and was easy enough for a child of nine to understand. Yet in the end it was turned down on the ground of being too difficult, and in fact the whole idea of chess fell through. Can you blame the B.C.F. for such lack of enterprise, and can you imagine this happening in U.S.S.R.?

Yours very sincerely,
    VERA STEVENSON

PART IV.
APPENDICES, NOTES,
BIBLIOGRAPHY, INDICES

Appendix 1:
The "Vera Menchik Club"

In 1929, at the Carlsbad Tournament, Vera Menchik lost her first game. That night Albert Becker proposed that anyone who lost to her should be inducted as a member of the "Vera Menchik Club." Those players who drew with her would become candidate members of the club. In the third round of the tournament Becker became the club's charter member. For a while Dr. Max Euwe the future World Chess Champion was recognized as the club's "President," owing to his score of +1 −2 =1 score, although I am inclined to award the title to International Master George Thomas who lost no fewer than 9 games and drew 13 to Vera.

Following is a list of prominent club members as well as candidate members. In all cases the players were recognized Grandmasters and International Masters as defined by the standards of the day.

Members

1. C.H.O'D. Alexander
2. Edgar Colle
3. Stefan Fazekas
4. Harry Golombek
5. Jacques Mieses
6. Josef Rejfíř
7. Ramón Rey Ardid
8. Jakob Adolf Seitz
9. Mir Sultan Khan
10. Karl Treybal
11. Frederick D. Yates
12. Eero Böök
13. Max Euwe
14. Paulin Frydman
15. Reginald P. Michell
16. Karel Opočenský
17. Samuel Reshevsky
18. [Friedrich]
19. Herman Steiner
20. Lajos Steiner
21. George A. Thomas
22. William A. Winter
23. Eugene Znosko-Borovsky

Candidate Members

1. E. Eliskases
2. Karl Gilg
3. George Koltanowski
4. Géza Maróczy
5. Vasja Pirc
6. Rudolf Spielmann
7. Salo Flohr
8. Ernst Grünfeld
9. Imre König
10. Miguel Najdorf
11. Akiba Rubinstein
12. Milan Vidmar, Jr.
13. Milan Vidmar, Sr.

Appendix 2: Women's World Chess Champions

From 1927 through 1939 FIDE held a Women's World Championship tournament in conjunction with its Olympiad. These events were single or double round robins (except Stockholm 1937). One match was held between the champion, Vera Menchik, and a challenger, Sonja Graf, in Semmering, Austria, in 1937. After World War II, FIDE held a round robin tournament in the winter of 1949-1950 in Moscow; the title was won by Liudmila Rudenko. Thereafter qualifying events determined a challenger to the champion. The 1956 "match" actually was a three way event with Rudenko, Bikova and Rubtsova.

In 2000 the women's cycle was again brought into conformity with the "men's" or open cycle and the champion was determined by 64-player knock-out tournaments. In 2011 the cycle went to a yearly system where in even years there are 64-player knock-out tournaments and in odd years there will be two player matches with a challenger meeting the reigning champion.

Reign	Champion	Country	Life Dates
1927–1944	Vera Menchik	USSR/Czechoslovakia/UK	1906–1944
1950–1953	Liudmila Rudenko	USSR	1904–1986
1953–1956	Elisaveta Bikova	USSR	1913–1989
1956–1958	Olga Rubtsova	USSR	1909–1994
1958–1962	Elisaveta Bikova	USSR	1913–1989
1962–1978	Nona Gaprindashvili	USSR	1941–
1978–1991	Maia Chiburdanidze	USSR/Georgia	1961–
1991–1996	Xie Jun	China	1970–
1996–1999	Zsuzsa [Susan] Polgar	Hungary	1969–
1999–2001	Xie Jun	China	1970–
2001–2004	Zhu Chen	China	1976–
2004–2006	Antoaneta Stefanova	Bulgaria	1979–
2006–2008	Xu Yuhua	China	1976–
2008–2010	Alexandra Kosteniuk	Russia	1984–
2010–2012	Hou Yifan	China	1994–
2012–2013	Anna Ushenina	Ukraine	1985–
2013–2015	Hou Yifan	China	1994–
2015–2016	Mariya Muzychuk	Ukraine	1992–
2016–	Hon Yifan	China	1994–

Appendix 3: Matisons Problem
(Based on Menchik Game)

In 1929 Menchik reached the position below against Milan Vidmar, Sr., after his (White's) 69th move. Play continued with 69. ... ♖a3+ 70. ♔d4 ♖a4+ 71. ♔e3 ♖a3+ 73. ♔d5 ♖a5+ 74. ♔c6 ♖a6+ 75. ♔c5 ♖a4 76. h×g6 and Black resigned 12 moves later.

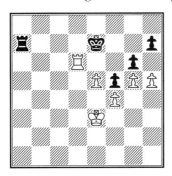

M. Vidmar vs. Menchik
Carlsbad 1929—after White's 69th move

On playing 69. ... ♖a3+, Menchik hoped for the reply 70. ♖d3 for then after 70. ... ♖×d3+ 71. ♔×d3 g×h5 72. ♔e3 ♔f7 would have led to an interesting draw, or so it seemed. Hermanis Matisons, who was playing in the same tournament, suggested to her that she should turn this idea into a study. She responded by inviting Matisons to do so as composing was not one of her interests. Matisons took this finale, added an introduction to it and dedicated the finished study to Vera. No one at Carlsbad noticed at the time that the projected draw was an illusion. After the study was published, however, the flaw was quickly spotted. Below is the problem as published (*Juanākās Zinas*, 1929) with the intended solution and the cook.

1. f6 [1. a5? d3 2. a6 d2 3. a7 d1♕ 4. ♔b7 ♕h1+ 5. ♔b8 ♕h2+ 6. ♔b7 ♕×a2 wins—RT] **1. ...
♚g6 2. ♔d5 ♚×f6** [2. ... d3 3. ♔e6 enables White to promote the f-pawn—RT] **3. ♔e4 ♚e6
4. ♔d3 ♚d6 5. ♔c2 ♚c6 6. ♔b2** [6. ♔b3? d3 wins—RT] **6. ... ♚b6** [6. ... d3 7. ♔c1 ♚b6
8. ♔d2 ♚a5 9. ♔×d3 ♚×a4 10. ♔c2 ♚a3 11. ♔b1 b3 12. axb3 ♚×b3 13. ♔c1 ♚×c4 14. ♔c2
draws—RT] **7. a3 ♚a5 8. ♔b3 d3 9. a×b4+ c×b4 10. c5 ♚a6 11. ♔b2 ♚b7 12. a5 ♚c6
13. a6 ♚c7 14. ♔b3 ♚c6 15. ♔b2** draws.

The fly in the ointment is that Black can win the ending if instead of 7. ... ♚a5, he plays 7. ...
d3 with the continuation of 8. a×b4 c×b4 9. ♔b3 ♚c5 10. a5 ♚d4 11. a6 d2 12. ♔c2 ♚e3 13. a7
b3+ 14. ♔c3 d1♕ 15. a8♕ ♕c2+ 16. ♔b4 b2 etc.

Appendix 4: Tournament and Match Results

Location	Date	Type	Section or Opponent	Win	Loss	Draw	Place
Russia–?	about 1920		"Boys"	unknown			2+
Hastings Christmas Cong.	Dec. 1923–Jan. 1924	RR	1st Class	3	5	1	8
Hastings CC	1924			3	0	3	Unknown
Hastings Christmas Cong.	Dec. 1924–Jan. 1925	RR	1st Class	4	1	2	2
Stratford on Avon—B.C.F.	Aug. 17–29, 1925	RR	1st Class	6	1	4	2
Edith Price Match #1	1925	Match		2	1	2	Won
Edith Price Match #2	1925	Match		3	2	0	Won
Hastings Christmas Cong.	Dec. 28, 1925–Jan. 5, 1926	RR	Major	1	4	4	7–10
London Girl's Champs	1926	RR	Champ	4	0	0	1
Hastings Christmas Cong.	Dec. 28, 1926–Jan. 5, 1927	RR	Major Res.	5	1	3	1–2
London Girl's Champs	1927	RR	Champ	5	0	0	1
Tunbridge Wells	Apr. 16–23, 1927	RR	Major	1	3	3	5
Hastings Christmas Cong.	Dec. 28, 1927–Jan. 6, 1928	RR	Major Open	3	4	2	7
Cheltenham	1928	RR	Major	6	0	1	1
Scarborough	May 26–June 2, 1928	RR		4	4	1	7–8
Tenby—B.C.F.	July 2–13, 1928	RR	Major Open	5	3	3	6
Hastings Christmas Cong.	Dec. 27, 1928–Jan. 5, 1929	RR	Prem. Res.	3	5	1	8
Ramsgate	Mar. 30–Apr. 8, 1929	Schev.		3	0	4	2
Paris	June 15–30, 1929	RR	Champ	2	7	2	7
Carlsbad, Czech.	July 31–Aug. 28, 1929	RR	Champ	2	17	2	22
Barcelona, Spain	Sept. 25–Oct 11, 1929	RR	Champ	4	4	6	8
Hastings Christmas Cong.	Dec. 27, 1929–Jan. 4, 1930	RR	Champ	2	4	3	9
Hastings CC Champ.	1930	RR	Champ	13	0	1	1
Hasting Master R.R.	April 14–18, 1930	RR	Champ	2	2	0	3
Canterbury	Apr. 19–26, 1930	RR	Champ	2	2	3	5
Scarborough	June 23–July 5, 1930	RR	Champ	0	3	8	10
Hastings Christmas Cong.	Dec. 29, 1930–Jan. 7, 1931	RR	Champ	2	5	2	8
Hastings CC	1931	RR	Champ	unknown			2
Worcester—B.C.F.	Aug. 10–22, 1931	RR	Major Open	7	0	4	1
Antwerp Match Tourney.	Aug. 1931	Schev.		3	3	0	6–7
Hastings Christmas Cong.	Dec. 28, 1931–Jan 6, 1932	RR	Champ	3	4	2	5–8
Cambridge	Mar. 26–Apr. 2, 1932	RR	Champ	1	2	4	5–7
London	Feb. 1–12, 1932	RR	Champ	3	5	3	8
London—B.C.F. Champ	Aug. 15–27, 1932	RR	Major Open	9	2	0	2

Location	Date	Type	Section or Opponent	Win	Loss	Draw	Place
Hastings Christmas Cong.	Dec. 28, 1932–Jan. 6, 1933	RR	Champ	2	4	3	8
Mnichovo Hradiště, Czech	Aug 6–19, 1933	RR	Champ	2	4	5	8–12
Hastings Christmas Cong.	Dec. 1933–Jan. 1934	RR	Champ	2	5	2	7–8
Groningen, Netherlands	1934	RR	Champ	3	0	1	1
Amsterdam, Netherlands	April 1–2, 1934	RR	Section 1	1	1	1	2–3
Maribor, Slovenia	Aug. 5–15, 1934	RR	Champ	3	1	4	3
S. Graf	1934	Match		3	1	0	Won
Semily	Aug. 20–25, 1934	RR	Champ	5	1	1	2
Hastings Christmas Cong.	Dec. 1934–Jan. 1935	RR	Champ	1	4	4	8
Moscow	Feb. 15–Mar. 14, 1935	RR	Champ	0	16	3	20
Margate	Apr. 24–May 23, 1935	RR	Champ	2	6	1	9
Yarmouth	July 8–20, 1935	RR	Major Open	6	3	2	3
Margate	Apr. 15–24, 1936	RR	Champ	2	4	3	7
Poděbrady	July 4–19, 1936	RR	Int'l Champ	6	9	2	13
Nottingham	Aug. 10–28, 1936	RR	Major Open	3	5	3	8
Hastings Christmas Cong.	Dec. 28, 1936–Jan. 6, 1937	RR	Champ	0	4	5	9
London	1937	RR	Champ	1	3	1	5
Eugene Znosko-Borovsky	1937	Match		0	2	2	Lost
Margate	Mar. 31–Apr. 4, 1937	RR	Champ	3	4	2	6
Bournemouth	1938	RR	Champ	0	1	2	3–4
Łódź	Mar. 20–Apr. 5, 1938	RR	Champ	1	9	5	15
Margate	April 20–28, 1938	RR	Champ	2	5	2	9
Engl. vs. Neth.—London	June 5–6, 1938	Team Match	Bd. 8	0	0	2	
Brighton	Aug. 8–19, 1938	RR	Champ	2	2	7	7
Plymouth	Sept. 5–10, 1938	RR	Champ	2	3	2	5
Margate	1939	RR	Champ	0	4	5	9
Montevideo	Sept. 21–29, 1939	RR	Champ	4	1	2	3
London—Hampstead	Dec. 1939	RR	Champ	5	4	2	5–7
London—Easter Cong.	March 19–28, 1940	RR	Champ	4	1	4	3
London—Nat'l Chess Cntr	1940	RR	Prelim. "B"	3	3	5	7
Jacques Mieses	1942	Match		4	1	5	Won
Sidcup	1942	RR	Champ	3	1	1	2–3
W. London Summer	1943	RR	Champ	5	1	3	3
W. London CC Champ.	1944	RR	Champ	?	?	?	6
				196	207	166	

Women's World Chess Championships

Location	Date	Type		Win	Loss	Draw	Place
London	1927	RR		10	0	1	1
Hamburg	1930	Dbl RR		6	1	1	1
Prague	1931	Dbl RR		8	0	0	1
Folkstone	1933	RR		14	0	0	1
Warsaw	1935	RR		9	0	0	1
Semmering	1937	Match	S. Graf	9	2	5	Won
Stockholm	1937	Monrad (SS)		14	0	0	1
Buenos Aires	1939	RR		17	0	2	1
		WWC Record		87	3	9	
		Total		283	210	175	

Appendix 5: County and British Team Match Results

In each case Vera Menchik represented Sussex, Hastings, the Imperial CC, Croyden, National Chess Center (London), British Chess Congress or the West London CC as applicable.

Date	Event & Site	Board	Opponent	VM Result	Source
04/01/23	Hastings CC vs. English Boys	Bd. 26B	N. Lambert	loss	HSLO 4-14-23
05/05/23	Hastings Women vs. Hastings 3rd Team	Bd. 3	F.A. Riley	win	HSLO 5-12-23
06/09/23	Hastings vs. Brighton	Bd. 28	H.M. Baldrey	drawn (adj)	HSLO 6-23-23
09/29/23	East Sussex vs. West Sussex	Bd. 39	A. White	drawn (adj)	HSLO 10-23-23
03/0/24	Hastings vs. Brighton @ Hastings	Bd. 17	G.E. Smith	win	HSLO 3-8-1924
05/03/24	Hastings vs. Brighton & Hove	Bd. 18	A.T. Watson	win	HSLO 5-10-24
06/06/24	Hastings vs. Rest of Sussex (-Brighton)	Bd. 16	G.J.D. Gregory	win	BCM 1924 p. 270
06/21/24	Hastings vs. No. London Carlisle Parade @ Lond.	Bd. 10	L.W. Cave	win	HSLO 7-5-1924
08/09/24	Hastings vs. Cranbrook	Bd. 4	D.C. Cozens	win	HSLO 8-16-24
11/01/24	Sussex vs. Middlesex	Bd. 23W	T.J. Camon	win	SDN 11-3-1924
02/14/25	Sussex vs. Essex @ St Bride's London	Bd. 27	M.F. Willis	win	BCM 1925 p. 117
02/21/25	Hastings Ladies vs. Bye CC	Bd. 1	E.R. Pigrome	win	HSLO 2-28-25
02/28/25	Hastings vs. Christ Church Brighton (informal)	Bd. 8	G.V. Butler	win	HSLO 3-1-1925
03/0/25	Hastings vs. Tunbridge Wells	?	J. Wilson	win	HSLO 3-28-25
03/27/25	Hastings vs. Thornton Heath and Norbury	Bd. 4 ?	A.H. Willott	win	HSLO 3-28-25
04/03/25	Hastings vs. Ibis CC	Bd. 9	W.W. Beresford	win	HSLO 4-4-1925
05/02/25	Hastings vs. Metropolitan CC (informal)	Bd. 7	M. Savage	win	HSLO 5-9-1925
05/16/25	Hastings vs. Rest of Sussex	Bd. 9W	A.E. Smith	draw	HSLO 5-23-1925
09/0/25	East Sussex vs. West Sussex	Bd. 9	H.T. Grover	win	HSLO 9-26-1925
10/03/25	Sussex vs. Kent	Bd. 15	W.H. Dobinson	draw	BCM 1925 p. 450
10/24/25	Hastings vs. Brighton	Bd. 6	Dr. Dunstan	draw	HSLO 10-31-25
11/07/25	Sussex vs. Surrey @ Brighton	Bd. 15	R.H. Birch	loss	HSLO 11-1925
12/0/25	Hastings vs. Tunbridge Wells (informal)	Bd. 4	N. Grace	win	HSLO 12-19-35
12/05/25	Sussex vs. Essex @ London	Bd. 16	R.H. Bayley	win	BCM 1926 p. 21
02/13/26	Hastings vs. Christ Church	Bd. 5	J.H. Jones	draw	BCM 1926 p. 116
04/24/26	Hastings vs. Brixton (informal)	Bd. 5	Dr.F.St. J. Steadman	win	BCM 1926 p. 271
10/02/26	Sussex vs. Kent	Bd. 11	B.W. Hamilton	loss	BCM 1926 p. 680
11/0/26	Sussex vs. Surrey		Dr. T.W. Letchworth	win	BCM 1926 p. 733
11/06/26	Hastings vs. Brighton	Bd. 5	Castle Leaver	win	BCM 1926 p. 737
02/0/27	Sussex vs. Essex	Bd. 8	W.G. Elsmore	draw	BCM 1927 p. 106

Date	Event & Site	Board	Opponent	VM Result	Source
03/08/27	Sussex vs. Middlesex	Bd. 9	W.H. Reagon	win	BCM 1927 p. 149
10/01/27	Sussex vs. Kent	Bd. 7	C.E. Taylor	draw	BCM 1927 p. 459
10/29/27	Hastings vs. Brighton	Bd. 4	J. Storr Best	loss	BCM 1927 p. 495
11/11/27	Sussex vs. Surrey	Bd. 10	G. Wernick	draw	BCM 1928 p. 70
02/18/28	Sussex vs. Essex @ St Bride's London	Bd. 9	G. Freeman	win	BCM 1928 p. 110
01/28/28	Hastings vs. Christ Church	Bd. 6	Castle Leaver	win	BCM 1928 p. 115
03/10/28	Sussex vs. Middlesex	Bd. 10	Dr. F.S. Duncan	win	BCM 1928 p. 149
09/29/28	Sussex vs. Kent	Bd. 6	T.M. Wechsler	draw	BCM 1928 p. 410
11/03/28	Sussex vs. Surrey	Bd. 6	A. Fletcher	win	BCM 1928 p. 452
02/02/29	Sussex vs. Essex	Bd. 6	E.J. Randall	win	BCM 1929 p. 94
1929	Sussex vs. Middlesex	Bd. 6	W.H. Watts	win	BCM 1929 p. 134
1929	Hastings-St. Leonard's vs. Brighton-Hove	Bd. 4	Dr. M.W. Varley	win	BCM 1929 p. 215
11/02/29	Hastings vs. Brighton @ Brighton	Bd. 3	E. Macdonald	draw	BCM 1929 p. 463
11/29/30	Sussex vs. Middlesex	Bd. 2	Wm. Winter	draw	BCM 1931 p. 19
01/31/31	Hastings vs. Christ Church Brighton	Bd. 1	A.T. Watson	win	BCM 1931 p. 111
02/21/31	Sussex vs. Kent	Bd. 2	H.H.Cole	win	BCM 1931 p. 107
04/18/31	Hastings and St. Leonard's vs. Brighton and Hove	Bd. 1	E. MacDonald	win	BCM 1931 p. 260
10/0/31	Hastings vs. Christ Church, Brighton	Bd. 1	W. Atkinson	win	BCM 1931 p. 490
10/03/31	Sussex vs. Kent	Bd. 2	O.C. Muller	win	BCM 1931 p. 487
10/24/31	Sussex vs. Essex	Bd. 2	C. Maxwell	win	BCM 1931 p. 521
11/14/31	Middlesex vs. Sussex	Bd. 2	M. Sultan Khan	loss	BCM 1931 p. 524
12/12/31	Imperial CC vs. National Liberal Club	Bd. 1	F. Salmony	win	BCM 1932 p. 16
02/13/32	Sussex vs. Surrey	Bd. 2	R.P. Michell	win	BCM 1932 p. 110
09/24/32	Imperial CC vs. Buck's County	Bd. 1	J.W. Ford	win	BCM 1932 p. 446
12/03/33	Sussex vs. Kent	Bd. 2	R.C. Noel Johnson	win	BCM 1934 p. 8
01/27/34	Sussex vs. Middlesex	Bd. 2	Wm. Winter	loss	BCM 1934 p. 111
04/28/34	Hastings vs. Brighton	Bd. 1	C.H. Stasey	win	BCM 1934 p. 243
04/06/35	Sussex vs. Middlesex		Wm. Winter	win	
02/20/37	Sussex vs. Kent		R.C. Noel Johnson		
12/18/37	London vs. Birmingham @ St. Bride's London	Bd. 6	B.H. Wood	win	BCM 1938 p. 21
11/01/41			J. Mieses	draw	WLCC Gazette #1
05/09/42	Sussex (Ladies vs. Gentlemen)		H. Streusler	win	BCM 1942 p. 131
08/16/42	Combined Armed Forces vs. Congress	Bd. 1	Lt. A.C. Bloom	win	BCM 1942 p. 199
09/12/42	Essex vs. Kent @ Stratford	Bd. 1	T.H. George	draw	BCM 1942 p. 226
01/01/42	Croyden Central CC vs. Kent	Bd. 1	R.A. Lester	loss (adj)	BCM 1942 p. 249
04/17/43	WLCC vs. Ilford		T.H. George	win	

Appendix 6: Simultaneous Exhibition Results

Date	Site	Source	Bds	W	L	D
01/01/42	Ilford NFS Station	*Chess* 12/42 p. 34	24	17	3	4
	Bournemouth		19	16	2	1
01/31/42	London	BCM 1942 p. 55	19	11	3	5
	Bournemouth	JGW: 789.691	22	15	3	4
11/10/36	Llandudno, WA		20	15	2	3
Spring '34	Zandvoort, NLD	Bikova	33	25	2	6
Spring '34	Bloemendal, NLD	Bikova	32	25	1	7
Spring '34	Netherlands-other*	Bikova	309	188	51	70
10/10/34	Harrogate CC	*Harrogate Herald* 10-10-34	?			
08/18/34	Semily, Czech.		25	19	4	2
1934	Lincolnshire Chess Assn	SCQ p. 352	25	22	1	2
11/07/33	Norwich	*Eastern Daily Press*	20	13	4	3
02/15/33	London	SCQ p. 260	18	17	1	0
12/01/31	London: Empire Social Club	BCM 1932 p. 15	16	14	0	2
11-0-28	Antwerp	HSLO 11-17-28	20	12	5	3
01/16/26	London	BCM 2/26	13	9	2	2
			615	418	84	114

No doubt there are many more exhibitions for which records could be found. Certainly Holland in March and April 1934 should be traceable. More difficult would be the exhibitions she gave in Britain both before and especially during World War II. In her era simultaneous play was a substantial part of the income of most prominent players. With the relative lack of tournaments, they offered a rare opportunity to see and play the elite. Given the strength of competition (as Bikova states in her book, many first rate players competed), Vera's record is not bad. On the other hand if we look to Capablanca and Blackburne's records of the time or Fischer's in the modern era, we can see that she was not exceptional.

In Bikova's book she notes that, "Vera Menchik often demonstrated her high chess aptitudes taking part in simultaneous exhibitions where she used to struggle against first class players. In March and April 1934 she made a tour of Holland playing simultaneous exhibitions. She played 16 exhibitions where she won 238 games, 83 were drawn and 54 lost. Very good results were achieved in Zandvoort (+25 −2 =6) and Bloemendaal (+25 −1 =7). We would like to sum up the results of some other exhibitions given in 1928–1944. 13 of them were played against men and one against women. 264 games were won, 35 were drawn and 26 lost." The present author has extracted the Zandvoort and Bloemendaal exhibitions and lumped the other 14 together above. The 13 other exhibits have not been included as it is not known which are included in the above listing.

Appendix 7:
Results by Opponent

Included in these two lists (men, then women) are only those tournament players who played against Menchik beginning in her first major master event, Cambridge 1928. Games played against earlier competitors are included only when they also showed themselves to be strong enough to play her at later dates. County and club match opponents are included when they also met in the appropriate tournaments. Not included are lightning/blitz games, casual games and others of the like. The results should approximate all serious games against masters and other worthy competitors.

The FIDE titles are given when appropriate as follows: WC = World Champion; GM = International Grandmaster; IM = International Master; WIM = Women's International Master. An "*" after the title indicates the player died before FIDE started awarding titles in 1950, but that the player is and was universally considered to be of that strength (e.g.: Frank Marshall). An "-e" after the GM title indicates that FIDE awarded the title on an emeritus basis after the player had ceased active competition (such as Golombek and Koltanowski). Needless to say there are a number of players who no doubt were of at least IM/GM strength who never received a title even after FIDE started awarding them, as they died too early for the process or because nobody lobbied for their cause (such as Mir Sultan Khan). Unless a solid source could be found the author has refrained from listing a title for them even when documented retroactive grading indicates they should have a title.

Although not listed below it is startling to note how many of these players also received the IA (International Arbiter) title.

Men	Title	Win	Loss	Draw	Games
Abrahams, Gerald		1	1	1	3
Aguilera, José		1			1
Ahues, Carl Oscar	IM			1	1
Aitken, James Macrae				1	1
Alatortsev, Vladimir	GM-e		1		1
Alekhine, Alexander A.	WC		8		8
Alexander, C.H.O'D.	IM	2		4	6
Alexander, Frederick F.		1			1
Appel, Izaak			1		1
Asztalos, Lajos	IM			1	1

(Men)	(Title)	(Win)	(Loss)	(Draw)	(Games)
Baert, Arthur			1		1
Baratz, Abraham		1	1		2
Beamish, E.A.		1			1
Becker, Albert	IM	1			1
Berger, Victor		3		3	6
Blažej		1			1
Blum, Martin			1		1
Bogoljubow, Efim	GM		1		1
Bohatirchuk, Fyodor P.	IM			1	1
Böök, Eero	GM-e	1			1
Booth, A.N.			1		1
Botvinnik, Mikhail M.	WC		2		2
Brierley, W.L.		1		1	2
Broadbent, Reginald J.		1			1
Braam		1			1
Brown, E.				1	1
Bruce, Ronald Mackay		1	1		2
Butcher, A.J.G.		1			1
Canal, Esteban	GM		1		1
Capablanca y Graupera, José	WC		9		9
Chauvet, Lt. M.		1			1
Chekhover, Vitaly A.	IM		1		1
Coggan, S.S.			1		1
Colle, Edgar	GM*	1	4	1	6
Collins, F.G.T.		2			2
Conde, Adrian Garcia				1	1
Craddock, James M.				3	3
Cross, Alfred Rupert		1		1	2
Damant, C.A.S.			1		1
DeMey, Emiel		1			1
Dewing, Leslie C.		1			1
Dobiáš, Josef			1		1
Drewitt, John Arthur James			2		2
Drezga, Tihomil		1			1
Duchamp, Marcel				1	1
Eliskases, Erich Gottlieb	GM		1	3	4
Euwe, Machgielis "Max"	WC	2	1	1	4
Fairhurst, William Albert	IM		1		1
Fajarowicz, Sammi				1	1
Farkas, Private Victor				1	1
Fazekas, Stefan	IM	2	2		4
Feigin, Movsa				1	1
Felderhof, H. William		1			1
Fine, Reuben	GM		2		2
Flohr, Salomon "Salo"	GM		7	3	10
Foltys, Jan	IM		3	1	4
Font, José María				1	1

(Men)	(Title)	(Win)	(Loss)	(Draw)	(Games)
Frydman, Paulin	IM	1	1		2
Gerstenfeld, Eduard			1		1
Gilg, Karl	IM			1	1
Goglidze, Viktor	IM		1		1
Golmayo de la Torriente, M.	IM		1		1
Golombek, Harry	GM-e	1	4	4	9
Groenevelt, J.		1			1
Grünfeld, Ernst	GM			2	2
Gulla, Luis Alberto		1			1
Hadač, Pavel				1	1
Heath, Christopher		2			2
Hounié Fleurquin, Carlos		1			1
Israel, Harold		1			1
Ivanoff, V.		1			1
Jackson, Edward Mackenzie		3	1	3	7
Jacobs, Herbert		1		1	2
Johner, Paul F.	IM*		1		1
Kan, Ilia	IM		1		1
Kashdan, Isaac	GM		2		2
Keres, Paul	GM		2		2
Kitto, Francis E.			1		1
Klein, Ernst Ludwig		1	1		2
Kolski, Josek				1	1
Koltanowski, George	GM-e		4	3	7
König, Imre	IM			1	1
Kovarik		1			1
Lacy-Hulbert, A.P.		1			1
Landau, Salo	IM*			2	2
Lasker, Emanuel	WC		1		1
Lazard, Frédéric		1			1
Lenton, Alfred			1	1	2
Levenfish, Grigory Y.	GM		1		1
Lightfoot, A.		1			1
Lilienthal, Andor	GM		1	2	3
Lisitsin, Georgy, M.	IM		1		1
List, Paul			4		4
Littlejohn, P.C.		3		2	5
Lundin, Erik	GM		1		1
Mallison, Harold Vincent		1	1	1	3
Maqy, Desider					0
Marín y Llovet, Valentín				1	1
Maróczy, Géza	GM		1	3	4
Marshall, Frank J.	GM*		1		1
Matejka		1			1
Matisons, Hermanis	IM*		1		1
May, Desider				1	1
Michell, Reginald P.	IM*	4	1	4	9

(Men)	(Title)	(Win)	(Loss)	(Draw)	(Games)
Mieses, Jacques	GM	5	3	6	14
Milner-Barry, Philip Stuart		5	3	8	16
Monticelli, Mario	GM-e		1		1
Morry, William Ritson		1		1	2
Mühring, Willem Jan	IM			2	2
Mulder, Emile A.J.M.			1		1
Najdorf, Miguel	GM			2	2
Nimzowitsch, Aron	GM*		1		1
Norman, George M.				1	1
Noteboom, Daniël			1	1	2
Oliviera, Alfredo		1			1
Opočenský, Karel	IM	1		2	3
Paroulek, Vít			1		1
Parr, Frank		1	1		2
Pelikan, Jiří (Jorge)	IM		1		1
Perquin, Walter				1	1
Petrovs, Vladimirs	IM*		2	1	3
Pirc, Vasja	GM		4	1	5
Podger, C.V.		1			1
Podhorzer, David				1	1
Pokorný, Amos				1	1
Price, Hubert Ernest		1	2	1	4
Prins, Lodewijk	GM-e		1		1
Rabinovich, Ilya	GM*		1		1
Rada, Josef		1			1
Ragozin, Vyacheslav V.	GM		1		1
Reeve, H.T.		2			2
Regedziński, Teodor				1	1
Reilly, Brian P		2			2
Rejfíř, Josef	IM	2	1		3
Reshevsky, Samuel Herman	GM	1	1		2
Rey Ardid, Ramón	IM*	1			1
Reynolds, Arthur		1	1		2
Rhodes, H.G.		1			1
Ribera Arnal, Angel		1			1
Richter, Emil	IM	1			1
Richter, Kurt	IM		1		1
Riumin, Nikolay	IM*		1		1
Roháček, Ivan V.		1			1
Romanovsky, Pyotr A.	IM		1		1
Roux Cabral, Luis		1			1
Rubinstein, Akiba Kiwelowicz	GM		1	1	2
Salik, Franciszek					0
Sämisch, Friedrich	GM	1			1
Sapira, Emanuel			2		2
Saunders, Harold			1		1
Schenk, Holger S.		2			2

(Men)	(Title)	(Win)	(Loss)	(Draw)	(Games)
Schlotens, C.		1			1
Schubert, František		1			1
Schwartzmann, Leon I.			1		1
Seitz, Jakob Adolf	IM*	1	4	2	7
Sergeant, Edward G.		3	4	4	11
Sergeant, Philip W.		1			1
Shernetsky, D.		1			1
Skalicka, Carlos		1			1
Skrbek		1			1
Soler, Plácido				1	1
Solomon, J.D.		1			1
Spencer, Edmund			1		1
Spielmann, Rudolf	GM*		3	1	4
Spitz, R.		1			1
Ståhlberg, Gideon	GM		4		4
Steiner, Herman	IM		1		1
Steiner, Lajos	IM	2	1	1	4
Stoltz, Gösta	GM		1		1
Stronach, Bernard H.		2			2
Stupan, Bogumir		1	1		2
Sultan Khan, Mir	GM*	1	6		7
Takács, Sándor	IM*		1		1
Tartakower, Saviely	GM		3	2	5
Thomas, George Alan	IM	10	6	13	29
Torres Caravaca, Joaquín			1		1
Treybal, Karel	IM*	1	2		3
Tsukerman, Iosif			2		2
Tylor, Theodore		2	1	7	10
Van den Bosch, Johannes			1		1
Veerkamp, J.			1		1
Vidmar, Milan, Jr.	IM			1	1
Vidmar, Dr. Milan, Sr.	GM		1	2	3
Vilardebó-Picurena, J.		1			1
Wallis, Philip N.		1			1
Watts, William Henry		2	1	1	4
Wenman, Francis Percival					0
Wheatcroft, George S.			1	1	2
Winter, William	IM	5	7	4	16
Wolthuis, J.A.				1	1
Wood, Baruch H.		2	1	1	4
Wright, G.		1			1
Yates, Frederick D.	IM*	2	3	5	10
Zinner, Emil			1	1	2
Znosko-Borovsky, Eugene	IM*	1	4	3	8
Known results against men		**138**	**190**	**148**	**476**

Women	Title	Win	Loss	Draw	Games
Andersson, I.		2			2
Bain, Mary	WIM	1			1
Benini, Clarice	WIM	3			3
Berea de Montero, Maria	WIM	1			1
Beskow, Katarina		5			5
Carrasco Araya, Berna	WIM	1			1
Daunke, M.		1			1
D'Autrement		2			2
DeVigil, M.		1			1
Fleröw-Bulhak, Barbara		1			1
Frigard, Marie Jeanne		1			1
Gerlecka, Regina		1			1
Gilchrist, Mary		3			3
Graf, Sonja	WIM	15	3	5	23
Harum, Gisela		5			5
Henschel, Wally		3	1		4
Hermanowa, Dr. Róża Maria	WIM	1			1
Holloway, Edith		4		1	5
Janečková, Blażena		1			1
Karff, Mona May	WIM	2			2
Kowalska, N.		1			1
Larsen, Ingrid	WIM	2			2
Lauberte, Milda		1		1	2
Lougheed, Anabelle		1			1
Mellbye, Elisabeth		1			1
Menchik, Olga		3			3
Michell, Edith		2		1	3
Mora Iturralde, María Teresa	WIM	1			1
Nakkerud, Ruth		1			1
Price, Edith		8	4	2	14
Reclauskiene, Elena		1			1
Reischer, Salome		1			1
Rinder, Elfriede (Friedl)	WIM	1			1
Roodzant, Catharina		2			2
Schwartzmann, Paulette		2		1	3
Shannon, A.M.S.		1			1
Skjonsberg, Catherina		1			1
Stevenson, Agnes		6			6
Stirling, F.H.		1			1
Stoffels, M.		1			1
Synnevaag, S.		1			1
Thierry, Helene		1			1
Thomson, F.		1			1
Trepat, Dora		1			1
Wolf-Kalmar, Paulina		4		1	5
Known results against women		*100*	*8*	*12*	*120*

Appendix 8: Key Players and Persons in Menchik's Life

Alekhine, Alexander (1892–1946) Fourth Official World Chess Champion (1927–1935 and 1937–1946). Alekhine was the first player to regain the world title after losing it as well as the only player to die while holding the title. Born in Russia of minor nobility, he left for France after the Russian Revolution. Married four times, his undisputed passion in life was chess. Willing to play whenever he had the opportunity, he opposed Menchik in eight tournament games, and noted that she had a real talent which the world had an obligation to nurture.

Capablanca, José Raúl (1888–1942) Third Official World Chess Champion (1921–1927). Probably the world's greatest natural talent, Capablanca played Menchik nine tournament games.

Drewitt, John Arthur James (1879–1931) A Hastings master of some ability, he was Vera's first formal teacher; he won against Vera in Tunbridge Wells 1927—their only major tournament game. Drewitt, who had poor eyesight, died when exiting a moving train.

Euwe, Max (1901–1982) Fifth Official World Chess Champion (1935–1937) Not only a world champion but later the President of the World Chess Federation (FIDE), Euwe was known as one of the great gentlemen of chess. He was also one of the few true amateurs to reach the top levels of chess. Not only did he join the "Vera Menchik Club" but with a lifetime record of +1 –2 =1 against her he was the only major grandmaster to have such a negative score.

Flohr, Salo (1908–1983) One of the top players of the 1930s, Flohr received the GM title in 1950 when it was first granted by FIDE and the IA title in 1963. Flohr was a "candidate member" of the "Vera Menchik Club" and wrote what is probably the most engaging obituary of her in 1958.

Graf (Stevenson), Sonja (1908–1965) IWM 1950. Quite possibly the second best female chess player in the world, Sonja played a match with Vera in Semmering, Austria, in 1937 for the title of Women's World Chess Champion. After the Women's Championship in Buenos Aires, in 1939, she remained in South America. Upon marrying Vernon Stevenson in 1947 she settled in the United States. She won the U.S. Women's Championships in 1957 and 1964. Shortly thereafter she died of liver failure. She wrote two autobiographical works in Spanish entitled *Así Juega una Mujer* (*This Is How a Woman Plays*) and *Yo Soy Susann* (*I Am Susann*).

Mansfield, Katherine (1888–1923) A prominent writer of short fiction. Born in New Zealand she was a friend of D.H. Lawrence and Virginia Wolfe. She lived a tempestuous life for the era and was an active bisexual. Her writings were among Menchik's favorite. She died of pulmonary tuberculosis.

Maróczy, Géza (1870–1951) A challenger for the world championship in the early 20th century; Maróczy was highly respected by the chess community for his impartiality. After World War I he lived for a time in Hastings, England, as "Grandmaster in Residence." While there he taught Vera, imparting his positional style and openings which became hallmarks of her play. In 1935 and 1937 he was the controller of the Alekhine vs. Euwe matches for the world title. In 1950 he was one of the original recipients of the FIDE GM title.

Menchik, František (?–c. 1936) Vera's father. Given that Czechoslovakia did not exist until 1918 after World War I, one has to assume that he was with the Austrian mission. Unfortunately there are far more questions than answers where he is concerned: for example, What did he do from 1918 to 1921 when the rest of the family left the USSR—and after. Evidentially he was a chess player, but not a strong one according to Vera in an interview in the *Sussex Daily News* on August 1, 1927. Evidently he was still alive in 1929, according to an interview with Vera, but by the time of her marriage in 1937 he was listed as deceased.

Menchik, Olga (c. 1885–1944) Vera's mother. She took her children, Vera and Olga, from Moscow to Hastings, England, in 1921. For some time they lived with the elder Olga's mother, Mrs. Marie Illingworth, in Hastings. Along with her daughters she died on June 26, 1944, in the V1 bombings in London.

Menchik (Rubery), Olga (1908–1944) The younger sister of Vera, she was also a chess player. Although not a very strong player, she was competent, and competed in a number of events both with and without Vera in attendance. Included in those would be the British Girl's Championships from 1926 to 1928 and the Women's World Championships of 1935 and 1937. Along with her sister and mother she died in the bombing of their house in Clapham (greater London), England. She married Clifford G. Rubery (died 1999) in December 1938.

Mieses, Jacques (1865–1954) One of the last romantics, he won many brilliancies. Although he generally lost in matches to the very best (e.g., Lasker and Tarrasch) he was still able to win a match against Gerald Abrahams at age 81. When FIDE started awarding titles in 1950 he was one of the original "Grandmasters." In 1951 he was awarded the title of "International Arbiter." As an organizer his great contribution was insisting that players be compensated for their travel and room-and-board at the San Sebastion 1911 tournament (of which he was the organizer)—a practice which only then became standard. Fleeing Nazi persecution at age 73, he settled in England, where he was an active part of the chess scene.

Stevenson, Rufus Henry Streatfield (1878–1943) A long-time chess administrator, Stevenson was the Hon. Secretary of the Kent County Chess Association for many years. In 1938, he was named Hon. Secretary of the British Chess Federation. He was married to Agnes Stevenson, one of the top British female players for many years, until her tragic death in Warsaw. She had just arrived to play in the 1935 Women's World Chess Championship when she walked into a propeller. In 1937, he married Vera. They remained married until November 10, 1943, when he died of a heart attack. By profession Mr. Stevenson was a pharmacist.

Thomas, Sir George H. (1881–1972) Two time British champion (1923 and 1924), Thomas was known for his model behavior and sportsmanship. He was awarded the IM title in 1951 and the IA title in 1952. Sir George played at least 24 tournament games with Vera, more than any other player.

Winter, William (1898–1955) A frequent opponent of Vera's, he started publishing the magazine *The Social Chess Quarterly*, which ran from 1931 until 1936 when it was incorporated into *Chess* magazine. Vera was the games editor. Although there is little if any evidence of a political symbiosis they had very similar leftist political and agnostic religious leanings. Winter received the IM title in 1950.

Wood, Baruch Harold (1909–1989) B.H. Wood founded and ran *Chess* magazine, the lighter of the two major British chess publication. In 1941 he hired Menchik to be the games editor for the journal. In 1974 he received the IA title.

Appendix 9: Obituary of Rufus H. S. Stevenson

In 1937 Vera married the husband of her formal rival, Agnes Lawson Stevenson, who had been killed by an airplane propeller at the Poznan airport while enroute to the 1935 Women's World Championship in Warsaw. Although 28 years younger than her husband, they apparently had a very strong marriage. He won the title of 1919 Kent County Champion and was a competent player, but was better known as an organizer and administrator. Having been the Secretary of the Southern Counties Chess Union for 26 years, he was from 1938 until his death the Secretary of the British Chess Federation. He also played major roles in starting the Hastings Christmas Congresses, the Margate Congresses and more. Sadly he was in poor health during much of the latter part of his life—a fact which prevented Vera from competing in the 1937-38 Hastings Congress.

Following are excerpts from a memorial to Mr. Stevenson printed in the April 1943 issue of *Chess* magazine.

In Memory of R.H.S. Stevenson

Dear Mr. Wood,

Your request asking me to send you an appreciation of the work my husband did for chess, sets a very difficult task before me. His activities in this sphere started long before I had even met him. No doubt someone else will deal with this, and deal with it more ably than I could. However, one fact stands out: for some 40 years he worked hard, with great enthusiasm, and often to the detriment of his health for the cause of chess. You may ask what did he achieve in this time? The answers could be many and varied; I could enumerate County Competitions he started, the Victory Congress of 1919, International and Team Tournaments he promoted, etc., but to my mind, all these are unimportant compared to the work he did for the ordinary, unknown and undistinguished players; welcoming them, encouraging them and making the lives of many a lonely person the happier for having learnt to play chess. This is no idle talk, it is a fact, to which in peace-time his Christmas mail largely testified. And that is not all; whenever it was necessary to raise funds for a chess function it was usually he who was asked to do it.— and he did it. Generous contributions from people little known in organized chess circles came from all over the country, accompanied by messages of goodwill. To see these was to believe that his work had not been for nothing.

Yours very sincerely,
VERA STEVENSON

* * *

"My deepest sympathy is with you in your sorrow, as will be that of every chess player in the country. The debt owed by British chess to your husband is one that cannot be expressed in words; not only because of the tremendous amount and the excellence of his work, but also because of the way in which he did it. I first met him over forty years ago and he was then—as ever since—an outstanding worker for the game he loved so well. It is difficult to imagine future B.C.F. Congresses without his guiding hand. It will indeed be hard to fill the gap he leaves; and he will be remembered in chess circles with gratitude and affection for many, many years to come."

G.A. THOMAS

* * *

"I feel that I must add my own humble acknowledgements to this guide, philosopher, and friend who was ever ready to assist the young and inexperienced player. Gifted with consummate tact in the ironing out of those occasional wrinkles which are apt to appear during Congress and match play, Mr. Stevenson proved himself a 'doyen' in chess diplomacy.

"Both Mr. Stevenson and Mr. William Winter will be sadly missed by their Kent colleagues, and I doubt whether such a gap will ever be filled again. It is very sad to lose two such kind friends in so short a space."

ELAINE SAUNDERS

* * *

"His loss will be a very heavy blow to British chess and, as far as the Margate Chess Congress is concerned, I am very certain that his absence will prove a very grave handicap. As you know he was Chairman of the Congress Committee from its inception and it was very largely due to him that the Margate Easter Congress was such an immediate success."

E.D. MAKEPEACE

* * *

"British chess has lost one of its greatest personalities and I, with many others, will mourn him as a friend. The memory of my long association with him as a fellow-official in county chess will always be among my cherished recollections."

H. MEEK

* * *

Appendix 10:
The V-1 Flying Bomb

The V-1 flying bomb, which was responsible for the death of the Menchik family, was essentially the first iteration of what we now know as the cruise missile. They were 27.3 feet long, had a wingspan of 17.6 feet and weighed about 4,700 lbs., of which the warhead accounted for 1,900 lbs. Powered by a pulse jet engine, they flew at a speed of 400 mph and had a range of 160 miles.

A simple autopilot regulated speed and altitude while an odometer driven by an anemometer on the nose would determine when the target area had been reached. Needless to say pinpoint accuracy was not achievable although rough area-bombing could be attained. The overwhelming number of casualties were civilian in nature. The weapon was essentially a weapon of terror rather than one of tactical military importance. V-1 attacks on London were launched only from June 13 until October 1944 as the allies after D-Day overran the launch sites.

One of the characteristics of these bombs was that when the engine stopped working they created a loud buzzing sound (they were known as "Buzz Bombs").

The attack on Clapham that killed the Menchiks was one of the first V-1 strikes. Ironically, the government had already built a 365 yard long shelter underneath the Clapham North tube station (which is still there). There was also an Anderson shelter in the backyard of the Menchik house. Sadly they chose to seek shelter in the basement of their home. Given the direct strike on their house they never stood a chance of survival.

Notes

1. London 1932 & Poděbrady 1936.
2. H.J.R. Murray, *A History of Chess*, Part II Chapter II pp. 434–5, Benjamin Press, 1913.
3. Aldredge, French, 197; Jefferson Papers 18: 168.
4. William Steinitz, *ICM* March 1886.
5. *www.Chessville.com/BillWall.*
6. Much of the information in this section is detailed in the 1981 BCM Survey on Women's Chess.
7. Death certificate FE077009, for Marie Illingworth, County Borough of Hastings 1934.
8. *Sachmaty*, 1928, p. 160.
9. "Legendary Vera Menchik" A memorial article by G.M. Salo Flohr, *64-Sachmatnoje Obozrenije*, 1983 no. 4.
10. The Bradley Marten Cup was a competition in which the competitors were grouped in small sections according to the players' strength on level terms and then the section winners had a playoff for the cup at handicap odds.
11. This is based on calculations at *www.dollar times.com,* a currency conversion and equivalency site.
12. *BCM* September 1927, p. 390.
13. *Hastings & St. Leonard's Observer*, 11 August 1928.
14. *Hastings St. & Leonard's Observer*, 4 August 1928 quoting the *London Observer*.
15. *Hastings & St. Leonard's Observer*, 9 June 1928.
16. Bikova, E., *Vera Menchik*, 1957, Moscow.
17. See Appendix 1 for a more comprehensive list of members.
18. *BCM*, January 1934, p. 8.
19. *Chess*, May 1937 p. 208.
20. *Chess*, June 1937 pp. 348–349.
21. *The Times*, 20 July 1937.
22. Following an error in Jeremy Gaige's book *Chess Personalia*, Mr. Stevenson's name is often misspelled as "Streatfeild." Vera's marriage and death certificates indicate a spelling of "Streatfield."
23. *Chess*, September 1939, p. 19.
24. *Chess*, October 1939, p. 26.
25. For a more detail on the N.C.C. see *BCM* 1939, pp. 56–58.
26. J. du Mont remembrance *BCM* 1944.
27. "Vera Menchik" by Brian Denman on the Hastings & St. Leonard's Chess Club web site.
28. *The Rating of Chess Players* by Arpad Elo, 1978, p. 193.
29. *Sussex Daily News* 1 August 1927.
30. *The Jewish Telegraphic Agency* of 29 July 1927 writes, "Vera Menchik, the young Russian Jewess who is a member of the British team in the International Chess Tournament, is 'carrying everything before her....'" Nowhere else have I found any reference to a religion or ethnic background for her.
31. *BCM*, August 1944, p. 178.
32. Needless to say this item did not make it into Elizaveta Bikova's book on Vera!
33. *BCM*, 1944, pp. 199–200.
34. *Chess*, August 1944.
35. *Chess Life*, October 2011, p. 24.
36. As calculated on *http://www.fx-exchange.com/currency-converter.html* and *http://gbp.fx-exchange.com/usd/1925-exchange-rates.html.*
37. *HSLO*, 5 September 1925.
38. *BCM*, February 1929, p. 93.
39. Information was taken from "*Ramsgate 1929*," A J Gillam, editor and from "*Vera Menchik*" by E. Bikova. Interestingly this event had not been published in its entirety until Gillam's work in 1995.
40. *BCM*, 1929, pp. 221 and 288.
41. *La Liberté*, June 24, 1929.
42. *New York Times* article by A. Alekhine, 25 August 1929, pp. 1–2 of the Sports Section.
43. Donaldson & Minev, *Akiba Rubinstein: The Later Years*, p. 184.
44. P.W. Sergeant, *A Century of British Chess* p. 284, 1934.
45. *The Times*, 22 April 1930.

46. *BCM*, February 1931, p. 53.

47. *The Times*, 1 April 1932.

48. *The Times*, 2 April 1932.

49. R. Eales, *Chess: The History of a Game*, London, 1985, p. 164.

50. Much of the information contained herein is from N. Krylenko, *Moscow 1935 International Chess Tournament* as translated by Jimmy Adams, Caissa, USA, 1998.

51. N. Krylenko, *Moscow 1935 International Chess Tournament* (trans. J Adams), Caissa, Yorklyn, DE, 1998, p. 29.

52. *BCM* 1935, p. 358.

53. *BCM* 1936, p. 214.

54. E. Bikova, *Vera Menchik*, 1957, Moscow.

55. Skinner and Verhoeven, *Alexander Alekhine's Chess Games 1902–1946*, p. 582, McFarland, 1998.

56. *The Times*, 1 January 1937.

57. E. Bikova, *Vera Menchik*, 1957, Moscow, p. 137.

58. *Chess*, May 1939, p. 334.

59. *BCM* 1940, p. 150.

60. *BCM* 1942, p. 199.

61. *Chess*, November 1943, p. 28.

62. E. Bikova, *Vera Menchik*, 1957, Moscow.

63. *BCM*, September 1927, p. 369.

64. *Chess*, November 1937, p. 260.

65. *BCM* 1937, p. 463.

66. E. Bikova, *Vera Menchik*, 1957, Moscow.

67. *BCM* 1944, p. 201.

68. *Chess*, March 1950, pp. 116–117.

69. Of course deals and minor manipulations have always been part of the system. A not well known fact, for example, is that when Mikhail Tal and Arthur Bisguier received the title they had not fully met the requirements and the result was part of a Soviet–USA deal.

70. It appears Vera missed Black's response of 13.Nb6+–.

Bibliography

There are a number of Miss Menchik's games that have been anthologized numerous times. Her 1932 win over Sir George Thomas alone was found in no fewer than 13 game collections and the 14th game of her 1937 match with Sonja Graf is not far behind. An attempt has been made to limit this bibliography to those items which contain substantial or unique material on her career or life. It is also limited to those volumes which the present author has been able to personally review. It does not include most of the items that people have sent in as partial photocopies or of books with isolated and commonly accessible data. Those items, when necessary, are referenced in the notes section.

Books on Vera Menchik

Bikova, Elizaveta I. *Vera Menchik*. Moscow, 1957. Russian.
G.P. *Vera Menchik-Stevenson: en vetbataloj virina saka mondcampioneco*. 1959 manuscript. Esperanto.
Kalendovský, Jan. *Program XI Ročníku Šachoveho Turnaje*. Brno, 1986. Czech.
Surhone, L.M. *Vera Menchik Women's World Chess Championship, Chess Tournament*. Mauritus, 2010.

Books on Women's Chess in General

Bikova, Elizaveta I. *Women's World Championship Chess*. Moscow, 1955. Russian.
Chidi, L.S. *The Greatest Chess Queens*. Privately published, 2013 (this book is *not* recommended).
Graf, Sonja. *Así Juega una Mujer*. Buenos Aires, Argentina: 1941. Spanish.
Graham, John. *Women in Chess: Players of the Modern Age*. Jefferson, NC: McFarland, 1987.
Shahade, Jennifer. *Chess Bitch*. Los Angeles, CA: Siles Press, 2005.

Tournament Books

Adams, Jimmy. *Second International Chess Tournament*. Moscow, 1935; Yorklyn, DE: Caissa Editions, 1998.
Aguilera, R. *Hastings 1934-35*. Madrid, 1975. Spanish.
Alekhine, Alexander. *London International Chess Tournament 1932*. London: David McKay, 1932.
Brandreth, Dale. *Hastings 1936/37*. Yorklyn, DE: Caissa Editions, 1992.
_____. *Margate 1938*. Yorklyn, DE: Private Publication.
Cload, Reg. *Battles of Hastings*. Sutton Coldfield, UK: Pergamon Chess, 1991.
Cordingly, E.G. *Hastings 1932-33*. UK: private publication, 1933.

_____. *Hastings 1933-34*. UK: private publication, 1934.

_____. *Hastings 1934-35*. UK: private publication, 1935.

_____. *Moscow Chess Congress 1935*, private publication.

_____. *Hastings Chess Congress 1936-37*. UK: private publication.

Gilliam, A.J. *Barcelona 1929: The Chess Player*. England, 1995.

_____. *Ramsgate 1929: The Chess Player*. England, 1995.

Golombek, Harry. *Scarborough 1930, BCM Quarterly #6*. London: 1962.

Kalendovský, Jan. *XIII sjezd UJCS: Mnichovo Hradiště 1933*. Brno, Czechoslovakia: self published, 1989. Czech.

Kashdan, Isaac. *Book of the Folkestone 1933 International Chess Team Tournament*. Leeds, UK: Whitehead & Miller, 1933.

Kent County Chess Association. *Vera Menchik Memorial Tournament*. October 1994.

Krylenko, N. *Moscow 1935 International Tournament*. Yorklyn, DE: Caissa Editions, 1998.

Lachaga, Milcíades A. *Łódź 1938*. Argentina, 1975. German.

_____. *Margate 1938*. Argentina, 1975. German.

_____. *Maribor 1934*. Argentina, German.

Lahde, Peter. *Hastings: Seven Christmas Chess Congresses 1932–1939*. Macon, GA: American Chess Promotions, 1994.

Nimzowitsch, Aron (et al.). *IV Internationales Schachmeisterturnier Karlsbad 1929*. Vienna, 1929.

Reinfeld, Fred. *Book of the Margate 1935 Tournament*. Private publication, 1936.

Schroeder, James. *International Chess Tournament Hastings 1934/35*. Cleveland, OH: 1970.

Spence, Jack. *Carlsbad 1929*. 2 vol. US: private publication.

Toth, L. *Schacholympiade von Hamburg*. British Chess Magazine. London, UK: 1973 (1931). German.

Wiener Schach-Zeitung: IV Internationales Schachmeisterturnier Karlsbad 1929. (231 games). Vienna, 1930. German.

Reference Books

Betts, Douglas A. *Chess: An Annotated Bibliography*. Boston, MA: G K Hall & Co., 1974.

Di Felice, G. *Chess Results 1921–1930*. Jefferson, NC: McFarland, 2006.

_____. *Chess Results 1931–1935*. Jefferson, NC: McFarland, 2006.

_____. *Chess Results 1936–1940*. Jefferson, NC: McFarland, 2007.

_____. *Chess Results 1941–1946*. Jefferson, NC: McFarland, 2008.

Elo, Arpad. *Rating of Chessplayers Past & Present*. New York: ARCO, 1978.

Fiala, Vlastimil. *Chess Biography of Marcel Duchamp* (1887–1968). Olomouc, Czech Republic: Publishing House Moravian Chess, 2004.

_____. *Chess Biography of Marcel Duchamp 1887–1968*. vol. 2. Olomoue, Czech Republic: Publishing House Moravian Chess, 2004.

_____. *Quarterly for Chess History #14*. Olomouc, Czech Republic: Publishing House Moravian Chess, 2008.

Gaige, Jeremy. *Chess Personalia*. Jefferson, NC: McFarland, 1986.

_____. *Crosstable Books*. New Jersey: self published, 1984.

Hooper, David. *Oxford Companion of Chess*. Oxford, England: Oxford University Press, 199?

Podgorný, Napsal Jiří. *Jan Foltys*. Prague, Czechoslovakia: 1956.

Polgar, Susan. *Breaking Through*. Everyman Chess, 2005.

Wildhagen, E. *Capablanca*. Hamburg, 1963. German.

Periodicals and Newspapers

Atputa, 1937 (Latvia). Latvian.

British Chess Magazine, 1924–1945 (St. Leonard's on Sea, UK).

Československý Šach, 1931–1936 (Czechoslovakia). Czech.
Chess, 1936–1945 (Sutton Coldfield, UK)
Chess Review, 1937–1945 (New York)
Hastings & St. Leonard's Observer (Hastings, UK)
Lada, 1934 (Czechoslovakia). Czech.
Poslednie Novosti, May-June 1929 (Paris). Russian.
Social Chess Quarterly
Tidskrift for Schack, 1942–1944. Swedish.
The Times (London)
Wiener Schach-Zeitung, 1927–1936. German.

Books with Substantive References to Vera Menchik

Golombek, Harry, and Bill Hartston. *Best Games of C.H.O'D. Alexander*. Oxford, England: Oxford University Press, 1976.
Polihroniade, E. *Campionii de Şah al Lumii*. Bucharest, 1980. Romanian.
_____. *Schachjahrbuch 1929/30*. Verlag von C. Brugel & Son, 1930. German.

Websites with Substantive References to Vera Menchik

www.Chessgames.com—A site containing a number of Vera's games
www.Hastingschess.proboards.com—Brian Denman biographical article on VM (May 24, 2013)

All of the above publications are in English unless otherwise noted.

Index to Opponents by Game Number

GM-e (Grandmaster-emeritus) represents people who were awarded the title Grandmaster many years after their career was over. GM* represents people who were bestowed the title of Grandmaster post-mortem. Games in which the moves are not known are not indexed.

Index to ECO Openings
by Game Number

Index to Traditional Name Openings
by Game Number

General Index to Page Numbers